A
LIFE
COMMITTED

Essop Pahad

A Life Committed

A memoir

Published by Real African Publishers
236 Frederick Drive
Northcliff
Johannesburg 2195

www.realafricanpublishers.com

First published in October 2023

© Essop G. Pahad

ISBN 978-1-7764567-1-0

Editor: Angela McClelland
Book Design: Reedwaan Vally
Cover Design: Adam Rumball
Index: Jackie Kalley

Printed and bound in South Africa

All rights reserved. Without limiting the rights under copyright reserved above, no part of this publication may be reproduced, stored in or introduced into a retrieval system, or transmitted, in any form or by any means (electronic, mechanical, photocopying, recording or otherwise) without prior written permission of both the copyright holder and the publisher of the book.

This book is sold subject to the condition that it shall not, by way of trade or otherwise, be lent, re-sold, hired out or otherwise circulated without the publisher's prior consent in any form of binding or cover other than that in which it is published and without a similar condition being imposed on the subsequent purchaser.

For my mother,
Amina Pahad,

and my father,
Goolam Hussein Ismail Pahad

Contents

Foreword	11
Family Tree	19
List of Abbreviations	20
Chapter 1: Early Years	28
Chapter 2: Into Exile	72
Chapter 3: World Marxist Review	122
Chapter 4: Focus on Africa	166
Chapter 5: International Solidarity	214
Chapter 6: My Mentors	260
Chapter 7: Return Home	324
Chapter 8: First Years of Our Democracy	372
Chapter 9: Minister in the Presidency	404
Chapter 10: Timbuktu, SADET and the FIFA World Cup	450
Chapter 11: Developments in the ANC and SACP	486
Epilogue	519
Postscript and Tributes	527
Index	532

Acknowledgements

I should like to thank my family, especially my wife Meg, and my friends. So many of you helped to refresh my memory and check some facts that time had blurred. Meg typed up my handwritten work and helped sort out the chronology of events, the names of protagonists, and the accuracy of quotations. Our children and grandchildren kept up my spirits so I could continue to write even when I was tired.

Professor David Monyae, the Director of the Centre for Africa China Studies at the University of Johannesburg and the Research Director, Dr Emmanuel Matambo, persuaded me to finish the book and prepare it for publication. They also provided me with an excellent editor in Angela McClelland, who clarified a few confusions, supplied useful footnotes, and most importantly made the book far more readable.

I have often consulted with Reedwaan Vally in relation to the work of other authors and was very happy to entrust this publication to him.

I am delighted that former President Thabo Mbeki graciously agreed to write the Foreword.

Foreword

The half-century from when the founders of the ANC Youth League became part of the national leadership of the ANC, around 1949, to when they retired from active politics, around 1999, is an exceptional period in the protracted struggle for the liberation of South Africa.

During this period, for the first time since its formation, the historic creation viewed by the oppressed indigenous majority as their authentic representative, the African National Congress, drew into its ranks as members thousands of Africans and thus became a mass movement.

It produced a defining Vision Statement of the South Africa their Movement, the ANC, and the masses of the people fought for, for over a century, the Freedom Charter, whose continuing relevance has remained and will remain during the lifespans of successive generations.

It proved capable of mastering a complex, challenging and dynamic situation which entailed combining different forms and stages of struggle, including peaceful mass struggles, armed action, global mobilisation and diplomacy and negotiations without losing sight of, or deviating from the one goal of the defeat of white minority rule and the transformation of our country into a non-racial and non-sexist democracy.

Similarly, it graduated with great panache from being a combatant in the trenches of struggle, denounced by its opponent as a savage terrorist, to assume political power and introduce a socio-political order our country had never seen – a democratic, non-racial and non-sexist South Africa, governed according to a negotiated Constitution which entrenched respect for human dignity, equality and human rights.

A central component of the leadership which took the ANC through this complex process, during a mere half-a-century, from the adoption of the Programme of Action in 1949, to the end of the first five years of democratic rule in 1999, was made up of the young patriots who had formed the ANC Youth League in 1944.

These former Youth Leaguers gave birth to the next generation of freedom fighters, who also started out as Members of the Youth League, the ones whose unique historical Mission would be to entrench the democratic order by the successful eradication of some of the main negative elements of the pernicious legacy of colonialism and apartheid.

The author of this autobiography, Essop Pahad, is a member of this younger cohort, a successor to the 1944–1999 generation. It is very interesting to read this book among other things to see how successful the '44–'99 generation was in bringing up a successor generation imbued with the same inspiration, courage, stamina, creativity and attachment to principle which informed its own conduct.

Indeed, to read about the political upbringing of Essop Pahad is to be exposed to an important historical account of what happened during vital years in the advance towards the victory of the Democratic Revolution.

Accordingly, the story of Essop's early political upbringing is told within the context of such epoch making events as the Defiance Campaign, the Congress of the People and the adoption of the Freedom Charter, the Women's March to the Union Buildings, the Treason Trial, the Sharpeville Massacre and the banning of the ANC and other organisations, the re-emergence in the underground of the South African Communist Party (SACP), the formation of Umkhonto we Sizwe (MK), the Rivonia Arrests and the Period of Extreme Repression.

Part of this book therefore tells a story of how a young nascent patriot, Essop Pahad, who was very fortunate to have been born in a family of freedom fighters and was therefore exposed to the leadership of our struggle from an early age, joined the mass activities connected with the Defiance Campaign at the age of thirteen.

From there the book tells the tale of Essop Pahad as he interacts with the historic developments of the time, including joining the Transvaal Indian Congress (TIC) and its youth wing, the TIYC, to when, after two arrests as the period of extreme repression began, he is forced to go into exile aged twenty-five.

During his twenty-six years of exile, he remained engaged in struggle to defeat the apartheid regime.

During some later years of our struggle, particularly the 1980s, false accusations were made that our Movement had promoted a slogan and campaign around the call – Liberation Now, Education Later!

This book tells an inspiring story of how the leadership of our Movement responded to a situation during the 1950s which threatened the education of the Indian youth in Johannesburg, by setting up the Central Indian High School (CIHS) which became known as "the Congress School".

What was most remarkable about the Congress School was its cohort of teachers. Its teachers were in fact the very leaders of the Movement, black and white, people who, to this day, we honour among our most eminent leaders – Michael Harmel, Duma Nokwe, Dan Tloome, Molly Fischer, Alfred Hutchinson, Diza Putini and others!

This story, told in this autobiography, emphasises the point that this was yet another element in the political upbringing of the younger generation – the inculcation of the imperative to respect the right of the young to quality education.

Even as our Movement worked hard to strengthen MK to carry out its combat tasks effectively, it also paid close attention to the training of its own intelligentsia, which joined MK after completion of its academic studies. This was done to ensure that when victory came, the Movement would have the cadres who could manage the democratic State.

Those who accused the Movement of promoting the slogan Liberation Now, Education Later! either did not understand the very character of the Movement or deliberately set out to misrepresent it.

I mention this one matter about education to make the point that this book is rich in specific instances which relate to the very making of our Movement over time, and I therefore advise that it should be read with an eye to understanding our Movement's evolution as well as the maturation of the struggle itself.

For instance, the book relates the story of the formation in London, England of the ANC Youth and Student Section in 1966. Young activists of our liberation struggle found themselves together in the United Kingdom. Some of these, including Essop, had worked together inside South Africa though they belonged to the various Youth Leagues of the ANC and the other organisations of the Congress Movement.

Together, in the UK, they decided that it was no longer necessary that they should work in these separate formations, but should come together as the Youth and Students of the ANC, regardless of colour or nationality. In this regard, they were following the example already set by MK, the people's army.

When these young people consulted the then Acting President of the ANC, O. R. Tambo, while he was visiting London, he promptly approved the initiative to form the ANC Youth and Student Section (ANC YSS). Later, the ANC National Executive Committee (in exile), joined President Tambo in supporting the formation of the ANC YSS.

It is interesting to note that it was only at its Consultative Conference held in Kabwe, Zambia in 1985 that the ANC decided fully to transform itself to function in the manner decided by the ANC youth almost 20 years earlier, when they formed the ANC YSS.

Located in Europe in exile, the ANC YSS played an important role in giving substance and entrenching the internationalism of the ANC. This it did by participating actively in struggles in solidarity with the peoples of Vietnam, of Zimbabwe including after Smith's UDI, of Greece after the Colonel's seizure of power, and of other nations.

The ANC YSS had also played a leading role in the formation of an International Students Society after the British Government had imposed higher University fees for foreign students. This enabled the YSS to act in solidarity with students and peoples from such countries as Iraq and Iran.

All this information, which constituted part of the political upbringing of the young Essop Pahad, is in this autobiography, exemplifying the many instances in the book which report the qualitative transformation of our Movement.

It is true that since the emergence in South Africa of an organised Socialist Movement, through the formation of the International Socialist League in 1915, three years after the formation of the ANC, the South African liberation movement contained two tendencies within it, both the nationalist and the socialist. Ultimately the collaboration between these two tendencies found its ultimate form and content in the Tripartite Alliance of the ANC, the SACP and COSATU.

As he grew up, the subject of this autobiography, Essop Pahad, became a member and leader of the South African Communist Party, SACP, and later participated in the ranks of the leadership of the World Communist Movement by joining the Editorial Board of the *World Marxist Review* based in Prague, in the then Czechoslovakia.

Much has be written and said, true and false, about the role and place of the SACP and the world Communist Movement relative to our Movement and struggle for national liberation.

Thanks to the account of the author of his involvement in both the SACP and the international Communist Movement, including his interaction with the Communist Parties of the Soviet Union, the German Democratic Republic, Cuba and others, we will get a glimpse of what the domestic and world Communist Movement meant to our struggle as well as the global progressive movement.

This, too, will help us understand yet more about the development of the cadres who succeeded the '44-'99 generation of South African liberators.

As we would surmise, these cadres, now mature members of our broad Movement, began to constitute an important component part of its leadership from about 1974, thirty years after the formation of the ANC Youth League. Representing the assumption of such leadership positions, Essop Pahad joined the Editorial Board of the *World Marxist Review* in 1975, after completion of his studies at the Lenin School in Moscow, which he had joined in 1973.

The two decades from 1974 to 1994 proved to be a period of momentous changes which would challenge the leadership of our Movement to live up to its responsibilities concerning the historic liberation of the people of South Africa from apartheid and white minority domination, ensuring the victory of the National Democratic Revolution.

During this period of two decades we experienced the epoch-making defeat of US imperialism in Vietnam, the collapse of the Portuguese Empire in Africa and therefore the liberation of the Portuguese colonies of Guinea Bissau and Cape Verde, São Tomé and Principe, Angola and Mozambique, marking the beginning of the final liquidation of colonialism and apartheid in Africa.

This was to be followed by the liberation of Zimbabwe, the defeat and eviction from Angola of the apartheid army of aggression by the combined Angolan People's Liberation Forces and the Cuban Army. While the struggle suffered a temporary setback with the signing of the Nkomati Accord in Mozambique, the defeat of the apartheid forces in Angola led to the independence of Namibia and ultimately the negotiations leading to the liberation of South Africa in 1994.

This period had also seen a progressive left turn in Latin America, marked by the victories of the Farabundo Marti National Liberation Front in El Salvador and the Sandinista National Liberation Front in Nicaragua, while also suffering a serious setback with the overthrow of the democratically elected Government of Salvador Allende by the Chilean Army, encouraged and supported by the CIA.

And, of course, this period saw the globally defining moment described by the collapse of the Soviet Union and the related defeat of socialism in Europe. Out of this was born the unipolarity in global affairs described by the fact that the USA emerged as the sole global super-power.

Our movement for national liberation and its leadership had to navigate through this complex two-decade period of fundamental change in Africa and the world and ensure the victory of the National Democratic Revolution after years of protracted struggle.

At last this victory was achieved, with the successors brought up by the 1944-1999 political generation playing their own and honourable part marked by the historic celebrations of May 1994, when that outstanding leader drawn from the '44-'99 generation, Nelson Mandela, was inaugurated as President of South Africa, after his historic Movement, the ANC, had won the April General Election, the very first democratic elections in our country!

Essop Pahad and others of his generation had proved their worth during the two decades leading to the democratic victory in 1994. They won the confidence of the people that they could lead the nation in establishing the new South Africa of which the people dreamt. This they did by helping to put in place the policies, including the Constitution, and the programmes to realise that dream, working hand-in-hand with the older generation which had led the struggle for half-a-century!

But obviously the story of Essop's generation cannot end there.

After all there is that promissory note, the Constitution, which this generation drafted. It solemnly promises among others, to heal the divisions of the past and establish a society based on democratic values, social justice and fundamental human rights, as well as improve the quality of life of all citizens and free the potential of each person.

The question arises naturally – how far has the successor generation to the '44-'99 cohort fulfilled the undertakings it formally inscribed in golden words in a binding compact, the Constitution, giving expression to the hopes of generations past, present and future?

The honest answer to that question will also give a firm indication of how well this successor generation has, for its part, also brought up its own successors who would be ready and prepared to fulfil the new Mission.

It is no wonder that the author of this biography, Essop Pahad, after more than sixty-five years of activism within the Congress Movement, and undoubtedly expressing the views of many of his peers, writes passionately about what is to him and his peers their most fervent wish.

He states that wish in these words – our country, Africa and the progressive forces throughout the world need a strong, healthy and cohesive ANC – an internationalist ANC that is free from corruption!

Essop Pahad makes this call fully aware that it is exactly through this kind of ANC that new Mission spelt out in the Constitution will be fulfilled as the earlier Missions, including as detailed in the 1949 Programme of Action, were realised.

The outstanding progressive historian, Eric Hobsbawm, has said:

> It is part of life and business to question ourselves about where the future is leading. Where possible, we all make an attempt at it. However, predicting the future must necessarily be based on knowledge of the past…Thus we must try to make predictions, albeit with certain reservations. We have to be aware of the danger of aping the fortune-teller.*

When Essop Pahad made the call about the future of the ANC, he was beginning to ask the question – where is the future leading? – without aping the fortune teller.

I am happy to commend this educative tour through many decades of exciting struggles for our liberation and a better world, as contained in this autobiography. I leave it to the reader to discover the future of hope which will be born of the actions of the Essop Pahad generation, working hand-in-hand with the successor cadres it has prepared for the new victories detailed in our Constitution.

Thabo Mbeki
Johannesburg June 2023

---

* Eric Hobsbawm: *On the Edge of the New Century.* The New Press, New York, NY 10036, 2000.

PAHAD FAMILY TREE

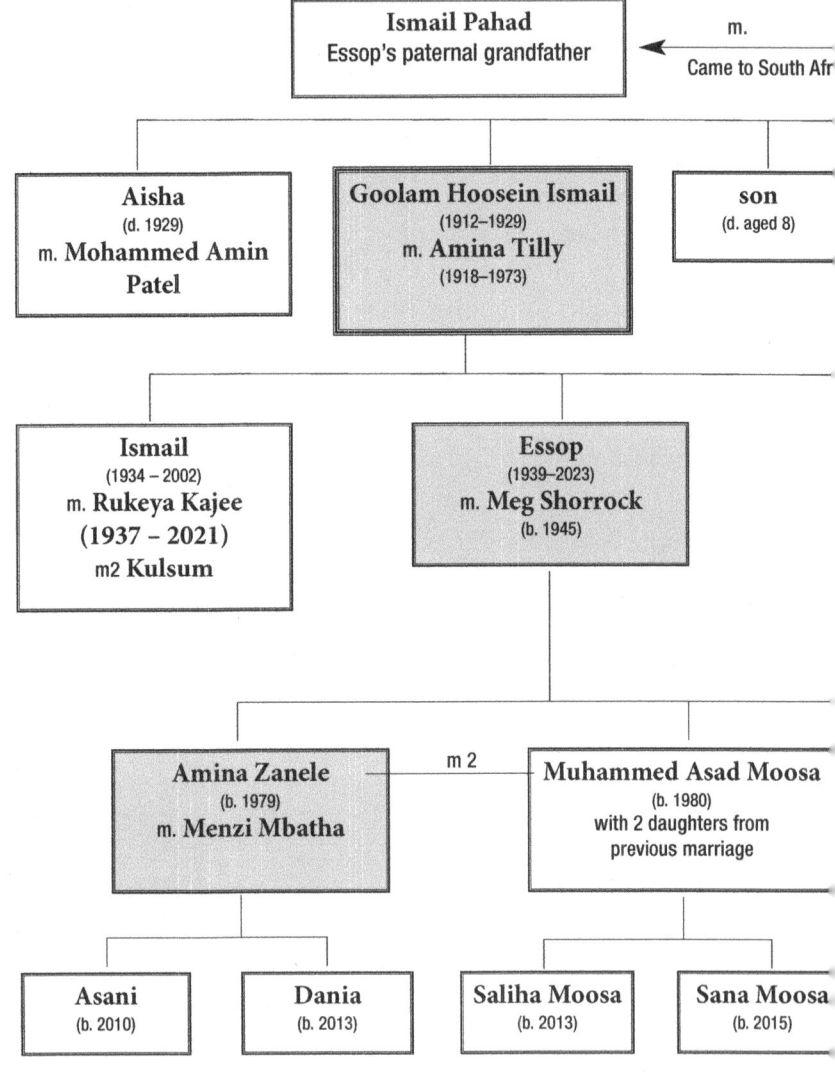

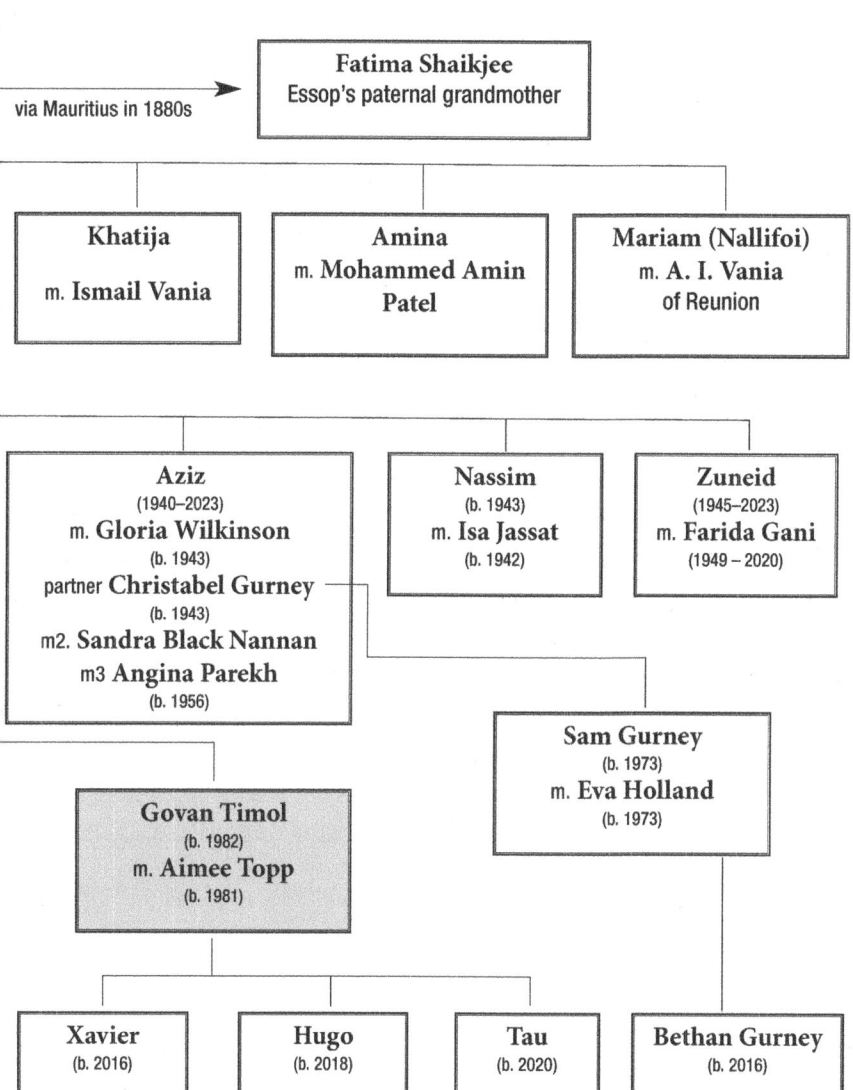

List of Abbreviations

AAM	Anti-Apartheid Movement
AAPSO	Afro-Asian People's Solidarity Organisation
ACP-EU	African, Caribbean and Pacific states and European Union
ACTSA	Action for Southern Africa
ACTT	Association of Cinematograph, Television and Allied Technicians
AIPSO	All India Peace and Solidarity Organisation
AIYF	All-India Youth Federation
AKEL	Progressive Party of Working People (*Anorthotikó Kómma Ergazómenou Laoú*)
AKFM	Congress Party for the Independence of Madagascar (*Antokon'ny Kongresin'ny Fahaleovantenan'i Madagasikara*)
AMPS	All Media Products Survey
ANC	African National Congress
ANC Y&S	ANC Youth and Students
ANCYL	ANC Youth League
APES	Animals, Plants and Environmental Sciences
AQIM	Al-Qa'ida in the Lands of the Islamic Maghreb
ASA	African Studies Association
AU	African Union
AWB	Afrikaner Weerstandsbeweging (Afrikaner Resistance Movement)
AZAPO	Azanian People's Organisation
BCM	Black Consciousness Movement
BCP	Bulgarian Communist Party
BJP	Bharatiya Janata Party
CAF	Confederation of African Football
CBD	Central Business District
CC	Central Committee
CEO	Chief Executive Officer
CFMAG	Committee for Freedom in Mozambique, Angola and Guinea Bissau
CGE	Commission on Gender Equality
CGT	The General Confederation of Labour (*Confédération générale du travail*)
CIA	Central Intelligence Agency
CIHS	Central Indian High School
CND	Campaign for Nuclear Disarmament
CNR	National Council of the Revolution (*Conseil National de la Revolution*)
COGTA	Cooperative Governance and Traditional Affairs
COMTASK	Communications Task Group
COP	Congress of the People
COPWE	Commission for Organising the Working People of Ethiopia
COSIR	Community Support Initiatives for Refugees
CPC	Communist Party of Czechoslavakia

CPGB	Communist Party of Great Britain
CPI	Communist Party of India
CPI(M)	Communist Party of India (Marxist)
CPL	Congolese Party of Labour
CPS	Communist Party of Syria
CPSA	Communist Party of South Africa
CPSL	Communist Party of Sri Lanka
CPSU	Communist Party of the Soviet Union
CPUSA	Communist Party of the USA
DA	Democratic Alliance
DFID	Department for International Development
DIRCO	Department of International Relations and Cooperation
DKP	Communist Party of West Germany (*Deutsche Kommunistische Partei*)
DPSA	Disabled People of South Africa
DTI	Department of Trade and Industry
EISA	Electoral Institute of Southern Africa
ESOF	Education Services Organisations Forum
FAPLA	People's Armed Forces of Liberation of Angola (*Forças Armadas Populares de Libertação de Angola*)
FDJ	Free German Youth (*Freie Deutsche Jugend*)
FEDSAW	Federation of South African Women
FET	Further Education and Training
FNLA	National Liberation Front of Angola (*Frente Nacional de Libertação de Angola*)
FRELIMO	Liberation Front of Mozambique (*Frente de Libertação de Moçambique*)
GBV	Gender-based violence
GCIS	Government Communication Information System
GDR	German Democratic Republic
GEAR	Growth, Employment and Redistribution
GETOA	Gauteng Education and Training Organisations Association
GP	General practitioner (medical doctor)
GTZ	German Technical Co-operation
HMB	People's Liberation Army (*Hukbong Mapagpalaya ng Bayan*)
HR	Human Resources
IBA	Independent Broadcasting Authority
IBSA	India, Brazil, South Africa
ICASA	Independent Communications Authority of South Africa
ICP	Iraqi Communist Party
ICT	Information and Communication Technology
IDASA	Institute for Democratic Alternatives in South Africa
IEB	Independent Examinations Board
IEC	Independent Electoral Commission
IFP	Inkatha Freedom Party
ILEA	Inner London Education Authority
ILG	Internal Leadership Group

IMC	International Marketing Council
IMF	International Monetary Fund
INC	Indian National Congress
IT	Information Technology
IUEF	International University Exchange Fund
IUS	International Union of Students
KZN	KwaZulu-Natal
LOC	Local Organising Committee
LSE	London School of Economics
MA	Master's degree
MCW	Military combat work
MDDA	Media Development and Diversity Agency
MK	Umkhonto we Sizwe
MPC	Multi-Party Committee
MPL	Member of the Provincial Legislature
MPLA	People's Movement for the Liberation of Angola (*Movimento Popular de Libertação de Angola*)
MPPC	Multipurpose Communication Centre
NAI	National Archives of India
NASREC	National Recreation Centre
NCOP	National Council of Provinces
NEC	National Executive Committee
NEDLAC	National Economic Labour and Development Council
NEPI	National Education Policy Initiative
NETF	National Education and Training Forum
NGM	National Gender Machinery
NGOs	Non-governmental organisations
NIC	Natal Indian Congress
NICRA	Northern Ireland Civil Rights Association
NLF	National Liberation Front
NPA	National Prosecuting Authority
NQF	National Qualifications Framework
NUM	National Union of Mineworkers
NUS	National Union of Students
NUSAS	National Union of South African Students
NUT	National Union of Teachers
NWC	National Working Committee
OAU	Organisation of African Unity
OBE	Order of the British Empire
OSDP	Office on the Status of the Disabled
OSW	Office on the Status of Women
PAC	Pan-Africanist Congress
PAIGC	African Party for the Independence of Guinea and Cape Verde (*Partido Africano para a Independência da Guiné e Cabo Verde*)
PB	Political Bureau (Politburo)

PCI	Italian Communist Party (*Partito Comunista Italiano*)
PDS	Senegalese Democratic Party (*Parti démocratique sénégalais*)
PEC	Provincial Executive Committee
PIT	Party of Independence and Labour (*Parti de l'Indépendance et du Travail*)
PKI	Communist Party of Indonesia
PKP	Philipine Communist Party (*Partido Komunista ng Pilipinas*)
PNLC	Party National Liaison Committee
PM	Prime Minister
PMAC	Provisional Military Administrative Council
PNLC	Party National Liaison Committee
POA	Programme of Action
PPP	People's Progressive Party
PRPB	People's Revolutionary Party of Benin (*Partie de la Révolution Populaire du Bénin*)
PS	Senegalese Socialist Party (*Parti Socialiste du Sénégal*)
RDP	Reconstruction and Development Programme
RPL	Recognition of Prior Learning and Experience
RPMC	Regional Political Military Council
RSA	Radical Student Alliance
RSS	Rashtriya Swayamsevak Sangh (the Sangh)
SAARF	South African Audience Research Foundation
SABC	South African Broadcasting Corporation
SACP	South African Communist Party
SACTU	South African Congress of Trade Unions
SAFA	South African Football Association
SAFCERT	South African Certification Council
SAIC	South African Indian Congress
SANDF	South African National Defence Force
SANROC	South African Non-Racial Olympic Committee
SAQA	South African Qualifications Authority
SASO	South African Student Organisation
SAWID	South African Women in Dialogue
SED	Socialist Unity Party (*Sozialistische Einheitspartei Deutschlands*)
SETA	Sectoral Education and Training Authority
SOAS	School of Oriental and African Studies
SOE	State-Owned Enterprise
SRC	Student Representative Council
SWAPO	South West Africa People's Organisation
SWFPN	Socialist Workers and Farmers Party of Nigeria
TAC	Treatment Action Campaign
TEC	Transitional Executive Council
TIC	Transvaal Indian Congress
TIYC	Transvaal Indian Youth Congress
TMF	Thabo Mbeki Foundation

UCL	University College London
UCT	University of Cape Town
UDF	United Democratic Front
UEFA	Union of European Football Associations
UIF	Unemployment Insurance Fund
ULU	University of London Union
UNHCR	United Nations High Commissioner for Refugees
UNISA	University of South Africa
UNITA	National Union for the Total Independence of Angola (*União Nacional para a Independência Total de Angola*)
UP	Popular Unity (*Unidad Popular*)
USIS	US Information Service
UWC	University of the Western Cape
WAY	World Assembly of Youth
WFDY	World Federation of Democratic Youth
WFTU	World Federation of Trade Unions
Wits	University of the Witwatersrand
WMR	World Marxist Review
WPC	World Peace Council
WPJ	Workers Party of Jamaica
WSIS	World Summit on the Information Society
YCL	Young Communists League

Chapter 1
The Early Years

Amina Pahad, left, her husband, and five boys when she went to jail during the 1946 Passive Resistance Campaign

The Early Years

Prior to the arrival of colonialism, imperialism and white settlers in South Africa, the land and mineral resources beneath the soil belonged to the indigenous communities. The colonial demarcation of provinces and boundaries within provinces was carried out at the expense of these communities through their occupation and domination. This was codified in the Act of Union 1910, passed by the British parliament, which gave economic and political power to the white minority. In the years up to 1885, the area now called Schweizer-Reneke was inhabited by the Tswana/Tlhaping and the Korana (Koras), descendants of the Khoikhoi. These groups competed for grazing and firewood, with sporadic fighting. Their relatively peaceful existence was shattered when the Boers (Afrikaans-speaking white immigrants), led by President Kruger, defeated the Koras in 1885. The capture and defeat of the original inhabitants led to the establishment of Schweizer-Reneke, named after Captain Schweizer and Field Cornet Reneke, who were killed in the fighting.

Schweizer-Reneke was in the old Transvaal and is now part of the North West Province.

The bitter laager mentality and harsh racist behaviour of many of the Boers in that area can be partly explained by the following extract from *South African History Online*:

> (Lord) Methuen's destruction of Schweizer-Reneke took place towards the end of the [Second Anglo-Boer] War [1899–1902], when the British were pursuing a devastating scorched-earth policy towards the Boer guerrilla forces to deprive them of local support in the form of food, water and shelter. During the course of the War, some 30,000 Boer farmhouses were destroyed and tens of thousands of cattle slaughtered. Inevitably, those most heavily affected were Boer women and children and the elderly, who were left destitute and starving. The British solution was to intern them in concentration camps, the first time the term was used ... The camps were overrun with diseases – whooping cough, measles, typhoid fever, diphtheria,

diarrhoea and dysentery – especially amongst the children.

Eventually, 26,370 Boer women and children (eighty-one per cent were children) died in the concentration camps. The British scorched-earth policy also displaced thousands of African farmworkers, and the British established 66 concentration camps for them, accommodating 11,500 people at the height of their existence. Mortality rates in Black camps were as high as in Boer camps. Half of the recorded Black deaths occurred in the three months between November and January 1901 (2,831 deaths were recorded in December 1901). Officially, 14,154 deaths were recorded, but as the records of the camps are unsatisfactory, the number could be as high as 20,000.[1]

It was in that nondescript, dusty dorp of Schweizer-Reneke that I was born on 21 June 1939, as were my three younger brothers, Aziz (1940), Nassim (1943) and Zuneid (1945). My elder brother Ismail was born in India in 1934, when my mother, following the custom of Gujaratis living in the diaspora, had returned to her family in her village of origin for the birth of her first child. She rejoined her husband in South Africa soon after the birth but left Ismail with his grandparents. As his paternal grandmother was particularly attached to him and could not bear to be parted from him, he stayed in India for four or five years until a close family friend, Abdul Haq (Freeman) Dadabhay, brought him home. Freeman would always tease Ismail and his family, saying, 'I should have thrown you overboard when I had the chance!'

So we were five brothers; no sisters. Ismail, the eldest, was later came to be known as the 'Fordsburg Fox' for contributing to professional soccer amongst Black people. He owned and ran the Dynamos Football Club. Sadly, he passed away in May 2002. I am the second child, and the third is Aziz, who, for many years, was Deputy Foreign Minister of South Africa. Fourth is Nassim, a self-employed businessman in shipping, forwarding and clearing. Nassim was involved in the resuscitation of the TIC (Transvaal Indian Congress) in the 1980s and the launch of the United Democratic Front (UDF). And Zuneid (Junaid on his birth certificate) is the youngest, an accountant who served two terms as an elected ANC local councillor for

---

1. 'Anglo-Boer War 2: Lord Metheun, British general, destroys the village of Schweizer-Reneke', South African History Online, 4 August 1901. Available at https://www.sahistory.org.za/dated-event/anglo-boer-war-2-lord-methuen-british-general-destroys-village-schweizer-reneke

Mayfair in the Johannesburg Municipality.

My father had a shop called Hollywood House, and our home was at the back. Already in the 1930s, Schweizer-Reneke was a hotbed of right-wing Afrikaner nationalism, chauvinism and racism, and there were only a few families of Indian origin. These included the Kathradas (Ahmed 'Kathy' Kathrada was born in Schweizer-Reneke); the Cajees – we called Amin Cajee 'Uncle'; he was a genial, generous man who became a deeply committed freedom fighter, a combatant of Umkhonto we Sizwe who, for his involvement, was arrested and brutally tortured – and the Patels, who were our neighbours.

When my parents and siblings moved to Johannesburg in 1946, I elected to stay on in Schweizer-Reneke to be with my best friend Ahmed Patel and his brother Iqbal. Ahmed and I went to school together (Grade 1), and, not surprisingly, had a few skirmishes with boys who used to call us 'Coolies' – a derogatory term applied to Indians in South Africa. It was an enjoyable year playing cricket and football with my friends in their yard, but I missed my family and I eventually joined them in Johannesburg in 1947.

When I returned, my family were living in Ophirton. Fortunately, in what would be a game changer in our lives, we moved into a flat our father rented – Number 11 Orient House in Becker Street (now Gerard Sekoto Street), Ferreirastown. I really cannot imagine how our lives would have panned out had we remained in Ophirton.

As Mila de Villiers describes Johannesburg in the 1880s: 'The wealthiest city in Africa was a dusty den of drunken debauchery. Greed was its ancestor, iniquity its matriarch, a metropolis its progeny.'[2] The discovery of gold in 1886 saw all types of people 'flocking to Ferreirastown (then known as Ferreira's Camp), where the first gold digging started and where the diggers first settled'.[3] When we moved to Orient House, Ferreirastown was still a rough, tough area with shebeens, retail shops, the Indian Market in Diagonal Street and gangsters. One of the most prominent and feared gangsters was Sherief Khan, who operated from Ferreirastown. He:

> was destined to become king of the South African underworld and owned or controlled many illegal gambling establishments in and around Johannesburg. ... In addition to drug pushing and extortion, [his] gang [the Sherief Khan Organisation] excelled at shop and

---

2. Mila de Villiers. 'Lust, dust and power: the somewhat sordid history of Johannesburg', Lifestyle, *The Sunday Times*, 19 July 2020.
3. Ibid.

> warehouse breaking which was performed after meticulous planning ... A feature common to both the 'Msomi' gang and the Sherief Khan Organisation was the close contact they appeared to have had with the police. ... When Sherief Khan was caught by the Pretoria police in Fordsburg while robbing a warehouse, there was a flying squad car in attendance to ensure that no one disturbed him during the robbery.

Throughout his reign of more than three decades as an organised crime leader, Sherief Khan frequently appeared in court on charges such as extortion, bribery and murder, but he and his gang were usually acquitted. The unexpected lapse of memory of state witnesses or the lack of evidence was the cause of this.[4]

Orient House, built in 1939, is a sturdy building that has stood the test of time. The Dadabhay family possessed the foresight and confidence to build what was, to us, an imposing building of seven floors. Our flat on the second floor had three bedrooms, one sitting-cum-dining room, a kitchen, and one bathroom with a shower and a separate squat toilet. Apart from two Chinese families, the rest of the occupants were Muslim and Hindu families who originated from Gujarat, India. Some 100 metres diagonally from Orient House is Kholvad House on Market Street, in which Ahmed 'Kathy' Kathrada resided at Flat 13, now memorialised in a myriad documentaries.

Becker Street is a narrow street intersecting several parallel main roads viz., Commissioner, Market, President and Fox Streets. Moving from Orient House, across Commissioner Street, one would arrive at the Johannesburg Magistrate's Court, and Chancellor House, where Nelson Mandela and Oliver Tambo opened their legal offices on the corner of Becker and Fox Streets, as well as a billiards saloon, which we frequented when we were old enough, and the Kosy Café.

Ferreirastown also housed the offices of the African National Congress (ANC), prior to its banning in 1960, along with the Transvaal Indian Congress (TIC) and the Transvaal Indian Youth Congress (TIYC). Nearby too was the Trades Hall, a venue for many trade union and political meetings. The area was also a bustling commercial centre which hosted the headquarters of the mining giant Anglo American.

After the banning of the ANC, the Congresses took over the top floor of Macosa House, an office building on the corner of Commissioner and

---

4. 'Organised Crime in South Africa – An Assessment of its Nature and Origins', Monograph No. 28, August 1998. Available at https://issafrica.s3.amazonaws.com/site/uploads/Mono28.pdf

Bezuidenhout Streets. The TIC office there was run by Mosie Moolla, the Dynamos football team had a club in the basement, and, for a while, my father had his office there, as did Walter Sisulu. We used Macosa House to meet ANC and ANC Youth League (ANCYL) members and leaders, and this was where I first met Thabo Mbeki.

If you crossed Market Street, you would encounter a large courtyard demarcated by flats all around it. In that Yard – variously designated 'The Yard', 'Scotland Yard' or even derogatorily *Goja* Yard – lived Ahmed 'Archie Boy' Bhayet as well as the Adam family. The latter family comprised five brothers (Mohammed, Goolam, Essop, Ebrahim and Suleiman) and two sisters. Their father had died at an early age, and their mother raised them under extremely difficult conditions in a one-bedroomed flat. Goolam Adam's daughter Feroza grew up to be an activist in progressive women's movements and in the UDF. She became an ANC Member of Parliament (MP) after the first democratic election in 1994, dying tragically young in a car accident soon after entering parliament. She was a great loss, both to family and to our nascent democracy.

When we formed Dynamos – inspired and led by my brother Aziz – Mohammed and Ebrahim Adam formed Young Tigers Football Club. For years, we had very tough derby matches, as important to us as perhaps Liverpool vs Everton, and on most occasions, much to the chagrin and disappointment of Tigers, Dynamos came out on top.

Although one can argue that Ferreirastown was part of the Central Business District (CBD), the city centre itself was the domain of the whites. No Black person was allowed to own or rent a property in the area, and the Johannesburg Public Library, along with the majority of cinemas, clubs, hotels, theatres and pubs were reserved for Whites Only.

As a youngster, I became part of the Becker Street gang, which consisted of a bunch of tough young guys led by Hamid Suliman 'Tossie' and Ebrahim Adam. They were rough street fighters who were also excellent football players. Most of these small gangs were territorial groups protecting their own, not serious criminals. The Becker Street gang were involved in fights with gangs from Fordsburg, Vrededorp, Newclare, Newlands, Sophiatown, Coronationville and Albertville. My brother Ismail was indirectly associated with our Becker Street group and was famed for his audacity and total lack of fear. There were many stories of his brushes with the police whom he attacked often to prevent them from arresting or harassing someone. In such cases, he seems to have had a flair for the dramatic, shooting at a policeman's feet and ordering him to 'JUMP' repeatedly, or, on one occasion, stabbing six policemen during a successful rescue attempt. On another occassion, a big burly Afrikaaner policeman had Ismail pointed out to him as the well-known local miscreant – but on seeing how short and skinny he was, did not believe he could have done the damage he was accused of and refused to arrest him.

Ismail's daughter Yasmin remembers that he was well-known for facing a policeman who had entered Kholvad House and punching him so hard that he was propelled backwards, breaking the glass door and ending up outside on his back.

Ismail was capable of terrifying our enemies, and his nerves were unshakeable, characteristics which won the respect of even the more serious gangs, like that of Sherief Khan. We could always use Ismail's name to save our skins if anyone threatened us.

We played football, cricket and other ball games on the pavement and in the street. From time to time, we even dared to play on the pristine lawns of the Magistrates' Court, which was dangerous, as the Marshall Street police station was nearby; we had to be alert to avoid arrest.

It was also in Ferreirastown where we made lifelong friends, and it was where our political activities started.

౮

Before continuing my story, I will contextualise the history of South Africans of Indian origin using some extracts from my PhD thesis for the University of Sussex.[5]

In 1843, Natal became a British Colony ruled from the Cape. By 1856, it was a separate colony with a partly-elected legislature offering manhood suffrage based on property qualifications. Virgin Natal offered tremendous opportunities to European planters and farmers – but they faced an acute shortage of labour since the African people were unwilling to work on European farms.

Therefore, a demand arose for indentured labourers from India, and 'after protracted negotiations between the Natal Government and the Secretary of State for the Colonies, the Natal Coolie Law, Law 14 of 1859, was passed.'[6] On securing the reluctant agreement of the Indian Government, the wheels of immigration were set in motion.

---

5. *The Development of Indian Political Movements in South Africa, 1924–46*, (July 1972, pp. 12–15).
6. https://www.sahistory.org.za/article/anti-indian-legislation-1800s-1959

The first batch of indentured labourers arrived in Durban on 16 November 1860. There were 342 persons, including 75 women and 83 children, mainly South Indian Hindus with a sprinkling of Christians and Muslims. Ten days later, another shipload, from Calcutta, disembarked with 351 passengers, including 61 women and 83 children, mainly from the South and East of India.

> No food, shelter or interpreter was provided, with the result that, on arrival, the Indians were in a confused and desolate state ... according to the dictates of chance, friends, relatives and members of the same family were parted and assigned to new masters.[7]

Even for the late nineteenth century, the working and living conditions of the labourers were miserable and disgraceful. Suffice to quote some of Fatima Meer's examples of the treatment received by the labourers:

> Ramsamy, caught out of bounds, was tied to the rafters and lashed with a sjambok and then jailed for desertion. Illama gave birth in the fields because her employer would not release her, and a little girl of 16 was found dying of anaemia on the roadside because she had not been examined on her arrival in Durban before being sent off 50 miles to her place of employment. ... [T]he Coolie Commission of 1872 found that on many estates, no medical care was provided, wages were withheld and illegal flogging was common.[8] The term 'indentured labourer' was clearly a euphemism for a type of slavery.[9] The main difference being that on the expiry of their contracts, these labourers were free to seek paid employment or become self-employed, and many in Durban initially used their skills to become market gardeners.

In 1869, a new wave of immigration occurred – of traders from the West Coast, mainly Gujarat. Referred to as 'passenger Indians'[10] as distinct from indentured Indians, these new immigrants, mainly Muslims, were attracted by Durban's rich potential for trade. Later, some moved into the interior,

---
7. Fatima Meer. *Portrait of Indian South Africans.* (Durban: Avon House, 1969).
8. Ibid
9. If you would like to know more about the living conditions of the indentured labourers, I can recommend *Inside Indian Indentured Labour: A South African Story, 1860–1914* by Ashwin Desai and Goolam Vahed, (Pretoria: HSRC Press, 2010). It is a well-researched book and eminently worth reading.
10. Skilled immigrants who paid for their passage to their destination.

following the main transport route from Durban to Johannesburg, which resulted in a settled Indian community in every major town along the way.

Of course, my family, like others from that group, were in regular touch with their extended families, and many regularly visited India and continued to speak their Indian languages for several generations. This was not usually the case with the descendants of the indentured labourers, who were originally mainly Tamil- and Telegu-speaking families. Hardly any of them were able to keep in touch with their relatives or use their languages under the slave-like conditions to which they were subjected.

One cannot deny the immense contribution of the Indian people to the economic development of Natal. In 1903, Sir Liege Hulett, ex-Prime Minister (PM) of Natal Colony and a sugar baron said that Durban had absolutely been built by the Indian people.

※

Now to return to my early life and introduce you to my mother, Amina, a very generous, caring and utterly unselfish woman who had a profound effect on our lives. She was also determined, principled and courageous, and we could rely on her at all times in all circumstances.

Amina Tilly's parents came to South Africa in the 1880s, and she was born in Klerksdorp in 1918. There, my grandfather had a very successful general store which was the subject of one of the many celebrated court cases resulting from the forced relocation of Indian businesses to designated segregated areas. Unfortunately, he lost the case. Later, when he was unable to run the business effectively, he went bankrupt and took his family back to Kholvad, the village in India where his parents had been born and raised. Amina preferred living in South Africa and was not pleased with the move back to the village. Zaibie Bhyat told us that Amina had sent her a couple of tear-stained letters from India, where she was a person of little importance in the family. In South Africa, she had felt independent, valuable and respected. When her family received a marriage proposal from Goolam Pahad (also originally from Kholvad), who was visiting India from South Africa, she was very happy to accept and return to her natural home.

My mother influenced us through her strength of character and unshakeable values, which were apparent from our earliest memories. Although she was forthright in her reaction to people, from everything we can recall and what others tell us about her, my mother had no racial prejudice; racism and other forms of intolerance were behaviours she would not accept. The following is an example of Amina Pahad allowing herself to rebuke a visitor.

In the early 1940s, several ANC leaders would visit our parents when passing through Schweizer-Reneke, and there was an occasion when Uncle J. B. Marks, a leader of the ANC and the Communist Party of South Africa (CPSA), was touring and came to stay with us. When a white Afrikaner friend of my parents walked into the house and saw Uncle J. B. and some other visitors sitting there, he became very agitated. 'Why are you sitting with these Blacks?' I think he used a more derogatory term. To which my mother replied:

> Now listen to me! You come to my house whenever you want, but this is J. B. Marks. He is one of our leaders. You will never talk about J. B. Marks and others like this. If you want to talk this way, get out of my house!

That is the kind of environment in which we grew up.

From the time we moved to Orient House, several ANC leaders were frequently in and out of our home. Many of the Indian Congress leaders were there almost daily because a lot of their important meetings took place in my parents' flat. One of the most frequent visitors was Dr Dadoo, who was also our family doctor. Soon, people like Mandela and Walter Sisulu also started coming to our place.

My mother was an exceptional human being with a heart of gold, making it very difficult for her to say anything negative about anybody. Because she instinctively expected people to be good, she brought out the best in those with whom she interacted.

In our sitting room were several photographs: one of Yusuf Dadoo, our hero, and one of Gandhi and Nehru together. But occupying pride of place was a portrait-sized photograph of ANC leader Chief Albert Luthuli, who regarded my mother as a daughter. On the few occasions when he came to Johannesburg and was invited to stay over, he would refuse and insist on going to 'my daughter's place'. And so the other bedroom would be given to Chief Luthuli, and that is how we got to know him personally: from a young age, we were accustomed to him staying in our flat. The last time he was able to travel, just after he had been banned, he came to Johannesburg from Cape Town. When Madiba took him to stay in a house in Orlando, he said, 'No, you take me to my daughter's house,' and Madiba did.

One strange day, two African guys barged into the flat to rob my mother. When they entered the sitting room, demanding money and other items, they saw Luthuli's picture and asked, 'Who is that?' My mother replied, 'That is my father.' 'How can that be your father?' 'No, it's Chief Luthuli, my father,' she replied, explaining who he was and that he used to stay with us. Suddenly, they said, 'Oh, we apologise, we are very sorry. But don't leave this room. Don't do anything!' Then they left, closing the door, and ran off to rob a neighbouring flat.

Another anecdote concerning about my mother occured in 1949, when the Indo-African riots erupted in Durban and something similar was brewing here in Johannesburg. Efforts made to avert it included some of the gangsters attending meetings at my parents' flat in the middle of the night; one of them may have been Peter Ntithe, who later became the president of the ANC Youth League. When they arrived, my mother would get up, welcome them and offer them refreshments; if they were hungry, she would cook for them.

Our flat was around the corner from Diagonal Street, which is where a lot of the Indian traders had their little shops selling fruits and vegetables. One day, while my mother was shopping, she walked into one of these shops where the shopkeepers knew her. Suddenly, an African guy, a bit of a gangster, grabbed my mother from behind and everyone froze. When my mother turned around to face him, he said, 'Mummy, it's you! Do you recognise me?' She said she did. Then he said, 'You know what? I have been in your house; we had meetings in your house. You woke up; you fed us. You are my mother!' He then said to the shopkeepers, 'Now you people, you must treat my mother properly. This is my mother.' They were all astonished at his reaction. But that is the kind of impact she had.

My mother became politicised very early on, and she participated in demonstrations, even one just before she gave birth to me – one of the largest ever held in Johannesburg by the TIC. It is estimated that about eighty per cent of the adult Indian population of the city in 1939 participated.

When I was seven and my youngest brother only sixteen months old, my mother was imprisoned for participating in the 1946 Passive Resistance Campaign. She had been one of the first to volunteer. As Mandela recorded:

> I often visited the home of Amina Pahad for lunch, and then, suddenly, this charming woman put aside her apron and went to jail

for her beliefs. If I had once questioned the willingness of the Indian community to protest against oppression, I no longer could.[11]

From my mother's recollection, a meeting was held at my parents' flat, and everyone was sitting in discussion while she prepared food and other refreshments. When Dr Dadoo emerged briefly from the meeting for a minute, she asked him, 'Why are you people sitting there and taking so long?' He replied, 'We are trying to get together a group of volunteers who will go to Durban and be part of the Passive Resistance Campaign we are launching.' To which my mother replied, 'That's fine, put my name.' Dr Dadoo asked her, 'And what would Goolam say?' My mother replied, 'No, Goolam won't go to prison. You put my name.' She then suggested that he add Ama Naidoo's name (mother of Indres, Ramnie and Shanthie Naidoo) and that of Miriam Cachalia, Molvi Cachalia's wife. 'Put my Auntie Ouma Bhayat there. Put your sister ...' And several other women were suggested.

The first group of women resisters from Johannesburg included Zaynab Asvat, who put on hold her studies for a medical degree to volunteer, Zohra Bhayat, Zubeida Patel and my mother.

The women travelled to Durban by car, knowing they would go to prison. When that happened, my mother left behind five children, the eldest of whom was twelve. One of my father's nieces, Aisha Saloojee (née Vania), whom we called Bigbhai, came and stayed with us to cook and take care of everything.

Although still very young, Ismail, Aziz and I were quite aware that our mother was in prison and conscious of the fact that she had gone there as a volunteer for the Passive Resistance Campaign. When she returned from Durban, I clearly remember her describing to other adults how white hooligans had physically attacked them when they were pitching their tents on Umbilo Road. Our mother didn't tell us these things directly; we eavesdropped in on her conversations. So I overheard about the ill-treatment she and the other women had endured and the abuse they had suffered at the hands of those white men. But she would just focus on the strength and resilience of all of them as women and how they resisted – not just herself but all of them.

Years later, Judge Jody Kollapen[12] told me that his mother, who at a young

---

11. From Nelson Mandela's autobiography, *Long Walk to Freedom*, quoted in 'The Father of the Nation Has Passed On', Mohamed Saeed, News24, 6 December 2013. Available at https://www.news24.com/news24/xarchive/voices/the-father-of-the-nation-has-passed-on-20180719

age also courted imprisonment in 1946, had spoken admiringly about how my mother took care of her in prison.

During the Passive Resistance Campaign, my mother courted imprisonment twice between 1946 and 1948. During one of these stays in prison, she contracted rheumatism, which rendered her right hand quite dysfunctional and severely restricted the movement in both her elbow joints. But that never stopped her from working, cooking and being constantly active. She was again one of the first to volunteer for the Defiance Campaign and again went to prison in 1952, in spite of being told that this would only make her rheumatism worse.

Ever ready to work and help anyone who needed it, my mother was greatly loved by all our neighbours. During the time we were growing up, almost an entire football team would sleep in our flat – in one bedroom. The next day, she would feed them all – even in the evening – and never complain about it. She had a great love for humanity, which she put into practice without theorising or philosophising about it, and even now, people in that community talk about my mother. Back in India, students who visited my parents at their flat in Bombay still recall her warmth and hospitality.

My mother was even polite to people who did not deserve it. Whenever raids by the Security Police were carried out, our flat was always included. At that time, when they came from Marshall Square – John Vorster Square was built much later – my mother was always very civil. She would welcome them; she would offer them tea or coffee – even if it was four o'clock in the morning. She never changed, even when we were grown up and banned and the Security Police came continuously to the house to harass her and threaten to arrest her children. Every single time, my mother would sit them down and offer them coffee or tea. Then I would quarrel and ask, 'Why are you nice to them?' And she would reply, 'Look, this is not your flat. It's my flat, and I will continue to be nice to people. And you, why are you doing … (the things they would report to her)?' She never, ever lost her humanity, not even when faced with the worst oppressors.

I can see in retrospect how strongly all of that influenced us, increasing our abhorrence of what was going on under apartheid. We grew up in that flat where our parents were already directly involved, where our father was a leader of the Indian Congress. My mother never held any formal positions, but she had a great impact on people. If you read Mandela's biography, he specifically talks about her. She also appears in Sisulu's biography and the

---

12. In 2021, Judge Kollapen was appointed to the Constitutional Court. He began his service the following year.

memoirs of both Kathrada and Ismail Meer. She was highly respected by the Congress movement, and every time we met Mandela after we returned from exile, he always talked about her. He remembered that she was the first non-African person who ever served him food or drink, and he always spoke of her with great love and admiration.

In his book *Memoirs*, Ahmed Kathrada writes:

> Aminabhai was an exceptional person: warm, friendly, always smiling, generous, compassionate and hospitable to a fault. Her hard work and hospitality became legendary among the countless friends, family members and political colleagues – many of whom were strangers – who visited the Pahads from all over South Africa. The generosity, kindness and hospitality of the Pahad family were unprecedented. There was seldom a mealtime when non-family members did not arrive unexpectedly; [then], as if by magic, an ever-smiling Aminabhai would rustle up enough delicious victuals to feed us all.[13]

My mother was an excellent cook, and even today, people who ate her food still talk about her cooking. Every day, she made sure that all of us had our breakfast, that our clothes were clean and ironed, that we were washed and ready and that we went off to school on time. When we came back in the afternoon, there was always food for us, even if there were a lot of other people she was feeding. And she was extremely active in assisting the Indian Congress, going out with Kathrada and Suliman 'Babla' Saloojee to collect money from people in the country towns.

She was very friendly with people like Albertina Sisulu, Adelaide Tambo, Doreen Motshabi and Rica Hodgson. despite never having attended a formal school. Her command of the English language was weak, although she could manage reading and writing in Gujarati, her mother tongue. In spite of that, she always managed to communicate with people from all backgrounds.

Another story reveals a lot about my mother's attitude towards other people. In August 1956, she was one of the women who marched to the Union Buildings. Afterward, I remember her saying that she had seen a white person opening the window and looking at them sympathetically and perhaps even trying to wave to them, which told her that not all white people are bad. We knew that also because Bram Fischer, Joe Slovo, Rica Hodgson,

---

13. Ahmed Kathrada, *Memoirs* (Cape Town: Zebra Press, 2004), p. 71.

Jack Hodgson and Michael Harmel, for example, were regular visitors to our flat. It has always stuck in my mind that even in the midst of that historical event, my mother could find someone who displayed a sense of humanity: a small but significant insight that was an important element of her experience.

That same attitude applied when she participated in the Defiance Campaign. After her arrest and time in Boksburg prison, she would tell stories about the ill-treatment and how they had to flush the toilet to obtain water to brush their teeth. Still, she always found something positive to say about people as she continually looked for the best in every human being, even the worst oppressor.

I must emphasise that my mother tried to instil in us her great love for humanity, no matter what colour a person's skin or the religion to which they belonged: Hindu, Christian, Muslim or atheist. We were brought up to deal with people on the basis that everyone is the same, for we were part of the resistance, involved in the freedom struggle, and that was what mattered to my mother, not race. Her commitment to the struggle was consummate, thus informing a prominent role in the development of my own world view.

Interestingly, although my mother conformed to the demands of the culture in which she had been raised, she was also able to look outside these customs and see that change was necessary. Although uncomplaining, she was by no means a doormat. She was a wonderful mother-in-law and would side with a daughter-in-law against her son if she felt that he was wrong. She accepted her sons' choice of wives wholeheartedly, regardless of race, colour, creed or nationality.

My mother joined her husband, two of her sons (Aziz and I) and her granddaughter Yasmin in London for a while, even though this was a hard decision. She was especially fond of her first two grandchildren, Yasmin and Shehnaaz, and treated them as the daughters she had never had. Sadly, half of her family remained behind when she decided to leave South Africa on an exit permit. The Security Police forced such decisions onto people who were not allowed to come and go freely.

In London, my mother approved of the arrangements agreed on in the flat rented by her husband, where all the men had to share in the cleaning, laundry, cooking, shopping and other housework. When this system was developed, there were only men and a very young Yasmin staying there, and since even our combined incomes could not pay for a helper, there was not much choice.

Although my mother accepted her husband's decision to have a long-term, openly acknowledged mistress, she confided to my wife that it hurt her terribly to see him in love with another woman. She said that neither Goolam nor Ingrid realised that although they respected her wisdom and understanding, the process was excruciating when they came to her to mediate their problems.

In London, my mother would insist on serving all the young people at the table, even though they begged her to sit down and eat with everyone else. She would say, 'I am too old to change now. You youngsters, though, you must change. You must help in the house and be faithful to your wives.'

Eventually, my parents decided to move to Bombay (now Mumbai), where, tragically, in 1973, my mother was struck by a car and killed, an unbearable loss for our extended family and friends. Dr Dadoo organised a memorial meeting for her at his home in North London, during which Robert Resha spoke in glowing terms about her. On 20 April 2006, Amina Pahad was posthumously awarded the National Order of Luthuli in Silver by President Mbeki. Ama Naidoo received that award at the same time. My mother's memory lives on, never to be extinguished.

༈

My father, Goolam Pahad, was the other primary influence on our lives growing up. He was a stable and reliable presence, often in the background, and he loved, honoured and respected our mother, working constantly to provide for our family.

Goolam was also a genuine humanitarian without racial prejudice. Deeply committed to the Indian Congress and later the Congress Alliance, he held leading political positions in the TIC and SAIC (South African Indian Congress), spoke at meetings and rallies and was particularly good at raising money and advising people on financial issues. He always managed to earn enough money to feed everyone who came to eat at our house, day after day. He was also calm and even-tempered and prepared to listen, discuss and offer advice, when asked.

My father's political activity and generosity, combined with my mother's hospitality and cooking, ensured that, from an early age, we all came into regular contact with some of the greatest political minds of the period.

My grandfather on my father's side had come to South Africa from India in the 1880s, via Mauritius. He and his wife lived for a while in Durban, where my father's elder sister Aisha was born. When the family later returned to India, Aisha stayed in South Africa, where she married Mohammed Amin Patel, the family of whom I will describe in more detail below, as we are still close to many of them. Mohammed Amin had also been born and raised in South Africa. See the family tree on page 18 and 19.

Aisha and Mohammed had five daughters: Zubeida (whom we called 'Apa') died in 1959. The second, Amina (whom we called 'Ben'), married Dawood Saloojee, and they had two children: Anver, who married Zuby, and Yasmin. The third daughter, Fowzia, married Dawood Karodia; the fourth was Zaibie (whom we called Goribhai), and she married Hamid Bhyat and had three children with him: Farouk Mohammed (who married Fatima Bhikhoo), Zaheer (who married Alice Sweetnam) and Shamim (who married (Dr) Mohammed Bhikhoo, brother of Fatima). The fifth daughter, Sharifa, married Yusuf Docrat, and they had two children, Rashid and Zarina.

After Aisha's death, that same Mohammed Amin Patel married my father's third sister, Amina, and they had four children: Farida (who married Yakoub Docrat, Yusuf's brother); Feriel (who married Dr Goga); Farouk, who died young; and Abdul (who married Rabia). Abdul and Rabia's family live near Durban, and their three children are Mohammed Amin, Ahmed and Anisa. After Rabia's death, Abdul married Rukshana.

My father's second sister married I. M. Vania, and they had two sons, Amin and Kader, and three daughters: Fatima (whom we called Goribhai), Aisha (whom we called Bigbhai and who married a Saloojee from Rustenburg), and Zayboon. His fourth sister (whom we called Nallifoi) married I. A. Vania of Réunion Island, and they had no children.

My father, Goolam Hoosein Ismail Pahad, was born in 1912 in Kholvad, India, in the state of Gujarat. He came to South Africa as a child in 1919 to join his father, who had a shop in Klerksdorp. At the age of ten, Goolam was sent back to India to school, where he stayed until his father died in 1926. During this period, he met Yusuf Dadoo, who would become his close friend later in life in South Africa and then in London. Dr Dadoo had an enormous influence on our family. In 1925, Dr Dadoo and my father met Gandhi, who had experienced the violence and humiliation of racism in South Africa in 1893–1894 as a young lawyer. They were both impressed by the philosophy of *satyagraha* (non-violent resistance to unjust laws).

After the death of his father in 1926, Goolam's elder sister Aisha asked him to return to South Africa to help in their shop in Bloemhof. There, he worked for three pounds a month, which he sent home to his mother and two sisters in Kholvad. Aisha also gave him food, clothing and one shilling-a-week pocket money.

When Aisha died in 1929, her husband left Bloemhof for Cape Town, and my father Goolam took responsibility for his two nieces, Zaibie and Sharifa. In 1930, my father returned to Klerksdorp to work for Ahmed 'Dadiseth' Tilly, my mother's father. And there he met my mother, who was just twelve years old at the time. She was soon to return with her father to India when his business suffered during The Great Depression.

Over the next few years, my father worked very hard for several Indian families and proved to have sound business sense. Gradually, he saved up enough money to open his own business. He was also popular and sociable and adept at cricket and football.

When Gandhi launched his passive resistance campaign in 1933, Goolam Pahad went to India to participate and met Gandhi again, who advised him to return to South Africa, explaining that militant youth were needed. Prior to returning, he married my mother, Amina Tilly, that same year. In 1934, he was elected secretary of the Kholvad Madressa back in Johannesburg.

Both of my grandfathers came from the small village of Kholvad in the Indian state of Gujarat, near to the town of Surat. The Muslims who had come to South Africa from India, especially from that part of Gujarat, became mainly traders and shopkeepers. When they first arrived in South Africa, they tended to associate themselves in terms of their village of origin. As this too applied to people from Kholvad, they formed an association called the Kholvad Madressa, which, in 2015, celebrated its 100th birthday and now has several thousand members. When Goolam and Amina Pahad returned to South Africa in 1934, he was a member of the Kholvad Madressa in the then-Transvaal until 1961, when he again left the country. From 1943–1958, he was its general secretary; in 1959, he was elected its president.

Since both our parents came from Kholvad, we were identified as Kholvadians. Dr Dadoo was also very active in the Kholvad Madressa, which raised money to improve conditions in the home village, including installing electricity and building a secondary school there. In 1942, the Kholvad Madressa built an impressive block of flats in Johannesburg, Kholvad House, just across the street from Orient House, designed by a brilliant young architect, Lionel 'Rusty' Bernstein. Rusty and his wife Hilda were already at that time very active in the Communist Party of South Africa. As mentioned earlier, Flat 13, Kholvad House, later became the home of Ahmed Kathrada and, like 11 Orient House, another unofficial meeting place for leaders of the Congress movement.

My father was a great activist and a leader of the TIC, and he was well-known amongst all the Indians, not only political activists. If somebody asked my name and I said, 'Essop Pahad,' they would ask, 'Which Pahad?' When I replied, 'Goolam Pahad,' there was immediate recognition – partly because of his work in the Indian Congress but also because he became an expert in company law, along with Molvi Cachalia. Although he had never been to a formal English school, his spoken English was fine, but he was not able to write fluently in it. After the Group Areas Act was passed in 1950, my father and Molvi became increasingly proficient in dealing with problems resulting from the Group Areas Act.

As a result, many people came to my father's flat seeking his help, but he didn't make any money because he was giving free advice. I don't think anyone had heard of a consultant in those days. People would just come to the flat and consult with my father at any time of day, any day of the week. The same thing was happening with Molvi Cachalia at his house. Of course, eventually they had to advise people on who to hire as a lawyer, which was essential if they needed to go to court. If people wanted to liquidate their shops, they would come to my father and he would advise them how to do it to best and save what little they had and protect themselves. He became an expert in those processes.

But Goolam had to work, and his main job was as a travelling salesman for several firms; he also worked in finance. As a salesman, he would go around the countryside taking orders, which were big enough to enable him to live a relatively comfortable life where his children didn't have to do without food or clothing. My parents were also able to feed any number of people – really large numbers – who would arrive at any time to take both lunch and supper, seven days a week.

Meanwhile, my father was already a leader of the Indian Congresses: the TIC and the SAIC. By the time of the 1946 Passive Resistance Campaign, although he was not a resister, he was part of the meetings between the Indian Congress and the ANC leadership. He was also in contact with the Mandelas, the Sisulus and the Tambos, who would always come to the flat, as did Robbie Resha, Tom Nkobi and many others.

The Defiance Campaign of 1952, in which thousands voluntarily invited imprisonment by breaking unjust apartheid laws, had a monumental impact on the ANC and the Indian Congresses. It laid the base for the ANC to become a genuine mass political movement and sealed the Congress Alliance led by the ANC and included the South African Indian Congress, the South African Coloured Peoples Organisation, and the Congress of Democrats – a small group of courageous whites who joined the resistance, many of them communists. The Alliance also gave impetus to the formation of the South African Congress of Trade Unions (SACTU).

Goolam Pahad was a member of the SAIC delegation (rebuffed by General Smuts in February 1946) who took the decision to initiate a passive resistance campaign. He served on the Passive Resistance Council and, from 1945 to 1960, was an executive member of the SAIC, primarily concerned with the Finance Committee. He was also a member of the SAIC delegation that met the ANC Executive Committee in 1946, laying the foundation for the 'Three Doctors' Pact' in 1947, signed by doctors Y. M. Dadoo (TIC), G. M. Naicker (NIC) and A. B. Xuma (ANC). Goolam was also a delegate to the meeting between the ANC and SAIC leaders following the 1949 Durban Indo-African riots in which many Africans and some Indians lost their lives.

In 1955, my father met a Mr McAlpine, with whom he planned to launch a credit card system. Back then, there was nothing but Diners' Club in Southern Africa, so my father raised £10,000 and began setting up the operating system for 'Global Express'. As the director of the business, he opened an office in Eloff Street and was the only Indian with an office in the city centre at that time. By 1958, the basis for the credit card system had been established and trialled throughout South Africa with a similar system based on cooperatives organised in Swaziland. Slowly, the idea began to pick up trust and credibility. But in March 1960, Goolam was arrested, and those who had signed up cancelled their contracts; the Swaziland scheme also failed.

My father's arrest, alongside other Congress leaders, was during the State of Emergency in 1960, and he was detained for four months. In 1961, he left South Africa to settle in London, following Dr Dadoo, who had already been asked by the SAIC and ANC in 1960 to go there to develop and intensify international support for the national liberation movement.

So on both sides, our parents inculcated in us a great love for the liberation movement, mainly the Indian Congress, but also the ANC, and a real hostility towards any kind of racism and sectarianism or religious bigotry. We grew up in that kind of atmosphere and didn't have the racial prejudices that a lot of Indian families had – even some of our own friends – against

Africans and Coloureds. Neither were we prejudiced, as some were, against Hindus, Christians or Jews.

Aziz and I were fortunate to have had regular contact with several extraordinary people who had a strong and positive influence over us: Dr Yusuf Dadoo, Nelson Mandela, Walter Sisulu, O. R. Tambo, Molvi and Yusuf Cachalia, and Ahmed Kathrada. Yusuf Dadoo was, for us, our guide and great leader. For me, Ahmed Kathrada, who was nearer to us in age, was a real mentor. He was like my mother's eldest son and, for us, like our eldest brother. Although he also came from Schweizer-Reneke, he is not related to us in any way, but my mother helped to bring him up when he came to stay in Johannesburg.

The Defiance Campaign consisted of many meetings, protests, demonstrations and other political actions, and many young people were attracted by these heady events and activities. Thirteen years old at the time, I joined several demonstrations, including those demanding the release of leaders on trial. I remember marching to Dr Dadoo's house in End Street, Doornfontein, a few kilometres from the magistrates' court. During those demonstrations, I always tried to walk behind Ida Mntwana, a leader of the Federation of South African Women (FEDSAW). She used to lead the singing of the ANC protest and revolutionary songs, and her beautiful melodious voice both attracted and enchanted me. I guess, in today's language, I was a groupie.

Participating in those demonstrations, protests and meetings enabled me to learn ANC freedom songs, even though I did not know the meaning of the words. When I was about fifteen or sixteen, Kathrada helped found the Central branch of the TIYC, and two of its first recruits were Aziz and me.

My first year in high school (Standard 6: now Grade 8) was at Johannesburg Indian High School, the only high school for Indians in this city. All the teachers were white, and one I remember was a Mr Brodie, a genial, gentle soul. The school was a rough, tough environment in which we were involved in a few gang fights. My elder brother Ismail had also attended that school before me and had a reputation to be feared. If older boys tried to bully me, I would threaten to call him, which helped a lot and put paid to that kind of intimidation.

Then, just before starting Standard 7, we were informed that we had to continue our studies at Booysens Indian High School, a temporary measure intended to pave the way for compelling our parents to send us to school in Lenasia. As an integral part of the famous Group Areas Act, designed to prevent Indians from living and trading in the segregated parts of Johannesburg to which they had previously been confined, Lenasia had been created for Indian settlement. Earlier, in 1953, the apartheid government had passed the Bantu Education Act since, in the words of Dr Hendrik Verwoerd, Africans should not seek pastures beyond being 'the hewers of wood and drawers of water'. This legislation was extremely damaging to future generations of Black South Africans. However, the move to compel us to move to Lenasia proved a blessing in disguise, for the TIC, which had led the struggle against the Group Areas Act, mobilised Indian parents to resist and set up an alternative school, the Central Indian High School (CIHS), which later became known as 'the Congress School'.

My father, a leader of the TIC, was in the forefront of that decision, and Ahmed Kathrada became the secretary of the parents' association. The CIHS was funded entirely by donations and school fees, but no student was turned away if their parents could not afford to pay. When it opened, we had a Standard 8, which included me, a Standard 7, which included Aziz, and a Standard 6. Standards 9 and 10 were added later. My brothers Nassim and Zuneid also attended the CIHS, which, in my view, remains one of the most remarkable schools in the history of South Africa. I doubt that we will ever see another school of its ilk.

Michael Harmel was the first principal of the CIHS. He wrote *Fifty Fighting Years*,[14] a history of the SA Communist Party, under the name A. Lerumo, and was a pre-eminent member of the Congress Alliance and a leading theoretician of the Communist Party. As a setwork book, he gave us *The Story of an African Farm* by Olive Schreiner and took us carefully through the whole thing. My Afrikaans teacher was Molly Fischer, wife of Bram, who would invite pupils to their home to use the swimming pool if they wished, though few could swim. Another teacher called Mrs Palmer invited matric pupils to her home in Emmarentia for a farewell party. Such racial mixing was a new experience for all but the most highly politicised students. Molly Fischer took over as principal from Michael Harmel.

Our history teacher was Alfred Hutchinson, a leader of the ANC who wrote the book *The Road to Ghana*.[15] He taught us two syllabuses: the first one we had to know to pass matric; the other was the truth from an African and anti-imperialist perspective. I remember writing an essay when I was in either Standard 9 or 10. Instead of the 'First Kaffir War', 'Second Kaffir War', I wrote the 'First African War', the 'Second African War', through which

---

14. A. Lerumo, *Fifty Fighting Years: The Communist Party of South Africa, 1921–1971* (London: Ikululeko, 1971).
15. Alfred Hutchinson, *The Road to Ghana* (London: Victor Gollancz, 1960).

Hutchinson struck with his pen and wrote in big letters, 'KAFFIR, KAFFIR, KAFFIR.' When I asked, 'What are you doing?' He replied, 'Look here, don't come and try to impress me. You have to write these people's exams, and if you put the 'African War', you are not going to pass. They call it the "Kaffir War".'

Our science teacher was Diza Putini, who was a role model, a leader of the ANC Youth League and later of the ANC. In 1957, when I was in matric, I was already an executive committee member of the Transvaal Indian Youth Congress. There was another group called the Youth Action Committee, which was made up of the TIYC, the ANC Youth League, a Student Organisation from the University of the Witwatersrand (Wits), some Coloured youth, and white youth from the Congress of Democrats. I was present at a few of those meetings. On one occasion after the lunch break, we were talking amongst ourselves and returned late to the classroom, where Diza was writing some formulas on the blackboard. We walked in like big shots and sat down at the back. Then Diza said, 'Those who have come late must leave.' We pretended not to hear. He said it a second time and then turned around, very angry, and shouted: 'I said, get out!' He kicked us out.

The next afternoon, Diza and I met in the ANC office, where he called me over and offered me a cigarette, which I took. Then he said:

> Now, listen to me. When we are in the Congress office, we are together. When we smoke a cigarette here, we are together. When we sit in the meeting, we are together. When you are in my classroom, I am the teacher. And never again will you do what you did.

And I replied, 'Yes, sir; yes sir.' And he said, 'So here we are fine. Now smoke a cigarette.' Those are the calibre of people we had as teachers.

Later, when we were in Standard 9, my bookkeeping teacher was Dan Tloome, a leader of both the ANC and the South African Communist Party (SACP). In Standard 8, our mathematics teacher was Duma Nokwe, who was about to become the first African lawyer in South Africa. Then we had an English teacher called Hazel Weiler, who later married Hutchinson, our history teacher. After meeting at the CIHS, they went into exile in Ghana, where they married (their marriage would have been illegal in South Africa because of the 'Immorality' Act). Later, they lived in Brighton in the UK, where Hutchinson read for an MA in African History at Sussex University. Our friendship rekindled there in later years when I was reading for a PhD.

Then there were people who came later, like Moosajee, who was very active in the TIC. He took over as principal from Thandaray, another leader of that organisation, who had succeeded Molly Fischer. After I left, Can Temba, the famous short story writer who had worked with many great journalists at *Drum* magazine, also taught there.

Amongst those who attended the Congress School were Abdul Bham and Abdul Minty, both lifelong ANC activists; Ebrahim Adam; Amrit Bhowan, an exceptionally talented sportsman and student; Yusuf 'Joe' Kajee, who became an underground cadre of the ANC; and Jivan Ramjee, who became one of the organisers of the annual Gandhi walk in Lenasia.

One day in 1956, the Security Police arrived to arrest Hutchinson at school while he was teaching us history. During the process, some students snuck out and stuffed paper in the petrol tank of the police car so it wouldn't start. Later, when I went to visit him at the Fort, Hutchinson told me a very interesting story. The Security Police had arrested him for treason, like many others who would become part of the Treason Trial, and put him in the car, which they eventually managed to start. While travelling from Fordsburg, those white Special Branch people asked Hutchinson, 'What are you doing here? *Wat doen jy met die Koolie kinders?*' And he replied, 'I'm teaching history.' 'What history are you teaching?' He said, 'I'm teaching them about the Anglo-Boer War.' He started talking to them about it, going into great detail. So engrossed were they in the discussion that they forgot they had arrested him for treason. They were so angry with the British in the Anglo-Boer War that all of their anger was directed at them and what had happened and how the Afrikaners had been treated. Only when they got to the Fort and had to get out of the car did they remember what they had been doing – arresting a man for High Treason. Some other pupils from the school also visited Hutch in jail.

One can assess from the quality of the teaching staff how unique Central Indian High School was – they were nearly all people in the Congress movement. It was also the only school in South Africa with a racially mixed staff: whites, Africans and Indians; and a range of religious beliefs: Muslims, Hindus, Christians and atheists. The teachers believed in what they were doing, but they never knew if they would get paid because, although people were donating and the parents who could afford it were paying fees, there was not always enough money to pay full salaries.

I still have a copy of the programme for the school end-of year event of December 1955, which includes a lot of songs and dances and a prize-giving by Father Trevor Huddleston. This was followed by a play, written and directed by Michael Harmel and Alfred Hutchinson, entitled *2005 – A Glimpse Into the Future*. In creating this multiracial future and supporting the school, the staff and their friends in the Congress movement involved their children in the production.

Here is the remarkable cast of the play:

Sipho	Boysie Makwana
Eileen	Barbara Harmel
William	Mark Weinberg
Tandi	Memory Mphahlele
Marie	Ilse Fischer
Peter	Max Sisulu
Ismail	Aziz Pahad
Nirmala	Bommie Govender
Tom	Larry Anderson
Roonie	Khairoonisha Patel

Announcer: Toni Bernstein
Chorus: Vincent Makhubu, Tembi Ncube, Sheila Weinberg, Simon Motaung, Madiba Mandela, Mancy Molife, Obed Ramurula.

Of course, we knew that our teachers were ANC leaders. While I was in Standard 8, there were a lot of political activities in the TIYC, and I was helping to distribute leaflets and such things. Sometimes my friends didn't understand what was going on, and one or two of them would say, 'What's wrong with him? He thinks his natives are cleverer than we are.' But those young Indian kids who went to 'the Congress School', many of whom were not very political, interacted with people like Duma, Alfred and Diza, which had a profound impact on them; they learnt to respect Black people at that school.

While still at CIHS, I attended meetings organised by the ANC, TIC and TIYC mobilising for the historic Congress of the People (COP) in Kliptown, which adopted the Freedom Charter in 1955: a far-sighted, advanced and progressive document which still serves as the framework guiding ANC policies.

In the fifties, the ANC office was in the basement of Minty's shop on the corner of Market and West Streets in Ferreirastown, very close to Kholvad

House and Orient House, which made it easy for us to spend a lot of time there. The night before the opening of the COP, a delegation arrived by bus from Natal, despite attempts by the racist regime to prevent them from doing so. As there was no sleeping accommodation, they slept on the floor without complaint. But they were also very hungry. Greatly moved by their resilience and discipline, I went home and, with the assistance of my mother, took them as much food as possible to relieve their hunger pangs.

It remains a badge of honour that, with the backing of my parents, I attended the COP – as a helper, not a delegate, for I was only sixteen. In recalling that time, I still don't know who gave me a lift to Kliptown or ensured that I returned home safely. My most lasting memory of that extraordinary event was the reaction of the delegates, including my parents, who remained calm in the face of the racist invaders, armed to the teeth with automatic weapons and surrounding them. During this most vicious provocation, the delegates sang freedom songs and adopted the Charter, clause by clause.

In my matric year, I failed Afrikaans and repeated it twice before succeeding. Prior to 1960, universities such as Wits, the University of Cape Town (UCT) and Natal still accepted a number of Black students. But in 1959, the apartheid regime passed the ironically dubbed Extension of University Education Act to prevent Black students from enrolling at 'white' universities and also dividing Black students by ethnicity. The Act contained the provision that Black students already registered would be allowed to complete their studies. Aziz and I registered as special students at Wits in 1959, which enabled us to do some courses that were not recognised for degree purposes. It also meant that we could apply and be accepted as full-time students.

I started my university studies proper in 1960, and because I had been there earlier, I already knew a lot of the Black students. Our political activities were enhanced by two leaders of the TIYC: Essop Jassat (brother of Abdulhai), studying medicine, and Herbie Pillay, studying for a law degree. (His sister Harlene later married Abdulhai.)

The year 1960 was a turning point in the history of the resistance movement in South Africa, for it was the year in which the ANC and the Pan

---

16. People have suggested for a while that South Africa's name be changed. The following are pull-out quotes from Stephen Grootes' 13 June 2017 interview with PAC General-Secreatry Narius Moloto on 702: 'Azania is the original name of the southern tip of Africa and the research by Professor Es'kia Mphahlele clearly reveals that the real name of South Africa is actually Azania; The name Azania is derived from the term 'Azanj', which is Arabic; It has its own historic referral rather than geographical ... This country did not have a real name, rather... a geographical name. Available at https://www.702.co.za/articles/260287/why-the-pac-wants-south-africa-renamed-azania

Africanist Congress (PAC) of Azania[16] were banned. Preceding the bannings were the Sharpeville massacre on 21 March 1960 and the declaration of a state of emergency, in which thousands were arrested, including my father.

The CPSA had been banned in 1950, but some of its leaders resuscitated it in 1953 as the SACP; however, they did not announce its existence until the aftermath of Sharpeville. When the ANC was banned in 1960, Aziz and I were involved in the laborious process of helping to reproduce leaflets by cyclostyle[17] in Ophirton. But the leadership decided against their distribution, and we were instructed to burn them. In 1961, we were again involved in the distribution of leaflets, this time announcing the existence of the SACP.

The PAC, formed in 1959 as a break-away group from the ANC, had hurriedly organised a number of anti-pass demonstrations, jumping the gun on the well-planned ANC anti-pass campaign. Robert Mangaliso Sobukwe, a lecturer in Zulu at Wits, was the leader of the PAC. He was quite popular amongst some sections of the African people, including African students.

Although the PAC's plan for demonstrations in places like Orlando went off like a damp squib, in Sharpeville, their call for people to gather at the police station and dispose of the hated *dompas* attracted a reasonable crowd. Tragically, and without proper warning, the trigger-itchy police opened fire on the demonstrators, including children, killing at least sixty-nine people. Most of the dead and injured had been shot in the back. This unprovoked massacre caused outrage in the international community and gave impetus to the ANC and PAC turning to armed struggle. But the PAC, with its slogan 'No bail, no fine', was left leaderless, as many, like Sobukwe, were in prison. So it was left to the ANC to take the initiative in mobilising the people, with Chief Luthuli publicly burning his passbook in defiance of the apartheid system.

At Wits, the Sharpeville killings led to intense, robust and heated debates about the revolutionary merits of the ANC and PAC and the role and place of Coloureds, Indians and whites in the struggle. At the same time, the intensified repression and increasingly draconian legislation made many people angry but also fearful of the might of the police state.

It should be noted that the opening sentence of the Freedom Charter, 'South Africa belongs to all who live in it, black and white', was anathema to

---

17. The cyclostyle duplicating process is a form of stencil copying. A stencil is cut on wax or glazed paper by using a pen-like object with a small rowel or spur-wheel on its tip. A large number of small short lines are cut out in the glazed paper, removing the glaze with the spur-wheel, then ink is applied. It was invented in the later 19th century by David Gestetner, who named it cyclostyle after a drawing tool he used. https://en.wikipedia.org/wiki/Cyclostyle_(copier).

the leaders, members and followers of the PAC. During this time, the Central Intelligence Agency (CIA) was busy in South Africa, creating and supporting alternatives to split and confuse the genuine liberation movements. One result of that was the PAC, which was formed in the US Information Service (USIS) in Johannesburg. Like the Liberal Party and the Trotskyite New Unity Movement, the PAC was anti-communist.

That a number of African students at Wits were hostile to the ANC and in support of the PAC did not sit well with me, so I went to Tata Sisulu, who had always shown the greatest respect for the Transvaal Indian Youth Congress. He thought we were one of the best-organised groups in South Africa, which we were, and he could give us any work to do and we would do it. So I vented my frustration and anger to Uncle Walter, who said to me, 'Tell me something. Have you ever asked them to join the ANC?' And I said, 'No, but why are you asking me this question?' And he said, 'You see, what you are doing is correct. Argue, quarrel, defend the movement. But with African students, don't ask them to join the ANC.' I asked, 'Why?' And he replied:

You see, if you ask them to join the ANC, they will think, 'This ANC, who is running this ANC? These Indians, these whites, these communists. Why don't the Africans themselves come and ask us to join?' So you defend Congress policy. But don't ask them to join the ANC.

That compelling advice.

But we agreed that something had to be done, and without delay, so I agreed to organise a meeting with the help of Martin Mabiletse, who was from Alexandra Township and was later to graduate as a lawyer. The meeting was predominantly attended by African students, and Duma Nokwe came and spoke to them. Duma was the first Black South African advocate, highly respected for a razor-sharp mind and for his logical approach in argumentation, accompanied by a profound understanding of politics. We just sat there and listened to him as he engaged with his audience. It was a good tactic and helped, especially with those students who were not yet committed to the PAC. There were quite a few who were unsure because the PAC message was quite appealing, with slogans like 'Africa for the Africans!' 'We do things for ourselves!' 'The ANC is too soft!' This approach was particularly attractive to students in the face of enormous repression and oppression – and one must remember that the ANC and the Communist Party had already been banned.

There were many white students who opposed apartheid, the overwhelming majority being liberals, but there were also racist students, most of whom were from the engineering faculty. They were vicious and would threaten to attack our demonstrations and protest meetings with violence. At one demonstration on the steps of the university, some of them threw stink bombs at us from the rooftop.

About ninety-five per cent of the white students who were good friends with Aziz and I and who went to parties with us, were Jewish. To mention a few: Marcel Berlins, who is now a media law expert in England; Martin Channock, who became a professor at Monash University in Australia; Adam Kuper, a professor of anthropology; Harry Rayjack, who was a professor of Law at Sussex University; Richard Kuper, who became a sociologist; and the Polansky brothers, who were outstanding students. Later was Robin Cohen, who became a professor at UCT, and his brother Stan. We were close friends with David Adler, who is very involved in education here in South Africa with non-governmental organisations (NGOs). He was CEO of the Independent Examinations Board (IEB) and instrumental in setting up the South African Qualifications Authority. David is the nephew of Ray Harmel (née Adler), a revolutionary trade unionist, lifelong communist and ANC member who was married to Michael Harmel, our former CIHS principal. Another friend was Jeff Lamb (who I do not think was Jewish), who married Barbara Harmel, Michael's daughter, who later worked at the World Bank. There were also some progressive white students who did not belong to any particular organisation. For example, in NUSAS, I remember Saul Bastomsky, who later went to Australia. He always played a very progressive role regarding the international positions and affiliations of NUSAS.

Another of our student contemporaries was Dennis Brutus, founder of the South African Non-Racial Olympic Committee (SANROC). He also spent time on Robben Island and later, while living in exile in London, spearheaded the international campaign to boycott apartheid sports and sportspersons. Later, Sam Ramsamy took over the leadership of SANROC, and under his guidance, the campaign to boycott apartheid sports made great strides and was hugely successful.

I knew Dennis from when he came to Johannesburg in 1958 or 1959 to kick-start SANROC. Ahmed Kathrada had instructed me to work with Dennis because of my great love of sports, especially football, so he and I formed SANROC in Johannesburg, bringing in Theo Mthembu and the Reverend Sigamoney, who ministered a little church in Vrededorp. Both men were active in football administration, and we started developing support for SANROC, mobilising amongst the Black players, sporting coaches and managers.

When Dennis was banned and wanted to stand for the Student Representative Council (SRC), I became his election agent because he couldn't attend or speak at meetings. We used the fact that he was banned as a mobilising point to get votes for him.

In 1960, in addition to my political activities in the TIYC and at Wits – and my involvement with Dynamos, who were emerging as a powerful football club – I fell in love with the card game Bridge. Instead of attending lectures and reading books, I spent a great deal of my time playing it, the upshot of which was that I failed my first year, passing only two subjects: Political Science and Classical Life and Thought. I tried to rationalise my failure in terms of my political activities and playing Bridge, but I didn't manage to convince even myself.

At Wits, we attended Marxist classes with a select number of trusted students. I remember Harold Wolpe was one of the lecturers. The banned Dennis Brutus also attended, as did Gerald Ludi, a white student. Dennis Brutus had been detained, and when the Security Police were interrogating him, they let slip that they knew who attended those meetings. So we started thinking: who among us would have given information to the Security Police? Some of us honed in on a particular white student (not Gerald Ludi) and organised a party at his house. When, during the party, a few of our group went to check out his bedroom, we decided it wasn't him. That was a shame because I think he knew he was under suspicion, as people kept away from him. Indeed, that showed how sometimes innocent people could be unjustly accused of working for the other side.

We should have looked more closely at the other people who attended that Marxist class, but we didn't. We only found out that Gerald Ludi *had* been spying on us when several people were arrested, including Bram Fischer, and when the Security Police were questioning people like Anne Nicholson and Sylvia Neame. It then became clear that Ludi was an informer, and a lot of things began to fall into place. But by that time, it was too late; the movement had sent him to the World Youth Festival in Moscow. Whether he had been recruited before we became friends or after he got arrested is unclear, but Gerald Ludi became a senior Security Police officer.[18]

I related that anecdote to make the point that the Security Police were very active in recruiting students to spy for them. But since our political work at university, except for the Marxist class, was essentially student politics, there was nothing they could do but keep a constant eye on us. Of course, the

---

18. Note the glaring typo in the headline of this *New York Times* article about Ludi:
https://www.nytimes.com/1964/11/27/archives/secret-agent-q018-unmasked-a-vetwoerd-spy-security-branch.html

African Resistance Movement was also recruiting at the university, and I presume they were also monitoring students. I was not too concerned because, speaking for myself, what we were doing was quite open.

In addition to the South African Security Service, there were people from the United States on university campuses trying to unearth information about student activists. In my view – at least in some cases – they were working for the CIA. Regardless of who they worked for, they were told who the student leaders were, and I was one. Their main concern was the South African Communist Party and its relationship with the Congresses. But of course, by that time, the organisations had been banned, so it was quite easy to ask: 'But the Communist Party is banned, so why are you asking questions about the Communist Party?' It was already clear at that time that intelligence agencies outside South Africa were very interested in determining the role and place and influence of the South African Communist Party within the national liberation movement.

Overall, I think student politics helped us gain a better understanding of strategy, assisted us in learning about mobilising other students and sharpened our tools of analysis.

Regarding the international situation, we had our differences, which made it essential to articulate our position clearly. We from the Congress were supportive of the World Federation of Democratic Youth and the International Union of Students; the others supported various organisations set up by the CIA after a period of unity following World War 2.

The National Union of South African Students was essentially an organisation of white students primarily interested in protecting the interests of white students, which raised the question about the kind of organisations it was worth working with and to what purpose. There had to be a shift from focusing only on issues of academic freedom towards building a broader base amongst white students against apartheid and racism. In the view of many of us, NUSAS did offer the opportunity for that kind of work.

So to summarise, the issues went beyond student politics. Sometimes, because we were dealing with the policies of the ANC and PAC, we were grappling with important matters of revolutionary struggle. This assisted us in developing and defining more clearly our political approaches and consciousness, which was vital then because we had to deal with a wide variety of people at various levels of political understanding.

One of the things that always kept me on track and prepared to fight against all forms of racism was seeing grown African men being arrested for not having a pass. As a kid, that really pained me. They would be handcuffed one to the other and made to sit in full view of the public, even on extremely hot days – sitting on the pavement until such time that the police had finished their raid in the particular area. I couldn't think of anything more humiliating for a person – and then they could also lose their jobs and face other troubles. I was glad that a lot of the ANC campaigns were focused on fighting the Pass Laws.

As I grew older, I had many arguments with the police. Fortunately for me, they never beat me up. But when they were arresting someone, I would try to intervene: 'Why are you doing that? What are you doing?' And I would ask the people who had been arrested: 'Are you working here? Give me your name.' And then I would go and phone their employers. Of course, the white police didn't like this at all, but fortunately, they only threatened to arrest me (which they never did) or beat me up. There was a point beyond which one couldn't go, and I would not push past that point.

Quite a few of our student friends at Wits lived in Douglas Smith House, a university residence for Black students. When they came to visit us at our flat, they would have to go home after curfew, which was specially imposed on Africans who were not allowed to be on the streets after a certain time. This was extremely humiliating. Sometimes, we couldn't give them a lift because the family car was unavailable, and they would have to find their own way back. Then, we would have to write them a letter like this one:

> To whom it may concern, Sir …
> Please excuse Mr Tom Madumo … (No, you don't say 'Mr'.) Please excuse Tom Madumo for being out after 9 p.m. He is late (or) He is violating the curfew (I can't remember the exact words) because he was working for us.

One had to write the letter in such a way that the white policeman wouldn't get upset and think, 'Who is this fellow?' What made our blood boil was that we had to write such a letter at all – just to invite someone to our house – that made us very angry, but it had to be done to protect the visitor. That experience contributed to our political consciousness, which wasn't just studying Political Science, which I did; it was the reality of oppression and repression that inspired and gave impetus to the commitment of many of the people involved in student politics and the liberation struggle. It also gave us a better understanding of the different forms resistance could take.

At university, I met Billy Nannan, who later became one of my closest friends. Billy was a very bright mathematician, and one time, when I was selling the *New Age* and organising, Billy was refusing to buy and refusing to be mobilised, so I launched a fierce verbal attack on him in the canteen at Wits. Fierce. There were other students sitting there. It was vicious. 'Who do you think you are? What kind of person are you? So you want to be a teacher and what are you going to do?' Now I did not, of course, know that Kathrada had asked Billy to lie low because they were organising him into the underground structure of the movement. Billy was also a very good friend and drinking partner of Aggrey Klaaste (of *Drum* magazine, *The World* and later editor of *The Sowetan*) in the shebeens. Of course, Billy didn't say anything because he was a disciplined member. He just sat there and withstood that fierce attack from me. Afterwards he went to see Kathrada and complained, saying, 'You told me to do this, but now look what has happened? Essop came and said terrible things.' It was true, I had said terrible things to him. He went on, 'And I'm sitting there, and I can't answer him because you told me that I'm not supposed to say anything.' And Kathrada said, 'Oh, and what did you do?' 'I didn't do anything.' 'Right,' he said:

> So Essop is right, and you are right. It's good if he is attacking the students who don't want to get mobilised, and you are right for not talking because he doesn't need to know that you are involved in the underground structures of the ANC.

This pacified Billy. I had known nothing about it until Billy told me the story much later. He had just held his tongue and kept a bit of a distance. Kathrada didn't say anything to me.

One of the issues the ANC and its Youth League had to address after the ANC was banned was whether or not we needed another organisation that could help to mobilise African students. As NUSAS was only for university students, we were also thinking about those who were still at school, especially the more senior learners. There had always been a kind of permanent tension between NUSAS and the non-European sections – especially students from Fort Hare and the University of Natal.

A decision was made to form the African Students Association (ASA) with Thabo Mbeki, later president of South Africa, and Sindiso Mfenyana, who became the South African High Commissioner to Tanzania, leading the move. I think Tata Sisulu had asked them to come and see me to discuss the formation of ASA because of the possible impact it could have on those of us mobilising in other institutions where there were still African students.

They explained that the priority at that time was mobilising African students and that involving Coloured and Indian students or organising progressive whites would distract from the main focus. African students faced specific problems, for example, at school, so one needed to mobilise without starting debates about who is Black and the role of NUSAS, and so on. I think that forming a student organisation for Africans only was the correct decision to make at that time. It was agreed that if any assistance were required from the Indian Youth Congress, that would be fine, but the membership and leadership would come from Africans themselves.

Many of the ASA people were instrumental in the formation of the first Black Consciousness student organisations. In subsequent discussions around the exclusion of white students, some of the ANC students were resistant to a Blacks-only organisation. There were people in the ASA who were also involved in the formation of SASO: Nkosazana Dlamini (later Dlamini-Zuma) and Barney Pityana, to name two, and they were ANC people. It was a complex situation with no easy answers.

Meanwhile, for the Pahad brothers, playing, watching, organising and following international football, especially the English football league, continued as a deep passion. From an early age, maybe ten or eleven, we had organised our own matches and even went by train to Roodeport and Krugersdorp. At that time, Aziz was busy forming a team, and under his initiative, we started Dynamos Football Club. My very good friend and neighbour, Aboobaker Saloojee – who was also an accomplished football player – and I, suggested the name, which we took from Moscow Dynamos and a team from Czechoslovakia which also had that name. The badge on our Dynamos blazers displayed the Russian satellite, Sputnik orbiting Earth with South Africa coloured red. It was designed by Ahmed 'Archie Boy' Bhayet.

Dynamos became a household name in Johannesburg and some other parts of the then-Transvaal province. We were well-liked in Soweto, as we also played there and had beaten two of their teams. The game forever etched in my memory and that of many Dynamos players and supporters is the one against Home Killers in Kliptown on the hallowed ground where the Freedom Charter was adopted. At the time, Home Killers were the champions of the Johannesburg Bantu Football Association. The other association was the Johannesburg African Football Association. To the consternation and surprise of Home Killers, and the great joy of the Dynamos supporters and players, we won 3-2.

Ismail, our eldest brother, who was dubbed 'The Fordsburg Fox', was instrumental in the formation of the first professional league for Blacks. Together with 'Archie Boy' Bhayet and Ali Mohammed, we drove to Durban and contacted Ramhori Lutchman, (who later became Secretary of the Natal Inter-race Soccer Board and President of the Durban Indian Sports Grounds Association) and another person. From our discussions arose the decision to form the first Black professional league in South Africa, and Dynamos negotiated with the two top African teams, Orlando Pirates and Morocco Swallows, to join that professional league. Without those two teams from Soweto, we would not have succeeded in our quest.

Unfortunately, Dynamos did not participate in the first professional league because we were prevented from using the Orlando stadium by the absurd racist regulation that only 'Bantus' could play there, and the only ground available to us that was fenced off (enabling us to charge an admission fee) was the old Natalspruit ground in Doornfontein. There, our problem was that the ground was under the control of people such as 'Chummy' Mayet (who ran an insurance company with its office in Orient House), who insisted that they would only let us play there if we formed a semi-professional league, including Dynamos, from which one team could be created to participate in the professional league. I was the chair of Dynamos at the time, and we had to make a tough decision since agreeing to the condition meant the team would only play in the semi-professional league. Because there were six or seven players, including me, who were not good enough to play for the professional team, we made the sacrifice, and that is how we formed Transvaal United.

Transvaal United were the first champions of that league, with Ismail Pahad as manager and the team featuring Haroon Patel from Dynamos and several other notable players such as Ebrahim Adam, Links and Pickie Padayachee, Fischer from Germiston and Bonke Ndamase who, in my opinion, remains one of the finest left-backs South Africa produced.

For the games in Durban, the team had to travel by combi on a Friday and leave Durban on the Sunday evening, with many having to be at work on Monday morning, straight off the combi. I travelled with the team, packed in with minimum room for comfort or manoeuvre, but such was our passion and love for the game that no one complained about it.

In the years that followed, Ismail took Dynamos to new and greater heights, and they joined the professional league, becoming one of the top teams with a solid loyal fan base. Dynamos also organised several popular football tournaments. Ahmed Timol, who was brutally tortured and killed by the apartheid regime in 1971, and Yusuf 'JoJo' Saloojee, who later became an ambassador in the democratic South Africa, played prominent roles in organising those tournaments.

*

My formative years of political education, training and activism were in the TIYC, which laid the basis for my advance to leadership positions within the ANC and SACP. It was fortuitous for me that the TIYC executive included Ahmed 'Kathy' Kathrada, Dr Essop Jassat, Paul Joseph, Herbie Pillay, Ebrahim Moola, Moosa 'Mosie' Moolla, Abdulhai 'Charlie' Jassat, Suliman Esakjee and Suliman 'Babla' Saloojee.

Ahmed Kathrada, Babla Saloojee, Herbie Pillay, Faried Adams, Mosie Moolla and Suliman Esakjee became known as the 'Picasso Club' for their painting of slogans and defacing and altering official signs. One such example by persons unknown was the altering of a road sign in the south of Johannesburg which announced 'DANGER, Natives Cross Here'. They had inserted an omission mark and one word so that it read 'DANGER, Natives *Very* Cross Here'. We still don't know who had that brilliant idea.

Of the amazing group of people in the TIYC executive, besides Kathy, Mosie Moolla influenced me most. He introduced me to the works of Howard Fast and Jack London and the folk music of Burl Ives and the Soviet Red Army Ensemble. Two books that made a great impression on me were Fast's *Spartacus* and his *The Passion of Sacco and Vanzetti*.[19] Fast's story of the slave revolt in ancient Rome embedded in me a deep commitment to being part of the struggle against all forms of national and class oppression and exploitation. Sacco and Vanzetti were two anarchists who were wrongly executed in the USA for their political activities, which ignited in me a deep hatred for American imperialism and injustice.

My first classes in Marxism-Leninism were those arranged by the TIYC, and my first lecturer was Rusty Bernstein, who took us through the works of Emile Burns. I was a novice since the others had undergone political

---

19. Howard Fast, *Spartacus* (New York: M. E. Sharpe, 1951).
    Howard Fast, *The Passion of Sacco and Vanzetti: A New England Legend* (London: Panther, 1959).
20. Moscow: Progress Publishers, 1960

education classes previously. Later, Ben Turok was my tutor working through *The Fundamentals of Marxism-Leninism*;[20] needless to say, this and the Burns books were banned. It was in the TIYC that I grew to love and defend at all cost the Soviet Union and the other socialist countries; at the same time, I developed an enduring hatred for colonialism, capitalism, racism, and national and class oppression.

Before my election to the TIYC executive in 1957, the Treason Trial took place, the culmination of mass raids conducted by security forces throughout the country in December the previous year, when 156 leaders were arrested. Amongst those were leaders of the TIYC – Ahmed Kathrada, Mosie Moolla, Paul Joseph, Suliman Esakjee and Faried Adams. Given that there were no hotels for Blacks in the Transvaal, Treason Trialists not residing in Johannesburg had to be housed in family homes. When Ismail Meer and Dr Chota Motala from Natal stayed in our family flat, I used that opportunity to have serious discussions with them on political developments in South Africa, Africa and internationally. They were very patient with my questioning on a wide variety of issues, and I am most grateful that I learned so much from those two humble freedom fighters and leaders of our movement.

On the opening of the Treason Trial, I joined the demonstrators with placards demanding the release of our leaders. Although it was a peaceful demonstration, it was broken up by the police opening fire on the protestors. To this day, I don't remember how I managed to scale the fence into the Drill Hall grounds and then get into the Drill Hall itself. The accused, seated in a cage-like construction, brought the proceedings to a halt by protesting and demonstrating when they heard the gunshots. Some of them were eager to hear from me what was happening. That was the day I met Brian and Sonia Bunting for the first time; I would later serve with them in the same SACP unit in London.

Following the State of Emergency in 1960, during which many of our leaders were arrested, leaders of the SACP and ANC decided it was necessary to advance from passive resistance to armed struggle, and Umkhonto we Sizwe (MK) was formed in December 1961. In those years, Aziz and I were very close friends with Shirish Nanabhai and Indres Naidoo, who were activists in the TIYC. Abdulhai Jassat, Shirish, Indres and Reggie Vandeyar were some of the first recruits to Umkhonto we Sizwe, and in 1963, the latter three were sentenced to ten years on Robben Island for sabotage. These brave freedom fighters had also been brutally tortured before their trial started.

As Indres records in his book *Island in Chains: Ten Years on Robben Island*:

> Hundreds of people queued to say goodbye in the cells below the court, and the crowd outside was so thick that when we were placed in the van it could not move. In fact, the van began to rock backwards and forwards, and the black policemen in it with us panicked and begged us to appeal to the crowd to let us through. The face of one of my closest friends (Essop Pahad) pressed up against the mesh. 'Don't worry, comrades,' he shouted, 'you'll never serve ten years, you'll be out long before then.'[21]

My optimism proved to be unfounded.

Incidentally, my wife Meg reviewed *Island in Chains* as told by Indres Naidoo to Albie Sachs in the August 1983 edition of *World Marxist Review*. Indres and Albie ended with an appeal:

> Our hope ... is that each reader will be stirred by the story it tells into thinking about the contribution he or she can make to ... the release of all political prisoners in South Africa and the ending of the system which results in the best sons and daughters of our country finding themselves behind bars[22]

In March 1961, all those before the court in the six-year-long Treason Trial were acquitted. But they were not left alone for long. Nelson Mandela was arrested in 1962, and some of the remaining leadership still inside the country were arrested in Rivonia in July 1963. At the trial's end, in June 1964, the Black revolutionary leaders from the Rivonia Trial – Nelson Mandela, Govan Mbeki, Walter Sisulu, Raymond Mhlaba, Ahmed Kathrada, Elias Motsoaledi and Andrew Mlangeni – were all imprisoned for life on Robben Island. Denis Goldberg was imprisoned in Pretoria Central, as he was white.

Mosie Moolla and Abdulhai Jassat had been detained in May 1963 under the new ninety-day law and were in the Marshall Square police station when they were joined by Harold Wolpe and Arthur Goldreich, who had been arrested in Rivonia. These four staged a dramatic escape from Marshall Square in August 1963, and the oppressed and exploited Black majority were overjoyed at hearing the good news.

---

21. Middlesex, England: Penguin, 1982.
22. Indres Naidoo, *Island in Chains*

Before I went into exile, I was arrested twice. The first time was during the three-day general strike called by the ANC in 1961 in the name of Mandela. Under legislation that allowed detainees to be imprisoned for two weeks without bail, thousands of political activists and leaders were arrested to defeat the strike. That legislation laid the basis for the more vicious and draconian 90-Day (later 180-Day) Law that allowed the regime to imprison people in isolation and incommunicado (without habeas corpus – no trial or legal representation), which gave the security forces carte blanche to inflict inhumane treatment, including torture, on those detained.

Along with Henry (Squire) Makgothi, an ANC leader, I was part of a group carted off to a prison in Boksburg known as 'Blue Sky'. Prisoners had given it this name because they were compelled to sit in the courtyard where all they could see was the sky. When our group arrived, the white prison official exclaimed in Afrikaans, 'What is this?' – referring to me. They had no Indian prisoners, but given the racist regulations, they decided that I could not be locked up with my African comrades and must be put in a cell reserved for Coloureds. That cell had several light-skinned Africans 'playing Coloured' because Coloureds got better food than Africans. These individuals were also the gang leaders of that cell.

When I was locked in with the Coloureds, I made it quite clear to them that I was a political prisoner, one of the thousands who had been arrested when the authorities had attempted to break the strike. Interestingly, ordinary criminals had great respect for political prisoners, and the cell leader proclaimed that I was excused from cleaning duties and emptying the ablution buckets placed there every evening.

During the day, our section of the prison was overseen by an unpleasant petty-minded white Afrikaans-speaking warder who, disregarding the regulations, had confiscated the cigarettes of the awaiting-trial prisoners. It was said that he used these cigarettes to pay prisoners he compelled to work on his farm.

Blue Sky had a system whereby inmates could complain to senior prison officials who made the rounds in the morning, and I decided to lay some complaints. To engage those officials, one had to stand aside in a designated spot. When asked what my complaint was, I deplored the conditions in the cell, to which the major replied, 'I am running a prison, not a hotel.' When I then pointed out that the officer in charge had confiscated our cigarettes, to which we were legally entitled, the major instructed the officer to return them. That officer never forgave me and constantly looked for an opportunity to charge me for violating prison regulations, but I did not give him the satisfaction.

Fortunately, I had relatives named Behra living in Boksburg, and one of their sons brought me homemade food whenever allowed. I also had the advantage of being a university student who could write well in English, which made me popular. I was happy to oblige fellow prisoners by writing letters to the authorities and lawyers regarding their demands and requests. When we political detainees were released, the entire section gave us a guard of honour.

Once I was out, I was put on trial – not with my fellow detainees but with Mosie Moolla. We were charged with calling on Africans to strike, which was illegal, but not Coloureds, Indians or whites.

Our lawyer was an exceptionally bright and sometimes brash young man, Ismail Mohamed. He was an outstanding law student and later joint chairperson of the CODESA (Convention for a Democratic South Africa) negotiations, which began in December 1991 at the World Trade Centre, and still later was appointed Chief Justice. That was the beginning of a friendship I valued until his untimely death from cancer in 2000. Ismail brilliantly demonstrated that we were legally entitled to call on Indians and Coloureds to strike. He pointed out that I had been arrested for putting up posters in that part of Ferreirastown inhabited by Indians and Coloureds, and Mosie and I were found not guilty.

My second arrest was in 1964 when Aziz and I were arrested for breaking our banning orders. We had both completed our BA degrees the year before. But then, in January 1964, we were summoned to the Special Branch offices in Marshall Street, Ferreirastown. When we got there, an officer named Van Tonder read my banning order to me and then read out Aziz's. These orders banned a person from all political activities for five years, from entering any educational institution or factory, and from communicating with any other banned person. Indeed, even married people were prohibited from communicating with each other without the permission of the so-called Minister of Justice. I asked, 'What do you expect us to do? We are brothers sharing the same bedroom. What do you mean I can't communicate with him?' Van Tonder's reply was short and to the point, 'I can't help you. You must go to the Chief Magistrate and get his permission to communicate with each other.'

Fortunately for us, the Magistrates' Court was in Becker Street, the very street in which we lived. As Aziz and I walked to the Chief Magistrate's Office, we kept a distance between ourselves because we knew we could be arrested if caught speaking to each other. When we arrived, we had to wait but were finally granted temporary permission to restore our communication.

We then wrote to that so-called Minister of Justice, who happened to be B. J. Vorster, and applied to carry on with postgraduate studies. I think Aziz's intention was to study Law, while mine was to do an honours course in Political Science. I asked people like Helen Suzman and others to support the application. When Vorster replied, he said, 'I acceded to your request to communicate with your brother Aziz, but you are not granted permission to continue your studies.'

So essentially, we were supposed to stay at home, but we were still able to do a lot of political work while we were banned. It didn't stop us, just as it didn't stop all the other people prohibited from continuing their political activities. We just had to be more careful about what we did.

At that time, there was a legal dispute about what the banning order meant by a 'social gathering'. Once, when Aziz and I briefly attended a student party in Fordsburg, there was a Coloured policeman present: Swartz, who was a goalkeeper in our Dynamos team. We naively assumed that since he played for Dynamos and even slept at our flat, he would not rat us out to the police. How wrong we were. He reported us, and we were both arrested for breaking our banning orders.

Ismail Mohamed, our lawyer, who loved to explore and challenge areas of dispute in the Group Areas Act and those pertaining to banning orders, asked me if I knew a credible person who would say in court that he had advised us about the possible legal loophole. So I went to a friend of mine from Wits by the name of Marcel Berlins, who had just finished his legal studies, was articled and later became a prominent media person in London, and I asked him, 'Marcel, are you ready to come to court to say that you gave me this legal advice?' Now of course this was difficult for Marcel, but he agreed: 'No problem.' And Marcel appeared in court to say, 'I advised them that in terms of the law, this matter was in dispute; therefore, attending such a party may not necessarily be breaking the law in relation to social gatherings.' There were always people who were ready to help. Marcel didn't have to do what he did, and I always appreciated his assistance. In any event, we were found guilty of breaking our banning orders.

That was a period when the ANC and the SACP were recruiting cadres to go abroad for military and political training, and Aziz and I were approached by Suliman 'Babla' Saloojee to consider leaving South Africa, if necessary by taking an exit permit. Babla was such a lovely, bubbly go-getter person, and he was in the thick of the struggle. Tragically, the Special Branch arrested him on 6 July 1964 and killed him under brutal torture on 9 September of that year. They claimed he jumped from the sixth floor window of their headquarters in Marshalltown, the same treatment they would mete out to Ahmed Timol at John Vorster Square, along with the same lies about the cause of his death in 1971.

We agreed with Babla to go into exile for training, and Ismail Mohamed argued in court that because we were ready to apply for an exit permit, we should receive a suspended sentence if found guilty. The court agreed.

At my request, Bram Fischer had most generously agreed to be the Senior Advocate to Ismail. Bram was well-known to us as a family friend and brilliant defender of many Congress accused. But just before our trial started, he was arrested. Bram had been instrumental in ensuring that the Rivonia Trialists received life rather than death sentences and was particularly hated by the apartheid regime, who considered him a traitor since he came from a prominent right-wing Afrikaner family, which included a Judge President and a Prime Minister.[23] Bram, too, among others, was defended by Ismail Mohamed, amongst others.

As our trial and his were in the same Magistrates Court, Bram and I bumped into each other in the corridors there, and he engaged me in a discussion about the situation in South Africa and my future intentions. Since we were both banned persons, we were prohibited from communicating. But how could I, who faced trial for breaking a banning order, and he, a long term of imprisonment or even a death sentence, suggest that under the circumstances we should not speak to each other? So we spoke, and I sought his advice on applying for an exit permit, to which he concurred.

Later, when Bram realised that I was also banned, he immediately sent Ismail to find me and apologise. This act of genuine concern for another person demonstrated to me the greatness and readiness to sacrifice of one of the most outstanding revolutionary and legal brains in the history of our country.

The outcome of our trial was that Aziz and I were going to leave behind our family, life, friends and familiar surroundings for an unknown future in

---

23. On 23 April 1908, Abram (Bram) Fischer is born in Orange Free State to an auspicious family that includes Abraham Fischer, Bram's grandfather, who was State Secretary of the Free State Republic and the only Prime Minister of the Orange River Colony in 1907, and his father Percy Fischer, who later became Judge President of the Orange Free State. Available at https://www.sahistory.org.za/article/abram-fischer-timeline-1908-1975

a strange country. We had decided to go to London because my father was already there, as were Yusuf Dadoo, Thabo Mbeki and Abdul Minty. Abdul had been in the same class as Aziz, and he and I had been, on many occasions, declared joint winners in our school debates. He had gone to London earlier where, with Dr Dadoo and Vella Pillay, he was instrumental in helping to form the British Anti-Apartheid Movement. So off to exile we went, to face a new life, new challenges and what would be a new turning point in our futures.

Chapter 2
Into Exile

Essop and Ahmed Timol outside the North End Road flat, 1968

INTO EXILE

Our flight to London was the first time Aziz and I had travelled on an aeroplane. As hand luggage, we carried a blanket our mother had insisted we take, and I had an overcoat bought for me by Ahmed Timol. Mine was a most uncomfortable journey, prompted, I guess, by my anxiety about what awaited us in London. Aziz, on the other hand, appeared to enjoy it.

On arrival at Heathrow airport, we had no problem with immigration or customs and were overjoyed to be met by our father. He informed us that we would first go to the flat of Ingrid Wier, his partner for many years, who lived in Streatham, for breakfast, and then on to Clapham South, where we were to live. Although I was always polite to her, I was not friendly with Ingrid, as I always wanted to defend and protect my mother. Ingrid's relationship with my father was long established, and my mother accepted it, so there was no point in opposing it. (Incidentally, my father and Ingrid were not formally married, and Ingrid moved on to another relationship later in the 60s.)

It was a cold, dark, bleak, windy morning, and the view from the car was unpleasant. I thought, 'Good grief, did I leave Johannesburg for this place?' As it turned out, I grew to love living in London and exploring it, particularly the West End with its cinemas, theatres and vibrant nightlife.

My father had rented a house for his niece Zaibie Bhyat, her husband Hamid and their children Farouk, Zaheer and Shamim. We occupied one bedroom on the first floor with a bathroom in the passage. Aziz and I shared a double bed, while my father had a single one. Although he generously kept the electric heater on all night, and we kept our jerseys and socks on, we still shivered.

We were lucky that the Bhyats lived with us for a while. We were like a family, with Auntie Zaibie cooking our familiar home-style meals and the enjoyable company of our cousins. But Hamid had decided that London was not for him and soon took his family to Toronto, Canada. Later, Dasoo Joseph and Herbie Pillay also came into exile and lived in Clapham, which was wonderful, as it enabled us to enjoy many political discussions with them.

At that time, Clapham South was a dreary suburb, and I did not enjoy living there. Over time, it gradually became a more desirable residential area and was yuppified in the seventies. In 1965, my father found and rented a flat in North End House, Fitzjames Avenue, West Kensington. North End House would become a home or second home to many South Africans and even friends of my father from India, just like 11 Orient House back in Johannesburg. We were delighted to be there. The flat had central heating, four bedrooms, two bathrooms, a good-sized sitting room and a large kitchen. It was luxury. West Kensington was wonderfully near to Kensington High Street, with all its shops, the famous Olympia, Earl's Court, Hyde Park, Fulham, Chelsea and Hammersmith, and we settled in very quickly. Since Aziz and I had secured bursaries from the International University Exchange Fund, financed mainly by the Swedes, we were able to contribute to the living expenses.

The day after our arrival in London, our father took us to the offices of Yusuf Dadoo in Charing Cross. We were both fascinated by the Underground Tube ride. After a lengthy debriefing from Uncle Doc, as we called him, he suggested that we should continue our studies and discuss this with Michael Harmel.

Harmel had a good friend (a South African) who was a senior lecturer at University College London (UCL), and thanks to his assistance, Aziz and I were enrolled in January 1965 as students, even though we had missed a term. Aziz enrolled for a law degree. I only had a bachelor's degree, so I was asked to write a qualifying exam that would enable me to do a master's (MA). It was a wonderful experience attending the seminars of post-graduate students in international relations.

One of those doing an MA at that time was Abraham Benatton Ramos from Honduras, who was familiar with the workings of the Central American Common Market. We became friends, and I learnt a great deal from him about Central and Latin America and the boorish, intimidatory behaviour of US administration officials. He told me that at international conferences, Central American countries would agree to common positions on contentious issues within the region and the views and positions of the USA. But after a night of visits by US officials, some of the countries would change their minds and support the US. This was a defining lesson for me about the domineering behaviour of the US and the weak-kneed response of some easily intimidated Central American countries. Many years later, I learnt that, following General Oswaldo López Arellano's non-violent military coup in 1972 in Honduras, Ramos was appointed Minister of Economic

Affairs. Unfortunately, that government was overthrown by another coup in 1975; however, he has survived and works with the Honduras Business Council.

Although I only spent seven months at UCL, I found it very stimulating. Aziz and I also engaged in extensive political discussions with Vella Pillay and Barney Desai. Barney tried to convince us to stop supporting the ANC but failed; he went on to join the PAC and became one of its leaders.

Several students from the Labour Party and the Communist Party of Great Britain (CPGB) enhanced our understanding of the political currents in the UK, along with the National Union of Students (NUS). University College London had other spin-offs: it was in the centre of London next to the students' University of London Union (ULU) building, where we enjoyed playing table tennis with a few top-class players from Nigeria. It was also not far from the London School of Economics (LSE), where we often went to student parties on Friday evenings.

Furthermore, there were two bookshops I loved. One was next to UCL, and the other was Collet's in Leicester Square. Collet's was a revelation, as there were books on Marxism-Leninism and others by a range of progressive writers, as well as pamphlets and booklets from a wide variety of left-wing groups, both local and international. I delighted in that bookshop. When Ahmed Timol came to live with us, I introduced him to Collet's, and he also relished the incredible extent of reading it offered. For us, this was fantastic because, in South Africa, almost all progressive literature was banned (including, I add, to illustrate the paranoia of the regime, Black Beauty, a story about a horse).

While at UCL, I applied to read for an MA in African politics at the School of African and Asian Studies (AFRAS) at the University of Sussex. Thabo Mbeki, who had just graduated, stayed on to do an MA in economics at Sussex, which made me even more eager to be accepted. The dean of that school, Professor Tony Louw, was a renowned historian of East Africa and India. As I only had a below-average BA degree, I was most apprehensive, but Professor Louw was warm, welcoming and sympathetic. To my relief, he accepted my application, explaining that I had two very impressive references: one from Professor Sir Robert Birley, former principal of Eton, one of the leading English public schools,[24] whom I had met when he was visiting Wits University, and the other from Professor Julius Lewin, who was Head of African Studies at Wits.

---

24. Such a school in South Africa would be described as an elite 'private' school.

At the same time, Kenny Parker, a student leader from the University of Cape Town, was admitted to read for an MA in English Literature. I met Kenny at the ANC office in Earl's Court, where he was assisting Lionel Ngakane (writer, actor and film director) and Anne Darnborough (from Anti-Apartheid) in setting up an effective and successful 'Artists Against Apartheid' campaign. Raymond Kunene, a writer of epic Zulu poetry, also played a prominent role as the ANC's chief representative.

Kenny and I decided to share a house in Spring Street, Brighton, which was used for many meetings, discussions and parties, with one of the most memorable hosted by Thabo Mbeki, Kenny and myself for the all-conquering West Indies cricket team who came to play Sussex in 1966. Our plan was to engage the players in discussing the campaign to ban apartheid sports and sports personalities. It was a most congenial evening with cricket stars of whom I was in awe; that our views were welcomed and well-received was even more pleasing.

My MA included a special course under Professor Walsh on the terms of trade between developed and developing countries. It was a stimulating year reading and analysing books and articles on African politics with intellectual luminaries like Professors Walsh, Tony Louw, Colin Leys, Bruce Graham, and the senior lecturer in African history, Richard Brown, who would later supervise me when I read for my PhD.

Student politics at Sussex was a sedate affair compared to the hurly-burly and rough and tumble of student politics in South Africa. At that time, Sussex was a hotbed of Trotskyite activities pursued by one of its factions, the Militants. 'The Trots', as we called them, labelled Thabo, Kenny and myself the BBs (the Black Bourgeoisie). We delighted in telling them that in South Africa, there was no Black bourgeoisie since apartheid politics and ideology precluded the development of such a class. In all my years at Sussex, I could not relate to the politics of the Trots. I found them full of revolutionary rhetoric, anti-Soviet to the core, lacking empathy for those on the Left who disagreed with them, and, with a few exceptions, having little of substance to contribute regarding political mobilisation and organisation. Despite my feelings at the time, I have to admit that the two main Trots, Alan Woods and Roger Silverman, have stuck to their politics and achieved much more than I would have predicted.

Alan Woods studied Russian at Sussex and was a leading member of the Militant Tendency (the Militant), which practised 'entryism' into the Labour Party. He speaks fluent Italian, Spanish, French and German, as well as

English and Russian. Woods and his family moved to Spain in the 1970s to support the struggle against Franco. In 1992, he left the Militant and became one of the co-founders of the International Marxist Tendency. He was seen as a close advisor to Hugo Chavez and a supporter of the Bolivarian revolution. Woods has written extensively and edited two Marxist journals. Roger Silverman also studied Russian and has edited a socialist journal and written a book and several articles. He has consistently supported the Marxist Tendency, which aims to transform the Labour Party into a socialist position.

To return to the three South Africans: Thabo, Kenny and I; we completed our MAs and attended the same graduation ceremony. My parents were thrilled and took great pride in my academic achievement.

I thoroughly enjoyed living in Brighton, a seaside town with pebble beaches, and loved walking along the seafront and in the town centre with its ancient Lanes[25] and the Royal Pavilion. Another monumental impact on my life emerged from Sussex when Thabo Mbeki introduced me to some of his friends who rented a lovely flat overlooking Brighton's West Pier. One of them was Meg Shorrock, who would later become my partner and wife, mother of our children and grandmother of our grandchildren.

Meg shared the flat with her friends Lesley Garner, Rhiannon Richards and Rhiannon's partner Mel Gooding. Mel and Rhiannon later married and lived in Barnes, where we often stayed in later years when visiting London. The daughter of Ceri Richards, the famous Welsh artist, and Frances Richards, a well-known embroiderer and painter, Rhiannon has created a wonderful home where friends are always welcomed as if part of the family, with many of these friends being South Africans. Mel became a renowned art critic and curator who has written over a dozen books. Sadly, Mel died in 2021, leaving the world a poorer place.

Another student with whom I formed a lifelong friendship is Peter Lawrence, who shared a flat with Thabo and later with Aziz and I in Brighton. Peter became a distinguished Professor of Economics at Keele University and is a founding editor of the *Review of African Political Economy*. He contributed many articles to my journal, *The Thinker*.

Earlier, when I shared a flat in Spring Street with Kenny Parker, Derek Gunby shared a house with Thabo and Peter, and he and his wife went to Zimbabwe after it won its independence. When they contacted the ANC there and offered to help, they were given a car with a false bottom filled with

---

25. The Lanes are a collection of narrow lanes in Brighton in the city of Brighton and Hove, famous for their small shops (including several antique shops) and narrow alleyways. https://en.wikipedia.org/wiki/The_Lanes

weapons to drive to Johannesburg and hand over to an underground contact. It was a harrowing experience, as not everything went according to plan, but they finally emerged unscathed. Derek also writes political and historical articles and supports the Left in the Labour Party.

Another person in that progressive group, who later became our excellent friend, was Mike Prior. He, like his parents, was a staunch member of the Communist Party of Great Britain. Mike studied at Durham and then Essex before attending Sussex for his MA in 1964–1965. He left just before I arrived but kept in touch with his friends from Sussex, including Peter and Thabo, so I also got to know him. For many years, he was a well-known consulting economist specialising in energy issues and contributed many excellent articles to my journal, *The Thinker*.

That group from Sussex have all remained good friends to this day.

Of course, we had many other friends there, and I shall mention two who will crop up again later: Jan Haxton, who, with her sister Wendy, were Meg's close school friends since the age of four, and Tony Bunzl who was a good friend of Rhiannon's since her teens.

Following my graduation, Uncle Doc recommended that I consider reading for a PhD, as that could benefit the movement as a whole. I agreed and approached Professor Louw, who had no hesitation in enrolling me, suggesting that I do it in history under his tutelage. But the problem was I had yet to study history as a specific academic discipline. To overcome that obstacle, Prof. Louw proposed that I first do one term of African history with Richard Brown and one term of Indian history with Peter Reeves. One of the areas I studied with Reeves was the rise of the Rashtriya Swayamsevak Sangh (RSS), a fascist-type organisation that started its work amongst the peasants in India. The RSS, with its obnoxious philosophy of Hindu chauvinism, is the bedrock on which the Bharatiya Janata Party (BJP) was built to become the ruling party in India under Atal Bihari Vajpayee and later Narendra Damodardas Modi at the beginning of the twenty-first century. Both of my lecturers gave me a strong recommendation, so I started another eventful academic journey on a solid footing.

In those days, there were no computers or word processors— and no Internet to make research more accessible. A thesis had to be typed manually, and making any major changes involved retyping the whole document. I used to write in my terrible handwriting, Meg would check the grammar, then Ahmed 'Ronnie' Suliman Kaka, who lived in North End House, would copy this out in his beautiful handwriting (for free), and Joan, who was the girlfriend of Kaliq Bhaba, a good friend of ours, would type it for me (at a small cost). How much easier these things are now.

At first, I worked under Professor Louw on Ugandan history and was keen to do further research on the impact of the 1949 strike on Uganda's anti-colonial history. However, since at that time it was difficult to go to Makerere University, Professor Louw agreed to my suggestion that I work on some aspects of South African history under the supervision of Richard Brown. I chose the thesis topic 'The Development of Indian Political Movements in South Africa, 1924–1946', which turned out to be a fortuitous choice since it enabled me to study, in-depth, multiple elements of South Africa's complex history. Although I did not realise it then, it also led to an opportunity to visit and work in India later.

Richard Brown was a beneficial supervisor who, in his quiet way, with admirable patience, would improve my research skills and writing ability. I owe him my immense gratitude for enabling me to obtain a PhD – but not before overcoming a serious hurdle.

A few months after I had submitted my thesis in October 1971, I had to undergo a viva voce, which was held in the offices of Dr Shula Marks, who had been appointed as the external examiner. The internal examiner was Dr Peter Reeves. Shula was a highly respected historian who taught at the Institute of Commonwealth Studies. It was a gruelling session, with Dr Marks posing probing questions about my understanding and interpretation of South African history. The two examiners pointed out a number of weaknesses. At the end, I was relieved that they did not reject the thesis but said that I must rewrite the last chapter to address their criticisms and the concerns they had raised.

With Richard's help, I completed the rewrite, and to my great relief, I was awarded the PhD early in 1972. Let me add that I was casually informed that Shula remained unhappy at what she considered my polemical writing, favouring, in no uncertain terms, the progressive forces within the Indian community led by Dr Dadoo and Dr Naicker.

During those years, much had been happening in North End House. Soon after we moved in, my brother Zuneid and his good friend Ronnie Kaka joined us (not on exit permits). Zuneid found a job at Barkers in High Street, Kensington, while Ronnie pursued his studies. Ronnie remains our close friend to this day. A little later, Vijay Rama, also from Orient House, joined us. Vijay was an excellent cook and built up a reputation as a chef, working initially at Ingrid's Stockpot restaurant near Oxford Circus and eventually becoming a chef at a Fleet Street pub celebrated for the quality of its food. He stayed with us for a few years until he got married. Ronnie and Meg also worked briefly as waiters at the Stockpot. When disappointed customers complained about the scarcity of prawns in the prawn risotto, Vijay would tell Meg and Ronnie to explain to the customers that it was a competition: 'Find a prawn and win a prize.'

Billy Nannan had come to London in 1965, and his family joined him a year later. He got a job at Abbey Life Assurance Company, owned and managed by Joel Joffee (the instructing solicitor for the defendants in the Rivonia Trial) and his partners Mark Weinberg and Ralph Sepple. Billy was a mathematics genius and became their principal computer systems analyst. When Mark and Ralph split from Abbey Life to form Albany Life, they took Billy with them, and he was a great asset to the firm. He worked there almost up until his tragically early death in 1992.

Paul Joseph and Harlene Jassat worked at Abbey Life for about eleven years, and Issy Dinat and Abdul Bham also worked there full-time for a long while. Several exiled South Africans were given work there for short periods to help them through gaps in employment or deployment by the ANC. These included Thabo Mbeki, Aziz, Yusuf 'Charles' Saloojee, Sobizana Mngqikana, Pallo Jordan, Alex La Guma, Ronnie Kaka and Wolfie Kodesh.

As my mother was pining to be reunited with her husband and sons, she visited us in 1966 with our niece Yasmin, aged eight. When Yasmin was born, my mother was over the moon, having given birth to five sons. Yasmin's parents, Ismail and Rukeya (Ruki), had their main meals with us, with Ruki helping to cook, and my mother more or less adopted Yasmin. Their first visit to London lasted for about six months, and after a few months back in South Africa, they returned and settled down to live with us. Then we were joined by Ahmed Timol, who had also decided to live in London, where he got a teaching job, so we had a full house.

After about a year, my mother decided to go to India with my father, who had an import/export business and frequently travelled between the UK and India. He rented a flat in Bombay's popular Peddar Road, and my mother decided to stay there. But Yasmin was happy living in London, so she remained with us in North End House and became our daughter.

I had enrolled Yasmin, aged nine, in a primary school in Fulham, and every day, she had to take a bus to school and back by herself. It was not easy, and I admired her courage and fortitude. Although she was only a little girl, Yasmin lived in a flat full of grown men for most of her time in London, where she coped wonderfully well and brought joy into our lives.

For about a year, a friend of my father's, Arthur Knox, a well-known criminal lawyer from Durban, also lived in that flat, and later came back for shorter visits. As if this were not enough, we had regular visitors from South Africa and India who lived with us for short periods. One such visitor was a famous screenwriter from Bollywood. A few days after his arrival, I took him into the kitchen and demonstrated how to wash and dry dishes since all of us living in the flat had to accept a place on the rota for performing various domestic duties, including cleaning the bathrooms and toilets. He never forgot that encounter. When Meg and I went to stay with my parents in Mumbai in 1980, my father took us to visit that gentleman who gave us a delicious meal. A bit later, he summoned his entire staff and recounted what I had instructed him to do in London. They could not stifle their laughter and surprise. He was a generous host and, at the end of the evening, offered us the use of his cottage on the beachfront in Madras (Chennai) – an offer we were most happy to accept.

My love and passion for football is enduring, so it was great that North End House was close to the home grounds of Chelsea and Fulham. Ronnie Kaka, Yusuf 'Charles' Saloojee, Aziz and I and others attended many games at Stamford Bridge, Highbury, and White Hart Lane to watch the home games of Chelsea, Arsenal and Tottenham Hotspur. My favourite stadium, however, was Craven Cottage, the home of Fulham. It was a small, informal, intimate ground, with the River Thames running behind it, and wonderful fans: well-behaved, typically British working class with their cloth caps and profound knowledge of the game and the players – unlike the hooligans who filled the 'Shed' at Stamford Bridge.

I also had the privilege of witnessing memorable games at the mecca of football, Wembley Stadium. I watched the World Cup final between England and Germany, the European Championship final between Manchester United and Benfica and a few FA Cup and Old League Cup finals.

During those years, Meg and I continued our relationship, and Aziz went out with Gloria Wilkinson. Meg had spent a year near Manchester with her family, where she and her brother Michael tried to give some moral support to their parents. Her father had had a nervous breakdown, and they were in financial difficulty, downsizing from their big house and garden to a flat. Meg was working as a teacher then and was able to hitch-hike down to London from time to time to see me. She got on very well with her brother Michael, who was a barrister and only two years older than her. When he was at

Cambridge and she was still at school, and later Sussex, he had taken her on a few trips to meet friends. They supported Manchester United and visited pubs together. Oddly, she had visited the Duke of York pub with him in London to listen to Chris McGregor and the Brotherhood of Breath. Michael was terrific company, well-read and witty. He is married to Marianne, and they have two daughters, Amabel and Rosie.

At this point, I should mention Meg's other siblings. Meg also has a sister Jill, five years older, who, by that time, was married to Geoffrey Faux. Geoffrey was a teacher who had been educated at a public school and began his teaching career at Gordonstoun, where his pupils included Prince Charles. However, he soon began to question the whole public school ethos and moved to the Left, outstripping his liberal wife and becoming a supporter of the left wing of the Labour Party. He kept on moving to new schools in search of more rewarding work, so they moved house frequently, resulting in Jill supporting or starting playgroups for her two sons, William and Andrew, so they could mix with other children wherever they lived. Jill became a national organiser for the Pre-School Playgroups Association and has always been known for her helpfulness to the whole family.

Geoffrey was, for many years, a respected maths advisor and very active in the Association of Teachers of Mathematics. He and his children have always been enthusiastic walkers, climbers and sailors, and for many years, Geoffrey was a judge in the Duke of Edinburgh's Award, a programme to encourage young people to pursue active interests and serve their communities. He is still a determined walker at the time of writing, aged 85.

Meg also has another brother, Chris, the eldest, who moved to Switzerland in 1960 to work as a research scientist at the Battelle Institute and is married to Heidi, a beautiful woman with striking red hair, clever, patient and athletic. Chris and Heidi love (and until recently excelled at) walking, running, skiing and mountaineering. They have three children, Luke, Celia and Matthew. At one time, Chris was the Assistant Director General of the International Union for the Conservation of Nature.

In 1968, Meg returned to London and joined her former flatmate from Brighton, Lesley Garner, in a rented flat in Whitfield Street above the Spaghetti House, near Goodge Street tube station. This was most convenient for me, as her flat was just a few minutes away from the ANC office in Rathbone Place, the Anti-Apartheid office in Charlotte Street, and Dadoo and Slovo's unofficial SACP office in Goodge Street.

In 1969, North End House became a little crowded when my brother

Ismail and his wife Ruki came to visit with their daughter Shehnaaz (Yasmin's sister). We already had Ahmed Pochee, Ayob Varachia and Ahmed Bulbulia, who had joined Aziz, Yasmin, Ronnie, Timol and me. Ismail, Ruki and Shehnaaz returned to South Africa in 1970.

In that same year, Meg and Aziz's girlfriend Gloria moved into North End House. Sometimes South Africans studying in the UK would stay for a couple of days when visiting London, for example, Mohamed Khota (the son of my father's friend 'Quarter') or Mohammed Timol (Ahmed's brother). When that happened, too many people had to sleep in the third bedroom, which became a dormitory for six or more.

Although these visitors did not live at North End House, we became very close to many of them, and these two have remained my friends up till today. Mohammed Timol is a true internationalist and we enjoy sharing information and opinions, for example about the war between Russia and Ukraine. And since my retirement Mohamed Khota and I have regularly spent time walking around Rosebank shopping centre on Saturday mornings, drinking tea and chatting to people we meet. This has been real pleasure for me, as I don't drive and Meg hates shopping centres. He has become a constant support and friend to myself and my three brothers.

At one stage, we cooked an evening meal for fourteen or more people daily, with Meg taking responsibility for the weekday meals and Gloria those on the weekends. Ronnie, Pochee and Yasmin always helped with the cooking and others with the food shopping. There was a kitty to which everyone contributed, so the provision of meals was quite a social process.

In 1971, Ismail returned to London with his friend Rashid 'Mousie' Adam, so Ronnie found a flat with Ahmed Pochee nearby in Barons Court. Yusuf 'Charles' Saloojee had been sent to school in London at the tender age of fourteen by his family, who had justified high hopes for his academic ability. When he had finished his Higher National Diploma and was working at University College London to become a Member of the Institute of Biology, he joined Ronnie and Pochee. When Ismail later decided to live in Barons Court with Ronnie, Charles obligingly agreed to move into North End House with us.

During that time, Yusuf ('Dada') Dadabhay, from the Dadabhay family who owned Orient House, visited London and stayed with Ronnie. Dada would later marry Yasmin.

In 1972, Aziz and Gloria moved into the same building in Barons Court for a short time and then later got a lovely flat in Tufnell Park in a building managed by a housing association which controlled the selection of tenants. Stephanie Kemp and Albie Sachs were living there and gave them a good reference. Anne Davies also had a flat in that building; she was a brilliant advisor to teachers in the Inner London Education Authority. Later, Anne and Aziz became partners.

Ismail met a couple of women, Sally and Nevin, and brought them to a party in West Kensington, where they met Ronnie and Charles, and they quickly became our friends. Sally lived in a building in Stoke Newington; Anne Nicholson lived in another flat in the same area. Anne had been held in solitary and tortured as the result of a trial in South Africa, where several white South Africans were prosecuted for being communists. She later attended the Lenin Party School with Thabo Mbeki and Ahmed Timol. Nevin Faik also lived in Stoke Newington and was an actively anti-racist infant school teacher who went to great lengths to create equal opportunities for poor and Black inner-London children and became very close to our group of ANC friends, especially the Nannans and Meg and I. Charles lived with Nevin for some time; later, she went out with Moeletsi Mbeki. She was always one of our close friends.

Following an extensive discussion with Uncle Doc and ANC leaders such as Alfred Nzo, the Movement agreed that Aziz and I could marry our partners, Gloria and Meg. Meg and I had not worried too much about getting married, but we wanted to buy a flat and, at that time, could raise a larger mortgage as a married couple. We visited Meg's parents at Christmas in 1970, and I formally asked for Meg's hand.

Meg's father, Jim Shorrock, was a barrister descended from yeomen, with ancestors who had supported Cromwell, a grandfather who had been High Sheriff of Westmorland, and a father who had built and owned a Lancashire cotton mill. Jim had been brought up with his sisters in Wharton Hall and then Morland Hall, a nine-bedroomed mansion on fifteen acres of parkland with the River Eden flowing through it, and educated at a well-known public school, Clifton College. Meg's mother, born Mary Lings, was also from a wealthy cotton family, her father owning the Fine Spinners in Manchester. As well as overseeing the business, he became a well-known ornithologist, taking part in expeditions in search of rare birds, collecting and classifying their eggs and feathers. The men of that family were also educated at Clifton, as were Meg's brothers. However, both families lost all their money in the cotton slump of the 1930s.

Mary Lings was an excellent cook, homemaker and a kind and loving mother to their four children. She and Jim Shorrock had been brought up in a world where all their friends had inherited money and, although sensible and never extravagant, they did not manage to save much for old age or a rainy day. They bought an old house on an acre of land just after Meg was born that had been used as HQ by the Home Guard in Cheadle Hume during the War, with all the windows painted black and the garden full of broken bottles and rusty barbed wire, and renovated it themselves. Meg's mother became an expert painter, wall-paperer and window cleaner and once even knocked down a wall single-handedly when everyone was at work or school. Together, she and her husband (without outside help) transformed the garden into one of the most beautiful in the area. It had lovely roses, a rockery with herbaceous borders, a grass tennis court, a massive vegetable garden, productive fruit trees and hens and geese. In the spring, people would peer through the hedge to look at the bulbs, particularly the magnificent display of crocuses. It was a wonderful place for children to grow up.

Meg had very bad asthma until she was about thirteen years old, which delayed her physical growth. Her mother was constantly looking after her at home and, luckily, her friend Wendy Haxton brought her homework to her almost every day if she was sick. When Mary Lings' mother got cancer, she and her husband moved in with them, and Mary nursed her mother until she died. She then had to look after her father, who had become bedridden and had all his meals in bed for several years. Mary was always kind and even-tempered and willing to help anyone who fell on hard times.

The Shorrock and Lings family politics were a strange mixture: the Lings family, in particular, included a number of 'eccentric' individuals who did not conform at all to the typical expectations of their class. Meg's grandfather on the Lings side was in the Lancashire cotton business and had a partner with a cotton plantation in the USA who used slaves. Her Great Uncle Eric had been sent to the US because he was 'causing trouble' in Lancashire among the mill workers, and once there, he had promptly 'caused trouble' amongst the slaves. He was then sent to Mexico, where he joined Emiliano Zapata's men and ended up in the British Embassy, which deported him back to England. The Lings family were *Guardian* supporters (*The Manchester Guardian* at that time) and had a considerable dose of liberalism mixed into their otherwise largely conservative views. The boys in the house were expected to do the same amount of housework as the girls, even though the boys went to public school paid for by a Lings family trust fund. The girls were sent to local schools, as there was not enough money for them to be privately educated, and it was hoped that they would marry well.

When I sought their blessing for our marriage, Meg's father wanted an assurance that I could keep her 'in the style to which she was accustomed'. When I explained that Meg fully understood that my first commitment would always be to the ANC and that she would be keeping me, it did not go down too well.

On 30 April 1971, a double wedding took place at Fulham Registry Office in the presence of Meg's family and our friends and comrades, with Uncle Doc acting as Aziz's best man and Sobizana Mngqikana as mine. We knew the evening wedding party would be chaotic, so we decided to cater for our wives' parents separately earlier. Gloria's parents had lunch with her and Aziz in North End House, while Meg's family and I lunched at Bertorelli's in Charlotte Street, hosted and paid for by her Uncle Martin Lings, keeper of Oriental Manuscripts at the British Museum, a brilliant scholar, linguist and Islamic philosopher. His Islamic name was Abu Bakr Siraj ad-Din, and he later became a Sufi, with followers all over the world, including a Muslim community in Cape Town, many of whom had been forcibly removed from District Six. He wrote several books, including *Muhammad: His Life Based on the Earliest Sources*.[26]

Meg and her uncle had many discussions, as they both strongly rejected rampant capitalism, consumerism and the obsession with accumulating wealth and possessions. He and his wife Lesley occasionally took us out for a meal or to one of the wonderful Kathakali dance performances, and he showed Meg around the Tutankhamun exhibition at the British Museum in 1972. It was very crowded during the day, so he took her to see it after the museum had closed – just the two of them – which was an unforgettable experience enhanced by his unique depth of knowledge about the history and civilisation of Ancient Egypt.

But Martin Lings regarded Marxism as a mistaken focus on the material things in life, to the detriment of the spiritual. He thought it was important for societies to create the possibility for certain people to devote their lives to spiritual rather than material concerns, which allowed him to see something positive in the caste system in India, for example. Meg, however, wanted justice and equality now on earth, echoing Joe Hill's parody of the Salvation Army's exhortation to the working class to find patience:

---

26. Vermont: Inner Traditions, 1983.

You will eat, bye and bye
In that glorious land in the sky
Work and pray, live on hay,
You'll get pie in the sky when you die.

The preparations for the wedding were minimal and informal, as we didn't have any money to spend on it. The evening before the celebration, Aziz and I went out with a couple of friends, Ronnie Kaka and Yusuf (Charles) Saloojee, to try to gather some sprays of cherry blossoms we wanted to use to decorate the wedding venue, which was a very unprepossessing Scout Hall behind the Olympia Exhibition Centre. Gloria and Meg stayed behind, hoping to receive a present of fifty chickens promised by a friend of my father living in Burnley. These never arrived, and we could not get hold of the would-be donor, so the two brides-to-be had to roast the twenty or so chickens we had bought at the last minute from a vendor who was selling them cheap because they were past their sell-by date. Meg and Gloria washed them thoroughly in water with vinegar to eliminate the unpleasant smell. This treatment fortunately, was successful.

Meanwhile, I was arrested for picking branches of cherry blossom growing in a nearby school. Because they were overhanging the wall, we thought picking them was acceptable but discovered too late that it was a criminal offence. However, we did manage to persuade the police not to arrest us after telling the sob story of the possible outcome – the cancellation of our proposed double wedding.

We had a fabulous wedding party in the end – even though we had told people to bring drinks and warned them there would not be much food, as we had no money. Invitations were by word of mouth and a notice in the ANC office. Literally hundreds of people came, including many from the ANC in London, colleagues, friends, and comrades from the British Left. We had the twenty roast chickens, dozens of baguettes, some cheeses and a wedding cake. There was great music and everyone danced. Sobizana organised a spectacular gumboot dance and announced the cutting of the cake, but when Gloria and Meg went to cut it, they found that it was already half eaten. People remembered that wedding for years.

We had made a monumental blunder in not personally inviting Mama Adelaide Tambo to the event, and until her dying days, she never tired of scolding me, at times in the presence of Comrade O. R. Her two sons had not invited her to their wedding; for Mama Adelaide, Thabo Mbeki, Pallo Jordan,

Aziz, and I were her sons.

Then, just six months after our wedding, in October 1971, we received shattering news from South Africa.

Ahmed Timol, our dear comrade and brother, had been brutally tortured to death by the apartheid security forces. Timol was an exceptionally close friend, and before I went into exile, we spent a lot of time socialising. He was always generous and, on many occasions, paid for my ticket so we could go to the Lyric or Majestic cinemas in Fordsburg. Indeed, when I went into exile, he bought me an overcoat I wore for many years. In London, we lived together in North End House and enjoyed each other's companionship. I was the one who saw him off when he left to return to Johannesburg. Timol's courage and devotion to the struggle were apparent, as he was conscious of the dangers that would confront him on his return to work for the underground of the SACP and ANC. He took that decision even though it meant breaking off his relationship with Ruth Longoni, the woman he loved.

In the book *Timol, A Quest for Justice* by Timol's nephew Imtiaz Cajee, Thabo Mbeki wrote in the foreword about the hatred and fear Ahmed raised in the regime by his very existence when they thought they had destroyed our underground: 'He was and remained, even after his death, the spectre that was haunting Africa.' Mbeki lauded 'the courage and humanity of this extraordinary African'.[27]

In the same book in a 'Note by a Friend', I wrote that for Meg and me, the memories of his death are 'graphic and poignant'. I remembered how he was always neat and tidy, had a dry sense of humour and was so kind-hearted that he found it difficult to say anything unpleasant about anybody. In paying tribute to that brave, indomitable hero of our revolutionary movement, I wrote:

> Timol died a wretched death at the tender age of 29. In his short life, he had accumulated knowledge that many do not store up in a lifetime. He was rigorous and informed, politically and theoretically, and showed acute insight into South African politics and international affairs and an exemplary commitment to our national liberation cause. Ahmed, though given glimpses of a freer and better life by travelling extensively abroad, was robbed of the opportunity to blossom to the full. He never had time to use the potential that we, his friends, knew existed in him. The movement for national

---

27. Johannesburg: STE Publishers, 2005.

liberation remained strong and will continue to be strong in our hard-won democracy.[28]

In 2019, Ahmed Timol was awarded the Isitwalandwe Medal, the highest award given by the African National Congress, only bestowed upon the bravest warriors, those distinguished by their leadership and heroism.[29] We shall never forget him.

⌁

I need to backtrack now to outline the focus of my political activities from 1964 to 1973.

From our arrival in London in December 1964, Aziz and I were acutely aware of the prevailing structural and institutional racism and participated in anti-racist and international solidarity demonstrations in support of progressive forces alongside the British Left and international exiles from other communist, socialist and workers' parties. I also had contact with prominent anti-racist activists from the Afro-Caribbean and Afro-British communities. However, my main focus was on the ANC Youth and Students, the ANC, the SACP and the British Anti-Apartheid Movement.

Soon after arriving in London, I met Thabo Mbeki at the ANC's one-room office in Earl's Court, Kensington. I had known and worked with Thabo at Macosa House when he came to Johannesburg from the Eastern Cape, and we struck up a friendship politically and socially. In London, he briefed me on political developments in the UK and Europe. His main concern was mobilising and organising South African youth and students studying or working in the UK and generating support for the ANC in Western Europe. He had already discussed this with Ismail Coovadia and Cap Zungu, and it was decided that we should consider forming an ANC Youth and Students Section that would include non-Africans. We, for this, needed the leadership's consent because membership of the ANC was restricted to Africans only at that time.

Then, as luck would have it, Comrade O. R. Tambo came to London. Mama Tambo had rented a flat in Highgate, and Thabo suggested we go

---

28. Ibid.
29. Isitwalandwe means 'the one who wears the plumes of the rare bird', in particular the blue crane, which is featured in both Zulu and Xhosa culture and is the national bird of South Africa. Known as the Isitwalandwe Medal until 1994, it is now known as the Isitwalandwe Award and spelled Isithwalandwe and Isithwalandwe/Seaparankwe. Available at https://aaregistry.org/story/the-isitwalandwe-seaparankoe-medal-a-story/

there to meet O. R. At that meeting, Thabo outlined our ideas about a youth and students section, and, typical of his outstanding leadership qualities, O. R. listened intently and merely responded, 'Thabo, Essop, what is the problem? Why are you asking? It needs to be done, so just do it.' When we raised the question of the ANC leadership needing to consent to membership from all races, his response was again pithy and to the point: 'You do what you have to do and leave the ANC leadership to me.' That was the go-ahead we required, so, with Cap Zungu, Ismail Coovadia, Aziz and a few others, we formed, without fanfare, the ANC Youth and Students Section in London, with Thabo in the Chair as our leader.

Some months after that, we received a tremendous boost with the arrival of Sobizana Mngqikana, who had been granted a scholarship to study for an MA in International Relations at University College London. Sobizana had been active in student politics at the University of Fort Hare and in ANC underground structures. He was a well-known rugby player, a lover of music and a good saxophonist. He was just what we needed: an asset in the areas of culture, sports and politics, and he assisted us in forming our choir and was an excellent choirmaster. The first choir included Sobizana, Billy Nannan, Vijay Rama, Thabo Mbeki, Cap Zungu, Theresa Maimane and myself. Theresa had a beautiful voice. We had many rehearsals in preparation for participation at the World Youth Festival organised by the World Federation of Democratic Youth (WFDY) in Sofia, Bulgaria in 1966. We also produced several political documents to be used by the ANC Youth and Student delegation to the Festival.

I was extremely excited to attend, as it was also my first visit to a socialist country. En route, we had to change trains in East Berlin in the German Democratic Republic, and the Free German Youth (Freie Deutsche Jugend: FDJ), the youth wing of the ruling Socialist Unity Party, was given responsibility for the train on which we would travel. We were most impressed by their enthusiasm, work ethic and efficiency. While we waited at the station, Sobizana entertained all the delegations going to Sofia by playing the saxophone.

The group from London included Thabo, Aziz, Billy Nannan and Abdul Bham. The entire delegation was led by Johnny Makathini.[30] At the very first meeting, the comrades from the Soviet Union, who included Joe Nhlanhla, later to be a Minister in Mandela's first government, queried Makathini's leadership. To resolve the question, it was decided that each separate

---

30. There are various spellings of Johnny's surname, depending on which source one consults: Makhatini, Makhathini and Makatini.

delegation would deliberate the issue. When the group from London, under Thabo's leadership, had no difficulty endorsing Makathini, everyone finally agreed.

The festival was an unforgettable experience. Attending seminars and discussion groups and meeting with delegations from other countries was exhilarating and inspiring and added to our political understanding of international issues and our experience of international solidarity.

My most memorable meeting was with the delegation from the United States. Joe Nhlanhla opened with Marx's statement that the 'spectre of Communism was haunting Europe'. Our choir was strengthened by those from Lusaka and Dar es Salaam, and our rendition of freedom songs and performances of the gumboot dance were very well received by all our audiences. It was at this World Youth Festival that I first met Poppy Nokwe, daughter of Duma and Tiny Nokwe. She had an awesome singing voice, and when she sang the songs of Aretha Franklin, if you closed your eyes you could believe it was the greatest singer of soul music herself.

Back in London, to strengthen our ANC office, I suggested that we ask Thami Mhlambiso to apply for a scholarship offered by the London School of Economics. Thabo and I engaged with some of those involved to lobby for Thami. He was an outstanding candidate with powerful credentials as an ANC student leader at Fort Hare, and we had been happy to welcome him into our ranks. Unfortunately, years later, he was to join the 'Group of Eight', who were expelled from the ANC for their divisive, sectarian and chauvinistic opposition to the Morogoro decisions and open hostility to Comrade O. R. Tambo as Acting President of the ANC.

In 1966, the ANC Office moved to Rathbone Place, near Goodge Street tube station. As mentioned, this was conveniently close to *The African Communist* office, Dadoo and Slovo's office and the headquarters of the Anti-Apartheid Movement. It was also happily near the famous Duke of York pub where Chris McGregor and the Brotherhood of Breath played regularly, as well as The 100 Club in Oxford Street, where all the great London-based South African jazz musicians like Dudu Pukwana, Louis Moholo, Mongezi Feza and Johnny Dyani were regularly featured. Those musicians, along with political and cultural activists such as Dumile Feni, John Matshikiza, Zakes Mokae (*The Comedians, Blood Knot, Cry Freedom*), Pallo Jordan and Sobizana (Bizo) Mngqikana rubbed shoulders with the British Left. The Duke of York and Finches in Goodge Street became meeting places for young South African exiles and activists to exchange ideas with progressive British activists. People like Mike Terry and Christabel Gurney, the leadership of the NUS and many from the CPGB and Labour Party, our friends Mel and Rhiannon from Sussex and several from North End House often mingled there to relax.

When the ANC decided to launch a monthly journal, *Sechaba*, its first editor was M. P. Naicker, a leader of the SACP and the Natal Indian Congress. The inaugural issue was published in January 1967, produced in Rathbone Place and printed in East Berlin in the GDR. Naicker was a hardworking, gentle person and a good mentor to inexperienced writers. After he died at the early age of fifty-six in 1977, *Sechaba* was edited by Francis Meli until December 1990. This journal left a proud record of achievement which influenced the thinking and knowledge of ANC membership and supporters throughout the world.

The ANC Y&S worked extremely hard to assist in the operations and work of the ANC, which had grown exponentially. We addressed many meetings, rallies and protests organised by ourselves and the Anti-Apartheid Movement at that office.

In the early sixties, the leadership of the British National Union of Students had shunned us, preferring to cooperate with the South African National Union of Students. This made it even more imperative that we get involved in student politics and work closely with progressive forces who were determined to change the outlook and positions of the NUS. We worked very well with the students from the CPGB, the Young Communist League, the left wing of the Labour Party, the Young Liberals and other radical students not affiliated to any political party. The CPGB's student organiser was a dour Scotsman named Fergus Nicholson, who was a master tactician and later led the Straight Left pro-Soviet faction of the CPGB which opposed Eurocommunism. This faction and many of the young people in the CPGB were close to the South African, Iranian, Iraqi and Greek Communist Parties and very active in international solidarity. The upshot of these activities by the progressive students was the ousting of the old NUS leadership and the election of a progressive slate, including Jack Straw, who later became Foreign Secretary in a Labour Government.

I consolidated my friendship with Mike Terry, who had emerged as an influential leader and one of the most consistent and committed supporters of the ANC and the other national liberation movements in southern Africa, Guinea-Bissau and Vietnam. After completing his studies, Mike became the executive secretary of the Anti-Apartheid Movement from 1975–1994. When he joined the CPGB, the leadership asked him to keep his membership quiet, as not everyone was happy with the predominance of communists in the leadership of the NUS and Anti-Apartheid Movement.

The period from 1963 to 1966 was exceptionally difficult, traumatic and depressing for the ANC and its supporters, both inside and outside South Africa.

A while after the Rivonia Trialists were imprisoned, the second high command of MK, including Wilton Mkwayi, Mac Maharaj, David Kitson and Laloo 'Isu' Chiba were arrested and sentenced to long-term imprisonment in what is known as 'the Little Rivonia Trial' in 1964. Another:

> Lionel Gay, a Member of the Central Committee of the SACP ... was [also] arrested and charged in that ... trial ... However, he turned state evidence and was released. He immediately went into exile. When he was living in England, he made contact with the ANC again and joined the Anti-Apartheid Movement.[31]

In that same year, three prominent trade unionists, Vuyisile Mini, Zinakile Mkaba and Wilson Khayinga were executed.

During those bleak years, Looksmart Ngudle, Suliman 'Babla' Saloojee, Caleb Mayekiso and Alpheus Maliba were among those who were tortured to death. Then, in 1965, to the glee of the apartheid regime, Abraham 'Bram' Fischer, who had been leading the SACP underground, was arrested and sentenced to life imprisonment in 1966.

The freedom struggle had suffered grievous damage, but to the consternation of the apartheid regime, the flames of resistance, however dimly, kept burning and could not be extinguished. For example, in 1969, twenty-two men and women were arrested separately in different parts of the country and kept in solitary confinement for seven months (some who had been arrested earlier were held in solitary for longer) and repeatedly tortured in a brutal effort to force them to make statements incriminating each other. These rarely remembered or mentioned people suffered with unbelievable courage and determination to protect their comrades and the cause in which they believed, so I include all their names here: Samson Ndou, Lawrence Ndzanga, Rita Ndzanga, Winnie Madikizela-Mandela, Shanthie Naidoo (Indres's sister), Nomwe Mamkhala, Joyce Sikhakhane, David Motau, Jackson Mahlaule, Elliot Goldberg Shabangu, Joseph (Snuki) Zikalala, David

---

31. 'Gay, Lionel', *O'Malley – The Heart of Hope*. Available at https://omalley.nelsonmandela.org/index.php/site/q/03lv03445/04lv03519/05lv03557.htm

Tsotetsi, George Mokwebo, Joseph Nobanda, Samuel Pholoto, Simon Mosikare, Douglas Mvemve, Venus Mngoma, Martha Dlamini, Owen Vanqa, Peter Magubane and Paulos Matshaba. All of them steadfastly kept their silence, despite not knowing who else had been arrested and being unable to communicate with each other or anyone else. The consequence was that the 'Trial of 22' activists collapsed.

Outside South Africa, the international solidarity movement went from strength to strength. That was evident in Africa, Scandinavia, the Soviet Union and other socialist countries, Anti-Apartheid Movements in Europe and Asia, and international bodies such as the World Peace Council, the Afro-Asian Solidarity Movement, the World Federation of Trade Unions (WFTU), the International Union of Students (IUS), and the World Federation of Democratic Youth. In addition, MK combatants were receiving training in the Soviet Union, and the ANC and SACP were regrouping in exile. In 1966, SACP leaflets (brought into the country by Vivian Higgs) were circulated, thus demonstrating that the ANC and SACP had yet to be destroyed.

Following discussions between ZAPU (the Zimbabwe African People's Union) and the ANC and their armed wings, ZIPRA (the Zimbabwe People's Revolutionary Army) and MK, combatants of the two armies entered Rhodesia. The Wankie and Sipolilo Campaigns from August 1967 to July 1968 gave rise to fierce battles between the Rhodesian forces backed by racist South Africa and the armed liberation fighters. Some of our combatants lost their lives, while others were imprisoned in Rhodesia or Botswana; Chris Hani was one of those imprisoned in Botswana. Those campaigns gave impetus to the struggle in South Africa and the international solidarity movement. However, there were some weaknesses and deficiencies in preparing the campaigns, which led to severe criticism from some MK participants in the Luthuli Detachment led by Chris Hani and those arrested and imprisoned in Botswana. Subsequently, a group of these people drew up what came to be known as the Hani Memorandum, which contained serious allegations against top officials of the ANC and MK, which, in turn, led to heated debates amongst the ANC leadership. It is often claimed that a military tribunal had been set up to investigate and that it went as far as proposing to execute those who drew up the memorandum, but this is not true. Proposals to discipline the signatories of the memorandum were categorically overruled through the intervention of O. R. Tambo and Mzwai Piliso, and Chris and the others were not expelled but suspended.

However, in the ANC camps, such as Kongwa in Tanzania, there was increasing dissatisfaction at the lack of armed and political actions inside South Africa. All this, combined with the growing unrest in MK, led to the correct decision to convene a special ANC Conference in Morogoro, Tanzania, on 25 April 1969. Morogoro was attended by more than seventy delegates, including Thabo Mbeki, who represented the ANC Y&S from London. The delegates represented units of the ANC and MK, leaders of the Coloured and Indian people, and white revolutionaries like Joe Slovo, who is credited with drafting the Strategy and Tactics document; Duma Nokwe and Joe Matthews played an essential role in editing the drafts.

After intense, heated debates, the following far-reaching decisions were taken: to open up membership of the ANC – except for its NEC – to non-Africans; to intensify political and armed actions inside the country; to establish a political underground to support armed struggle; and to set up a Revolutionary Council headed by O. R. Tambo with Yusuf Dadoo as his deputy. These decisions helped consolidate Tambo's leadership and that of the ANC-SACP alliance.

However, some who disagreed with those decisions – especially opening up ANC membership to non-Africans – embarked on an anti-communist and chauvinist campaign laced with virulent poisonous personal attacks on Tambo. Dubbed the Group of Eight, this lot included two leading SACP members, Tennyson Makiwane and Alfred Kgokong, who had tried to mobilise ANC structures in exile, in prison and known people inside the country. They made no headway – except to the dustbins of history.

Post-Morogoro, a special unit was set up to manage the movement's propaganda campaigns in the face of high-level police and security activities in South Africa. An important and integral part of that work was the recruitment of courageous non-South Africans, all white, to go to South Africa to prepare and distribute leaflet-bomb pamphlets proclaiming the existence of the ANC and SACP and exhorting the people to continue the struggle. Under the leadership of Yusuf Dadoo and Joe Slovo, that unit, which included Ronnie Kasrils and Jack Hodgson, later augmented by Aziz Pahad and Dr Ronnie Press, did a marvellous job. For readers interested in that important work, I recommend *The London Recruits*, edited by Ken Keable (Merlin Press, 2012). The introduction by Ronnie Kasrils is a riveting account of how the recruits were prepared to risk their freedom and possibly even their lives to give our freedom struggle a much-needed boost.

The Morogoro Conference documents and decisions leant greater energy and vigour to our work in the ANC, the ANC Y&S and the broader Anti-Apartheid Movement, and we addressed numerous meetings, large and small, and organised and participated in protest demonstrations outside South Africa House, Trafalgar Square, come rain, cold or sun.

A memorable debate for me was one at Leeds University. The hall was packed, and my opponent was a Jewish member of the University Council. He tried to argue that he opposed racism and apartheid but that sanctions on apartheid South Africa would not work. I decided to take him on with no holds barred, so I put it to the audience that as a Jewish person, he should not even dare to suggest that Hitler and his Nazis should have been treated softly, softly. I argued that the best way to fight apartheid was to intensify the struggle inside South Africa and impose economic, cultural, academic and sports boycotts on the obnoxious regime and its supporters. At the end of the debate, the audience of more than 500 students voted in favour of my position, while my opponent could not muster a single vote. That was when I first met Mike Terry; our friendship lasted until his untimely death in December 2008.

As the ANC, we had regular meetings of our members at which we discussed and debated openly and honestly the challenges facing us inside the country and in exile. The Y&S section organised regular study groups in which leading members took turns giving input on a topic and smaller groups discussed and reported back their views. Many found this quite challenging but beneficial.

The ANC organised fundraising activities, including an annual bazaar, which became quite a popular event, selling good-quality new and second-hand items at ridiculously low prices, including Makonde carvings[32] and donated goods from the Soviet Union. For the first five or six years, May Brutus, Maud Phillips, Harlene Jassat, Theresa Nannan, Ramnie Dinath, Gill Marcus, Shanthie Naidoo, Meg, Tommy and Bobby Vassan, Herbie Pillay and a few other volunteers would cook pots and pots of mince curry, dahl, rice, and carrot salad, which people always expected to buy at a very reasonable price, as part of the event.

Although chief representatives of the ANC in London came and went, one important person at the London Office was permanent: Abdulhai Jassat, who came to London with his wife Harlene in 1971. While in prison, he had been brutally tortured, with epilepsy as one of the after-effects of the electric

---

32. The Makonde people from Tanzania and Mozambique are famous for their ebony carvings, often depicting the human form. Makonde carvings are one example of the African art that profoundly influenced twentieth-century European artists like Picasso.

shocks he received. Abdulhai was absolutely incorruptible and extremely strict with the petty cash. He kept a hawk-eye on every penny, and nothing ever went missing. People would beg him to let them in free to a fundraiser or just have a few shillings for a sandwich, but he was absolutely unshakeable: the answer was always NO; the ANC's money was untouchable. In contrast, he and his wonderful wife Harlene could not be more generous and hospitable.

I regularly played Bridge with Issy Dinat, Billy and Theresa, Mannie Brown and (after his release) Indres Naidoo. At one stage, we had regular weekend parties at the homes of Issy and Ramnie or the Nannans, with Aziz and Gloria, Meg and me, Bizo Mngqikana and his wife Lindiwe, and a few others, including Nevin Faik who, as previously mentioned, was a wonderful infant school teacher of Turkish Cypriot origin who became and remained our friend for years. Meg's and my friendship with Issy and Ramnie and Billy and Theresa became stronger and stronger, and we grew to love their children. We also remained very close to Mel and Rhiannon Gooding and had some lovely get-togethers at their house in Barnes.

The work we did extended far beyond that of the ANC. Thabo, with the invaluable assistance of a female British comrade, Nicola Seyd, who was very close to the Iraqi students, was instrumental in forming an international student body which included students from Iraq (mainly from the Communist Party), Iran and other countries. As the ANC Y&S, we learnt a lot about the challenging work facing them in their fight against repressive and authoritarian regimes. We participated in meetings and demonstrations in favour of the Cypriots, the progressive forces in Greece against the coup of the Colonels, and against fascism in Spain. We also utilised the student uprisings in Western Europe in 1968–69 to enhance our contacts with radical and militant students and their leaders.

We also participated with enthusiasm in organising and supporting demonstrations against US imperialism's murderous military onslaught on the National Liberation Front (NLF) in South Vietnam and the Communist Party-led North Vietnam.[33] Representing the ANC Y&S, Thabo and I were on the organising committee which mobilised one of the biggest demonstrations ever witnessed in London – about Vietnam – and, despite

---

33. The Saigon regime dubbed the NLF the 'Viet Cong', a pejorative contraction of Viet Nam Cong San (Vietnamese Communists). The NLF's military arm was the People's Liberation Armed Forces (PLAF). In February 1965, the PLAF attacked US Army installations at Pleiku and Qui Nhon, which convinced President Lyndon B. Johnson to send the first US ground troops to South Vietnam a month later. Ultimately, more than 500,000 US troops were sent to Vietnam to fight the PLAF and the People's Army of Vietnam (PAVN, or North Vietnamese Army). Available at: https://www.history.com/this-day-in-history/national-liberation-front-formed

the antics of a few Maoist groups and anarchists, it was hugely successful.

After the demonstration reached the US Embassy in Grosvenor Square, many of the demonstrators, including our group, sought to breach the large police cordon around it, but our efforts were not successful. Then, as we were leaving the square, Thabo Mbeki, who was carrying our banner, disappeared. Later, we learnt that the police had grabbed him and the banner in a swift move in which he lost half a tooth and a shoe. Thabo has never had that tooth repaired, as it is a reminder of that hugely successful demonstration. When later I had the honour of addressing a meeting in Pretoria at which the Vietnamese Prime Minister was the main speaker, I encouraged him to ask Thabo when he met him the following day about how his tooth had been broken. He was most interested and indeed did ask him.

Our work with anti-racist, anti-fascist freedom fighters around the world and progressive forces in the UK left an indelible mark on me and strengthened my resolve to always remain true to the principles of international solidarity.

༄

In the early 1970s, the Inner London Education Authority was finding it hard to attract and retain teachers to work in its toughest schools, some of which had been placed in a category known as 'areas of special social difficulty'. Teachers who were prepared to commit to working in such schools for a minimum of three years were offered council flats as an incentive. St Stephens School in Westbourne Park, where Meg was teaching, fell into this category, so she was offered a centrally heated duplex in Braemar House, Edgeware Road, Maida Vale, close to the tube station and on many bus routes. It had three bedrooms (one of which was tiny), a bathroom, a kitchen just big enough to eat in, and a sitting room, and the rent was very low. Maida Vale was a pleasant suburb with easy access to such areas as Marble Arch, Notting Hill and Oxford Street.

Meanwhile, Ismail had returned home to South Africa to settle down with his new wife, Kulsie, and my parents remained in India. The flat in North End House was kept in the name of Goolam Pahad but was rented out.

After I had resubmitted my thesis in early 1972, I needed to find employment while waiting for my results. Through a friend, I contacted Jane King, the ballet critic at the *Morning Star* who was Head of the English

Department at Hammersmith College of Further Education. A member of the CPGB, Jane was a remarkable person, kind, warm and passionate about her work. She offered me a job teaching English and liberal studies to young working-class people who came to college on day release every week.

But on my first day of teaching, I received a rude shock. In the classroom were all white males and one very young woman from the Caribbean. As I introduced myself, one of the students shouted, 'There ain't no f***ing Paki going to teach us English,' and the entire class, with the exception of the one woman, walked out. They stood outside the room talking loudly and making racist comments. I concluded that it was a battle of wills and was in no mood to lose, so I approached that rowdy group and, using some well-chosen expletives, made it clear that they either entered the classroom or left the premises. They left, and I politely asked the young woman also to go.

Jane King was superb in the way she dealt with that incident. She asked me to stay calm and continue teaching the next class as scheduled. In the meantime, she upbraided that group for their terrible racist behaviour with the upshot that they attended classes the following week.

But when recording their attendance, the students gave names of well-known football players from leading London clubs, thinking that I wouldn't realise they were playing games with me. Since employees who were sent by their employers on day-release to attend further education classes received full salaries if they did so, I played along, recording their fake names and informing them that their pay would be docked for not being marked as 'present'. Possibly the football stars who earned quite well would not need the extra income. That had the desired impact, and they rather meekly gave me their real names.

Since English was their home language, which most of them read and wrote rather badly, I realised that I would not improve their command of it by teaching them formally once a week and instead devised word games and discussion groups around their passionate interest in football. I even managed to get them to write and hand in some work – and at times, with the consent of Jane King, I would take one of the classes for football games on an adjacent pitch. As a result, I was able to achieve something and earn a little bit of money.

Still seeking to supplement my meagre income, with the help of Ben Turok, I obtained a part-time job teaching liberal studies at a Police Cadet College in Welwyn Garden City. Again, I was lucky to find a warm and welcoming head of department. Trying to interest young people, some of whom, in my view, would become thugs or gangsters if not police officers, was a difficult but interesting challenge. After a while, I established a good working relationship with that group. Then, something unexpected happened. After participating in a sit-in at the SAA offices in Oxford Street, unaware that it would be shown on BBC News, the next time I entered that class, there was a chorus of, 'We saw you! We saw you! You're a demonstrator!' So then and there, I decided to talk to them about why people demonstrate, illustrating my talk with examples from the Anti-Apartheid Movement (AAM), demonstrations against the US war in Vietnam, and the annual Campaign for Nuclear Disarmament (CND) marches in England. I thought I had made a good impression. How wrong I was.

The following week, the Head of Department gave me a lift to the railway station and asked me what I had said to the class. I told him the whole story, and he listened very attentively. Then he reminded me that my students were police cadets, many of whom were politically conservative, and a few might even be racists. He said that one or more of them had laid an official complaint about my political views on demonstrations. He only asked that I be more cautious when discussing some of the more sensitive issues in the UK. It worked out quite well, and at the end of the year, the class gave me a present and some kind words about what they had learnt from me. My experiences at Hammersmith and Welwyn Garden City made me much more appreciative of the work Meg was doing teaching at the tough schools in Inner London.

In 1972, Meg and I moved to Maida Vale with Yasmin and at last had a family home. The three of us even visited Meg's family in the Lake District for a holiday. Meg's parents were pleased that I was working for money, despite having refused to promise to support my wife. We had many memorable and enjoyable times with our friends in Braemar House, and I have to admit that sometimes we allowed the music to go on rather late, perhaps offending our neighbours. It was a very happy period that did not last long, for our little family would soon be broken up.

On 26 May 1973, my mother Amina was killed by a dangerous driver. She had been walking peacefully in Mumbai when a car mounted the pavement and caught part of her clothing in its wheels. Not realising what he had done, the driver proceeded down the road, dragging our mother to her death. That left a vacuum in our family which could never be filled. Her death was a devastating loss.

Then, from 28 July to 5 August of that year, our ANC Youth and Students

(ANC Y&S) section once again sent a delegation to the World Festival of Youth and Students in East Berlin, German Democratic Republic (GDR). Meg joined the British delegation led by Mike Terry, which included Nick Wright, at that time a leading light in the 'Straight Left' faction of the CPGB, so we went with different groups but on the same train along with several other small delegations. Our ANC group from London included Billy Nannan, Sobizana, Abdul Bham, Tony Seedat and me. Joining us from Toronto were our cousins Zaheer Bhyat and Anver Saloojee, who I was very pleased to see and introduce to Meg. Yusuf 'JoJo' Saloojee, Ahmed Timol's close friend, also came from Toronto.

When entering West Germany from the Dutch border, the train was stopped at a station called Aachen, where West German officials arrested some Iraqi delegates, removing them from the train. When Mike Terry alerted the ANC delegation and many of the other delegates, we got off the train and refused to continue until the Iraqi comrades were released and allowed to rejoin us. We have photos of our group protesting at the station. Finally, we were all (including the Iraqis) allowed to continue to East Berlin.

The Festival was huge, with about 250,000 delegates accommodated from all over the world demonstrating, singing, dancing and discussing under the slogan 'Peace, Friendship and International Solidarity'. The official leader of our delegation was Joe Nhlanhla, but Chris Hani also played a leading role. The Festival's focus was solidarity with those fighting anti-imperialist struggles, like those in Vietnam, Palestine and Southern Africa. Our choir was very popular with its freedom songs. Erich Honecker presided over the event, and one of the chief guests was Angela Davis.

When we returned to London, we were met with a shock. It had been arranged that Yasmin (who was sixteen years old and doing her O levels) would use her school holiday to visit her sister and parents in South Africa from the end of July. But the apartheid regime took the opportunity to spitefully revoke her passport, and she was unable to return to us in August. We were deeply grieved and disappointed because we loved her like a daughter and still do.

Then, in September, it was decided that I must attend the Party School in Moscow for about a year. Aziz had already left for eight months of specialised training in military combat work (MCW) in Moscow, telling people he was going to India to help my father reorganise his life after my mother's death. He was there from about May until December. Of course, those training programmes were always conducted clandestinely, so we had to make up a cover story for Meg's family and others who asked them to explain why I was not around in London anymore. I had to leave Meg on her own.

Meg had joined the Communist Party of Great Britain after Timol was murdered in 1971 and was secretary of the North Paddington branch. She was also the convenor for the primary school section of Teachers Against Racism and was the National Union of Teachers (NUT) representative for her school. With her friends and work as a teacher, her life was still busy.

The branch meetings of the local CPGB all took place in our flat, with some wonderful people involved, such as branch chair Tom Wolfenden, who was a great raconteur. He and Charlie Doyle had worked at Battersea Power Station and were instructed by Bert Ramelson, the industrial organiser of the CPGB, to ensure that they organised the unions throughout London to control the power and switch off the capital city by calling a strike if so instructed. Harold Wilson held Bert responsible for the 1966 Seamen's Strike, blaming it on a 'tightly knit group of politically motivated men'. Tom proudly related how they organised after their initial meeting (just the two of them on a park bench) until they achieved their goal, just a year or two later. He had a wealth of beautifully expressed slogans like: 'If they won't give us bread, we'll take the bloody bakery.' His wife, Nina, and Charlie's wife, Micky Doyle, were also wonderful people and great supporters of the *Morning Star*. We became good friends with many of the people employed there, including Billy's wife, Theresa Nannan, who worked for a while as a bookkeeper.

Brian and Mary Filling came from Glasgow to London from 1971–74, when Brian was appointed editor of the Young Communist League (YCL) magazine, *Challenge*. When they moved into our area in 1973, they joined the North Paddington branch. Brian was the YCL delegate to the Preparatory Committee for the World Youth Festival in Berlin in 1973. During one of the meetings, I appealed for donations to the International Solidarity, and Brian pledged a substantial amount from the YCL; that infuriated its leadership, as they did not wish to make any contribution. Consequently, Brian was prevented from attending the Festival.

Brian had also been active in the Anti-Apartheid Movement since the early 1960s, and he founded the Scottish AAM in 1976 and chaired it until 1994. I shall have more to say about Brian Filling later in this memoir.

Nick Wright was also a member of the North Paddington branch, and, like Brian and Mary, supported the Straight Left group. When David Triesman and Colin Roberts, both Eurocommunists, joined, there were fierce debates in the branch. David later became a life peer, Baron Triesman, in 2004 and was Tony

Blair's Under-Secretary for the Foreign and Commonwealth Office in 2007. In 2008, he became the first independent Chairman of the Football Association.

Meg and I became good friends with many British communists, including Christabel Gurney, editor of the *Anti-Apartheid News* and treasurer of the Ladbroke Grove branch of the CPGB, Ken and Tess Gill, and Mike Seifert. Ken Gill was a leading trade unionist, a supporter of the AAM and the *Morning Star*, and a strong defender of the Soviet Union. He was expelled from the CPGB in 1985 when it broke ties with Moscow and adopted a Eurocommunist position. Mike was a great lawyer from the left-wing firm Seifert Sedley, whose clients included the CPGB, the National Union of Mineworkers, the Greenham Common women, and the ANC. He was a true internationalist and friend of the working class as well as a generous, amusing and witty host.

※

If I remember correctly, I was recruited into the SACP in late 1966 or early 1967. At that time, Reg September was the chief representative of the ANC in the UK. One day, he called me into his office and suggested we go for a walk. It was an unusual request, but I assumed he wanted to say something that should not be heard by anyone in the ANC Office or the British and South African Secret Services, who may well have been bugging our phones.

On that casual walk, he gave me great news: I had been recruited into the Party and, at a certain date and time, should go to the home of Brian and Sonia Bunting for my first Party meeting. I was told in no uncertain terms that my membership was a secret which must be known only to the Party leadership and others who were members of the same unit. I guess Aziz was recruited in a similar manner at about the same time. I was overjoyed but could not share my happiness with anyone.

On the appointed date, I made sure I was on time and was delighted to find that, besides Brian and Sonia, M. P. Naicker and Ronnie Kasrils were there. I also recall other members of that unit: Johnny Sachs, Tony O'Dowd and Mary Turok. Later, Herbie Pillay was transferred to join us. We met once a month at the Buntings'.

At those meetings, Brian would lead a discussion on developments in South Africa, based mainly on South African newspapers, which he read assiduously. Those were interesting and thought-provoking discussions and debates, as the unit members brought their own understanding and experience to bear. They also enabled us to keep in touch with what was happening within the various political, trade union and civic organisations inside the country.

As a unit, we were at times asked to read, analyse and comment on documents prepared by the Central Committee on wide-ranging issues in South Africa and internationally in preparation for crucial meetings, such as the Augmented Meeting of the Central Committee held in East Berlin, GDR, in 1970. I was very pleased when informed that I had been selected as a delegate; it was the first time I had been invited, and I was both elated and nervous. At that meeting were the luminaries of the Party and also Aziz, Billy Nannan, Antonio Mongalo and Thabo Mbeki. I spent a lot of time outside the official sessions with Billy, Aziz, Antonio and Thabo. We had countless chats – for the first time as Party members – which helped solidify my friendship with Billy and Antonio.

It was a fresh learning experience listening to delegates discussing the 'Call to the South African People', which had been written so as to be readily understood by all the people of South Africa. We first discussed the international situation with a firm condemnation of imperialism and praise for the heroic resistance of the Vietnamese people, which we described as 'an inspiration to us'. We then recorded the successes of FRELIMO in Mozambique, ZAPU in Zimbabwe, MPLA in Angola, PAIGC in Guinea-Bissau and Cape Verde, and SWAPO in Namibia as close allies and comrades-in-arms. As the document was a call to the people of South Africa, there was a special mention of 'The Socialist Way of Life'. An analysis of South Africa was offered, which declared that 'the greatest organisation of the South African democratic revolution is the African National Congress, undisputed leader of the majority of our population.' The message was clear: we needed a 'people's war': guerrilla warfare. As the document pointed out:

> Yes. It is true that the enemy is powerful. They have the armoured cars and the tanks, the planes and the command of the roads and the railways. But there is a way to fight, to beat the enemy. It is the way of people's war.[34]

In a rousing appeal to the people, the document calls for the building of and support for the illegal ANC and SACP to act militantly for higher wages, land

---

34. 'Call to the South African People', SA History.org, p. 19. Available at https://sahistory.org.za/sites/default/files/Freedom%20Can%20Be%20Won%20-%20A%20Call%20to%20the%20South%20African%20People.pdf

and freedom and to fight the national liberation war to the finish.

As Lerumo (Michael Harmel) explains in his book *Fifty Fighting Years – The South African Communist Party 1921–1971*:

> Emphasis was laid on the character of the fighting force as one of political cadres subordinate to the political movement and based on conviction and commitment rather than traditional bourgeois-type military discipline. Political and military leadership must be coordinated and eventually integrated. (The meeting) also devoted much of its attention to the complex and exacting problems of organisation, propaganda and the maintenance of high standards of conduct and discipline in the present testing conditions.[35]

That meeting, coming as it did not long after the Morogoro Conference, had a profound impact on the cadres, including me, and the leaders of the SACP, ANC and SACTU. That clarion call to the people was illegally distributed inside the country and, from the reports that emerged, it was well received.

Within the party, I grew as a disciplined revolutionary, and my commitment to the freedom struggle and building and strengthening the ANC was reinforced. The party unit was my special political home in which I learnt a great deal of the theory and practice of Marxism-Leninism, revolutionary struggle, and international events and developments. My love and support for the Soviet Union, Vietnam, Cuba and the other socialist countries became an irresistible force. In the party unit, all were encouraged to express their views and disagreements. I found this refreshing and a rebuttal of those anti-communist writers and scribes who claimed that the party was anti-democratic, bureaucratic and a network of conspirators.

From my party membership came another responsibility and opportunity: in 1970 or 1971, I became a member of the board of *The African Communist* (AC), a magazine which operated from a small office in Goodge Street for nearly twenty years. In the beginning, it was run by Michael Harmel, the founding editor, and Sonia Bunting. After Harmel's deployment to Prague in 1972 as the SACP representative on the Editorial Council of *World Marxist Review* (WMR), Brian Bunting took over as editor and held that position with great distinction until 1990.

Meanwhile, Sonia Bunting ran the AC office (the only address the SACP had) single-handedly. Her selfless hard work handling correspondence,

---

35. Ibid. p. 111.

receiving visitors and helping to prepare every issue ensured that the AC was printed in the GDR and distributed to readers throughout the world. At the same time, Sonia was an active member of the SACP, the ANC and the Anti-Apartheid Movement. She, like Brian, was always very kind to me and, on numerous occasions, invited me to their house for an evening meal before a Party unit meeting. Sonia should be celebrated as a true hero of our struggle.

Any person who wishes to write on the history of the SACP from the 1960s to the present time would do well to read and critically analyse the editorials, articles and book reviews contained in *The African Communist*. It remains a treasure trove of the views, policies and positions of members and non-members of the SACP. In retrospect, I feel proud of some of the articles I contributed.

Although the CPSA had been banned in 1950, it was reconstituted illegally under its new name, the SACP, in 1953. However, its existence was only made public in 1961, prior to which it had been decided to produce *The African Communist* – not in the name of the party but in the name of 'a group of Marxist-Leninists'.[36]

In its first issue in 1959, *The African Communist* declared that 'Africa needs Communist thought as dry and thirsty soil needs rain',[37] profound words which have reverberated within me ever since. When Kathrada gave me a copy of its first issue, he did so with the strict instruction to keep it in a safe place but not at home. Together with many cadres in the movement, I was greatly inspired by that inaugural edition and understood that it was published by the Communist Party.

After 1959, the board of *The African Communist* featured some of the ablest Communist Party thinkers and leaders, including Govan Mbeki, Rusty Bernstein, Joe Matthews, M. P. Naicker, Joe Slovo, Brian Bunting, Yusuf Dadoo, Thabo Mbeki, Alan Brookes, Francis Meli, Barry Feinberg, Ronnie Kasrils, Jabulani 'Mzala' Nxumalo, and 'Phineas Malinga' (Tony O'Dowd).

Looking back on my appointment to the board of the AC, I felt excited and honoured but initially somewhat nervous about being in the company of Michael Harmel. Michael was a warm, compassionate comrade with a fine sense of humour who knew how to work with younger comrades and was ever ready to encourage us to read and learn more about the theory and practice of Marxism-Leninism. I have always remembered two of his sayings. When he wanted to invite you for a drink, he would say, 'Let us lift a few

---

36. 'Avenge the Martyrs of Coalbrook', Editorial, *The African Communist*, 1 October 1959, p.2. Available at https://disa.ukzn.ac.za/sites/default/files/pdf_files/Acn159.0001.9976.000.001.Oct1959.pdf
37. Ibid. p.2.

elbows,' and if someone said or wrote something unintelligible or ambiguous, he would describe it as being 'as clear as mud'.

Alan Brooks and I were given a lift to my first board meeting by Joe Slovo. There, we joined Harmel, the Buntings, Rusty Bernstein, Ronnie Kasrils and Tony O'Dowd. The AC Board met regularly and discussed the sociopolitical and socio-economic situation in South Africa, the continent and internationally. We also discussed the immediate past issue, forthcoming articles and who we could ask to contribute, and any responses we had received from the party leadership and our readers. I thoroughly enjoyed those discussions and participated as well as I could. I still maintain that we produced a journal accessible to cadres of our revolutionary movement and non-South African readers. Although the language had to be clear and simple, as a Communist Party journal, it used Marxist-Leninist terminology and included numerous quotes from Marx, Engels and Lenin.

Undoubtedly, the AC influenced many cadres and was particularly helpful in raising the level of consciousness and understanding of the young revolutionaries who joined the ANC following the Soweto and connected uprisings of 1976. The AC was read and critically analysed in MK camps in Tanzania, Zambia and Angola and underground units in the Frontline States. Special efforts were made to distribute it at home: when posted from London, it had false covers. We were always heartened to hear reports from inside South Africa about the responses of those who had obtained it under extremely difficult conditions. If found with a copy or copies of the AC, they would have faced a lengthy prison sentence.

In his article in the AC in October 2009, Ronnie Kasrils gave a very useful account of the journal's launch and the endeavours made to get it to the people inside the country. He records that the last AC Editorial Board to operate from London 'consisted of Brian and Sonia Bunting, Rusty Bernstein, "Phineas Malinga", Frances Meli, Essop Pahad and Barry Feinberg'.

My first article for the AC was in the 4th Quarter 1971 edition on Indians in South Africa, published under the pseudonym Ahmed Azad. I chose Ahmed in deference to Ahmed Kathrada and Azad because it means 'freedom' in Urdu and was the name of one of India's great freedom fighters and leaders, Maulana Kalam Azad. My pseudonyms varied from this to Ahmed, AA, and Vusizwe Seme; sometimes I used my real name.

From 1973 to 1988, I did at least six book reviews. My reviews of a book by Bridglal Pachai called *The International Aspects of the South African Indian*

---

38. Cape Town: Struik, 1971.

Question, 1860–1971[38] and Ben Turok's *Strategic Problems in South Africa's Liberation Struggle: A Critical Analysis*[39] were harshly critical. In the latter, I wrote rather melodramatically, 'It is neither scientifically analytical nor constructively critical.' My review of a book by Nosizwe (Neville Alexander) was equally critical. I also reviewed *Socialism and the Newly Independent Nations* by R. Ulyanovsky,[40] a high-ranking official of the Communist Party of the Soviet Union (CPSU) and leading scholar on Africa; *Non-Capitalist Development: An Historical Outline* by V. Solodnikov and V. Bogoslovsky;[41] *Revolutionary Democracy in Africa: Its Ideology and Policy* by N. Kosukchin;[42] and *Marcus Garvey, Anti-Colonial Champion* by Rupert Lewis.[43] Rupert was, for a few years, the representative of the Workers Party of Jamaica (WPJ) at the WMR, and his book gave me a new insight into the politics and work of Garvey. Meg also contributed a book review in 1989 under the pseudonym GEM, on *Matigari* by Ngũgĩ wa Thiong'o.[44]

My most frequent contributions to the AC were in its 'Africa Notes and Comment', where I wrote as Ahmed Azad. That was a daunting task, as I was aware that Thabo Mbeki had contributed to the same column as Jabulani before me. Between 1981 and 1988, I wrote seventeen of the 'Notes', covering Sudan, Central Africa, Uganda, Egypt, Gambia, Senegal, Chad, Ghana, Liberia, Mali, Angola, Somalia, Burkina Faso, Libya, Cameroon, Algeria, Nigeria, Mozambique, Tunisia and Kenya.

An example is No. 104 First Quarter 1986 when, in the 'Africa Notes and Comment' section, I opined on Burkina Faso in an article titled 'No Easy Road to Social Progress'. After lauding some of the positive achievements of Sankara and the National Council of the Revolution (Conseil National de la Revolution: CNR) from 1984–1985 and the plans to improve the conditions and status of women, I concluded:

> Quite naturally, revolutionaries in Africa follow with close attention developments in Burkina Faso. A successful revolutionary transformation of Burkinabe society would have a profound effect on the revolutionary process unfolding in Africa. But this requires the unity in action of all the revolutionary forces. Any division will be exploited by local and foreign reaction. In the case of the latter,

---

39. Richmond, British Columbia: LSM Information Center, 1974.
40. Moscow: Progress Publishers, 1974.
41. Moscow: Progress Publishers, 1975.
42. Moscow: Progress Publishers, 1979.
43. London: Karia Press, 1987.
44. Oxford, UK: Heineman, 1987.

French imperialism is still working to make Burkina Faso dependent once again on neocolonialism and US imperialism. Its agencies such as the CIA are working to destabilise the country.⁴⁵

On 15 October 1987, President Thomas Sankara was tragically murdered in a coup no doubt engineered in Paris and Washington.

In the years 1971 to 1988, I wrote thirty articles covering countries such as Cuba, the Soviet Union, Chile, Ethiopia and Somalia and dealing with issues like world peace, proletarian internationalism and anti-Sovietism and the contribution of people like Yusuf Dadoo, Ahmed Kathrada and Henry Winston to the struggle against racism in SA and the USA. During that time, I also organised and participated in a round-table contribution on culture chaired by Brian Bunting which included Ngũgĩ wa Thiong'o, Mongane Wally Serote and Mandla Langa. There may have been more contributions, but not all editions of the AC are available for review.

For this memoir, I have selected quotes from seven articles I contributed. The first is from 'Lessons of the Chilean Revolution', First Quarter 1975. In September 1970, the Popular Unity Government under President Salvador Allende of the Socialist Party and its close ally, the Communist Party of Chile, were voted into power through a democratic election. In September 1973, US imperialism and its primary instrument, the CIA, engineered a coup that overthrew the Popular Unity (*Unidad Popular*: UP) government and brutally murdered Allende. For over fifteen years, the people of Chile were subjected to the most gruesome detention and torture and murder of progressive political figures, intellectuals and artists. Pablo Neruda's famous words about Guernica were now horrifyingly appropriate for his own country, Chile:

> You will ask: why doesn't his poetry speak of dreams and leaves and the great volcanoes of his native land?
> Come and see the blood in the streets.
> Come and see
> The blood in the streets
> Come and see the blood
> In the streets!⁴⁶

In the concluding paragraph of the article I wrote:

---

45. The article starts on page 67 of Issue No. 104 with the featured quote appearing on page 69. The entire issue is available online at https://disa.ukzn.ac.za/sites/default/files/pdf_files/Acn10486.pdf
46. Available at https://disa.ukzn.ac.za/sites/default/files/pdf_files/Acn6075.pdf

> Three years of Popular Unity government have given not only the people of Chile but all revolutionary forces a wealth of experience. Its successes and gains should not be underestimated and likewise its mistakes should not be overestimated. ... It is a tragic but temporary defeat suffered by the brave and heroic people of Chile and their revolutionary organisations.[47]

In the Second Quarter of 1976, I wrote 'The Island of Freedom' about the First Congress of the Communist Party of Cuba and was utterly surprised but overjoyed when the editor and management of the WMR asked me to join the deputy editor as a delegate from the WMR. In that article, I wrote:

> For me as a South African revolutionary, the 1st Congress was an unforgettable political and emotional experience. To experience first-hand how racialism has been eradicated and relegated to the dustbins of history, how proud the Cubans are to have flowing in their veins the blood of Africa, Asia, [Native] America and Europe. To feel that great love of friendship, brotherhood and militant comradeship that ties our oppressed people to the free people of Cuba.[48]

The article continues to describe how, at the end of that Congress, a Congress of the People – more than a million strong – was held near the José Marti Memorial in Revolution Square. I wrote:

> As Fidel approached the podium, the vast crowd burst into great shouts of 'Fidel! Fidel! Fidel, hit the Yankees hard!' The discipline of the crowd and their enthusiastic support for the decisions adopted by Congress are indescribable. When the various speakers spoke on behalf of the mass organisations pledging their support to the Congress resolutions, you could hear a pin drop, such was the silent attention of more than a million people.[49]

In the Third Quarter of 1976, I wrote about the torrent of anti-Soviet, anti-Cuban and anti-communist tirades following the defeat of the apartheid army in Angola in an article entitled 'No Room for Anti-Sovietism in Africa'.

---
47. Ibid.
48. Available at https://disa.ukzn.ac.za/sites/default/files/pdf_files/Acn6576.pdf
49. Available at https://disa.ukzn.ac.za/sites/default/files/pdf_files/Acn6075.pdf

The major imperialist powers threatened the Soviet Union, claiming it was putting in jeopardy the policy of détente and peaceful coexistence. I wrote:

> In South Africa, the anti-communist hysteria was most evident. ... The arrogant and vainglorious White South African army, saturated by racial prejudice and attitudes, had assumed that no 'backward ignorant' black people would be able to defeat them. However, the sharp and victorious counter-offensive of the MPLA soldiers and their Cuban allies ... rudely shattered the myth of white superiority.[50]

In that same article I declared:

> For communists, proletarian internationalism is the cornerstone of Marxism-Leninism ... The ideologues of imperialism are now paying special attention to the apparent contradiction between the national struggle and internationalism. But there is no such contradiction; communists are at one and the same time patriots and internationalists. ... Internationalism is no abstract concept but arises from the objective conditions of the life of the workers and peasants which propel them to combine their forces in order to resist on an international scale the attempts of the imperialists to hold back social and national liberation.[51]

In the article 'The Horn of Africa – Defeat for Imperialism', Third Quarter 1978, I wrote:

> However, the days when the imperialist powers could with racist arrogance consider Africa as their own backyard are over. Africa is on the move and constitutes a vital part of the worldwide forces which are busy making history.[52]

In that article, I condemned Somali aggression in the Ogaden region of Ethiopia. In attempting to understand that complex conflict between Somalia and Ethiopia and the reversal of progressive policies in Somalia, I warned about the danger of imperialism, saying:

---

50. Available at https://disa.ukzn.ac.za/sites/default/files/pdf_files/Acn6676.pdf
51. Ibid.
52. Available at https://disa.ukzn.ac.za/sites/default/files/pdf_files/Acn7478.pdf

> It is unpleasant but true that the imperialist powers, particularly US imperialism, still possess great reserves of economic, political, ideological and conspiratorial power which they use unscrupulously to undermine not only revolutionary democratic states but also socialist countries.[53]

I also commented:

> The recent events in Somalia graphically demonstrate that chauvinism is absolutely incompatible with socially progressive policies. Chauvinism arises from a belief in national exclusiveness and superiority and a refusal to have a class standpoint on national and international politics. The myth of creating a 'Greater Somalia' was taken to absurd levels.[54]

I was fortunate to attend the World Assembly for Peace and Life and Against Nuclear War in Prague in June 1983. In the article entitled 'Humanity Yearns for Peace and Life' in the Fourth Quarter of 1983, I noted that there were 3,625 participants from 132 countries covering a diverse spectrum of peace fighters and peace defenders. I also criticised some sections of the Western media, including the BBC, for distorting the whole nature and character of the Assembly. In the opening paragraph, I wrote:

> To prevent a nuclear holocaust is the most burning question facing all humanity. This is because the Reagan administration continues to poison international relations, believes in a first-strike nuclear policy, and, against all the evidence, holds that a limited nuclear war between the USA and the USSR is an option, which, in certain circumstances, must be seriously considered.[55]

I was most impressed by the peace rally of 200,000 people held in Prague's historic Old Town Square and was particularly moved by the speech of Fenner Brockway, a lifelong fighter against colonialism, racism, fascism and for world peace and national liberation. He was ninety-four, and I wrote admiringly, 'His youthful optimism and his deep commitment to peace, freedom and national independence inspired everyone.'

---

53. Ibid.
54. Ibid.
55. https://disa.ukzn.ac.za/sites/default/files/pdf_files/Acn9583.pdf

There was also a Solidarity Forum addressed by, among others, Yasser Arafat; Luis Echeverría, former President of Mexico; and Alfred Nzo, Secretary-General of the ANC.

~

I will now backtrack to another event which profoundly affected my life. In September 1973, Uncle Doc informed me that I had been selected to attend the Lenin Party School in Moscow. I was beyond happiness, for, not only was I going to what I considered the most prestigious international communist school, but also to the Soviet Union, a place I had wanted to visit since my earliest introduction to political life. Thabo Mbeki, Anne Nicholson and Ahmed Timol were the last South Africans to study there (in 1969).

The SACP made all the travel arrangements, and Uncle Doc impressed on me that I had to use the opportunity to learn as much as I could and always be a disciplined student to protect and enhance the reputation of the SACP in the Soviet Union and the World Communist Movement.

It was in September 1973 that I arrived in Moscow, full of excitement and raring to go. But after clearing passport control and customs, I found to my disappointment and astonishment, that there was no one there to meet me. With my suitcase in hand, I was a lost soul in a city I had never seen and knew not a word of the language. Given that my mission was secret, I could not approach the information desk at Sheremetyevo Airport.

After many failed attempts, I found someone who could speak English and asked him to inform the relevant authorities that I was a guest of the CPSU, but for some reason, there was no one to meet me. Not long after, a grey-haired man who spoke a smattering of English took me to the VIP lounge. He was warm and kind and, responding to my obvious anxiety with reassurances that all would be well, gave me tea and biscuits. An hour or so later, I was collected and taken to a 'dacha' (a country home) run by very friendly people. But they spoke no English, and I spoke no Russian, so we communicated by sign and body language. I felt very lonely. What a welcome to my mecca of communism!

Later that day, a group of Iraqi students arrived, and to my great relief, one of them spoke English. He was really pleasant, and with his help, I was able to communicate with the entire group. Then the following day, a group of Chilean students arrived. They had finished their studies and were on a seven-day practice so they could visit one of the Soviet republics and learn something about life there while having a short rest before returning to their home countries. Fortunately, one of the Chileans also spoke English, which enabled his colleagues to communicate their excitement about returning home to help build a new socialist Chile. I was so happy for them but also envious because, while they were building a new society, we were still looking for light at the end of a tunnel.

But life and its unfolding can sometimes be cruel and unforgiving. On 3 September 1973, disaster struck when a CIA-inspired and fully supported coup overthrew Salvador Allende, murdered him, and put in place the fascist monster, Augusto Pinochet. Joy and optimism about realising a socialist dream were replaced by despair, despondency and fear for the fate of comrades, friends and family living in Chile. Pinochet's brutal regime immediately arrested thousands of socialists, communists and others from various progressive forces, and political and civic activists, intellectuals, artists, scholars and academics were rounded up, imprisoned and subjected to the most vicious forms of torture and death.

The Communist Party of Chile now had to begin the long walk of anti-fascist underground struggle. To their credit and our admiration, they kept alive the unity and cohesion of the party and its alliance with the socialists and other progressive forces under the extremely harsh conditions of a tragic and deadly reversal of fortunes.

Two days later, after a medical test, I was taken to a building that housed the Lenin Party School: Number 49, in a street named after Lenin; it was often referred to as '49' (in Russian). There, I was given a room by myself in the main building; there was also a separate residential annexe about ten minutes' walk away. On my arrival, I was lucky to meet four students from the Philippines: Sammy, Ali, Abdul and Tristan. We became close friends and comrades, spending many days and hours together and playing volleyball and football in the main hall.

A day later, an unusual incident occurred when I was taken by Alexei, an interpreter, to a photographer who, instead of taking photos, just stared at me. I was perplexed, to say the least, and when I asked Alexei what was happening, he burst into laughter. Apparently, the photographer was in love with Pushkin, one of Russia's greatest poets, who was of Ethiopian ancestry, and I resembled him, which enthralled the photographer. Alexei suggested I visit the famous statue of Pushkin to see for myself. So with the help of my Filipino comrades, I found the statue, and to my delight, there was a definite similarity. I guess my long curly hair contributed to the resemblance. Thereafter, I would joke that either Pushkin or my ancestors had been up to something naughty.

Since I was the only student from South Africa and had a PhD from Sussex University, the rector and his management team decided I should study on my own and not with the English-speaking students from India, Australia or New Zealand.

After a brief course on media studies, I concentrated on political economy and philosophy. My tutor for political economy was Professor Randina, who had written extensively on the topic, and we started with Marx's volumes on capital and later moved to socialist economies, especially in the Soviet Union. Then, as luck would have it, I was assigned a philosophy lecturer named Arkady Grigorian, who had also tutored Thabo, Timol and Anne. From our first encounter, we got on like a house on fire. He was an extraordinary human being – warm, compassionate and humble with a sense of humour – embodying all the finer points of empathy. He always had a ready smile, treated his students with care and attention and instilled in me a lasting love and appreciation of the philosophy of Marxism-Leninism. We became very close friends and comrades, and I visited his home – first a flat near Oktyabrskaya metro station and later one within walking distance of the Lenin Party School. It was a two-bedroomed flat he occupied with his wife Nadia and their two- or three-year-old daughter of the same name. There I experienced Russian hospitality first-hand.

After a few months, Arkady suggested that I extend my stay from six months to a year to complete the philosophy module on the same level as a Soviet PhD: a Candidate of Science. As this would also entail a dissertation, which would take more time, the matter was raised with officials from the CPSU and the SACP leaders. Both sides agreed, and my stay was extended to eighteen months. As the extension would entail a long absence from London, the party leaders arranged for Meg to meet me in Moscow, where we stayed for a week in the party hotel, Oktyabrskaya. I would later visit that hotel on many occasions as a guest of the CPSU.

Working toward the Candidate of Science was extremely challenging as my reading assignments increased, and I was expected to explain the texts I studied in depth. We also spent some time discussing and analysing bourgeois philosophy. Working with Arkady was an unforgettable experience. In addition to our work, he taught me a lot about life in the Soviet Union and the CPSU.

Arkady also influenced me to review my former admiration for Stalin. While telling me about the many crimes Stalin had committed during his reign as head of the state and party, Arkady recounted how his father, then a high-ranking Red Army officer, had been imprisoned by Stalin with many other officers. With pride, he related that when Nazi Germany was on the outskirts of Moscow, Stalin released those officers, including Arkady's father, and asked them to go to the front. Without hesitation, they agreed and helped the Red Army to repulse the attack on Moscow and other cities in the USSR. As a mark of our friendship, he gave me his soldier's belt from his time in the Red Army, a gift that I treasure to this day.

Before I continue, I have to tell you this story. Opposite the Party School was a small dim-looking bottle store, and when walking around the area, I was fascinated by an individual who would often come to stand outside it and put up three fingers. As soon as he did that, three others would join him in quick succession. Once they were four, and without exchanging a word, they would disappear into the bottle store, emerging a few minutes later, looking happy, and disperse without any communication. This ritual made no sense to me, so I asked Alexei about it. Well, he could not stop laughing but eventually explained that a bottle of vodka cost four roubles, and since those individuals were short of cash, they would each contribute one rouble and gulp down the vodka on the premises.

As I had to experience that, I can tell you how it works. You stand in the queue, and once there are four of you, you enter the bottle store together and give one rouble each to the person collecting the money, who then buys the vodka and is given four plastic cups. Without hesitation, he pours four equal portions into the cups; then, you gulp your share and, without a word to the others, leave the store. I would not recommend this ritual to anyone, but it did alert me to what I would call the Soviet underclass, some of whom were unemployed, did not fit in with Soviet society and indulged in petty crime.

Now, back to the Party School, which was very close to the Dynamos metro station and the home of Dynamos Football Club. Given that we had taken the name of our South African Dynamos from the Moscow and Czech Football clubs, I just had to attend some of the games at that stadium.

A valuable part of my learning experience at the Party School resulted from the fact that the students came from all over the world. There was a long-standing tradition that on special occasions, such as the anniversary of the founding date of a party, the relevant group from that party would organise a lively get-together. One representative from each of the other parties would be invited, and since I was the only South African, I was invited to all of the celebrations and had to make a speech on behalf of the SACP at each one. Attending those functions contributed to my political understanding, maturity and development. I learnt a great deal about the history and activities of many different communist parties and, from Brazil in particular, about fascist-type repression and anti-communism.

In addition to the Filipino comrades, I developed close personal and working relationships with the students from India. Some of them would cook curries in the style of the areas they came from. One such student was Rajah, who used the pseudonym Stalin and later rose to become National Secretary of the Communist Party of India.

I also enjoyed going to Gorky Park some Sundays. I would go on my own, sit on a bench and observe how young Soviet citizens walked, talked, laughed and socialised, which gave me a small insight into their behaviour patterns. I recall an incident much later when I was visiting Yerevan in Armenia. An interpreter from Moscow accompanied me, and the local party organisation provided an interpreter from Armenia. One day, they were surprised when I requested to visit the main park in Yerevan and even more surprised when I suggested that we just sit there and observe people walking around in it.

After a while, I noticed something peculiar: people in small groups, the composition and size of which rapidly changed, engaging in animated discussions. I asked the Armenian interpreter if we could stand near enough to those groups to find out why they were so excited. We did so, and he explained that the previous year, the football team from Yerevan had been crowned champions of the Soviet Union, but now, it was not doing so well. Everyone seemed to be exchanging views and criticisms about their beloved team's performance, and like fans all over the world, they had numerous suggestions about how they could improve. I thoroughly enjoyed this experience, and both the interpreters now understood why I had wanted to visit a park. I recommend this approach to anyone who wants to observe behaviour patterns and gain insight into everyday life in a country.

Another highlight of my stay at the Party School was watching the ballet *Spartacus*, which was the most moving experience. I saw other ballets at the Bolshoi Theatre, but it was *Spartacus* that I enjoyed the most.

While I was at the Party School, Aziz was also sent to Moscow for special training, so our time there overlapped for about three months. Since our mother died just before we came to Moscow, the Party leadership permitted us to meet on compassionate grounds. Depending on our work programmes, we would get together on a Saturday or a Sunday and have tea or coffee and ice cream. One day, Aziz asked why, since there were no monopolies in the Soviet Union, so many of these places were called Pectopah. I was unsure if he was taking the mickey, but I explained that the word for 'restaurant' in Russian, written in the Cyrillic script, looks to English-speaking people like Pectopah. It was great to meet Aziz and share our views and experiences of the Soviet Union.

I invested a great deal of my intellectual, academic and political capacity in my studies and worked extremely hard. Never before had I spent so much of my time and energy studying; it was tough but rewarding. As was the norm at the School, at the end of the course, students had to sit for examinations – not written but an interview and interrogation. Some twenty minutes before an exam, we would be given the questions to peruse so we could refer to relevant basic materials. The political economy exam was no problem, but in philosophy, I was expected to respond at the level of a post-graduate student studying at a university in the USSR. I was very pleased to hear that I had scored excellent marks.

My mini-thesis was on the rise and practice of fascism in South Africa, and to my great regret, I have lost the only copy I had of it. Arkady tutored me on the theory and practice of Nazism and fascism and secured permission for me to use the famous Lenin Library. He also took the time and trouble to translate my mini-thesis into Russian for the other examiners. Since I was unable to meet all the requirements for the post-graduate degree, including a working knowledge of Russian, they could not confer the degree on me. But this did not concern me, as I was not looking to add to my existing academic qualifications. I was happy, however, to be told that my work had met the standards required for the degree of Candidate of Science.

At the Lenin School, I was fortunate to have met and had regular discussions with a close friend of Arkady who was a professor of philosophy. One encounter with the two of them revolved around a transistor radio I had purchased with the decent stipend given to all students. In the evenings, I would listen to the BBC World Service for information on South Africa and the world. When I complained to those two that, at times, the Soviet authorities were jamming the BBC, Arkady's friend smiled and said that, in his view, the Soviet authorities were wasting a lot of resources by jamming radio signals from the West, as within a few years, developments in the field of Information Technology (IT) and electronics would enable satellites hovering in the sky to transmit information, pictures and stories directly into the homes of Soviet citizens. It was a salutary lesson on the pointless nature of the obsession of the Soviet authorities with preventing their population from accessing the admittedly anti-Soviet, anti-communist propaganda. They should have had more confidence in their peoples' consciousness, understanding and support for socialism in the USSR and utilised their resources for better purposes.

During that wonderful, exhilarating eighteen months of living and learning, I received permission to do two additional classes. One was on underground, illegal work, and the other on the history of the CPSA (SACP). The latter class was given by Professor Apollon Davidson, who was not a member of the CPSU but one of the finest historians, studying, amongst other things, the history of the CPSA. He was what the English would call 'a true gentleman': humble, warm and very likeable. He taught me a great deal about the history of the CPSA[56] using primary sources, and we developed a close friendship that has endured.

My tutor in the work of the underground was a former Red Army officer with extensive experience working covertly in areas occupied by the murderous anti-communist German army. We did a lot of practical work, including how to set up dead-letter boxes.[57] From him, I got first-hand accounts of the courage and heroism of the underground operatives, especially members of the CPSU. I am so appreciative of the school authorities for organising those two additional classes.

The Lenin Party School also gave me the confidence to engage in serious discussions and robust debates on the theory and practice of Marxism-Leninism and the history of the CPSU, the Soviet Union and the World Communist Movement. I remain indebted to the SACP and the CPSU for making that possible, and I will forever treasure my interaction with and memory of the four students from the Philippines and Arkady Grigorian.

Regarding Arkady, let me recount a miserable experience meeting him some years later.

When Thabo Mbeki was Deputy President, I accompanied him as his Deputy Minister on an official visit to Moscow. With the help of Shubin[58] and

---

56. Professor Davidson headed the African Section of the Institute of General History of the USSR Academy of Sciences and wrote several books on British colonialism in various parts of Africa.
57. A dead-letter box is a covert location where messages or other items are deposited for retrieval by other intelligence operatives. Also called a dead drop, it is most often used as a means of transferring documents and messages but can also be used to funnel equipment and money to agents in the field. Available at https://www.encyclopedia.com/politics/encyclopedias-almanacs-transcripts-and-maps/dead-letter-box
58. Vladimir Shubin, member of the Soviet Union's Afro-Asian Solidarity Committee. He later worked for the CC of the CPSU with responsibility for South Africa.
59. Dr Vyacheslav Tetekin.

Slava,⁵⁹ who was, at that time, a leader of the Russian Communist Party, I was able to meet Arkady at a place outside Moscow. The Soviet Union had collapsed, the CPSU had been disbanded, and he had a poorly paid job as a lecturer in philosophy for the party in the area where he lived. He was divorced from Nadia and survived in a one-roomed flat with a tiny kitchenette. I was shocked and distressed to witness his working and living conditions. Despite losing his incredible zest for life and living, he tried very hard to be a good host. When I told Thabo about my shock and sadness at Arkady's condition and arranged for the two to meet, Arkady was most pleased.

For me, those who assumed power in Russia and reduced so many outstanding communists like Arkady to poverty were inhuman, violating fundamental human rights and dignity.

I was sad to leave the Lenin Party School but happy to return to Meg and my other comrades. I was battle ready, politically and ideologically, more disciplined, and better equipped to continue the long and unfinished journey as a freedom fighter.

Chapter 3
World Marxist Review

At a World Marxist Revue Editorial Board meeting

WORLD MARXIST REVIEW

After nearly eighteen months in Moscow, I was back in London with Meg and my friends and my ANC and SACP comrades. Although my future work in the movement was still uncertain, I continued my efforts in those organisations, with the former kindly agreeing to pay for my travel fares and giving me lunch money. Meg continued to bear the full cost of the flat, running our household, and additional personal expenses incurred by me. This lasted for about six months, until I was informed by Uncle Doc that I would be deployed to the *World Marxist Review* (WMR) to represent the SACP on its Editorial Council.

The WMR was based in Prague, Czechoslovakia, and I was delighted with the news, although my joy was mixed with trepidation since I was succeeding Michael Harmel, a giant of the party.

Michael died in Prague on 18 June 1974 at the age of fifty-nine, which dealt a hammer blow to the revolutionary alliance since he was one of our foremost theoreticians. To summarise, Michael helped found and edited *The African Communist* from 1959 to 1972 and played a leading role in drafting the *Road to South African Freedom*,[60] which developed the influential concept of 'Colonialism of a Special Type'. He had a lovely flowing writing style that was easy to read and digest – and I must remind you that he was the first principal of the CIHS and my English teacher when I was in Standard 8. Michael had a good rapport with younger comrades and worked with them in a way which helped them develop as communists and revolutionaries. He was a very sociable man who loved Irish pubs and poetry. His second partner, Kate O'Callaghan, an Irish communist, remained in Prague for about a year after we arrived, and she and Meg enjoyed each other's company.

In August 1975, I arrived in Prague alone. Meg had a teaching job and had applied for a year's leave of absence but had to make arrangements regarding our flat in Maida Vale. I was taken by a Czech staff member to a furnished flat with some basic kitchen utensils and bed linen in Arabskà in a suburb called Červeny Vrch (Red Hill), given some Czech crowns and shown where

---

60. Policy Document (London: Ellis Bowles, 1962).

the nearest shops were. I duly went shopping for my breakfast and supper the following day and, without a word of the local language, selected some essential foodstuffs, paid with the Czech money and pocketed the change.

The next day, I was taken to the offices of the WMR in Thakurova Street where, with the help of Slava, a Soviet interpreter, I was shown to my spacious office and given a briefing on the work of the journal and some articles to read. Slava also showed me how to use the beautiful metro and took me to the city centre. With his help, we identified Bulgarian, Hungarian and Russian restaurants I could frequent until Meg came to Prague. Those supplemented the Czech food provided in the WMR restaurant at lunchtime on weekdays, which I found bland and tasteless. Unfortunately, there were no Indian restaurants or even fast-food outlets, so I soon developed the habit of carrying a small bottle of Tabasco Sauce in my pocket. After about a month, Meg joined me, and we waited another month for our trunk full of Indian spices and lentils to arrive to set us up again with the food we liked best.

The *World Marxist Review* was called *Problems of Peace and Socialism* in many of its language editions. Its working language was Russian, and it was the only permanent collective institution serving the World Communist Movement with representatives from Communist and Workers Parties from Asia, the Middle East, Latin America, North America, the Caribbean, Europe and the Socialist World. From Africa, we had Algeria, Senegal, Sudan and South Africa. In 1982, the WMR had sixty-five representatives on the Editorial Council, which was regarded as a vital decision-maker where, among other responsibilities, current and future problems and challenges were discussed, as well as long-term plans.

There was a smaller Editorial Board of fifteen Parties, including those from India, the US, France, Italy and Great Britain, who were responsible for overseeing the work of the journal and links with the international communist movement and revolutionary national liberation movements. To assist in the working of those structures, there were regional and problem-orientated commissions; I chose to sit on four: class struggle in capitalist countries; problems of theory; problems of peace and democratic movements; and national liberation struggles in Asia and Africa. I played a more prominent role in the latter commission. All but one of the posts were held by Soviet citizens appointed by the CPSU; the exception was Pavel Ausberg from the Communist Party of Czechoslovakia (CPC), one of the two executive secretaries.

During my time at the WMR, we had three editors-in-chief: Konstantin

Zaradov; Yuri Sklyarov; and Alexander Subbotin. The Soviet comrade with whom I worked most closely was Vsevolod Rybakov, an always helpful intellectual with a deep understanding and passion for Asia, Africa and the Middle East. There was also a group of highly competent simultaneous interpreters covering Russian, French, Spanish, Arabic, German and English from the Soviet Union. Their assistance to the party representatives was immeasurable, and without them, we would not have been able to communicate with each other. They were also ready to assist with numerous mundane matters.

While at the WMR, I had the privilege and pleasure of meeting some amazing, courageous, caring and dedicated communists. I cannot mention all these wonderful people here, so include below those with whom Meg and I interacted most. Two others, José Lava and Amath Dansokho, will be covered later in the chapter on my mentors.

John and Margrit Pittman were the first people Meg and I made friends with when we were lucky enough to be allocated the flat in Arabska on our arrival in Prague. They lived in the same building.

John Pittman (1906–1993) was an African-American intellectual and exceptionally gifted journalist whose articles were a pleasure to read. Although he was older than me, we struck up a wonderful relationship and shared the view of the need to intensify the struggle against racism in the US, South Africa and the world. He had been born and brought up in Atlanta, Georgia, at a time when, as a Black child or man, you could be beaten, for example, for not getting off the pavement when a white person was walking towards you – and lynched for something considered worse. In our interactions, you could not help but feel the deep scars of slavery and racism, still prevalent today, that impact the lives and livelihoods of Black Americans in the USA.

John earned an MA in Economics from the University of California in 1930, lived through the Cold War and the McCarthy era in the US and had worked in all kinds of jobs. He was editor of the Communist Party of the United States of America's (CPUSA)'s paper *People's World* and a regular contributor to its monthly journal *Political Affairs*. He was unpretentious, smart, even-tempered and patient, with a very lively sense of humour. Often when we walked together and he noticed an attractive young woman, he would say, 'Now, Essop, you're never too old to look!' He was also the best shaggy-dog storyteller we have ever met, and when others tried to repeat his stories, it was a total flop. John had a perfect sense of timing and a wicked twinkle in his eye.

One example of a story he would spin for about fifteen minutes, building up to the climax, was about a memorial to General Custer commissioned by his admirers to be erected on the site of Little Bighorn. The artist was very famous and only consented to create the memorial if no one interfered with his project and everyone waited to view it on the day it was unveiled. Everything was agreed, and eventually the monument was revealed by the mayor. Well, the centre of the work was an enormous fish with a halo, and the massive border portrayed scores of Cheyenne and Sioux in a veritable Kama Sutra of possible positions of sexual intimacy. The horrified audience protested and demanded to know how this commemorated Custer's Last Stand. The reply was simple: It's based on Custer's last words: 'Holy mackerel! What a load of fucking Indians!'

If he wanted to discuss something with me, he would say, 'Essop, please come and see me – I need to pick your brains.' He was an excellent raconteur of the politics of the US and a passionate and dedicated fighter against racism and sexism. I learnt so much from John.

Margrit Pittman, née Adler (1919–2013), was a German Jewish refugee from Nazism whose aunt and cousins had been murdered in the Holocaust. She was also a prominent member of the CPUSA and a fine journalist, writing for the *Daily World* and *People's World*. Margrit commuted between Prague and East Germany, working as a correspondent for the communist media in the GDR and the US. She was a dedicated communist, an anti-racist and anti-fascist fighter, intelligent, compassionate and witty.

John and Margrit often invited people for a meal and went out of their way to ensure that all their guests were treated with equal respect and interest, not just the official representatives of the parties concerned. They were both genuinely anti-sexist and would encourage shy and modest women to discuss their political views and activities. We reciprocated their invitations and spent many enjoyable evenings together. They also shared their English-language paperbacks with us and introduced Meg to a few unfamiliar crime writers like Rex Stout, Maj Sjöwall and Per Wahlöö, as well as novelists like Barbara Kingsolver, who was not so well-known at that time. They were up-to-date in their concerns about world peace and humanity, with awareness, for example, about the dangers of carbon emissions, climate change and the possible abuses linked to genetically modified seeds.

We discussed and debated issues of race, class and gender and the achievements and shortcomings of the socialist countries, especially the GDR and Czechoslovakia. Margrit had deep insight into developments in the GDR and its ruling Socialist Unity Party.

John and Margrit remained active until their deaths and were involved in many campaigns and struggles for social and economic justice; they were fierce opponents of racism, sexism and fascism and fighters for world peace. They were close to Charlene Mitchell and Angela Davis, and, from 1991, they supported the group of members of the CPUSA who left to found the 'Committees of Correspondence', a broadly Marxist, democratic socialist, progressive group. In 2002, John and Margrit's children Carol and John Peter were involved in setting up the progressive publication *Portside*.

After John left the WMR, he was replaced by Jim West. Meg and I got on very well with him and his wife, Audrey. After Meg gave birth to our son Govan, the two of them were moved to a specialist hospital for sick babies on the second day of his life. There they had to stay for about six weeks, leaving me to look after our firstborn, Amina, who was three. Audrey was a great help to me during that time, assisting in all kinds of useful ways.

Sarada Prasad Mitra had been involved in politics in India, especially in the Communist Party of India (CPI), since his youth. At the first congress of the All-India Youth Federation (AIYF) in 1959, he was elected as its first General Secretary. The AIYF played a sterling role in the WFDY and mobilised international solidarity in India for anti-colonial, anti-imperialist struggles in Africa and Asia. It also played a prominent role in the Anti-Apartheid Movement and in building support for the ANC in India.

A mild-mannered pipe smoker with an infectious smile and a lovely sense of humour, Mitra deeply understood the complex class and national questions in India and the region. He was a member of the Editorial Board, chaired the Commission on The National Liberation Struggle in Asian and African Countries, and set a fine example of how to chair a meeting of diverse individuals from different countries in a pleasant and democratic manner. He was also patient and listened attentively to the various and sometimes conflicting views and positions articulated in that Commission, which enabled him, when the need arose, to summarise the discussions in a

---

61. Vaghar is a technique of pan-frying spices before adding them to a dish. In English, this would be called 'tempering'. The frying of the spices toasts them and brings out the aromatics. A vaghar is a mix of spices prepared in this way. Knowing what spices to use and how to vaghar is one of the most basic skills of Indian cooking. ... Ayurvedics would also say vaghar opens up the spices, improving their nutritional and medicinal value when consumed. Available at https://indiaphile.info/how-to-do-a-vaghar/

manner that satisfied all the participants.

Mitra was also a good West Bengali cook who was proud of the *vaghar vaghar*[61] he made as a garnish to enhance the scent and flavour of his curries. He would often invite a group of us, including his very close comrades, Sudiman from Indonesia and Agamemnon Stavrou from Cyprus, to enjoy his food and share some drinks and convivial discussion. Our conversations would cover the socialist countries, world peace and disarmament, the class and national liberation struggles in Africa, Asia and Latin America and ongoing developments in the more advanced capitalist countries. Mitra's wife was from the GDR, and their son, who had been born and raised in that country, was a member of the Socialist Unity Party (*Sozialistische Einheitspartei Deutschlands*: SED). The GDR remained their home while Mitra lived permanently in Prague, although his wife visited him regularly. That gave him an insider's understanding and assessment of the GDR and its ruling party, the SED.

Mitra often expressed his disagreement with the prevailing view that the CPSU and the Soviet government had to be on a par with the US in the arms race, with its destructive and debilitating impact on the economy and social life of the Soviet Union. He insisted that, since the USSR possessed enough nuclear weapons to inflict untold damage on the US in the event of the unthinkable – a nuclear war between the two superpowers – it did not need to match the US in the arms race. For him, and I fully agree, the Soviet Union could have utilised the saved resources to improve the living and working conditions of its people.

Unfortunately and most unexpectedly, Mitra had a heart attack alone in his flat, and by the time his comrades Sudiman and Stavrou went to call on him, he was dead. His death was a great loss to his family, the CPI and all who worked at the WMR.

Agamemnon Stavrou was an alternative Central Committee (CC) member of the Progressive Party of Working People (*Anorthotikó Kómma Ergazómenou Laoú*: AKEL), one of the two most powerful and influential political parties in Cyprus. He was exceptionally courteous, generous, mild-mannered and graced with a permanent smile. He spoke in a gentle, quiet voice, even when discussing the Turkish military occupation, which, today, still divides that lovely island. Agamemnon's wife Dana was from Romania, and he was always finding ways of assisting her family in coping with the regular food shortages in that country. When our daughter Amina was born,

Agamemnon gave her a huge teddy bear which we named after him; when she turned one, he arrived at our flat with a lovely rocking horse. I thoroughly enjoyed his company, and years later, when I visited Cyprus, I had the opportunity to meet him and swap memories about our time in Prague. By then, he was a full CC member of AKEL and editor of their paper.

Satyadjaya Sudiman represented of the Communist Party of Indonesia (PKI) at the WMR. He was a thoughtful person, somewhat serious, who carried the pain and anguish of the massacre of his party with fortitude and courage. Post-independent Indonesia was led by Sukarno, an anti-imperialist leader who worked closely with the PKI. He was also instrumental, with the great Nehru of India, in convening the Bandung Conference in 1955, which laid the basis for the formation of the Non-Aligned Movement. In 1965, the PKI was the largest communist party in the world, after those of the Soviet Union and China. That was anathema to the US Administration, which, through its murderous instrument, the CIA, inspired, funded and orchestrated a coup against Sukarno and installed the right-wing, authoritarian and sadistic General Suharto. Suharto, with the backing of Washington, unleashed one of the most horrific massacres of left-wing people in the history of humanity. From 1965 to early 1966, about one million left-wing patriots, mainly communists, were brutally murdered and another million locked up in concentration camps.

The PKI was highly respected and admired for the way it worked with Sukarno and the overwhelmingly Muslim population, and I was in awe of its courage and heroism and the way it worked with the Muslim majority and its faith-based institutions. As someone born and brought up as a Muslim, I had a lot of discussions with Sudiman about how to mobilise and organise deeply religious people and work with outstanding non-communist revolutionaries. We attended several party conferences outside Prague, which helped to cement our friendship. His courage, dedication and commitment to the PKI under extremely difficult conditions, including living in exile, were exemplary. The tragedy enacted on the PKI and the other progressive forces in Indonesia haunts me to this day.

Yacoub Garro and **Nawal Yazeji** from Syria also had a flat in our building. We bonded as close family friends and shared many meals together, discovering much in common and learning a great deal about each other's countries and problems and different ways of mobilising people according to the specific context.

Yacoub was a CC member of the Communist Party of Syria (CPS), which he represented on the Editorial Council of the WMR. He was a seasoned activist, well-acquainted with Marxism-Leninism, and he spoke English but was more comfortable in Arabic and French. I benefited from his wisdom and astute reading of the situation in Syria, Lebanon and the Middle East. He was a warm, friendly person who hardly raised his voice, even when provoked by the representative of the Communist Party of Lebanon, following the Syrian intervention in that country. With admirable patience, he would unravel for us the complex state of affairs in Syria under the rule of Assad, such as the precarious existence of the CPS, an ally of Assad without full democratic rights to operate. Yacoub and I had some differences of opinion about Arab unity; I thought they were exaggerating the reality and were not as united as they liked to proclaim.

On his return to Syria, Yacoub was involved in the inner-party battles against the overbearing and, at times, autocratic long-serving leader of the Party, Khalid Bakdash,[62] and in 1986, participated in the breakaway faction led by Hanin Nimir and assumed a leading position.

Nawal was a party member and leader in the women's movement in Syria. For her, the struggle for the empowerment and emancipation of women was inextricably linked to the national and class struggle in her country, the region and the world. She was fluent in Arabic, French and English, which made it much easier for us to communicate, and was warm, friendly and generous, with a wealth of empathy.

Nawal and Yacoub collaborated in Syria so she could work amongst the women in her community. If she were seen out in the evening without her husband, people might start gossiping maliciously about her, so Yacoub would stand on the balcony when he expected her to come home and greet her loudly and affectionately to make sure everyone knew she was acting with his knowledge and permission. Another example of their awareness of the psychological impact of patriarchal customs was apparent in the upbringing of their daughter Hala. After her birth, they followed the custom of letting themselves be referred to by their friends and family as Abu-Hala and Um-Hala. But when a second child (a boy) was born, custom dictated that they should become known as the mother and father of the boy's name (Abu-Boy's name and Um-Boy's name), as boys take precedence over girls. They decided not to follow this tradition to prevent Hala from feeling that

---

62. Also Bekdache.

she had somehow been replaced in their affection by the newborn baby. Both of them were prominent supporters of the Palestinian resistance movement and against patriarchy in any society.

Nawal also told us about the frequency with which rape was used in Syria and Iraq as a weapon of war and how often this led to the girls and women who had been raped – and thus seen to be dishonoured – being put to death by their families in so-called 'honour killings'. One couple she and Yacoub knew had killed themselves in a suicide pact after the wife had been raped in prison. They could not bear the future facing her, and he would not let her suffer alone.

Nawal has continued to keep in touch with the situation of women in Syria and fight for peace in her home country. In 2015, she became a member of the Women's Advisory Board at Geneva III, the Geneva peace talks on Syria.

When I went on an official visit to Syria as Minister in the Presidency in 2007, Meg joined me, and Nawal took a whole week's holiday to spend time with her and show her around. Syria was a beautiful country, and even though Assad's leadership was not fully democratic, he was not as dictatorial or oppressive as many of the leaders in the Middle East who receive the full support and financial and military backing of the US. The Syria we visited was a relaxed and happy meeting place where people with different religious and ethnic backgrounds intermingled with ease. No one could have imagined the tragedy that would soon engulf that country and destroy its people's lives.

Elean Roslyn Thomas (1947–2004) was, in her own words, 'a Black Caribbean Communist woman'. She represented the Workers Party of Jamaica at the WMR, and, from our very first encounter, we were enchanted by her. She became like a sister to us, and we spent a lot of time together. She was a journalist, novelist and a wonderful performance poet. Elean was very proud of the colour of her skin and a fierce opponent of racism and sexism. She would bristle at the slightest hint of such attitudes and would not mince her words in responding to transgressors. It was a joy to be in her company. When she spoke, you could feel her hatred for the exploitation of workers, peasants, women and Black people. She expressed her views very strongly, pulling no punches.

Whenever we had comrades and friends at our flat or at other social functions, we would implore Elean to perform her poems, which she did brilliantly. How we loved to hear her exclaiming 'Ain't that a shame', a conscious use of bathos in an account of the heroism of women in the struggle being rewarded by patronising excuses to avoid giving them any real authority. Lamenting the fact that the endless oppression of women in all spheres is widely accepted as 'natural', even by their own comrades, the poem ends with the lines:

Ain't it a shame
That so many
Still think it
NATURAL
For the woman to go FIRST
Yet remain LAST

And ain't it a shame
That so many
WOMEN
Still agree
ITS NATURAL

NOW – Ain't *THAT* (Elean's emphasis)
A SHAME?

Another of our favourite poems which she performed with energy, drive and vigour was 'Liberation Beat – to a South African Freedom Fighter', which begins:

Moving through the bushes
Your AK in your hands
Surrounded by your people
Your heart and theirs
    Beat
Boom di di Boom
Boom di di Boom
Boom di di Boom
A BEAT OF LIBERATION.

After leaving Prague, Elean lived in London for a while, where she met and married Lord Tony Gifford, a well-known and respected left-wing lawyer.

Together they moved to Jamaica, where Gifford opened a legal practice, and Elean continued her political work. Their marriage broke up in 1994.

Elean visited us in Johannesburg, where she became a friend of Wally Mongane Serote. Against our advice, she would take off and go to Alexandra Township alone. That was Elean – fearless and defiant.

In his foreword to her book, *Before They Can Speak of Flowers* (Karis Press, 1988), one of Africa's greatest writers, Ngũgĩ wa Thiong'o, wrote, 'Elean Thomas has stitched for us an intricate pattern of thought and beauty in our fight for human liberation.' It was with great sadness that we learned of her untimely death at the young age of 56.

Elizabeth (Betty) Sinclair (1910–1981) was born in the tough Ardoyne area of Belfast in Northern Ireland. She became a member of the Communist Party of Ireland in 1932 and remained a communist to the end. Betty was indeed committed for life and was a no-nonsense, feisty, tough nut on the exterior with a warm, caring, passionate heart. Hardened by growing up in Belfast as a witness to the horrors of sectarian violence and discrimination directed against the Catholics, she was a fearless fighter for justice and human rights and against the exploitation of workers' labour.

Betty founded and worked diligently and strenuously in the Northern Ireland Civil Rights Association (NICRA) and the local Trades Council and was admired and respected by the Protestant and Catholic communities for her hard work, courage and fearlessness in the cauldron of violence and hostility that engulfed Northern Ireland.

Betty came to the WMR as the representative of the Communist Party of Northern Ireland, and given her dynamic interest in the struggle in South Africa, we very quickly became friends. She was a true internationalist and a firm and unyielding supporter of the Soviet Union and the freedom struggle in South Africa. I thoroughly enjoyed the time we spent together and learned a great deal from her. However, Betty was a doer and a non-stop activist who could not settle down to a life of reading, debating and discussion. She pined to be involved in the day-to-day battles in Ireland and was happy when she was allowed to return to Belfast.

Niall Farrell and later Tommy O'Flaherty succeeded Betty, and Meg and I got on well with both of them. I was able to help Tommy in a rather unusual way. Since his Irish accent was so strong, hardly any of the English speakers could understand him, so I often volunteered to 'translate' his words into English with 'received pronunciation'.

Clement Rohee (born in 1950) was the Representative of the People's Progressive Party (PPP) of Guyana on the editorial council of the WMR from 1979–1983. Prior to his deployment, Cheddi Jagan, founder of the PPP, sought my view as to whether or not the organisation should send a representative; without hesitation, I replied in the affirmative, saying that whoever comes will learn a great deal about Marxism-Leninism and the World Communist Movement. By the end of his or her deployment, he or she would be ready to play a more mature role in the life of the Party and the politics of Guyana.

Rohee was very interested in international affairs and sought to advance his thinking and understanding of world developments. He was a proud Afro-Guyanese, sensitive to any sign of racism and a firm supporter of the ANC and the SACP. He was insistent on learning more about the ANC, its policies, strategy and tactics, and the divisions in our organisations he had heard about from other people and would not be fobbed off with simple answers. He would probe me with questions and doubts about my responses – those discussions were demanding, and my respect for his understanding of South African politics grew steadily. In turn, I learnt a lot about the politics of Guyana and the divisions between the Indo-Guyanese and the Afro-Guyanese so assiduously fomented and encouraged by the British and American authorities. These nefarious activities were intensified after Cheddi won the election in 1953. After just 133 days, he was removed by the British government. I shall write more about Cheddi in the section on my mentors.

Rohee would come to my office daily, and we would have tea or lunch together. Despite his serious demeanour and dedication to his Party and to Cheddi and Janet Jagan, he was quite chatty and relaxed. Rohee was really close to Janet and would relate stories about how strict she was with the comrades in the PPP, demanding discipline and dedication at all times. In his view, Janet, more than any other leader, had helped to keep the Party focused, united and cohesive.

On his return to Guyana, Rohee was elected to the Executive Committee of the PPP and became Secretary of the International Committee and Convenor of the Race Relations Committee. In the PPP Government, he served as Minister of Foreign Affairs from 1992–2001, as Minister of Foreign Trade until 2006, and, from 2006–2015, as Minister of Home Affairs. I am grateful to him for our continued friendship and happy that he held such vital positions in the government of his country.

Donald Ramotar (born 1950) replaced Rohee at the WMR and represented the PPP from 1983–1988. He was warm, gentle and modest, with a ready smile and a lovely sense of humour. We became very close family friends, and Meg, Amina, Govan and I spent many happy days and evenings with Donald and his wife Diolatchmee and their children Lisavita, Alexei and Alvaro, until we left Prague in 1985; then I continued to meet him and his family regularly on my visits to the WMR. Donald was articulate and well-versed in the politics of Guyana and the Caribbean and was keen to imbibe as much knowledge as possible on the theory of Marxism-Leninism, the world communist movement and the struggle in South Africa. He was liked and respected by the other party representatives and Soviet staff working there.

In 1997, on the death of Cheddi Jagan, Donald was elected as General Secretary of the PPP and served in that role until 2013 – a resounding endorsement of his wonderful leadership qualities. He was President of Guyana from 2011 until 2015. When the PPP had been one short of a parliamentary majority, he had the arduous task of navigating that position with opposition parties determined to unseat him. But Donald was also a tough negotiator and survived those attempts to lead the government with some distinction. However, owing to the pressure of being president, he resigned as General Secretary of the PPP and nominated Rohee as his successor. Rohee was elected in August 2013.

While I was writing this book, I spoke to Donald and asked him if he could recollect a little about his time in Prague and our enduring family friendship. Here are parts of his response:

> It was in Prague that I met Comrade Essop Pahad, who was the representative of the SACP. I was introduced to him by Comrade Rohee. Even though I was meeting him for the first time, I already knew something about him. He was highly regarded by Dr Cheddi Jagan, the General Secretary and foremost founder of the PPP. Cheddi told me before I left Guyana that Pahad was a solid comrade and that I should work closely with him.
>
> Comrade Pahad was also well-known to the leaders of the PPP, who had met him at various conferences. Among them was Comrade Feroze Mohamed, who was one of our leading comrades on theoretical issues. He, too, had a very high opinion of Comrade Pahad and asked me to seek him out when I got to Prague. So when

we met, [Comrade Pahad] was not a stranger to me, and soon, I found he was everything I had heard about him. He was very intelligent, and his knowledge of Marxist theory was deep. That was on full display at meetings of the Editorial Council of the WMR ...

This debate [on dogmatism] began, and Comrade Pahad was one of the leading advocates calling on us to look at theory in the light of the many changes that were taking place. Another outstanding comrade in this pursuit was the late Semu Patheguey of Senegal.

Those of us who were proposing to take into consideration the changes in the world and developing our theory were quite enthused when Mikhail Gorbachev became the leader of the Soviet Union. It was like a breath of fresh air. However, it soon began to dawn on some of us that there appeared to be a throwing out of the baby with the bath water. That eventually proved to be the case as the leadership of the Communist Party of the Soviet Union began losing control of the process. The rest, as they say, is history.

Apart from the political and ideological affinity that developed between Comrade Essop and myself, we developed a strong personal friendship that became a friendship of our families.

My family was often a guest at Cde Essop and Meg Pahad's home in Prague. We also hosted them from time to time. Our conversations were not confined to ideological/political subjects but on a wide array of issues, family challenges and other personal matters and, of course, sports.

I recall I was once very concerned about Pahad's health. He went to Angola on his party's assignment, and there he contracted malaria. When he came back to Prague, he was immediately hospitalised. [When] I accompanied Meg to see him in the hospital, I was shocked to see how much weight he had lost. All I recognized was his huge smile and large, rather bulging eyes. The malaria had damaged his body but his spirit, enthusiasm and optimism were undimmed.

[When] we talked for a while about the situation in Africa and the prospects for victory of the ANC-led liberation movement, he had no doubt that 'victory was around the corner'.

I remember at one time asking him how the unity of the ANC, COSATU and the SACP was maintained in such good order. He told me that the SACP was very careful not to take decisions for the movement in its own ranks and then try to impose it on the ANC. In fact, he related that in some ANC NEC meetings, it was not unusual to see two members of the SACP arguing vehemently against each other.

That lesson stayed with me, and when I became General Secretary of the PPP, I followed the same principle with our partners from civic society. Our alliance is still intact today and has matured.

Our friendship was bolstered by us meeting each other after we left Prague. Pahad visited Guyana in 2000 or 2001, and I was delighted to take him into our jungle to see the majestic Kaieteur Falls, the highest single-drop waterfall in the world.

I also met him in South Africa in 1993/94, when I attended an ANC Conference inside South Africa. That, too, was the last time I met Joe Slovo in Essop's home. I met Essop on other visits in the first decade of this century, when I attended a Joint Parliamentary Assembly of the ACP-EU countries (African, Caribbean, Pacific states and European Union) held in South Africa.

In 2005, I travelled to South Africa to receive the Oliver Tambo Gold Award given to Cheddi Jagan posthumously for his contribution to the fight against apartheid, and we met in Johannesburg when President Nelson Mandela passed away in 2013. We spent quite a while together on that occasion.

I was surprised and delighted to meet him in India in January 2015, when we were both presented with the Pravasi Bharatiya Samman Award by the Indian Government for our achievements in our respective countries as persons of Indian origin.[63]

---

63. Donald was the guest of honour.

[Comrade Essop and I] have stayed in contact through all these years, and I consider him and his family among my dearest friends.

Our family friendship has endured the test of time and geographical separation. In my life, I have met and interacted with many remarkable people from all walks of life. Among these, I treasure very highly my friendship and comradeship with Donald Ramotar.

Dr Naziha Jawdet Ashgah al-Dulaimi (1923–2007) was the representative of the Iraqi Communist Party (ICP). A formidable freedom fighter, she was committed to the empowerment and emancipation of women in Iraq, the Middle East and the world. She helped found the Iraqi Women's League and was its first president. She was also a practising medical doctor who studied at the Royal College of Medicine when there were very few female medical students and worked in a hospital in Baghdad and then in clinics, where she offered free medical treatment to the poor. The monarchy's security apparatus harassed her during this period.

In the 1950s, Naziha was active in the Iraqi Peace Movement and a member of the World Peace Council. As a result of her intellectual capacity, organising abilities, deep understanding and knowledge of the Iraqi political landscape and her talent for working with people across class and ethnic divides, she became the first woman cabinet minister in Iraq and the Arab world. She succeeded in clearing slums and creating a massive housing project and also changed the marriage and inheritance laws in a manner that protected women's rights.

Naziha was quiet, humble and friendly, had a lovely smile and was a wonderful host. On many evenings, she would invite us to share the sumptuous Iraqi food she made, of which our favourite was her oven-baked fish.

From Dr Naziha, I learnt a lot about how the Iraqi government functioned and the historical ebb and flow of the attitude of the Ba'athist leadership toward communists and other progressive forces. Her position and life experience had required years of stamina, patience and fortitude in a patriarchal world dominated by men, many of whom had little or no respect for a single independent woman. Naziha told my wife how she had reluctantly decided that she could never have a close relationship with a man or become a mother in the particular context in which she operated. The respect she had won was too tenuous to withstand any perceived weakness, and she could never let down her barriers, even for a second.

Abu Wushdan (full name unknown) is another Iraqi I met and befriended at the Lenin Party School in Moscow. His party had sent him to Prague as a member of the WMR staff to assist with the Arabic edition. He was some years older than me, always cheerful and smiling and was an excellent cook. His bedroom in the WMR building contained a kitchen, where he taught us to cook carp (the main fresh fish available in Prague) with many spices, which transformed it into something we could really enjoy.

From Abu Wushdan and Iraqi representatives and others from the region, we learned of the sheer horror and sadistic ways of successive Iraqi regimes. The Iraqi Communist Party was legal under the monarchy from 1937 to 1958 and under Qasim until 1963. When the Ba'ath Party overthrew Qasim in that year, they executed thousands of communists, lining them up outside abattoirs for slaughter. When the men could not be found, their wives, mothers and daughters were subjected to brutal beatings, rape and torture.

The regime which took over from 1966–1968 suppressed both the Communists and the Ba'athists. In May 1978, after an interlude of comparative calm, the ruling Ba'ath Party executed twenty-one communists, once again forcing many Iraqi communists into exile. The ICP was officially outlawed again in 1985.

Members of the ICP had been subjected to horrendous treatment on an even larger scale than that unleashed on us by the apartheid regime, which was why I could not countenance meeting representatives and leaders of the Ba'ath regime, including Saddam Hussein. On one occasion, when Deputy President Zuma hosted a high-level Iraqi delegation and I refused to attend, I was told, 'You have no choice. They are here at our invitation.' So I attended but avoided all interaction except observing the necessary protocols.

Idris Cox (1899–1989) represented the Communist Party of Great Britain at the WMR. He was a Welsh miner, a prolific writer and editor, and Secretary of the Party's International Department from 1951–1970. He was highly respected internationally and active in the Movement for Colonial Freedom. Two of his best-known works are *Socialist Ideas in Africa* (1966) and *The Hungry Half – A Study in the Exploitation of the 'Third World'* (1970).[64] Idris Cox got on very well with Michael Harmel.

---

64. Both published by Lawrence & Wishart in London, UK.

Bert Ramelson (1910–1994), born Baruch Rahmilevich Mendelson in the Ukraine, was the National Industrial Organiser of the Communist Party of Great Britain from 1965 to 1977 and a member of the Editorial Board and Council of the *World Marxist Review* from 1977 to 1990, replacing Idris Cox. Prior to 1977, I had no connection or interaction with Bert but was aware of his role in the British Labour Movement and his condemnation of the Soviet Union's intervention in Czechoslovakia in 1968. The CPGB, with Bert at the forefront, had given their full support to the 1966 Seamen's Strike and later to the 1984–1985 Miners' Strike led by Arthur Scargill. As mentioned in Chapter 2, at the time of the Seamen's Strike, Harold Wilson had dubbed Bert and his communist colleagues a 'tightly knit group of politically motivated men'. Wilson's accusation certainly elevated the status of Ramelson in the eyes of many on the left, including me.

When Bert came to Prague for about a week every month, he would visit us and enjoy playing with Amina. One evening, when she was about three, Amina was wearing my 'delegate' badge from a meeting, and Bert commented that he saw she was a delegate. For some reason, Amina was most indignant and upset, denying that she was a delegate and bursting into tears.

Our debates and discussions about what was going on in the Soviet Union and other socialist countries were at times robust but friendly. I grew to like Bert and respected his deep knowledge of the British Labour Movement, which enhanced my understanding of the Trade Unions in the UK. I concur with John Daniels who, in a review of the book *Revolutionary Communist at Work: A Political Biography of Bert Ramelson* by Roger Seifert and Tom Sibley,[65] wrote:

> The one thing that does come out of this book is Ramelson's formidable personality. He was a vigorous and accomplished orator, convivial in manner, knowledgeable and still committed to an optimistic Marxist vision of the possibilities for socialism – and obviously quite a character.

Salim Ahmed Salim and **Thoraya** were also close friends with whom we shared many evenings, along with the Garros, Rohees, Dansokhos, Pittmans and many others. Salim and Thoraya were their pseudonyms, but we were all aware that Salim's brother, Abdel Khaliq Mahjub, Secretary-General of the

---

65. Also published by Lawrence & Wishart, London, 2011.

Sudanese Communist Party, had been executed by hanging by the reactionary Nimeiri military regime in July 1971. Many other communists were also executed under Nimeiri. Salim was deeply affected by those terrible events, but he never dramatised their situation. He stressed the need for communist parties to be ever-vigilant to power shifts and changes in the local and regional contexts and was a resolute opponent of all military regimes. Salim was usually serious and somewhat stern, but when with his closest friends, he relaxed and warmed up.

Thoraya was a revolutionary communist, an indomitable fighter for women's liberation and a leading member of the Sudanese women's movement. She was vehemently opposed to female genital mutilation, which was not against the law in Sudan and quite a common practice there. Babette Dansokho (a medical doctor) and Nawal Yazeji were also well-informed about that issue, about which neither Meg nor I had previously known very much. In many countries in Africa and the Middle East, it is a long-standing cultural tradition organised, performed and enforced on little girls by women. It is continued by families who have emigrated to countries where the practice is illegal, so the girls are taken 'home' for a 'holiday' to be cut. Thoraya and Nawal had actively campaigned against the unfair discrimination and abuses suffered by women in their countries and pointed out that this fight for women's rights was complex, for patriarchy was deeply embedded in the society, and many women were complicit in supporting patriarchal actions and attitudes.

The first few times we had dinner at their flat, Thoraya spent most of the time in the kitchen preparing and serving an endless series of delicious Sudanese dishes and did not really join us till later in the evening. Meg and I objected that this was unfair on her – and us since we enjoyed her company very much. After some persuasion, they reorganised the approach so that most of the preparation, serving and eating could happen in the sitting room with all of us enjoying the food and the company together.

Salim taught me a great deal about the politics of Sudan, working in an illegal party, the clashes between North and South Sudan and the inner workings and disputes within communist parties in the Arab world and North Africa. He also gave me further insight into the experience of Sudanese communists working with Muslim believers, recruiting them into the party and treating Islam with respect. I used to tease him about the way the Sudanese at the Party School in Moscow would pray regularly and take time off on Fridays for prayers. He took my jokes very well but often reminded me that in our African context, it would be unwise to follow the route of the CPSU, since the majority of our populations were Muslim, Hindu or Christian believers.

Amath Dansokho, Salim and I were deeply involved in drafting the document of the Communist and Workers' Parties of Tropical and Southern Africa entitled 'The Communist Call to Africa'. Salim, in his quiet and thoughtful manner, made a notable contribution to the document, which I shall discuss in the next chapter.

After the collapse of the Soviet Union and the WMR, Salim, Thoraya and their daughter moved to Sweden. Later, I was greatly saddened to hear of his death in that country. His loyalty, discipline and dedication to his party were admirable.

Raja and **Chandra Collure** were also friends of ours. Born in 1938, Raja was the representative of the Communist Party of Sri Lanka (CPSL) on the Editorial Council of the WMR and a firm defender of the Soviet Union and other socialist countries. His wife Chandra is a charming hostess, a strong, intelligent woman and a caring and sensitive mother. We often got together as families with their two children, sharing our different versions of curries and talking about our own and other countries and their problems.

Raja was unaware that he had an amusing ritual when speaking at a meeting or conference. When he thought he was making a telling or important point, he would slowly and deliberately remove his spectacles and put on a serious face. We had wide-ranging discussions, but the most intense debates were about India's attitude towards Sri Lanka, of which Raja was critical, and Sri Lanka's problems. The politics of Sri Lanka were consumed by the demands of the Tamil minority for greater autonomy in the areas where they lived (in two provinces they were actually the majority) and for the proper recognition of their language and cultural rights. Raja felt that the positions and postures of the Tamil organisations were divisive and a threat to the unity of the country. My view was that the Sinhalese majority, including the Communist Party, needed to be more sensitive to the national question in their country.

After returning to Sri Lanka, Raja was elected as an MP, Secretary-General and then Chairperson of the CPSL. Some years later, when I attended a conference in Sri Lanka, I had an enjoyable visit to the Collure home. At the 21st International Meeting of the Communist and Workers' Parties in Izmir, Turkey, in October 2019, Raja said, 'Today, the communists in different countries seek to establish alliances with anti-imperialist forces for the attainment of certain common objectives and often for the overthrow of dictatorial and authoritarian regimes backed by imperialism.' He continues to support socialist countries and, in January 2020, attended the 61st Anniversary of the Cuban Revolution in Sri Lanka as Governor of the Uva Province and Chairperson of the Communist Party. In September 2020, aged eighty-two, Raja was appointed Governor of the North Western Province.

As I cannot list everyone here, I have mentioned just a few of the representatives of communist and workers' parties with whom we became friendly – there were many others I knew well and worked with daily, for example, the Latin Americans, who mainly communicated with each other in Spanish.

During my years at the WMR, I also established warm personal relationships with representatives from socialist countries, some of whom I mention below.

Raúl Valdés Vivó (1929–2013) arrived at WMR in the late 1970s as the representative of the Communist Party of Cuba (CPC) and had an extraordinary history in the fight against the Batista regime. When he joined the party in 1946, he met Fidel and Raúl Castro, beginning a strong political and comradely friendship that endured until his death. His bravery and courage were demonstrated not only in the freedom struggle in Cuba but also when he was the Cuban ambassador to the National Liberation Front of South Vietnam in 1967. He lived and worked in the liberated areas of South Vietnam, and on several occasions, his office and the surrounding area were bombed by the US aggressors.

Raúl Vivó was impressive and inspirational, humble and friendly with a happy expression and an easy sense of humour. From our first encounter, we found that we had a lot in common and really liked each other. One day in 1980, when our daughter Amina was a baby, he volunteered to babysit. When we took him up on this offer, he was very disappointed when she slept the whole time we were out, as he had wanted to play with her.

It was a pleasure to be in Raúl's company and draw from his encyclopaedic knowledge of the Cuban revolution, the relationship between the CPC and Castro's army of liberation, and the dynamics of building a socialist society in the face of the most dangerous intrigues, plots, invasions and sanctions, orchestrated by the most powerful country in the world, the USA.

When relating stories about his stay in Vietnam, Raúl gave one a vivid impression of the personalities involved in that struggle, bringing to life the heroism and unprecedented creative resistance of the Vietnamese fighters and their families, including the building and effective use of schools and hospitals in underground bunkers in the struggle to survive and the venomous bombing of the invading US war machine. Together, the people of North and South Vietnam achieved the greatest victory in the history of all national liberation struggles.

Raúl was also very well informed about the communist parties of Latin America and armed resistance groups in countries like Nicaragua, and I relished our meetings and all that I learnt from him. In turn, he would probe me about our South African revolutionary struggle, relations between the ANC and SACP, the combat readiness of Umkhonto we Sizwe (MK) and our opinion about developments in Angola, Namibia, Mozambique and Ethiopia.

Raúl was appointed Director of the Cuban Party School by Castro after the 5th Congress in 1997, when Fidel said it was necessary to re-establish Marxist Leninist values in the country. He was highly respected and acknowledged as a leading intellectual, writer and journalist – well beyond the shores of Cuba. On the four occasions I visited there, I always successfully sought him out and, although usually very busy with his work, he was always friendly and engaging, and he expressed his happiness at my appointment as Minister in the Presidency.'

When he died on 19 November 2013, wreaths from Fidel and Raúl Castro accompanied his coffin to the Veterans Pantheon at Havana's Colon Cemetery. Jorge Risquet, a member of the Central Committee of the Communist Party of Cuba, spoke in his honour: 'Valdés Vivo devoted his entire life to the cause of the Cuban Revolution and to the dissemination of progressive and revolutionary ideas.' My friendship with Vivó has left an indelible impression on me that I shall always cherish.

Roland Bauer (born in 1928) was an intellectual of note with a doctorate in history. His father was interned by the Nazis in the Dachau and Mauthausen concentration camps, which, combined with his own experience, led him to be a fierce opponent of racism and fascism, wherever or whenever it raised its ugly, brutal face. In 1971, he was elected to the CC of the Socialist Unity Party of the GDR. From 1978–1990, he was the SED representative on the Editorial Board of the WMR.

It was a pleasure and an education interacting with Roland. He was open about some of the shortcomings of his country and a fountain of knowledge about the history of communism in East and West Germany, as well as ideological questions and problems. For me, the drawback was that he spoke no English, so we required the assistance of an interpreter when we wanted to converse. We shared a number of common positions and ideas on the measures necessary to make the journal more accessible in content and form to its readers inside and outside the socialist world.

Roland was most approachable and never avoided expressing his opinion, even if the issues were sensitive and unclear. I recall that at the time, the Solidarity Movement in Poland was gaining influence and strength, and political shifts in Hungary allowed GDR citizens to go to the West via Hungary, but Roland remained confident that the GDR would ride the storm. After Roland attended a CC meeting of the SED, I arranged to meet him, as I, like many other representatives, was concerned about those rapid developments. He assured me that the Party was in control but that the absence of SED leader Erich Honecker from the meeting had led to some paralysis in decision-making. He was certain the party would arrive at the correct solution to stem the building tide of opposition that was aided, abetted and funded by the USA, West Germany and other major Western powers.

Shortly after our meeting, Roland attended an emergency meeting in Berlin where, to his amazement, the decision was taken to remove Honecker from all his positions in the party and the state. It was said at the time that Gorbachev had played a part in his removal. On his return from that meeting Roland was disappointed and had lost his ebullience and optimism. He was also genuinely upset to learn that the GDR authorities at different levels were doctoring the statistics to make the country look better economically and politically. I was very sad to see him in that state, as he was a good comrade and kind to me. The fall of the Berlin Wall and collapse of the GDR was a great shock and tragedy to all of us in the ANC, SACP and SACTU. The GDR, its ruling party and solidarity organisations were great and effective supporters who gave us tremendous material assistance.

After Roland and I had left Prague, I was informed that he was well and living in his flat in Alexander Platz.

Dimitar Stanishev (1924–2000) represented the Bulgarian Communist Party (BCP) on the WMR Editorial Board in the mid-1970s, where we developed a friendship that lasted for many years. He was friendly and easy-going, and Meg and I had many get-togethers with him and his wife, Dina, a well-respected intellectual and philologist in Bulgaria and the Soviet Union. We could chat with them informally, as their English was excellent. Dimitar's history as a guerrilla fighter in the resistance to fascism gave him a deep understanding of our armed resistance movement and continuing need to strengthen the capacity of MK to provide further impetus to the armed revolutionary struggle.

Dimitar had met Dina in Moscow, but under Stalin's laws, marriages to foreigners were illegal. Although their first child was born in 1952, they were not able to marry until the ban on mixed marriages was lifted after Stalin's death in 1953. From 1958, Dina lived with her husband in Bulgaria. In 1979, she was fired from her job at the Institute of Bulgarian Languages for insisting that the Macedonian language should be recognised. At that time, the existence of a Macedonian minority in Bulgaria was denied.

After returning to Sofia, Dimitar Stanishev was elected Secretary to the CC of the BCP from 1977 to 1990. We kept in touch, and, in 1980, he invited Meg, Amina (aged nine months) and I for a fabulous holiday in a CC place in Sunny Beach. Even though there were several other guests from other parties and he had work to do, he took the trouble to meet us and ensure everything was fine.

In the 1980s, when our camps in Angola were running short of goods and equipment, Antonio Mongalo, the ANC Chief representative in the GDR, contacted me and asked me to speak to Stanishev for emergency assistance. With the agreement of the CC, he arranged for supplies to be sent to Angola via the GDR, which had organised planes to convey the emergency stock.

During those years, I also met Dimitar's son Georgi, who was studying in Moscow and later became an architect, and his younger son, Sergey Dmitrievich, who was only about ten years old. At the time of writing, in November 2020, Sergey is a member of the European Parliament and President of the Party of European Socialists.

Girgin Girginov (1921–1998) succeeded Dimitar Stanishev as the BCP representative and, given my relationship with Stanishev, knew about me and made contact on arrival. He was friendly and good company. His wife was a leading cultural figure in Bulgaria, and they had two wonderful daughters who spoke fluent English. We became family friends.

Girginov was a professor of philosophy at the Bulgarian Academy of Sciences and at the Party School and was a member of the CC. He enriched my knowledge of contemporary Bulgaria and its history as well as the philosophy of dialectical and historical materialism. Through his family, we developed a better understanding of the cultural and student life in Bulgaria.

However, with Girginov, I had a disagreement. My view was that the ANC and our struggle should be characterised as revolutionary nationalism, while he argued that nationalism, by its very nature and content, could be progressive but not revolutionary. We settled our difference by invoking the assistance of Yevgeny Panfilov, who was Secretary of the General Commission on Theory. Panfilov agreed with my view, and Girginov was persuaded to change his mind.

In spite of our close friendship with the Girginov and Stanishev families and our liking for the country, its people, its food and its history, I did not agree with the attitude of the Bulgarian Party and government with respect to what they called the 'Bulgarianisation' of their society, which occurred in the late eighties. It entailed, for example, expecting Bulgarians of Turkish descent to renounce their Turkish names and adopt Bulgarian names. They were also discouraged from using their language and practising their cultural and religious beliefs. When this was explained to me at an official meeting in 1989, I held the very firm position that this policy was divisive and dangerous and contrary to a Marxist-Leninist approach to the National Question.

Badamyn Lhamsuren represented the Mongolian People's Revolutionary Party on the Editorial Board of the WMR. He was a member of the CC of his party and a gentle, modest, soft-spoken comrade. We established a firm friendship early on, even though he was shy to use his English, of which he had a limited command. Sometimes we talked on a more complex level with the assistance of an interpreter. We had many convivial dinners together at each other's flats, and his wife would spend hours preparing and cooking the most delicious dumplings I have ever tasted.

At this time, I was no longer living in Prague but still represented the SACP on the Editorial Council. While Lhamsuren was visiting, the WMR organised a conference in Ulan Bator, the Mongolian capital, which I attended.

Once, before our plane took off from Ulan Bator for a rural area, Lhamsuren approached me with a friendly smile and informed me that I should not be worried as our pilot was the best in Mongolia. I had not been concerned, just somewhat baffled by this information, but when it was time to land, there was no landing strip – just an open field. After landing intact without incident, we taxied to a small unpretentious building. That was my first surprise.

The second was when we visited an elderly comrade at his 'yurt' – a spacious living, dining and sleeping space – where he lived with his family. I was most impressed by the yurts, the original moveable accommodation of nomadic Mongolians, similar to tents. Traditionally, they would have been circular homes with a central pole and flexible framework of attachable poles covered in animal skins or waterproof animal felt. The modern versions are much improved, with many having iron stoves with chimneys and some having doors and windows instead of flaps in the material to be raised and closed. Some even have TV antennae attached to them. At our meeting, the Mongolian comrade gave us an overview of the socio-economic dynamics of that area and a lesson in the theory and practice of Leninism. We were also given a light meal of Mongolian food.

None of us knew that the April 1988 conference on the work of the WMR would be the last, for the Soviet Union and the European socialist countries would collapse the following year. Uncle Dan Tloome, Chairman of the SACP, attended that conference, and I prepared his input, which he accepted fully. I quote one paragraph here, which refers to the report on the work of the WMR from December 1984 to February 1988:

> In setting out its assessments of the most important issues facing humanity, the report treats in the most cursory manner the struggle against racism. The political and ideological struggle against racism is and should be of the greatest significance for the international communist movement. It involves and effects every part of our globe. There can be no real advance in the fight for a better, safer and saner world without a consistent, passionate and thorough-going struggle against all forms and manifestations of racism. It is, to put it bluntly, shameful that this burning question is just tagged on in the section dealing with the national liberation movement in Africa and Asia. We therefore urge the editorial collective to pay more attention to this question.

By 1985, I had spent ten wonderful years at the WMR but needed to be more directly involved in the day-to-day practical work of the SACP and ANC. So by agreement with the party, I returned to London with my family, staying on as the SACP representative to the WMR until a replacement could be found. It was agreed with the editor and the Secretariat that I would commute monthly from London to Prague.

It took longer than anticipated to find a replacement, but in 1988, the political bureau decided that Comrade Mzala Nxumalo should be that person. When consulted, I concurred that Mzala would be more than competent to fill that vacancy. He was young, a prolific contributor to *The African Communist*, a good theoretician, dedicated and disciplined. He would also benefit from the experience of working at the WMR and would make an even greater contribution to strengthening the party. But something horrific occurred.

Mzala arrived in Prague determined to do his best and was given the usual medical check-up, which showed he was HIV positive. To his horror and disappointment, the Czech authorities, instead of accepting his condition and giving him the necessary medical support and treatment, advised the WMR that he was persona non grata. The WMR wrongly took this advice and refused to accept him as the SACP representative. I was bitterly disappointed at what I considered their unacceptable reactionary decision.[66]

As it turned out, at the end of 1989, the WMR was dissolved.

While at the WMR, my knowledge and understanding of Marxism-Leninism and communist and workers' parties worldwide significantly increased. Working there also helped me better understand and appreciate positive and negative developments in Czechoslovakia and the other socialist countries. The comrades and friends I got to know helped immeasurably in making me a more mature and better person, and I remain eternally grateful to the SACP for giving me that extraordinary opportunity and all those who made my time there fruitful and beneficial.

There were three other influential international organisations with their headquarters in Prague at that time: the International Union of Students, the International Organisation of Journalists, and the World Federation of Trade Unions (WFTU). Below I mention three of the comrades who worked at the WFTU and greatly impacted our lives.

Eric 'Stalin' Mtshali (1931–2018) represented the South African Congress of Trade Unions at the WFTU, and it was said that he was dubbed 'Stalin' because of his admiration for that leader. Mtshali had a proud record of involvement and leadership in SACTU, the ANC, SACP and Umkhonto we Sizwe. Following in the footsteps of other giants of our movement – Wilton

---

66. I would recommend the book *The Lost Prince of the ANC – The Life and Times of Jabulani Nobleman 'Mzala' Nxumalo 1955–1991*, Mandla J. Radebe (Johannesburg: Jacana Media: 2022).

Mkwayi, Mark Shope and Moses Mabhida – he came to the WFTU in the late seventies.

Mtshali was a teetotaller but a heavy smoker, and we shared an addiction to Benson and Hedges cigarettes. He was a good companion with a ready smile and an infectious chuckle when amused. He related wonderful stories about his experiences in all our Congress Alliance organisations over the years, with his stories often following a circuitous route, making a point somewhat obliquely, but finally doing so with great clarity and usually humour. In one story, John Gaetsewe was trying to persuade a group of people on a particular course of political action, but they wanted to be reassured that there was no risk. 'Are you sure that it will work out like you say?' someone asked. 'I am not a watchmaker – I don't give guarantees,' he replied, giving a broad smile.

Mtshali's involvement in trade union activities began at a young age. One story he told was about a time he was tasked to meet members of a certain trade union in Natal. Upon his arrival, although they recognised him, they refused to converse with him and insisted that he bring Billy Nair along to introduce him. His pleas were in vain, so he eventually returned with Billy Nair and only then did the workers accept his credentials. This illustrates Eric's honesty and modesty, the respect the trade unionists had for Billy Nair, and their maturity in accepting the leadership of a person of Indian origin.

Another anecdote Mtshali told was about the time he accompanied Uncle J. B. Marks on a visit to the Soviet Union. On the first day or two of the visit, he noticed that wherever they went, Uncle J. B. was warmly embraced while he was totally ignored. When he told the Soviet comrades that, as a member of the CC and part of the official SACP delegation, he didn't understand those rebuffs, their response was swift. Because he would always stand directly behind Uncle J. B. out of deference, Mtshali had been mistaken for the security officer, who, according to Soviet protocol, always stands directly behind the principal guest. When he told Uncle J. B. this story, they had a good laugh and were careful to stand next to each other in the future. After that, Mtshali never stood behind the leader when part of an official delegation.

At Mtshali's request, Jeff Radebe and his first wife Zinto, who were then students in the GDR, stayed at our flat for about two weeks, and I was asked to have extensive discussions with them about our history, our movement and the theory and practice of Marxism-Leninism.

In 2015, Eric Mtshali was awarded one of South Africa's National Orders:

the Order of Mendi in Silver. He died three years later.

Haider Hassani (1938–2008), whose full name was Haider El Hassani El Djazaïri, was a fighter in the Algerian Liberation Movement, a member of the banned Algerian Communist Party and a passionate trade unionist. He was born in Damascus, Syria, where his great grandfather, the Emir Abdelkader of Algeria, had been exiled by the French for his military and religious leadership of the opposition to colonial rule.

Haider was an intellectual of note, well-read and well-informed about political developments in Algeria, France, the Middle East and South Africa and was equally at home reading, writing and speaking Arabic, French and English. He studied economics and political science at Manchester University (1958–62), returning to Algeria, where he was active in the Communist Party and the unions. Owing to his opposition to the 1965 military coup that ousted the great Algerian revolutionary Ben Bella, he was imprisoned for two years. He then worked in France and joined the French Communist Party and the General Confederation of Labour (*Confédération générale du travail*: CGT).

At that time, Haider's cousin, who was at Leeds University, introduced him to fellow student David Rabkin and his girlfriend Sue, and they quickly became close friends. David and Sue travelled regularly to Paris to see him, and it was a matter of great pride to Haider that he was largely responsible for the two of them joining the ANC and later being recruited into the SACP. In 1973, David and Sue returned to South Africa to become part of the ANC underground machinery, a dangerous undertaking, with the ever-present prospect of arrest, detention and torture. Following their trial in 1976 under the Terrorism and Internal Security Act, they were convicted and imprisoned. Sue, at the time eight months pregnant, was sentenced to one year but was released after their baby (Franny) was born, while David served his term until 1984. Tragically, he died in Angola that same year while training in an MK camp.

I met Haider in Prague, where he had been sent (from 1977–1986) by the CGT as the advisor to Pierre Gensous, General Secretary of the World Federation of Trade Unions (WFTU). Haider and Amath Dansokho were my two bosom friends and comrades in Prague. Haider was ebullient, charming, loyal to his party and friends and generous to a fault. He was an incessant talker, empathetic, fun and a joy to be with – but his moods were erratic: from wild enthusiasm, he could descend into depression. I witnessed this when he came to stay in our flat in Arabska in 1977 when Meg was in London for a year. I was sometimes worried that he could be suicidal, given his depression. He stayed for many months and, except when he cooked one of his favourite Algerian couscous dishes, we ate at restaurants most of the time, with Haider always insisting on paying.

After our first year together in Prague, Meg went back to London, where her one-year leave of absence from the Inner London Education Authority was about to expire. I had originally been asked to go to WMR for a year but soon realised that the SACP would likely extend this period again and again, which I explained to Meg. Unfortunately, foreigners could not get a job in Czechoslovakia unless with an international organisation, and she wanted to work.

When I told Haider that Meg wanted to find a job in Prague before returning, he immediately spoke to Pierre Gensous at WFTU. When they found her a position in the editorial department of the *Trade Union News*, she happily came back to Prague and started work there.

Unfortunately, however, that department fell under Boris Averyanov (always referred to in the Western press as 'a fully fledged colonel of the KGB'), who had decided from day one to ignore Meg and not invite her to any department meetings or give her any work. That was because she had obtained the job through Pierre Gensous, while the French Party was taking Eurocommunist positions and was sometimes critical of the Soviet Union. Also, Meg was from the CPGB, which was also Eurocommunist. The fact that Meg belonged to the 'straight left' faction of the Party, while Haider and I were very pro-Soviet, made not a scrap of difference: Meg was a spy the French CGT had imposed on Boris's turf. Boris, an overweight, boorish bully, fitting well with the Western caricature of a Soviet bureaucrat, tried all sorts of pathetic complaints against Meg, which were laughed at by Louis Tenerini from the CGT, who was in charge of Human Resources. Eventually, Meg was delighted to be transferred to work in the library reviewing English and French-language newspapers for information about trade unions around the world. There, her boss was a calm, intelligent, disciplined and caring man called Atchutan, a communist from Kerala in India.

I recall with fondness how much I loved my time and friendship with Haider. We would talk late into the night, fortified by a few drinks, which would sometimes degenerate into a shouting match but never a rupture. For me, then and now, those disagreements, vigorous as they were, were a measure of our friendship. Haider was very emotional, hated imperialism in all its guises and loved his friends and comrades.

On a whim, as only best friends can, we decided that Haider would drive to France from where I would travel on to London. Although it was winter and we had a harrowing journey across snow-covered mountains, we survived, and so did our friendship, despite the bickering about who had made the foolish decision.

In the early 1980s, Haider met and fell in love with an Iraqi student, Maj, and they married. Meg and I were overjoyed to attend that function in the Old Town Square in Prague and see him happy at last. After leaving the WFTU, he returned to Algeria to head up the publications department of the Ministry of Culture and Tourism. But that did not last long, as he found both the job and Algerian politics stifling, so he returned to Paris, where he continued his work with the CGT and remained until his death a member of the National Union of Journalists. Maj gave birth to a daughter, Sarah, in 1991, and both were doting parents.

Unfortunately, after my return to South Africa, we lost contact for some years. However, Dansokho kept me abreast of Haider's health and well-being. I tried to persuade him to visit us in South Africa, but to my great regret, I failed. The news of his death at the age of seventy was a shocking matter of great sadness, for I had lost a wonderful, charming, exceptional friend and comrade. An article in *l'Humanité*, the newspaper of the French Communist Party, recorded his death with these words: 'The progressive world, in France as in Algeria, has lost a man of conviction – honest, loyal, true to his value system and his commitments.'

Noel Harris (1937–2014) was larger than life, a strong personality with a cheerful round face and an engaging smile. He was a committed communist and lifelong trade unionist in Belfast, Dublin and London. In 1967, he led the formation and launch of NICRA, which would play a vital role in defending and fighting for human rights, freedom and democracy and against sectarianism in Northern Ireland. At the launch of NICRA, Noel was elected chairperson, and Kader Asmal, who would go on to be South Africa's Minister of Water Affairs and Forestry, was one of the main speakers. Later, when Noel and his wife Rhona moved to Dublin, they formed a close personal relationship with Kader and Louise Asmal, who were instrumental in forming the Anti-Apartheid Movement in Ireland. In Noel, they found a willing and committed anti-apartheid activist and leader.

Noel and Rhona came to Prague in October 1979 with their sons Kevin and Brian and stayed less than two years but had a big impact on our lives. Noel was Head of the Social and Economic Department of WFTU, and from our very first meeting, we took to each other. Meg and Rhona also hit it off with shared interests in race, class and gender in education, and our family friendship was cemented by our common positions on working-class politics in Ireland, South Africa and the world. Amina was a new-born baby at the time, while Kevin and Brian were at secondary school. Their parents sent them to the Russian School in Prague, which obviously used Russian – of which they did not know a word – as the medium of instruction for all subjects. To our delight, they coped wonderfully and became fluent very quickly. Moreover, the time spent in Prague did not set them back academically when they returned to school in England.

We visited each other's homes regularly, which was difficult for the Harris children since they had to endure hours in the company of adults. Rhona told us that the children said they would only go to the Pahads' if Auntie Meg cooked her chicken curry.

Noel had a beautiful baritone voice, very similar to that of the great Paul Robeson, and whenever we were together with other friends, we would ask Noel to sing for us. He had a great repertoire of revolutionary and working-class songs and needed no accompaniment. One of my favourites was a song dedicated to Kevin Barry, a member of the IRA who was hanged by the British at the age of eighteen in November 1920. The song begins:

> In Mountjoy jail one Monday morning
> High upon the gallows tree,
> Kevin Barry gave his young life
> For the cause of liberty.
> Just a lad of eighteen summers
> Still there's no one can deny,
> As he walked to death that morning,
> He proudly held his head on high.

The chorus, which we joined in singing (not always in tune) goes as follows:

> Shoot me like a soldier.
> Do not hang me like a dog,
> For I fought to free old Ireland
> On that still September morn.

Noel knew at least four verses, and his powerful performances would move some of us to tears.

When they returned to London, Noel was appointed National Organiser of the Association of Cinematograph, Television and Allied Technicians (ACTT), and Rhona returned to teaching. We continued our firm family friendship until I left for South Africa in July 1990. True to his international solidarity commitment, Noel assumed the role of General Secretary of COSIR (Community Support Initiatives for Refugees), which campaigned for peace, human rights and democracy in Iran. He and Rhona visited us twice in South Africa, and we kept loosely in touch. When he became ill, they decided to return to Ireland, where he died at his home in Donaghadee, County Down.

At the time of writing, Rhona is still strong at 84, Brian is a full-time union negotiator at Prospect in the UK, and Kevin is a highly successful cloud computer technologist. Since both men are the spitting image of their father, every time we see their photos, we are reminded of the wonderful times we spent with their family.

Other people with whom Meg became close at WFTU include Steve and Sue Arloff, English translators who joined for the adventure and experience. Steve once gave Meg a free non-stop lift to London on condition that she chatted with him all the way – with only a break for the car ferry – so he could stay awake. Cde Atchuthan and his wife gave advice and support about traditional Kerala exercises and diets for babies when Govan was born sick. There was also Anton Hanna, a Palestinian from Syria who spoke Arabic, French, English and Czech fluently. Hélène Bouneaud, his wife, was a brilliant simultaneous interpreter in French, Spanish and English and later head of the CGT's international department for the Americas. Although they are now divorced, they have visited us in South Africa separately.

My primary contact with the Communist Party of Czechoslovakia was Drabek, who headed the Southern Africa Desk in its International Department. I had a lot of meetings with him in his office, discussing the issues and challenges confronting the national liberation movements in Southern Africa. Drabek was a true friend to our movement, as illustrated by the following anecdotes.

The first was when a Czech ambassador, either in Ethiopia or Tanzania, wanted permission to further develop his contacts with the PAC. When he raised the matter with me, I persuaded him that such a move would counter the interests of the socialist world, the ANC and SACP. Once convinced, he assured me, 'Don't worry, it won't happen.' Through the International Department, the ambassador was told not to follow up his contacts with the PAC.

The second anecdote concerns the South West Africa People's Organisation of Namibia (SWAPO). On an official visit to Czechoslovakia, Sam Nujoma requested a supply of various weapons, including the Scorpion, one of the most popular handguns internationally. Since it brought a lot of income to their coffers, the Czech Army chiefs were most reluctant to give it away free of charge. Once more, Drabek assured me that the Party, not the Army, was in control and that the request would be met. And indeed it was.

༄

That was a broad overview of some of the special people I knew through my work in Prague. Now I shall tell you about the most important events for us – the births of our children, who were born there: Amina Zanele in 1979 and Govan Timol in 1982.

We had been trying to have children for some years, so the birth of those two brought us great joy and happiness. Meg had strong views about the importance of natural birth, the role of midwives, breastfeeding, and physical contact and bonding between parents and children from day one, so the situation in Prague in 1979 was difficult and frustrating for her.

I was not allowed to be present when Amina was born. Against her specific instruction, the medical staff gave Meg an episiotomy, insisting it was their standard policy for all births. Almost as soon as she was born, they removed Amina and only brought her in with all the other babies at what they had decided were the correct times for her to be fed. Lying on a trolley, she had a number attached to her, which was the same as Meg's. When that number was called, Meg had to put up her hand to claim Amina.

I was also not allowed to visit the maternity ward, but they let Meg bring Amina to a window through which I could look at her. The nurses did not give Meg enough time to feed Amina, removing her forcibly, with the result that Meg's breasts became engorged, which made it worse. When a nurse pinched Amina's nose to make her let go of the nipple, Meg lost her temper and slapped the nurse's face. A senior hospital manager then gave Meg a lecture on her bad behaviour. Thankfully, Meg and Amina were allowed home on the third day, and Amina's life became one of calmness and love, and we could hold our child to our hearts' content.

Meg's parents came to Czechoslovakia to help when Amina was born. Her father, Jim Shorrock, a retired barrister who pretended to be more conservative than he really was, admitted there were things he could admire about the socialist system in place. Both Meg's parents appreciated the beauty of Prague and its wonderful historic buildings. When asked how he managed with the language, he explained that it was easy to communicate: 'You only need to know three things in Prague: no means yes, Pivo means beer, and horseshit is mustard.' (The word for *yes* is *ano*.). He said there was beer almost everywhere you went, and if you were hungry, there was always someone selling hot dogs. All you had to do was point, and they would start to prepare the roll and look at you questioningly, eyebrows raised and ask: 'Hořčice?'. Then you must answer 'No' and nod, and you would get the mustard.

Meg's parents were incensed that Amina could only obtain British citizenship through me, as at that time, the children of British women who gave birth abroad were not automatically entitled to it. Meg's father then went to the British Embassy and told the consul in no uncertain terms what he thought of the ridiculous situation (and the people who enforced it), where a British-born woman from a family that had been British from time immemorial could not pass on her nationality to her child.

As opposed to the horrific Czech hospital experience, we enjoyed the wonderful childcare system in Czechoslovakia. Mothers were encouraged to stay at home with their children for the first three years by being paid seventy-five per cent of their salary if they did so. If they preferred to go back to work, there was universal free provision of a crèche or *jesle*. Children could be dropped off any time between seven and ten a.m. and picked up between three and five p.m. Amina usually attended from nine until about four-thirty. The infants were given breakfast, a snack, lunch (soup and a meal of meat plus two vegetables) and another snack and kept until the agreed time. Every day, even if it was minus twenty degrees Celsius, the children were taken out for at least an hour's exercise. Parents provided three complete changes of clothes and five muslin nappies on the first day to the jesle, the staff of which kept them clean and ready for replacement. Outer clothes were worn to and from school and kept clean by the parents. For winter, these had to include an 'eskimo' suit, gloves and a hat which covered the ears and was tied under the chin for winter. They sang and danced a lot, learnt how to blow their noses and tie their shoelaces, and how to share and help each other. The only thing Amina didn't like was sleeping after lunch. She was in perpetual trouble for refusing to do this and had to be put in a room by herself because she would not be still or quiet. She made friends at that school, and we were told that her Czech was as good as her English.

After *jesle* came *mateřska škola*, for children from three to six. The Czechs believed in nurturing children and disapproved of pushing them into formal lessons in reading, maths and so on. Of course, they read lots of stories, discussed the world around them, played counting games and learned through play. The Czech people we spoke to (not only the teachers) were aware that childhood is a special time that need not be rushed: a precious time. While in Prague, we never saw anyone hitting a child or screaming at one. It shocked us when we returned to London and realised how common this was in the UK.

Fortunately, when Govan was born (three years after Amina), the maternity ward situation had greatly improved, and after his birth, when they had both been cleaned up, Govan was put in a cot next to Meg's bed in the maternity ward, so the contact and feeding were perfect. But from the first day, Govan vomited the colostrum and then the milk, and on the third day, he vomited excessively in a projectile manner. When Meg explained this to the doctor and nurse, they said it was impossible, as it was too early for pyloric stenosis. So Meg fed Govan and then held him up facing the clean white wall onto which he performed a classic projectile vomit with a cartoon style SPLAT! When the doctor and nurse saw this, they put him in an incubator in intensive care for a day's observation.

They became very concerned, and when Govan was just one week old, they decided he might need an operation so moved him with Meg to the only hospital in Prague that performed surgery on babies. They were fascinated by Govan's problem and performed endless tests on him, never giving him any peace. Eventually, they discovered he had a twisted stomach and a urinary tract infection and had been weakened by being given antibiotics too soon. After about five weeks, we were really worried, but we had a wonderful paediatrician called Dr Pačes, who had been Amina's doctor, and he visited Meg and Govan and discussed the case with us. He said the hospital was the worst place for Govan and advised us to discharge him and take him home. He promised to visit us regularly and monitor Govan's progress. So we took his advice.

Although only for a few weeks, my experience being a single parent to

Amina has made me always appreciate and sympathise with those who raise children on their own.

After he got home, Govan gradually put on weight and became healthy. For about a year, he was fed on demand and held upright after feeding for about thirty minutes to allow the food to slowly trickle around the twist, which gradually straightened out without any surgical intervention. We believe that Dr Pačes saved his life. Until he was about fifteen, he was approximately three years shorter than other boys his age, but he caught up as a teenager, again without medical intervention – although many people tried to persuade us to give him various drugs to 'help' him grow faster. In reality, after the first year of his life, he was strong and healthy and is now average height and very fit.

Before I move on, I must say a little more about Prague and add another family who was unconnected with our places of work.

When Amina was at *jesle*, we had the good fortune of finding out about a local family interested in looking after another child at their home during working hours. When we met them, they seemed perfect. The mother, who offered to be the caregiver, was Eugenie Bidenkova, one of the warmest, most caring people we have ever met. She was devoted to her children Jiří (now Georgi) and Evuška (now Evelyn) and later also to Aminka (Amina) and Govski (Govan). She asked us all to call her *Teta* (Auntie) and was frequently assisted by her mother (*Babička*, which means grandmother) and sometimes by her father (Dědeček: grandfather). *Teta* and her mother took care to prepare good quality, fresh and tasty food for every meal and were very disappointed if the hearty meals were not finished. *Teta* took the children out for walks – whatever the weather – and they climbed trees in the cherry orchard, played in the communal sandpits, and ran and kicked balls. No one ever seemed to be stressed or angry.

Teta's husband, Ivan Bidenko, was equally welcoming and good-natured. He was a Bulgarian engineer, highly qualified and innovative, already at that time an expert in water supply and sewage systems whose work was respected internationally. His mother was a paediatrician in Bulgaria who worried that the Czech diet was too laden with fat and carbohydrates and made sure that *Teta* included lots of fresh fruit and vegetables in her grandchildren's food.

Govan only went to *jesle* for a short time because, when he was about eighteen months old, Meg was able to return to work, and he joined the Bidenko family with Amina. Jiří, their eldest, now holds a senior position in his father's highly successful engineering and construction company in the environmental sector. Evuška is the same age as Amina and works in the banking sector. Her English is excellent, so she was able to help her mother communicate when they came to Johannesburg for Amina's wedding. Jiří and Evuška are both married with two children.

Amina and Govan were so lucky to have been cared for by that family: overflowing with love, patience and kindness. We will always be grateful for the role they played in our lives.

༄

Prague is a spectacular city with numerous Gothic towers, magnificent baroque churches and many bridges arching across the Vltava River, notably Charles Bridge, lined with statues of Catholic saints. Towering above it is Prague Castle, and in the Old Town (*Staré Město*), the amazing mediaeval clock with its hourly performance and *sgraffito*-decorated buildings. [67] When we lived in Prague, there was no advertising (no capitalism, so no economic competition), and the mediaeval part of the city appeared to be time-locked in the past. One could sit in the Old Town or the Small Quarter (*Malá Strana*) on a snowy day, and the scene appeared to be part of a Bruegel painting – people wrapped warmly carrying a jug of beer or some freshly baked bread across a square to their home. Cobbled streets, no motorised traffic, no neon signs, just people eating or drinking or shopping; visually, only the occasional banner reminding us of the Great October Socialist Revolution betrayed the period in which we were living. When the film *Amadeus* was made, not enough parts of Vienna looked old enough for Mozart's time, so Prague was used instead.

Life in Czechoslovakia was pleasant and stress-free for most citizens. There was a full employment policy, so everyone was guaranteed a job and a place to live appropriate to the size of their family, and bus and tram and underground travel were so cheap as to be almost free. Childcare and education were free and accessible to everyone. However, there were some things about the way socialism was interpreted and applied that were irrational and absurd. For example, small businesses supplying artisanal

---

67. Sgraffito is a technique of wall decor, produced by applying layers of cement plaster tinted in contrasting colours to a moistened surface. 'Sgraffito' and 'sgraffiti' come from the Italian word *graffiare* ('to scratch'), ultimately from the Greek γράφειν (gráphein) 'to write'. Related terms include graffito and graffiti. For more information on this technique, visit http://web.nationalbuildingarts.org/collections/cementitious/sgraffito/background-on-sgraffito/

services, such as motor mechanics, and service industries like small shops and restaurants, were strictly regulated to avoid competition, so every concern had an approved list of what they could offer and the price to be charged – which made sense in many but not all contexts. For example, at the beginning of strawberry season, when there were hardly any strawberries, the queues would be long and the berries would be sold quickly for the same price that would later be charged when there was a glut and the fruit was beginning to rot. The laws of supply and demand were not allowed to influence price. Because of this, a skilled artisan might be tempted to sell his services illegally because he was not allowed to charge more for his competent and efficient services than a colleague who was lazy, careless and unreliable.

Skilled professionals were paid less than their counterparts in the West, whereas technicians and manual workers were better paid and had complete job security. A television repairman who came to our house explained that if there were not an 'iron curtain', he would want to stay in Prague, whereas his daughter, a medical doctor, would definitely join the 'brain drain' to the West.

Even if it was freezing cold or there was a cloudburst, people were forced to queue outside a shop (except for one big supermarket in town) to wait for a basket before entering, even though they would be happier to queue inside to pay before leaving (which I suggested to Drabek). When Meg and her friend Barbara Sukupova took their children to a country restaurant near a wood full of bilberries, the waitress whispered to them that bilberry pie was available but not on the menu. They bought this delicious dessert but were reminded not to tell anyone, as the restaurant could get into trouble for selling something not on the approved list.

Another view I expressed to Drabek and others is that in a socialist society, while the main means of production and leading industries can be in control of the state, the retail and service sectors should be open to private ownership. That would result in better-quality service and more contented citizens.

A more serious aspect to that kind of problem was that people who complained about those silly regulations could be victimised. Meg occasionally came across taxi drivers, window cleaners and manual workers who had once been university lecturers, senior professionals or managers but had been fired or demoted – also artists who were refused support – for not toeing the line.

During all our time in Prague, Meg worked, except for the first year and the year Govan was born. As the general staff at WFTU were Czech, whereas at WMR they were Soviet, she got to know more Czech people than I did. She once went to a party where a number of Charter 77 supporters tried to convince her of their cause. Two of them soon revealed their true colours – near to fascism in Meg's opinion – with one of them wanting to see the US 'bomb Vietnam back to the stone age'. Given my political and ideological orientation and work at the WMR, I refused to meet anyone connected to Charter 77.

However, there were many who supported the idea of socialism but were irritated by the government's attitude to criticism. Some people told Meg that the Czech communists and trade unionists who had fought the Nazis and people like the South Africans fighting apartheid were 'real communists', who they respected, but they were disillusioned with the current leadership of their country, many of whom they regarded as fakes. They said that a lot of communists were simply members of the Communist Party because they had to join if they wanted promotion at work and an easier life. Many people confirmed this.

One day, Meg's friend Barbara asked for help with an English paper she had to write. She said, 'I feel so ashamed showing you the stupid title of this essay,' which was: 'Explain why you think that the Great October Socialist Revolution is the single most important event in world history.' Barbara asked, 'Why do they pretend to ask a question while telling you the answer?'

Although some people owned their homes, this was unusual, as almost all property belonged to the state. As circumstances changed, people could be moved from their homes – like when Govan was born and we were moved from our one-bedroomed flat in Arabskà to a two-bedroomed one in October Revolution Square. The state also had the responsibility of maintaining the property. People in homes provided by the state could not depend on staying there permanently until death or passing the property on to their children, so they were naturally reluctant to spend time and energy on improving or even maintaining their homes. At some stage, the government made it relatively easy to purchase a weekend cottage or holiday home, just like the USSR government allowed people to own a dacha.[68]

The Bidenko family owned a *chata*[69] just outside Prague with a fair-sized garden where they could grow some fruit and vegetables and spend some of

---

68. A dacha is a seasonal or year-round second home, often located in the exurbs of post-Soviet countries, including Russia. A cottage or shack serving as a family's main or only home, or an outbuilding, is not considered a dacha, although some dachas recently have been converted to year-round residences and vice versa. In archaic Russian, 'dacha' means 'something given'. Available at https://en.wikipedia.org/wiki/Dacha
69. A recreational cottage or cabin

their energy making it attractive and comfortable. For energetic, intelligent and family-orientated people, it was wonderfully fulfilling, investing personal effort in the future, and it also made us realise that banning private ownership brings its own problems.

Teta and Ivan were always respectful about my political views and only ever voiced mild criticisms to us and indeed appreciated the positive aspects of socialism in both Czechoslovakia and Bulgaria.

So our children had a happy start to their lives, with a safe and healthy environment and lots of love and care from us and the Bidenko family. I remember the layers of clothes we had to put on Amina whenever we went outside and the effort of pushing her around, first in an old-fashioned pram and later a pushchair. Also how, by the time she was two-and-a-half, she would walk along the little rough path to the swimming pool in Šarka Valley when Meg, who was pregnant, couldn't carry her. Amina was so strong and never complained. On the weekends in winter, she wore me out when she tobogganed down a nearby hill and I had to pull the toboggan back up for her to repeat the ride about thirty times before she would agree to stop. Later, when Govan joined in those adventures, it was even more exhausting but nevertheless wonderful.

By the time I was sent back to London, both children could speak Czech as well as they could English, but they were only three-and-a-half and six-and-a-half, so, with no one else in their extended families speaking any Czech, we reluctantly decided that it was not feasible to keep up their proficiency. If it had been Russian or Arabic or French, we might have thought the effort worthwhile.

Chapter 4
Focus on Africa

Focus on Africa

During my time at WMR, I was still concerned about keeping a focus on Africa within the broader context of internationalism. The most important work I did in that regard relates to the 'Communist Call to Africa', which started soon after I arrived in Czechoslovakia and continued in different phases, off and on, for another twelve years. Here is a brief summary.

In February 1976, the 25th Congress of the CPSU was held in Moscow. Utilising the opportunity afforded by their attendance at that Congress, some of the leaders of the Communist and Workers Parties of Tropical and Southern Africa decided it would be useful to hold a meeting to exchange views and discuss developments on the continent, in the world communist movement and internationally, among other topics of mutual interest.

It was agreed that the Senegalese Party of Independence and Labour (PIT), the Sudanese CPS and the SACP, which had representatives at the WMR in Prague, should establish an organising committee to draft a document that could be presented for adoption by the parties concerned and the Congress Party for the Independence of Madagascar (AKFM), the Communist Party of Reunion, the Socialist Workers and Farmers Party of Nigeria, and the Communist Party of Lesotho. The committee was composed of Amath Dansokho (PIT), Salim Ahmed Salim (CPS) and myself (SACP).

A month or two later, we held our first meeting, and it was decided that the draft document should be in English and that I should be the main drafter. We started with a clean slate and had extensive discussions on a wide range of topics, challenges and problems confronting the African continent, the Marxist-Leninist parties and the revolutionary process. On the basis of those discussions, I was to produce a working draft which would be analysed, criticised and improved by the three of us. We also agreed to consult with academics and leaders from the SED of Germany and the CPSU. From the GDR, we were assisted by Professor Maerdhal and from the Soviet Union by Ulyanovsky and Manchka from the International Department of the CPSU, who were also prominent scholars on Africa and Asia. Both the SED and

CPSU also provided logistical support for our work.

From the Soviet and GDR comrades, we received and considered inputs and analyses of socio-economic developments on the continent, including in Angola, Mozambique, the Democratic Republic of Congo, and Benin, whose ruling parties were guided by Marxism-Leninism. Everyone agreed that the draft should reflect the collective views of the participating parties and be authentically African in form and content.

At the beginning, Amath would speak in French, which would be interpreted into Russian or German and then into English. This was cumbersome, and some of the nuances in his inputs would be missed, so I prevailed on him to speak English, and I endeavoured to reflect his views as accurately as possible. After I had prepared a draft, it would be dissected, criticised and improved; I would then redraft it for further discussions until we were satisfied. Once we agreed, we would send it, with the help of the CPSU, to the other parties for their criticisms, suggestions and alternative formulations.

By the middle of 1977, we were ready to organise a meeting of the participating parties, and the CPSU and SED were keen that it be held on the African continent. But this was not possible, as no African country would agree to host a meeting of communists and workers' parties at that time, so the meeting took place in Leipzig, GDR, once more with the SED and CPSU making all the logistical arrangements. The following parties attended the meeting: the AKFM of Madagascar; Communist Party of Reunion; PIT of Senegal; Workers and Farmers Party of Nigeria; Communist Party of Sudan; and the SACP.

The atmosphere was cordial, the discussions intense, and many new ideas were suggested. In particular, Paul Virges, General Secretary of the Communist Party of Reunion, argued forcefully and persuasively that the draft document must take into account the movement of people from the rural areas into the city centres, which had a developmental impact on the rural and urban economies and human settlements. This trend was absent from the draft but using my extensive notes, I was able to incorporate it into the document.

Following that meeting, Dansokho, Salim and I, as the Committee, were invited to meet with Hermann Axel, Member of the Politbureau and Secretary of the SED Central Committee in East Berlin. Hermann received us warmly and called our draft a historic document. He also said that, once adopted, it would have a positive impact and influence on the GDR state and the Party. The three of us then met in Prague to fine-tune the document in line with the inputs made in Leipzig. Eventually, we circulated our improved draft to the central committees of all the participating parties (including that of Lesotho, which had not been in Leipzig) to be finalised and formally adopted at a meeting of the top leaders. Once again, we could not hold this meeting in Africa, and instead, the SED and CPSU arranged for it to take place in Moscow in May 1978. This led to further changes, so after a discussion between Dansokho, Salim Ahmed Salim and me, I again fine-tuned the document, and we had a final draft for adoption. I sat up all night, and, with the help of the Soviet staff, we had it printed out and ready for the next day.

When 'The Communist Call to Africa' was adopted, Boris Ponomarev, a highly respected figure in the World Communist Movement, Member of the Politbureau and Head of the International Department of the CPSU, was present. He expressed his support for a document that was, in his words, prepared and produced by Africans for the African continent. He also said some kind words about me and the amount of work I had put into the project.

After two years of hard work by the three of us and the contributions of the participating parties, we had our document, 'A Communist Call to Africa for the Freedom, Independence and Social Progress of the Peoples of Tropical and Southern Africa.' It was published in full in The African Communist edition of the fourth quarter of 1978.

That document also served as the basis for discussions with the ruling Marxist-Leninist parties of Angola, Mozambique, Congo, Benin and Ethiopia. At a personal level, I was satisfied that I had contributed to the adoption of a historical document, the first of its type on the African continent. I quote a few paragraphs below to indicate our assessments and analyses of socio-economic developments in our region at the time:

> ... By means of economic and financial levers of the world capitalist market, the most excessive monopoly over maritime transport and freight rates, and by dictating the prices of technology, international imperialism not only continues to rob substantially the peoples of the fruits of their labour but also increases its economic and financial pressure on them. ...
>
> ... It is impossible to ensure real social progress for a long period without taking into account the very serious problem of the

peasantry, without responding to the aspirations of the peasant masses for socio-economic progress, without the active support of the peasantry. ...

... The process of urbanisation has also led to the growth of the middle and some transitional strata, which includes elements dislocated from the rural areas, small traders, artisans, office workers and intellectuals. These strata also take part with varying degrees of intensity in the struggle for democracy and national and social progress. It is from these strata that such an influential force as revolutionary democrats, more or less clearly shaped, is emerging and which in the socialist orientated countries controls state power.
...
... This stratum plays a role of the first importance in the relations between the domestic bourgeoisie and imperialism while performing a regulating function between the diverse groups of domestic exploiters. ...

... Being in control of the economic and political levers of state, the bureaucratic bourgeoisie is carrying on capitalist accumulation at a high rate to the detriment of the national interest. In practising institutionalised corruption and frittering away the natural resources and public property, it combines explicit submission to the imperatives of the neo-colonialist policy of imperialism with extensive nationalist demagogy. The control it exercises over the state apparatus provides this narrow group with [the] powerful means of gearing key economic mechanisms to the development of all the domestic exploiting strata.[70]

With the assistance of the SED and CPSU, we asked Amath Dansokho to visit some of the parties to apprise them of the document's contents and seek their agreement for a meeting between the ruling socialist-orientated parties on the continent and those which had adopted the 'Call'. His interactions did not produce positive outcomes, and the matter was left for further consideration.

However, a breakthrough came for a meeting of twelve parties during the International Scientific Conference in Berlin in October 1980, organised by the CC of the SED and the WMR. On the opening day of the Conference,

---

70. 'A Communist Call to Africa for the Freedom, Independence and Social Progress of the Peoples of Tropical and Southern Africa', *The African Communist* No. 75, 4th Quarter 1978, p. 5. Inkululeko Publications. Available at https://www.sahistory.org.za/sites/default/files/archive-files4/Acn7578.pdf

Sergio Vierra from FRELIMO reprimanded me in an offensive, boorish manner for adopting the 'Call to Africa' without consulting the ruling Marxist-Leninist parties. Somehow, I managed to keep my cool and arranged for Yusuf Dadoo, who was leading the SACP delegation, to meet Vierra, who was respectful to Dadoo, and they agreed that Dadoo should convene a meeting. That took place on 23 October 1980, and representatives from the seven parties that had adopted the 'Call' attended, as well as representatives from the MPLA, the Congolese Party of Labour (CPL), the Commission for Organising the Working People of Ethiopia (COPWE), and the Liberation Front of Mozambique (*Frente de Libertação de Moçambique*: FRELIMO). Representatives from Benin did not attend that international conference.

That meeting began uneasily and uncomfortably when Vierra, in a rude and arrogant manner, implied that the seven non-ruling parties had benefited from assistance given to them by the communist parties of the coloniser countries, whereas, they, in Mozambique, had to go to a toilet to read any Marxist literature. Obviously, he was deliberately ignoring the role played by the Portuguese Communist Party in the overthrow of the brutal fascist Salazar regime and in supporting MPLA in the very first days of independence. But all the representatives ignored those insulting and provocative remarks, and, Dadoo, as chair, was patient and calm. His even-tempered mature chairing of the meeting and the positive interventions of the other delegates led to a successful conclusion, and it was decided that all the delegates would report to their central committees and examine the possibilities of calling a follow-up meeting which would also include the party from Benin.

The twelve parties did indeed meet in Berlin, GDR, in 1981 during the 10th Congress of the SED. It was a meeting held in a spirit of frank and honest discussion and debate and led to the setting up of an International Preparatory Committee composed of the SACP (convenor), FRELIMO and the CPL. Although follow-up meetings were held in Moscow and Berlin, progress was slow. In an attempt to speed up the process of greater bilateral cooperation, a meeting held in Moscow during the Jubilee Celebrations in 1987 agreed that the initial group should be assisted by an implementation committee based in Prague, composed of the relevant representatives from the WMR and the ambassador of Ethiopia to Czechoslovakia. Sudan was the convenor and, although I had been living in London since 1985 and only going to Prague monthly, I was part of the Committee.

By that time, both Dadoo and Moses Mabhida had passed away, and Joe

Slovo was the General Secretary of the SACP. He was then living and working in Maputo, which facilitated interactions with FRELIMO as part of the Contact Group, as the Committee was now called. They had the responsibility, together with the Congolese Party of Labour (CPL), of preparing a document entitled the 'Maputo Manifesto, Africa and the Struggle for Socialism'.

As part of that process, an 'African Inter-Parties Seminar' of the twelve parties was organised in May 1988 in East Berlin. The SACP delegation, led by Slovo, consisted of M. Sere (pseudonym), Jessica Jacobs and me. The FRELIMO delegation was led by Oscar Monteiro and included Vierra. That was my first encounter with Oscar, whom I found highly intelligent, politically astute, warm and mature. We struck up a friendship that has continued to the present time, and whenever he comes to Johannesburg, we still meet and discuss political and other challenges facing our movements and governments.

The other parties represented at that meeting were the MPLA, CPL, AKFM, Workers' Party of Ethiopia, PIT, Sudanese Communist Party, Socialist Workers and Farmers Party of Nigeria (SWFPN), Communist Party of Lesotho and the PRPB (*Partie de la Révolution Populaire du Bénin*). The Communist Party of Réunion sent apologies.

At that friendly and comradely meeting, it was agreed that we should intensify the work on the Maputo Declaration and organise our next meeting on African soil. We did not know then that this planned meeting would never happen. In November 1989, Joe Slovo contacted other members of the group with a proposal to meet in January 1990, preferably in an African country. But seismic events in the latter part of 1989 led to the collapse of the Soviet Union and other socialist countries in Eastern Europe, followed by the unbanning of the ANC, SACP, and PAC in South Africa by President F. W. de Klerk in February 1990 – all of which changed the situation and resulted in the proposed meeting not taking place. It was unfortunate that we were unable to build on the platform created in Berlin in 1988 and that the draft Maputo Manifesto was never adopted but left to gather dust.

The preparatory meetings leading to the adoption of the 'Call to Africa' afforded me the opportunity to meet some remarkable communist party leaders, three of whom I mention here: Wahab Goodluck and Dapo Fatogun of Nigeria and Mokhafisi Kena of Lesotho.

Wahab Goodluck founded and led a number of trade unions, and is widely recognised as one of the finest trade union leaders in the history of

Nigeria. At the founding conference of the Nigeria Labour Congress (NLC) in 1975, he was elected its national president. Successive military regimes failed to intimidate Goodluck into silence. Indeed, the NLC was banned in 1976, and a year later, the military regime attempted to restructure the trade union movement minus Goodluck and some other communist trade unionists. But to the chagrin of the regime, many of the restructured trade unions were led by protégées of Goodluck, one of whom was Hassan Sunmonu, the first president of the new NLC and later General Secretary of the Organisation of African Trade Union Unity (OATUU). At a lecture to the Kolagbodi Memorial Foundation in 1999, Sunmonu said of Goodluck that he was 'almost the most honest trade union leader I had come across' and described him as 'a fantastic organiser ... a courageous leader' who 'had integrity ... never lied ... and devoted his life to workers' struggles'.

Goodluck was always very friendly, comradely and kind to me. He was keen to know more and understand better the trade union movement in South Africa, the ANC, SACP and our struggle for national liberation, human rights and democracy. I learnt a great deal from him about trade unions in Nigeria and the African continent as well as how to outsmart and out-manoeuvre repressive regimes.

Dapo Fatagun was genial, patient and unpretentious with an ever-present smile. Like Goodluck, he was a solid supporter of the ANC, the SACP and the Anti-Apartheid Movement. When we last met in Berlin, he was the leader of the Socialist Workers and Farmers Party of Nigeria (SWFPN). Whenever we met, we had intense discussions about the political, economic, social and cultural developments of the African continent and the challenges facing the international communist movement. He was a courageous opponent of the military regimes and, like Goodluck, could not be silenced. He was also founder of the magazine *New Horizon* and constantly sought information on how we produced and distributed *The African Communist*. He had a high opinion of the calibre of the contributing authors and the quality of their published articles. I thoroughly enjoyed my encounters with Fatagun and benefited from his vast experience of our continent and his optimistic vision of the future of his own country and the world revolutionary process.

The third leader I must mention is Mokhafisi Kena, who was General Secretary of the Communist Party of Lesotho (CPL) when we met in Berlin. When the Party divided over the Sino-Soviet split, he was part of the pro-Soviet group. The CPL was banned in 1970, and Kena and some others continued to work underground; due to their unrelenting struggle, it was legalised in 1991.

Kena was tall and well-built, quietly spoken, caring and passionate about the struggles in Lesotho and South Africa. He was always interested and appreciative of the work I was doing, and we both enjoyed our discussions about political developments in Southern Africa. Often, when he remarked that his abiding wish was to return to life on a farm, I would tease him that from a peasant he became a worker, then a leader of the working class in his country, and now wanted to turn the clock back and become a farmer.

The CPL produced some really good intellectuals and also assisted our underground structures in Lesotho.

More than thirty years after meeting Goodluck, Fatogun and Kena, I have fond memories of our discussions and comradeship, and I feel privileged and honoured to have known and worked with those courageous African leaders.

༄

While at the WMR, I visited many countries, but I shall mention visits to the following African countries as being of interest: Somalia, Ethiopia, Mozambique, Botswana, and later, Angola, where I did my training.

Somalia

At the First Congress of the Communist Party of Cuba in December 1975, I had the good fortune to meet the delegation from Somalia. From our first encounter, we took to each other and got along extremely well. We had intense discussions on the revolutionary process unfolding in that country and their endeavours to pursue anti-imperialist socio-economic policies and positions, including fraternal relations with the Soviet Union and other socialist countries. I was impressed by their determination and conviction. We also discussed the possibilities of initiating and sustaining relations between Somalia and the WMR.

I reported that discussion to the editor at the WMR and expressed the firm view that we should enter into a working relationship with the Somali comrades. Then, in October 1976, I was invited to visit Somalia to continue the discussions we had started in Cuba to give form and content to the relations between their party and the WMR. The editor and management of the WMR welcomed the invitation and fully supported my visit.

The Somali comrades received me warmly and arranged the necessary meetings with other Somali political leaders. I also engaged in long and worthwhile discussions about a range of issues, including the theory and practice of Marxism-Leninism and revolutionary democracy. They were keen to learn from me and formalise the relationship with the WMR. I was equally interested to learn from them about their country and its future development and the wider region. I learnt a great deal from those interactions but did express my serious misgivings about the President of Somalia's expressed desire to work to bring about a 'Greater Somalia'.

Unfortunately for the progressive forces in Somalia and Ethiopia, my misgivings were confirmed when President Mohamed Siad Barre of Somalia ordered the invasion of Ogaden, a geographic entity of Ethiopia. In an article in *The African Communist*, 3rd Quarter 1978, I condemned that and wrote that 'the myth of recreating a "Greater Somalia" was taken to absurd levels with Barre launching a chauvinistic campaign to justify his aggression'. That action also marked the start of a retreat from progressive policies. As it transpired, over the following years, a number of revolutionary Somali leaders, some of them my friends and acquaintances, were arrested, with some executed.

My experiences concerning Somalia also taught me a lot about the power of clans and clan politics in that country. Barre himself was from one of the most powerful clans. It was as true then as it is now that to fathom and understand Somali politics, you have to give the greatest consideration to the politics of clans. I came to understand and appreciate in greater depth the national question and its interaction and interconnectedness to the class question in South Africa and elsewhere in Africa.

Ethiopia

At around that time, I also visited Ethiopia. Following the military overthrow of Emperor Haile Selassie in September 1974, a Provisional Military Administrative Council (PMAC), headed by General Aman Adom, was set up with Mengistu Haile Mariam as First Vice President. Adom was killed within a few months and replaced by Teferi Benti, but it was widely accepted that the real leader was Mariam. I was in favour of the military coup but not fully aware of the violence gripping that country or of the confusion and divisions within the ranks of the revolutionary left.

My first visit to Ethiopia was in 1976, the same year that the Afro-Asian People's Solidarity Organisation (AAPSO) in the Soviet Union organised the International Conference on Apartheid, covering the travel and accommodation costs for all of the delegates. Those delegates from Europe and other parts of the world travelled on Aeroflot from Moscow to Addis Ababa. One of them was a CC member of the Communist Party of Malta who, when we stopped in Yemen, bought food and distributed it to many of the delegates. Given the not-so-palatable food served on Aeroflot flights, his generosity was much appreciated. During the trip, we became friends and, on our arrival in Addis, I warned him about respecting the night curfew imposed by the military regime and not to leave the hotel, as violence from the regime and its opponents was a regular feature of life in that country.

In the early hours of the next morning, there was a loud knocking on the door of my bedroom. On opening it, I found the Maltese comrade looking extremely worried and sweating profusely. He told me that, despite my warning, he had gone out that night and on his return was manhandled outside the hotel. The officer in charge was extremely rude in demanding an explanation for his violation of the curfew. He also pushed his sub-machine gun into my friend's chest and threatened to kill him. No wonder he was mortified and in mental anguish. I offered him a glass of whiskey, which he gulped down, and it took me nearly two hours to calm him. Needless to say, he never left the hotel at night again.

The second incident I recall from that trip was when Alfred Nzo, leader of the ANC delegation, asked to see me at his hotel. He wanted me to help him write his speech, as he was one of the main speakers. He assured me that he had spoken to the relevant military authorities, who had authorised me to violate the curfew, and said that an officer would accompany me back to my hotel. After we had finished, I waited in the lobby for more than an hour for my military escort. When it arrived, the officer in charge rudely berated me for being out so late. I responded rather tetchily that it was him, not me, who was late and that I did not need a lecture from him on the importance of revolutionary discipline.

At that conference, where I represented the WMR, one of my tasks was meeting the relevant people to open discussions on developing mutually friendly relations between the WMR and the Ethiopian administration. I managed to arrange a meeting with an officer in charge of communications and briefed him about the WMR and our desire to develop close relations. He listened to me, but it became clear as we talked that he was more inclined toward the ideology of Maoism and not favourably disposed toward the Soviet Union. Although that was not a helpful meeting, it confirmed my opinion that the military leaders and officials held differing and conflicting political and ideological viewpoints, which led to a lack of unity and cohesion within their ranks. I had a brief meeting with a few of the PMAC leaders, including Mengistu Mariam, who would emerge as the leader of the PMAC until 1991.

After that trip, I made a special study of Ethiopia, reading up on its rich history and contemporary developments. I became more aware of the political contradictions within the PMAC and, lower down its machinery, the personality clashes and ongoing heightened violence from all sides of the conflict. I made other visits to the country, and the dangerous environment could not be ignored. When people you knew and liked or perhaps had only met briefly just disappeared, you were discouraged from enquiring about them. Some media spoke of 'Red violence versus White violence'.

Despite those weaknesses, I became a firm supporter of the revolutionary process in Ethiopia, and, although I found Ethiopians wary and even suspicious at first meetings, they gradually warmed up, and some even trusted me and became real comrades. Once that happened, they expressed their views directly without diplomatic niceties or nuanced hidden meanings, and once they had made an undertaking, they would do their utmost to implement it.

On reflection, I can now see that I was hugely optimistic about Ethiopia's future and consciously and subconsciously ignored signs and incidents I should have seen as indicators of unacceptable political processes and injustice. The ruling party was steeped in a military confrontation where the opposition had the support of major imperialist powers and, instead of seeking a political solution, they were driven to attempt to solve their problems through military action. Nevertheless, my experience working with comrades from Ethiopia enhanced my understanding of the difficulties of the transition from autocracy to democracy. It also highlighted the importance of not ignoring internal political and personal contradictions and clashes, the insidious impact of external conservative and reactionary forces and their agencies, and the critical importance of mass mobilisations and continually striving to ensure that the people are supreme. Without their direct involvement in decision-making at all levels of government administration, the revolutionary process is in danger of derailment.

Mozambique

Similar historical lessons can be gleaned from Mozambique.

Portuguese colonial Mozambique and racist South Africa had close economic and political ties for nearly a century. Many Mozambicans worked in South African mines, factories and homes, and the port Lorenzo Marques (Maputo) was used by South Africa for imports and exports.

The fraternal and political relations between FRELIMO, the ANC and the SACP – as well as the close friendship between O. R. Tambo and Samora Machel, leader of FRELIMO and the first president of independent Mozambique – had developed into a powerful political alliance. One outcome was that in 1969, a group of MK combatants under Lennox Lagu (Mongameli Tshali) entered the Tete Province at the invitation of FRELIMO to conduct reconnaissance to ascertain the feasibility of infiltrating MK comrades into South Africa from that province, which was coming under the control of FRELIMO. Lennox reported that, given the distance from Tete to the South African border and the hostile terrain they would have to traverse, that option was not feasible.

In 1968, Lord Tony Gifford, Polly Gaster and Basil Davidson (a distinguished historian of pre-colonial Africa) formed the Committee for Freedom in Mozambique, Angola and Guinea-Bissau (CFMAG) in London, and the ANC immediately offered its support and assistance. I worked closely with Gaster and Gifford, offering my experience and that of the ANC in building a strong solidarity group. At anti-apartheid meetings and rallies, I always made sure to mention the CFMAG and called upon the audience to offer them support, which strengthened my friendship with the two.

Progressive forces in South Africa, together with the ANC, SACP and SACTU, welcomed the independence of Mozambique in 1974 with joy and excitement. Meanwhile, the South African regime's response was to ban meetings and rallies called to celebrate that great African victory and arrest some of the organisers. The collapse of the Portuguese colonial and fascist empire was the result of the sustained and dangerous struggle conducted by anti-fascist and anti-colonial organisations working together. The banned and hounded Portuguese Communist Party and progressive military officers and soldiers played a prominent role, but most important were the unrelenting and courageous armed struggles waged by FRELIMO, the MPLA and the African Party for the Independence of Guinea and Cape Verde (*Partido Africano para a Independência da Guiné e Cabo Verde*: PAIGC.)

My burning wish to visit independent Mozambique was fulfilled in September 1975, when I had just started work at the WMR and was invited to attend an AAPSO conference in Maputo. Soon after our arrival at our hotel, an ANC comrade and I decided to walk the streets of independent

Mozambique and breathe the air of freedom. We walked for about an hour, taking care to note our route so we could return to the hotel without any difficulty. When we did so, we were met by an angry Joe Nhlanhla, one of the organisers. He didn't mince his words about what he considered a serious breach of discipline for venturing out without consulting him or taking an escort, as counter-revolutionary elements were already active in Maputo. I protested his humiliating words and insulting attitude and reminded him that we had known each other since the late fifties and, with other Congress comrades, had rebuffed attempts by pro-fascist Hungarian refugees who had tried to disrupt a meeting called by the 'Friends of the Soviet Union' in the Gandhi Hall in Ferreirastown. That had the desired effect of calming him down, and we agreed that, in the future, we would inform the relevant people before leaving the hotel.

I took the opportunity of phoning my brothers Nassim and Zuneid to find out if they had any contacts in Maputo, as I wanted to buy some artefacts and cashew nuts, which were a Mozambican speciality. Through a family friend called Amin Laher, they arranged for someone to help me do my shopping. Laher and I were going to meet again, but the second time he came to the hotel, the security at the entrance refused to let him in. He felt insecure and intimidated, so I agreed to meet him later outside the hotel. He kindly asked me to his home for supper, but that was not possible due to other commitments.

Josiah Jele, who also attended the conference, took me to visit an old friend I had not seen for many years, Pam dos Santos. Pam had married Marcelino dos Santos, one of the leading figures in FRELIMO and the democratic government. She was very friendly, invited Meg and I for dinner and took us to see various parts of the city. It was a wonderful visit and fortified my resolve to witness the demise of apartheid South Africa. As it turned out, it would be nearly fifteen years before I returned to that city.

The racist South African regime engaged in a counter-revolutionary offensive against the FRELIMO government while supporting and assisting the terrorist group RENAMO with military equipment, training and funds. For many years, RENAMO carried out guerilla destabilisation activities, while the apartheid military and security forces stepped up their aggressive actions. In 1981, they attacked an ANC house in Matola, a suburb of Maputo, killing fifteen of our comrades. One of those was William Khanyile, a leader of SACTU and member of the ANC and SACP, whose wife Eleanor was living and working in London at the time. As O. R. Tambo stated at the Matola memorial service in 1982:

> The Matola invasion was a raid which insulted the sovereignty of the Mozambican people, defiled their national dignity, violated their territorial integrity and challenged the very concept of African independent statehood.[71]

In August 1982, Ruth First, a South African revolutionary, renowned writer, journalist and wife of Joe Slovo, was killed by a letter bomb in her office at Eduardo Mondlane University. Pallo Jordan, a leading member of the ANC, who later held ministerial posts in the Mandela and Mbeki governments, was injured in that blast.

Although FRELIMO had declared its unconditional support for the ANC and SACP and allowed leaders and members of both organisations to live and operate in Mozambique, the unrelenting pressure and severe attacks by the apartheid political, security and military forces had an impact and influence. In March 1984, Samora Machel and P. W. Botha signed the 'Nkomati Accord', a poisonous non-aggression, good-neighbourliness pact the racist regime had no intention of honouring. On its side, FRELIMO ordered all ANC and SACP personnel (bar ten) to leave Mozambique. The ten were allowed to continue to run the office but severely limited in what they could do. It was a bitter blow that was almost impossible to contemplate, never mind comprehend; for many of us, it was an act of betrayal.

The leadership of the ANC and SACP, though bitterly disappointed, took a mature and responsible position. They did not condemn FRELIMO or Machel publicly and said they understood the dilemma confronting Mozambique. It was also important to retain the comradely alliance between the ANC and FRELIMO, as was done, to continue to use underground methods to infiltrate cadres through Mozambique to Swaziland for operations inside South Africa.

As I write this memoir, my disgust and disappointment with the Nkomati Accord remain, and, to this day, I fail to understand why FRELIMO and its government thought the evil, duplicitous apartheid regime would stand by that agreement. They continued to support RENAMO by all possible means, and, in my view, some members of the South African security apparatus were responsible for the plane crash on SA territory that led to the death of Machel in October 1986.

---

71. Available at https://www.thepresidency.gov.za/national-orders/recipient/matola-raid-martyrs-1981

A few months earlier, on 7 April of that year, Albie Sachs, a member of the ANC and lecturer at Eduardo Mondlane University, lost an arm and the sight in one eye when his booby-trapped car exploded. Apartheid security agents had once more violated the territorial integrity, dignity and sovereignty of Mozambique, despite their promises in the Nkomati Accord. Albie survived that attack and went on to become a distinguished judge at our Constitutional Court.

Botswana

Botswana shares a long border with South Africa and is land-locked, with Zimbabwe and Namibia as its other two significant neighbours. Angola and Zambia are also quite close to Botswana. There are family, clan and tribal relations between the Batswana and South Africans, and prior to independence in 1996, many Batswana worked in South Africa. Botswana's economy depended on South Africa before and after independence. The British colonial authorities had cordial relations with the apartheid regime but refrained from expelling South African political leaders and activists who had entered that country on their way further north.

A few Batswana leaders played an important role in our struggle. Among them were Michael Dingake and Fish Keitseng. Keitseng made a vital contribution by helping ANC leaders and members find refuge in Botswana and go further north to Zambia and Tanzania. I knew Dingake in the late 1950s and, although he was eleven years older, he always treated me with consideration as a comrade. In 1987, he wrote one of the best accounts of living in apartheid South Africa and working in the legal ANC and underground called *My Fight Against Apartheid* (Kliptown Books). He was illegally sent from Rhodesia to South Africa in 1965 and subjected to severe torture before being sentenced to fifteen years imprisonment in 1966. He served his term on Robben Island before being released in 1981. When he came to London for his book launch, we had wonderful talks about old times at Macosa House and his term on Robben Island.

My first visit to Botswana was in June 1963. My father (who left South Africa in 1960) had found his way from London to Francistown, and my mother, three brothers and our first cousin Farouk Patel, who drove the car, went to meet him. At that time, one did not need a passport to and from Botswana. Nevertheless, a British administrator in Lobatse questioned us about our reasons for entering the country. I guess he was just being difficult.

My second trip to Botswana was in June 1977, during which I spent about five months in Gaborone. Uncle Doc had asked me to go there to ascertain the feasibility of meeting South Africans of Indian origin living in Johannesburg and the Transvaal province. Without hesitation, I agreed and once more left Meg on her own. On arrival, I was taken to Bontleng Township, where the ANC had a house with several occupants, two of whom were Snuki Zikalala and Keith Maope, who had arrived in Botswana in 1974 and 1975, respectively. The house had three bedrooms, a garage and two rooms at the back, which Snuki and Keith used to store arms before transportation to South Africa. I shared a bedroom with Snuki. On many occasions, he and Keith would be out till late at night, so we got to know each other during the day. Their work – recruiting young South Africans to join the ANC and MK – escalated tremendously after the Soweto uprising of 1976, when thousands of young South Africans found their way to Lobatse and Gaborone with a view to joining the liberation struggle. In Botswana, there were members of the ANC, the PAC, the BCM, the South African Student Organisation (SASO), the Azanian People's Organisation (AZAPO) and the Unity Movement, which illustrates the tremendous pressure Botswana was under.

Amongst the young people Keith and Snuki encountered were Welile Nhlapo and Tebogo Mofolo, who both joined the ANC and MK. After 1994, Tebogo headed Mbeki's office when he was deputy president, and Welile, after a stint at the Department of Foreign Affairs, joined the Office of the President as a special representative for the Great Lakes region. Welile is a treasure house of information about that area and the ANC in exile and post-1994. I first met him when he came to work at the ANC office in London in the seventies, and we have retained our friendship, meeting at times at the home of Aziz and his wonderful third wife, Angina Parekh (married in 2011), who are both very close to Welile.

Snuki and Keith worked tirelessly and with some success at recruiting cadres and infiltrating personnel and arms into South Africa. I was not part of their work or operations but did suggest at times that they were too relaxed and not sufficiently security conscious. They assured me that they were as interested as I was that they should survive.

The community in Bontleng were very supportive of the ANC and would report any suspicious vehicles or people they spotted in the township. Furthermore, whenever an ANC car was spotted, young children would run after it, shouting 'ANC! ANC!'

Most mornings, I would walk from the township to the city centre, which generated some amusement and curiosity, for the Bontleng community was used to the small number of Indians in Gaborone riding in cars, not walking. Once they worked out that I was living in the ANC house, they would greet me with a smile.

Others I met there were Uncle Dan Tloome, Henry Makgoti and the Chief Representative of the ANC office, Isaac Makopo. On Fridays, I would go for lunch to the house of Ismail Bhamjee, who later became a leading official at the Confederation of African Football (CAF) and the International Association Football Federation (*Fédération Internationale de Football Association*: FIFA). This was until he was alleged to have fraudulently sold 2010 World Cup tickets he received as a FIFA official.

Ever-present was the danger that the house would be attacked at night by the apartheid security forces, so we decided that one adult should stay awake with the curtains drawn shut and now and then do a quick surveillance with a torch. I dutifully carried out my responsibility but was unsure about the point of it. With the curtains drawn, we would only be able to alert others in the house once an attack had started, and that would be too late. My views were noted, but the guard duty continued in the same manner, at least while I was there.

I remember one of the recruits I had identified: Saad Cachalia, who was related to Molvi and Yusuf Cachalia. He was studying at a High School in Gaborone and preparing to enter university. He was intelligent, engaging and very interested in joining the struggle. After I left, Snuki and Keith kept in touch with him. He qualified as a lawyer and, as I am writing (February 2021), he is South Africa's Ambassador to Qatar.

While in Botswana, I met Thabo Mokwena, a lecturer in natural science at the local university and friend of Thabo Mbeki. He and I spent many hours discussing political issues relating to South Africa, Botswana, the African continent and the world. Since he was in contact with Snuki, there was no need to discuss his role and responsibilities as an ANC member. Indeed, he helped the ANC in many different ways.

One day, my tranquillity was shattered when I was informed that the Botswana Special Branch had ordered me to go to their offices. There, I was interrogated about my reasons for visiting Botswana and gave the same reply to their incessant questions:

> I am a member of the ANC, but I am not here on behalf of the ANC or to do any of their work. I came here to see some members of my

family who I had not seen since December 1964.

When the head of the local police joined the meeting, he exclaimed loudly from the side of the room where we were sitting, 'Balderdash!' I could only respond, 'It is not balderdash, but the truth.'

It seems likely that the apartheid security forces had informed their Botswana counterparts about my involvement in debriefing a comrade who had been arrested while on a mission inside the country. But I had not been involved.

After a few hours of interrogation, I was allowed to leave. I then contacted my family, and my niece Yasmin agreed to come immediately. But before she could get to me, my cousin Yusuf Pahad from Cape Town arrived, and we had a long chat in his car. He was clued up about events in South Africa and in my mind was a potential recruit.

Then Yasmin and her husband Yusuf Dadabhay (Dada) arrived with their daughter Zakkiya, whom of course I had never met, and they stayed for the long weekend at the Holiday Inn. It was wonderful seeing each other, and we enjoyed trading stories about family, friends and Dynamos Football Club. Dada was an outstanding player who played professionally for Dynamos. It was brave of Yasmin and my other relatives to come to meet me, as there was the risk of them getting into trouble.

When it was time for me to leave Botswana, I noticed that the passport stamp was smudged and I had misread it and overstayed for a few days. When I requested a short extension so I could exit the country without difficulty, the official at first refused and threatened to declare me a prohibited immigrant. That I wanted to avoid, as I had hoped to return at some point; eventually, I persuaded the official to give me the necessary extension on the firm promise that I would leave on time.

There are two more things I want to mention about that trip to Botswana. One is about Pinky, a Batswana woman with whom Snuki was in love. They considered marriage, but like all of us struggle comrades when we were young, Snuki insisted that he was married to the struggle and was not free to commit marriage to Pinky. I told Snuki that since Pinky understood his commitment to the ANC and he was not fooling her with false promises, there was no reason they should not ask for permission to get married. I explained that Aziz, Thabo Mbeki and I had all received permission to marry, but he would have to contact Comrade Alfred Nzo for permission. As it happened, he and Keith were kicked out of Botswana, so Pinky visited him monthly in Lusaka, where they tied the knot. They then went to Bulgaria together to study, where Pinky became a medical doctor and Snuki achieved a PhD in media studies. It was good to see them again when they visited us in Prague and stayed in our flat for about a week, and I can happily report that they are still together.

Snuki, currently President of the ANC's Veterans's League, told me an interesting addition to that story. Pinky was from a well-known middle-class family, and her mother was highly esteemed. Unknown to Pinky's family, Snuki and Keith had surreptitiously used the family's garage to store weapons. After an ANC operation in Zeerust, an ANC operative who had become an *askari*[72] brought the apartheid security forces to that home, where they found a large cache of weapons. Fortunately, they did not harm the family or blow up the house, presumably because they believed the family knew nothing about the concealed weapons. Luckily for Snuki, that incident did not interfere with his relationship with Pinky, but it once more highlighted the dangers of *askaris* and other apartheid agents infiltrating our ranks. That is a problem we have never solved, and even now, we still do not know who in our organisations worked for the other side and might still be involved in counter-revolutionary acts.

In addition to the immense pressure on the Botswana government to come out in support of the apartheid regime, to denounce sanctions and, critically, to restrict the activities there to the barest minimum, the racist regime bombed targets and killed a number of people, including Batswana citizens. Of those many attacks, the most horrendous took place on 14 June 1985 in Gaborone, and several South African refugees and Batswana citizens were brutally murdered. One of those was Thamsanqa (Thami) Mnyele, an artist with great potential and a member of the Medu Art Ensemble, a cultural group set up by Wally Serote and others to promote South African culture and interact with cultural workers from Botswana. Wally Serote and other ANC comrades were lucky to have survived that gruesome attack. The ANC house in Bontleng was also demolished.

As South Africans, we should always remember the sacrifices, including loss of life, made by innumerable Batswana citizens in support of our liberation.

On my return to London, I reported my observations on Botswana to Uncle Doc, including the activities of the ANC and the promising possibilities of meeting South Africans of Indian origin for possible

---

71. In South Africa, the word 'askari' describes a member of the liberation movement who was 'turned' by the apartheid regime's security branch and used to supply information, betraying his former comrades.

recruitment and smuggling propaganda into South Africa. I indicated my readiness to return to Botswana, but that did not happen.[72] My next visit to that country was in the early 1990s, when Thabo Mbeki, Aziz, Sydney Mufamadi and I travelled by car to watch South Africa play Botswana in a friendly football match.

Angola

Now back to my time in Prague – via Angola, where, in 1984, I was sent for military training. Earlier, Uncle Doc had suggested that I go to our camps in Angola as an instructor in political education, and I agreed. But that changed, and it was decided that I should go for military training as an ordinary soldier for about three months. I was forty-five years old then, with two children: Amina, aged five, and Govan, aged two, but Meg agreed immediately, even though she would temporarily become a single parent. The WMR had no objections and paid my full salary in my absence.

When I arrived in Luanda in June, I visited Marius Schoon and met his wife Jeanette, who was very friendly and welcoming. Then I was taken to Caxito, some two or three hours away. It was a harrowing drive with dire warnings about what to do in the event of an attack by Unita forces.

While at the camp, I learnt on 28 June 1984 that the Schoon family had suffered a terrible tragedy: Jeanette and her daughter Katryn, aged six, had been assassinated. They had opened a parcel bomb in their kitchen in the presence of three-year-old Fritz, who had seen his mother and sister blown to pieces and splattered on the walls. Marius found Fritz wandering about outside the house; he did not speak for more than a week and was haunted by that horror for years. The bomb had been arranged by Craig Williamson, a spy granted amnesty by the Truth and Reconciliation Commission, but I and many others, particularly Marius and Fritz, feel that decision was a grave injustice.

In Angola, I had the name Mohammed. On arrival at the camp, I was taken to my sleeping quarters in a tent, which hosted eight to ten people, and instructed how to fold my uniform and make up the bed. The following day, I was waiting to meet the Camp Commander, Thabang Makwetla, when a platoon commander saw me and ordered me to join a political education class that was underway. As I entered, the instructor paused and asked me if I knew the four stages of human development as enumerated by Marx: slavery, feudalism, capitalism, socialism. I said 'Yes' and found a rock to sit on.

---

72. Possible reasons include enough comrades in Botswana and the danger of my assassination by the racist regime.

I was physically unfit and struggled with the strenuous military exercises and drills. Thankfully, when the instructor saw my discomfort, he very kindly suggested that I should just do as much as I could.

A short while after I got there, Chris Hani, Chief of Staff of MK, came to the camp. There was palpable excitement amongst the leadership and the trainees, and Chris made a rousing speech which was received rapturously. There was no doubt how popular he was. In his speech, he pointed to me and said that I was well-versed in theory and the history of our country and movement and encouraged them all to utilise my presence and benefit from my knowledge and experience. Unsurprisingly, my status rose after that, and I was asked to give political education classes to the trainees as well as the instructor. In a one-on-one meeting, Chris said that I should work with Comrade Makwetla to identify a few comrades who could be recruited into the SACP.

Makwetla, as the Commissar, and the other camp leaders were living in a separate building called the 'White House' by the trainees – a label that he winces at to this day. The two of us would meet at night and, at our first meeting, I kept falling into the trenches that had been dug to guard against the possibility of a Unita attack. When I explained to him that I suffered from night blindness and could hardly make out any shapes or holes, he made sure that a torch lit the way for me. Makwetla was well-informed about the theory and practice of our struggle but had extremely high standards about the qualities required to be recruited into the party. The upshot was that he disposed of my recommendations when I pointed out to him that, based on his stringent criteria, there would be only two communists, Moses Mabhida and himself. He understood, and by the time I left the camp, we had identified three potential recruits. Makwetla later became Deputy Minister of Defence and Military Veterans.

To put it mildly, life in the camp was harsh, and I continue to have great admiration for the commitment, discipline and hard work of the trainees, the commander and instructors. I was particularly impressed by the women comrades, who were able to do everything the men did without complaint or hesitation and were better shots than some of the men. Their strength and endurance seemed limitless. I felt immensely proud of them but was disturbed to notice that some of the men found it hard to acknowledge that they were more than equal to them in practice and theory.

The camp was infested with mosquitoes, malaria was rife, and a few comrades succumbed to the disease. I contracted malaria twice and lost considerable weight. A young medical officer with no previous training in health tried his level best to assist those afflicted by malaria and other conditions. When I told him that I was taking anti-malaria tablets I had brought with me, he shrugged his shoulders and said in a jovial manner, 'But Comrade Mohammed, your European tablets are no match for the Angolan mosquitoes.'

In spite of the harsh conditions, I was enjoying my stay and interactions with the MK combat trainees. Sunday was the day to wash your uniform and yourself with soap at the river flowing by the camp. It was also a day for football and volleyball. In the latter game, I was a player, while in the former, I was the referee. Moreover, on appropriate days, cultural events would be staged, and it was an eye-opener to witness the intelligence and competence of those who wrote the scripts, directed, produced and participated in those productions.

Chris Hani came for a second visit, this time with Joe Slovo, and the camp was thrilled at seeing them. Following the speeches, Chris called me over and said, 'Pack your bags, you are returning with us to Luanda.' I asked to be allowed to stay a few more weeks to finish my course, but his response was as swift as it was emphatic, 'No. You look terrible. You are coming with us now. We didn't send you here to die.'

When we arrived in Luanda, I went into the bathroom and looked in a mirror for the first time in weeks. What I saw was shocking. Chris was correct. I was horribly thin with hollow cheeks and an unpleasant skin colour. That evening, Joe Modise, Joe Slovo and Manto Tshabalala (born Mali and later Tshabalala-Msimang), a doctor in our camps and well-acquainted with the unsuitability of the Caxito environment, came to the house. After Manto and I described the conditions to Slovo and Modise, it was agreed that the Caxito camp should be evacuated, a decision that was implemented within days. Manto had a wealth of experience treating tropical diseases and told me that my white blood cell count was very low and that I must be hospitalised as soon as I returned to Prague.

After an uncomfortable journey via East Berlin, I was most happy to land in Prague. Meg was shocked at my appearance but remained calm and unemotional, as she did not want to upset the children. My hospital stay was successful, as the Czech doctors had experience dealing with similar malaria cases when Czech volunteers and their families kidnapped by Unita soldiers in parts of Angola returned home in need of treatment. Meg and the children were given permission to visit me, which made things easier, and after a few days, I was cured and allowed to go home.

⚘

To flashback briefly, at the NEC meeting in 1980, it was decided to convene a consultative conference, in preparation of which, all ANC structures and departments throughout the world participated in discussing the issues, challenges and problems confronting the organisation. The result was the Kabwe Conference, which opened on 16 June 1985.

I was elated to have been invited as a delegate to that historic conference, where some 250 delegates converged on Lusaka and, from there, were conveyed by bus or car to Kabwe. Most delegates were MK combatants who had swelled the ranks of our movement following the Soweto and connected uprisings of June 1976.

In the bus in which I was travelling, Billy Modise, one of the organisers, announced that all liquor was prohibited, and anyone in possession of alcohol had to dispose of it before arriving in Kabwe or it would be confiscated. Some of us had whisky, which we at the back of the bus started consuming. At one point, I took a bottle to the front and offered a drink to Joe Slovo and Joe Modise. They were enthusiastic about the singing that came from the back and remarked on the high spirits of the delegates. I smiled and wondered if they were aware of the other spirits doing the rounds.

In Kabwe, I was allocated a room to share with Kader Asmal, Dean of the Law Faculty at Dublin University at that time and recognised as an influential international law expert. He could talk and talk, and we had some lovely robust discussions. One of the many topics at the Kabwe Conference was the idea that membership to the NEC should be opened up to non-Africans, a radical departure from the position held by the ANC since 1912. Kader was ambivalent about that idea, whereas I was in full support. Unable to convince him, I suggested he meet some of the younger delegates to probe the issue. After meeting them, he returned, positively gushing about their political maturity and consciousness. They had convinced him that opening up the leadership to non-Africans was not only correct but more accurately reflected the mood of our people, in particular the Mass Democratic Movement inside the country.

There were heated debates and discussions in which Johnny Makhatini, an NEC member, and Brian Bunting, a CC member of the SACP, argued for the retention of the old position. Brian was promptly put down by Jack Simons, who argued the opposite case in a cogent, logical and articulate manner. Jack had already established an enormous reputation and was highly respected amongst MK cadres who had received political education classes from him in the camps.

When ANC President Tambo came into the hall, flanked by the NEC, the applause for him was deafening. Delegates broke out into boisterous songs, one of which was *Tambo, skokela Tambo* (Tambo, lead us, Tambo). The awe, admiration, love and respect that Tambo evoked in the ANC membership and amongst the MK combatants was unanimous.

The main person working behind the scenes was Thabo Mbeki, who was instrumental in preparing Tambo's NEC report to the Conference and Tambo's influential report on the mistakes and excesses made by our security forces in executing their tasks. Thabo was also responsible for drafting the main resolutions to be debated and endorsed or amended by the Conference. To carry out that arduous task, he roped in Albie Sachs, me and one or two others. Thabo distributed the work and edited all the resolutions. Albie was the main drafter of the 'Call to the People of South Africa', and I played an important role in drafting the 'Call to the People of the World'. At one point, Thabo took me aside and said, 'Essop, you must stop drafting as if you were in the WMR.' He meant that I mustn't use communist jargon or slogans in an ANC document, so I took his point. When Thabo presented all the resolutions to the Conference, he was interrupted by rapturous applause in recognition of his brilliant preparation for that day. I was also asked to be the rapporteur for the ideological commission. The inputs from those present were most impressive and included the need to intensify the battle of ideas and set up a political school.

The Kabwe Conference, which we declared would be the last one in exile, dealt with several delicate and complex issues, such as the paramount need to intensify the armed struggle and the strategy and tactics required to do so while mobilising the mass of our people. That entailed the examination of hot topics such as the characterisation of the balance of forces inside and outside South Africa and the call for a redefinition of soft and hard targets.

At the end of that impressive and highly successful conference, a new NEC was elected. To assist the delegates, it was agreed that President Tambo would present a list of forty names from which thirty would be elected. The Conference had the power to go beyond the names submitted on the list, and when the new NEC was elected, it included one white person (Joe Slovo), two

Coloureds (Reg September and James Stuart [Hermanus Loots]), and two Indians (Mac Maharaj and Aziz Pahad). There were only three women: Florence Moposho, Ruth Mompati and Gertrude Shope. Oliver R. Tambo was elected president, Alfred Nzo secretary-general, and T. T. Nkobi, treasurer-general. The remaining twenty-seven elected members, in alphabetical order, were:

4. Steve Dlamini	18. Anthony Mongalo
5. Chris Hani	19. Florence Moposho
6. Pallo Jordan	20. Joe Nhlanhla
7. Moses Mabhida	21. John Nkadimeng
8. Mac Maharaj	22. Aziz Pahad
9. Simon Makana	23. Mzwai Piliso
10. Johnny Makatini	24. Reg September
11. Cassius Make	25. Gertrude Shope
12. Henry Makgothi	26. Sizakele Sigxashe
13. Robert Manci	27. Joe Slovo
14. Thabo Mbeki	28. James Stuart
15. Francis Meli	29. Dan Tloome
16. Joe Modise	30. Jacob Zuma
17. Ruth Mompati	

But before Kabwe in June 1985, I had attended the Sixth Congress of the SACP held in Moscow in November 1984, where Moses Mabhida was elected General Secretary and Joe Slovo, National Chairperson. Unfortunately, Mabhida died from a heart attack in March 1986, another great loss to the ANC, SACP and SACTU. At that Congress, a new central committee was elected and an electoral commission set up with the power to re-order the elected on the grounds of security or considering the national, class and gender composition.

Vladimir Shubin, a Soviet academic and functionary of the International Department of the CPSU, a solid and loyal friend of the movement who personally helped so many of us, wrote a book entitled *ANC: A View from Moscow*. In it, Shubin records that only one amendment was made to the elected list: 'An exile veteran was dropped in favour of a representative of the Soweto generation.'[74]

About a year after the Sixth Congress, I was informed separately by

---
74. Johannesburg: Jacana Media, 2008.

Mabhida and Tloome that the dropped veteran was me. Both assured me that the Party was very happy with my work and contribution and that I would soon be elected to the CC. If my memory serves me right, I was co-opted onto the CC in 1986, and my first CC meeting was in Budapest in 1988.

I returned to Prague from the Kabwe Conference in 1985 fully energised and thoroughly convinced that we could see the light at the end of the tunnel and would soon liberate our country and break the yoke of racism, apartheid and the super-exploitation of Black labour power. But I was also more determined to be in the ranks of our fighting forces and return to London to be active in the structures of the ANC and SACP. My wish was granted, and it was agreed that our family should move back to London that same year.

༄

I had been in Prague for ten years and Meg for nine, so moving back to the UK was quite a challenge. Although we had lived comfortably in Prague, we earned our incomes in the Czech currency, and our savings were not convertible into any Western currency. However, we took back to London (and later South Africa) the Czech china, glassware and lovely set of Slovak cupboards and bookshelves we had purchased.

For a few months after our return, the British Inland Revenue harassed us constantly about why we had not paid tax in Britain on the Czech money we had earned while living in Czechoslovakia. When they asked me why the money was not convertible to the English currency, Meg was most amused when I replied, 'I believe that was a decision of Her Majesty the Queen.' After that, they never bothered us again with that question.

Fortunately, we had retained our council flat, fully furnished, and when Meg returned to London and her job in 1977, after her year's leave of absence, John Matshikiza rented Yasmin's room. Later, Dumile Feni stayed there rent-free, where he painted the enormous canvas, 'Don't Mourn, Mobilise!' in honour of M. P. Naicker for his memorial service. That message graced ANC funerals for many years.

But when Meg returned to Prague, we had to let the flat out long-term to friends (which was not strictly legal), and they had to pay our rent in Meg's name. The first person to assist with this plan was Dulcie September.

Dulcie had left South Africa for England at the end of 1973 on an exit permit after serving a five-year prison sentence for conspiracy to commit sabotage, followed by a five-year banning order. Soon she went to work for the International Defence and Aid Fund and, in 1976, joined the ANC, where she worked in the Women's League. In 1983, she was appointed ANC Chief Representative in France. In March 1988, at the age of fifty-two, Dulcie was assassinated outside the ANC office in Paris: shot five times in the head with a 22-calibre silenced rifle. To protest what was clearly an action orchestrated by the South African and French Secret Services and to mourn Dulcie's death, 20,000 people gathered in Paris.

When Dulcie left for Paris, Nick Wright of the 'Straight Left' faction of the CPGB took over our flat and stayed there until we asked him to move when we knew we were returning from Prague. So we had no money, but we did have a furnished flat big enough for our family with very low rent and enough possessions for our needs.

Meg's childhood friend Jan Haxton had married Max McColl, who had a degree in history but decided he preferred working as a builder, at which he was very competent. Since Max had a bakkie (light truck) and wanted to see Prague, he agreed to visit us and take all our possessions back to London. I was able to get the relevant documents approved and signed to assist him with getting through customs, and we managed to pack everything onto the bakkie, which eventually arrived in Maida Vale. We were lucky that our niece Yasmin and her husband Yusuf Dadabhay (Dada) were visiting London. They and Yusuf (Charles) Saloojee and Max came to help us carry everything up three flights of narrow stairs since, unsurprisingly, the lift was out of order.

In London, I was appointed to the ANC's Regional Political Military Council, headed by Aziz. That took up most of my time, and I will go into more detail about it in a later chapter.

Our next task was getting the children (aged three and six) into a suitable school and finding a job for Meg. Pallo Jordan and his wife Carolyn Roth recommended that I visit the local school which their daughter Nandipah attended, but the school secretary told me to come back in September at the start of the school year, as there were no waiting lists. Meg had informed the Inner London Education Authority (ILEA) that she was returning and would need a job from around June, but they also told her they would only consider her request in September.

As soon as she had unpacked and settled in, Meg went to the recommended school to try her luck. The secretary, Hanna Pascucci, said they might be able to fit in Govan, but there was no room for Amina. Just then, Gareth Thomas, the headmaster, came in and stared at Meg in shock. 'Meg! Where have you been? What are you doing here?' After a few hugs and exclamations, Hanna said, 'I've just been telling your good friend there is no room here for her daughter.' 'Oh,' said Gareth, who had been a teacher with Meg at St Stevens School in Westbourne Park Road and a guest at our wedding, 'I'm sure we can manage something.' When Gareth discovered that Meg had not yet found suitable work, he immediately phoned the officer in charge of ILEA Division 2 and told him that he wanted Meg to be given a job at Paddington Green as soon as possible. 'Are you mad?' he asked the officer, 'Turning away an experienced London teacher like her when you send me people who can't cope with the inner city?'

After about forty minutes, Govan had a place in the nursery, Amina one in the infant school and Meg had a job.

Gareth said Amina must go into the Red Class with teacher Elaine, as Meg and Elaine would get on well, which showed he was an excellent judge of character. Aside from Elaine Simpson in the infant school, Meg soon made friends with some of the other teachers there, such as Marlene Wardle (Deputy Head) and Micky Garvey, who taught in the junior school like Meg. Micky's maiden name was Marietje Beukes (sister to the famous violinist Gina Beukes and percussionist brother Johan). When Micky had arrived in London as a white South African, she met such hostility that she started using her husband's surname and called herself Micky for convenience. She was already divorced from her husband, and we never knew him. Gareth, Marlene, Elaine and Micky were all actively anti-racist and firm supporters of ILEA's stance on race, class and gender – which made it easy for Meg to fit into Paddington Green. Elaine also had a daughter, Chloë, who was about the same age as Govan, and we all got on well together.

Paddington Green had an interesting catchment area. There were a few left-wing professionals (teachers, social workers, journalists), who wanted their children to go to a local state school, and many respectable working-class families. But there were a lot of parents who were more difficult to manage – racist whites who ran market stalls or drove taxis, flashy drug dealers with smart cars and expensive clothes, and a few prostitutes. There was also a fast turnover of immigrants who started off their new lives near Paddington Station and then moved on. At one stage, the school of about 1,350 children included families with about thirty-five different first languages.

Amina learned to read properly in about a week, as soon as she saw that most of the children her age could do so. She and Elaine got on perfectly, and Amina settled down and did excellent work. She also developed a love for gymnastics. Later on, she and Govan went to a gymnastics club with their friends Lily and Jenny McNeil, where they made more good friends and had lots of fun. The school was very rough, and some of the little ones were already in training for a life of crime and violence, but Amina adapted fast and took no nonsense from any of them. One of the toughest boys in her class decided he liked and respected her, which helped.

Govan joined Amina in the Red Class at the end of summer 1986, as the infant school practised family grouping (children from 'rising five' to seven, inclusive, with one teacher for three years and siblings following each other). The next year, Amina progressed to the junior school, so it was fortunate for Govan that he was in Elaine's class. He was capable and intelligent but worked at his own speed and only made an effort if he was interested. He often carried on diligently, focused on a task for half a day, while other children were moving on after ten minutes or so. Elaine gave him the time and space he needed, while encouraging him to comply with rules which were necessary for the good of the class or school as a whole. We think it is likely that Govan would have been a school refuser if he had been less fortunate in his introduction to formal schooling. At Paddington Green, the only 'silent sitting in rows' occurred in the morning assembly, where talks were short, songs were plentiful and a couple of children might perform something of which they were proud. In the classrooms, activities took place in groups and the teachers moved around, rarely sitting at their desks except for roll calls.

When we got back to London, we found it hard to live in a flat where it was not safe to send the children out to play, which we had been able to do in Prague. Meg desperately wanted a place with a garden, however small, so the children could get some fresh air and exercise while she was busy preparing work or food and I was out. A tenant of a council flat was allowed to swap with another tenant if they both wanted to do so, so Meg went every week for about six months and gradually put a note requesting an exchange through the doors of all the terraced houses the Council had bought in the area and converted into flats. The ground floors of each had a small garden, which many of the tenants did not use. Meg offered a modern centrally heated flat near to Maida Vale tube station in exchange for an old flat with no heating but a garden. Eventually this paid off, and we moved to a flat in Shirland

Road, West Kilburn. Elaine and Micky and Lily and Jenny and their parents, Anne and George McNeil, lived nearby, as well as Chris Curran (adult educator) and his wife Maryvonne, who worked for *The Guardian*, whose daughter Stephanne also went to Paddington Green.

The house needed a lot of work, and Max once more proved a valuable friend, helping us with alterations and installing central heating. He helped Meg carry out the old fridges, car engines and broken appliances from the garden. Then she slowly dug over everything, removed the remaining rubbish and grassed the centre of the area, carrying the turf pieces through the house to get to the garden. She put up swings and a garden shed, dug and lined a tiny pond and used the soil to build a rockery. She fan-trained a peach tree to the shed and planted roses and wisteria at the street entrance by the bus stop. Soon it really was a garden. Not long after we made those improvements, Westminster City Council's Conservative Lady Porter started selling off Council houses cheaply to the occupiers in what was exposed later as the 'Homes for Votes' scandal. Although the CPGB and Labour Party opposed those sales, they advised their supporters to purchase their own homes since they were being sold anyway. With help to make up the initial deposit from my brothers Nassim and Zuneid, we took advantage of that and bought our home on a mortgage.

Fortunately, we still had a lot of old friends in London, and we managed to find time to see most of them, though less regularly than before. Aziz was now living with Anne Davies, a brilliant educator working for ILEA, supporting mixed-ability teaching in groups and working with teachers of bilingual under-fives. Anne was very politically active and well-informed. She was also caring and psychologically astute and encouraged Aziz to play a more active and supportive role in the life of Sam, his son by Christabel Gurney. We always visited Sam and Christabel when we came on our annual visit from Prague, and because Sam's birthday was on 19 December, we were usually able to attend his birthday party. Now, Christabel and Sam spent time with Meg and our children, and we strengthened our family ties.

While we were away, Billy Nannan and Theresa split up, and Billy moved in with Sandra Black. Billy and Sandra seemed very happy and had a daughter together named Zinzile. Then, tragically, Billy had a stroke and was paralysed down one side and unable to speak for several months. Sandra looked after him well and gradually helped him communicate better and keep in touch with his friends in the ANC. Nevin Faik was a constant help during that difficult period. When we got back to London, we also kept in touch with and tried to help Theresa and the children: Vanessa, Nadine and Nicky.

Nevin was also a great friend to Meg. She also had two children, Zed and Shay, and was friends with the same group of people as us, so they had a lot in common. We still saw Ronnie Kaka and Yusuf (Charles) as well as Ramnie and Issy Dinat and their children, Natalya and Sean. We had missed major events in those people's lives but gradually caught up.

We kept in touch with Mel and Rhiannon while we were in Prague and often stayed at their house in Barnes when we visited the UK. Mel had become a highly respected and well-known art critic, curating exhibitions and writing several books, with Rhiannon contributing a lot to his work. They had also visited us in Prague, where they developed friendships with artists who were frowned upon by the government. They were always good company, well-informed, especially about arts and culture, and were lively and amusing. They willingly hosted some of the other friends we had in London, with Rhiannon making the most delicious meals. Their two boys, by then teenagers, had developed very distinct personalities and added to our enjoyment of staying in their household. Francis, the elder one, became an expert on South African jazz.

Mike Seifert was another loyal and charming friend, who regularly hosted us at his favourite restaurant when we visited London, inviting our friends for a wonderful feast of great food and plenty to drink. Included were usually Mel and Rhiannon, Christabel and Sam and several others. I have already mentioned Mike's epic support for the National Union of Mineworkers (NUM) during the great miners' strike and his many other left-wing clients. He was also active in and gave legal advice to the Cuba Solidarity Campaign, the *Morning Star*, the Marx Memorial Library, the Anti-Apartheid Movement, the CPGB, Greenpeace, the ANC and almost all progressive trade unions. When he died in July 2017, Arthur Scargill of the NUM wrote, 'The working class has lost a true warrior, and I have lost a true friend.' I echo this statement and record that I also lost a unique, witty, passionate and genuine friend.

We also became friendly with Amin and Susi Mawani and sometimes went for picnics and outings with them and Anne Davies and others with children, like Nevin or Christabel. Amin was a communist from Uganda, expelled by Idi Amin for the crime of being of Indian descent – a very skilled carpenter/cabinetmaker and a wonderful human being. His wife Susi was a graphic designer from the GDR and was very intelligent and friendly. They were both founder members of the Ealing Anti-Apartheid Movement, and Amin was later its secretary. In 1988, he was elected to the AAM's National Executive Committee, and Suzi took over as Chair of Ealing. Together, they organised numerous concerts and social events to raise money for the AAM. They were most hospitable, and together they regularly cooked wonderful Indian meals for us.

I was busy and could never take time off for a holiday, so Meg relied on our friends a lot for support. Fortunately, in the late 1980s, Meg's sister Jill's job with the Pre-School Playgroup Association made it necessary to spend about a week every month in London, so Meg was always delighted to put her up and have company and help for a few days, and Jill paid her the allowance she was given for accommodation. Jill and her husband Geoffrey have a holiday cottage on the Isle of Mull in the Inner Hebrides off the west coast of Scotland which they let out, and Meg and the children went there quite a few times at no cost. It was a perfect spot for children, right on the beach. Meg also took the children to visit Jill and Geoffrey in Carlisle, which is close to the Lake District and many beautiful holiday spots.

Meg also reconnected with her childhood friend, Wendy Haxton, who had a daughter, Hélène, just a little older than Amina; they also went to Mull together and to a few other places. Meg and Wendy instantly became close friends again, in spite of the long gaps when they had not been in touch. Wendy had spent many years in West Africa, and her second husband had worked for Doctors Without Borders. She was a teacher but also did counselling and liaison with parents, and she and Meg had much to discuss.

Meg's most frequent holiday spot was a caravan she sometimes hired at Pennard in South Wales, near to Rhiannon's inherited family cottage. Usually, she just went with the children if there was a long weekend or half-term break. They could get the bus to Paddington, a train to Swansea and another bus to Pennard, where the caravan was, and spend a few days walking on the cliffs and playing on the beach.

Several South Africans came to see us on short visits to London. These included my brother Nassim, who stayed with us; my cousins Yusuf and Ismail (Zombie) Pahad; Jay Naidoo of COSATU, who bought the children Rummikub and played with them; and numerous people from the ANC who helped me to keep in touch with events at home, like Jakes Gerwel and André Odendaal.

One visit I remember clearly was that of Harry Gwala. Imprisoned for life on Robben Island, he was released because he suffered from motor-neuron disease. His failing physical health did not diminish his determined and (at times) aggressive spirit, and when he visited us, we had a lovely day with a few friends round to celebrate. These included Elean Thomas and her husband (Lord) Tony Gifford, Amin and Susi Mawani, Jimmie Corrigall and our neighbourhood friends Chris and Maryvonne Curran and their daughter Stephanne.

We had all recently seen the film *Mapantsula* and broadly supported its optimistic assumption that it was possible for a self-centred petty criminal to be transformed after confrontation with injustice into a more responsible human being who could, in time, play a positive role in the liberation struggle. When that question arose, the Lion of the Midlands did not hesitate to give his verdict, which amounted to a severe piece of advice: a person like that will always end up selling you out; don't trust him an inch. For him, the film's optimism was merely romantic fantasy.

Another important event for our family was Govan Mbeki's release from prison on 5 November 1987 after serving nearly twenty-four years on Robben Island. Our son Govan was named after him, and our children always sent birthday cards to him on Robben Island. Unfortunately, we were not able to see him until 1990, when he visited our flat in Shirland Road and I went with him to Glasgow. I shall speak more about that in the chapter about my mentors.

On my return to London, I was integrated into the ANC and SACP structures, including the board of *The African Communist*. My deployment to the Regional Political Military Council (RPMC) was most pleasing, as it afforded opportunities to be directly involved in the important workings of the ANC. The RPMC in London was headed by Aziz, who was also the secretary and on the national Political Military Council (PMC). The other members of the RPMC were Reg September (also on the PMC), Wally Serote, Billy Masetlha, Tito Mboweni and Poloka Nkobi (administrative secretary).

After an ANC delegation headed by O. R. Tambo visited Vietnam in 1978, major resolutions were made to overhaul and streamline the political and military aspects of the struggle, such as setting up the Politico-Military Strategy Commission. Other critical measures were put in place to strengthen the underground structures and mass mobilisation within South Africa, and military actions, political activities and mass mobilisation were closely coordinated. The Revolutionary Council set up at the Morogoro Conference in 1969 was replaced by the PMC, which had to coordinate the work of the political, military and intelligence structures inside South Africa and the Frontline States.[75] The PMC structures were given the necessary powers to recruit new cadres and combatants and intensify the all-round struggle inside the country. In an informative account, made all the more interesting by his insider view, Aziz Pahad writes:

> The PMC in Lusaka met regularly at least once a month and was mandated to deal with broad strategic planning and to continuously assess developments in the country. The Executive Committee of the PMC, in turn, met on a daily basis. Various higher organs in the Frontline States were replaced by regional political and military committees and their new mandate gave them the authority and responsibility to make 'operational decisions', including the selection of targets. Previously, such decisions could only be made from the ANC headquarters in Lusaka.
>
> The regional PMCs were mandated to coordinate political and military activities in all the 'forward areas' for which they were responsible but also to establish area PMCs in South Africa. These area PMCs had to be responsible for providing local leadership on both political and military matters, as well as collecting intelligence and training political and MK cadres inside South Africa.
>
> London was designated a 'forward area', and I became secretary of the RPMC.[76]

As a member of the RPMC, which met Monday to Friday, one of my main tasks was to take cadres and leaders from inside South Africa for intensive political education classes and two-way discussions, during which we endeavoured to raise their political consciousness and improve their understanding of the history of the ANC and SACP and important documents such as the Freedom Charter. I also gave lectures on Marxist

---
75. The Frontline States were those bordering on or in close proximity to South Africa, including Angola, Botswana, Lesotho, Malawi, Mozambique, Swaziland, Tanzania, Zambia and Zimbabwe. For more information on the Frontline States, visit https://omalley.nelsonmandela.org/index.php/site/q/03lv03445/04lv03446/05lv03471.htm
76. Aziz Pahad, *Insurgent Diplomat – Civil Talks or Civil War?* (Penguin South Africa, 2014).

philosophy and political economy. At the same time, we learnt a great deal from the first-hand experience, knowledge and understanding those comrades had of the rapidly evolving political, economic, cultural and social developments in South Africa and the mood of the people.

It was an exhilarating experience, and I certainly benefited from my interactions with those comrades who included Barbara Schreiner, Barbara Creecy, Fazel Ismail, Derek Swart, Moss Ngoasheng, Ketso Gordhan and Roy Padayachee. I also interacted with Muff Andersson and Riaz Saloojee, who were already active in structures linked to the PMC and RPMC.

For my clandestine meetings, I had the use of the home of Victoria Brittain, a noted journalist and writer and committed fighter against apartheid and the Israeli occupation of Palestinian land. Meg and our close friends Mel and Rhiannon Gooding also opened their homes and were very helpful and understanding, never enquiring about the strangers coming over. At other times, I would take comrades to a cemetery in North London. There, we would find a bench appropriately located with a good view of people entering or leaving. This was par for the course, as we were continually on guard to protect comrades from the prying eyes of the apartheid and British intelligence services.

The political discussions and reports back in the RMPC were most interesting and highly valuable. We worked as a collective, united by our determination to discharge our tasks to enhance the struggle inside South Africa and international solidarity. Identifying women and men for our underground structures and MK was demanding work.

One day, Wally Serote asked me to join him in meeting and preparing Yvonne Muthien for recruitment; she was reading for a PhD at Oxford University and fit the bill comprehensively. Highly intelligent, incisive in her analysis and understanding of the socio-economic situation in South Africa, she had a humble, pleasant personality and was courageous in her readiness to contribute to the dangerous work of an underground cadre. As I will point out later, she also played an important role in post-apartheid South Africa. But from the beginning, we faced a conundrum. She was married to Krish Naidoo, a facial surgeon, who was doing a Master's degree at a medical college in Oxford. He was unaware of our secret meetings with Yvonne, and she had to find reasons for her absences. Wally and I discussed the matter with her, as we were concerned that a suspicious husband could lead to serious marital problems. We then agreed that the best way forward would be to recruit Krish Naidoo as well. It was a correct decision, as his courage, understanding and maturity matched Yvonne's.

Following our meeting in July 1987 with an IDASA (Institute for Democratic Alternatives in South Africa) delegation in Dakar, Senegal, it was agreed that I and Tommy Bedford, a former highly rated Springbok captain, would liaise to set up a meeting with Danie Craven. Craven was the boss of white rugby in South Africa and ran that union as an autocrat. Back in London, I met with Tommy again, and we arranged a date and venue for the meeting. But when Craven suffered a heart attack and could not travel, he asked Louis Luyt to meet us. Luyt was a wealthy businessman who had founded the *Citizen* newspaper with slush funds from the apartheid regime as a front for National Party propaganda. He was a tall, well-built person – like a rugby lock – and overweight. He spoke his mind and said things as he saw them but lacked diplomatic skills. Luyt arranged his own accommodation at a posh hotel in Mayfair, London, and booked and paid for the boardroom where we met. The ANC delegation led by Aziz included Wally Serote, Francis Meli, Tito Mboweni and me. It was a useful meeting in which conflicting views were aired, albeit in a friendly manner. The upshot was that it laid the basis for our later meeting with Craven and Luyt in Harare, Zimbabwe. I remain convinced that Luyt did not fully understand that we had in our delegation two NEC members (Aziz and Francis) as well as Wally Mongane Serote, one of the greatest poets to come out of our country.

At the end of the meeting, the delegation agreed that I should stay behind and have lunch with Luyt and Bedford. We continued our discussions and talked about how rugby could be an important factor in bringing about change in South Africa. During the informal conversation, I discovered, to my great surprise, that Bedford had never been invited to the VIP lounge – not even at his home ground in Durban. When Luyt heard that, he condescendingly informed Bedford that whenever he wanted to be invited to the VIP lounge in any of the rugby stadiums, he would arrange it. Bedford and I continued our meetings, which led to another ANC delegation meeting with Luyt and Craven in 1988–1989.

At that meeting, the ANC delegation was led by Secretary-General Alfred Nzo and included Thabo Mbeki, Barbara Masekela, Steve Tshwete and me. We also invited Ebrahim Patel, whom I knew before I went into exile. He was head of the non-racial SA Rugby Union (SARU). I don't think Patel was at all happy with such a meeting taking place but did not show it and participated in the discussions. I did point out to him that, as the ANC, we thought it necessary to hear his views and underline the position that, as far as the ANC was concerned, he had the same status as the white rugby bosses.

It was a successful meeting at the end of which a joint statement between the three participating parties was agreed upon and made public. It was also a recognition of the importance of the ANC in the unfolding struggle inside the country, but the National Party Government led by De Klerk was most unhappy about the meeting and its outcomes. Craven and Luyt told them in no uncertain terms that the National Party Government had to meet with the ANC and emphasised that their contacts with it would continue. Craven was clear that for the Springboks to play international rugby, from which they had been barred, the ANC would have to give its consent.

Throughout that period, I was attending a lot of anti-apartheid meetings in Europe. One particularly interesting trip was organised by the Communist Party of Ireland (Eire CPI) and the Communist Party of Northern Ireland.[77] In Dublin, I was happy to see Kader Asmal, a sharp legal mind who was Dean of the Faculty of Arts at Trinity College, Dublin, at the time. He specialised in human rights, labour and international law and was also one of the main founders and current chairperson of the Irish Anti-Apartheid Movement. His wonderful wife Louise was a welcoming hostess and the core person in the day-to-day management of the movement, working with a vibrant group of loyal activists.

It was a most enjoyable visit, and my guide, who was a councillor from the CPI, took me to many different parts of Eire, some of which are stunningly beautiful. In one place, I was accommodated in a small hotel which had no receptionist after eleven p.m. Before retiring, I went to the bathroom, which was just down the hall near the bedroom, leaving my bedroom door open. Somehow it closed itself and locked me out – so I improvised and slept on the floor of a room which had been used for a wedding reception. Everyone laughed off the incident and no one made a fuss.

During that trip, while driving, my guide noticed someone he explained was Gordon Winter, an apartheid spy who had written the book, *Inside BOSS: South Africa's Secret Police – An Ex-Spy's Dramatic and Shocking Exposé*,[78] and asked me if I was willing to speak with him. I readily agreed and asked Winter if he would tell the ANC more than what was already recorded in the book, and he agreed. I reported that to the RPMC, and it was decided that Billy Masetlha should meet Winter and debrief him. They met, but

---

77. Eire is independent Ireland; Northern Ireland is part of the United Kingdom of Great Britain: England, Scotland, Wales and Northern Ireland.
78. Harmondsworth: Penguin, 1981.

Winter unfortunately gave no real new information and tried to fob Billy off with anecdotes.

In many ways, my visit to Belfast was an eye-opener, as there was a vast difference between Belfast and Dublin. The latter was peaceful, with robust political debate, and one felt safe and secure walking the streets or going to a pub. In contrast, Belfast was highly militarised, with heavily armed British soldiers patrolling the city and occupying many street corners. You could feel the tension, and the fear etched on people's faces was palpable. There were also no-go areas in that city. The political forces representing the Protestant majority were hostile to the minority Catholics, and there was blatant discrimination against Catholics in housing, education, health and political representation.

In the meetings I addressed, I was careful about how I explained our armed revolutionary struggle, as I did not want to be regarded as a supporter of IRA violence in Northern Ireland or London. While there, I was constantly reminded of what Betty Sinclair and Noel Harris had told me about the politics of Northern Ireland, including the duplicity of the British Government regarding the treatment of the Catholic minority. It also reminded me of the information we had been given by Niall Farrell, who represented the CPI at the *World Marxist Review*, about the way his sister Mairéad Farrell had gradually been convinced that the violent actions of the Provisional IRA were necessary. Recruited at the age of fourteen, she had taken part in some IRA activity and been sentenced to fourteen years in jail at the age of nineteen. She spent ten years in Armagh prison in appalling conditions, humiliated and strip-searched regularly. She and two of her fellow women prisoners initiated a hunger strike to coincide with the famous strike led by Bobby Sands at Long Kesh. Two years after she was released, Mairéad was shot dead by British special forces in Gibraltar at the age of thirty-one.

That Belfast experience reinforced my determination to fight relentlessly against religious bigotry and chauvinism and never underestimate the critical National Question. In all my visits to different countries, I had never felt such tension and threat of impending violence as I did in Belfast. That visit also made me appreciate even more the work of the communists in Northern Ireland.

Another memorable trip was to West Germany at the invitation of the DKP (Communist Party of West Germany). For some years after the Second World War, the DKP had been operating in a semi-legal manner and was subject to a torrent of anti-communist, anti-GDR, anti-Soviet propaganda and abuse. Communists were barred from certain jobs and faced heavy discrimination.

Despite its small membership, the DKP organised many meetings, small and large, in different parts of the country. This was great as it took me to various cities and gave me the opportunity to meet dedicated communists who had sacrificed the possibility of finding well-paid jobs in the public service, business or academia for their membership of the DKP. What surprised me was that in the meeting hall, the audience would sit around trestle tables, smoking and drinking lots of beer. They were well-behaved and respectful and were mainly DKP members who were well-informed about the atrocities of apartheid but hungry for more information about the ANC, the SACP and the trajectory of the struggle in South Africa. I spoke about the growth and development of trade unionism in a fascist environment, which was well-received, and contrasted the GDR with the West German government, which supported the racist regime and assisted it in acquiring nuclear weapons. Such an acquisition was a threat not only to the people of South Africa and the African continent but also to world peace and nuclear disarmament. My visit was an invigorating learning experience which enhanced my understanding of German politics, the Holocaust, German revanchism and the ever-present danger of the revival of fascism in that country.

At some point during 1986, I was co-opted onto the CC of the SACP. In an interesting and well-written book entitled *The South African Communist Party: Exile and After Apartheid*,[79] Eddie Maloka points out that in 1986, six members were co-opted but without voting rights. Since my first CC meeting had been in Budapest, Hungary, in 1987 or 1988, I assume I was one of those six. That was also the first CC meeting attended by Joel Netshitenzhe. Thereafter, I formed part of the CC Committee in London with Brian Bunting, Aziz Pahad and Francis Meli. Later, when we were convinced that Meli had been recruited by the apartheid regime, he was excluded and, with the help of O. R. Tambo, not invited to the 7th SACP Congress in Cuba.

During those years, I also had the pleasure of working with Mzala Nxumalo, who had been very active in his party unit in the work of *The African Communist* and the ANC. Through my interactions with him, I became increasingly impressed by his passion and deep commitment to the party and the ANC, his voracious reading of political literature, his growing

---

79. Johannesburg: Jacana Media, 2013.

maturity as a Marxist theoretician, his writing and skill as a rapporteur. Had he not tragically died at an early age, I am convinced he would have occupied a leading position in the party and possibly become editor of *The African Communist*.

Mzala invited Wally Serote and myself to meet Blade Nzimande, who was delivering a paper on education at the School of Oriental and African Studies. After that meeting, Mzala and I agreed that we should recruit Blade into the underground machinery at home. That was important for us as the SACP was keen to have in its ranks African intellectuals. At one of our CC meetings, I proposed that we recruit Blade, and Aziz was tasked with contacting our underground structures to ascertain their views. The response from one unit was negative, suggesting that he was a 'workerist', referring to a group of ultra-leftists in London and South Africa who had sharp political differences with the SACP.

However, in our CC discussions, I stood my ground. Although in making a decision we had to give the most serious consideration to the views of our underground comrades, my position was that, while always an important factor, it could not be decisive in all cases. I do not know if Brian had solicited the view of Mzala, but we finally agreed that Blade should be recruited.

According to Maloka, at the time of the 7th Party Congress, the SACP had about 609 members, of whom 494 were in exile. Given the membership of the ANC, the population of South Africa, and the growth and high level of political consciousness of the Black working class, that membership figure was very low. However, the Party was cautious and only recruited those they considered to be the most politically conscious and mature cadres in the ANC, MK, trade unions and student formations. Notwithstanding its small number, through sheer hard work and dedication to the building and strengthening of the ANC, MK, UDF, trade unions and other civil society structures, the SACP had a profound influence on the conduct, trajectory, pace and direction of the freedom struggle in South Africa.

I must offer a resounding rebuttal to the anti-communist lies and propaganda so assiduously peddled at that time by the mainstream print and electronic media, white politicians and their Black fellow travellers, large numbers of business people, academics, intellectuals and cultural figures who all sang the same tired old song: that communists entered the people's organisations to subvert them in the interest of foreign powers such as the Soviet Union. Let me emphasise that the SACP always insisted that it was a communist's responsibility to promote, defend and work to strengthen the unity and cohesion of the ANC, SACTU and any other progressive organisation for which they worked in South Africa. Communists were expected to respect and defend the independence and integrity of those organisations.

It was an injunction that party members and leaders had to be fierce opponents of sectarianism, chauvinism and factionalism. I am fond of repeating that, in exile, when a lot of ANC NEC members were communists, the most heated debates and controversies arose amongst party members. We clearly understood that as communists, we did not conspire to get a position or positions adopted by the ANC and other organisations. We participated as members of that organisation, expressing our own views and positions. We understood then that the liberation of our people depends on maintaining a strong, viable, well-organised and disciplined ANC free from the scourge of corruption and factionalism. That is even more important to understand today, when those twin scourges are wreaking havoc. Not for one moment do I claim that all members of the SACP followed the injunctions to the letter, even at that time. In exile, some bad eggs and self-centred individuals existed in the party, but they were a small minority.

One of my important tasks as an ANC member in London was to contribute to the work of the Anti-Apartheid Movement and support its campaigns. I shall describe some of that work in the chapter on international solidarity, but here, I shall note that I was happy to be involved in the work for the Free Nelson Mandela campaign and related concerts.

After the first Mandela concert, I was part of a panel on the show *After Midnight* with that great singer, anti-racist freedom fighter and internationalist, Harry Belafonte, Ismail Ayob (Mandela's lawyer) and Denis Worrall, South African Ambassador to the UK. As Worrall was known to be smart, patient and an articulate defender of the apartheid regime, I decided that the way to deal with him was not to be diplomatic but to attack and expose him as a defender of the indefensible. He was rattled, and, while retaining his demeanour, aware that he was on the losing side. Thereafter, many people who had seen that show and those in South Africa who had seen copies smuggled into the country, praised me for my input.

From about the time we returned to London in 1985 there were many signs that change was coming. Aziz Pahad, in his book *Insurgent Diplomat – Civil Talks or Civil War?* gives an interesting account of negotiations and the woefully weak ideas of the National Party in starting those talks. They were intent on insisting that the ANC must renounce armed struggle, and sever its links with the SACP and the Soviet Union; and equally they demanded the defence and protection of white privilege under the euphemism of 'group rights'.

I was not involved in any of those meetings, except the ones in Dakar, Senegal and Burkino Faso in July 1987 and in Paris late in 1989 organised by IDASA (the Institute for Democratic Alternatives in South Africa) and founded and led by Van Zyl Slabbert and Alex Boraine, former MPs of the all-white parliament.

Prior to that, an ANC delegation led by O. R. Tambo met with a group of white business leaders and influential editors such as Harald Pakendorf, Tertius Myburgh and Hugh Murray. Their leader was Gavin Relly, a director of Anglo American, a mega-mining company with a substantial stake on the Johannesburg Stock Exchange.

Fortunately for me, whenever Thabo Mbeki came to London he informed me about those early talks. By 1985, he was convinced that the political prisoners would be released and that these talks would soon lead to negotiations between the sides without preconditions. However, there were many in the ranks and leadership of the ANC, SACP and MK who were sceptical and determined that we should continue to strive for an armed seizure of power. This view had prevailed at the Kabwe conference in 1985 and was still strongly held by many at the 7th Congress of the SACP in Cuba in 1989. Thus, those who were participating in such talks, and others like me who were not, had to tread cautiously in raising the possibility of a negotiated settlement. The 1987 meeting in Dakar was a sign that Thabo's optimism was well-grounded.

During that time, Nelson Mandela, an apartheid prisoner, was conducting secret talks with apartheid leaders such as Kobie Coetzee, 'Minister of Justice', and Niel Barnard, head of the apartheid intelligence agencies. It is noteworthy that both Mandela and the ANC, without consulting each other, categorically rejected the demand to sever their links with the SACP. This insistent demand was absurd and ironic, as they would have known from their intelligence structures that Thabo Mbeki, Jacob Zuma, Aziz Pahad and Joe Nhlanhla were all members of the SACP. Moreover, the first three of the above were also members of the CC.

My lingering reservations about the probability of impending negotiations were laid to rest at the Paris meeting in 1989, organised by IDASA and including UDF leaders such as Trevor Manuel, Cheryl Carolus and rising businessman Wiseman Nkuhlu. At that meeting, held in a warm and friendly environment, we broke into smaller groups to facilitate broader participation in debating the main issues and challenges confronting us while searching for common ground. In my group, which featured the late Eddie Funde, Professor Breyten Breytenbach of Stellenbosch University made a most impressive intervention predicting future events in the National Party and its government. In a breathtakingly fresh assessment, he foreshadowed closely the speech that De Klerk would soon make, which would unban the ANC and other organisations and pave the way for the release of Nelson Mandela. When I rather impishly asked whether the SACP would also be unbanned, a recently retired and respected judge, Laurie Ackerman, retorted, 'But Essop, you are a communist, and you know that if only the ANC is unbanned the communists will nevertheless enter the country on the coat-tails of the ANC. So, yes, the SACP will also be unbanned.'

At the plenary that followed, I was asked to report back from my group and responded that since Professor Breytenbach's input had been so far-reaching, he should be requested to repeat what he had said to our group. I was now fully convinced of Mbeki's assessment of future developments in South Africa: that soon, we would be going home. What a beautiful and exhilarating feeling! But the sentiment was not unanimous. At least two of the participants in the IDASA delegation kept repeating the slogan 'Long Live the Spirit of No Compromise!' The ANC delegation just shrugged and ignored their provocative stance.

A few weeks after that Paris gathering, F. W. de Klerk, in opening the all-white parliament on 2 February 1990, unbanned the ANC, SACP and other organisations and promised that Mandela would be released. On that morning, I received a phone call from a friend in Cape Town who informed me that they were outside Parliament demanding the unbanning of the peoples' organisations. My response was: 'Change your tune – F. W. is going to lift the ban.'

Nevertheless, there were some – indeed many – who remained sceptical and doubted the sincerity of De Klerk and the apartheid machinery. However, the leadership of the ANC and SACP fully understood the gravity of De Klerk's speech and started making preparations to bring its leading cadres back into the country and started working with organisations and individuals at home to prepare for the legal opening of our structures. Soon thereafter, noting the reservations of some within our ranks, the CC, at a meeting in Lusaka, decided to seize the opportunity to open and build a legal

SACP inside South Africa. It was also decided that Jeremy Cronin and I as CC members, along with Geraldine Fraser-Moleketi as administrative secretary, should do that work on a full-time basis. Jabu Moleketi was deployed to head the party structure in the Transvaal.

After forty years of being banned – with its members and leaders hounded, and if caught, brutally tortured and even murdered, as in the case of Ahmed Timol – the SACP was legal. Our task was made easier by the preliminary work done by Mac Maharaj and Ronnie Kasrils, who had entered the country illegally, and the underground units.

Meg was as excited as I was, and we had long chats about how we would cope. She was very supportive and encouraging, readily agreeing that I should return to South Africa as soon as possible while she stayed behind in her teaching job to be a single parent to Amina, then eleven, and Govan, eight. Exactly when and how they could join me would be assessed as the situation at home became clearer. Her understanding and strength were most helpful to me.

Prior to my return, Aziz and some other leaders, such as Jacob Zuma, Henry Makgothi and Penuell Maduna, had already returned and were preparing the ground for the historic Groote Schuur talks, which led to CODESA (Convention for a Democratic South Africa) and the return of the exiles.

In July 1990, I packed my bags and took the flight home to prepare for the legal launch of the SACP later that month. My excitement at returning to work in the legal structures of the SACP and ANC and seeing my extended family and friends, many of whom I had not met for nearly twenty-six years, was beyond description.

Home at last, ready for further advances and victory – but I was also nervous and apprehensive. Would I be able to put to the best use the experience, political consciousness and maturity I had acquired in exile?

When I returned to South Africa, it was clear that Meg and the children would join me, but we wanted them to feel that they were part of the decision-making. Meg would have to sell the flat, work out her notice and organise the move, and we needed to find some way of earning money, as we basically had no savings, so they couldn't just get on a plane as I did, even if they had wanted to. Meg had had a very tough year at school where, for some time, she was acting head, as Marlene had been sent on a training programme after the Westminster Education Authority replaced the Inner London Education Authority. Journalists who would often phone me for information about South Africa now called Meg to find out if Jeremy or I had been arrested like Mac Maharaj or gone underground like Ronnie Kasrils. It was a worrying time, and the children seemed to have permanent colds and chest infections.

We organised a Christmas holiday for December 1990, the plan being for Meg and the children, with Anne and Sam, to come to South Africa together to join up with Aziz and me. Tragically, however, Anne was diagnosed in August with a virulent form of stomach cancer which could not be treated and was unable to join us. She died in January 1991. Nevertheless, Meg, Amina, Govan and Sam did come, and we went together with Yusuf (Charles) Saloojee to Knysna and stayed with Yasmin, her husband Yusuf and their three children, Zakkiya, Zayd and Mohammed, in her mother Ruki Kajee's two-bedroomed family home. Shehnaaz and her husband Georgie were also there with their daughter Zeenat, so all the children and some of the adults slept on roll-down mats on the living room floor. The group from England found it unbelievable to be able to swim in the sea at Christmas time, having never previously left the Northern Hemisphere. We had a lovely holiday and convinced Amina and Govan that it was a good idea to join me and move to live in South Africa in 1991.

So Meg put the flat up for sale, and her brother Michael and sister Jill helped by finalising the sale after she left for South Africa. The money we got was enough to buy a house in Bellevue East (between Yeoville and Observatory), and I began that process. We got support from the United Nations High Commissioner for Refugees (UNHCR) to transport our possessions in a container to South Africa in which there was enough space to fit our second-hand Ford Fiesta, which Meg had recently bought after learning to drive in Prague. A friend, Tony Bunzl, who had also studied at Sussex University, donated £5,000 for my initial support in South Africa. I was very grateful for that generous gift, which meant that I didn't draw a salary from the SACP for nearly a year.

Meg noticed on her visit that when she told people she was a primary school teacher, they appeared to think this was a part-time job for those who couldn't find anything better to do. So at the age of forty-six, she decided she needed to do a Master's degree if she wanted to be taken seriously, and I managed to get funding for her studies, which was another help for us financially. I also organised for the children to register at Sacred Heart College, which we had been told was the most multiracial and progressive school in Johannesburg. The school's director was Brother Neil McGurk, who had always taken a strong anti-racist stance and was happy to ease the way home for many of the returned exiles. He said that Amina and Govan could attend for free until we began earning enough to pay school fees. With all that support, we thought we could manage for the first year.

And so, on 23 August 1991, Meg, Amina and Govan said goodbye to their life in London and flew off to their new home in South Africa.

Chapter 5
International Solidarity

Brian Filling presents Chris Hani with money raised by Scottish Anti-Apartheid for the SACP, London.

INTERNATIONAL SOLIDARITY

From the late 1950s, when I became more involved in the work and activities of the TIYC, I was made acutely aware of the importance of international solidarity. It became clear that an appreciation of internationalism would lead to a better knowledge and consciousness of many aspects of our struggle in South Africa, and we knew international solidarity was a key weapon in our arsenal.

We members of the TIYC were brought up to be active in support of anti-colonial, anti-imperialist struggles in Africa and Asia and in opposition to neocolonialism, racism and monopoly capitalism – and also to be ardent and faithful supporters of the Soviet Union and other socialist countries in Europe, Asia and Latin America. I was fortunate to have had many leaders, such as Dr Yusuf Dadoo, Ahmed Kathrada and Mosie Moolla, to guide me in those formative years.

As a student at Wits University, I was vociferous, and on occasions aggressive, in my support of organisations dubbed 'pro-Soviet' or 'communist', such as WFDY (the World Federation of Democratic Youth) and the IUS (International Union of Students). Even at NUSAS (National Union of South African Students) conferences, I vehemently opposed those pro-West leaders who were only interested in forging links with such organisations as the World Assembly of Youth (WAY), which was founded and financially supported by the US administration and its agencies such as the CIA.

My initial interest and thirst for knowledge about the powerful impact of international solidarity was greatly enhanced by my experience living in exile.

Marx and Engels clearly articulated that their theory would remain on paper without the agency of political organisations based nationally and internationally, and they were instrumental in forming the International Working Men's Association in 1886 (later called the First International). In the *Communist Manifesto*, they coined one of the most inspiring and enduring slogans, 'Workers of all lands unite,' which Lenin enhanced as 'Workers of all lands and peoples subjected to oppression unite.'

The First International gave rise to political parties based on the working class and the theories of Marx and Engels as well as the objective of realising a socialist society. After its demise, the Second International was founded in 1889, but it broke up at the start of the First World War in 1914, when leaders of the Second International sided with their respective national leaders in a war that led to the death of millions of workers and peasants.

The victory of the Bolsheviks under Lenin in the Great October Socialist Revolution of 1917 opened up new vistas, opportunities and possibilities for working-class solidarity and support for anti-colonial and anti-imperialist movements in different parts of the world. Under the leadership and guidance of Lenin, the First Congress of the Communist International – the Comintern – was held in Moscow in 1919. Socialists from South Africa joined the Comintern, and later, two leaders of the Communist Party of South Africa, D. Ivan Jones and Bill Andrews, served on its executive. The Comintern made it obligatory for its members to support and assist the subject nations under colonialism. It was run on strict democratic centralist lines, and its affiliates were bound to implement its policies and strive for its objectives unconditionally. But by 1943, such practices on an international scale were increasingly impractical, particularly in the context of the Second World War, and consequently, the Comintern was dissolved.

I would argue that the Sixth Congress of the Comintern, held in Moscow in 1928, had a positive impact on our struggle, as the resolution it adopted called for an 'independent native republic with simultaneous guarantees for the rights of the white minority and struggle in deeds for its realisation'.[80] Only then, would the conditions be present for the transition to a socialist society. It also called on communists to work closely with the oppressed African people and their political organisations.

That resolution laid the basis for the powerful theory of 'Colonialism of a Special Type' contained in the SACP's *Road to South African Freedom* adopted in 1962. In that programme, the Party made a clarion call, which also expressed a critical methodological principle that 'the main content of this revolution will be the national liberation of the African people', which is 'the key for future advance to the supreme aim of the Communist Party: the establishment of a socialist South Africa, laying the foundations of a classless communist society.'[81]

The resolutions of the Sixth Congress and the 1962 programme of the

---

80. Brian Bunting and Moses Kotane. '2. The National Question', South African Revolutionary. Available at https://www.marxists.org/subject//africa/bunting-brian/kotane/ch02.htm
81. 'Programme of the South African Communist Party 1962: The Road to South African Freedom' (Ellis Bowles, London), South African History Online. https://www.sahistory.org.za/sites/default/files/Programme%20of%20the%20 South%20African%20Communist%20Party%201962-%20The%20Road%20to%20South%20Africa%20Freedom.pdf

SACP paved the way for the ANC-SACP alliance, which has endured to this day in the face of hostility from all stripes of anti-communist ideologues, politicians, media and business people.

I have given this brief and inadequate potted history of the various Internationals here because they had a powerful impact on the development and history of the working class and national liberation movements in South Africa and on me. To conclude this section, here is a paragraph from my article 'What proletarian internationalism means to Africa' in *The African Communist*, Third Quarter 1977.

> Class consciousness of workers is exceptionally complex and includes phenomena such as sociopolitical, sociopsychological, ideological and ethical factors. Whatever the complexity, the highest form of working class consciousness is the understanding of the common interests of the worldwide proletariat. Thus, proletarian internationalism is the very core and heart of the relations between the component parts of the World Communist Movement and the three basic revolutionary streams of our time – the world socialist system, national liberation movements and working class movements in the advanced capitalist countries.[82]

In this section of the memoir, I reflect on some of the key international contributors to our struggle: the Soviet Union, Cuba, the GDR, the OAU and its Liberation Committee, the Frontline States and the British Anti-Apartheid Movement.

The Soviet Union

All my political life, until the Gorbachev and Yeltsin meltdown years, I remained a firm, uncritical, determined and dogmatic supporter of the Soviet Union. I fought anti-Soviet statements, positions and policies vigorously, passionately and at times aggressively. For me, as for many comrades in the SACP, ANC and SACTU, the Soviet Union was the bulwark against racism, colonialism, neocolonialism and imperialism. Incidentally, I was also a keen supporter of Moscow Dynamos – and especially of Lev Yashin, one of the greatest goalkeepers in the history of world football.

My thoughts, ideas and positions on the role of the USSR are reflected in an article I wrote as Ahmed Azad: 'No Room for Anti-Sovietism in Africa' in

---
82. Available at https://disa.ukzn.ac.za/sites/default/files/pdf_files/Acn7077.pdf

The African Communist, Third Quarter 1976.

For me, the struggle against anti-Sovietism was central in the ideological battles between the forces of socialism and those of capitalism. As an example of the unstinting all-round support given to progressive forces in Africa, I cited that given to Egypt under Nasser when they defeated the combined military aggression of Britain, France and Israel in 1956. I wrote confidently that the imperialist world was:

> ... unable to act with impunity as the existence of the world socialist system offers the African countries an honest, reliable and disinterested alternative source of supply. No longer has independent Africa to rely exclusively on the capitalist countries for machinery, equipment, manufactured goods, military supplies, loans, credits and technical assistance.[83]

The same article also makes the following points:

> ... We in Africa know from our own bitter experience that without the support of the Soviet Union, it would not have been possible to defeat Portuguese colonialism backed by NATO and to bring closer the final liquidation of racist and colonial rule in South Africa and Rhodesia. Our liberation movements have been armed, fed and clothed by the socialist countries. This assistance is not new. Throughout the period of the liberation struggle – the dark days as well as the bright ones – the Soviet Union has remained a faithful friend and ally. ...

> ... At no time has the Soviet Union attempted to interfere with the internal affairs of our movement or to impose conditions and restrictions on its vital material assistance. It is not the so-called 'Soviet intervention' that threatens our independence but the interference of the imperialist powers. Let us state unequivocally that those who by their actions give succour to our enemy and benefit from the super-exploitation of our working people have no right to advise us on our relations with the Soviet Union and other socialist countries. ...

---

83. Available at https://disa.ukzn.ac.za/sites/default/files/pdf_files/Acn6676.pdf

... It is precisely the disinterested practical assistance of the socialist world, especially the Soviet Union, which has enabled some African countries to break away from dependence on the world capitalist system. Above all, it must be emphasised that the Soviet Union exports no capital to Africa, owns no factories, exploits no workers, does not own one inch of African soil and has no military bases in Africa.[84]

Lest we forget, the Soviet Union trained a large number of MK combatants as well as political leaders of the ANC and SACP for nearly twenty-five years. In 1969, when Tanzania summarily expelled the MK combatants still in Kangwa camp and no other African country was ready to receive them, the USSR stepped in and retrained those soldiers. The refresher courses lasted until at least June 1971, and it is generally agreed that this unusual assistance helped to prevent the possible disintegration of Umkhonto we Sizwe.

That unselfish all-round material, military, financial, diplomatic and political support from the Soviet Union played a critical role in enabling us to free our country and our people from the shackles of apartheid, racism, national oppression and the super-exploitation of labour power.

To our dismay and that of many of our supporters in the Soviet Union and other socialist countries, the Gorbachev years from 1989 led to a weakening of support from the USSR. Under Yeltsin, it deteriorated still further. This was reflected in the writings and assessments of academics such as Gleb Starushenko, Viktor Gonsharov and Boris Assoyan. Amongst these newly promoted academics, Assoyan was the least supportive of our liberation struggle.

Vladimir Shubin and Marina Traikova inform us that at a meeting of the CPSU International Department, Assoyan 'tried to convince the meeting that the apartheid state should not be abolished because white minority power guaranteed the preservation of the highly developed South African economy and the Afrikaaner nation'. He even had the temerity to pose the question, 'Why do we need black majority rule?' and belittled the ANC.[85]

That outrageous, reactionary and racist view was one that even many of the conservative critics of the ANC and SACP in the West would hesitate to express in public.

The Gorbachev and Yeltsin years led to the collapse of the Soviet Union

---

84. Available at https://disa.ukzn.ac.za/sites/default/files/pdf_files/Acn6676.pdf
85. *The Road to Democracy in South Africa, Vol. 3*: International Solidarity, Part 2, SADET (Pretoria: Unisa Press, 2008), p. 1,050.

and the other socialist countries in Europe as well as the CPSU and other ruling communist parties. This was a devastating blow to communists, socialists and other progressive forces all over the world. There are many varied and complex reasons for that collapse, but I am still astonished that, somehow, many millions of members of the CPSU seem to have disappeared into thin air.

However, the struggle to bring about a socialist Russia remains. Vyacheslav (Slava) Tetekin, who worked at the Southern Africa desk of the Soviet Afro-Asian Solidarity Committee from 1981–1996, has kept in touch with me, written articles for The Thinker and stayed with us several times in Johannesburg. He keeps me informed about the Communist Party of Russia, the second-most powerful party in that country, and in their view, they would win many local, regional and national elections if it were not for the manipulation of the electoral system and the fraud and machinations of the ruling party led by Putin. Slava has been the MP for the Communist Party representing Siberia and the chief advisor to the General Secretary. He received the Order of the Companions of O. R. Tambo in Silver from President Ramaphosa in 2018.

Cuba

I was eighteen-and-a-half years old on 1 January 1959, a historic date because it marks the defeat of that tyrant and US puppet Fulgencio Batista by Cuban revolutionaries led by Fidel Castro. Despite the reactionary anti-communist media reporting in South Africa, activists and leaders of the Congress Alliance received the news with much joy and excitement. A successful revolution had taken place just ninety miles from that mighty predatory power, the USA. Our admiration for the Cuban revolution grew in leaps and bounds when the Cubans defeated the US-organised and inspired invasion in *Playa Giron*, the Bay of Pigs, in April 1961. I still remember how inspired I was by that victory and Fidel Castro's declaration that Cuba was a socialist country.

Many of us young activists in the Congress Alliance, whenever we met at parties or get-togethers would sing 'Take the country the Castro way' with great enthusiasm and gusto. At that time, the thought of ever visiting Cuba seemed no more than a pipe-dream.

One of the most glorious chapters in the history of international solidarity is about the support of the people, party and government of Cuba for Angola under the leadership of the MPLA. In April 1974, the Portuguese fascist regime was overthrown by progressive military leaders, including some who had close ties to the Communist Party of Portugal.

The relentless anti-colonial revolutionary struggles led by the PAIGC, the MPLA and FRELIMO in Guinea Bissau, Angola and Mozambique contributed a great deal to that historic event. In 1975, Mozambique, Guinea Bissau, Cape Verde and São Tomé won their independence. But Angola, with its rich oil, mineral and agricultural resources and important geopolitical position, was too great a treasure trove to be relinquished by imperialist forces. So US imperialists, South African racists, and the corrupt, thieving kleptomaniac Mobuto of Zaire conspired and worked in concert to thwart the MPLA and install in power Holden Roberto of the National Liberation Front of Angola (*Frente Nacional de Libertação de Angola*: FNLA) and Savimbi of the National Union for the Total Independence of Angola (*União Nacional para a Independência Total de Angola*: UNITA). The latter two acted as instruments of those who opposed African independence, sovereignty and integrity and were, of course, the enemies of not only the MPLA but also the ANC and SWAPO of Namibia.

Angola would be declared independent in November 1975, but by October that year, the apartheid war machine had penetrated deep into that country and was poised to capture its capital, Luanda. However, early in November, Cuba agreed to the request from the MPLA for military assistance, and Operation Carlotta, named in honour of a woman slave who led an uprising in 1843, was set in motion from the 5th. On 9 November, special troops of the Ministry of the Interior landed in Luanda and immediately began to repulse the South African regime's invasion and save the capital. This helped stabilise the situation and enabled the MPLA to be recognised as the ruling party in Angola by the Organisation of African Unity (OAU) in January 1976, and the People's Armed Forces of Liberation of Angola (Forças Armadas Populares de Libertação de Angola: FAPLA), the MPLA's armed wing, became Angola's official armed defence force.

That was the beginning of the war waged by Cuban and FAPLA troops against the racist South African National Defence Force (SANDF) invaders, which would last until the decisive defeat of the SANDF in March 1988 in Cuito Cuanavale. From preparing for and carrying out Operation Carlotta, Cuban internationalists were involved for fifteen years and four months in promoting, defending and stabilising the MPLA government. In addition, they gave invaluable assistance to the ANC and SWAPO and their military wings.

During that period, more than 30,000 Cuban combatants and internationalists of the highest order served voluntarily and selflessly in Angola, and 2,077 lost their lives. Even today, grieving Cubans are very proud of the sacrifices made by their family members and citizens.

Cuban blood was shed and lives lost to nourish the soil of freedom in Angola, Namibia and South Africa. We, in this country, region and continent, must never lose sight of that enormous contribution. It is painful to witness some people's ignorance of this history, and we must oppose all attempts to belittle and undermine Cuba and its achievements.

My second visit to Cuba was in 1992 as part of an SACP delegation led by Chris Hani. The politbureau had agreed to Hani's recommendation that we include trade unionists and a woman, so Sam Shilowa, Gwede Mantashe and Nosizwe Madlala formed part of the delegation. None of those three were at that time members of the Central Committee. It was a wonderful visit during which we experienced Cuban warmth and hospitality of the highest order. We had many meetings with Cuban officials and paid a visit to Raúl Castro. Our pride and joy at meeting the mercurial Raúl was crowned when he took us on a tour of his office and showed us the room with its secret encrypted machinery that allowed two-way communication with the Soviet Union, defeating the attempts of the US intelligence agencies to monitor and record conversations between the two governments. But that joy was nothing compared to our feelings when Fidel Castro made a surprise visit to our guest house on the morning of our departure. He was hearty, friendly and very chatty. That was my first and unforgettable personal encounter with one of the greatest revolutionaries and political leaders in the history of humanity.

From the mid-1970s, the fraternal relations between Cuba, the ANC and SACP grew from strength to strength. In December 1978, the ANC opened its mission in Cuba, the first in Latin America and the Caribbean, and the Seventh Congress of the SACP was held there from 7–12 April 1989 at Yumuri Village. I was a delegate, and all of us were deeply appreciative of the care and assistance we received and the support given by Cuba to the SACP. At that Congress, which was attended by what we call the Soweto Generation, I was once more elected to the Central Committee.

After my appointment as Deputy Minister, and later Minister in the Office of President Mbeki, I had the pleasure and honour of making official visits to Cuba. On every visit, I would request a meal at La Bodeguita restaurant, where I relished the typical Cuban black beans and lively atmosphere. This restaurant's fame is partly the result of the signatures left on the wall by its customers, which include those of Ernest Hemingway, Salvador Allende, Pablo Neruda, Nat King Cole and Gabriel García Márquez.

However, my most memorable visit was in 2008. After being appointed Minister in the Presidency, I tried, whenever possible, to take a member of staff who did not occupy a top position in my office as part of the delegation. In that case, I asked Vathiswa Mafana to join us. She was overjoyed to go to Cuba and had never travelled abroad before. Vathiswa had been with me since my time as Parliamentary Counsellor to Thabo Mbeki. When she started, she had no experience working in an office, but through sheer hard work, dedication and a willingness to learn, she improved her skills considerably. By the time I resigned later that year, Vathiswa had become a valuable member of staff with a good understanding and knowledge of working in the presidency.

Before we arrived in Cuba, a mishap occurred. Our itinerary had us travelling first to Madrid, then to Caracas in Venezuela and then on to Havana. But when we arrived in Madrid, we discovered that Vathiswa had left our passports in the VIP Lounge at Jan Smuts Airport (now O. R. Tambo) in Johannesburg: mine, my daughter Amina's, Anver Saloojee's (advisor) and Louis du Plooy's (Chief of Staff). Fortunately, our Ambassador to Spain met us at the airport in Madrid, and with the kind assistance of the Spanish customs and passport officials, we were allowed entry. We contacted our people at Jan Smuts, who arranged to send our passports to Madrid on the next flight, and we were able to continue our journey.

In Caracas, I met an old friend from Prague, Jeronimo Carrera, then-General Secretary of the Communist Party of Venezuela. In Caracas, I attended a seminar that started after a delay caused by the late arrival of that charismatic leader, Hugo Chavez. As late as he was, he first shook hands with all the hotel staff who had lined up to welcome him and then proceeded to make a lengthy speech. The delegates did not mind and were just happy to listen to him and meet him at the end of his address. Caracas was interesting, not least because our ambassador absolutely refused to allow me to visit the working-class areas dotted around the central business district (CBD). He said it was too dangerous and that even the CBD was unsafe at night.

Our Cuban hosts were very kind and hospitable and took special care of Amina, including visiting night clubs. The discussions we had with the Cuban officials covered multiple areas, including the complexities and challenges of being a ruling party.

One of the leaders I met was Esteban Lazo Hernandez, a Cuban African member of the Politbureau of the Communist Party and the President of the National Assembly of People's Power. He was tall and well-built with grey hair and a lovely smile. Our discussions lasted much longer than the usual one hour, during which he posed many sharp and intelligent questions concerning racism in South Africa in the past, present and future, as well as in the rest of the world. We also shared opinions on the necessity for the Cuban authorities to intensify their anti-racist educational programmes, which were already good, and to be on the alert for any signs of racist behaviour or language. It was a thoroughly enjoyable discussion, and I learnt a great deal about how they were trying to overcome the serious challenges facing the Cuban Party and Government as a result of the collapse of the Soviet Union and other European socialist countries. That was particularly severe, as they were still subjected to the economic blockade and continuing destabilisation programmes and projects emanating from the USA.

That was the height of my visit, but then came another surprise. A former Cuban Ambassador to South Africa phoned me to say that I was to have a meeting with 'the Chief'. I said, 'But I have not asked for such a meeting, as I am aware of the very busy programme of comrade Raúl Castro.' He laughed and said, 'But the Chief wants to see you.'

I was most elated at that honour and privilege. Raúl Castro was warm and friendly and informed me that Comrade Hernandez had spoken to him about our meeting and suggested that he might find it useful to have a discussion with me, in particular about the issues, problems and challenges of racism.

The meeting again went beyond the allocated time and, in response to my query about the health of Fidel, Raúl assured me that Fidel was still actively involved and persistent in being informed about developments in the CPC, the government and international relations. He remembered meeting our delegation led by Chris Hani and once more gave me a tour of his office and the room with the encrypted equipment, which now lay dormant since the disintegration of the Soviet Union. He also asked his son and two friends to come to the office and introduced us. It is a meeting that will always remain close to my heart – one of the best I have ever had in my life.

For sixty-two years, Cuba successfully resisted and rebuffed endless heinous plots to assassinate Fidel Castro, as well as invasions, destabilisation, aggression and the most harmful economic blockade and sanctions in history. Its bitter enemy, the most powerful economic and military power in the world, has failed to destroy Cuba, and indeed still fears what Cuba stands for and perceives it as a threat to their safety and security. How absurd and foolish.

The German Democratic Republic

Most of the information and assessments given in this section are based on a comprehensive article by Hans-Georg Schleicher entitled 'The German Democratic Republic and the South African Liberation Struggle' in *The Road to Democracy in South Africa, Vol. 3*, International Solidarity, Part 2.

The attitude of the Socialist Unity Party (SED) and the Solidarity Committee was in stark contrast to that adopted by the major political parties in the Federal Republic of Germany (West Germany). While the latter had extensive economic, political, diplomatic and military ties with apartheid South Africa, the GDR imposed economic, trade and other sanctions against the regime, at some cost to their economy. Unlike their West German counterparts, political leaders in the GDR held numerous high-level talks and discussions with the leaders of the ANC and SACP. Our leaders were treated with respect and accorded similar status to that given to representatives of ruling parties from other countries.

The solidarity and assistance provided by the GDR was given across a wide range of areas, some of which I mention below.

Information and propaganda play an essential role in political struggle. When the ANC started publishing its official mouthpiece, *Sechaba*, in 1967, the GDR agreed to print the original 6,230 copies per month at no cost. This generous commitment continued, even as the print runs increased, first to 10,000 and later to 20,000 a month. The GDR also paid for two assistants to be stationed in Berlin, one of whom was an old friend of mine, Eric Singh. Until his death, M. P. Naicker, as the editor, would prepare the journal and then take it to Berlin for printing and distribution.

Later, the SACP requested similar assistance from the SED, and from July 1979, *The African Communist* was also printed in Berlin, including the copies for clandestine distribution in South Africa. From an initial 7,000 copies, the number grew over the years. First Michael Harmel and then Sonia Bunting would take the final version to Berlin for printing and then to its London office for distribution. Without that support, it would have been prohibitively expensive for the ANC and SACP to produce and circulate their two most vital publications. In addition, a number of other ANC and SACP materials were printed at no cost to us in the GDR. Interestingly, the print workers who performed this work did so with passion and regarded it as their solidarity contribution to our struggle.

Military assistance to MK and the ANC was considerable, and from 1976 to the late eighties, about 1,000 MK combatants were trained in the GDR. It should be noted that the GDR also bore the cost of flying those trainees in and out of the country, mainly from Angola, and supplied military equipment and uniforms to MK. They always responded swiftly when the ANC requested emergency assistance for its camps in Angola and airlifted the requirements, despite the expense, even when the GDR was suffering its own financial difficulties.

One of those trained in the GDR was Siphiwe Nyanda, who later became head of the democratic South African National Defence Force.

The GDR also paid for many South African students to study at their universities or their political school. Graduates include Francis Meli, Zola Skweyiya and Jeff Radebe. Zola and Jeff became cabinet ministers in the governments of Nelson Mandela and Thabo Mbeki.

When ANC President Tambo opened the ANC mission in East Berlin in 1978, Anthony Mongalo, a very dear friend, was the first ANC representative there and remained in that post until 1984. That mission proudly flew the ANC flag in the area designated for foreign embassies. During the many visits I made to East Berlin, I always met with Anthony, who spoke highly of the relations between the ANC and the Solidarity Committee, the SED and other political parties as well as the mass organisations of women and youth. I have no doubt he played a key role in maintaining that goodwill.

From my first visit to the GDR for the World Youth Festival in 1973, I was a great admirer of the people, the party, the government and the Solidarity Committee. I attended many conferences, seminars and consultative meetings in the GDR over the years, and I loved staying at the Party Hotel, which overlooked the famous Speer River, where we received the most wonderful hospitality. I found it easy to engage in discussions with the political leaders in the GDR, as they always treated me and my views, opinions and positions with respect. Here, I will recount three treasured memories.

On one of my official visits, I had a guide/interpreter, a female comrade whose name, to my shame and regret, I cannot remember. She confided how she and her husband were facing a difficult problem. Their son, who was ten or eleven years old, wanted to watch Westerns broadcast on West Berlin TV and transmitted to East Berlin. He was most insistent that he felt left out at school when the other children played cowboys and Indians. Eventually they gave in, but explained to their son that in real life, the cowboys were the 'baddies' and the Indians were Native Americans who were persecuted in their own country. The son then joined in but insisted on being an 'Indian' and explaining their side of the story to his peers.

The second was when Francis Meli joined me in the work of the drafting committee on the 'Call to the Communists'. Because of the status given to the delegations represented there, we were given full security. Previously, neither Francis nor I had ever been offered security. One evening, Francis decided to visit a woman friend he knew from his student days. I advised against that visit because of the security we had been afforded. When he got into the official car at our disposal, a security officer joined him, and Francis, who spoke fluent German, could not get rid of him. Eventually, he decided to go on his visit, regardless of the unwanted company. After spending a few hours with his friend, Francis was surprised to find that the security officer was waiting across the road outside her flat to escort him back to his hotel. When he expressed his surprise that the man had waited on the open street for him for such a long time, the officer replied, 'But Comrade, that is my job. I am given the task to ensure your safety, and even if you had stayed all night, I would have waited.'

The third memory is a story I was told. Pemba was a SACTU leader, a very affable comrade with the nickname 'Ben Bella',[86] who was noticeably overweight. On one his visits to the GDR for SACTU work, he was on his way to his car when a group of children ran up to him, pointing at him and chanting, 'Capitalist! Capitalist!' It seems that they believed capitalists were overfed from exploiting the workers.

Schleicher estimates that the assistance given to the ANC by the GDR from 1975–1989 amounted to about 37,306,400 German Marks.

When the GDR collapsed in 1989–1990, it was a great shock and cause of distress for many of us in the movement. We loved and admired that country, its people, party and Solidarity Committee. I personally witnessed one such reaction to the bad news. Harry Gwala, the fierce 'Lion of the Midlands' of our struggle, who was suffering from motor neuron disease, was on a visit to London after a trip to the GDR. He came to London full of enthusiasm and joy at what he had seen, but when I informed him that the GDR was on the verge of collapse, he looked at me in disbelief. On several occasions after that,

---

86. Variously known as Aaron Pemba or Alvin Bennie. A *New Age* picture identifies him as Alvin Bennie, but in exile he used the name Aaron Pemba. 'Ben Bella' is probably the 'Ben' from Bennie plus the 'Bella', named after the Algerian socialist revolutionary who later became President of Algeria.

when we met in South Africa, he would stand ramrod straight with his arms hanging at his side, look me in the eye and sternly ask: 'Why did you have to tell me that the GDR would collapse?'

In reflecting on the selfless, unstinting support and solidarity offered to our struggle by the GDR, we should always bear in mind the role of the other Germany as one of the principal backers and supporters of apartheid South Africa. How sad that the 'reunification' of Germany was actually the takeover of the East with its internationalist and socialist ideology by the imperialist West. I will always respect, admire and love what the GDR stood for and what it did to help us.

African countries and their contribution to the struggle against apartheid

The support, solidarity and assistance given to the ANC and PAC by the people and countries of Africa, the OAU and, most importantly, the Frontline States, was invaluable and highly commendable. It certainly played a decisive role in the imposition of international sanctions and the isolation of racist South Africa.

In the world of sports, those people, countries and organisations were instrumental in ensuring that apartheid sporting codes, personnel and teams were not only excluded but expelled from major international events and organisations. To achieve that, they had to overcome the resistance of many sports leaders and players from countries such as the USA, the UK, France, West Germany, Australia and New Zealand. The supporters of apartheid were forced to accept the exclusion of apartheid South Africa from prestigious events like the Olympic Games, the Commonwealth Games, the FIFA World Cup and international cricket tournaments. They also gave the South African Non-Racial Olympic Committee valuable support in its campaign to isolate the racist regime.

In the previous chapter, I wrote about my military training in Angola, a country I return to briefly now. Should you wish to read more about Angola, recommend an article entitled 'The Role of the Organisation of African Union Liberation Committee in the South African Liberation Struggle' by Elias C. J. Tarimo and Neville Z. Reuben in *The Road to Democracy in South Africa, Vol. 5*, African Solidarity, Part 1. There is also a well-researched book by Hugh Macmillan, *The Lusaka Years: The ANC in Exile in Zambia, 1963 to 1993*.[87] Another I recommend highly is *Beggar your Neighbours: Apartheid*

---
87. Johannesburg: Jacana Media, 2013.
88. CIIR in conjunction with James Currey and Indiana University Press, 1986.

Power in Southern Africa by Joseph Hanlon.[88]

Hanlon estimates that in 1984, the accumulative cost of apartheid aggression and destabilisation of the SADC countries came to US$10 billion, which he extrapolated to US$18.7 billion by 1986. These shocking figures demonstrate the heavy burden borne by our neighbours. Let those who harbour ill feelings or xenophobia relating to our sisters and brothers from Southern Africa take note of what those countries have suffered on our behalf.

Hanlon also estimates that, at the very least, apartheid aggression and destabilisation cost Angola US$12 billion and displaced at least one-tenth of the population, turning nearly a million people into internal refugees. Let us recall that by November 1975, the apartheid military machine had penetrated deep into Angola and was ready to enter the capital, Luanda. Only the intervention of the Cubans made it possible to repel that invasion. While the racist regime fully supported UNITA in its war against the MPLA government, UNITA was ambushing and attacking MK combatants and convoys, causing injuries and deaths.

The apartheid war devastated the Angolan economy, potentially the richest in our region, and prevented the MPLA from implementing its policies of building socialism, peace, democracy and development. Yet, even in the face of apartheid savagery, the MPLA government gave the ANC permission to operate MK camps to house, train and equip its soldiers. It was this selfless assistance that enabled the ANC to offer military training to the many young fighters who left South Africa after the Soweto and connected uprisings. The racists' army and air force also bombed the military camps of the ANC and SWAPO in Angola.

Furthermore, during the mutinies in our camps,[89] the MPLA government stood by the ANC and MK and assisted them in quelling the rebellions. They also allowed ANC officials to operate without hindrance at the airport, enabling ANC and MK personnel to enter and leave the country without difficulty and, at times, without any documentation.

There is no doubt that the Angolan solidarity with the ANC and SWAPO ranks as the most powerful and influential international solidarity in the history of our continent. Namibia and South Africa owe eternal gratitude and thanks to the people of Angola and its ruling party, the MPLA, for without their solidarity and support, our freedom from apartheid and race tyranny would have been seriously delayed.

---

89. Triggered by agents of the apartheid regime, difficult living and working conditions, and the frustration of waiting for action.

Sweden, our main supporter among the Western governments

A great deal of the information, assessment and analysis of Sweden's international solidarity with and support of the ANC and the broader freedom struggle in South Africa can be found in 'Sweden and the Nordic Countries: Official Solidarity and Assistance from the West' by Tor Sellström in *The Road to Democracy in South Africa, Vol. 3*, International Solidarity, Part 1, Chapter 6.

My first visit to Sweden in 1965 was as part of an ANC delegation to a summer camp organised by the Social Democratic Party. The following year, Aziz and Sobizana Mngqikana also attended, and in early 1974, Sobizana was appointed to lead the ANC mission in Stockholm. At that time, I was neither politically nor ideologically well-disposed to social democracy; I was a convinced Marxist-Leninist, a communist and a firm supporter of the Soviet Union.

However, I was impressed by the way the Social Democratic Party was organised, its influence on Swedish society, its anti-racist positions and its extensive social assistance programmes. Interestingly, there were not many Black people in Sweden on my first visit, and our delegation had to adjust to people staring at us in the streets.

The Social Democratic Party had been the ruling party in Sweden for forty-four years. Then, in 1976, the Centre Party assumed power in a coalition government. Swedish support for the ANC cut across ideological and political divides, and thus, in 1976, the Centre Party Government's official assistance to the ANC was increased. In 1978–1979, the Swedish minority government led by the Liberal Party was the first government of a highly developed economy in the West to ban investments in apartheid South Africa and occupied Namibia. In addition to those three main parties, support for our struggle was shared by the Left Party (Communist Party), their own anti-apartheid movement, students, churches and other civil society organisations. However, it should be noted that many big business interests in Sweden were opposed to that assistance and the call for boycotts and sanctions.

The Swedish-ANC relationship was assisted by the deep and abiding friendship between former Prime Minister Olof Palme and O. R. Tambo. Before becoming prime minster in 1982, Palme had been a student activist and internationalist, and his forthright support for the Vietnamese freedom fighters against US imperialist bombing and aggression was a milestone for any leader of the West. He was a determined and convinced anti-colonial fighter. In an interview with a French journalist he said:

> ... it was in Asia that I concretely experienced what colonialism [stood for] ... In Singapore, I spent ten days in a university compound where Chinese, Malays and Indians lived. The silent contempt they all displayed for 'White supremacy' made a strong impression ... it was easy to discuss. We did not only have the same value opinions but we also shared the will to take practical steps. We wanted to reform the world ... Basically, all the discussions ended with the same idea. The folly of imperialism must be defeated and poor peoples must themselves be allowed to form their destiny.[90]

Tambo and Palme met as brothers, both enjoying each other's company and sharing many ideas and positions on South Africa, Sweden, Africa and the world. Tambo visited Palme's home and was impressed by his warm and cosy manner of interaction.

In 1986, from 21–23 February, more than 1,000 delegates attended the 'Swedish People's Parliament Against Apartheid', probably the most representative gathering of its kind in the history of Sweden. Olof Palme and Tambo both attended it and had discussions on a wide range of issues, including an initiative taken by Tambo that the ANC had to start giving serious consideration to a post-apartheid South Africa. So, even though many in the world could not see the light at the end of the apartheid tunnel, Tambo had the foresight to consider that question and ask Sweden for financial assistance.

A week later, while strolling home from the cinema with his wife through the streets of Stockholm, Olof Palme was assassinated, and his wife was slightly wounded. This brutal act shocked not only Sweden but the ANC and progressive forces all over the world. It is my contention that the apartheid security forces had a hand in that assassination, but to date, the Swedish government and its security agencies have not been able to establish to their satisfaction who the perpetrators were.

The close relationship between Palme and Tambo was amply demonstrated when, after his release from prison, Mandela visited Stockholm in 1990, where he was formally treated as a head of state.

In December 2002, President Mbeki awarded the National Order of the

---

90. Tor Sellström, *The Road to Democracy*, Vol. 3, p. 526.

Companions of O. R. Tambo in Gold to Olof Palme, Mahatma Gandhi and Kenneth Kaunda. I was very happy to participate in that event.

Now let me go back a few years to 1967, a time when the ANC was in financial distress and urgently needed funds to pursue its campaigns inside and outside South Africa. Their initial attempt to obtain financial assistance was unsuccessful, despite the efforts of the Central and Liberal Parties. Only in February 1973 did the Swedish International Development Cooperation Agency (SIDA) finally agree to allocate the modest sum of SEK 150,000 to the ANC, a modest beginning that would grow over the years. The ANC engaged in extensive bilateral discussions relating to the assistance it required for its operations in Southern Africa and what the two sides called the 'Home Front'. Tor Sellström gives a detailed account of that and calculates, in what he calls current figures, that from 1973 to 1994, the allocation to the ANC grew to SEK 127 million. He then points out that 'Counting only the support granted directly by the Swedish government, at the time of the 1994 elections in South Africa, it had reached, in current figures, a total of SEK 896 million.'[91]

As O. R. Tambo said, the Swedish assistance was 'absolutely decisive for the organisation's existence'.[92] Similar sentiments were expressed by many ANC leaders, including Thomas Nkobi and Kay Moonsamy from the ANC Treasurer-General's office.

But there was also a negative side to some of the organisations – such as the International University Exchange Fund (IUEF) – that were heavily subsidised by Sweden. I was a recipient of a scholarship from the IUEF which made it possible for me to complete my studies, and my brother Aziz and many other ANC students also benefited in that way. The director of the IUEF was a Swede named Lars-Gunner Eriksson, who ensured that organisations such as the Black Consciousness Movement and SASO received nearly twice as much as the ANC. Lars was also associated with attempts to build the BCM into a 'third force' and recruited the notorious apartheid spy Craig Williamson as Deputy Director of the IUEF. As detailed earlier, Williamson was involved in the assassination of Ruth First in Maputo in 1982 and Jeanette Schoon and her daughter in Angola in 1985.

In 1977, the IUEF got involved in trying to set up a meeting between O. R. Tambo and Steve Biko. At that time, Olof Palme was scheduled to visit Botswana and would have been part of that meeting, information Craig Williamson relayed to the South African Security Services. As a result, Biko was arrested, brutally tortured and murdered. The blood of our martyr Steve

---

91. Tor Sellström, *The Road to Democracy, Vol. 3.*
92. Ibid.

Biko drips from the fingers of that despicable fascist murderer Williamson, who still walks free after (wrongly, in my opinion) receiving a pardon from the Truth and Reconciliation Commission. He alone knows if he played a role in the assassination of Olof Palme.

Before Williamson was exposed as an apartheid spy, Lars-Gunnar Eriksson was exposed as a CIA agent, causing grave embarrassment to the Swedes. He had good contacts with many Social Democrats and was heavily funded by the Swedish authorities. In my view, his being a CIA agent is also an indication of the close links between the CIA and the apartheid security machinery.

Notwithstanding those devastating blemishes concerning the IUEF, it must be recorded that the financial, political and moral assistance offered by respective Swedish governments was exceptionally helpful in keeping the ANC alive, hastening the demise of the apartheid regime and ushering in a democratic dispensation.

The Anti-Apartheid Movement in Britain

International Solidarity was one of the four pillars around which the ANC led and conducted the struggle against racism, colonialism and apartheid in South Africa. The ANC and its allies, the SACP and SACTU, worked tirelessly and with tremendous vigour to assist in building the international Anti-Apartheid Movement, which covered Western Europe and North America and developed into one of the greatest sustained acts of international solidarity in the history of the world. The other was the international solidarity extended to the people of Vietnam.

Although I was involved in many AAM activities in Western Europe, I shall concentrate on Britain in this memoir and later touch on Italy (because of Reggio Emilia), which gave the ANC a home in that country and has continued their cooperation with us to this day.

For a comprehensive and informative account of the birth, growth and development of the British AAM, see the article by Christabel Gurney, 'In the Heart of the Beast: the British Anti-Apartheid Movement, 1959–1994', in *The Road to Democracy in South Africa, Vol. 3*, International Solidarity, Part 1, SADET, Unisa Press, 2008.

In 1965, a few weeks after my arrival in London, I visited the AAM offices in Charlotte Street, London, to get to know more about its activities and see if I could be of any assistance. There, I met with Ethel de Keyser, who had also started working in the AAM office that year, and subsequently devoted ten years of her life to that movement. She was a pillar of strength and made a significant contribution to the promotion, growth and success of the British AAM.

After some discussion, Ethel suggested that I address a meeting of Liberal Party supporters just outside London. I agreed, not knowing what to expect or what to say, as this was my first speech in England. The meeting was in a house where I found a number of elderly white women in a sedated atmosphere. As I was addressing them, some were doing their knitting. It was disconcerting, to say the least, and could not have been more different from the types of meetings I was used to in Johannesburg. However, my disappointment was short-lived, as the women phoned Ethel and said how impressed they were by 'this young man' and pledged to intensify their support for the AAM. That taught me a valuable lesson – a solidarity movement is built by people across race, colour, gender, class, religious and age divides.

The British AAM was founded in March/April 1960, and South Africans such as Vella and Patsy Pillay, Abdul Minty, Kader Asmal, Mac Maharaj, Tony Seedat, Mana Chetty and Nandha Naidoo played an important role. They were also assisted by Dr Dadoo, who had arrived in London early in that year. From those humble beginnings, the AAM grew into a powerful and influential solidarity movement not only in Britain but across Western Europe.

Over the years, the British AAM drew its support from a base comprising students, religious groups, trade unions, academics and branches of the Labour Party, Liberal Party and Young Liberals, the Communist Party of Great Britain (CPGB) and Young Communist League (YCL), as well as artists, writers, musicians, sculptors, actors and poets. But its main weakness was that it failed to make meaningful contact or alliances with organisations representing the anti-racist battles of people from the Caribbean, Asia and Africa.

The Labour Government was a profound disappointment, as it rebuffed the efforts of the AAM to impose a meaningful arms boycott and sanctions on apartheid South Africa. Individual MPs and even Cabinet Ministers played an important role in building the AAM, but their demands also fell on deaf ears. Indeed, under Harold Wilson, the British Government refused to have any official contact with the ANC while it continued its relations with the racist regime. Joan Lestor, a vice president of the AAM and a junior minister in Foreign Affairs from 1974–1975, once told me after we had addressed a meeting together that she was firmly rebuffed by Wilson when she sought his permission to meet SWAPO officially.

Although small in number, members of the CPGB and the YCL and its newspaper, the *Daily Worker*, later renamed the *Morning Star*, played an invaluable role in helping to build the AAM and offering solidarity and assistance to the ANC and SACP. For me, they are a shining example of how a small number of dedicated, determined, hard-working people can have a political influence and impact far beyond their numbers. I recall that at one time, there was a regular daily lunchtime picket outside South Africa House which was always attended by Gordon McLennan, General Secretary of the CPGB. He would come and leave by public transport or on foot from their offices to offer his and his party's support.

In the mid 1960s, the National League of Young Liberals were a wonderful, dedicated group of anti-apartheid fighters who developed a good working relationship with the ANC Y&S section. I worked very closely with those impressive young activists.

I was also an active participant in the Stop the Seventies Tour against the apartheid rugby and cricket teams. That was also when Peter Hain emerged as an organiser and leader. Regarding the boycott of apartheid sports, I was involved first with Dennis Brutus and later with Sam Ramsamy and recall two incidents.

In 1965, when the white cricket team claiming to represent South Africa were going to play at the Lord's Cricket Ground, a group of us – three or four AAM volunteers – were happily putting posters up on the wall of that ground when we saw the police coming. We carried on and, to our surprise and disappointment, were arrested. Abdul Minty came to the police station and secured our release, and the following day, we had to appear at the Marylebone Magistrates' Court. We were advised to plead guilty, which we did, and the magistrate found us guilty but let us off.

The second incident was at a large demonstration outside Twickenham, the home of English rugby. While some of us, including Aziz, were able to gain entry and disrupt the game, most of us were outside, vociferously demanding that the racists go back home. One policeman thought I was one of the leaders of the demonstration, but I was not, I was just very vocal. When the British police stood in front of us with their legs apart and their arms behind them, I experienced their well-drilled tactic as they gave us hefty kicks on our shins. That one policeman kicked me and continued to threaten me, so I called the superior officer in charge and asked him to instruct his junior to desist and said that if he did not, I would lay charges against them both. The officer in charge complied with my request, but to no avail, for as soon as we left the demonstration, that policeman followed me. I asked the group of comrades I was with to stick with me until we got to the tube station, and, thankfully, there, he stopped following us.

During my time in the UK, I attended scores of meetings in England, Scotland and Wales. At all of them, large or small, I was commended for my speeches and assured that the attendees were inspired to redouble their efforts to defeat apartheid.

In Glasgow, on 16 June 1986, I had the honour, together with Robert Gray the Lord Provost, to rename St George's Place, where the apartheid consular offices were situated, as Nelson Mandela Place. This put the apartheid regime in the embarrassing situation of having their formal address in Scotland named after their most famous political prisoner. As a result, they would only accept their mail through a post office box. After the renaming ceremony, I and Brian Filling, who headed the Scottish AAM from his home in Glasgow, addressed a meeting in the banqueting hall of the city chambers. Despite continuous heavy rain, a large crowd attended the naming event. In fact, years later, a woman told me that she had participated in that meeting with her child in a pram, determined to express her support for our struggle – despite the downpour and her toddler's discomfort.

Those are the kinds of people who enabled the AAM to grow and develop into the force it became.

Another significant encounter in Scotland also took place in 1986, soon after my visit to Glasgow. The Labour Party had just won the local government elections in the beautiful city of Edinburgh, and at one of its council meetings, they decided to fly an ANC flag on the council building and invite the ANC to send a speaker, which was me.

As usual, it was raining, but I received a warm reception from the Labour councillors. However, just as the session started, a councillor from the Tory Party started making animal noises, rudely insulting me. The Labour councillors were very angry and about to remove him from the chambers when I interjected, addressing the Tory as 'the Honourable Member for Johannesburg South'[93] and said:

> I really do not understand this lowly Conservative with no manners refusing to listen when high-ranking Conservatives like Malcolm

---
93. In other words, closely associated with the apartheid regime.

Fraser, Prime Minister of Australia, is talking to the ANC. So let us continue with our meeting and ignore this uncouth, rude and ignorant Conservative.

The Council erupted in applause and laughter, and that Conservative left the meeting in a huff, followed by a Labour councillor, and went through the rain to the roof of the building to lower the ANC flag, after which the Labour man got into a physical confrontation with him to protect it. We were very happy to report that he succeeded and the ANC flag continued to fly proudly from that building.

Another event that remains fresh in my memory is the NUS Conference in 1970, which I attended as an observer from the ANC Y&S. There was no money for my accommodation, so the Radical Students Alliance (RSA), with Mike Terry playing a prominent role, found me a bed to sleep in since the main delegates were up all night planning their strategy and moves to change the leadership and also pass a tough resolution on apartheid South Africa. As an observer, I participated in lobbying the delegates about the apartheid regime and in support of the RSA slate for the elections. The RSA succeeded on both counts, a really good resolution was passed which included support for the armed struggle in Southern Africa, and their candidate Jack Straw was elected leader. Years later, Straw was appointed Foreign Secretary in a Labour government.

My various activities supporting the AAM helped mould my political maturity and gave me a deeper appreciation for the place and function of international solidarity. They also honed my public speaking skills. I learned to judge the response of an audience by focusing on a few people. If they looked bored, I would shout a slogan or change the direction or tone of my remarks to regain their attention. I also acquired the ability to size up an audience and tailor my approach, form and content to those present. It usually went well.

An essential task of the ANC and SACP in London was to give input into the work of the AAM and support its campaigns – one of the largest and most successful being the Free Nelson Mandela campaign and related concerts. To mark Mandela's upcoming 70th birthday,[94] the ANC chose 11 June 1988 as the date for international celebrations and fully supported the AAM's decision to organise a massive birthday concert at Wembley Stadium. Father Trevor Huddleston, Mike Terry and Bob Hughes, a Labour Party MP,

---

94. Which is on 18 July.

played key roles and persuaded a young, energetic Tony Hollingsworth, brimful of ideas and a tremendous negotiator, to produce the 'Free Nelson Mandela Concert'. Jerry Dammers, who composed and sang the hit song 'Free Nelson Mandela', and later, with Dali Tambo, formed the organisation 'Artists Against Apartheid', also played an important role. Tony Hollingsworth convinced the BBC to broadcast the concert live to the USA and the rest of the world, giving it an international dimension. When a committee was set up to organise the event, the ANC asked me to be part of it.

Tony was adamant that the event should be free of politics, which I did not understand and pointed out that the Free Mandela campaign was, in essence, political, but we eventually agreed that we would not have ANC slogans or other openly party political statements. Tony correctly predicted that the BBC would not agree to be the conduit for worldwide broadcasting, unless the event could be described as a celebration of Mandela's 70th birthday, rather than a political event. Margaret Thatcher and other Tories exerted pressure on the BBC to refuse to become involved. In reality, the event itself was an unequivocal political statement, simply because Mandela's freedom was not a personal question but an issue of international political significance.

Previously, Jim Kerr of Simple Minds, at that time one of the most popular music bands in the UK, had agreed to perform. However, Mike Terry informed me that Jim was expressing political reservations about the concert. I went with Mike to see Jim, and after long discussions, persuaded him that the ANC was fully behind the concert and that it would have a powerful impact, not only regarding the release of Mandela and other political prisoners but also on the heightened struggle inside South Africa. At the same time, Hollingsworth was in discussions with Kerr, and to the relief of all of us, he agreed. Once we had Jim, it was possible to convince other artists such as Whitney Houston, Dire Straits (with Eric Clapton), Stevie Wonder and Sting to participate, soon to be joined by Annie Lennox, Sly and Robbie, Joan Armatrading, UB40, the Bee Gees, Peter Gabriel, Tracy Chapman and many others. Gabriel already had a big hit with his song 'Biko', as had Jerry Dammers with his hit Mandela song. The addition of Salif Keita from Mali and Youssou N'Dour from Senegal gave us two great international African stars.

The concert's widespread appeal was extended by the speakers, notably Harry Belafonte, Whoopi Goldberg, Richard Gere, Graham Chapman and Richard Attenborough. Of course, our own Miriam Makeba and Hugh

Masekela performed, and there was a wonderful South African jazz session which included stars like Jonas Gwangwa, Caiphus Semenya, Letta Mbulu, Julian Bahula, Lucky Ranku and Pinise Saul. Mahlathini and the Mahotella Queens were also featured.

Thus, on 11 June, the Wembley Stadium was rocking, not with football supporters but over 100,000 joyous young people enjoying the music and shouting 'Free Mandela!' It was a magnificent event, with an opening speech by Harry Belafonte who demanded that Mandela be released from prison, and many of the musicians and their songs sending the message that racist South Africa should be boycotted. This was beamed to countries all over the world with an audience of hundreds of millions who were won for the cause. In one day, Mandela became perhaps the most famous person in the world.

The credit for one of the world's greatest concerts must go to Tony Hollingsworth, Trevor Huddleston, Mike Terry and all the artists who performed. Wally Serote was also involved in producing that concert and ensuring the participation of South African artists. My personal satisfaction was having played a role as a member of that organising committee.

In April 1990, a second Mandela concert was held with Mandela as the guest of honour and main speaker. He came to London with Winnie Mandela, Ahmed Kathrada, Barbara Hogan and Zwelakhe Sisulu; Murphy Morobe augmented the delegation. That event was another resounding success, with Mandela cheered to the rafters. Meg and I attended with our daughter Amina and her friend Nandipah, daughter of Pallo Jordan and Caroline Roth.

The Mandela delegation stayed in a hotel with strict procedures in place to prevent it from being overrun with people wanting to meet and greet them. Given my work for the ANC, I could enter the hotel and rooms occupied by the delegation and was overjoyed, as that gave me the chance to have long chats with Kathrada, Hogan, Sisulu and Morobe and the opportunity to interact with the Mandelas.

༶

By that time, we, as the ANC, had established good working relations with a few Black MPs, organisations and individuals from the Caribbean community. I was approached by two leading activists from the Notting Hill area who were also involved in the popular Notting Hill Carnival. When they pleaded with me, I was able to arrange for them to meet with the Mandelas and take a photo with them. The Mandelas were really friendly and hospitable, and my friends were over the moon with happiness and couldn't stop thanking me for what they said had been the experience of a lifetime. Everyone the Mandelas met reacted this way, which demonstrated their aura and how much they meant to people from all walks of life.

During my involvement with the AAM, I visited many places in the UK and met some wonderful people. Two who became very close comrades and friends were Mike Terry and Brian Filling. I have previously mentioned Mike, and our friendship lasted for many years, with his visiting us in South Africa after our liberation, right up to his sudden and untimely death in London in 2008 from a heart attack. But he needs elaboration.

Mike Terry studied physics at Birmingham University, where he was elected president of the student union in 1969 and joined demonstrations against the Springbok rugby tour. He became national secretary of the NUS and was elected to the Executive Committee of the AAM. In 1972 the younger members of the AAM's EC organised to get Mike elected as the AAM's Vice Chair, replacing the existing Vice Chair, Labour MP Joan Lestor, who had the support of the older members of the committee. The incident was part of the upsurge of youth and student activism which favoured direct action over parliamentary lobbying. Joan Lestor was in fact a dedicated anti-apartheid campaigner, who was quickly appointed as one of the AAM's Vice-Presidents. Three years later in 1975, Mike became the Executive Secretary of the AAM.

With Mike at the helm, the movement grew in strength, emphasising the military, sporting, political and economic isolation of the racist regime and support for the ANC and freedom for political prisoners. The membership grew from 2,500 in 1984 to 20,000 in 1989, with 1,300 affiliated organisations. After the two Wembley concerts, the release of Mandela and the victory of the ANC, Mike was instrumental in setting up Action for Southern Africa (ACTSA), as AAM members expressed a wish to continue to play a constructive role in the future of Southern Africa. He then decided that it was time for him to indulge in his passion for teaching, which was his main focus for the rest of his life. In 2001, he was awarded an Order of the British Empire (OBE) for his work in the AAM.

Brian, whom I met in London early in my exile years, had been active in the Anti-Apartheid Movement since the early 1960s. We also knew him and his wife Mary through the Straight Left group of the CPGB. He founded the

Scottish AAM in 1976 and chaired it until 1994. He also served on the Executive Committee of ACTSA until 2011 and is now the Honorary Consul for South Africa in Scotland. In lighter moments, I would call him the Honourable Member for Johannesburg South, reminding him of the Glasgow event. He was awarded the National Order of the Companions of O. R. Tambo in Silver in 2012 for outstanding solidarity work. That is the highest honour bestowed on non-South Africans by the Republic of South Africa. The same Order in Gold can only be awarded to a Head of State.

I am still in awe of the many thousands who refused to buy South African products in supermarkets and who came out to attend meetings, rallies and demonstrations, come rain, shine or snow. They gave their time, energy, money and commitment voluntarily and with good humour. We owe those hundreds of thousands our deep gratitude and appreciation.

Here, I would like to say a few words about Christabel Gurney.

Christabel was a member of the CPGB, and, like many of our friends was opposed to the Eurocommunist line adopted by the Party. She was Treasurer of the Eurocommunist-dominated Ladbroke Grove branch. In the mid-1980s, the divisions in the CPGB became very unpleasant and Christabel was officially suspended from holding office. However, she remains close friends with those who shared her political views, and these friendships continue to this day.

From 1969 to 1980, Christabel edited the *Anti-Apartheid News*, did the layout, collected the long galley, Letraset the headings and organised the whole printing process (so much more work in those days than now) – all as a volunteer without pay. The printing was done by Jim Nichol at Feb Ed, the printing press of the Socialist Workers' Party. Christabel was Secretary of the Dambusters Mobilising Committee, which gave rise to the campaign to persuade Barclays Bank to pull out of South Africa, and also Secretary of the Notting Hill Anti-Apartheid Group.

In 1973, Christabel was briefly employed full-time with a salary by the AAM but had to give up that job when her baby Sam was born the following year. Sam's father is my brother Aziz, and Meg and I and the rest of the Pahad family have always been close to Sam and Christabel. Sam is now married to Eva, and they have a delightful daughter, Bethan. He is now Regional Secretary for London, East and South-East England for the Trade Union Congress. The Gurneys and the Pahads continue to get together for at least one visit a year.

When the AAM closed its doors and created ACTSA, it also set up a voluntary archives committee with Mike Terry as secretary and Bob Hughes as chair. When Mike died, Christabel took over as secretary. She is a writer and historian and still plays an active role as an archivist of the AAM. In the 2014 Birthday Honours List, she received an OBE 'for political service, particularly to Human Rights'. Christabel was awarded The Order of the Companions of O. R. Tambo in 2023.

In concluding this reflection on the AAM, I shall quote from Christabel's article, 'In the Heart of the Beast: the British Anti-Apartheid Movement, 1959–1994', to which I referred earlier:

> In the 1980s, the AAM grew into a movement which transcended party politics and won support across wide sections of British society. From being a small pressure group on the fringes of British politics, it built a coalition of political parties, trade unions, local authorities and churches behind the demand for the isolation of apartheid and support for the democratic forces in South Africa. At the same time, it reached out to people who had no other political or organisational involvement but who joined in its campaigns in a multitude of ways, from joining a demonstration to wearing an anti-apartheid T-shirt or badge. ...
>
> The AAM's achievement in the 1980s was to find forms of expression that enabled people who would never have become involved in a formal political organisation to give voice to their gut feeling that apartheid was wrong.
>
> Apartheid became a burning issue in every sphere of public life. The AAM turned the multiplicity of British links with South Africa into a weapon against apartheid by challenging them at every level. Its campaigns were framed in such a way that everyone was faced with choices in their personal, social and working lives: whether to buy South African oranges, bank with Barclays, fill up with petrol at a Shell garage, question their pension fund's investment policy or challenge their employer's use of contractors with interests in South Africa.[95]

Anti-Apartheid Movements in many countries gave tremendous support to

---
95. *The Road to Democracy in South Africa, Vol. 3*, Part 1, Chapter 4, p. 350.

our struggle for freedom and democracy, with the movements particularly powerful and effective in the Nordic countries, Holland, Ireland, Italy, France and Portugal. I have not been closely involved in those, so I shall not attempt to give the history of their efforts and achievements here but leave that to those who know their stories better.

I do, however, want to mention the support we received from Italy, where we have a strong connection over many years with Reggio Emilia.

Italy and the city of Reggio Emilia

In recognising the role played by this medium-sized Italian city, we have to note the sterling part played by Anthony Mongalo, the ANC's representative in Italy, in developing the enduring relationship between Reggio Emilia and the party. Reggio Emilia is in the Emilia Romagna province, which, together with Tuscany, Marche and Umbria, forms part of Italy's 'red belt'. The region was a stronghold of the Italian Communist Party (*Partito Comunista Italiano*: PCI) from 1945 to 1989 and subsequently of left-wing social democrats.

Reggio Emilia is also where a liberating, original approach to early childhood learning and development originated. The Reggio Emilia approach empowers children to explore the world and express themselves in various ways. It also adapts to the local environment and each child's particular strengths and weaknesses, and the children participate in the learning process and help to create it, rather than being expected to respond to directions given by a teacher. Two of our grandchildren attend a Reggio Emilia school (Small World) in Johannesburg, where their mother, our daughter-in-law Aimee, is a teacher. Incidentally, that part of Italy is also famous for producing Parmigiano Reggiano and balsamic vinegar as well as communists – so it clearly knows what it is doing.

Reggio Emilia had established close fraternal relations with FRELIMO, the national liberation movement of Mozambique, and its leader, Samora Machel. When Mozambique gained its independence, Machel requested the city authorities to intensify their solidarity with the ANC. In 1976, Tambo, Mongalo and Giuseppe Soncini, who was Councillor for International Relations of the Municipality of Reggio Emilia and a member of the PCI, agreed on an action plan which included the signing of an agreement between that city and the ANC. On 26 June 1977, Oliver Tambo signed the historic Solidarity Pact in the presence of José Luis Cabaco, a Minister from Mozambique. Reggio Emilia invented this unusual but innovative agreement, which allowed the city to formally recognise the ANC as a movement committed to the struggle for a free and democratic South Africa.

In December 1977, the UN Centre Against Apartheid published the text of the Pact of Solidarity with an introduction by Leslie O. Harriman, Chairman of the Special Committee Against Apartheid. In 1978, the International Anti-Apartheid Year,[96] Reggio Emilia hosted the National Conference of Solidarity for the Peoples of Southern Africa Against Colonialism, Racism and Apartheid. The speeches made by Oliver Tambo and Sam Nujoma laid the foundation for organising Italian solidarity, and the city of Reggio Emilia was appointed to chair the National Solidarity Committee. Following that conference, the two African leaders were received in Rome by the President of the Republic, Sandro Pertini, and Pope John Paul II.

In the same period, the city of Reggio Emilia began publishing an Italian edition of the ANC magazine *Sechaba*, and 5,000 copies of that and the English edition were distributed throughout Italy until the end of 1984. Oliver Tambo considered the Italian version of *Sechaba* to be of particular importance:

> It ensured an ideal and operational link between the most diverse forces in Italy that wanted to do something for the people of Southern Africa. It put [people] in contact with each other, stimulated new [forces] and finally became the promoter and organiser of more demanding initiatives.

Reggio Emilia also published Nelson Mandela's *The Struggle Is My Life* in the Italian language in 1980. It had not previously been available in Italian.

During those years, Giuseppe Soncini led the National Committee for the Fight Against Apartheid, coordinating internationally important initiatives. In 1980, the first Ship of Solidarity, named *Amanda*, left Genoa with a cargo of aid for the ANC headquarters in Lusaka and educational materials for the Solomon Mahlangu Freedom College. In 1983, Soncini organised the Second National Conference Against Apartheid in Rome, where the City Council bestowed honorary citizenship on Nelson Mandela.[97] And in 1984, the second Solidarity Ship, *Rea Silvia*, sailed from Livorno to support cooperation projects in South Africa.

Another historic event was the three-day hosting of a meeting of various representatives of the ANC who discussed the organisation of international

---
97. Available at https://studylib.net/doc/9007294/office-translation-from-italian-to-english-quote
96. It began on 21 March of that year.

solidarity. The meeting was also attended by Secretary-General Alfred Nzo, Thomas Nkobi (treasurer), Josiah Jele (Director of International Affairs) and Johnny Makhatini (Deputy Director of International Affairs and Permanent Representative to the UN).

Over the years, Reggio Emilia has hosted, cared for and welcomed numerous members of the African National Congress passing through Italy, including representatives from ANC missions such as Ruth Mompati (United Kingdom), Neo Mnumzana (France), Godfrey Motsepe (Benelux), Tony Seedat (Federal Republic of Germany), Anthony Mongalo (German Democratic Republic), Yusuf (JoJo) Saloojee (Canada), Max Moabi (World Peace Council), M. D. Naidoo (International Committee for Solidarity with the Peoples of Southern Africa), Thami Sindelo (Italy) and Frene Ginwala (London Research Department).

In 1985, during the Second National Consultative Conference of the African National Congress held in Kabwe, Zambia, the city of Reggio Emilia was declared 'an established force against the apartheid regime', the only city in the world mentioned. On 24 October 1987, the Reggio Emilia City Council approved two honorary citizenships for Albertina Sisulu and Desmond Tutu and the naming of two city streets after Albert Luthuli and the Martyrs of Soweto.

Reggio Emilia's commitment was also acknowledged by the ANC after the release of Nelson Mandela, when the city's mayor was invited to and participated in the first International Solidarity Conference held in Johannesburg in 1993 and again in May 1994. Reggio Emilia was also the only European city invited to the celebrations of Mandela's inauguration as the first democratically elected president of the new South Africa.

The untiring work of Giuseppe Soncini and Anthony Mongalo (who was replaced in the Italian mission first by Thami Sindelo, then by Benny Nato and finally by Stephen Gawe) and the relationship between Reggio Emilia and the African National Congress was lauded by its leader Oliver Tambo. In 1978, during the National Conference at Reggio Emilia, he said:

> The people of Reggio Emilia have a heroic past of struggle against foreign domination and fascism [and] for freedom, democracy and social progress. They have made an extraordinary contribution to the victory of FRELIMO and the fall of the Portuguese government. The ANC is honoured to embrace the City of Reggio Emilia, its employees, young people and intellectuals, as comrades in the

struggle of the people of South Africa [and] allies in the cause of justice.[98]

In 1982, after the conference in Rome, Oliver Tambo sent a thank you message to the city of Reggio Emilia:

> A big river always comes from a smaller source. The great wave of solidarity with our struggle which now flows in all of Italy has its source in Reggio Emilia. This great wave passes through Reggio Emilia. We came to Rome, we have witnessed the great success of the Conference, we have seen how the weight of the Conference is all on your shoulders, and we know that you work every day for our cause, carrying out the day-to-day commitment to our struggle for southern Africa. Time passes, but these things are not forgotten ... On behalf of myself and Comrade Sam Nujoma and the people that we represent, we express heartfelt thanks, because you feel like real friends who believe in our struggle and the objectives that we want to achieve.[99]

In 1983, upon a suggestion from Tambo, Armando Giuffredi, an artist from Reggio Emilia, designed and produced the Isitwalandwe medal, which is the highest honour awarded by the ANC.

Tambo personally invited Giuseppe Soncini to participate in the historic conference in Arusha, Tanzania, which took place from 1–4 December 1987 in recognition of Soncini's enormous contribution to building the Anti-Apartheid Movement in Italy.

Over the years, Tambo visited Reggio Emilia several times, the last being in 1989, two years before Giuseppe Soncini's sudden death. A few weeks before Tambo's death in 1993, he met representatives of the city on the sidelines of the International Solidarity Conference and left a video message in which he underlined the role of Reggio Emilia: 'We can never thank you enough, but we promise that we will never forget you.'

During the run-up to South Africa's first democratic elections, Stavros Nicolaou, an internationalist and successful businessman of Greek-Cypriot origin, approached the ANC with a proposal to form an organisation of South African people whose origins were Hellenic (Greek or Cypriot), Italian or Portuguese to provide electoral support to the ANC. He discussed this

---

98. *The Road to Democracy in South Africa*, Vol. 3, Part 1, Chapter 4, p. 350.
99. Ibid

with Thabo Mbeki, Aziz, Gill Marcus and me, and his offer from the Hellenic, Italian and Portuguese Alliance of South Africa (HIP), of which he is chair, was accepted. I have become close to Stavros over the years, and the HIP has given consistent support to the ANC. The leader of the Italian section of the HIP, Maurizio Mariano, is also one of the organisation's founders and a childhood friend of Stavros. Maurizio also continues to provide tireless assistance to the ANC.

Since that time, I have grown to know Maurizio Mariano personally. He is a gregarious, generous and engaging lawyer, and we have become firm friends, meeting regularly. Maurizio is the only South African of Italian heritage to have been bestowed both honours of Knight Commander of the Order of Merit of the Italian Republic (in 2017) and Grand Officer of the Order of the Star of Italian Solidarity (in 2001) by the President of the Republic of Italy.

In 2012, during the celebrations of the ANC Centenary, the Italian section of the HIP Alliance and the City of Reggio Emilia worked together on a project to create an exhibition dedicated to the friendship between Reggio Emilia and the ANC. Maurizio was instrumental in arranging for Deputy President Kgalema Motlanthe to visit Reggio Emilia in October of that year, where he officially opened the exhibition.

Also in 2012, the Italian section of the HIP invited the Mayor of Reggio Emilia, Graziano Delrio, and a delegation to South Africa. During this visit, the same exhibition that had been shown in Reggio Emilia was set up in the Gauteng Legislature and was opened in Johannesburg by David Makhura (then Premier of Gauteng), Baleka Mbete and Graziano Delrio. I was asked to be the main speaker.

That incredible story of friendship and solidarity continues, and in 2013, Reggio Emilia named a park after O. R. Tambo in the presence of his daughter, Ambassador Nomatemba Tambo, and Ambassador Anthony Mongalo, a pillar of the liberation struggle. On 27 April of the same year, Giuseppe Soncini was awarded the Order of the Companions of Oliver Tambo in Silver. In April 2015, the city inaugurated Nelson Mandela Park in the presence of Mandela's widow Graça Machel.

Today in the park dedicated to Oliver Tambo, a few metres away from each other, stand a statue of O. R. waving the Freedom Charter and a monument dedicated to Giuseppe Soncini, two men who united the people of South Africa and the people of Reggio Emilia forever.

India – The Jewel in the Crown

I grew up in a home and political environment in which India held a prominent place. As detailed in Chapter 1, my family's ancestral home village is Kholvad, just outside Surat, a bustling port and commercial city in the state of Gujarat. Given that both my parents and many of my relatives had family and friends living there, Kholvad was always a familiar topic for discussion. Yusuf Dadoo and my father were also leaders of the Kholvad community organisation in South Africa. Owing to the financial contributions of Kholvadians in this country, Kholvad was one of the first villages in India to have access to electricity, and a school and madressa were opened which catered for students from the surrounding areas. My mother frequently spoke about her father, stepmother and siblings living there and the lovely house they occupied. Kholvad was a foreign place, far from Johannesburg, but it did stir interest in me, and I wondered if I would ever see it or my relatives there. For many years, I was fascinated by India and its leaders, such as Mahatma Gandhi and Jawaharlal Nehru.

Thus, when the opportunity arose in 1969 to go to India to do research for my PhD thesis, I was excited. The suggestion was first made by Professor Louw, Dean of the School of Oriental and African Studies at Sussex University. He also raised some money for the air-fares and advised me that on arrival at the National Archives of India (NAI) in Delhi, I should approach Miss Keshwani, a deputy director there. It was also most fortunate for me that Alfred Nzo and Molvi Cachalia were the representatives of the ANC Asian mission in Delhi.

Molvi and his wife Miriam had a two-bedroom apartment at South Extension, about ten to fifteen kilometres from the city centre, and had indicated that I was most welcome to live with them. Later, their grandson Ahmed joined them, and we were like a family. Miriambhai, as I called her, looked after me as a son. She always heated water for the morning bath, and every evening there was a lovely home-cooked meal.

On my first day at the NAI, I introduced myself to Miss Keshwani and tried to understand how the records were catalogued and kept. I also immediately struck up a friendship with someone referred to as a 'peon', one of the lowest-ranking officials working there, whose job was to bring you the documents you needed, which had to be requested on a special form. Not knowing where to start, I decided to look at the section under 'P&J' (Politics and Judiciary), but none of those thick volumes had anything on South Africa. I was most discouraged and sat there holding my face in my hands.

The worker noticed and asked 'What is the matter?' I explained my predicament and, without hesitation, he said 'Mr Pahad, you should look at 'EH&L' (Education, Health and Land) and went and brought me a number of large volumes. To my great delight, they contained a lot of useful information on South Africa. I thanked him and told him how grateful I was.

At the NAI, they had a little place at the back of the building where you could have tea, and many of the archivists frequented it. As I was talking to one of them, I boasted about realising I needed to focus my research on EH&L (missing out the role of the peon). To my surprise and distress, he explained to me that if I wanted to use EH&L, I would have to once more obtain permission. All of my pleas about having to finish in six months made no impression. Totally distressed, I went back to my seat and once more sat with my head in my hands.

Again, the peon came to my rescue, saying that, since Miss Keshwani had taken a liking to me, I should go to her office and ask her to help me. So I went to see her without an appointment and explained my plight. I had already told her about my work in the ANC and how I was yearning to work for it full-time. As we were speaking, the archivist who had told me to apply for permission came into her office but tried to beat a hasty retreat when he saw me. I immediately said, 'That is him!' She asked him to what regulation he was referring, but there was none. She also told him that both I and Frene Ginwala, who was also doing research for her PhD, had special permission to go to the Department of Foreign Affairs and study documents beyond the stipulated thirty-year period. That was my first salutary lesson in India: don't show off, beware of bureaucratic persons, and remember there are wonderful people – like the peon and the deputy director.

The amount of relevant material was vast, even excluding material on Gandhi and South Africa, which I paid to get typed. There was no way I could plough through that material in six months, so back I went to Keshwani, asking for permission to get the material on microfilm. She was most sympathetic and explained that they only had one machine and already faced a backlog of requests from scholars from the USA, Australia and the UK, including Professor Louw. I pleaded and explained my position regarding time frames and my determination to work for the movement. She then suggested I go to the director's office and explain my predicament and predicted that he would repeat what she had just said about the backlog. She followed that with the idea that I undertake a Gandhian form of resistance, a *gerou* or sit-in, in his office. And that is what happened. I did just that for a few hours until he asked Keshwani for help. Then out she came and, after rebuking me for violating the director's office, suggested that, owing to my special circumstances, my request be prioritised. To my great relief, he agreed, and on the day of my departure for London, I collected my last reel. There were twenty reels which came to about 10,000 pages. What a lesson that was in human kindness and behaviour – from the lowest-ranked worker to the deputy director.

On that first visit, I had other experiences that live on in my memory. One was a visit to Mumbai (Bombay) at the request of Molvi Cachalia to meet South African students studying there and look at potential recruits for the ANC underground. I stayed with a student called Jeeva, and after many meetings, decided to recommend him and M. H. Moola, who was studying dentistry. My suggestion was accepted and both were recruited. Moola became a good friend of mine and Aziz and later assumed the post of Dean of the Dental School at the University of the Western Cape (UWC).

The second was my visit to Kholvad, where my grandparents (my mother's parents, the Tilly family) had a lovely home overlooking the Tapi River and were most welcoming. Their four sons, Ebrahim, Suleiman, Essop and Ismail, and their daughter Zohra were also very friendly and helpful.

One notable episode involves my youngest uncle, Ismail, who was then a teenager. Every morning, he would take me around the village, and when I enquired why we were not going in a certain direction, he merely shrugged and said, 'But the Hindus live there.' My indignation on hearing that was palpable, and I gave him a real dressing down. He cried and pleaded that I should not say anything to his father, as Papa had warned them that my mother had told him I was a communist and they must be careful about what they said and did in my presence. That was an eye-opener regarding Muslim-Hindu relations in India, and other incidents in Kholvad attested to that.

I enjoyed visiting the village and seeing my grandparents and other relatives and was surprised at how much some of those residents knew about Kholvadians in Johannesburg. They could describe in detail what our places of residence looked like, who owned which businesses and other details I was unaware of.

A third memorable experience was my visit to Kolkata (Calcutta), a politically vibrant and progressive city with two leading communist parties, both very active: the Communist Party of India (CPI), which had always been a staunch ally of the Soviet Union, and the Communist Party of India

(Marxist) (CPI(M). Indeed, the CPI(M), which had split from the CPI at the height of the Sino-Soviet conflict, became the governing party there for at least twenty years. I spent a week there at the home of Chinmohan Sehanavis and his wife Uma, two intellectuals with a love and deep understanding of Bengali culture and literature. Chinmohan had joined the CPI in 1941 and been imprisoned and participated in an eight-week hunger strike when the party was outlawed. He was a prolific writer of books and journal articles in Bengali and English and covered many topics, including Rabindranath Tagore, the links between the Soviet Union and India, Lenin, the Russian Revolution and the history of the CPI. I learned so much from my discussions with them.

However, one incident stands out. Kolkata was a city in which you had street traders occupying pavements and street children using the gutters as toilets. In addition, my visit coincided with a strike, and at a distance, what looked like little huts, on closer inspection, turned out to be mountainous piles of garbage. It was hard to bear the awful scenes and disgusting stench. There were many other weird and upsetting sights and experiences during that first visit, and I began to understand that to really know and appreciate India in all its diversity, positive and negative, one must see it as a continent, not a country.

Now for a bit of background on the Indian National Congress (INC).

On 28 December 1885, the INC was founded in Bombay. It was the first national liberation movement to cover the vast Indian landscape, and it is interesting that a white civil servant, A. O. Hume, was one of its founders. From its early years, after Gandhi returned to India to lead the INC and the struggle for independence, the INC supported the Congress Movement in South Africa and grew from strength to strength. We can say with confidence that the bilateral relations between the Congress Movements of South Africa and India comprise the longest sustained and enduring relationship between two parties in the history of the anti-colonial, anti-imperialist and anti-racist struggles in the world.

Under the leadership of the INC, India was the world's first country to impose a trade embargo on racist South Africa in 1946 at some economic cost. Since then, India and the INC imposed economic, trade, financial and sporting sanctions on racist South Africa. India was also the first country to raise the South African issue at the United Nations, singling out its treatment of people of Indian origin in South Africa, a move that marked the beginning of UN involvement against the racist apartheid regime.

In 1947, India became one of the first British colonies to win independence, and the jewel in the crown of British colonialism and imperialism was lost forever, putting paid to the boast that the sun never sets on the British Empire.

In 1967, following discussions between the INC and the ANC, and with the full support of Prime Minister Indira Gandhi, the first Asian mission of the ANC was opened with Alfred Nzo and Molvi Cachalia as its first two representatives. They were followed by, amongst others, Mendi Msimang, Agnes Msimang, Moosa (Mosie) Moolla, and Sidney Molefe.

The All India Peace and Solidarity Organisation (AIPSO) played a critical role in mobilising support for solidarity and assistance for the ANC, with mammoth input from members of the CPI. From my first visit, I worked with some of them and addressed meetings organised by AIPSO in various parts of the country. Molvi, and later other representatives of the ANC, had a wonderfully warm and fraternal relationship with that organisation. In 1985, with the full suppport of Rajiv Gandhi, Anand Sharma, then a young INC MP, founded a massive anti-apartheid movement based in the Indian Youth Congress. Since then, Anand, who is married to South African Zenobia Asvat, has played and continues to play a leading role in growing and cementing the ties that bind the INC and ANC together, as well as the peoples of the two sister countries. When Mandela visited India in 1990, Rajiv Gandhi's government donated US$5 million and 5,200 million rupees worth of material assistance to the ANC. My friendship with Anand is solid and binding, and whenever I visit India, we always spend time together. Likewise, he always arranges to meet me when visiting South Africa, and we have spent many happy times together.

Mandela and other ANC leaders have received numerous rewards from academic and other institutions in India, and I was most pleased to accompany Thabo Mbeki to Delhi when he received an honorary doctorate from the Jawaharlal Nehru University in December 1996. On that visit, the Prime Minister of India accepted a proposal from Mbeki that the relationship between the two countries be raised to a 'strategic' level, a first for both sides.

Since 1969, I have made many official trips to India as minister or deputy minister to attend meetings and conferences such as the Congresses of the CPI and CPI(M). I shall mention a few below.

At a time when Vajpayee of the right-wing BJP was prime minister, I was asked by President Mbeki to make a visit to see him as Minister in the

Presidency. My first response was to ask why, since I never ask to meet presidents or prime ministers, as I know from experience how busy they are. Mbeki's reply was that he had spoken to the PM, and I was to brief him on the plans to form IBSA (India, Brazil, South Africa) to consolidate our relationship and lay the basis for a more powerful movement representing the interests of what was called the 'Third World'. Joel Netshitenzhe, then CEO of the Government Communication Information System (GCIS), was part of that delegation and joined me at the meeting with the PM. When we got to Vajpayee's office, he opened by saying that he had spoken with Mbeki and agreed with the founding of IBSA.

Since there was now nothing to discuss, I requested that Vajpayee ask all his officials to leave, as I wished to raise a delicate matter. Joel stayed behind. I then brought up the issue of bilateral relations between the BJP and the ANC, a topic I had cleared with Mbeki before leaving, pointing out that Vajpayee was well aware of the enduring bilateral ties between the INC and the ANC and that that would not change. But since the ANC does not elect the PM and the Government of India, for that is the sole prerogative of the people of India, and since the governing party of India was the BJP, our government-to-government relations would be strengthened by party-to-party relations. He agreed and set up a meeting with the leaders of the BJP at their headquarters. At that meeting, it was decided that the BJP would send an official delegation to meet the ANC to confirm the relationship. For reasons unknown to me, this never happened, and the idea just faded away. I also had to brief Anand Sharma and a few leaders of the INC about our proposal to the PM. They were reluctant to agree but understood its importance for relations between our two countries. I assured them that our partner of first choice would remain the INC.

Another visit was to attend a conference organised by the CPI(M) in Kolkata in 1993, soon after the assassination of Chris Hani and before our first democratic election. The conference was interesting, and my discussions were fruitful; however, the icing on the cake was when they took me and a few other international delegates on a trip to various parts of West Bengal, including the rural areas. The power, reach and influence of that party on the people of West Bengal was most impressive. Wherever we went, even to the most remote areas, members of the CPI(M) would come out in their hundreds and shout with gusto and enthusiasm, 'Long live Chris Hani, long live! Long live Chris Hani, long live!' I must say, I was taken aback. Given the circumstances of Chris's assassination, it was not surprising that, of all those who spoke at those meetings, I received the loudest cheers and longest ovations. The whole visit was a revelation, showing how, with meagre resources but deep passion and commitment, one can mobilise thousands, if not millions, of people.

The most memorable meeting I addressed in India was in Kolkata. The AIPSO had organised a mass rally against apartheid and racism in support of the ANC with Krishna Menon as the main speaker. He was a legendary freedom fighter, former Minister of Defence and a friend of Dr Dadoo since the 1930s. A million people attended that rally. Mosie Moolla told me that a few years later, he also addressed a similar rally of a million people in Kolkata.

Since my first visit to Kolkata in 1969, I have retained a deep love of the CPI, CPI(M) and other progressive forces in that part of India. When I became Minister in the Office of the Presidency, I was happy to arrange a visit by Jyoti Basu, leader of the CPI(M) and former Chief Minister of West Bengal. In one of our meetings, he mentioned that the one country he wished to visit was democratic South Africa. After discussions, and with the agreement of President Mbeki, I invited him as a Cabinet Minister so he would be received with the appropriate protocol. Thereafter, on the few occasions I had the pleasure and honour of meeting him, he remembered his visit and thanked me graciously. I should add that Basu was a legendary figure in India, an immensely popular politician across party lines, a towering intellectual, a committed internationalist and a warm and generous host.

The third event I shall highlight is the symposium held in Delhi in November 2014 to launch a year-long commemoration of one of the greatest leaders in the history of the world, Jawaharlal Nehru. It was organised by the INC, and the invitations were sent out in the name of Sonia Gandhi. Several other ANC leaders, such as Ahmed Kathrada, Barbara Hogan, Jessie Duarte and Ebrahim Ebrahim, also attended that symposium. I was asked to prepare a presentation and chair one of the important sessions. Anand Sharma, who was one of the organisers, later edited a book entitled *Remembering Jawaharlal Nehru*, which includes contributions from many renowned Indian and international figures. I am happy that he included my speech, in which I said:

> Jawaharlal Nehru is one of the most outstanding anti-colonial anti-imperialist freedom fighters in history. His extraordinary

---
100. Anand Sharma (ed.) *Remembering Jawaharlal Nehru* (New Delhi, India: Academic Foundation, 2016).

contribution to the struggle for peace, democracy, justice, freedom and human rights for people across the globe should never be forgotten. Nehru, a profound thinker and great intellectual, had an amazing knowledge and understanding of world history and socio-economic development from the 1930s.[100]

In 2005, I made at least three or four trips to India in connection with our attempts to resuscitate arms sales to that country. At that time, the Government of India had suspended arms trade with us, as they were interested in obtaining information about corrupt arms deals concluded by a middleman from England employed by Armscor. Alec Erwin was then Minister of Trade and Industry, but even with his intervention, Armscor categorically refused to supply the information required. I made trips to engage Sonia Gandhi, leader of the INC, Anand Sharma and other leaders of government, but we were unable to provide satisfactory responses to their questions, which left a bitter taste, and the arms trade remained suspended. My cabinet colleagues had a running joke: 'Cde Pahad spends more time in India than in South Africa. Perhaps he should join the Indian Cabinet.'

In addition to those official visits, Meg and I took a holiday to India in 1980, when Amina was only a few months old, leaving her with Meg's parents. It was a memorable visit, including a trip to Kholvad. But somehow, Meg had left her handbag in the waiting lounge at the Mumbai airport with our passports, air tickets and money in it. Once more, I was astounded by India. We contacted my father, who went to the airport and reported the loss, and the helpful officials in Bangalore also reported it. We were thrilled and amazed when my father phoned to say that a worker had found the bag and handed it in, and nothing had been touched.

Kholvad was a pleasant surprise for Meg because she hadn't realised that the people would be so friendly or that the old houses the Muslim merchants and traders had built there were so beautiful. Although rather run down and lacking modern facilities, such as Western toilets and bathrooms, they were most elegant and well designed. Each was built around a big courtyard with plenty of covered seating areas and a few large swing seats for gentle motion. The front entrances from the street were also covered, with the roofs supported by stone pillars, and the façades included decorative stone carvings. But the greatest pleasure was being escorted around the main part of the village by the school teacher and a small crowd of interested people and having the family homes of so many of our friends in South Africa proudly pointed out: Dadoo, Timol, Saloojee, Kaka, Pochee, Dadabhay, Bhyat, Tilly and Pahad. At that time, they also kept photos of relatives living in the diaspora (later, this was considered by some to be a form of idolatry). Everyone was so anxious to help and please us; it was most heart-warming. And they cooked the very best, most special food for every meal.

From December 2003 to January 2004, Meg and I took Amina and Govan with us on a trip to India. In addition to the usual tourist sites such as the Taj Mahal, we visited Anand Sharma in his home and then went to Kholvad to visit my relatives. Both children enjoyed the visit, and their cousins went out of their way to make them feel at home and took them around on their motorcycles to see some places around the Kholvad area. We were also shown around the pleasant mosque overlooking the river and once again went to my mother's grave. The children were fascinated to see the ancestral village of so many people they knew.

Because of the key role played in the ANC and SACP by people such as Dr Dadoo, my father and others from that village, and the brutal murders by the security police of Suliman (Babla) Saloojee (1964) and Ahmed Timol (1971), the village of Kholvad is well-known to South African freedom fighters. When Ronnie Kasrils was visiting India as Deputy Minister of Defence, he was asked by his counterpart if there was anywhere in particular that interested him in India. Ronnie replied that he would like to know more about Kholvad. To his astonishment, they had never heard of it and brought out a map and searched for it, eventually finding a tiny spot, a place of no consequence to them, with one little river. Ronnie's response was, as usual, quick and witty: 'It may be a little river for you, but it produced one of the biggest rivers in South Africa.'

My last trip to India was in January 2015 to receive an award from that country. I agreed to go and asked Menzi Mbatha, my former son-in-law, to accompany me. Our visit and travel arrangements were made by Randhir Jaiswal, Consul General of India in South Africa at the time. He is a wonderful, generous man, very experienced and full of the most interesting tales of the history of India and remains for me one of the finest representatives of the Government of India in South Africa. His wife, Dr Abha Jaiswal, a public health specialist, is also a marvellous person. We had a deep friendship and occasionally hosted each other. They had been stationed in Cuba, which they adored, and Abha had mastered the cooking of a number of her favourite Cuban dishes, amongst which was my favourite: Cuban black beans.

On the flight to India on Qatar Airlines, I had a serious mishap when my passport fell out of my jacket and lodged down the side of my seat. The only way the staff could retrieve it was to remove the seat, after which the passport was utterly mangled and no longer an acceptable proof of identity. At the passport office in Qatar, the official was friendly and allowed me to proceed. In the meanwhile, Randhir had been in contact with the airports in Delhi and Gujarat, and they allowed me to enter without any difficulties. Problems arose later in Doha when an unfriendly passport official was reluctant to accept my passport. However, after an overnight stay, they allowed me to continue my journey to South Africa.

On 9 January 2015, President of India, Praneed Mukherjee, conferred on me and others the Pravasi Samman Award, given to people of Indian descent for 'promoting the honour and prestige of India and fostering the interests of overseas Indians', in Gandhinagar in the state of Gujarat. Amongst the many awardees was my good friend Donald Ramotar, then-President of Guyana. Given his high position, he was treated as a special guest, but he still made time to see me. Another special guest was Maite Nkoana-Mashabane, then-Minister of International Relations and Cooperation of South Africa. Unfortunately, she was unfriendly. I guess she was still fighting the battle of Polokwane, where Zuma was elected President of the ANC. As a result of her behaviour, I did not raise my passport problem.

Since we were in the state of Gujarat, I wanted to visit my mother's grave, as this was likely to be my last opportunity to do so. Also, Menzi had not met my relatives in India, so I expressed a wish to visit Kholvad. Randhir was most helpful and arranged for a car and a driver to take us there. My guide was a middle-aged man who was very friendly, but he was unable to travel with us, so he arranged for his son to come along. It took us nearly seven hours to reach Kholvad. After a lovely visit, which Menzi thoroughly enjoyed, we had to return to Gandhinagar, which took about nine hours because of rush hour traffic, and we arrived late at night, exhausted. However, the visit had been well worth the journey.

When we were at the airport in Gandhinagar for our departure, Menzi realised that he had forgotten his expensive watch in the hotel room. The chances of getting it back were slim, but I phoned my guide and the hotel to alert them. The guide went immediately to the hotel and, to Menzi's great relief, informed him that the watch was in his safekeeping. Once more, Randhir offered to assist and arranged for the watch to be taken to Delhi and from there to Johannesburg.

Essop Pahad in 1964 – 'non-whites' were not allowed to attend the whites-only graduation ceremonies at Wits University so the family arranged for 'fake' graduation photos for Essop and Aziz. They were both also banned at the time.

Standing: Nassim, Zuneid, Essop, and Aziz. Seated: Ismail, Goolam holding Shehnaaaz, Amina, Ruki and Yasmin in front

Leaders of the Congress Alliance: Yusuf Cachalia, D U Mistry, Dan Tloome, Goolam Pahad, O R Tambo, David Bopape and Molvi Cachalia on the roof of Kholvad House.

Above: In 1979, Essop and Meg visited the Tilly family in Kholvad. To the left of Essop (white beard) is Ebrahim and slightly in front of Essop is Suleiman.

Right: Visiting with more members of the extended family.

Below: Visiting the grave of his mother

Dynamos Officials: Extreme left: Goolam Cajee, Extreme right Hamid Sarang.
Dynamos Team: Back row: Archie Essack, Kimaal Nanabhai, Haroon (Froggie) Patel, Abdul Samed Allie (Skelly), Seaun (Policeman), Essop Pahad; Middle: Aboobaker Saloojee (Buks), Ismail Pahad, Cas Saloojee (Captain), Joe Isaacs Bhayet; Front: Aziz Pahad

The famous Dynamos team badge which was designed by Ahmed 'Archie Boy' Bhayet

Essop Pahad and Abubaker Saloojee in foreground, playing for Dynamos on the 'Chinese Ground'

Passive Resistance Campaign, 1946. Centre: Zainab Asvat, right: Amina Pahad

Demonstration outside the Drill Hall, Johannesburg, on opening of the Treason Trial in 1956. Essop is the tall one at the back

Essop and Meg's wedding in 1971. Left to right: Jim Shorrock, Meg's dad, Sobizana Mngqikana, Vivian Rama, Mary Shorrock, Aziz Pahad, Dr Dadoo
Below: It was a double wedding with Aziz and Gloria who were also married at the same time. Sobizana Mngqikana, Yusuf (Charles) Saloojee, Dr Dadoo, Meg and Essop

Top: L to R: Jenny Pochee; Jill and Geoffrey Faux; Yusuf Saloojee; Peter Lawrence; Rhiannon and Mel Gooding; Ismail Pahad; Mohammad Timol. Middle: Winnie Dadoo, Marianne and Michael Shorrock; Next: Lesley Garner, Mary Shorrock, Aziz and Gloria, Gloria's parents.

Left: Minty, Yusuf Saloojee, Rashid 'Mousie' Adam, Yasmin Pahad, Ronnie Kaka; Front: Jenny, Mohammad Timol, Ahmed Pochee, Ayoub Varachia

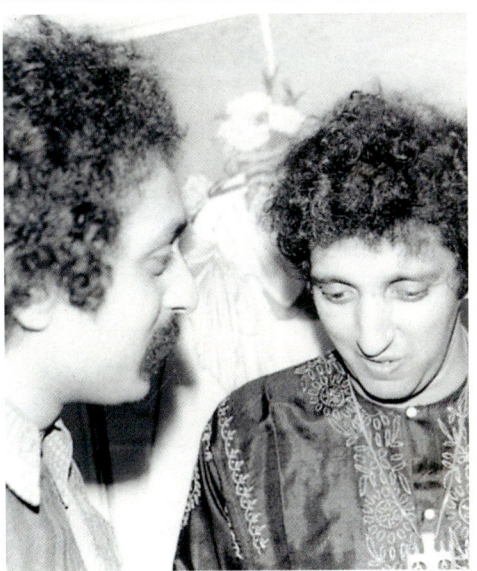

Vijay Rama and Aziz

Essop with Thabo Mbeki in the Pahad flat, West Kensington, about 1966

Class of 1967. Graduation from Sussex University. L to R: unknown, Kenny Parker, Thabo Mbeki, Amina Pahad, Essop Pahad, Goolam Pahad and Alfred Hutchinson

Left: Essop's PhD graduation, with Goolam Pahad, Meg and Dr Dadoo, 1971.

Yasmin with Meg and Essop in the Lake District, 1971.

The wedding of Thabo Mbeki and Zanele Dlamini in 1974. Left, Karen Fields; Essop is the best man, and Mendi Msimang is in place of Thabo's father. (Govan Mbeki was incarcerated on Robben Island along with Mandela, Sisulu and many other leaders.)

Essop spoke regularly at conferences, meetings and rallies. The photo below shows him speaking at Speakers' Corner, Hyde Park, against the celebration of the 600 years of friendship between Britain and Portugal, 1973.

World Youth Festival. From left: Tony Seedat, Albert Dlomo, unknown, Conco, Essop Pahad, Billy Nannan, Zaheer Bhayat, Anver Saloojee

Essop and Arkady Grigorian (centre) with the friends from the Filipino Party at the Lenin School in Moscow 1973

Top: Essop with Clement Rohee, representing the PPP of Guyana at WMR.

Left: Essop and Meg (left) with (right) Mitra from India and Yacoub Garro from Syria at our flat in Arabská. Above right: Margrit Pittman who worked both in Prague where she stayed with John, and also in the GDR. John Pittman, representative of the CPUSA, on the Editorial Board of WMR. These two and the Garros from Syria stayed in the same block of flats in Arabská.

Essop with Agamemnon Stavrou representing AKEL from Cyprus at his flat in Prague.

Essop with Satyadjaya Sudiman from Indonesia.

Semu Patheguey (Senegal), Essop, Feroz Mohamed (Guyana), Donald Ramotar (Guyana), José Lava (Philippines), at a conference at World Marxist Review.

Essop with Moses Mabidha in a Conference at WMR.

Walking the baby outside the flat in Arabská.

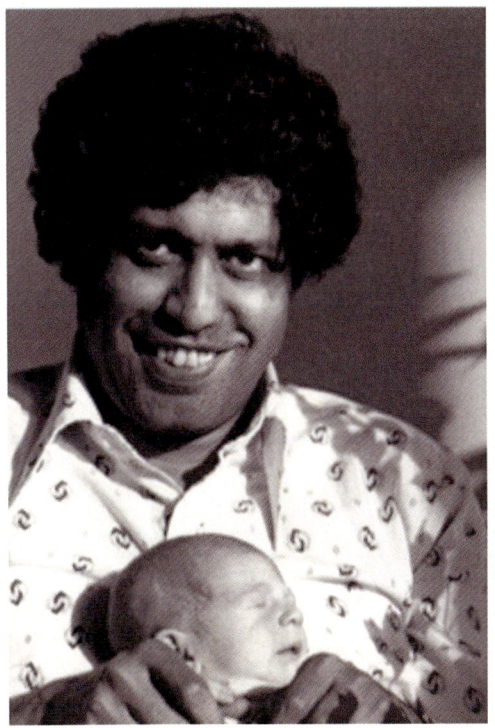
A proud father at last! Amina is born 1979.

José Lava is delighted.

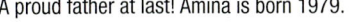
Haidar Hassani is almost as excited as Meg and Essop.

Above: We can see Essop, Ian Robertson and Hilary Rabkin amongst the demonstrators outside South Africa House, London

Demonstration outside South Africa House, London, 1979, against the execution of Solomon Mhlangu. Far Left, Theresa Nannan, then Essop Pahad.

A visit from Harry Gwala to our flat in Shirland Road, London, 1988. From left: Chris, Maryvonne and Stephanne Curran; Meg with Amina in front of her; Harry Gwala seated with Govan; at back: Jimmy Corrigall, Amin Mawani, (Susi took the photo) Elean Thomas, Tony Gifford, unknown and Essop.

Essop and Meg's flat in Shirland Road 1990: Karl Mbeki, Govan Pahad, Govan Mbeki, Amina Pahad, Zinzi Nannan, Meg and Essop behind.

IDASA, Dakar, 1987: Essop, Harold Wolpe, Manana, Tony Trew, Maduna, Frances Meli, Aziz, Lindiwe Mabuza; Front: Kader Asmal, Barbara Masekela, Thabo Mbeki.

Ahmed Kathrada and Zwelakhe Sisulu in London for the 2nd Mandela Concert, April 1990.

Launch of legal SACP in 1990. From top left: Valli Moosa, Ronnie Kasrils, Nelson Mandela, Limpho Hani, Essop Pahad, Joe Slovo, Pallo Jordan, Jeremy Cronin, Ray Alexander, Josiah Jele; Front: Chris Hani.

Essop was part of the SACP delegation to Cuba: Fidel Castro greets Chris Hani, 1992.

Meeting with Raúl Castro and Esteban Lazo Hernandez.

Essop and Amath Dansoko when he visited Essop in Johannesburg.

Meeting Yasser Arafat when he visited South Africa.

Wally Mongane Serote and Mara Louw at our house in Observatory.

Visit to India: Essop and family, with Louis du Plooy, visit Anand Sharma's family in Delhi.

Big business working group, 2003: Alec Erwin, Trevor Manuel, Essop Pahad, Thabo Mbeki, Patrice Motsepe, Artie du Plessis.

President Mbeki's cabinet of 2004. Many of the serving ministers resigned when President Mbeki was recalled. Phumzile Mlambo-Ngcuka, Mosiuoa 'Terror' Lekota, Essop Pahad, Ronnie Kasrils, Ngconde Balfour, Alec Erwin, Mosibudi Mangena, Thoko Didiza, Sydney Mufamadi, Geraldine Fraser-Moleketi; and deputy ministers, Aziz Pahad, Jabu Moleketi and Loretta Jacobus all resigned.

Geraldine Fraser-Moleketi, Essop and Sankie Mthembi-Mahanyele.

Essop with Gertrude Shope during a march in downtown Johannesburg.

Essop with Zanele Mbeki.

With Angela Davies at a party hosted by Trevor Fowler and Thelma in Observatory.

Frene Ginwala sharing a thought with Essop.

Sonia Gandhi was received at the airport by Essop when she visited South Africa.

In January 2005, Essop at the book launch of *Timol: A Quest for Justice*, at the notorious John Vorster Square Police Station where Ahmed Timol was killed. This was hosted by Essop, Aziz, Ronnie Kasrils, Charles Nqakula, Imtiaz Kajee and Reedwaan Vally.

Zuneid Pahad accepts the 'Order of Luthuli in Silver', awarded posthumously to our mother Amina Pahad, from Thabo Mbeki.

Some of the guests for the 1999 inauguration at our home in Observatory: Mike Seifert, Rhiannon Gooding, Adrian Mitchell and Meg.

Sussex friends invited for holiday with Thabo and Zanele Mbeki: Derek Gunby, Jenny, Mel Gooding, Meg, Thabo, Rhiannon, Essop, Zanele.

Carol Marshall and Tonio Fernandes, Frelimo and ANC Veterans

Mohammed Khota and his wife Cheryl

Amina, Essop and Govan

Family photo: Shenaaz Pahad, Shehnaaz Dadabhay, Eva Holland, Sam Gurney, Mayur Lodhia, Amina Pahad, Christabel Gurney, Yasmin Dadabhay; Front row: Essop, Isa Pahad, Angina Parekh, Aziz, Meg.
Inset: Bethan and grandfather Aziz on her birthday.

Staff of *The Thinker*: Neo Sithole, Liesel van der Schyf, Zain Dindar, Meg and Essop Pahad

Ahmed Kathrada and Barbara Hogan with Pahad family: Yusuf (Georgie) Dadabhay, Kulsie, Farida, Menzi Mbatha, Ruki, Shireen, Meg, Govan, Shenaaz, Amina, Barbara, Rikki Barnes, Zuneid, Yusuf (Jo) Pahad, Yusuf (Dada) Dadabhay, Shamim and Mohamed Bhikhoo, Aziz, Angina, Isa; Aimee, Asani, Kathy, Dania, Essop, Xavier, Shehnaaz.

Amina's wedding: Eunice Cross, Lily McNeil, Essop, Amina, Ntsiki Adonos.

Govan's wedding: John and Ann Topp, Meg and Essop; Front: Aimee and Govan.

Enjoying good company: Essop and Meg with Amina Frense and Ronnie Kasrils, 7 April 2023.

Aimee with Tau, Govan, Amina, Muhammed (Mo) Moosa, Angina; Essop with Hugo and Asani, Meg with Dania and Xavier, Aziz, Shenaaz.

Walter Mokoena and Maurizio Mariana greet Essop and Aziz at an early birthday party for Essop, organised by Amina for June 16 2023.

Family party 2023: Shenaaz Pahad, Tau, Govan, Hugo, Amina, Rikki Barnes; Saliha Moosa, Tau, Asani, Aimee, Waruna Adonisi-Kgame, Sana Moosa; Meg, Nolitha Adonisi-Kgame, Essop, Dania, Xavier.

Although that was my last visit to India, academic institutions have kept in touch. The Department of African Studies at the University of Delhi under the aegis of the Government of India, in collaboration with the Department of Education at Wits University, organised an international webinar in September 2020 on the topic 'The Relevance of Gandhian Philosophy in the Covid-19 Crisis'. I was the chief guest and asked to be the first speaker after the official opening. According to the Indian hosts, my contribution was much appreciated.

As I wrote earlier, I think of India as a continent. It is a fascinating place with its diversities, contradictions and large gap between the haves and have-nots. In my time as a member of the NEC of the ANC, I spoke about the achievements, trials and tribulations of the INC and what lessons we should draw from that experience. I remain convinced that the ANC should take the necessary steps to avoid the fate of the INC, which went from being the most powerful political force in India to the opposition benches. In 2021, it remains an opposition party, having suffered several splits as the result of factionalism and bitter infighting. For me, as for many millions in our country, that fate would be a tragedy.

The national and provincial elections in 2024 will show whether the ANC has lost the support of the people of South Africa.

Chapter 6
My Mentors

My Mentors

In the course of my political life, I have had the privilege, honour and pleasure of meeting and knowing some of the most wonderful anti-racist, anti-colonial, anti-imperialist and anti-capitalist freedom fighters. In various ways, they have enriched my life and my political consciousness, understanding and knowledge. To each I remain eternally grateful, and in this chapter, I write about some of them, in alphabetical order, as they cannot be rated or compared in importance: Dr Yusuf Dadoo, Amath Dansokho, Cheddi Jagan, Ahmed Kathrada, Jose Lava, Nelson Mandela, Govan Mbeki, O. R. Tambo and Henry Winston. Thomas Paine once said, 'Use your common sense.' All the mentors I mention were great leaders, profound thinkers and remarkable personalities because they did just that.

Dr Yusuf Mohamed Dadoo (1909–1983)

In 2009, when I was marking the centenary of Uncle Doc's birthday, I wrote an article about him for *The Thinker*, entitled 'A Simple Musket Bearer'.[101] I reproduce that article below, with minor changes, as an introduction to my mentor, Dr Dadoo. It begins here:

> In the course of the protracted, dangerous and exceptionally complex struggle for national liberation and socialism in South Africa, many outstanding leaders emerged. They are recognised as exemplary for their fearless and selfless contribution to the people's struggle. But amongst such leaders there are a few whose contributions were a cut above the rest. These include such luminaries as O. R. Tambo, Nelson Mandela, Inkosi Albert Luthuli, Moses Kotane, J. B. Marks, Bram Fischer and Yusuf Dadoo.
>
> At the funeral ceremony in London on September 24, 1983, then-President of the ANC, O. R. Tambo, said:

---

101. This was published in *The Thinker, Vol. 7*, 2009. Although Essop Pahad has a copy of every volume of *The Thinker* (from Volume 1), the University of Johannesburg only has archived issues from 2016 to the present. These are available at Journals.uj.ac.za/index.php/The Thinker/index

Loved and admired throughout the movement, 'Doc' – as he was popularly known – combined the best qualities of a revolutionary patriot and dynamic leader of the working class; because of his clear understanding of the factors underlying national oppression and the economic exploitation of the black South African masses, he was able, in his own unassuming manner, to guide and inspire others to commit themselves fully in the struggle for the noble ideals of freedom, democracy and a just social order. Most important of all, he led by example.[102]

Yusuf Mohamed Dadoo, popularly known as 'Mota' – a Gujarati term of respect and endearment – or 'Doc', was born on 5 September 1909 in Krugersdorp. After qualifying as a medical doctor in Edinburgh, he returned to South Africa in 1936. Upon his arrival, he set about the mammoth task of transforming the Transvaal Indian Congress, Natal Indian Congress (NIC) and the South African Indian Congress from moderate insular bodies into mass militant organisations. He worked in tandem with other leaders – in the Transvaal, for example: Nana Sita, Molvi Cachalia, Jasmat Nanabhai, Goolam Pahad, Naransamy Naidoo and Yusuf Cachalia, and in Natal with Dr G. M. Naicker, H. A. Naidoo, M. P. Naicker, J. N. Singh, Debbie Singh, Dr Sader, Ismail Meer and M. D. Naidoo, amongst others. He organised tirelessly, traversing the country, attending and addressing scores of meetings and demonstrations to mobilise the Indian Community into an integral part of the broader liberation movement led by the ANC.

The worldwide upheavals caused by the Second World War had a profound impact on political developments in South Africa, and while the erstwhile leaders of the National Party gloried in their awe and admiration for the Nazis and their leader, Hitler, progressives, communist and non-communist, denounced the war as an imperialist one. Dadoo, who had joined the Communist Party of South Africa in 1938, was in the forefront of the anti-war mobilisation campaigns. For his role and activities, he was harassed and then imprisoned for printing and distributing NEUF leaflets which declared: 'We answered the call in 1914–1918. What was our reward? Misery, starvation and unemployment. Don't support this war, where the rich get richer and the poor get killed.'[103] However, when Nazi Germany invaded the Soviet Union in June 1941, the CPSA and other progressive

---
102. *The African Communist*, No. 96, 1984. Available at https://www.sahistory.org.za/sites/default/files/DC/Acn9684/Acn9684.pdf
103. *Indian Opinion*, 13 September 1940. Also available at https://www.sahistory.org.za/people/dr-yusuf-mohamed-dadoo

forces changed tack and characterised the war as a 'people's war'. This abrupt change was not well received by many activists and people in the country, including in the Indian Congresses, and the daunting task of winning over the critics and doubters fell on the shoulders of Moses Kotane and Yusuf Dadoo. That they succeeded is testimony to their capacity for providing strong, persuasive, inspiring and brave leadership on contentious and controversial issues.

By 1946, the progressives had succeeded in routing the moderate leadership of the TIC and NIC and convinced their membership that all Black South Africans must fight a united struggle against oppression, rebuffing attempts to divide Indians from the African majority. In the same year, those organisations embarked on a Passive Resistance Campaign against the racist Asiatic Land Tenure Act. It was the first mass resistance campaign since the Satyagraha struggle conducted by Mahatma Gandhi in the early 1900s, and it is noteworthy that the first volunteers from the Transvaal were all women.

That resistance campaign laid the basis for the signing of the Dadoo-Xuma-Naicker pact in 1947 (the 'Three Doctors' Pact', in which the Indian congresses and the ANC pledged to work together) and later the emergence of the more formal Congress Alliance. At that time, Dadoo was also instrumental in the formation of the Non-European United Front. The solidarity achieved was strong enough to survive the negative impact of the 1949 riots in Durban between Africans and Indians in which eighty-seven Africans and fifty Indians lost their lives. Those riots were aided and abetted by the racist administration and individual whites.

In just over a decade, Dadoo, who came from a middle-strata background with limited political experience, became a highly respected, even revered, political leader with a large support base. Given that there was no television at that time and no serious coverage on the airwaves of the political activities of the national liberation and working-class movement, his popularity was phenomenal. A correspondent of *The Guardian*, the one media outlet that was radical, militant and an outright supporter of the progressive forces, wrote of Dadoo:

> This man was destined to become the storm bird of the South African revolution, the symbol of sacrifice and courageous resistance to the tyranny of colour in his native land ... Whether his political opponents like to acknowledge it or not, Dr Dadoo is a South African

of very considerable eminence not only among millions of his fellow countrymen in the Union, but also in wide circles abroad ... And, by the way, he is one of the most charming men I have ever met. (15 December 1949)

He also had an international profile in other parts of Africa, India, the Soviet Union and other socialist countries.

Throughout the turbulent fifties, in which the ANC, the Indian Congresses, the South African Coloured Peoples' Organisation and the South African Congress of Trade Unions embarked on mass militant resistance campaigns, Dadoo was actively involved, leading from the front. Repeated banning orders, arrests and trials did not prevent him from making his contribution to the work of the Indian Congresses, the SACP, the ANC and the Trade Union Movement. His stature and popularity was such that at the Congress of the People on 26 June 1955, together with Chief Albert Luthuli and Father Trevor Huddleston, Dadoo was bestowed with the Order of Isitwalandwe, the highest honour given to outstanding political figures by the ANC.

As a leader of the SACP, the Indian Congresses and the broader Congress Alliance, Dadoo was acutely conscious of the sensitive and complex interconnectedness of the national and class struggles in the South African revolution. An article he penned for the *World Marxist Review* in July 1978, to which I contributed, succinctly sums up his view and approach. He wrote:

> From the cradle, the African people are daily humiliated, their skin colour ridiculed and their cultures and traditions destroyed. Daily, thousands of African people are imprisoned or banished to remote areas under one or other of the vast battery of obnoxious racist laws which litter the South African statute books. Racist legislation is a key element of the system of national oppression in our country.
>
> In the conditions operating in South Africa, national oppression constitutes an exceptionally significant factor in the super-exploitation of the African people. The national income gap between whites and Africans is 14:1. African workers are denied even the elementary rights of collective bargaining, prevented by law – except when it suits the racist regime and monopolists – from doing skilled jobs, and have no social security and unemployment benefits. They

are regarded as mere 'labour units' to be dispensed with once they have served the 'needs' of the white minority. Africans in the rural areas are compelled to work on white farms for starvation wages – some are 'paid' in kind and not cash – and are not allowed to own even a small plot of land in 87 per cent of the territory of the country. In the 13 per cent – the co-called Bantustans – the poverty of the land and the destitution of their lives compel the Africans to become migrant labourers. The African middle strata, such as they are, have very limited scope for development since they are as much the victim[s] of racist laws and racial discrimination as all other sections of the Black population.

Thus we see that in racist South Africa, since the national aspect is not 'secondary' or mere form, the chief mobilising factor for the African people is their response to national and racist oppression. Proceeding from this, the ANC and SACP are deeply involved in stimulating and injecting a greater depth and content to the confidence, assertiveness and pride of the African people. As Lenin taught us, we should never underestimate the psychological factor in the national question.[104]

During the 1960 State of Emergency, Dadoo was asked to join O. R. Tambo and others abroad to strengthen the movement in exile. He was reluctant to leave South Africa, but as a loyal, disciplined member and leader, he accepted the decision.

In London, until his death in 1983, Dadoo served the SACP, ANC, Umkhonto we Sizwe, the World Communist Movement, World Peace Council (WPC), Afro-Asian Solidarity Organisation (AAPSO), and the Anti-Apartheid Movement with great dedication, distinction and loyalty. Throughout those exceptionally difficult years, when it seemed to many that the juggernaut apartheid war machine had crushed the liberation movement, Dadoo never lost his bearings, never wavered in his commitment and determination to continue the struggle, and remained firm in his conviction that a primary aim of the SACP was to build and strengthen the ANC and the trade union movement.

Dadoo played an important role in ensuring the unity and cohesiveness of the ANC at the historic conference in Morogoro in 1969. There, he was

---

104. Also available in 'Yusuf Mohamed Dadoo – South Africa's Freedom Struggle: Statements, Speeches and Articles including Correspondence with Mahatma Gandhi', compiled and edited by E. S. Reddy, with a foreword by Shri R. Venkataraman, President of India, pp. 142–143. file:///Users/rv/Downloads/Dadoo-speeches book full, and additions in SA edition.pdf

elected Deputy Chairman of the Revolutionary Council, which, under the leadership of O. R. Tambo, was set up to intensify the struggle on all fronts and all levels. Dadoo fulfilled that new and onerous task with his customary passion, zeal, dedication, political instinct and commitment.

An internationalist in every sense of the word, Dr Dadoo loved India and had close political and personal relations with leaders of the Communist Party of India and the Indian National Congress, including Mahatma Gandhi, Jawaharlal Nehru and Indira Gandhi. On the occasion of his 70th birthday, he was showered with awards from the socialist countries and international organisations.

Yusuf Dadoo was an unflinching, uncritical, staunch supporter of the Soviet Union and other socialist countries. Together with his comrades in the SACP and many in the ANC, he ignored or turned a blind eye to the many weaknesses manifested in the work of the ruling parties and the building of socialism. They were thoroughly convinced that the Soviet Union was indestructible and that, notwithstanding all the difficulties and challenges, socialism would triumph.

Dadoo was an extraordinary revolutionary, and his warmth, reassuring manner, medical skill, advice and patience made him an immensely popular general practitioner. He was in such demand that patients would refuse to consult another doctor even if they knew he would not be available for weeks.

A generous, genial personality with a good sense of humour and enjoyment, Dadoo had a wide circle of friends inside and outside the South African liberation organisations. He loved the progressive aspects of Indian culture, music, art, literature and, in particular, Urdu poetry. He was fond of cooking and followed avidly international competitions in cricket, soccer, rugby and ice hockey. A brilliant fundraiser, he was meticulous in ensuring that every cent donated to the movement was properly accounted for. He was so trusted by Indian businessmen that they would merely ask him to fill in the required amount in their cheque books.

Dadoo was a charismatic leader, a good listener and patient with even the most annoying interlocutors and opponents. He showed respect for the views of others and tried to win an argument or a dispute with the logic and persuasiveness of his ideas and approach. At committee meetings, he would puff away at his pipe, listen attentively, rarely intervening, except when necessary to find a synthesis of the contrary and contradictory views that had been canvassed. In his younger days, he was admired as a powerful orator able to command the attention of thousands without recourse to demagogy or cheap rhetoric.

Under very difficult conditions, he tried to keep in contact with the prisoners on Robben Island and later Pollsmoor, and, in turn, they always enquired about his health and whereabouts. On his 70th birthday, he received a card from Nelson Mandela addressed to 'My dear Motabhai' (big brother) with this message:

> I often think of September 5 and to wish you many happy returns! We think of you with far more pride than words can express. Those birthday parties we used to hold for you are amongst the memorable occasions Ahmed (Kathrada) and I often talk about ...

Dadoo was thrice married. His third wife, Winnie, was a member of the SACP and ANC and an indefatigable freedom fighter who was also the breadwinner in the family. His years in exile were made more comfortable, bearable and stable due to the love, care and attention paid to him by Winnie and their daughter Roshan.

A fierce fighter against all forms of discrimination, sectarianism and exclusivism, Dadoo's contribution to the creation, building and promotion of the unity in action of the ANC, SACP and SACTU is immeasurable. He sought no cheap popularity, did not actively canvass for positions of leadership and always put the interest of the struggle first. He remains by far the most remarkable and eminent political leader and activist produced by the Indian community in South Africa.

To the very last breath of his life, Yusuf Dadoo remained a loyal, dedicated, incorruptible and principled cadre and leader of the ANC and SACP.

In a moving message to a meeting of the Central Committee, written and signed hours before his death on 19 September 1983, he wrote:

> Our strength in the past has been built upon the depth of our Party's and cadres' ideological knowledge and understanding ... We must frankly, honestly and realistically provide direction for enhancing our work in the testing time that lies ahead. We are the revolutionary party of the working class, whose clear role is that of the vanguard in the fight for socialism. The working class, in essence the black working class in our country, is the pivotal force in the struggle for a revolutionary overthrow of the entire apartheid

system. As such, our Party must place its main focus and emphasis in organising, uniting and giving clear guidance to this class, which forms the backbone of our struggle. Included in this task is assessing our strengths and weakness[es] in the trade union movement as a whole, assessing (re-defining if necessary) the role of SACTU, and ensuring our future working in this vital field meets the demands of the time.[105]

Dadoo was buried in Highgate Cemetery, very close to the grave of Karl Marx. His headstone is inscribed, 'Fighter for national liberation, socialism and world peace.' As Joe Slovo pointed out in a tribute given in 1991, Dadoo himself would have probably preferred the words 'simple musket bearer', for this is the way he saw and described himself.

༄

Yusuf Dadoo treated Aziz and I as his sons, and in my case, if he thought that I was misbehaving or ill-disciplined, he would reprimand me in his quiet but firm voice. A reprimand from him was always taken seriously.

As part of our work to mobilise the Indian community (South Africans of Indian origin), Dadoo set up a committee composed of M. P. Naicker, Frene Ginwala, Mohammed Tikly, Aziz Pahad, Billy Nannan and me. Dadoo was chairman. Our responsibility was to keep abreast of developments within that community and produce a regular pamphlet, *Jana Sakthi*, which was distributed from London and clandestinely inside South Africa.

I recall an incident when Uncle Doc had been asked by Alfred Nzo to prepare a document on whether or not Indians should participate in the tricameral racist election in South Africa. There was a group of activists and leaders in Durban who were in favour of participating. When Billy Nannan and I were asked to draft a document for our committee, we took the view that because those in favour of participation used examples from the 1908 Russian Revolution to bolster their position, we should respond to that and quote Lenin to prove our point. We were quite proud of our contribution and confidently presented our paper.

At the end of our presentation, before any discussion could ensue, Doc (unusually for him) spoke immediately. He was adamant that what we had

---

105. E. S. Reddy, 'Yusuf Mohamed Dadoo – South Africa's Freedom Struggle', p. 261.

produced was not what Comrade Nzo had requested and was way off the mark. He said that while Lenin's quotes were interesting, they were irrelevant to our task, and there was no point in discussing our paper. He said that Billy and I should rewrite a document consistent with what was required. It was a slap-down, even though delivered in a soft-spoken voice.

That fulsome rejection shocked the two of us, as we had wrongly assumed that a leader of the SACP would be impressed by our references to the Russian Revolution and Lenin. We sheepishly accepted the criticism and rewrote the paper, which was presented, discussed and then finalised for presentation to Nzo. In the end, we were very pleased that the ANC leadership agreed that the Indian community should boycott the racist tricameral elections.

When my father was in London, he used to visit Uncle Doc, and they would cook their favourite recipes together, often including either trotters or dahl, and share a few glasses of whisky. Winnie Dadoo would later clean up the kitchen, observing good-naturedly to Meg and I that they didn't seem to be able to use a whisk without splashing food all over the wall.

After Michael Harmel's death, I felt that Uncle Doc was at times lonely, and I encouraged him to join me and a few others in going to cricket test matches at Lord's. If the West Indies team were up against England, he would be elated if they got the better of their opponents. He really enjoyed those outings and demonstrated his knowledge and appreciation of the finer points of cricket.

On many occasions, Aziz and I would meet him for a drink at a local pub near his office after he had finished his work. He preferred whisky but sometimes joined us in a pint of lager. Those were wonderful times since Uncle Doc was relaxed and spoke openly about our struggle and our shortcomings, the demands on the movement, the politics of the UK and international events. His assessments and analyses of what was happening in the UK and the world were insightful, thought provoking and refreshing. Often in our exchanges, he would crack a joke or make humorous remarks. We learnt a great deal from those informal encounters. When he asked me to write a few of his speeches and articles, I was thrilled and proud.

Whenever we asked him to go home by taxi rather than by tube and even offered to pay part of the cost, he would smile and turn down our request. For him, it was important not to waste the movement's money and to make clear that he did not think that, as a leader, he should travel by anything other than public transport.

Uncle Doc was my leader and mentor and one of the finest and most amazing people I have met in my life. Even when he admonished or criticised me, I never felt aggrieved, only remorseful that I had let him down. He remains one of the greatest South Africans to have graced the soil of our scarred but beautiful country.

Amath Dansokho (1937–2019)

Amath was one of the closest friends and comrades I have had in my life. He taught me more about the African continent than any other individual – more even than the books and articles I have read. He was a committed, passionate, courageous communist – a Pan-Africanist, anti-imperialist, anti-racist freedom fighter.

Born in Senegal, Amath joined the African Independence Party, the first communist party in French West Africa at a young age. He was a member from 1957-1959. He later left that party and with Seydou Cissokho formed the Party of Independence and Labour (PIT). Due to repression and bannings, he lived in exile from 1960–1977. For most of those years, he lived in Prague, which is where I met him and began our lifelong friendship.

Cissokho was the Secretary-General of the PIT, but for many years, he was in a hospital in Moscow suffering from TB. Amath was the recognised face of the PIT and assumed the role of Secretary-General after Cissokho's death in 1984, where he remained until 2010. Amath was a scathing critic and opponent of President Léopold Sédar Senghor and later became disillusioned with first Abdou Diouf and then Abdoulaye Wade. We shared similar views and criticisms of Senghor's vision and attempted practice of negritude.

After his return from exile, Amath was a member of the National Assembly, Mayor of Kégoudou, his place of birth, Minister of Urban Planning and Housing from 1991–1995 and again briefly in 2000. He had little time for the status and perks of serving as a minister and resigned from his first ministerial post because he felt the government was reneging on its election promises and mandates. Later, Amath played a prominent role in ensuring the victory of the erratic Abdoulaye Wade. But in November 2000, some six months after Wade appointed him minister, he resigned; when I asked him why, his response was that he could not serve an administration run by an arrogant, unpredictable personality who was too close to the French government.

I attended Wade's inauguration, held in a stadium packed with mainly young people. It was impressive, but then they played an anthem, which went on and on and was much longer than our national anthem. At the end of the ceremony, I asked Amath why the anthem had taken forever. With his characteristic loud laugh, he answered, 'But I have always been telling you that you do not know what he is going to do. That was not our national anthem but his own composition dedicated to African Unity.' That evening, we attended the reception, with Amath as the minister-designate.

In our discussions during my visit, Amath made it clear that if Wade misbehaved and acted contrary to the expectations of his party and the people, he would resign. And true to his word, he did, which made him unpopular with Wade and his party but popular amongst sections of the population for his integrity, honesty and principled stand. It was, and still is, unusual for a leader to resign as a matter of conscience and return to the opposition benches.

From our very first meeting at the WMR in September 1965, I was blown over. Amath gave me a bear hug while laughing and welcoming me. He was so experienced and well-informed about the strengths and weaknesses of the WMR, and he enquired about the ANC and SACP leaders he knew and about my likes and dislikes. He immediately invited me to dinner at his flat, which he shared with his wife Babette and two daughters, Laurence and Yacine, who were still small (about seven and nine).

Dansokho was immensely proud of his daughters and commented on their political acumen when they noted that there were a lot more lovely things for sale in the shops in Paris than in Prague: 'But lots of people in France can't afford to buy them, whereas in Prague, everyone can buy the things in the shops.'

Earlier in this memoir, I wrote about the crucial role Amath played in drafting the 'Communist Call to Africa'. Without his insights, understanding and analysis, we would have produced a weaker and poorer document.

Amath and I spent many hours debating the issues and challenges facing our continent, including the class composition of progressive and conservative states, the role and place of the national bourgeoisie, the importance of working with faith-based groups as well as potential allies and our work at the WMR. Amath was erudite and well-informed about the World Communist Movement and sociopolitical and socio-economic developments in both our countries. He was also well-connected to the French Communist Party and was a firm and dedicated supporter of the ANC and SACP, the Soviet Union and other socialist countries.

We got together often, visiting each other's homes and hosting dinners. Amath and Babette were good cooks of French and Senegalese cuisine. One evening, when Meg was in hospital with Govan, I tried my hand at cooking chicken curry with a recipe she had given me. I invited Amath to 'make history' by tasting the first curry I had ever dared to make. Without hesitation, he accepted my invitation and after eating, praised my culinary skills. That was Amath – always ready to make kind remarks – even though my curry was just palatable. When Meg came home, he told her, 'Don't listen to his excuses anymore – he is perfectly able to cook!'

Amath loved Senegalese music and would play it whenever we visited him and his family. On one occasion, he surprised me with an LP of Manu Dibango and suggested I should spend hours listening to that great musician and singer.

After Amath's return from exile to Senegal in 1977, he was deeply involved in building PIT structures, criss-crossing the country, developing appropriate strategies and tactics. He took the lead in forming and operating alliances with other parties to build a strong opposition with a view to deposing the sitting president, Senghor. During the government of President Abdou Diouf, he was appointed Minister of Urban Planning and Housing from 1991–1995. Later, he and the PIT became increasingly critical of Diouf and opposed his re-election. Notwithstanding his critical views of Abdoulaye Wade, Amath supported him in the 2000 presidential elections and, with the support of the PIT and other left forces, Wade won. Amath was once more appointed as a minister but resigned after only six months, convinced that Wade was unreliable and erratic.

Years later, for the 2007 presidential elections, the PIT was an important component of the alternative front coalition with Moustapha Niasse as their candidate. Dansokho was responsible for heading the coalition's list for the parliamentary elections in 2007. Prior to those, Wade accused Dansokho of corruption and threatened him with prosecution. Indeed, except for Wade's supporters, the people of Senegal refused to entertain those accusations. Amath Dansokho was known and admired for his integrity and honesty. He was also the main spokesperson for the twelve opposition parties, and they categorically rejected Wade's attempts to besmirch Amath's character. The opposition parties boycotted that election, but the PIT and their coalition parties continued their united opposition, and in 2012, their candidate Macky Sall defeated Wade. Sall had no hesitation in appointing Amath as 'Special Advisor to the President' with the rank of Cabinet Minister in recognition of his political acumen, insights, knowledge and deep understanding. His appointment had widespread support in Senegal.

Amath was larger than life with a beaming smile and irrepressible, delightful sense of humour. He was a tough but undogmatic negotiator, an absolutely reliable friend and comrade and an unflinching leader of his party. He was a wonderful raconteur, equally at ease with small talk or high-level discussions and was an incorruptible political figure who suffered imprisonment and exile and had no time for hypocrisy. With him, you got what you saw. He enriched my life in every sense, and I am eternally grateful and appreciative. I regret with pain and sorrow that when I was in Dakar, Senegal, just a few months before he died, I was unable to visit him, as I was told that he was too ill to receive visitors.

After his death on 24 August 2019, millions of Senegalese and all of us who had known and worked with Amath, were in deep mourning. Tributes poured in from all over Senegal and abroad. Le Monde, the highly rated French daily, recognised him as 'a major figure in Senegalese politics for more than 60 years'. President Macky Sall praised him for playing an eminent and remarkable role in linking together generations of political figures in the modern history of Senegal and described him as 'a great, tireless unifier' and a 'great fighter for freedom, democracy and the progress of peoples'. Alioune Tine, well-known as a defender of human rights in Senegal said, 'It is a baobab that has fallen, a man who has been involved in all the struggles for democracy and fundamental freedoms.' A former prime minister and political opponent, Idrissa Seck said, 'He was a great patriot, who, throughout his life, was at the service of Senegal and Africa.'

Meg and I had the pleasure of hosting Amath at our house in Johannesburg when he was still full of life, laughter and stories. He said that for him, a visit to a non-racist, non-sexist, democratic South Africa was one of the highlights of his life.

Cheddi Jagan (1918–1997)

Cheddi was a Guyanese of Indian descent, whose family were poor and worked on the sugar cane plantations. However, he went on to graduate as a dentist from Northwestern University in Chicago and become a founding member and leader of the People's Progressive Party (PPP), which led the anti-colonial struggle for independence and remains a powerful political force in Guyana and the Caribbean to this day.

In the 1953 elections conducted by the British colonial authorities, the

PPP won a resounding victory, and Cheddi assumed the position of Chief Minister of British Guyana. Winston Churchill's government sent in British troops to overthrow Cheddi in a military coup of their own government on the spurious grounds that he and the PPP were a communist threat to that country and the region. Anti-communism and anti-Sovietism were the staple diet of successive British and US administrations; however, the PPP and Cheddi were formidable and popular freedom fighters, and despite the intrigues, shenanigans and outright hostility of those two governments, Cheddi became Premier of British Guyana from September 1961 to 1974. The rich, persistent and enduring struggles of the PPP and the Jagans can be gleaned from Cheddi's book, *The West on Trial – My Fight for Guyana's Freedom*,[106] published in 1966 and reprinted in 1972, 1975 and 1980, as well as his other books, numerous articles and pamphlets.

In the face of hostility and opposition from the British government, political forces and the mass media, Jagan remained steadfast in the quest for a free, independent, politically and economically stable Guyana. Throughout his life, he was also a proud internationalist, supporter of the Soviet Union, Cuba and other socialist countries, as well as the anti-colonial struggles in Asia and Africa. His call for a new Global Human Order was adopted by the UN General Assembly in 2002, and his call for a global tax on energy, pollution taxes and debt relief resonate to this day.

After over forty-five years of unrelenting struggle, Cheddi took up his rightful position as President of Guyana in 1992. Unfortunately, the toll of those years of sacrifice led to his death from a heart attack on 16 March 1997.

Since my youth, I had heard about Cheddi from Uncle Doc, Kathy, my father and other leaders of the TIC and TIYC, and as I grew politically, I followed his and the PPP's trials and tribulations. Thus, when I first met him, I was nervous, as I was in awe of this inspiring revolutionary communist. At that first meeting, he noticed my nervousness and put me at ease with a warm embrace and a broad smile. He wanted to know about the ANC, the SACP and the development and conduct of our armed struggle. I tried my best to answer his questions, and he thanked me and said he was impressed by my input.

After that first meeting, whenever Cheddi was at an international conference or symposium where I was also present or visited Prague or Moscow when I was there, he would seek me out, and we would spend time together. We discussed the political and economic situations in our respective

---

106. London: Michael Joseph, 1966.

countries, regions and continents, as well as the socialist world. We exchanged views on the struggle against racism, sexism, chauvinism, the national question, and the pros and cons of forms of non-violent struggle versus the need for armed struggle.

We engaged in intensive discussions on the prospects and content of national democracy in the developing world, with specific reference to Guyana and the African continent, and debated the theory and practice of a national democratic state. From early on, Cheddi had a clear view and perspective of the policies the PPP would implement once they had assumed the reins of government. He was sure that, even in the face of electoral fraud and rigging, aided and abetted by the UK and US governments, truth and justice would prevail, and that either on its own or in a coalition government, the PPP would be a governing party.

Cheddi was so humble that I had no hesitation in expressing my views on national democracy, racism, ethnic politics and the interconnection between the national question and the class factor in both our countries, regions and continents. By that time, the gender dimension had become integral to the politics of our movements.

At our first encounter, Cheddi probed me on my work and responsibilities at the WMR. He had been thinking about sending a representative to the WMR but was unsure it was wise to release a leading comrade when the PPP needed all hands on deck. I expressed my view that a representative from their party would not only enhance the work of the journal but that the PPP itself would benefit greatly: their representative would learn a great deal about international affairs, the World Communist Movement and the theory and practice of Marxism-Leninism and would return home a better, more informed and more mature communist.

My response struck a chord, and he said he would propose such a move to the leadership of the PPP. In 1979, Clement Rohee was deployed to the WMR with special instructions to spend a lot of time with me and take my advice. In Chapter 3 of this memoir, I have written about Rohee and his successor, Donald Ramotar.

Cheddi was always warm and friendly, and I enjoyed all of our conversations. He treated me with respect and at no time made me feel inferior in age or understanding or in relation to the gulf between the positions we held in our respective parties. He was a good listener, which was evident in the questions he posed and the responses he gave. I still remain grateful that a seasoned communist, well-known internationally, the foremost leader of his party and country and a former chief minister treated me with such courtesy and respect and as an equal. He remains in my view one of the greatest communist, anti-racist, anti-imperialist freedom fighters the world has seen, and I cherish my memories of everything we shared.

One cannot talk or write about Cheddi without mentioning Janet Jagan (née Rosenburg). She was a nurse, and after meeting in 1942, she and Cheddi married the following year and had two children. She was, in some respects, the opposite of Cheddi – a strict disciplinarian – and woe betide those comrades in the party who failed to fulfil their role and responsibilities as comrades and leaders of the PPP.

After Cheddi's death, Janet kept the party together through the most difficult times. It amazed me how a white American woman, through her commitment, determination, discipline and strength of character was able to contribute so significantly to the unity, cohesion and purpose of the PPP inside and outside the country. Janet and Cheddi, with their contrasting but complementary approaches, made a formidable couple and team. Janet was appointed as the first female Prime Minister of Guyana in 1997 and served as Guyana's president from December 1997 to August 1999.

Cheddi Jagan was awarded the Companion of O. R. Tambo Award in Gold by President Thabo Mbeki in 2005.

Ahmed 'Kathy' Kathrada (1929–2017)

Kathy had an exceptionally rich history of involvement in the struggle from the age of about seventeen. For those interested in reading more about this courageous freedom fighter, my comrade, fellow MP, fellow parliamentary councillor, and above all mentor who taught me so much and inspired and sustained my political activism, I strongly recommend his *Memoirs*[107] and *Letters from Robben Island*.[108]

When he was eighteen, my mother unofficially adopted him as her eldest son. She loved and cherished him as much as she did her five other sons. My other siblings and I were not offended by my mother's choice. In fact, we were always proud of our special relationship. When Aziz and I began our involvement in the struggle, our mother would admonish us if she thought we were behaving incorrectly or were not sufficiently disciplined: 'Why can't you be like your Uncle Kathy?' Kathy took his responsibility as an elder brother seriously and would give us a good dressing down if he thought we deserved it. That was more evident when I was part of the executive of the TIYC, and he was the chairperson.

In *Memoirs*, Kathy writes, 'My second mother, Aminabhai Pahad, had a devotion to her husband and children matched only by her dedicated fight against racism and injustice.'

When Kathy and others were charged for organising the Defiance Campaign, Aziz and I attended a demonstration in support of them. Kathy instilled in me a deep commitment to the struggle and an appreciation of international events and developments.

After visiting the evil, deathly Dachau concentration camp where so many Jewish people were murdered by German fascists, Kathy brought home some bones of the victims, which he used to forcefully demonstrate the inhumanity of fascism and illustrate the atrocities committed in its name, making the point that the South African regime's leaders were moving in that direction.

When I was about seventeen, there was a Congress meeting in our flat of twenty to thirty people. My mother sent me to ask Uncle Kathy who wants tea, coffee, soft drinks or water. I knocked on the door and said, 'Uncle Kathy, Mummy wants to know who wants what to drink.' That whole room burst into laughter as this tall young man called him 'Uncle'. I closed the door and he came out fuming and said, 'Don't call me Uncle! Just say Kathy or Comrade Kathy.' That was the last time I called him Uncle Kathy.

Kathy's elder brother attitude carried on even when Aziz and I were at university. Kathy was well-known for organising parties at his flat, No. 13 Kholvad House, and would invite, amongst others, Billy Nannan and Bobby Vassan, who were our contemporaries at Wits, but refused to let us join them. When we remonstrated that we were old enough, he would smile and ask, 'What would Mummy say?' and that was that.

I will never forget the two occasions when I was at the end of a tongue lashing. The first was in 1960 or 1961, when Dynamos was to play an important game. The match clashed with the annual general meeting of the TIYC, which had to be attended by all sitting members of the executive. In my absence, to my relief and joy, I was re-elected to the EC, but the storm was still to come. At the next executive meeting, a furious Kathy lectured me on the absolute need for discipline and commitment as a leader of the TIYC and asked the executive to record its displeasure. I sat there silently and then apologised to the executive.

---

107. Zebra, 2004.
108. Michigan State University Press, 1999.

The second time was when Gora Ebrahim,[109] a fellow student at Wits, convinced me that we should consider setting up an alternative to NUSAS. I took his ideas and documents and raised it at the executive on which Herbie Pillay and Essop Jassat, who were Wits students, also sat. But when I had finished, Kathy, who was chair, did not call on anyone to respond. Instead, he tore into me, saying, 'What is wrong with Comrade Essop? Why does he come here with Trotskyite rubbish?' Other members also did not mince their strong criticism. I felt ashamed that I had fallen for that Trotskyite plan and undertook never to repeat that mistake. Kathy records both incidents in *Memoirs*.

Kathy had a history of bannings, house arrests and imprisonments and was one of the leaders arrested in the famous Rivonia raid in 1963. During the Rivonia Trial, my mother insisted that I take food to him, as he was imprisoned, like the other trialists, in Pretoria Central. However, Kathy also asked me to bring him *russo* (*rasam*), a South Indian tamarind soup prepared by Mrs Pillay, the mother of Herbie and Harlene. So I would go to Fordsburg, often walking there and back, collect the *russo*, and take the bus the next day[110] to Observatory, where Rusty and Hilda Bernstein lived, and catch a lift from Hilda to the prison.

Hilda Bernstein was also an active member of the SACP underground, so for her, time was of the essence. She asked me why it took me so long to see Kathy, as she always had to wait for me after she had visited Rusty. I pointed out that she was white and a woman, so they would not delay her, whereas I was always kept waiting. I also pointed out that Caroline Motsoaledi, wife of Elias Motsoaledi, sometimes had to wait a long time before seeing her husband. Hilda raised the matter with the prison officers, who thereafter did not keep me waiting for long. Clearly, they were prepared to avoid inconvenience for a white woman, but unfortunately there was no such consideration to help Caroline Motsoaledi.

It was difficult to keep my emotions in check, as we were aware that the Rivonia trialists faced the death sentence. However, Kathy was always cheerful and chatty. He wanted to know how our family was and the Pillays and other people he knew well. His bravery in the face of adversity made it easier for me to talk to him calmly, but I still struggled to keep my tears in check.

That year was 1963, and I was in the final year of my BA degree and most anxious not to fail. But for my mother and me, visiting Kathy in prison and

---
109. He was a Trotskyite then, and later, in 1961, a leader of the PAC.
110. Indians and Coloureds, but not Africans, were allowed to occupy the last two rows on the top.

talking to him was more important than passing my exams. As it transpired, I did pass my exams and attended some sessions of the Rivonia Trial.

Kathy's courage was once again demonstrated when he openly admitted to his membership of the illegal SACP and refused to appeal any sentence, even though he was told by the defence team that he had a reasonable chance of getting a reduced sentence compared to most of his comrades. But Kathy and the rest of the Rivonia Trialists had taken a unanimous decision not to appeal against any sentence, even if it was the death sentence. For political prisoners, 'Life' meant life: not leaving jail alive. That trial also showed the capacity of the accused to give enthralling evidence justifying their involvement in the struggle and also provided the opportunity for Mandela to give his famous closing address to the court.[111]

At the age of thirty-four, Kathy was sent to Robben Island for life and only released at the age of sixty: for twenty-six years, he was imprisoned on Robben Island and in Pollsmoor Prison.

The political prisoners on Robben Island demonstrated great inner strength and personal integrity, courage and determination when, supported by other prisoners, they refused to buckle under pressure and retained their dignity and revolutionary zeal.

Kathy acquired several degrees while in prison and developed into a fine writer of letters, sharpened his knowledge of South African history and deepened his theoretical insights. Many of his letters to family and friends were published in a book entitled *Letters from Robben Island* edited by a dear friend of his, Robert (Bobby) D. Vassen, in 1999. Amongst the published letters was one written to me in April 1968. It was meant for Aziz and our friends and comrades who were in exile in London. His encouraging words were:

> You can't imagine how happy and proud I am of your academic achievements. What pleased me even more is the subject of Essop's thesis. How often have I not wished, outside and inside jail, that some of our younger graduates should get stuck into research on different aspects of our history.[112]

The title of my PhD thesis was 'The Development of Indian Political Movements in South Africa, 1924–1946'.

---

111. Available in full at http://db.nelsonmandela.org/speeches/pub_view.asp?pg=item&ItemID=NMS010&txtstr=prepared%20to%20die
112. Ahmed Kathrada, *Letters from Robben Island* edited by Robert D. Vassen (Cape Town: Mayibuye Books in association with the Robben Island Museum and East Lansing: Michagan State University Press, 1999).

After returning from exile, I served on the Internal Leadership Group of the SACP with Kathy. However, once elected to the NEC of the ANC, he resigned from that position.

Kathy and I were part of the ANC list elected to go to parliament, and it was reported that he was part of Mandela's original list to be a member of the executive (either a minister or deputy minister). But after discussions in the NEC or NWC, Mandela had to revise the list. As happens in situations like that, it is easier to drop someone you are very close to, and Mandela dropped Kathy for someone else. What I never understood, and still don't, is why Mandela did not simply add another name to his executive of national unity. Kathy put a brave face on it, but those close to him knew that he was disappointed, not for himself but for the Indian community, who assumed he would occupy some position in the executive.

Deputy President Mbeki raised the question of Kathy with me, and my suggestion to him was that they consider the British system, where some ministers have a parliamentary councillor. Kathy could be Madiba's parliamentary councillor. I guess he discussed this with Madiba and De Klerk, who was the other deputy president. They agreed, extended it to the two deputy presidents, and Mbeki appointed me as his parliamentary councillor. My initial suggestion was that the position should be at the level of a deputy minister, which would give it the necessary status and gravitas. But Mbeki said that because it was a parliamentary position, the matter should be decided in conjunction with the Speaker of the National Assembly. In the end, it was decided that the parliamentary councillor to the president should be at a slightly higher salary notch. I was very happy with my appointment, and Kathy was also satisfied, especially as it meant he would be serving Madiba directly and constantly in touch with him.

The duties and responsibilities of a parliamentary councillor included being the eyes and ears of the principal and liaising with ANC MPs, but notably with opposition MPs to be able to advise the principal on positive and negative developments inside the National Assembly Chambers and in the corridors. That meant talking and listening to MPs from both sides of the aisle. In my view, Kathy was not doing that, so I raised the matter with him. His response was simple and to the point: 'My boss does not regard my job in the way you do. He has given me other tasks, and those are what I am going to do.'

I really enjoyed that work, as it also gave me the opportunity to be in frequent contact with Kathy, inside and outside parliament. Kathy declined the offer of standing for a second term.

Fortunately for his partner Barbara Hogan and his best friends, Laloo (Isu) Chiba and Ismail Vadi, Kathy had a flat in the same block as them. On several occasions, I visited, and we shared many memorable moments, with Isu often cooking an excellent meal.

I remain indebted to Kathy for taking me under his wing and giving me a reproof when he thought my work or ideas were out of line. In *Memoirs* he writes:

> Perhaps I was too stringent in my treatment of those enthusiastic young activists, whom I love as brothers! One of my more significant contributions to the political education of the Pahad brothers was showing them, by example, that though I was married to the struggle, I nonetheless made time to socialise with friends and family and build a rich and multifaceted life for myself.[113]

Obviously, he conveniently forgot that he refused to invite Aziz and I to the parties he had at Kholvad House!

I am aware that he was very proud of the fact that Aziz and I held ministerial posts and leadership positions in the ANC and SACP. However, the two of us were even prouder of Kathy's achievements, history, commitment, discipline and courage. We were always happy to be recognised as Kathy's younger siblings.

Kathy, our eldest brother, you will always remain in our hearts. We loved, admired and adored you. Your death was extremely painful to accept, and I shed rivers of tears.

I thank Barbara for giving a replica of the key to Kathy's cell on Robben Island, which Kathy treasured, to my grandson, Asani Mbatha. Kathy had suggested that she do that because he had been deeply moved by the devotion displayed by three-year-old Asani, who told his schoolmates in great detail the story of Nelson Mandela, showing the pictures from his book. When Madiba died, Asani went with his mother Amina to place flowers outside his house with everyone else's offerings and then insisted on also leaving his gingerbread man biscuit 'in case Nelson Mandela feels hungry in the night'.

---

113. Ahmed Kathrada, *Memoirs*.

José 'Peping' Lava (1912–2000)

José Lava was one of the most humble people I have ever met and worked with: one of six remarkable brothers and three sisters from a small landowner family. Three of those brothers, Vicente, José and Jesus, were in the forefront of the armed struggle, first against the Japanese occupation and later against the US imperialist occupation of the Philippines. Vicente completed a PhD at Columbia University before returning to the Philippines with his family. José was a lawyer and Jesus a medical doctor.

The socialist and communist parties of the Philippines merged into a single communist party in 1938, with Vicente elected onto the Central Committee, becoming General Secretary in 1942. He was one of the first leaders of the People's Army Against Japan (*Hukbong Bayan Laban sa Hapon: Hukbalahap*), which was established in 1942. Many of the leading cadres of that liberation movement were members of the Philippine Communist Party (*Partido Komunitas ng Pilipinas*: PKP), which also included non-communist patriots, organised peasants and workers.[114]

When the Japanese were defeated, the name was changed to the People's Liberation Army (*Hukbong Mapagpalaya ng Bayan*: HMB), and its members became known as Huks. When Vicente died in 1947 from complications arising from the time he spent as a guerrilla fighter and leader, his brother José Lava was elected as the new General Secretary of the PKP.

William Pomeroy, a soldier in the US army stationed in the Philippines, married Celia Mariano in 1948. The two of them were recruited by José Lava to 'enter the forest' and join the Huks in 1950 to fight for the freedom and independence of the Philippines and against the US military and political machine which fully supported the reactionary and repressive Philippines regime. Pomeroy's book, *The Forest*,[115] is a most enthralling, informative and inspiring book on guerrilla warfare. Even today, I would recommend it to anyone interested in understanding the difficulties and severe tribulations of fighting in a guerrilla army.

When José became the leader of the PKP, he also became supreme commander of the peoples' army. José was highly respected for his outstanding political and intellectual capacities. When he was captured and tried on multiple charges in 1950, the judge, heavily influenced by the regime and the US occupation forces, found José guilty of 'rebellion, complexed by murder, robbery, arson and kidnapping', and sentenced him to life

---

114. Not to be confused with the splinter group Communist Party of the Philippines.
115. Berlin: Seven Seas, 1965.

imprisonment. Pomeroy records that at the same trial, six other accused were sentenced to death and several others to life imprisonment.

When José was sentenced to life imprisonment in 1950, his brother Jesus was elected General Secretary of the PKP.

After spending twenty years in jail, José was released and went into exile in Prague, Czechoslovakia, for another twenty years. He joined the editorial council of the WMR, and I had the good fortune to meet him and his wife (under the names of Philip and Maria Malaya) and develop an enduring relationship with him until the end of 1969.

Before I was sent to the WMR, I had heard wonderful stories about José from my Filipino fellow students at the Lenin School. Thus, when I arrived in Prague, he was one of the first representatives I arranged to meet. Although I was so eager to meet him, I was not sure how he would receive me. Unlike Amath Dansokho and me, José was not one for bear hugs and exuberant welcomes, so I was greeted with a gentle smile and a warm, firm handshake. From our first meeting, we took a liking to each other, and he said he would always be happy to see me in his office. He also invited Meg and I to his flat, where his wife Maria cooked lovely Filipino food; she was exceptionally warm and friendly. They visited us at our home, too. When José was released from prison after twenty years on condition that he went into exile, Maria willingly agreed to go with him, leaving behind their grown-up daughter. José and Maria's daughter and her husband were active militants in civil society organisations and leaders in the PKP. They had a son who went to live with his grandparents in Prague, attended the Russian school, and later graduated as a medical doctor from Charles University. José and Maria rarely saw their daughter and son-in-law, but, from time to time, they managed to organise a visit.

In all my interactions with José, I found him humble, gentle and soft-spoken, choosing his words with great care. Whenever I was upset or angry at the WMR or our own movement and struggle, he would be a calming influence, insisting that outbursts of anger are no substitute for rational thinking and assessment. I remember talking to him about my disgust and disappointment with certain men and women (mainly men) who would sell their souls and dignity, revealing details about underground cadres and even participating in murderous raids inside and outside South Africa, leading to the tragic deaths of many comrades. Those were known as *askaris*, and a few had infiltrated our ranks. While some were persuaded by fear to betray their friends to escape torture or imprisonment, others sold out for money.

In his quiet voice, José would make me understand that such behaviour was to be expected in any revolutionary struggle and would offer examples of betrayal in his own ranks. Pomeroy mentions some of those in his book, including even uglier forms of betrayal, such as the decapitation of a district secretary, whose head was taken to the army for a reward, or a Huk who, in the silence of the night, killed his two companions, trading their heads for his freedom and money. As Pomeroy says:

> Betrayals seldom occur when the tempo is high, when victory is a talked of thing. They happen when the ground gives way, and uncertainty yawns. Then the weak run to make their accommodations with those who appear to be strong.[116]

Whatever the reason or motives, I still regard such behaviour as despicable and believe that we should not hesitate to expose the culprits if we have the knowledge and are able to back up the accusation with evidence.

José would probe me with insightful queries about the prospect of MK escalating armed actions and about the strengths and weaknesses of our underground structures and those participating in such dangerous activities. He listened very carefully when I spoke about our leaders on Robben Island, such as Mandela, Sisulu, Kathrada and Mbeki, and the campaign to release Mandela and all other political prisoners. Although he seldom spoke about his years of hardship and incarceration – or the fact that there was no campaign inside or outside the Philippines demanding the release of Filipino political prisoners – he was very proud, not of himself, but of other Filipino communist and non-communist Huk freedom fighters who sacrificed their freedom, safety and even their lives for a just cause. He always spoke about others and very rarely about himself.

José would caution me about the difficulties of underground armed struggle, telling me not to underestimate the enemy and their powerful allies, the US and other major imperialist powers. I would then point out our success in invigorating the trade union movement and encouraging and inspiring the formation of the United Democratic Front as highlights of our revolutionary struggle at that time.

José, from bitter experience, was a harsh and uncompromising critic of Maoism, but he discussed this in a calm and dispassionate way. We shared common views on Maoism, and he found it amusing that Maoists in Europe

---

116. William Pomeroy, *The Forest*.

and Africa dubbed Dansokho and me as 'running dogs of Soviet imperialism'. But his criticism was laced with an endeavour to understand better its origins and continued existence, and he would often ask me, 'Are you not concerned that Maoist China is speedily moving towards capitalism?' And I would reply that the ownership of the means of production was still in the hands and under the control of the Communist Party of China (CPC). However, I learned a great deal from him about China, the CPC and the how and why of seeking to make informed criticism and not rushing to judgement.

José Lava made a significant contribution to the WMR Commission on National Liberation and the meetings of the WMR Editorial Council. His input was valued and respected because it was methodical, logical and carefully argued – a consequence of his being trained as a lawyer.

Lava and I discussed between us, and at the WMR, Gorbachev's ideas and plans for perestroika ('restructuring') and glasnost ('openness').[117] In our own engagement, I said that the Soviet Union and the CPSU needed glasnost – at the very least, a more open and transparent society. In his view, Gorbachev was moving too fast. While the intelligentsia supported him, he was not sure about the position and opinions of the working class in urban and rural areas. He raised the spectre of the possible collapse of the Soviet Union and the disastrous consequences for the World Communist Movement and the socialist world. His assessments and insight helped me take a more critical view of what Gorbachev and the CPSU were seeking to achieve.

All these years later, I must say that José was unfortunately proved right. Gorbachev, and later Yeltsin, presided over the collapse of the Soviet Union and the European socialist countries.

What a privilege and an honour it is to have known well that gentle and remarkable revolutionary.

Nelson Rolihlahla Mandela (1918–2013)

Nelson Mandela, 'Tata Madiba' to many of us in the movement, was an icon of South Africa, Africa and the world and charismatic in every sense of that word. His early life, political and ideological beliefs, involvement in the struggle, arrests and imprisonment, and his life after release from prison are vividly and illuminatingly captured in his autobiography, *Long Walk to*

---

117. For more information on these two planks of Gorbachev's policies, go to
https://www.britannica.com/place/Russia/The-Gorbachev-era-perestroika-and-glasnost

Freedom,[118] a 'must read' book for anyone interested in the politics of South Africa.

As a young boy of seven years, I was fascinated by that tall, handsome man who used to pat me on the head and enquire about my school. During the Treason Trial (1956–1961), I visited the court on several occasions. On seeing him, I would greet him, and he would acknowledge me but not say anything. He was kept well informed about my parents and our home, 11 Orient House, by Ahmed Kathrada, Ismail Meer and Chota Motala. The latter two lived in our flat during the Trial.

In 1944, Nelson Mandela, Anton Lembede, A. P. Mda, William Nkomo, Oliver Tambo, Walter Sisulu, David Bopape and several others launched the ANC Youth League, the formation of which would change the composition and trajectory of the ANC. Although it had communists like William Nkomo and David Bopape at its founding meeting, the Youth League adopted a manifesto which Mandela felt was:

> an implicit rebuke to the Communist Party, which Lembede and many others, including myself, considered a 'foreign ideology' unsuited to the African situation. Lembede felt that the Communist Party was dominated by whites, which undermined African self-confidence and initiative.[119]

And thus began the active political life of Mandela, Tambo, Sisulu and others. Mandela, a powerful orator with a magnetic personality, grew in stature and popularity, and by 1952, he was volunteer-in-chief of the Defiance Campaign, with Molvi Cachalia as his deputy. In August of that year, Mandela opened his legal office, and after a few months, Tambo joined him. The Mandela & Tambo legal firm had its offices in Chancellor House on the corner of Becker and Fox Streets, about 100 metres from Orient House. By the time the Treason Trial took place, Mandela was already a hero to millions of oppressed and super-exploited Africans.

The Sharpeville Massacre of 21 March 1960 was a decisive turning point in our struggle, and the demand for a radical shift in the strategy and tactics of the movement was gaining strength. Mandela, Sisulu, Govan Mbeki and others, in conjunction with the SACP, were instrumental in forming MK, signalling the beginning of the armed struggle.

---

118. Boston, MA: Little, Brown & Co., 1994.
119. Nelson Mandela, *Long Walk to Freedom*.

Before returning to lead the armed struggle, Mandela secretly left the country for military training in Ethiopia and Algeria, and while operating in the underground, became apartheid's most wanted man. I had the opportunity to meet him at an underground meeting not far from Ferreirastown. He came dressed as a night watchman, and his gravitas, posture and firm voice were mesmerising. He explained to us the turn to armed struggle, the difficulties of operating an illegal ANC and called on us to utilise the legal operations of the TIC and TIYC to continue the struggle and find ways and means to propagate the views and positions of the ANC.

In 1962, Mandela was arrested after meeting Chief Luthuli while on his way from Durban to Johannesburg. Before the trial could start, a Free Mandela Committee had been set up, and, together with other TIYC comrades, we wrote Free Mandela slogans on some public buildings in our area. Madiba elected to be his own lawyer, with Joe Slovo as his advisor. When Slovo was banned and could not go to Pretoria, he was replaced by Bob Hepple. In a moving plea in mitigation, Mandela used the platform to make a powerful speech outlining his history and active involvement in the legal and the illegal ANC and said:

> I am prepared to pay the penalty … [and] when I come out from serving my sentence, to take up again, as best I can, the struggle for the removal of those injustices until they are finally abolished, once and for all.[120]

That was a precursor to his famous stirring address at the Rivonia Trial in 1964, at the end of which he was sentenced to five years imprisonment with no parole.

In his autobiography, Mandela describes how he and three other prisoners were shackled together and driven through the night to Cape Town with one sanitary bucket for their use. In an amusing and vivid account, he writes: 'It is not an easy or a pleasant task for men shackled together to use a sanitary bucket in a moving van.'[121]

At the Rivonia Trial, the accused collectively took a decision that they would not appeal any sentence that was imposed, even if it were the death sentence. In his closing address, Madiba once more used a plea in mitigation on behalf of all the convicted (himself, Walter Sisulu, Govan Mbeki, Ahmed

---

120. Available at https://www.un.org/en/events/mandeladay/court_statement_1962.shtml
121. Nelson Mandela, *Long Walk to Freedom*

Kathrada and Denis Goldberg) as a platform to address the court and the world about the need to fight apartheid. His moving and inspiring three-hour speech ranks with the very best prisoner statements in history. Let me repeat the famous last paragraph of his address, which has been quoted over and over again throughout the world:

> During my lifetime, I have dedicated my life to this struggle of the African people. I have fought against white domination, and I have fought against black domination. I have cherished the ideal of a democratic and free society in which all persons live together in harmony and with equal opportunities. It is an ideal which I hope to live for and to achieve. But if needs be, it is an ideal for which I am prepared to die.[122]

※

Fast-forward twenty-six years to a few interactions I had with Madiba after his release from prison.

In June 1990, on his way to the United States, Nelson Mandela spent two days visiting the Tambo family in London. Thabo Mbeki asked me to join the Mandela delegation and assist him and Ngoako Ramathlodi with writing some of the speeches he had to make on that whirlwind tour. That trip was an eye-opener. Wherever we went, the Mandelas were greeted with such warmth and love by the people, particularly the Black Americans. The streets were lined by thousands of people just wanting a glimpse as our convoy of cars drove past them. In New York, there may well have been a million people in the streets, and the famous ticker-tape welcome was awesome.

Thabo wrote the main speeches, such as the Joint Sitting of Congress, and Ngoako and I alternated doing the others.

There were many thrilling moments on that visit, but I will mention just a few. We were aware that the speech to Congress was the most critical, and Thabo sat in his hotel room with Zanele to draft it. On the morning, he was still busy drafting as our delegation made our way to Congress. At the Capitol, we were ushered into a VIP holding room, and while waiting, an overbearing official came and asked me and Chris Dlamini, a trade union leader, to leave. Not wanting to make a fuss and disturb Mandela, we

---

122. Available at https://www.nelsonmandela.org/news/entry/i-am-prepared-to-die

complied and waited outside. When Mandela noticed we were not there, he asked that we be found and brought in. I then explained that this particular official had asked us to leave. Mandela was not amused and said that we were part of his delegation and were to stay. He kept asking me where Thabo was with the speech, and I tried my best to reassure him that he was on the way. However, I also started fretting and went outside and spoke to a security officer and informed him that Thabo was in a nearby hotel and we were worried that with the tight security in place, he might be delayed from bringing the speech to Mandela.

Many American citizens have a healthy respect for speech-writers, and the security officer immediately spoke into his mouthpiece, instructing that Thabo's trip should not be impeded. By that time, we were all concerned, as the deadline was imminent. Then, just as we were leaving for Congress, Thabo arrived with the speech, looking cool and calm. To say that Mandela was relieved would be an understatement. It was a powerful speech, which Mandela read as if he had written and rehearsed it. He received rapturous applause, with numerous standing ovations.

We were travelling on a private plane, which gave us opportunities to meet both the Mandelas – but we were careful not to disturb their peace and leisure. I had to draft the speech Madiba was to give in Detroit, and luckily for me, the Black American stewardess talked to me about a Marvin Gaye song that was immensely popular amongst Black Americans. She quoted some lyrics in which he came out against drug abuse, and I wrote them into the speech. In my view, the speech was well-received, and Mandela was very happy with the reference to Marvin Gaye.

Another incident I recall was when we were in Chicago staying in a hotel with more than sixty floors. I had been so engrossed in drafting a speech that, when I prepared to leave, I discovered that Mandela had already left his room and was on his way to the event. The difficulty was that the security personnel had stopped all the lifts except the one Madiba was using. I was sweating and afraid that I would miss them; moreover, if you were not ready to be part of the convoy, you would be left behind. I approached one of the security officers guarding the lifts and informed him that I was one of Mandela's speech-writers and had his speech in my hand. Fortunately, he contacted one of his colleagues, who sent a lift that took me to the foyer of the hotel as Mandela was leaving. I assured him that the speech was ready, and he smiled and thanked me. Once again, although he did not have time to peruse it before delivery, he read it with assurance, and I was most pleased with how it was received.

We visited many cities, including Atlanta, but did not have time to see much. There, we met with Coretta Scott King, widow of the legendary Martin Luther King. In some ways, it was shambolic, as all those permitted into the building wanted a photo op with Mandela. He obliged without a murmur, but you could sense that it was most tiring and overwhelming. On that trip, Mandela also met with Muhammad Ali, one of the greatest athletes history has ever witnessed, and I was over the moon to meet and shake hands with one of my heroes.

I was glad that Thabo had asked me to join that delegation, as it was wonderful to be with the Mandelas on almost a daily basis. The delight, love and admiration shown to them by the thousands of Americans who turned out to see them and the manner in which they responded to the adulation shown was breathtaking. During that trip, my respect for them grew and grew. They took all the stress and strain, buffeting and demands on their time with composure, serenity and patience. Not once, to my knowledge, did they complain about the tough schedule and pressure to endlessly shake hands and pose for photographs.

The Convention for a Democratic South Africa (CODESA) began with a plenary session on 20 December 1991, almost two years after the unbanning of political parties and the release of Nelson Mandela.

Together with Joe Slovo and Enver Daniels, I was part of the SACP delegation at the CODESA negotiations and was one of those lucky to be present when Mandela responded to De Klerk's intemperate and undiplomatic speech criticising the ANC. Mandela had indicated to Judge Ismail Mohamed, who was chairing that session, that he wished to speak once more. Then, Mandela tore into De Klerk, and his anger was palpable. That was the moment the ANC ascended, and most of the participants were jubilant at Mandela's response and sensed the significant shift that had occurred. I could not stop talking about Mandela that evening.

Once the date was set for the first democratic elections in April 1994, Mandela was the face and leader of our campaign. He worked tirelessly, crisscrossing the country and addressing meeting after meeting. Once during that campaign, I was active in the North West province, and Mandela had come to electioneer in Potchefstroom. I was busy in another part of the province but was instructed to join the ANC team in Potch. After I declined the nomination to be premier, Popo Molefe was the favoured candidate. But Malebane-Metsing, who rose to fame for his part in the coup against Mangope, insisted on electioneering to be the premier. He did not enjoy the support of the majority of ANC members in that province, and Mandela was disappointed in his divisive role. For some reason, Mandela thought that I had also been electioneering to be premier. When I saw him, he hardly acknowledged my presence, and in the mass meeting that evening, pointedly referred to several comrades of Indian origin, including his host, Rupiah, an ANC member. Equally pointedly, he did not even give me a glance and did not refer to my mother, which he did on so many occasions. I then spoke to Jessie Duarte, who was with Madiba, and she informed him that I was on the election campaign for the ANC and that my decision not to stand for premier was final. Thereafter, he calmed down and greeted me warmly. But that showed me how, when he was angry at someone's behaviour (or perceived behaviour), he would demonstrate his disapproval.

With Mandela at the helm, the ANC won the first democratic election in our history by a landslide. When we gathered at the old Carlton Hotel to celebrate, we broke out in rapturous applause when Mandela and Mbeki entered the venue, and many of us could not hold back our tears at this precious moment of victory. As pointed out earlier, I was very pleased that I had played a role in that triumph as a member of the ANC's election war room and the many meetings and rallies I had addressed in the North West.

Mandela's inauguration was an unforgettable event made even more memorable by the spectacular display of jets and helicopters and a South African Airways plane that flew low over the crowd with our new South African flag. The crowd flinched for a second at the jets, but then realised they were no longer a threat, and my wife said, in relief and joy, 'They're ours, now! They are ours!' We were sitting with Aziz and a lot of other ANC MPs and were jubilant to witness the reaction of the crowd to the foreign dignitaries as they were introduced on their arrival, with by far the biggest cheers going to Fidel Castro and Yasser Arafat. We all joined in exhuberantly (with our not all melodious voices) singing freedom songs and, following the inaugurations of De Klerk as second deputy president, Mbeki as first deputy president and Mandela as president, I said to myself, 'Free at last ... Free at last!'

Mandela's concluding remarks in his inauguration speech were met with thunderous applause from all those present, including the international guests:

> We are both humbled and elevated by the honour and privilege that you, the people of South Africa, have bestowed on us, as the first president of a united, democratic, non-racial and non-sexist government.
>
> We understand it still that there is no easy road to freedom. We know it well that none of us acting alone can achieve success. We must therefore act together as a united people, for national reconciliation, for nation building, for the birth of a new world.
>
> Let there be justice for all.
>
> Let there be peace for all.
>
> Let there be work, bread, water and salt for all.
>
> Let each know that for each the body, the mind and the soul have been freed to fulfil themselves.
>
> Never, never and never again shall it be that this beautiful land will again experience the oppression of one by another and suffer the indignity of being the skunk of the world.
> Let freedom reign.
>
> The sun shall never set on so glorious a human achievement!
> God bless Africa!
> Thank you.[123]

And with those words ringing in our ears, we strolled off to a sumptuous lunch.

As president, Mandela was determined to pursue the ANC's policy of reconciliation: of forgiving but not forgetting our hideous past. He was also of the view that we should lower the voting age to sixteen and re-examine our electoral system of pure proportional representation. Penuell Maduna and I

---

123. Available at http://db.nelsonmandela.org/speeches/pub_view.asp?pg=item&ItemID=NMS176&txtstr=inauguration

arranged to see him to discuss those matters, as they would have a profound impact on our constitution and the electoral system, and we were concerned that they should be resolved without public controversy. President Mandela listened to our arguments against those two proposals attentively and with interest. We then responded to a number of his queries, after which he said that he would no longer, for the present, raise those issues. A few years later, however, we would have to return to those questions, as he was convinced that his views were in the best interest of our country and political system.

In 1996, Mandela appointed me as Deputy Minister in the Office of Deputy President Mbeki, which was an unexpected honour and privilege. Then, Mandela refused to stand for a second term and, in 1999, when Mbeki led the ANC to an even bigger victory, he appointed me as Minister in the Presidency on the evening of his inauguration.

Mandela, in his so-called retirement, was as busy as ever. There was a continuous stream of visitors to his home, and Jakes Gerwel, who had been director general of his presidential office and then headed his office and foundation, asked Aziz and I to visit Madiba as often as possible. He was concerned that too many people were approaching him and raising serious issues and challenges confronting the ANC, more or less asking him to intervene. That put Mandela under undue pressure since his concern for the ANC and the government remained undimmed. Jakes was happy that Aziz and I spent a lot of time with Mandela, discussing the past and talking about my parents. Whenever I saw him, he was always friendly and warm and regaled me with stories and anecdotes about former days and teased me about how he and the others had used strong-arm tactics to break up CPSA meetings when J. B. Marks was the main speaker. Joe Modise led the disrupters and repeatedly told me that at one packed meeting in Soweto, he realised that J. B. Marks was very popular. To counter this he went on to the platform and deplored that there were two bulls, one white and one black, in the kraal. The audience understood that Marks represented the white bull, and Mandela and his group won the day.

During the course of our conversations, Mandela would call some member of his staff, his family or some other visitor present and say, with a huge smile on his face, 'You see, here is my boss,' referring to me, 'and I knew him when he was still a child. Now he is a minister.' To say the least, I was embarrassed, but managed to laugh and respond, 'Not true, Tata. You were my leader since those days and you remain my leader.' It was a pleasure to visit him and learn so much about the history of our movement.

When my father died in 2001, Mandela was one of the first to visit our family at my brother Nassim's house to express his sympathy and condolences. Prior to that, I had managed to get Mandela to visit our home in Observatory, as we wanted to pay our respects to the memory of my mother. My father, who had not seen Mandela for many years, and my brothers and their families were overjoyed. We spent a wonderful afternoon with him, during which he talked about my mother and teased my father about how he and the other ANC leaders had bankrupted him. At his playful best, Mandela made some jokes and commented on his pride that Aziz and I had become leaders of the ANC and government. Mandela had appointed Aziz Deputy Minister of Foreign Affairs in 1994, a post he retained until Mbeki's recall in 2008. He then resigned.

Mandela was very special to millions of people, and I regard it as a privilege and honour to have known him, served in his government and been able to visit him after he retired from active politics.

I have mentioned this anecdote previously, but must raise it again in more detail. When Madiba died, my grandson, three-year-old Asani Kalusha Mbatha, was in deep sorrow and spoke about him. One evening, his mother Amina and I went with him to Mandela's house. Prior to the funeral, there were scores of people outside his home, and admirers left flowers on the pavement as a mark of respect. Asani had a gingerbread man to eat, but when we got to Mandela's house, he said, 'I'm going to leave my gingerbread man outside for Tata Mandela so he can have something to eat if he is hungry when he wakes up.' On hearing that, I felt so proud of my grandson. Asani also accompanied his father Menzi when he was part of a group of younger people holding a march in honour of Mandela.

The outpouring of grief in South Africa and internationally was a tribute to a great, great person and leader. To repeat my opening sentence, Nelson Mandela was an icon of South Africa, an icon of the African continent and an icon of the world.

Notwithstanding the rift between Nelson and Winnie Mandela and their divorce, Winnie retained the love, admiration and adoration of the masses of South Africa and people internationally. She was usually friendly and warm towards me, but when she was angry, she would show it by calling me to admonish me. At many meetings, she would mention my mother in glowing terms. Unfortunately, she had a habit of arriving late at public meetings and rallies and would make a point of drawing attention to her entrance in a triumphant manner.

I remember the day we relaunched the legal SACP and a few of us went to the Mandela home to brief them. I had an SACP badge on my lapel, and when Winnie saw it, she said, 'Please give me that badge. I want to wear it.' She had a lot of respect for the SACP and leaders such as Moses Kotane, J. B. Marks, Yusuf Dadoo and Chris Hani.

Winnie's bravery and courage in the face of the evil brutality of apartheid remains unforgettable. She endured the loss of her husband to prison, her enforced separation from her small children, bannings, banishment and imprisonment with strength, dignity and fortitude. She would not allow the regime to break her fighting spirit, and in the most difficult days of our struggle, she kept the flames of resistance alive along with the name of the ANC.

But Winnie made several dreadful mistakes, especially regarding the so-called Mandela United Football Club, but she never lost faith in the ANC or the capacity of the masses to wage a sustained struggle. She was a revolutionary, and I witnessed myself the love she inspired in thousands of people in South Africa, the USA, the UK and other places all over the world.

One evening when, at some reception, Winnie criticised me for something she thought I had done, her daughter Zindzi, who was with her, said, 'No, Mummy, Comrade Essop is a good person.' Winnie then apologised.

She was without doubt a controversial political figure and leader. Nevertheless, I feel proud to have known her.

Govan Archibald Mvuyelwa Mbeki (1910–2001)

Govan Mbeki was popularly known as 'Oom Gov', which is what I used to call him. 'Oom' is 'Uncle' in Afrikaans.

Oom Gov was a writer, journalist, editor, educator and renowned intellectual, who was a member of the SACP and the ANC from the mid-thirties and remained so until his death. He held leading positions in both organisations and also in Umkhonto we Sizwe.

As a consequence of his political beliefs and affiliations, Oom Gov was fired from his teaching jobs. He was imprisoned during the Defiance Campaign of 1952 and the 1960 State of Emergency and sentenced to life imprisonment at the end of the Rivonia Trial. In November 1987, he was released, having served twenty-three years and four months. He received numerous awards, including an honorary Doctorate of Social Sciences from the University of Amsterdam; the naming of the health building at the Glasgow Caledonian University in his honour; and the ANC's highest award,

Isitwalandwe, in 1986. He has a rich and proud history of relentless and fearless commitment to internationalism and the struggle for democracy, human rights and freedom in South Africa and Africa.

Despite the demands of his overstretched life as a political activist and leader and his long imprisonment, Oom Gov wrote two seminal books which had an influence and impact on many people: *Transkei in the Making*[124] and *The Peasants' Revolt*.[125]

For information and assessments about his political life, I have relied on a Jacana Pocket Biography called *Govan Mbeki*[126] by Colin Bundy, which is easy to read and absorb.

Oom Gov was a prolific writer for progressive newspapers and journals such as *The Guardian*, *Spark*, *Fighting Talk*, and *Liberation*. With Harold Strachan, he edited a newsletter, *Izwe Lomzi* (Voice of the People). His articles were incisive and provided a window into the lives of working people in rural and urban areas in the Transkei and Eastern Cape. Given his training, understanding and knowledge of Marxism, his ability to apply class analysis was apparent in all his writing, which gave his work its great strength. Edward Roux, author of *Time Longer than Rope*,[127] an outstanding history of the revolutionary movements in South Africa, lit the fire that led to Mbeki's lifelong devotion to Marxism-Leninism. Not surprisingly, he and his wife Epainette (Piny) Mbeki named their first son 'Thabo' after Thabo Mofutsanyana, a leading member of the CPSA.

Oom Gov spent five months in prison during the State of Emergency (1960) in Rooi Hell prison in Port Elizabeth. As in other places, thousands were arrested, and Rooi Hell became so overcrowded that, to quote Bundy, 'No-one was able to lie on his bac[k]' with 'bedding infested with lice, food – bitter pap – served in tin cans, the warders jumping and hostile.'[128]

While in prison, Oom Gov kept a prison diary he was able to pass on to Mary Benson. When she gave evidence to the United Nations Committee on Apartheid in 1964, she quoted excerpts from it. In it, he wrote that when he and his comrades in the Eastern Cape had discussed the essential qualities of leadership, they agreed on 'personality, dignity, alertness, intelligence, sincerity, perseverance, determination, restraint and humility' – all qualities that can easily be ascribed to Oom Gov.

Undeterred by the banning of the ANC, Oom Gov attended the

---

124. Natal: Verulam, 1939.
125. Written in 1958 and first published by Penguin African Library in 1964.
126. Johannesburg: Jacana Media, 2012.
127. Victor Gollancz, 1948.
128. Colin Bundy, *Govan Mbeki*.

consultative conference in December 1966, which called for an 'all-in conference representative of the African People', and attended a secret meeting of some SACP members. At that meeting, they agreed to a break with the strategy and tactics of the past and decided to move towards armed resistance. Similar sentiments permeated the ranks of the ANC, and MK was formed, with Oom Gov as one of its founders.

Bundy writes, 'The first generation of MK combatants w[ere] high on courage, commitment and bravado.'[129] I disagree with the use of the word 'bravado', which to me implies recklessness, boastfulness and self-advertisement, a suggestion that is wrong and offensive. More apt words would be brave and courageous.

Oom Gov was a participant in the first acts of sabotage undertaken by MK in December 1961, and a few weeks later, he was arrested with Harold Strachan and Joseph Jack. Bundy records that, while in solitary confinement:

> He staved off boredom by practising all the dance steps he could recall, playing tiddlywinks with maize seeds and an empty cup, dredging up English and Latin verse, and by drafting what became the second version of *The Peasants' Revolt* on scraps of toilet paper obtained by barter.[130]

Oom Gov worked tirelessly in the underground structures of the ANC, SACP and MK and chaired the first ANC Conference in exile in Lobatse, Botswana, in 1962. In 1963, he was one of the most senior leaders of the ANC, a CC member of the SACP and in the High Command of MK. In that year, he went underground and was living at Liliesleaf Farm, Rivonia, with other leaders of the movement. Because the security was weak and there were too many visitors, Oom Gov, Walter Sisulu and Raymond Mhlaba were to be moved to Trevallyn. When it was decided to call everyone together to discuss the document 'Operation Mayibuye', the three were persuaded against their wishes to attend one last meeting in Rivonia, which, tragically, would be their last.

In July 1963, that place was raided, and all the leaders present were arrested. There, the security police found Operation Mayibuye, which they considered a highly incriminating document. The debate continues whether that controversial document had been adopted by the leadership of the ANC, SACP and MK before the police found it. I agree with those who argue that

---

129. Ibid.
130. Ibid.

there is no documentary evidence of its adoption.

During the Rivonia Trial, Walter Sisulu, Oom Gov and Ahmed Kathrada gave evidence that thoroughly annoyed the Chief Prosecutor, Percy Yutar, as it was a powerful demonstration of the depth of understanding, knowledge and consciousness of the accused. They were all found guilty and, to the relief of the oppressed masses in South Africa and our international supporters, sentenced to life imprisonment on Robben Island – not to death as many had feared. In fact, the huge international outcry against the possible death sentence probably averted its happening.

From 1965 to 1972, the high organ of the ANC on Robben Island consisted of Mandela, Sisulu, Mhlaba and Oom Gov. Bundy, Kathy and some others have written about the differences between Mandela and Oom Gov regarding a number of issues and challenges concerning strategy and tactics and the national democratic revolution. Although the differences between those two highly respected ANC and MK leaders were sharp and sometimes even acrimonious, to the great relief of the ANC prisoners on the Island, they were always resolved amicably without causing dissension or a split in the ranks of the organisation.

I first had the pleasure of meeting Oom Gov after returning home from exile, when the SACP had set up an Internal Leadership Group (ILG) with him on it. I had heard about his exploits and life, read his writings and avidly followed his history. We had named our son after him and learnt the origin of his name from his son, Thabo. Govan Mbeki had been named after the Reverend William Govan, a progressive Scottish missionary who was the first principal (1841–1870) of Lovedale College, which he founded under the Glasgow Missionary Society as a place of higher education for Africans. Govan argued that Black people should be educated to a level where they could access the professions, writing many polemical documents attacking those who opposed his views.

From our first meeting, my admiration for him grew until, by the end of his life, I adored him. At the inaugural meeting of the ILG, Oom Gov and Mhlaba were flying to Johannesburg economy class. After discussions with Slovo and a few others, it was decided at my suggestion that, notwithstanding the parlous financial position of the Party, they should travel business class, an offer they both accepted.

From 1990, I had a lot of meetings, interactions and discussions with Oom Gov, and on at least three occasions, accompanied him on overseas visits. The second of these was to the Royal African Society's Conference on Sub-

Saharan Africa in April 1991 at St John's College, Cambridge, which was attended by 210 participants. I remember helping to prepare his paper. The third was to the People's Republic of China when he was Deputy President of the Senate, later renamed the National Council of Provinces, one of the two post-apartheid Houses of Parliament. In this memoir, I shall only write about his visit to Glasgow, which was his first.

Oom Gov was invited to deliver the Opening Address to the Sechaba International Conference and Festival: Cultural Resistance to Apartheid in September 1990. As I had only returned to South Africa in July, I was reluctant to go abroad so soon. But the pull of seeing Meg, Amina and Govan and many friends and comrades in London proved irresistible.

The children had heard about Oom Gov all their lives and sent cards to him and Kathy on Robben Island and often seen his photograph. Eight-year-old Govan, still very small for his age, was standing with Meg in a group waiting for Oom Gov to arrive. When he saw him, he broke away from his mother and, to our surprise and joy, ran to jump into his namesake's arms. Oom Gov caught him and gave him a big hug.

We spent a day or two in London, and Oom Gov was happy to visit us at our home in West Kilburn, where we also invited his grandson Karl (Moeletsi's son) with his mother Dorothy. Govan and Amina behaved as if he were their grandfather too, and Oom Gov was very affectionate with them and Karl, really enjoying himself after all those years deprived from human touch.

Our old comrade and friend Brian Filling was one of the main organisers of the Sechaba Conference and Festival, and I had been asked to draft the opening address, so in South Africa, before we left, and again in London, he and I held intensive discussions about what the speech should contain. Oom Gov had a great deal to say on various aspects of South African and universal culture and on the basis of his extensive input, I drafted the address. When we arrived in Glasgow, I asked Brian to review and edit it, which he did and made some important suggestions, which we incorporated.

The speech was well received and has been published in the book *The End of a Regime? An Anthology of Scottish-South African Writing Against Apartheid*, edited by Brian Filling and Susan Stuart. On rereading it, I feel a little proud that I was the main writer. Below I quote a few excerpts.

> Without a deepening of our cultural life, there can be no real deepening of our political life, and therefore only a superficial deepening of the revolutionary dynamic ...

The ANC and its allies – both in the prelude to their assumption of power and as a government – must work to ensure that, on the one hand, universal culture becomes the common possession of all South Africa's cultural groups, while on the other hand, promoting the development of all or particular cultures so that the finest fruits they can bear become part of the universal treasury of mankind ...[131]

And on the role of the masses, Oom Gov said:

Without their creativity, energy and faith, nothing will be possible. Everything depends on them, for it is their culture, their traditions, their life-world which we are proposing to assert against the claims of apartheid. But they have carried us on their shoulders in every other phase of the struggle. They will not let us down.[132]

During Oom Gov's tenure as Deputy President of the Senate, I visited him frequently at his Groote Schuur residence. When I missed a visit, he would phone and enquire if I was ill or too busy. I really enjoyed those visits and chats. We discussed the role, place and function of parliament in a democratic society, and we agreed that it should be a people's parliament influenced by the masses of our country that should strive to represent their interests, grievances, hopes and desires.

Oom Gov was very vocal about the lack of interest shown by the ANC, SACP, the government and representative institutions about how initiation ceremonies were conducted in the Eastern Cape, with consequent loss of lives. He would enquire about my work and Thabo's approach to various issues and challenges in South Africa, Africa and the world, and where he thought we were falling short, he was stern but fair in his criticisms. One evening, he said to me he thought Thabo's posture when delivering his speech to parliament left a lot to be desired, going on to say that Thabo should learn to look up at the audience from time to time and not just read from the script. Also that the rich content of Thabo's speeches was lost by the form of delivery because reading an address in a monotone can lose the attention of the audience. I agreed, with the qualification that the content of his speeches was so rich and the prose so beautiful that he did not usually lose

---

131. B. Filling and S. Stuart (eds), *The End of a Regime? An Anthology of Scottish-South African Writing Against Apartheid* (Aberdeen, Scotland: Aberdeen University Press, 1991).
132. Ibid.

his audience. As asked, I appraised Thabo of Oom Gov's view, and he took it in his stride and agreed to consider it.

Many who didn't know Oom Gov or were prone to malice and prejudice have circulated their opinion that he joined the struggle late, was dogmatic, a strict disciplinarian in the form of a schoolmaster and could be ruthless and unforgiving. All these so-called criticisms are devoid of truth. Instead, he instilled in the ANC, SACP and MK comrades the importance and necessity of discipline in their work and conduct and had a refreshingly open mind about Marxism and other revolutionary theories. He was compassionate, dignified, gracious, kind and forgiving. He played rugby at school and learnt ballroom dancing. His love for music included indigenous music, instrumental and dance music, freedom songs and workers' songs, and Western classical music. He was thrilled when he was asked to be patron of the Cape Town Symphony Orchestra.

Govan Mbeki was one of the greatest, most illustrious revolutionaries ever produced by our people and our movement. I learnt and benefited a tremendous amount from reading about his past and interacting with him later. He had a powerful influence on my thinking, understanding and analysis of our history, the democratic dispensation and the arduous, complex and multifaceted demands of building a non-racial, non-sexist, democratic and prosperous South Africa.

We cannot talk or write about Oom Gov without mentioning his partner from the thirties until his death, Epainette, known as Piny. Piny joined the SACP before Oom Gov, the second African woman to join. She was short in stature with a proud and dignified bearing and bore with courage the loss of her husband to the struggle and prison and her two older sons, Thabo and Moeletsi, to exile. Her other son, Jama, who had completed a law degree at Leeds University, disappeared in Lesotho in 1982, believed to have been assassinated. Until her dying day, she tried to find out what had happened to Jama and her beloved Kwanda, a son Thabo left behind as a baby when he went into exile. Kwanda had lived with Piny from the age of ten to seventeen when he and a cousin left in 1976 to join the struggle and disappeared. They are also thought to have been killed by the South African Security Police.

Fortunately, they also had a daughter, Linda, who was a year older than Thabo and a great help to her mother in every way, particularly with running the store and the household, providing company, support and affectionate grandchildren.

Oliver Reginald Tambo 1917–1993

In my view, O. R. Tambo is the greatest South African our country has produced. From his earliest schooldays and at the University of Fort Hare, Tambo excelled in his studies. His extraordinary leadership of the ANC can be traced back to September 1944 when, under the leadership of Anton Lembede, Tambo, together with others including Nelson Mandela, Walter Sisulu, William Nkomo and A. P. Mda, founded the ANC Youth League (ANCYL), and he was elected national secretary. The ANCYL would go on to play a significant and militant role in building the ANC into a powerful mass movement that would lead the struggle against colonialism, racism and apartheid.

Two of those young lions, Mda and Lembede, were elected to the NEC of the ANC in 1945, and in 1947, Tambo was elected to that high office. The ANCYL was instrumental in the ANC's adoption of the Programme of Action (POA) in 1949, which galvanised the ANC into taking more militant mass-based actions to confront and challenge apartheid and seek freedom for the oppressed and super-exploited African people.

Already then, Tambo's leadership qualities were evident. Not surprisingly, when Walter Sisulu was banned from undertaking all political activities in 1954, Comrade O. R. was elected to replace him as Secretary-General. In 1957, he was elected deputy president to Chief Albert Luthuli. When Luthuli died in 1967 under suspicious circumstances – supposedly accidentally hit by a train while taking a walk – Tambo was elevated to acting president. In 1969 at the Morogoro Conference, he was elected president, and at the National Conference of the ANC in 1991, he was elected chairman. No other individual in the history of the ANC has held all those positions.

I remember Tambo coming to my parents' flat when I was a young boy. Orient House was very near to the Tambo Mandela legal office in Chancellor House where, at that time, Mendi Msimang, who would later be elected treasurer-general of the ANC, was working there for no pay. Mendi related to Luli Callinicos how, when he and O. R. were hungry, 'they would drop in at the ever hospitable Pahad family ... or find Ahmed Kathrada ... where they might enjoy a spicy curry'.[133]

For anyone interested in the life and times of O. R. Tambo, I recommend Luli Callinicos's fascinating biography, *Oliver Tambo: Beyond the Engeli Mountains*,[134] which should be read together with *Oliver Tambo*

---

133. Luli Callinicos, Oliver Tambo: Beyond the Engeli Mountains. Cape Town: David Philip, 2004, p. 192.
134. Ibid.

Remembered, edited by Pallo Jordan[135] and *Oliver Tambo Speaks*, compiled by Adelaide Tambo.[136]

Following the Sharpeville massacre on 21 March 1960, the banning of the ANC and PAC and the declaration of a state of emergency in the same year, the ANC had the foresight and presence of mind to ask Tambo to leave the country. His task was to set up ANC offices abroad, mobilise international solidarity and generally assist the banned organisation.

Thus began O. R.'s long, arduous, stamina-sapping journey into exile that would last for three decades. Back then, he and the ANC were unaware that the mantle of leading the ANC and the resistance to an increasingly arrogant and murderous regime would fall on his shoulders. During those thirty years, the ANC faced the most challenging times, and by 1963, with the Rivonia arrests and those of the second High Command of MK, the apartheid regime gleefully boasted that it had broken the back of the ANC.

Inside the country, active resistance had come to a halt, and the international Anti-Apartheid Movement was still taking shape. Several African countries supported the PAC, as they incorrectly insisted that the ANC had to be 'Africanised' since it was too influenced by whites, Coloureds and Indians. In addition, more and more South Africans were going into exile, with many joining MK, and preparations had to be made to provide military training. All of that added to the heavy burden Tambo was carrying.

Comrade O. R., however, was tougher than nails: a highly disciplined, incredibly hard worker who gave his all to retain and promote the unity and cohesion of the ANC so the organisation could assist in building international solidarity against apartheid.

Comrade President kept us together in exile – one of the most challenging tasks for any leader to accomplish – in the dimmest moments of our struggle when the apartheid regime seemed unbeatable, and resistance inside the country was at its lowest ebb. He was more than the glue that bound us together: he criss-crossed the world, drumming up support for the ANC. With the help of Moses Kotane, Dr Dadoo and J. B. Marks, he convinced the CPSU and the Soviet Union to support our armed struggle, and at critical moments, he was there to inspire and help MK combatants. When the Wankie and Sipolilo campaigns were initiated, Comrade O. R. was there to see the combatants off. Then, after the debilitating fighting inside MK and when the Chris Hani memorandum threatened to tear the ANC apart, O. R. was there to calm people down, listen attentively to the different views and

---
135. Johannesburg: Pan Macmillan, 2007.
136. *Oliver Tambo Speaks*, edited by Adelaide Tambo. London: Heinemann, 1987.

present a voice of reason to find just ways of solving problems. He steadied the ship and rallied the troops. An important outcome of that sensible search for solutions was the Morogoro Conference of 1969.

At that watershed conference, Tambo offered to resign, following harsh criticism of the ANC leadership by some of the delegates. However, Kotane, Dadoo, J. B. Marks, Moses Mabhida, Joe Slovo and others persuaded him to return to the Conference, where he was elected President of the ANC and Head of the Revolutionary Council. Dr Dadoo was elected as his deputy.

In the decade and a half following that conference, the ANC increased its influence inside and outside South Africa. Internally, we had seen the Soweto and connected uprisings of June 1976, the workers' strikes beginning in Durban in 1973, followed by strengthened union activity over the next twelve years and the founding and growth of the UDF from 1983, which took resistance inside the country to new heights. In addition, the post-Soweto generation swelled the ranks of MK, giving it a much-needed injection of militancy and dedication.

During those years, the apartheid regime and its lethal security forces continued their violent assault on the people. In the early eighties, funerals of young people killed by that criminal state were held regularly; ironically, those funerals bred new freedom fighters and became sites of struggle.

After an extensive period of open and intense discussions within ANC structures throughout the world – including in the MK camps, which was unprecedented, especially in a banned organisation – the time was ripe for another consultative conference, and Tambo once more offered his wise and astute leadership.

That conference was the Kabwe Conference of 1985, which O. R. Tambo opened to rapturous applause from the delegates, most of whom were from the post-Soweto uprising generation. One of the issues raised for consideration was whether to open elections to the NEC to non-Africans. In his political report, Comrade President indicated his preference for such a decision, and, as detailed earlier in Chapter 4, five non-Africans were elected.

When Oliver Tambo was elected unopposed as President of the ANC, there was thunderous applause, with delegates giving him a standing ovation. Many of us who had the privilege and honour of attending Kabwe shed tears of joy and happiness. Tambo was the undisputed leader of the ANC, the Tripartite Alliance and MK – a recognition of his qualities as a person and leader.

Tambo was humble, self-effacing, cool, calm and an excellent listener. He had a fine intellect and was capable of grasping the finer points of the strategy and tactics of revolutionary struggle; he could work with people, young and old, cutting across race, class and gender, was unafraid to assert his leadership and, when necessary, could be a strict disciplinarian. He had a lovely smile accompanying his fine sense of humour. As he loved his immediate family, it troubled him that he was rarely able to offer quality time to his wife and children. He was always kind to me, engaging in discussion, asking about my family and treating me with respect – not only me, he dealt with all the members and cadres of the movement in the same manner.

But Tambo could also be a tough taskmaster. Many of us remember how at conferences, we would be drafting a speech for him, and he would read each draft carefully, including inserting or changing commas and full stops before suggesting changes, a process that could go on for hours. I remember one occasion, when he was dissatisfied with our final draft; without saying anything to us, he just spoke from notes he had made. Interestingly, Thabo Mbeki, who later wrote so many of O. R.'s speeches and documents, recalls:

> Many a time, I had to live with the embarrassment of O. R. completely rejecting my draft texts and, on a number of occasions, using his own notes to deliver addresses radically different from the draft speech I had prepared.[137]

At NEC meetings, O. R. would listen to all the speakers with interest and patience, only making his contribution at the end. He had a great ability to sum up the discussions, taking into account the sharp differences, even contradictory opinions, in a manner that was a fair and honest reflection of the debate. At the end, the NEC would accept his summation and reflections unanimously. He was generous with his time and would listen to people's views and problems, even on private family issues. Tambo was thoughtful and considerate. Very seldom did he show any anger or animosity, even to his opponents.

Comrade O. R. gave his all to the movement, and when the time came to consider the possibilities of negotiations, he felt that the Frontline States might take a position and impose their views on the ANC. To prevent that, he set up a group of ANC people to draft the Harare Declaration, which contained the ANC's precise position on several issues, including engaging with the apartheid regime while intensifying the struggle on all fronts. That was not without dissent in the ranks of the ANC, the Tripartite Alliance and the MK

---

137. Z. Pallo Jordan, *Oliver Tambo Remembered*. Johannesburg: Pan Macmillan, 2007, p. xvii.

camps, but, as always, Tambo used his persuasive skills to win over the sceptics. That document was also circulated to ANC leaders and structures and the UDF inside South Africa. To ensure that it would be adopted by the OAU and other international organisations, O. R. decided that it should first be taken to the Frontline States for their approval.

Kenneth Kaunda made his personal aeroplane available to Tambo and his delegation to visit those countries, and O. R. was accompanied by Thabo Mbeki, Pallo Jordan, Steve Tshwete, Penuell Maduna and Ngoako Ramathlodi. On that trip, Tambo patiently and carefully spelt out the Harare Declaration, listening intently to the critical views of his interlocutors and figuring out how to integrate their opinions into the document. Again, devoting his energy and time to the task at hand, he did not spare himself. Returning to Lusaka, in spite of his fatigue, he briefed the National Working Committee (NWC), which, after intense discussions, adopted it. That day, he had more meetings. Then, in the evening, disaster struck when Comrade President had a stroke. Mama Tambo was about to leave for Lusaka when Kaunda informed her that he had arranged for a plane to take O. R. to London for treatment. That plane belonged to Tiny Rowland and had been about to leave for London.

In London, O. R. received the best medical care and was lovingly tended by Adelaide. But it was a debilitating attack which left one arm paralysed and his speech impaired. Fortunately, his mental prowess and capacity remained intact. He slowly recovered and then went to a hospital in Stockholm. September 1989 will live forever in our minds, as at a most critical juncture in our struggle, we were without our pilot, our leader, our mentor.

Then, 2 February 1990 arrived, and we were unbanned, and political prisoners, including Mandela, were to be released. Tambo's foresight in preparing the Harare Declaration proved prescient and correct.

When Comrade President O. R. returned home to attend the ANC's Consultative Conference in Johannesburg from 14–16 December 1990, he received a hero's welcome at the airport and at the Conference, which was attended by over 1,500 delegates. I attended as a representative of the SACP. The ANC had held consultative conferences in exile, but the main purpose of this 1990 conference was to discuss policy and prepare for a properly constituted National Conference the following year. In his autobiography, Mandela records that Tambo's speech to the Conference, in which he called for a re-evaluation of sanctions, was 'met with indignation by ANC militants'.

Immediately thereafter, the ANC had to prepare for its first National Conference since its banning in 1960, which had to be attended by delegates from properly constituted ANC branches who could elect their new leadership. In July 1991, more than 2,000 delegates elected by branches inside and outside South Africa descended on Durban for the ANC's 48th National Conference (2–7 July), and once again, I was happy that the SACP had asked me to be one of the five invited delegates from the party. This conference had the huge task of preparing the ANC for the critical transformation from an illegal organisation to a legal one with branches throughout the country. It also had the responsibility of electing new office bearers and the NEC.

At that conference, Comrade President handed the baton to Nelson Mandela – and he did it with the grace and goodwill, warmth and comradeship characteristic of the O. R. Tambo we loved and cherished. In recognition of his mighty contribution to the ANC, he was elected chairman of the organisation, a newly created post. Walter Sisulu was elected deputy president, and Cyril Ramaphosa defeated Alfred Nzo for the position of secretary-general.

At that time, it was such a pleasure to go to the ANC headquarters, where the magnificent three, Mandela, Sisulu and Tambo, had their offices on the same floor, next to each other.

But in April 1993, two events would rock the ANC, SACP and the masses of our people. The first was the dastardly assassination of Chris Hani, General Secretary of the SACP, NEC member of the ANC, and leader of MK on 10 April.

Oliver Tambo was severely affected by the assassination and went to Hani's house every day and attended all of the funeral proceedings, despite his ill health. Sadly, that took its toll, and two weeks later, Comrade O. R., Comrade President, hero of heroes, passed away.

Upon hearing that deeply distressing news, I immediately thought of Jawaharlal Nehru's memorable phrase on the death of India's icon, Mahatma Gandhi: 'The Light has Gone Out.' For me, as for countless others at home and abroad, the light that so illuminated our fight for freedom, the light that kept us together during the most difficult and dreadful days of our struggle, the light that inspired and sustained the international anti-apartheid solidarity movement, the light that led us to freedom – had gone out. Comrade Oliver Reginald Tambo, our leader, guide and mentor, was no more.

In summing up some of O. R.'s qualities, I would like to quote some of the other people who have expressed themselves so eloquently.

In his autobiography, Nelson Mandela wrote:

Oliver was pure gold; there was gold in his intellectual brilliance, gold in his warmth and humility, gold in his tolerance and generosity, gold in his unfailing loyalty and self-sacrifice.[138]

At Tambo's funeral on 2 May 1993, Mandela said:

> A great giant who strode the world like a colossus has fallen. A mind whose thoughts have opened the doors to our liberty has ceased to function. A heart whose dreams gave hope to the despised has forever lost its beat. The gentle voice whose measured words of reason shook the thrones of tyrants has been silenced ...[139]

Walter Sisulu, the much loved and venerated leader of the ANC and SACP and mentor of so many ANC leaders, said:

> O. R. has qualities of his own ... [he] is one of the best in assessing a position. He speaks less. He observes and comes to a conclusion when everybody has spoken, everybody has expressed an opinion. This, I think, is the characteristic that made him so successful in mobilising the exile; in bringing about stability to a community ... you hardly come across anybody who was hostile. I think he was the most loved leader.[140]

Thabo Mbeki summarised what distinguished O. R. as follows:

- an unwavering commitment to serve the people of South Africa with no expectation of any personal benefit ...
- a sustained determination to conduct himself in his personal life so that ... he would never betray the ethical standards ...
- the commitment ... of his enormous intellectual capacity and personal energy to pursue the objectives of the National Democratic Revolution;
- his ability as an outstanding strategist ...
- his flexibility as a master tactician ...
- his capacity to communicate well-thought-out, clear and relevant messages ...

---

138. Nelson Mandela, *Long Walk to Freedom*, p. 601.
139. Z. Pallo Jordan, *Oliver Tambo Remembered*.
140. Luli Callinicos, *Oliver Tambo: Beyond the Engeli Mountains*, pp. 622–623.

- his ability to ensure the cohesion of the forces of revolution ...[141]

Gertrude Shope, a leader of the ANC and its Women's League, wrote:

> As a person, Oliver was humble in character, very down to earth and always ready to assist, including in our personal lives ... Oliver played the role of father in the absence of our parents.[142]

Gertrude points to Tambo's deep commitment to the involvement of women in our struggle and to the objective of the empowerment and emancipation of women. She quotes from a speech he made to the first conference of the ANC Women's Section in Lusaka, where he said:

> Women in the ANC should stop behaving as if there is no place for them above the level of certain categories of involvement. They have a duty to liberate us men from antique concepts and attitudes about the place and role of women in society and the development and direction of our revolutionary struggle ... The struggle to conquer oppression in our country is the weaker for the traditionalist, conservative and primitive restraints imposed on women by man-dominated structures within our movement ... We need to move from revolutionary declarations to revolutionary practice.[143]

He called on Black women:

> more oppressed and more exploited than any section of the population, to take up this challenge and assume their proper role, outside the kitchen among the fighting ranks of our movement and its command posts.[144]

Under Tambo's leadership, the ANC became more sensitive to the critical importance of women at all levels of the organisation.

Pallo Jordan, in his appreciation of O. R., raised the question of leading a diverse movement. He writes:

---

141. Oliver Tambo, *Oliver Tambo Speaks*, 2nd edition (Cape Town: Kwela, 2014), pp. 19–20.
142. *Oliver Tambo Remembered*, p. 209.
143. Ibid. p. 212.
144. Z. Pallo Jordan, *Oliver Tambo, Remembered*, p. xxviii.

O. R., perhaps better than many others, understood that it was not possible to suppress and silence the contradictions inherent in such a diverse movement. He mastered the art of giving political leadership to such a movement by the creative management of those contradictions, permitting open and free debate within the movement's ranks ... However, he never permitted such debate to impair the movement's capacity for united action. ... The practice he encouraged was a continuous search for consensus accompanied by an insistence on disciplined united action.[145]

In an article in *The Thinker*, Dali Tambo recalls a childhood memory which provides insight into Comrade O. R.'s great compassion, love and patience:

> My father was one of the greatest and first environmentalists. Because his whole philosophy was that if you were created by God, your right to life was self-evident, was a given.
>
> So we were taught not to kill insects and animals, bees, wasps, flies, moths – to the point where one time he was on the phone, [and] I was chasing this moth trying to hit it, and he came off the phone, and I was about to stomp it, kill it, and he said to me, 'Why are you doing that, take that moth gently outside and put it on a leaf so it can eat.'
>
> And then another time, there was an ants' nest. I had deliberately spilled some fizzy drinks around it and things they would like, and they were all over this food, and then I put some paraffin and set them alight. And he was watching me from the window of the house and again he came down and challenged me and explained to me that I had destroyed a city with a whole life system going on and that these ants have mothers, fathers, brothers, sisters. He told me in a way that a child can understand that I must respect their life, and I felt guilty about it.
>
> The next day, I wrote a poem about that, about how I didn't just destroy some ants, I committed genocide. And I gave him that poem as an apology.[146]

---

145. Ibid.
146. Dali Tambo, 'A partnership forged in Struggle', *The Thinker*, Vol. 58, December 2013. Available at https://docplayer.net/89950803-December-2013-volume-58-the-thinker-lest-we-forget.html

Mongane Wally Serote, one of South Africa's greatest poets and our country's current poet laureate, crafted an epic poem, *Sikhahlel'u-OR: A Praise Poem for Oliver Tambo*, which should be read and studied in our institutions of learning but also treasured and read often by those who loved that great man. Here are two extracts from his poem:

> i do not know if dadoo still needs his pipe
> his pipe dangling from his clenched teeth
> does he need it
> to smoke and ponder the distances travelled
> does he need it to stop and be still
> to ponder
> do you O. R.
> need your spectacles to see into distances far and near
> do you still need your pondo marks
> which made you glow and gave you a presence
> of the mapondomise who erased the distance they travelled
> and mingled the many languages
> of where they had been
>
> you strode the world after you learnt from them ...[147] (p. 67)

And
> O. R.
> showed us wisdom as it flowed
> like clean transparent water over rocks
> human beings
> oh humans
> with so many shades and sights looking this way and that way
> these beings which can be anything
> can also be so grandiose and deep with truth
> how did you fathom this to make it your own
> what knowledge
> what belief
> what understanding
> how did you reach out to become them
> we ask

---
147. Cape Town: Kwela, 2019, p. 67.

you who learnt to befriend hope and patience
O. R.
you who held love with your glittering eye
gave without second thought and any expectation
on the same way
your anger at nonsense was as sharp as a lion's claws
you pursued freedom for the people because
you were one with them
and they with you
such granite-hard love
you gave and left us
you
the tall man
the handsome man
broad shoulders and watchful dancing eyes behind glasses[148]

Amongst the many honours and accolades bestowed on Tambo at home are the renaming of the official home of the Deputy President of South Africa to O. R. Tambo House, a National Order: Companion of O. R. Tambo, and the renaming of the Johannesburg airport to O. R. Tambo International Airport in 2006; it had previously been named after Jan Smuts. And in the UK, the local Haringey Council unveiled a memorial to O. R. in 2007; in 2019, a statue; and in 2021, they renamed the recreation ground, a few hundred metres from the Tambo family home in London, The O. R. Tambo Recreation Ground.

However, no reflection on Comrade O. R. would be complete without mentioning the role and place of Mama Adelaide Tambo, an ANC revolutionary cadre and leader in her own right. Born in 1929, at the age of eighteen, Adelaide joined the ANCYL and trained as a nurse. Later, while exiled in London, she was a professional health worker, at times working two shifts to earn enough money to keep the family together. Mama Adelaide died at her home in Johannesburg in 2007.

In addition to her son Dali and two daughters, Tselane and Thembi, Mama Adelaide maintained that she had four other sons – Thabo (her favourite), my brother Aziz, Pallo Jordan and me. She also mothered several young women in the ANC who were studying and living in the UK, referring to some of them as her daughters. She took that role seriously, and many of

---

148. Cape Town: Kwela, 2019, pp. 76–77.

us were rebuked if she thought we were not behaving appropriately or working diligently. Mama Adelaide constantly reminded me that she had not been invited to Aziz and my double wedding, and on one occasion, when I met her and O. R. at the Party Hotel in Moscow, she berated me during dinner for not being on the front line of the struggle, which had escalated following the Soweto uprising. Comrade President listened patiently and, after about ten minutes, said quietly and with a smile, 'Adelaide, leave Essop alone; he is doing good work where he is.'

A few weeks after Comrade O. R.'s death, I would go daily to their home to pay my respects. On one occasion, Adelaide was sitting on a sofa receiving visitors. When I went to greet her, she motioned for me to come close to her and whispered in my ear, 'You are Thabo's friend. You must look after him.' I imagine she said that since she was aware that there were some in our broad alliance who were not friendly to Thabo Mbeki.

Zanele Mbeki, in an interview with Lindiwe Mabuza, says of Mama Tambo:

> She had an open house for the ANC youth ... At one time, she worked around eighteen hours a day because she had a day and night job ... [By looking after her children, family and other ANC members], she was making it possible for O. R. to be the leader he was.[149]

Adelaide was a wonderful, charming host to the many visitors to their home, even when Comrade O. R. was recovering from his debilitating stroke. Wally Serote recounts how, in 1990, when they were organising the enormous cultural event 'Zabalaza' on five consecutive days, they met with Tambo at this home. At times, there were twenty to thirty visitors, but Mama would welcome them graciously and, at O. R.'s request, ensure they were served with tea and cake. Tambo would sign twenty or more copies of his book *Oliver Tambo Speaks* with his unaccustomed left hand, as his right one had been incapacitated by the recent stroke.[150]

In 1987 or 1988, Frank Chikane, then-General Secretary of the South African Council of Churches, came to London accompanied by Mary Ntswaki Mxadana, Lenki Khanyile and Thembi Sekgaphane, and I arranged with Mama for them to visit Comrade O. R. at home. Although it was his birthday and they had decided on a private family get-together, she agreed to

---

149. *Oliver Tambo Remembered*, pp. 118–119.
150. Ibid. P. 207.

my request. As always, she gave the visitors a warm welcome, and Comrade President really enjoyed the evening, especially the choral songs by the three women in their beautiful melodious voices and Frank's accounts of developments in South Africa. When I reminded Frank about that encounter, he told me:

> It was one of the most exciting moments – to meet O. R. Tambo at home. It left an indelible mark on me. Oliver Tambo remains my reference point about what the ANC, South Africa and the world should strive to be.[151]

Mama Tambo served as an ANC MP for one term, from 1994–1999, when she sat next to Lindiwe Mabuza. The two were hard-working MPs who diligently attended all the sessions of the National Assembly and, when requested, addressed them. Adelaide was awarded the Order of the Baobab in 2002. She and O. R. had shared a wonderful partnership since their marriage in 1956.

Henry Winston (1911–1986)

Henry Winston was a Black American who was proud of his race, colour and political affiliation. For over fifty-five years, he served the struggle for Black human rights, equality and democracy with distinction, courage and intellectual rigour.

When he died, I wrote an article entitled 'Henry Winston: A Man of Vision' in *The African Communist* under the pseudonym Vusizwe Seme. I should like to open this part of my memoir with that thirty-four-year-old tribute, which I believe still holds true.

> Henry Winston, National Chairman of the Communist Party of the USA, an outstanding and internationally renowned fighter for racial equality and justice, peace, national liberation and socialism, died in Moscow on 12 December 1986 at the age of 75. A grandson of slaves, he grew up in Mississippi at a time when that state was ravaged by racism and racist lynchings. In 1922, the family moved to Kansas City to join his father, who had found employment as a steel worker. Winnie, as he was popularly known, attended a segregated school, the Abraham Lincoln High School. But he was forced to seek work before

---
151. From a conversation I had with Frank.

he could complete his secondary education. It was then that he made contact with the Communist Party of the USA for the first time. At the age of 20, he led a group of unemployed people to join the Hunger March of 1931 in Washington, DC.

Two years later, he joined the CPUSA and from then on devoted his indefatigable energy and boundless enthusiasm to the cause of liberating humanity from the evils of racism, national oppression, imperialism and capitalist exploitation. His courage and commitment were put to a severe test during the Cold War period. In 1948, 12 members of the Political Bureau [PB] of the US Communist Party were indicted under the notorious anti-communist Smith Act. Justice US-style was not for communists, and four members of the PB, including Gus Hall and Henry Winston, were forced to go underground. For five years, Winnie worked in the underground, eluding all efforts of the FBI to apprehend him. After his arrest, he served 5 years in prison where he completed his secondary education at the age of 50. Released in 1961, he had suffered from headaches and dizzy spells in prison, but, owing to the wilful negligence of the prison authorities, he received no treatment until 1990, when a tumour was removed in a New York hospital. Although he was left permanently blind, the government still refused to release him for another year.[152]

On his release from prison, Winston, unbowed and undaunted, declared at the first mass meeting he attended, 'They robbed me of my sight, but not my vision.' This vision of a world free from racial discrimination, class exploitation and war helped him to overcome the terrible hardships endured by blacks in the USA and the additional disability of blindness. In so-called free and democratic USA, the Afro-Americans continue to suffer from racism. They are the last hired and first fired, and on average, the wages of black workers are still lower than those of their white counterparts.

Comrade Winston was a warm-hearted, generous and compassionate human being. He possessed the admirable quality of making any person, irrespective of age, sex and position, feel at ease. On meeting someone for the first time, he would ask his wife Fern, or

---

152. In a 1961 debate with President John F. Kennedy, Fidel Castro called for the release of Winston and other political prisoners.

the person accompanying him, for a description of the individual to whom he had just been introduced. At times, he would display an uncanny sense of recall. For example, I met him for the first time 12 years ago. Two years later, I had the pleasure of meeting him once again. On hearing the name and voice, he not only recalled my physical and facial characteristics, but also the conversation that we had had. For me, Winnie combined the theoretical depth and organisational strength of Moses Kotane with the ebullient and loveable personality of J. B. Marks. In discussion, Winston listened attentively to all points of view. Yet, he could be merciless in polemicizing with his ideological and political opponents. His remarkable output of articles, speeches and reports was supplemented by two major books, *Strategy for a Black Agenda – A Critique of New Theories of Liberation in the United States and Africa*[153] and *Class, Race and Black Liberation*.[154] In both books, he takes issue with those who seek to dilute the purity of Marxism-Leninism, reduce or eliminate the leading role of the working class, turn African nationalism into narrow chauvinism or link it with black capitalism. He also took issue with those who make superficial comparisons between the oppression of the Black American minority in the US and that imposed on the peoples of present and former imperialist dominated colonies. On the latter point, he wrote:

> Those who talk of taking over the economy of the ghettos either through 'Black Revolution' or 'Black capitalism' fail to understand the fundamental difference between the position and demands of a colonial people and the oppressed Black people in the US.
>
> When freed of imperialist control, the colony has the possibility of developing a separate, viable economy on its own territory. But the ghetto enclaves across the country cannot form the basis for a viable economic life apart from the nation's total economy – either on a capitalist or a socialist basis.
>
> Unlike colonies, the ghettos scattered across the country have

---
153. New York: New Outlook Publishers, 1972.
154. New York: International Publishers, 1977

no economy and territory that can be separated from the monopoly-controlled economy dominating every nook and cranny of the country, including the ghettos. Moreover, unlike colonies, there are no riches in the form of oil, minerals, and agricultural products to be extracted from the ghettos.[155]

In one of the chapters in his second book, Winston exposes the dangers and weaknesses inherent in the arguments of those who suggest that 'the primary contradiction is between white and non-white workers instead of between imperialism and workers and peoples of all colours'. Furthermore, he points out:

> It is the bourgeois nationalist class orientation of Holden Roberto, Jonas Savimbi and Roy Innis – not skin colour – that determines 'code of conduct'.[156]

He also emphasises:

> In the era when the central contradiction is between the socialist system and the declining capitalist system, the liberation of emerging nations is intertwined with the ascendency of the international working class.[157]

Comrade Winston was an internationalist who never wavered in his admiration of and support for the Soviet Union and the countries of the socialist community. From their victories, progress and development, he derived optimism and confidence in the capacity of working people to shape their own future. He linked the fight for world peace with the defence and propagation of the peace policies and initiatives of the Soviet Union.

In the US solidarity movement, he worked consistently to consolidate and increase support for the ANC and SACP. No matter how busy he was, he was always ready to meet any ANC member who happened to be in New York. The comradely, warm meetings between him and leaders of our revolutionary alliance were characterised by serious discussions spiced with mutual affection and humour.

Elected National Chairman of the CPUSA in 1963, Winston was known

---

155. Henry Winston, *Strategy for a Black Agenda*, p. 303.
156. Henry Winston, *Class, Race and Black Liberation*, p. 67.
157. Ibid.

and loved by communists of other parties throughout the world. He was not only a deep theoretical thinker but also a superb organiser. Over nearly four decades, he played a prominent role in all the major struggles of the US working class, in particular of the Afro-Americans. If a comrade undertook some task, he would be exacting in checking whether or not that task had been accomplished. If not, he would be very critical. However, all comrades, young and old, knew that Winnie was always ready to offer a sympathetic ear to their problems – political or personal.

No tribute to Winston would be complete if it did not give due credit to his wife Fern. A wonderful, sensitive and warm-hearted person, she is an important political figure in her own right. A member of the National Council of the CPUSA, she is deeply involved in the difficult and complex struggles taking place in the United States. Over and above her own work, she helped Winnie in a myriad ways. In recognition of Fern's immeasurable contribution, Winston dedicated both his books to her.

To Fern, daughter Judy, two grandchildren, mother and sister, and to all his comrades, South African revolutionaries extend their deepest condolences.

The political, theoretical and ideological contribution of Henry Winston will continue to inspire and influence revolutionaries throughout the world. The Black Americans have produced some of the most outstanding thinkers, political activists, and cultural figures of the last century. It is not an exaggeration to rank Henry Winston with Frederick Douglass, W. E. B. Du Bois and Paul Robeson.

One of Winston's favourite poems was Robert Hayden's 'Frederick Douglass'. Lines from this poem make an equally appropriate elegy for comrade Henry Winston:

> When it is finally ours, this freedom, this liberty, this beautiful
> and terrible thing, needful to man as air,
> usable as earth; when it belongs at last to all,
> when it is truly instinct, brain matter, diastole, systole,
> reflex action; when it is finally won; when it is more
> than the gaudy mumbo jumbo of politicians:
> this man, this Douglass, this former slave, this Negro
> beaten to his knees, exiled, visioning a world
> where none is lonely, none hunted, alien,

---

158. Vusizwe Seme, 'Henry Winston: A Man of Vision', *The African Communist*, 2nd Quarter 1987, p. 93. Available at https://www.sahistory.org.za/sites/default/files/archive-files4/Acn10987.pdf

this man, superb in love and logic, this man
shall be remembered. Oh, not with statues' rhetoric,
not with legends and poems and wreaths of bronze alone,
but with the lives grown out of his life, the lives
fleshing his dream of the beautiful, needful thing.
(Robert Hayden, 1966)[158]

As you saw, I wrote, 'Winnie combined the theoretical depth and organisational strength of Moses Kotane with the ebullient and loveable personality of J. B. Marks.' In this memoir, I take the opportunity to add 'and the sharp political insight of Dr Yusuf Dadoo'.

⌘

When I first met Winston at the Party Hotel in Moscow in 1975, I was both excited and nervous, as I was already impressed by his book *Strategy for a Black Agenda*. As I greeted him and his wife, he asked Fern to bring me close to him, and he put his hands on my face, feeling it with tender care. Once he had done that, he said to Fern, 'He is a good comrade, warm and likeable.'

During the worst years of the Cold War, when anti-communism, anti-Sovietism, and racism were rampant in the political, economic and media operations in the USA, Black American communists stood up to be counted, and I am fortunate to have met and worked with some of those outstanding comrades. I have already written about John Pittman at the WMR; others I admired were James Jackson, Charlene Mitchell and Angela Davis.

Jackson's work and articles on racism in the USA and the struggle for a non-racial society free from capitalist ideology and domination influenced my thinking. He and Charlene Mitchell were both active in the World Peace Council and attended many of its meetings and those of the Afro-Asian People's Solidarity Organisation. Charlene was a staunch and unflinching supporter of the ANC and SACP. I met her and James at several international conferences, and it was a pleasure to share thoughts and discussions with them. We also shared many memories of Henry Winston.

Charlene was a leading member of the CPUSA until she, Jackson and Angela Davis left the Party, partly because of Gus Hall's authoritarian leadership, to form what they called the Committees of Correspondence,

---

158. Vusizwe Seme, 'Henry Winston: A Man of Vision', *The African Communist*, 2nd Quarter 1987, p. 93. Available at https://www.sahistory.org.za/sites/default/files/archive-files4/Acn10987.pdf

which also won the support of John and Margrit Pittman, our friends from the WMR. Gus Hall refused to pay Jackson his pension after he left the Party.

Angela Davis is a brave Black American Communist who took on the mighty US imperialist state from within the belly of the beast. A renowned philosopher, she wrote the highly commendable book *Women, Race and Class*.[159] While a student, she was active in a communist party branch and the Black Panthers. Angela was an active member of the Soledad Brothers Defense Committee.

In 1970, George Jackson's younger brother took a judge, a prosecutor and three jurors hostage at gunpoint and demanded the release of the Soledad brothers.[160] He was one of several people, including the judge, killed in a gun battle as they fled the scene. Angela was accused of complicity in the killing and charged with murder. She went into hiding and, at the age of twenty-eight, was put on the FBI's 'Ten Most Wanted Fugitives' list. When she was finally arrested, that obnoxious and disgraced President Nixon hailed the 'capture of the dangerous terrorist, Angela Davis'. That gave rise to the massive international 'Free Angela Davis' campaign in which Aretha Franklin, the Queen of Soul music, offered to pay her bail, and the Rolling Stones and John Lennon and Yoko Ono wrote songs about her. Angela spent sixteen months in jail, and the campaign helped to save her from the gallows.

When released from prison, Angela was much in demand as a guest speaker by many communist parties, and the CPGB, which had been active in the campaign to free her, also invited her. She agreed to go to the UK on the condition that she was a joint guest of the CPGB and the SACP. She was given an escort/minder from both organisations, and it was my honour to be allocated to her by the SACP. I made the most of the opportunity to benefit from her experience, and she was equally keen to learn about our struggle. She is an ardent admirer of Winston.

Angela Davis remains a towering intellect and powerful orator and is still active in the struggle against racism and sexism for a better life for all humanity and the reform of the US prison system. We remain in contact and see her occasionally when she visits South Africa through Trevor Fowler, who is still her close friend.

Those four comrades – Winston, Jackson, Mitchell and Davis – enriched my political life, ideological standpoint and commitment to the struggle against any form or manifestation of racism and sexism. With them, I had

---

159. New York: Random House, 1981.
160. For more info, visit https://freedomarchives.org/Documents/Finder/DOC513_scans/Soledad_Brothers/513.Soledad.Brothers.Support.the.Soledad.Brothers.pdf

extensive discussions about Henry Winston.

In a lecture to Communist Party organisers in 1971 Winston said that:

> ... all democratic and anti-monopoly forces, with the working class and Black liberation in the van, can effectively defend the interests of the vast majority of people when they actively further the struggle against racism. This is an essential precondition for the development of a fighting alliance which will unite all democratic and anti-monopoly [anti-capitalist] forces in the country.
>
> Marx wrote long ago that 'labour in a white skin can never be free while labour in the black skin is branded'. This profound observation points up the fact that racism is the consciously employed weapon of the white imperialist oppressors, who use it to create division in the ranks of the working class. And Marx correctly suggests that white workers must take the lead in the struggle against racism. This is the path that can lead to unity of Black and white workers in struggle, which can achieve Black equality and a real improvement in the conditions of all workers.

In my review of his book, *Class, Race and Black Liberation*, I write that Winston, 'with piercing clarity', shows that the denial of the class struggle and anti-imperialist solidarity in the USA and Africa:

> ... lead eventually to collaboration with the very forces of racial oppression which they claim to be fighting against because they repudiate the only effective anti-racist force in the world – the great alliance of the oppressed nationalities, the world working class and the socialist countries.[161]

As an internationalist, Winston constantly called for the imposition of economic, political and military sanctions against racist South Africa, condemned the nuclear build-up and war-mongering policies of the US administration and its rapacious and violent interventions in Latin America, and also the misguided policies of Maoist China. He stood firm in his belief in world peace, was against the nuclear arms race, and for the unity of the working class – Black and white – and solidarity with the anti-colonial, anti-

---
161. *The African Communist*, First Quarter 1978.

imperialist and anti-racist fighters in every corner of the globe.

Winston also had a fine sense of humour. One of his favourite jokes had to do with the growing influence of science and technology. He would say:

> You see, Essop – no matter the scientific advances, they will not be able to invent a computer that will be able to make an accurate translation. For example, some scientist fed the following phrase into a computer, 'Out of sight, out of mind,' and after a lot of clicking, the translation came back, 'The blind man is mad.'

I shall forever treasure my memories of my mentor Henry Winston.

Chapter 7
Return Home

Return Home

Flying home on a direct flight from London in July 1990, my unbounded joy at returning after twenty-five-and-a-half years in exile was tinged with uncertainty about my future and the work we were expected to perform in launching and building a legal SACP. The Party needed to become an influential player in a complex political environment where some people had been suffocated by the virulent anti-communist propaganda spread by the ruling apartheid regime and mirrored through the mass media, private sector and conservative faith-based organisations. However, we were bolstered by the knowledge that the majority of our people supported the SACP and also by its close links to the ANC and COSATU.

My arrival was low-key, and I had no problems with passport control or customs. My brother Ismail met me at the airport with a warm embrace and a comforting hug and then drove us to his home in Mayfair, which had gradually been transformed from a whites-only suburb to one with a growing number of Indian residents. Kulsie, Ismail's second wife after he and Ruki divorced, was wonderful, and she and their two children, Reyad and Yumna, welcomed me with open arms. Yumna had willingly given up her bedroom, which had an en suite bathroom, to me. Kulsie looked after me with patience, care and attention, and whatever I needed or requested was given.

Ismail died in June 2002; Reyad and Yumna are now parents with their own children, and Kulsie heads up a large extended family.

Over the next few days, I met my Dad, Nassim, Zuneid, Yasmin, Shehnaaz and their families and some old friends. It was like a dream come true.

Before I go on, I must say a little about my brother Nassim's life while I was in exile. Nassim Pahad, born in 1942, was directly involved in reviving the Transvaal Indian Congress (TIC) on 1 May 1983 at a meeting in Lenasia attended by about 1,500 people. At that meeting, he was elected joint treasurer with Kadir Saloojee, and Essop Jassat was elected president. In his book, *The Compassionate Healer: A Biography of Dr Essop Jassat*,[162] Haroon Aziz describes Jassat's intensive tours of the Old Transvaal to inform people

---

162. Johannesburg: Nadim Books, 2021.

of the revived TIC and the formation of the UDF. As a leader of the TIC, Nassim accompanied Jassat on those visits, using his own car. Haroon Aziz describes the aims and objectives of the TIC thus:

> to strive for a united, democratic, non-racial South Africa on the basis of universal adult suffrage; ... to resist all social, political and economic discrimination on the basis of race, colour, sex or creed; ... to cooperate with other organisations striving for democracy, and to strive for equal economic, political, social and educational freedoms for all the inhabitants of South Africa.[163]

Both the TIC and the UDF popularised the Freedom Charter adopted in Kliptown in 1955. The racist authorities, fearing the influence of the TIC, banned some of its meetings and its first newsletter, which paid tribute to Dr Dadoo. They also banned its poster, which proclaimed: 'Yusuf Dadoo (1909–1983) He Fought for Freedom – He Died our Leader'; a pamphlet entitled 'Yusuf Dadoo – Portrait of a Freedom Fighter'; and a Dadoo commemorative meeting organised in Lenasia for 24 September 1983.

Before his death, Dadoo, and those of us involved in keeping in touch with the Indian community in South Africa, welcomed the resuscitation of the TIC and the formation of the Transvaal UDF. We were particularly pleased to see the names of old TIC activists along with the new vibrant young activists from the Indian community.

Many years later, Roy Padayachee, formerly a leader of the NIC and an underground activist, told me that there had been a move to rework the Freedom Charter, as it was assumed it could not be circulated because it was a banned document. But Nassim would not consider that and insisted they reproduce the original Freedom Charter and test its legality. Nassim was correct – it was not a banned document.

Nassim is now a successful businessman, focusing on forwarding and clearing. He and Isa (née Jassat) have three children, Rouhana, Ahmed and Arshad. Rouhana has an MA in African Literature from Wits University and is married to Albert Pestana. They have no children but play a huge role in looking after everyone in the family. Rouhana works for Nassim and is also a good cook, and it seems that Albert is following in her culinary footsteps. Rouhana is very friendly and full of life and continues to provide a strong link between our families.

---

163. Haroon Aziz, *The Compassionate Healer*, p. 156.

Ahmed works for his father, is twice divorced and has two children. His eldest, Azad, has elected to stay permanently with his father, while his daughter, Iman, divides her time between her parents. Arshad, who is an attorney, is married to Faeeza, and they have two children, Aadam and Hala.

༄

Now, back to my life in 1990. Ismail was just great and offered to take me to any place I wished to visit or event I wanted to attend. The day after I arrived, he took me to the SACP's temporary office, which NUM had offered to us rent-free. Thereafter, for the next month or so, Ismail took me to the SACP office in the morning, which was initially in Marshallstown and later in Braamfontein, and at the end of the working day gave me a lift home.

Daddy and all my other brothers were also living in Mayfair at the time. Aziz and Yusuf (JoJo) Saloojee had rented a house in Mayfair with Yusuf (Charles) Saloojee and were later joined by Trevor Manuel when he came to live in Johannesburg.

Zuneid (born in 1945) was also in Mayfair, and I will fill you in a little about his life. From an early age, he was a keen and enthusiastic footballer and, under his initiative, together with Ronnie Kaka, Yusuf (Charles) Saloojee, Hamed Saloojee and Tickey Dadabhay, they formed Junior Dynamos. They were a very good team, and a few of them later became professionals.

Zuneid met Farida Gani in Fordsburg when he was eighteen and she was fourteen; they got married in 1970 and have no children. For many years, they have lived in a semi-detached house in Mayfair with the other half occupied by Farida's brother Farouk and his wife Zaida, who have four children: Ahmed, Zayd, Aaminah and Raisa. Farouk and Zaida very kindly allowed Farida and Zuneid to bring up Aaminah as their own daughter. Later, when Aaminah married Mohammed Loonat, Zuneid and Farida jointly hosted the ceremony with her birth parents, and Zuneid gave Aaminah away.

In 2001, at the suggestion of Ronnie Kaka, the local ANC branch in Mayfair selected Zuneid to be their candidate as local councillor for Ward 58. He served two terms, was hard-working, diligent and supported his constituency with distinction.

Farida was a wonderful host, always smiling, welcoming and cooking the most delicious food. At her request, we (and Aziz and Angina) always had lunch at their house on Eid. Sadly, Farida died from Covid in 2020, and we all miss her dearly.

After working as a bookkeeper for many years for the same firm, Zuneid and a fellow employee took over the business. Unfortunately, Zuneid is not in good health and his nephew Zayd is now in charge of the company. Aaminah is a qualified and experienced teacher, and she and Mohammed have a son, Yusuf, who was born soon after Farida's death. It was a very traumatic period for the family, as Yusuf's lungs were not fully developed and he was kept in hospital for some time. Aaminah was not allowed to stay with him because of Covid restrictions. Although Yusuf still has health problems, he is now blessed with a little sister called Maryam.

Aaminah was very close to Farida and Zuneid, and since Farida's death, spends a lot of time and energy tending to Zuneid's needs. Farouk and Zaida are also very good to Zuneid, and Farouk insists on keeping up the Eid lunch tradition, which we enjoy very much.

Yasmin and Shehnaaz were living in Becker Street when I returned to South Africa, in Eadie House and Orient House, respectively.

Thanks to my family, I settled down easily and was able to concentrate on my Party work without having to worry about paying for rent or food.

Interestingly, when I walked in the streets, I would be stopped by people who I had last seen thirty or forty years ago, and they would ask me, 'Do you recognise me? We were at primary/high school together.' In some cases, it was easy to answer, as most Muslim men then had beards, so I could respond, 'Not with that beard!' In a few cases, when I admitted that I did not recognise them, there was disappointment. And some Africans would stop me and ask me if I was Ahmed Kathrada or Mac Maharaj or even Kader Asmal.

Aziz and our dear friend the late Yusuf 'JoJo' Saloojee were working under Thabo Mbeki at the Department of International Affairs (DIA) at the ANC Head Office, and I would sometimes walk from the party offices to spend time with them at the DIA. Later, Aziz bought a house in Mayfair West, which he shared with JoJo, who enjoyed cooking and made delicious meals. Many evenings, Thabo and I would join them for good food, drinks and lively political discussions.

Among the friends I spent time with were Ahmed (Quarter) Khota, Ahmed Dadoo, Ahmed (Popeye) Coovadia, Willie Pochee and Mohammed Moolla. The latter two only had soft drinks, and even when they took me to pubs on many weekends, they would not allow me to pay my share. After I rented a flat in Kholvad House, prior to the arrival of Meg and the children in Johannesburg, they used to come there instead of going to a pub. I recall one evening answering a knock on the door. Outside was a group of young Muslims who were visiting people and asking them to be pious and go to mosque. Once I realised who they were, I merrily said, 'I am a Hindu,' and they beat a hasty retreat.

In the following years, Yasmin gave birth to a third child, Mohammed (Mo D.), to join Zakiya and Zayd, and Shehnaaz gave birth to Zeenat and Zaeem. They are now grandparents with very close family ties and everyone getting together at least once a week (barring Covid restrictions) – except for Zakiya, who lives with her family in Australia but gives and receives regular visits from her South African family and shares everything almost daily through social media. Yasmin and Yusuf have also had their Australian grandchildren stay with them in South Africa for long periods, so they are very much part of the close family. When separated, Yasmin has even done long-distance childminding and helped with homework from across the oceans.

At the end of Chapter 4, 'Focus on Africa', I recounted how we arranged for Meg and the children to come to South Africa with Sam for a holiday in December 1990, to demonstrate to Amina and Govan that moving here would be fine and that there were lots of friends and family who would make them feel at home. There were some very tense minutes for Meg, as she came through the customs and passport control with the two children on their British passports with holiday visas, as she expected a reaction to the names. However, the passport people obviously saw nothing unusual or suspicious about this English family with the names 'Govan Timol Pahad' and 'Amina Zanele Pahad' and said, 'Welcome to South Africa. Have a good holiday.'

The plan to make them feel at home definitely worked, with a warm welcome from my brothers and their families in Johannesburg, followed by a great holiday with Yusuf (Charles) Saloojee driving us all in his car to Knysna, encouraging the children to improve his car's performance by making brrmm-brrmm noises. There we stayed with Yasmin and Shehnaaz and their children. Somehow, we managed to fit into the little house Ruki had inherited in the Coloured quarter – which had a sea view but had been spurned by the whites because it was above the sewage works, with the consequent disadvantage of unpleasant odours from time to time. The children all slept in rows like little sausages on mattresses on the floor of the sitting/dining room. We all had a marvellous time and got on together perfectly. Amina and Govan really enjoyed the long car trip and the beauty of Knysna, Nature's Valley and Plettenberg Bay, and after the wonderful welcome from the family – especially Yasmin and Shehnaaz – they began to look forward to moving to South Africa.

Meg handed in her notice at Paddington Green and put the London flat up for sale. After paying off the mortgage, we got enough money from that to buy a house in Johannesburg, and I started looking and found a suitable place in Bellevue East that would be convenient for the children attending Sacred Heart College. Fortunately, house prices were very low at the time. Meg served her notice and packed up everything for the UNHCR container, leaving behind only the fridge and washing machine and some furniture for her nephew Andrew. She cancelled the insurance, and she and the children said goodbye to their friends and left the country. But the day before the transfer went through, someone broke into the empty flat and stole the appliances, two decent panelled doors and the tiled cast iron Victorian fireplace and smeared the walls and contents with excrement and ketchup. We suspected that our racist neighbours were responsible. Meg's sister Jill travelled down to London to sort it all out, and thanks to her, the sale went through as planned.

Meanwhile, my focus was on my work in the party.

At one of our first party meetings in the NUM boardroom, chaired by Joe Slovo, it was decided that Jeremy Cronin would edit *The African Communist* in addition to his other duties. Geraldine Fraser-Moleketi was the administrator and PA to Slovo, and I was to be responsible for international affairs and finance. The latter suggestion was made by Slovo, and I half-jokingly asked if it was because I was 'an Indian'.

To my dismay and disappointment, I was the treasurer of a party with limited finances and resources. But then, a few months later, Slovo gave me a bag full of money. It was about R300,000, the proceeds of our funds in London, and I didn't sleep that night for fear of a break-in and the money being stolen. The next morning, I took it to the bank and asked the manager to count it in my presence to make sure it would be accurately recorded and deposited. It was a mighty relief when all that money was safely deposited in the party account.

Since the SACP had very little money, the staff, including Pule Buthelezi (later ANC General Secretary, who passed away in January 2022), were paid less than the ANC staff. I took no pay for the first six to nine months since I was living with Ismail and Kulsie and had been given some money in solidarity with my work in the struggle by our friend in London, Tony Bunzl.

After a successful launch of the CPSA as a legal party on 29 July 1990 at a packed-to-capacity Soccer City stadium, we had the arduous task of regularising the application forms we had handed out at the rally. There were many thousands, but a large number of them could not be followed up as most of the addresses gave only the name of the township or location but no street name or number. However, with the assistance of the NUM, we were able to trace many of the applications and enrol them as party members waiting to be formed into viable, working branches. With Geraldine at the helm, we were quite successful. At my suggestion, we employed Indres Naidoo to assist Jeremy with the marketing and distribution of *The African Communist* and other party materials and Shirish Nanabhai as a driver and general office worker.

From August 1990 to December 1999, I participated in several interviews with Irish international peacemaker, author and professor Padraig O'Malley,[164] in which I expressed my views and opinions on developments in the SACP, the ANC and South Africa. In this memoir, I shall insert chronologically some quotes from what I said in those interviews, as they represent my thinking and attitudes at that time. All were recorded as part of The O'Malley Archives, which are hosted by the Nelson Mandela Foundation.

Prior to South Africa's first democratic elections, I did three interviews: in August 1990, September 1991 and August 1992.

In August 1990, when COSATU was demanding a 'living wage', I argued for a 'minimum wage'. On the economy I said:

> ... there is no way in which a new democratic government is going to be able to deal in any meaningful way with the fundamental socio-economic problems facing our country without a lot of government intervention – well beyond what the business people are talking about – which is just to create the necessary infrastructure and climate.[165]

I also emphasised that one of the tasks of a democratic government must be to try and give effect to the policy guidelines of the Freedom Charter and that economic policies should be about how you empower the masses – the workers and the trade unions – including discussing the possibilities of worker representation on the boards of directors of private companies. I

---

164. O'Malley specialises in the problems of divided societies, such as South Africa and Northern Ireland.
165. '23 Aug 1990: Pahad, Essop', *O'Malley – The Heart of Hope*, O'Malley Archive, Nelson Mandela Foundation. Available at https://omalley.nelsonmandela.org/index.php/site/q/03lv00017/04lv00344/05lv00389/06lv00487.htm

pointed out that COSATU was going to be an important major player and that we needed a powerful trade union movement.

Already at that time, I said we should move away from labels such as 'federalism', 'confederalism', and 'unitary state' but find a way to bring government democracy closer to the people, creating strong local authorities with powers to raise revenue.

Four years before the first democratic elections, I called for an ANC-led electoral front with the ANC symbol being the main one. Looking at future elections, I suggested that we needed to make inroads into white constituencies, and in respect of the white army and police, argued that what they probably wanted was some kind of confidence that they were not going to lose their jobs or their pensions. But in response to a question on De Klerk and power-sharing, I said: 'If by power-sharing, they mean the right of a particular national group they define as a minority to veto legislation of the sovereign party (the ANC), that is unacceptable.'[166]

On the prospect of socialism, my view was that it would be a process with three distinct but interlinked phases: an interim government, a democratic government, and then socialism. I explained that this is what distinguished the Party from the ANC. The ANC must, out of necessity, be a multiclass organisation, otherwise it would not be able to play its role in getting rid of apartheid.

In the interview in September 1991, I argued that the ANC entered into an alliance with the SACP because it was a revolutionary organisation that:

> will have to articulate the interests and aspirations of the masses of this country ... Nobody has a God-given right to the support of the people for all time. You have to earn this right ... by your policies, by your programmes and by what you do.[167]

In response to the issue relating to the threat of banning the Communist Party of the Soviet Union following a failed coup attempt, we strongly condemned the suspension of the CPSU and its banning in a number of republics:

> ... as a party that has been banned for 40 years ... we are opposed to [the] banning of political organisations, and we think it shows very

---
166. '23 Aug 1990: Pahad, Essop', *O'Malley – The Heart of Hope*.
167. '03 Sep 1991: Pahad, Essop', *O'Malley – The Heart of Hope*, O'Malley Archive, Nelson Mandela Foundation. Available at https://omalley.nelsonmandela.org/index.php/site/q/03lv00017/04lv00344/05lv00511/06lv00598.htm

> little about the democratic credentials of those in the Soviet Union who helped to defeat the coup, to talk about democracy when your next step is to actually ban a political party. ...
>
> ... you have people in SA, you have people in other parts of the world, who were horrified at the attempted coup, but these same people are silent when the CP is attacked, and it is this discriminatory approach to democracy which is extremely worrying. ... For our own country, SA, it is necessary for all of the people who claim to be in favour of democratisation to come out and say we are in favour of a multi-party system in our country, we are in favour of a political environment in which you have free political activity, freedom of political association, freedom of political movement; and if that is the case ... we must apply these standards to everybody.[168]

'Everybody' includes the CPSU. I also stated that the collapse of socialism in Eastern Europe and the profound crisis besetting the Soviet Union had certainly altered the balance of forces between the US and Russia. Moreover, it weakened the democratic anti-imperialist forces throughout the world.

I explained that I thought the European socialist countries had ignored the basic Marxist methodological principle that objective laws of development operate independently of the will of an individual, and I felt they had ignored the market factor – the laws of supply and demand.

On the future of socialism in South Africa, I pointed out that this was still a long-term objective and that the final arbiter of our survival in this country would be the working class. They will decide, they will pass judgement on us. If they like us and think we are worth having, we will thrive in this country.

I was also asked about democratic socialism and the possibility of an advanced form of social democracy. In this context, I suggested that we should study very closely the various forms of democracy and the Scandinavian countries. I said:

> As I am sitting here now, on [the] 3rd of September 1991, if we could have the social welfare system that Sweden has today, in SA now, I would be a very, very, very happy man. I think on issues like the gender question they are very advanced.[169]

---

168. '03 Sep 1991: Pahad, Essop', *O'Malley – The Heart of Hope*
169. Ibid.

I stressed that the gender issue was an important element in our struggle for socialism.

In an interview on 26 August 1992, in response to the SACP hosting a delegation from the Communist Party of China following the events in Tiananmen Square and what O'Malley termed 'the brutal execution of people who were defending human rights and democracy', I pointed out that the US and South African governments were keen to deepen business ties with China. I said that the SACP was very happy to receive the delegation and we would continue to see how best we could develop our relations further. 'Those 1.16 billion people are a reality, and they are also a powerful force in world politics.'[170]

In covering the period 1990–1994, I will deal mainly with the SACP and mention some developments in the ANC. I will also cover the Peace Accord and the CODESA negotiations in which I participated as an SACP representative.

A few months after 2 February 1990, in Johannesburg, we held our last meeting of the Central Committee elected at the 7th Party Congress in Cuba in April 1989. A few participants have made personal observations as to what transpired at that meeting and what decisions were arrived at. My recollection is that the meeting was somewhat tense but conducted in a warm, friendly manner. One critical issue was about what would happen when we openly declared members of the CC. One proposal that came up during the discussions was that the party consider having both open and underground operations. That was rejected on the grounds that it was neither viable nor feasible to have dual party membership and that all members of the party should be openly registered and acknowledged. Another proposal was that CC members such as Thabo Mbeki, J. Z. Zuma and Aziz Pahad should decide for themselves whether they wanted their membership to be made public. Those three, and a few others in leading structures of the ANC, decided to opt out of their party membership, which had been acquired while the party was banned and operating underground. They were concerned that the ANC would be compromised and attacked by many powerful forces in Africa and the world as an organisation under the control of communists. Some of the old CC members were unhappy about that decision.

My view then, as now, was that any SACP member recruited into a banned organisation and operating in secret has the right not to operate in the

---

170. '26 Aug 1992 – Pahad, Essop', *O'Malley – The Heart of Hope*, O'Malley Archive, Nelson Mandela Foundation. Available at https://omalley.nelsonmandela.org/index.php/site/q/03lv00017/04lv00344/05lv00607/06lv00712.htm

organisation when it becomes legal. They greatly contributed to strengthening and building the SACP under enormously difficult conditions. Thus, while they left us, we should never forget their contributions to developing the SACP's strategy, tactics and policies. We should not label them as anti-SACP or anti-communist because they were not.

Prior to the launch of the legal SACP, the party had a fruitful and, for me, inspiring meeting with the leadership of COSATU in Harare in March 1990. There, I met and exchanged views and ideas with Jay Naidoo, Alec Erwin and other COSATU leaders. At that meeting, we agreed that we should have one trade union federation in South Africa, which would mean disbanding SACTU and integrating its members and leaders into COSATU's structures.

Before finalising our list of the Internal Leadership Group (ILG) of the SACP, which we wanted to announce at the launch rally, Mac Maharaj resigned in reaction to the nomination of Harry Gwala. Mac was critical of what he considered to be Gwala's role in stoking the violence in KwaZulu-Natal (KZN).[171]

After a hectic period organising and mobilising, we launched the legal SACP on 29 July 1990. The mass rally in Soweto was attended by about 50,000 people who sang and danced and acclaimed the leadership of the party. When Chris Hani was introduced, the stadium was rocked by a deafening roar. Many ANC luminaries also attended to show their support for the legal SACP, including Nelson Mandela, Walter Sisulu and Winnie Mandela.

Following the launch, those of us working in the party office had the daunting task of forming SACP branches and offices throughout the country, which entailed visits to the various provinces to assist them, including offering our meagre financial help. The old elected CC coexisted with the ILG, and it was their responsibility, relying on the few of us who were working full-time, to prepare and organise the 8th Party Congress in December 1991. The politbureau also continued to function, and I was elected as one of its members.

A highlight of that mobilisation was the mass rally organised in Port Elizabeth in November 1990. More than 200,000 people attended, and Chris Hani was the main speaker. On the day of the rally, I was taken to a house where I met Chris. He gave me the speech that had been prepared for him for my comments and critique. My view was that it was a good speech for a more intimate gathering, but that a mass rally required him to be at his most

---

171. Gwala was instrumental in organising ANC members in the Natal Midlands into armed self-defence groups.

eloquent. I suggested that he rather speak from notes which would enable him to respond to the audience in a spontaneous manner. That approach was agreed upon, and I was asked to prepare the notes. Chris was electrifying, and the massive crowd erupted in response. In the audience were two of the Eastern Cape's and our country's political and revolutionary legends, Oom Govan Mbeki and Raymond Mhlaba.

What a rally! I felt so proud to be a communist that day and was fortified in my conviction that the SACP was here to stay and had a role and a future in our country.

Prior to the 8th Congress, earlier in December 1991, we had organised a national party workshop attended by fifty participants from the various regions of the country. In his book *The South African Communist Party – Exile and After Apartheid*,[172] Eddy Maloka points out that a programme of action was adopted which emphasised a membership recruitment campaign and some mass mobilisation activities. We had to run and supervise those campaigns from party headquarters on a very tight budget. As the person in charge of finance, this was particularly difficult, as I had to continually decline demands for financial assistance; it also prevented me from doing other important work.

In the Eastern Cape, Oom Gov and Oom Ray had rented office space well designed and furnished. When they asked me to come and look at it and to defray some of the expenses, I pointed out that the party could not afford such an office and that they would have to raise the funds to finance it. I explained that we had six regions, all of which were short of money and making demands on the party officials to help them meet their expenses. Fortunately, they understood my position and raised the necessary funds independently of the party officials.

At the 8th Congress, I gave a weak financial report, which was criticised by some delegates – mainly from the Western Cape, who then convinced Kesval 'Kay' Moonsamy to stand for the position of treasurer, even though I had already been proposed for it. On hearing about Kay, I approached him, confirmed that he was standing and immediately congratulated him as the newly elected treasurer of the SACP. When he expressed his surprise, I explained to him that I was not interested in that position and if there were an alternative candidate, I would withdraw so they could be elected unopposed. I then informed Slovo of my attitude and stance and was overjoyed that Kay was taking over the position of treasurer since that would

---

172. Johannesburg: Jacana Media, 2003.

give me more space and time to perform the various other tasks assigned to me.

An important part of my work was representing the SACP at various seminars, conferences and meetings called by the ANC, COSATU and other civil society structures, including the private sector.

One such important initiative was the National Peace Accord (NPA) of 14 September 1991, the signing of which was the culmination of numerous meetings of various political formations to discuss the merits of such an accord. The ANC was represented by Thabo Mbeki and Aziz Pahad, COSATU by Sydney Mufamadi, and the SACP by me. As the Alliance partners, we were deeply committed to doing all in our power to stem the growing tide of violence engulfing the country at that time.[173] Under the chairpersonship of John Hall, a prominent business leader, we worked with the National Party led by Roelf Meyer to pave the way for an NPA.

As an alliance team, we endeavoured to meet on Friday evenings at the offices of the attorneys Cheadle, Thomson and Haysom to evaluate developments and sharpen our positions, guided by the legal advice they offered. Azar Cachalia, a partner in the firm at that time, chaired our meetings and guided our discussions. It was a pleasure to work with him.

That the NPA was signed and delivered is testimony to the work and determination of the partners involved to find some way forward in dealing with the raging violence. Two civil society activists, Phiroshaw Camay and Anne J. Gordon, in assessing the strengths and weaknesses of the NPA, wrote in 1993:

> Overall, the NPA made a significant contribution to building communication and political tolerance amongst the contesting parties prior to the 1994 elections, allowing those elections to take place in an environment of comparative peace and stability.
>
> The direct and tangible impact of the NPA included the establishment of a National Peace Secretariat, eleven regional peace committees and more than 200 local peace committees. Approximately 15,000 peace monitors were trained across the country, drawn from all sections of society. The peace structures themselves, and the cooperation of key elements in government,

---

[173]. In my view, that violence was wrongly characterised as 'Black on Black violence'. It was, as I said earlier, instigated and stoked by the old apartheid regime and its agencies such as the South African Defence Force.

political parties, business and civil society, enabled considerable progress in reimposing the rule of law and bringing peace to many strife-torn communities.[174]

Our alliance delegations made a sterling contribution to the adoption and necessary, if uneven, implementation of the Accord. Mbeki, Aziz, Mufamadi and I then continued to serve on the main structure that arose from the NPA. That was my first involvement in a negotiating forum, and I learnt important lessons on how to work with other parties and structures outside our alliance, including the National Party. The NPA also contributed to the holding of CODESA.

⁓

The Convention for a Democratic South Africa opened with a plenary session on 20 December 1991, and Joe Slovo, Enver Daniels and I represented the SACP during the negotiations. At the opening plenary session, the SACP delegation was led by Chris Hani and included Enver Daniels, Ronnie Kasrils, Thenjiwe Mtintso and me. As an alliance, we were proud that multiparty negotiations had been organised and conducted by South Africans without any foreign involvement or mediation.

Chief Justice Michael Corbett opened the Convention, and Judges Petrus Shabort and Ismail Mahomed presided over the proceedings. The friendly and even jovial atmosphere during the first day was seriously disrupted that evening by an intemperate, undiplomatic speech by then-President of South Africa, F. W. de Klerk. Mandela was supposed to have been the last speaker, but he graciously agreed to De Klerk's request to speak at the end. In response to that polite gesture, De Klerk launched an attack on the integrity of the ANC and questioned whether it would abide by any agreements to which it was a party. To say that I and the majority of the other delegates were shocked by that would be a gross understatement. One could see from Mandela's face that he was upset, and when he motioned to the Chair, Ismail Mahomed, that he wished to speak once more, Ismail agreed.

Mandela's anger was palpable, and he did not mince his words criticising De Klerk and his government. Being Mandela, however, he ended his

---

174. 'The National Peace Accord and its Structures', South Africa Civil Society Governance Case Study No. 1, O'Malley Archive, Nelson Mandela Foundation. Available at https://omalley.nelsonmandela.org/cis/omalley/OMalleyWeb/03lv02424/04lv03275/05lv03294/06lv03321.htm

intervention by leaving the door open to continue working with De Klerk. In that exchange, even many of the other parties represented at CODESA supported Mandela, and I realised that the balance of power had shifted to the ANC and its allies.

Mandela then proceeded to have one-on-one meetings with some of the other delegates, and he asked me to find Amichand Rajbansi and set up such a meeting. I did so, and Rajbansi was beaming that Mandela wanted to see him. That evening, the ANC and its alliance partners enjoyed the dinner as we were now in the driving seat. I could not resist telling everyone how proud I was of Mandela and boasting about the difference between the two party leaders.

Chris Hani spoke on behalf of the SACP, a speech to which a few comrades and I had contributed; concerning the negotiations, it was the first time the SACP was speaking in its own right. Chris regarded it as a victory and committed the SACP to pursue the process that would lead to the formation of a new government elected by the people of South Africa.

The first Convention for a Democratic South Africa (CODESA 1), consisting of eighteen or nineteen participants, broke up into four working groups. I represented the SACP in Working Group 1, where the National Party was represented by Minister of Justice Kobie Coetzee and Hernus Kriel, Minister of Police. We were not fazed by these so-called heavyweights, and when necessary, I would express our disagreement in a calm, measured tone and suggest alternative approaches.

Unlike Working Group 2 on the constitutional principles, which had reached a deadlock owing to the intransigence of the National Party, Working Group 1 was able to reach agreement on a number of issues. As Sifiso Mxolisi Ndlovu points out, 'That group agreed to the speeding up of the release of political prisoners and the return of exiles and their families ... There was also agreement that discriminatory laws would be repealed and that the use of military means to pursue political objectives would end.'[175]

Working Group 1 also agreed on enabling political parties to have fair access to the SABC and the broadcasting corporations in the 'homelands' and Bantustans. Later, Joel Netshitenzhe, representing the ANC, and I, representing the SACP, were locked in negotiations with Danie Schutte of the NP concerning the South African Broadcasting Corporation (SABC). It was difficult to negotiate with Danie, as he was unwilling to accede to our reasonable request for access to the SABC and that the state broadcaster cease

---

175. *The Road to Democracy in South Africa*, Vol. 6, Part 2, Chapter 17, SADET (Pretoria: Unisa Press).

acting as the mouthpiece of the National Party. Only after intense discussions and the intervention of Cyril Ramaphosa and Roelf Meyer were we able to find an acceptable agreement.

I really enjoyed the negotiations in Working Group 1 and think I developed a good working relationship with two rabid anti-communists, Coetzee and Kriel. We treated each other's views with respect and sought to find a way forward, notwithstanding robust debates. I recall one occasion when two young white journalists approached me and sought my help persuading Kobie Coetzee to give them an interview. When I approached him with their request, he refused. But I persisted, pointing out that I had given them an interview outlining the position of the Alliance with respect to issues in Working Group 1 and explained that if he did not provide the view of his party, the journalists' report would be biased in favour of the Alliance. He understood, and to the surprise of the journalists, gave them a substantial interview.

Along with some failures, that first CODESA had its successes – such as those of Working Group 1 and the adoption of some of its reports. Slovo and I regularly reported to the politburo and CC of the SACP and, at party meetings in various parts of the country, gave them detailed briefings on the negotiations. The politburo and CC agreed with the positions of the Alliance and made suggestions on how to take the process forward to guide the negotiations. It was difficult to convince Harry Gwala at times, and I recall a heated CC meeting after Slovo had proposed the Sunset Clause to the NEC of the ANC. That proposal, which had earlier been put forward by Thabo Mbeki and Joel Netshitenzhe, angered Gwala, and at the CC meeting, he laid into Slovo and fiercely attacked the Sunset Clause as tantamount to selling out. After his outburst, which lasted for nearly an hour, I took the floor and supported Slovo's position. Thereafter, other CC members came out in support, and an irate and disappointed Gwala walked out of the meeting in a huff.

The ANC had set up a negotiations committee which met as often as required to review the process and the weaknesses and strengths of our positions and those of the National Party and other participants. Slovo and I represented the SACP at those meetings, which proved useful in sharpening our attitudes and positions and reviewing and, where necessary, changing our strategy and tactics. We were well advised by our legal experts on technical and complex issues, including specific formulations that would form the basis of agreements to be reached.

I was an active participant and learnt valuable lessons on the intricacies of finding the words and concepts that would best reflect our common positions on the issues and challenges confronting us. We proved more than a match for the National Party and were able to win over many of the other delegates to achieve sufficient consensus on some of the more intractable differences. During CODESA, the balance of power had shifted to the ANC, and even though the NP was still the governing party, they had to concede on a number of sticking points.

The second CODESA started in May 1992, and I was once more selected to represent the SACP with Joe Slovo. But in June 1992, the Boipatong Massacre occurred, in which forty-five people were murdered by armed gangs of Inkatha-aligned impis, encouraged and supported by apartheid security forces. The Inkatha Freedom Party (IFP) is a South African political organisation established by Chief Mangosuthu (Gatsha) Buthelezi, which encouraged a resurgent Zulu nationalism and created a platform for Buthelezi to advance his political ambitions.

I remember at that time we were having a CC meeting in Soweto, and Chris Hani came late, informing us that Mandela had called him to a meeting that morning and been very clear and determined that we could not under those circumstances continue to negotiate with the NP governing party. Mandela said that we had to send a message that the violence perpetrated in Boipatong could not be condoned and we thus had to call off the negotiations. The CC was in full agreement with Mandela's call. In supporting Mandela, I did, however, point out that it seemed to me that the manner of our withdrawing from the negotiations should be such that we leave open a window, however slight, for the resumption of the negotiations. This view was consistent with that held by many leaders of the ANC and SACP, and on 22 June 1992, the ANC withdrew from the negotiations.

Rolling mass action, spearheaded by the ANC and fully supported by COSATU, the SACP and other civic organisations, was intensified. I participated in that, including a massive demonstration in the streets of Johannesburg and a very successful stay-at-home on 3–4 August 1992.

In September 1992, the rolling mass action extended to the Bantustans when the Alliance partners decided on a mass march to Bisho, capital of the Eastern Cape Ciskei Bantustan (a nominally independent state recognised only by South Africa). Among the leaders deployed to the Eastern Cape were Chris Hani, Ronnie Kasrils, Steve Tshwete and Cyril Ramaphosa. Prior to the march, which was set for 7 September (the first anniversary of the Peace

Accord), Chris asked me to join them and assist in the mobilisation. I was down with a nasty bout of flu but agreed to go for a few days and miss the march. Chris agreed, and I was actively involved in the mass mobilisation campaign; then, with the consent of the organising committee, I returned to Johannesburg, still suffering from the flu.

The mobilisation was hugely successful, with about 80,000 people joining a peaceful march to hand over a memorandum asking for the Gqozo regime to step down.[176] But when they entered Bisho, the Ciskei defence forces opened fire, killing twenty-eight marchers and injuring over 200. The Bisho massacre of unarmed peaceful demonstrators was the last time the killing machine in Ciskei was released upon its citizens. Jeremy Thompson of Independent Television News, reporting live from Bisho, described it as 'a piece of cold-blooded savagery that could set back South Africa's peace process by months if not years'.

That event led to talks between Cyril Ramaphosa and Roelf Meyer, which culminated in a meeting between Mandela and De Klerk on 26 September 1992, during which they ratified the agreement reached by Ramaphosa and Meyer and signed a record of understanding. Suspended since June 1992, the negotiations resumed, and a joint commitment was made to elect a constituent assembly and set up a transitional government. I fully supported the agreement and was confident the door had opened for us to secure free and fair elections and broaden the scope for mass political activity. My role in the negotiating process as a representative of the SACP continued, while I also worked in the party's head office.

The party leadership were concerned that we still needed a full-time national organiser, and Ronnie Kasrils suggested we appoint Charles Nqakula in that role. Charles proved to be a capable, dedicated, hard worker who never shirked his duties and responsibilities, and along with others at the party head office, he and I helped ensure a successful 8th Party Congress in December 1991. Eddie Maloka's *The South African Communist Party: Exile and After Apartheid* includes a useful resumé of that Congress.

We, as the party leadership, were fully aware it would be a difficult Congress, the first in South Africa since 1962, with a membership of about 25,000 and over ninety per cent of the delegates new members with little experience of SACP history and work in the areas of ideology, theory, practice, and political education. But we were excited at the prospect of laying the foundation for a strong and viable SACP that would make an

---

176. Brigadier Joshua 'Oupa' Gqozo was the military ruler of the Ciskei Bantustan.

important contribution to liberating South Africa from racism, sexism and national oppression. Furthermore, we would continue our comradeship and solidarity with sister communist parties around the world, which was an important part of my work. To augment the staff at head office, we roped in leaders and members from the Gauteng region, where Jabu Moleketi and Trish Hanekom would play an invaluable role. An experienced and committed Party member, Trish was an efficient administrator who ensured the speedy registration of delegates, which enhanced the work of the Credentials Committee.

From the opening of the Congress, there was a clamour from the majority of delegates that Chris Hani should stand and be elected as General Secretary, a demand about which the incumbent Central Committee of the SACP had to have an emergency meeting. With many other CC members, I argued that Chris was the choice of the delegates, and we needed to hear and heed those voices. As a CC, we confronted the issue of what the attitude of the ANC would be to the election of Chris, who was one of the most popular leaders of the ANC and MK.

In the end, the CC decided to send a delegation composed of Dan Tloome, Oom Gov, Raymond Mhlaba and John Nkadimeng to ascertain the views of Walter Sisulu and Nelson Mandela. Chris decided that he would respect the wishes of Congress but be guided by the responses from Sisulu and Mandela. To our great relief and joy, they came back and reported that, while Chris Hani's new deployment would impact upon the work of the ANC and MK, they could not stand in the way of implementing a Congress decision.

To rapturous applause and acclaim, Chris Hani was elected General Secretary, Joe Slovo Chair and Charles Nqakula as Deputy General Secretary. From those at Head Office, Geraldine Fraser-Moleketi, Jeremy Cronin and Essop Pahad were elected onto the new CC. Also included were Govan Mbeki, Raymond Mhlaba, Ronnie Kasrils, Thenjiwe Mtintso, John Nkadimeng and Blade Nzimande. Other trade unionists and working-class leaders elected included Chris Dlamini, Sydney Mufamadi, John Gomomo and Sam Shilowa. I was elated to be re-elected to the CC and later by the CC to the PB.

Under Chris Hani, we now had an elected leadership with tremendous experience working in the SACP, ANC and COSATU. Being part of that leadership was an honour, and I was excited by the prospect of working directly with Chris.

Chris Thembisele Hani (1942–1993) is without doubt one of the most outstanding freedom fighters in the history of our revolutionary struggle. His dedication, discipline, fearlessness, intellect and understanding, combined with his mature political and ideological insight, are legendary. Having worked under his leadership, I will forever treasure my memories of that great human being. In this memoir, it is unfortunate that I cannot provide a fuller description of his extraordinary contribution to our history. What I have included, I reference from three books about Chris: *Voices of Liberation – Chris Hani* by Gregory Houston and James Ngculu;[177] *Thami Mali Remembers Chris Hani: The Sun That Set Before Dawn* by Thami Mali;[178] and *Hani: A Life Too Short* by Janet Smith and Beauregard Tromp.[179]

Chris Hani was a brilliant and accomplished student who started school at seven and matriculated at sixteen. At seventeen, he entered Fort Hare University to major in Latin and English. At the same time, he had an interest in Greek literature. In 1962, when he was nineteen, he graduated. In his youth, he was mentored by Govan Mbeki, who had a profound and lasting influence on his political trajectory. Hani, who had joined the ANC Youth League in 1957, worked closely with Andrew Masondo, a lecturer in mathematics at Fort Hare, to revitalise the ANC branches in Alice. Masondo was a leading member of the ANC, SACP and MK and served thirteen years on Robben Island. After graduating, Hani moved to Cape Town, where he worked with Archie Sibeko, a leader of SACTU and the ANC, and Looksmart Ngudle, who was brutally tortured and murdered while in detention in 1963.

Chris was a delegate to the underground conference in 1962, which adopted the 'Road to South African Freedom' document, and also to the first ANC conference after its banning in 1960, held in Lobatse, Botswana. After the conference, he and Sibeko were arrested at the Lobatsi border and sentenced to eighteen months in prison under the Suppression of Communism Act. While on bail and in hiding, Govan Mbeki sent the two of them for military training, and they arrived in Tanzania in June 1963. In exile, Hani developed into an extraordinary cadre, fighter and leader of the ANC, SACP and MK.

After receiving military training in Moscow in the Soviet Union, Chris was

---
177. Pretoria: HSRC Press, 2014.
178. Johannesburg: SACHED Books, 1993.
179. Johannesburg: Jonathan Ball, 2009.

sent to the MK camp in Kongwa, Tanzania, where he met and formed a formidable comradeship with another brave and outstanding MK combatant, Lennox Lagu (Mongameli Tshali). In 1967, the ANC and ZAPU had concluded a pact to set up bases within Rhodesia and be ready to fight Rhodesian forces if confronted. The longer-term goal was that MK would proceed into SA to establish bases there and revive the underground presence that had been smashed by the Rivonia arrests and subsequent repression of the ANC. For some time, the struggle had been stalled and our trained comrades, including Hani, had been languishing in Kongwa, desperate for action.

On 31 July 1967, under cover of darkness, a combined force of 79 combatants comprised of MK's Luthuli Detachment and fighters from the Zimbabwe People's Revolutionary Army (ZIPRA) of ZAPU crossed the Zambezi River from Zambia into Rhodesia in what became known as the Wankie Campaign. Hani was the Commissar, and Lennox the Chief of Staff. After eighteen days of gruelling survival, the MK combatants had their first military encounter with Rhodesian troops, killing two of their officers and forcing the other Rhodesian soldiers to retreat, leaving behind very welcome food and weapons. That outcome was repeated in the second encounter, but the enemy forces regrouped and, using their air superiority with spotter planes and helicopters, killed two MK combatants and compelled Hani and his detachment to retreat into Botswana. That first military encounter had a profoundly positive impact on the spirit and consciousness of all of us in the movement and the majority of our people at home.[180]

As they had agreed prior to entering Rhodesia, the Hani group voluntarily surrendered to the Botswana authorities in October 1967. However, instead of being repatriated to Zambia, the twenty-four guerilla fighters were arrested and charged. Chris was sentenced to two years imprisonment, and others to either three or four years. Under pressure from O. R. Tambo, in the name of the ANC and the OAU, Chris was released on 9 December 1968; those not released on that day were released four days later. Among other matters related to their experiences in Wankie and Botswana, Chris and his group were unhappy at how they had been treated on their arrival in Lusaka, and drew up what came to be called the Hani Memorandum.

That memorandum is published in full in the book by Houston and Ngculu. It decries 'the frightening depths and the rot in the ANC and the disintegration of MK accompanying this rot'. Their criticisms of the

---

180. For more detail on Wankie and Sipolilo campaigns, see *Umkhonto we Sizwe: The ANC's Armed Struggle* by Thula Simpson, Penguin Random House, South Africa, 2016.

leadership included careerism, attending too many international conferences, globetrotting, the opening of mysterious business enterprises and MK being run independently of the political organisation. They also criticised 'secret trials and secret executions' and 'reactionary methods of punishment' within MK. The anger, despair and anguish felt by the signatories is reflected in the untrue assertion that 'sons of leaders are sent to universities in Europe and groomed for leadership positions' and, after MK has 'overthrown the fascists, will come home after everything has been made secure and comfortable for them'.[181] While some of the allegations were well-founded, many were exaggerated or simply untrue.[182]

Of the twenty-four who were in prison, only six (including Chris) signed the Hani Memorandum, which had an enormous impact on the ANC, SACP and MK cadres and leaders. The main complaint was that the leadership was not paying sufficient attention to MK and the struggle at home, and this valid criticism was heard. Fortunately, the intervention of O. R. Tambo and Mzwai Piliso, among others, prevented the expulsion of the signatories from the movement, thus enabling Chris to continue to play his critical role in the struggle for freedom, democracy and human rights.

As mentioned in Chapter 2 of this memoir, the Hani Memorandum also played an important role in the NEC's decision to convene the Morogoro Conference in 1969, which laid the basis for an intensification of the struggle inside South Africa and a blossoming of the ANC-SACP alliance. Morogoro also officially opened the membership of the ANC, but not its NEC, to non-Africans. That latter decision was only taken at the Kabwe Conference in 1985.

Before returning to South Africa, Hani was deployed to Lesotho in 1974. There, he was a magnet for many young people coming into exile to join the ANC and MK. He entered Lesotho after illegally crossing two borders: from Botswana into South Africa and from there to Lesotho. The racist regime tried to kill him on a number of occasions but failed. After some years, he was forced to leave Lesotho on the advice of its government.

I remember first meeting Hani in late 1969 in London. Sobizana and I were walking in the street near the ANC office and the office of Dadoo and Slovo when a person greeted Bizo, and they hugged and laughed together. It was Hani, and we spoke our greetings. I had recognised him but was surprised and thrilled when he called me by name. That was the beginning

---

181. Houston and Ngculu, *Voices of Liberation – Chris Hani*. You can also read it here: https://www.sahistory.org.za/archive/original-chris-hani-memorandum
182. One such example was the opening of front businesses. Star Furniture, which was the business they criticised, was a front company for smuggling weapons into Botswana. These were hidden in the furniture exported to Botswana.

of a friendship and comradeship that lasted until his untimely assassination. We kept in touch through mutual comrades and, with Sonia Bunting, provided him with the works of Shakespeare he requested.

My next meeting with Chris was at the World Youth Festival in Berlin, GDR. Together with Joe Nhlanhla, he led the ANC Youth and Students' delegation. I was roped into the leadership committee, which gave me many opportunities to meet and discuss not only our participation but also the many challenges facing our movement, the struggle and the World Communist Movement.

Chris was always cheerful and friendly with a lovely smile and a readiness to make jokes. As a leader of the party, he was aware that I was going to attend the Lenin Party School following the Festival and took the opportunity to introduce me to one of MK's commanders, Julius Mokoena, who was part of our ANC Youth and Students' delegation, explaining that Julius was going to attend the Party School at the same time as me. Julius and I had some discussions about our impending studies, but it then transpired that he was given another assignment and was unable to attend the Lenin School.

My friendship with Chris and our respect for each other solidified in Berlin, where my admiration for him became deeper and stronger; it would be reinforced further when we worked together later when he was the General Secretary of the SACP.

To conclude this section, Chris Hani was assassinated by a rabid right-wing anti-communist called Janusz Walus, a heinous crime that robbed our people, country and revolutionary movement of one of the most admired and loved leaders of the ANC, SACP and MK.

At the time of the assassination, I was having a short break with my family and good friends Carol Marshall and Antonio Fernandes, who had invited us to join them at the Wits Rural Facility in Hazyview, from where we intended to visit the Kruger National Park every day. Their children, Mario and Miguel, got on very well with Amina and Govan, so we were all feeling happy driving around on 10 April 1993.

Then, in the evening, I turned on the news, and to my utter horror, there was the story of Chris's killing. It was devastating, and tears rolled down my face. Govan saw my distress and ran to find Meg, telling her, 'Mummy, Daddy is crying!' The whole group hurried in to watch the news, and Meg also broke down. Chris had been murdered in the driveway of his home, right in front of his fifteen-year-old daughter Khwezi. The shock was overwhelming; the consequences were incalculable. As Mandela said that evening in his critically important national address to the nation as ANC President:

> Today, an unforgiveable crime has been committed: the calculated cold-blooded murder of Chris Hani. It is not just a crime against a dearly beloved son of our soil, it is a crime against all the people of our country.

We decided to return to Johannesburg early the next morning. On arrival, I went straight to the Hani home in Dawn Park, Boksburg, and joined the committee tasked with organising his funeral. The assassination put the country on a knife's edge, with the prospect of unbridled violence breaking out. Fortunately, Mandela was able to calm the situation through an extraordinary speech on radio and TV.

Chris Hani's funeral at the FNB stadium was attended by thousands of mourners, including the Mandelas, Tambos, Sisulus, Thabo Mbeki and other leaders of the ANC, SACP and COSATU. In spite of Mandela's efforts and the strong position taken by the Alliance leaders, the situation in the country was tense, and the anger amongst some of the mourners was palpable. Meg told me later that, as she and Carol were driving to the carpark inside the stadium, one such group surrounded their car and blocked their way. She and Carol then wound down the windows and shouted, 'Amandla!' and 'Viva, Chris Hani, Viva!' and the angry group smiled and let them through.

The stadium that had hosted the joyous launch of the legal SACP in 1990 was now a sombre place. To this day, when I recall Hani's evil killing and funeral, I am unable to hold back my tears.

Two weeks after Hani's death, Comrade President O. R. Tambo died from a stroke. As detailed in Chapter 6, he had been badly affected by the assassination and sat through the entire funeral proceedings as unwell as he was. A giant towering above other giants in our history had left us.

Shortly after Tambo's death, I found myself at death's door. After going to a Nedbank branch near the Supreme Court to negotiate a mortgage for a house we were interested in buying, the party driver who was supposed to collect me and take me to the negotiations at the World Trade Centre failed to arrive. So I decided to walk to the shop of my sister-in-law, Farida Pahad (née Gani), which was nearby. On the way, I was accosted by a group of young men who pinned my arms behind my back and took my attaché case, which had no money in it but documents relating to the negotiations. As they had me in a stranglehold, one of them pulled out a stiletto-type knife and carefully and deliberately stabbed me in the heart. I felt the blood running down my chest and managed to enter an office, where I collapsed. Fortunately, I was conscious and able to ask the helpful people who were working there to phone the SACP office and inform them that I would not be at the meeting. They summoned an ambulance and spoke to Jeremy Cronin. Jeremy then phoned Meg and told her that I had been stabbed and taken to Hillbrow Hospital (now Hillbrow Community Health Care Centre).

When Meg arrived there looking for me, she was told she was at the wrong place. When she insisted on searching through the people waiting for attention, she found me lying on a stretcher with my head falling off one end, next to an overflowing bin full of used dressings. The denial of my being admitted as a patient was based on the fact that she was white and forgot to mention that I was not. When I had to stand for an X-ray, Meg was asked to try to support me and hold a bucket to catch my vomit. I was then taken to an operating theatre that had an open door. People were walking in and out, and Meg could see what was happening. Inside there, someone was smoking a cigarette while a doctor from Bangladesh saved my life, draining blood from my lungs, which was excruciatingly painful. I swore profusely to fight the pain. I was told that the knife had missed my heart by one centimetre. I will always be grateful to that doctor.

Meanwhile, Meg had contacted Fazel Randera, our GP and very old friend and comrade. She told him the place was filthy and I would die from an infection if I stayed there and asked if he could help. Fortunately, Fazel came and organised for me to be moved to the Milpark Hospital, which had good heart surgeons should another operation prove necessary.

Meg accompanied me to the Milpark, with instructions from Fazel to make sure the drip feeding fresh blood stayed up and the one draining blood out of the lungs stayed down, assuring her that we would be admitted without problems. However, when we arrived, I was left on a trolley in a passage for quite a while. Then a senior nurse asked Meg, 'What is this?' to which she replied, '"This" is my husband, and he's waiting for a bed.' The nurse replied, 'Well, he can't come in here. He's bleeding; this is a recovery ward.' After more objections, I was given a bed, and Meg was whisked away to sign a document taking full responsibility for any costs not covered by my medical aid. No one was friendly.

That same day, I was visited by Thabo Mbeki, Walter Sisulu, Joe Slovo and other leaders of the ANC and SACP, and the mood changed remarkably quickly. The following day, when the staff heard that Mandela was about to arrive, I was given a private room with no mention of extra charges and, from that moment, I was the most popular patient. It was all smiles, Meg and the children were most welcome, and nothing was too much trouble. To this day, I have no idea why I was stabbed. They did seem to be more interested in killing me than robbing me, as they didn't take my watch or wallet, only my briefcase.

After about a week, I was discharged and happy to rejoin the negotiations.

In both the ANC and SACP negotiating teams, we were concerned that we had not yet agreed on a number of sticky points. However, on 3 June 1993, Slovo took the initiative and set a confirmed date for the elections. As we had discussed that in the SACP negotiating team, I suspect that Slovo already had the backing of the ANC leaders, so there was no room for retreat. The National Party had to agree, and the date was now cast in stone: 27 April 1994. Just over four years after our unbanning, we had a definite date that would be a defining moment for the people of South Africa.

But that same month, another dramatic incident occurred. The extreme right-wing *Afrikaner Weerstandsbeweging* (Afrikaner Resistance Movement, commonly known as the AWB), broke through the glass entrance in an armoured car and occupied the World Trade Centre, the negotiation site. The National Party got the police and some soldiers to guard the delegates, who were taken to a room, but there was a nervous tension in the air since none of us knew what the AWB's motive was. I felt reassured when it became clear that the white police officers and soldiers were prepared to open fire if the intruders came to break down the door of the room in which we were ensconced.

All of us respected the order that we should stay where we were and remain calm. Only Rajbansi, in his foolishness, decided that he would speak to the right-wingers, and for his impudence, received a resounding *klap* across the face. After a few hours, the intruders left without having achieved anything but breaking some glass. But they did unite the will of the negotiators to bring the talks to an end as speedily as possible.

By November 1993, we had ratified the Interim Constitution, set up the Transitional Executive Council (TEC) and other structures to oversee the process leading up to 27 April 1994. The culmination of years and years of unremitting struggle, we had at last succeeded in negotiating the basis for the first free, fair, non-racial and democratic elections in our history. Those of us who were in the talks that day (3 June 1993) were aware of the milestone we had reached. I felt proud to be part of the SACP and ANC teams who had helped to bring about that fantastic achievement.

The next important step we had to take was organising and conducting successful fair and free democratic elections.

To that end, the Independent Electoral Commission was set up with Justice Johann Kriegler as chair and Dikgang Moseneke as his deputy. They made an excellent team with other members of the Commission, South African and non-South African. From the beginning of the process, they set up a party liaison committee with which they could consult and take decisions, even on controversial issues. In the first Liaison Committee, I represented the SACP. But later, it was decided that only parties registered and contesting the elections would be part of it. The ANC chose Azhar Cachalia (later a Supreme Court judge) and myself to represent it. We knew each other well and worked as a team. Azhar was invaluable for his fine legal brain and astute political insight and mediating capacities. The concept of a party liaison committee has endured and is now part of any electoral mechanism.

So the two major parties were the National Party, which was still the governing party, and the ANC. While sitting on the Liaison Committee, I was also a member of the ANC 'war room' set up to run their election campaign. The war room reported to the National Working Committee (NWC) and the NEC of the ANC. The other representative of the SACP was Geraldine Fraser-Moleketi, Deputy National Elections Coordinator. The war room consisted of, among others, Terror Lekota, Popo Molefe, Pallo Jordan, Joel Netshitenzhe, Gill Marcus and Marcel Golding (from the National Union of Mineworkers). The campaign and war room manager was Ketso Gordhan. That formidable team, together with representatives from the provinces, led the campaign.

Our sessions consisted of working on strategy and tactics, the election manifesto, campaign themes and slogans, publicity material and a special unit allocating speakers for the numerous meetings and rallies held throughout the country. We met weekly, receiving updates from the provinces, pursuing our media offensive, and studying and analysing polls conducted by private companies. We hit on the campaign slogan 'Now is the Time', which proved effective and popular.

In addition to my work on the Liaison Committee, my SACP responsibilities and the ANC war room, I spent some time on the election campaign, mainly in the North West Province. Prior to the election, I was one of the few national leaders to address meetings and rallies in the old Western Transvaal organised by the ANC, SACP or NUM. Travelling to cities such as Potchefstroom and Klerksdorp, I could see the vast tracks of land owned by mining giant Anglo American, and I well remember one incident. When James Motlatsi, leader of the NUM, and I were travelling back to Johannesburg from Klerksdorp, he suggested we enter a mining compound to witness first hand the living and working conditions of the workers and meet and greet them. He was obviously well-known and was met with happiness and enthusiasm. Then we got word that the police had been called to arrest trespassers. James was fine, but he worried about my security, so we made a hasty retreat to safety. That was another salutary lesson in the control exercised by mine managers over one of the most exploited sections of our working class.

୭

For the December holidays, Tony Fernandes and Carol Marshall invited us to stay with them for a holiday in Maputo. They were friends with a family from Belgium working in Maputo as *cooperantes* – progressive individuals from other countries working in Mozambique to assist in the post-independence reconstruction and development. It was also an opportunity for me to recover from the near-fatal stabbing.

After travelling to the Mozambican border in our old Ford Fiesta we had brought from London in the container, we met up with Carol and Tony and split up so that each car had an adult in it who could speak Portuguese and knew the way.

Meg travelled with Carol and Govan in our car, and I went with Tony and Amina in his four-by-four. We had been warned that parts of the route were dangerous, as there were still sporadic raids from the remnants of RENAMO, whose CIA-funded soldiers had opposed FRELIMO, our ally. About halfway to Maputo, Tony's car got a puncture, his second on that trip, so his spare tyre was already in use. Then a massive thunderstorm broke out, and we were stranded, and of course, those were the days before cell phones. Tony was very calm, but I was concerned about Amina; however, at the age of fourteen, she was cool and sensible. Fortunately, another car came by and stopped to help. They had a spare tyre which was not completely compatible with Tony's car, but they managed to fit it and felt it would get us to Maputo.

Meanwhile, Meg found the driving harrowing. The roads were full of giant potholes, with several car wrecks abandoned on the roadside. When it grew dark as they approached Maputo, it was apparent there was a power cut and none of the traffic lights or street lights were working. Carol asked when Meg had last seen the headlights of Tony's car in the rearview mirror, and she said, 'Not for ages.' Carol then explained that on that road, one needed to keep together like a convoy, and they should turn back to make sure we were okay. To the great relief of us all, we found each other and proceeded slowly to Maputo together.

We had a lovely holiday in Maputo with Tony's family and all of their friends welcoming us warmly. The place in which we stayed was close to where Tony's mother lived with one of his brothers, so we all ate together and enjoyed the Goan-style Mozambican food and the famous peri-peri prawns and chicken at restaurants.

On New Year's Eve, Tony and Carol took us to a party at the Navy Club. Pam Beira, whom I mentioned in Chapter 4 when I visited Maputo fifteen years earlier, was also there. At that time, her marriage to Marcelino dos Santos, one of the foremost leaders of FRELIMO, was on the rocks. During the evening, she took me into one corner of the outdoor venue and engaged in a long discussion about South Africa, FRELIMO, the ANC and Mozambique and briefly touched on her personal problems. Then, as the party was ending, she insisted on continuing our chat and that I should accompany her to her house. I was reluctant, but she was persistent, so with Meg's permission, I went with her in her official car and made sure Tony wrote down their official address.

Marcelino dos Santos had already developed a reputation which led to people he visited locking up their daughters, as the saying goes, and Pam needed to talk, but I was extremely concerned that my visit in the early hours could be misinterpreted by her husband's security officers and was neither sensible nor safe for me. Eventually, after about two hours, I managed to convince Pam that I had to leave, and she asked her driver to take me to where we were staying. Meg was relieved to see me but annoyed that I had made everyone worry.

As Maputo was still suffering from the long civil war, there were power cuts, but our borrowed house had a generator, so they were no problem for us. There was also a rubbish collection strike and massive heaps of refuse lying around. The kids roamed about the area, and one day, when Miguel and Govan were climbing a tree, Miguel fell from it into a pile of garbage and cut his hand very badly on a dirty tin can. That was an eye-opener for us because, even as well-known and respected doctors, Carol and Tony had to use all their contacts to get their son's hand safely cleaned and stitched up. But soon Miguel was fine again, and they arranged for us all to go together to the seaside in Bilene, where the children had a great time on the beach. At the end of that holiday, we felt refreshed and invigorated and were happy to go home and take on our South African challenges.

༄

While in Maputo, we did not follow developments in the ANC or SACP, so I was in for a big surprise on our return. The day after we did so, Charles Nqakula phoned to congratulate me on being nominated as premier-elect for North West Province. My response was that I needed to give it serious consideration before I could accept the honour. I had no clue why I had been elected by the Provincial Conference of the ANC but later learnt that Rocky Malebane-Metsing, who had been involved in a coup attempt in 1988 to overthrow Mangope, leader of the Bophuthatswana Bantustan, was a strong candidate. However, because of his erratic and bullying behaviour as the NEC representative deployed to that province, he was unpopular with many structures in the provincial ANC, including the Women's and Youth Leagues. At a critical moment, they decided that I would be the best candidate to defeat Metsing, and so, unable to contact me, they nominated me anyway. As I was informed, Metsing was defeated by a large majority.

Metsing was very upset and started mobilising to reverse that decision, enrolling the help of a few traditional leaders from Bophuthatswana to lobby Mandela and Sisulu, arguing that in those rural areas, a communist leader of Indian origin would be a losing candidate. They agreed with him and asked Slovo to speak to me to turn down the offer. My response was to thank Slovo for that information and explain that I was seeking advice and would give serious consideration to what he said but make my own decision.

After consulting a few people, including Thabo, I arrived at my decision. His response demonstrated tremendous political insight and thinking. He had asked for a few days to consider the matter and consulted with a few comrades and friends in the North West province and eventually advised me not to accept the nomination. We agreed that in light of the large rural areas that had been relatively well serviced under Lucas Mangope (compared to other Bantustan leaders) regarding housing, education and other services, a communist candidate would be anathema to many voters. He added that if I decided to accept the nomination, he would support me. However, by the time I met Mbeki, I had already given that dilemma a great deal of thought and had decided to turn down the nomination. Thus, Thabo's advice confirmed that I had made the correct decision.

I was a known leader of the SACP, a person of Indian origin who did not know even a few words of Setswana and had only been born in that province and resided there as a small child before leaving for Johannesburg. While it would have been an honour and a privilege to be a premier, my candidacy might have resulted in the ANC losing support to Mangope's party.

Once I had made that decision, I communicated it to the CC of the SACP and then to the NEC of the ANC. Both sets of leaders at the national level accepted my decision, except for Yawa, who was a leader of the NUM, the PEC of the ANC, and of the SACP in North West. Another person unhappy with my decision was the Queen of the Bafokeng nation, whom I had met when attending a meeting of the councillors and other members of the Bafokeng. She was friendly and promised me the full support of the Bafokeng King and her people. She insisted on meeting me again and came to our house in Bellevue East with the King and expressed her rejection of my decision in very strong terms. My best endeavours to explain my position cut no ice with her, and she repeatedly assured me of the full support of the Bafokeng. She was disappointed and, for years after, whenever we met, would express her displeasure.

The PEC, led by Reverend Tselapedi, who had also organised the meeting with the Bafokeng, refused to accept my position, too. Indeed, even at the last minute at the national conference organised to finalise the ANC election list, they tried to convince me to change my mind. But I politely refused and assured them that, working with the ANC leadership, we would find another candidate, and that person was Popo Molefe, who covered most of the bases.

In the meanwhile, Metsing continued to campaign for himself. He had hired or been offered the use of a luxurious limousine which prominently displayed the slogan 'The Eagle Has Landed'. I well remember one incident, when Mandela was in Potchefstroom to address a rally and meeting and Metsing arrived in that limo. He came with Joe Modise, presumably hoping to prove his popularity to the ANC leadership. That evening, I was scheduled to address a meeting in Klerksdorp but was ordered to go to Potchefstroom instead. In Chapter 6 about my mentors, I wrote about Mandela, describing his coldness towards me that day and how, after Jessie Duarte explained that I was there at the request of the ANC and was not a candidate for the position of premier, he greeted me warmly and with a big smile.

I addressed many meetings and rallies in the North West province, and my speeches were well received amid the chanting of 'Viva, Comrade Pahad, Viva!' But I must record here two incidents which were also part of the election campaign. Baleka Mbete and I were asked to go to the Boputathswana Bantustan (Bop), where our first port of call was the university. When we arrived, the students were having a sit-in, and I felt that, despite the heavy presence of the Bop army, who were refusing to allow anybody into the university grounds, I should try to go in on the basis of a free and fair election, which eschewed any no-go areas. But as I walked towards the entrance, a soldier put his sub-machine gun against my chest and threatened to shoot me if I entered the university. Baleka and I decided to withdraw.

Later, when we were in a rural area to address farm workers and were listening to other speakers, a young man approached Baleka and informed her in Setswana that the women in the area wanted to see her. We agreed that she should meet them. When she came back, she told me that the women had said to her:

> You and your comrade come here and talk about issues, challenges and problems. But do you understand that our main problem is our husbands or male partners? On weekends, after a bout of drinking, they harass, intimidate and beat us.

So Baleka and I decided that in our speeches we would address that problem directly by spending time talking about the empowerment of women. We also called on the ANC structures to prioritise the problems and challenges confronting women, especially in the rural areas.

Those were exciting times, during which we could feel the strong support for the ANC, and as the campaign unfolded, our confidence in our ability to win by a handsome majority grew.

When reviewing the preparations for the elections and their safe and fair conduct, it is important to remember the widespread violence and insecurity of that period. In addition to Chris Hani's assassination, there were the Boipatong and Bisho massacres, the frequent open fighting between the IFP and ANC, the violence instigated by the third force, and the attacks on individuals, such as the shot fired from the Observatory telecommunications tower at Joe Slovo. As late as March 1994, there had been extensive unrest following Mangope's announcement that Bophuthatswana would boycott the elections, culminating in the televised shooting to death of three AWB members, who had killed several Black people at random.

The situation in many parts of South Africa was far from stable: it was very tense.

When Justice Johann Kriegler heard that I was writing a memoir, he agreed to be interviewed about my contribution to the election process. Below are some extracts from that interview which illustrate the exceptionally difficult environment in which that first election was held. They also give a good picture of the difficulties organising such an election and the vote counting that followed. After Chris's assassination, we could not afford to consider a postponement, and the result needed to be conclusive enough to ensure that it was accepted and uncontested.

Meg conducted the interview with Kriegler in September 2019 and began by saying, 'Essop Pahad is of the opinion that if it were not for you, the 1994 elections might not have been as successful as they were. Please comment on the work of the Independent Electoral Commission (now the Electoral Commission) and your contribution to its work.'

> Well, I can return the compliment. If it weren't for Essop and the way he managed the Party National Liaison Committee, the election certainly wouldn't have been anywhere near as successful as it was. In fact, one of the major, if not the only contribution we made to international electoral administration and knowledge was the benefit of a liaison committee to anticipate and avoid or ameliorate disputes as and when they arose in the run-up – and there are umpteen things people disagree on in an election. To turn more specifically to the question, I'm neither vain nor unduly modest; I think it's correct to say it was a very, very difficult job …
>
> I don't think we would have accepted the mandate if we had known exactly how difficult it would be to do a three- or four-year job in three or four months. But everybody wanted it to work; the

momentum was there; the political will was there. And I, in some ways, represented a part of the desire on the part of the common folk to have the thing work. I think I also represented some sort of an in-between, a bridge that everybody could accept – that nobody liked but nobody could reject as being part of the enemy. I think the idea to pick a judge was good. I think if it weren't for Mandela, there would not have been that kind of respect for the judiciary. But I thought that it was a good move to have a senior judge chair the electoral commission. To have taken an Afrikaner was a risk, but I think it was a calculated risk because I wasn't an Afrikaner's Afrikaner: they had rejected me as being a 'communist'.

I think that in retrospect, my identity did contribute to the acceptability of the process – only for what I was; never mind for what I did. Purely the choice of a particular person showed political astuteness and a preparedness to seek common ground. Which I think is one of the major reasons why the elections took place at all and why the elections, notwithstanding their manifest shortcomings, were accepted as being substantially free and fair.

The IEC set up a multi-party committee as a means to involve the participating parties in the preparations for the first democratic elections in our history. What was the rationale behind this decision, and did it do what you, your team and the IEC commissioner expected of it?

We had had several years of initially secret discussions, and, thereafter, more frank and peripheral discussions between interest groups and then several years of give and take, rough and tumble and the baited argument in and around CODESA. So, by the time the election came around, the body politic was used to compromising, used to talking to one another, used to accentuating what we had in common and minimising that which divided us. I think that is part of the selection of the body to organise the election. Part of the spirit in which the adversaries went into the process and the manner in which, by and large, certainly the more visionary of the leadership saw the outcome. It's not good; it's not perfect; it's far from perfect. But it's a darn sight better than the alternative, and as my grandfather (rural Afrikaner) would have said, 'If your foot is in the stirrup, you

must ride.'
And I think that's the spirit [with] which most people in the leadership core approached the election. That's certainly the manner in which we in the commission did so. I very much was of the view that there would be no postponement. The date is carved in stone, it's not of our making – it's part of the given. I think having been a barrister for many years, I was used to accepting a brief for what it was – not because I chose it but because that was the brief I was given. You've got to do the best that you can with what you've got. I approached the election that way, and I suppose that added ultimately to the pragmatic 'let's make a plan' approach – scotch tape and a little bit of chewing gum here, and a lick and a promise there, but let's move. So, I think that's the answer to that question.

There was very little time, which made it very hard.

It made it extremely difficult. What made it even more difficult was that much of the preparation that had been done – I have no doubt in good faith – was badly done. For instance, we were told that we needn't worry about the identification of polling sites – that had been done by Home Affairs and it was all in hand. When we turned to look at that in early February, we found to our horror that the list of addresses that they had given was useless in many respects. The addresses were wrong, the coordinates didn't figure, and many of the places no longer existed; others were wholly unsuited. And in many instances, they had not spoken to the owners of the property to obtain consent to having their hall used [as] a polling station. You know, at that stage there was a potentially violent election process which could legitimately have elicited declinations from landlords, so unless you had it tied and signed up, it was no good. Anyway, we had to, for instance, start from scratch with that. We also found that the offices that they had selected for us near the airport where CODESA had been were wholly unsuited. There wasn't sufficient room for our staff, but much more seriously, it was electrically unsuited. We could not link up with a network of connected counting or polling stations, and telephonically, it wasn't capable of carrying the traffic. So, we had to move, and we moved also in mid-February, which was a greatly disrupting exercise.

And, of course, the political roleplayers were still negotiating and plans changed and agreements were changing, and the form of the election changed – whether there was going to be one ballot paper or multiple ballot papers changed three-quarters [of the] way through the process – and if you [are] planning an election … I don't know, have you ever done an election?

No…

Well, one of the simplest things to start with is how many people do you need in your polling station and which operations are to be performed by each one and in which sequence; and the layout of your polling station. And if you have one ballot paper, you need x number of reporting points and staff members, but if you need two ballot papers, then you need x plus perhaps three quarters of x for the next one. Some places would have been big enough for merely one ballot-paper station, but once you needed to fit in two separate polling sections, one for provincial and one for national, you had to change your polling stations, so that made it tricky.

They didn't know, didn't decide whether prisoners would be allowed to vote and then whether some wouldn't be allowed to vote and then whether all prisoners would be allowed to vote. And then whether foreigners would be allowed to vote if they had been here for x number of years and then whether South Africans abroad would be allowed to vote. And whether you'd have ex-pat voting and, if so, where? And how many polling stations and which ex-pats? Did they still have to have their South African ID documents? … So, yes, the process was messy.

Yes, very messy, I'm surprised we managed to get through it as well as we did.

Well, you know, if the truth be told, the success is in part due to the fact that we had so little time. Debates on issues that were divisive that could have held us up for days or weeks and could have had political parties at daggers drawn rushing to court to get all sorts of court orders and interdicts … and Lord knows what else … There wasn't time for that ... You can say, 'Sorry guys, you may be right, but we've got a vote 6 to 4 so let's go.' So, the shortness of the time had its advantages.

Your intervention at the National Recreation Centre (NASREC) counting centre made it possible to put aside for the time being disputes over comparatively small problems so as to allow the vote counting to continue. This averted what seemed to be a stalemate situation created by those who were not happy with the ANC's overwhelming victory in what was the PWV region, remember? Could you explain what happened?

Yes. Let me preface it. Until quite recently, I still had nightmares about that day. I still, if I think about it now, I have an incipient goose bump ... and there's a particular ringtone on a telephone that was in the office in the IEC. I haven't had a phone with that ringtone since. If I get to somewhere and the phone rings and it's that ringtone, I get all jittery. It really was the critical point. The Saturday afternoon five days after the election, and they haven't counted a single ballot paper and in fact they have not opened a single ballot box. We were looking at something like twenty per cent of the votes of the country there at NASREC. If that counting centre failed, it would not only have precipitated failures at other counting centres where there were comparable but not necessarily identical problems. If we had not held the line there, there was a very serious risk of it sliding everywhere. But even if it was only there, it was twenty per cent or eighteen per cent, I think, of the country's vote, without which the election could not conceivably have been regarded as credible.

That was part of the background. Another part of the background, a major cause of the hold up, was the inherent dicey security situation in the country, which nobody wanted to speak about at the time. But it effected our planning: I think we had to make do with fifty-four per cent of the polling stations that we had wanted in Soweto. The police said we simply could not secure that number and they forced us to contract and combine and coalesce, which led to the overflow, the deluge of ballot papers, which was the basic problem at NASREC. This was exacerbated long before we got to the counting point. It was already at the polling station. Stations were overloaded – there were too many people. Ballot boxes couldn't hold. I don't know if you knew this at the time ... but there was one instance where a polling station presiding officer had used his trousers – and he knotted the bottoms of the trouser legs and emptied the ballot box into that and pulled the belt tight and used that ballot box again. Because it had reached [the] overflow stage and he didn't have another ballot box. But if you think about the amount of regulations which had been written, inter alia by the Canadians, who had elections – Canada are the nitpickers of the world and rightly so, elections have got to be done technically so that everything is checkable and reportable and visible and auditable.

And then there was no way on God's earth, by the time we got to that Saturday afternoon, we could retrace our steps. To get to the more technical part – part of the verification process is that the presiding officer at the polling station must put inside the ballot box an identification sheet signed by himself and the party representatives to identify himself and the polling station and its number and put his stamp on it. And then he's got to seal the ballot box and put another label on the outside so that if you receive the ballot box you could say, 'Well, this is a ballot box coming from such and such a polling station, and if there's a query, I know I must go to so and so who is the presiding officer or I can say to the party representatives that you must get Shabalala and you must get Dingfoot if they were your representatives; there's this dispute.'

Once you have an anonymous ballot box, you can't do that kind of back-checking; you can't do an audit at all. You certainly can't do a paper trail, so the opposition was not necessarily malign. Certainly, some of it was ball-achingly law-abiding. The rules are the rules, never mind what the rules are there for, the rules are there, and they must be obeyed. And if you say that we can't obey these rules now, what do we do? They say, 'Don't ask me, all I can tell you is these are the rules.' So there were people like that; I can remember some by name. But here we are with this mountain that had been dumped by polling station presiding officers who had done forty-eight hours and seventy-two hours, and they were at the end of whatever tether they ever had. And they said you say I must stand in [a] queue and hand in my box and get my receipt and sign it over because that had to be done at every voting station. There had to be a receipt, a bookkeeping and a delivery note, and this was at three o'clock in the morning, and these guys had been going since ... Some just said 'Take them. I never want to see them again!' and they piled up and piled up. There was no way you could ever identify them again. There are a very large number that fell into this category. But as soon as you can't do all, doing some is no good. It's no good to say the ship is only leaking in some parts.

Maybe if it was one or two anonymous boxes, but it was hundreds ...

You didn't know how many, as you know – you were there. You realised what the atmosphere was becoming, it had become more and more confrontational. It hadn't quite reached the combatant state, but it was already quite abrasive.

I found that party reps who were counting actually had a CODESA spirit, but there were people who kept on coming from outside who were trying to stir things up.

And that is exactly why we never ever wanted top people on the Liaison Committee, the moment you have the *makulu baas* ... they can't compromise ... And those are the people that came from outside. It helped a great deal that Helen Suzman was there. The main objectors were her former party mates, but the decision itself was perfectly straightforward: there was no alternative, if you have to jump across the chasm or fall over, well it's pretty damned easy ...

But you were able to explain that 'this is the situation, and these are the items which are disputed ... so put them aside and sort them out later because at this moment in time there's only one way forward.

In fact, long before we got to the election, we had a fairly difficult technical issue about the printing of the ballot papers. The ballot papers had to be printed abroad, and we didn't want to do that. Parties insisted – your party insisted.

In retrospect, it seems ridiculous.

In retrospect, a lot of it seems ridiculous, but at the time, it made perfect sense; it had to be done by De la Roux in the UK with security features like they were bank notes. Each polling station presiding officer had a unique stamp, to which we had the index. And every ballot paper as it was issued to you as it was torn out of the book had to be stamped on the reverse side and handed to the voter. No ballot paper without that stamp was counted. No ballot paper with that stamp could be rejected because it had come out of the hands of the presiding officers. So, whether the ballot box had gone to Louis Trichardt and had been dumped in the Vaal dam and then preserved and brought back and dried out ... If the ballot papers had the identification stamp on the back, those were valid ballot papers that had been issued at the voting station to voters and they had to be counted. Never mind what the box looked like or whether they were in a box or came in somebody's tied up trousers.

So, yes, the identification and the paper trail and the receipts and the delivery notes are important, but when the chips are down and you say ultimately every ballot paper that was issued has the stamp and is here and every ballot paper here must have been issued by a polling station presiding officer, then what are we fighting about? It wasn't a constituency-based election where two votes or five votes this way or that way could make any difference, whether the votes were cast here or in Houghton or in Diepkloof, it didn't matter. They're in this election on this ballot paper – end of the news. We then went back to the board and said that if all else fails, we must do without all those proceedings. We went and amended the law, retrospectively. And nobody wanted to look at those ballot papers again – nobody ever wanted to look at them again.

Fortunately, the result was so overwhelming.

It was going to be.

Can you say anything specifically about Essop's role?

On many occasions, I have said that when we started that major contribution to the international knowledge of running elections in difficult places ... that you [must] have [a] negotiating body, [a] mediation body, and I've also said that it is essential that the staffing of that body should be by the political parties themselves. It's not for the electoral management body to try to run the negotiation and the liaison – that's for the parties. The competitors must run that process. And in fact, in a number of places where I have worked (I have worked in many strange places since), the identity of the participants on the Liaison Committee is crucial. It's not only that they should not be the Electoral Commission in disguise but that they actually be independent, act independently but also act cooperatively with one another. They should have the vision, the idealism, the commitment to the process to be able to surmount party political differences. The immediate need is to have people with that sort of commitment but also the wisdom and the vision to be able to see the difference between trivia and substance.

I have seen time and time again in South Africa [that] it worked. At the national level, which was the most difficult, the person who led that body was a man by the name of Essop Pahad, who was a committed party agent, a very, very committed freedom fighter, but he put his party interest ostensibly, if not in fact, aside sufficiently to be able to chair a liaison committee and facilitate the process. We could not have managed many of the disputes had it not been for the identity of that one particular person.

You know him. He is a tough sod, but he is also a very sociable one – he has a way with people. He can be very, very domineering if he wants to be, but he can also be very ameliorating if he wants to be. And he ran that body beautifully like a conductor running a symphony orchestra, and indeed it was a major factor in the success. You know at times during the counting process, the election darn near came unstuck long before we got to the actual main calculation of seats. Up in what's now Limpopo, the counters went on strike, and down in Durban at the city hall, they went on strike and wanted more pay. It was with the help of the Liaison Committee that we managed to avert those obstacles. I also think the fact that the Liaison Committee worked so well may have played a role in Buthelezi's decision to come into the process at the eleventh hour. He saw that the bus was going to leave without him and he'd better run and catch it. A part of that impression was because the IEC had said, come hell or high water, on [the] 27th of April, we are going to the polls. But the Liaison Committee had the parties speaking from that same hymn sheet.

Was it called the Multi-Party Committee?

The Liaison Committee had various levels. We couldn't call it the national party liaison because one of the parties was the National Party, so it was the Party National Liaison Committee (PNLC).

I understand that, after the election results were announced, Jacob Zuma, then leader of the ANC in KZN, approached you with his comrades in that province to declare the elections null and void there because of rigging and other alleged misdemeanours by the IFP, and you turned them down in a decisive manner. Would you comment on this incident?

That's true. It was not only Jacob Zuma, and it was after the close of the polls but before the announcement of the result. The days before the Friday when we announced the result, that Thursday night I had in my office Zuma, Peter Leon, and someone from the National Party. Each one had been there in succession; each one had a complaint. Each one not only on the Thursday night but also on the Tuesday, the Wednesday. Some of them had gone to the commissioners, and we had decided as a matter of policy that we were not going to listen to generalities. If people brought forward actual evidence (what this was we didn't say) of finagling, fraud, election stealing, we would investigate. But without actual evidence, only mere general allegations, the caravan would move on.

Leon's party had objected very strongly to having been excluded from electioneering in, for instance, the East Rand and Southern Gauteng townships. The ANC had complained bitterly that they had not been allowed to electioneer in KwaZulu; the IFP couldn't complain, but the Nats complained that they could not campaign in the Transkei. There were no-go areas – we knew that, and everybody knew that there were no-go areas. Our attitude was, and my attitude still is, that it mattered very, very little: overwhelmingly in deep KwaZulu, they were going to vote IFP, and in deep Transkei, they were going to vote ANC, and in the Platteland, they were going to vote NP ... and whether or not they had been able to conduct meetings in Diepkloof mattered not a jot.

It was that kind of country, so we took those complaints with a major pinch of salt. And we said, 'Bring us the evidence.' And in the end, we did take action in some places – for example, we docked the ANC some 300,000 votes in the Transkei because there was clear evidence that in some places, they had actually blocked the road.

Okay – Zuma wanted the Natal votes nullified, and the Democratic Alliance (DA) wanted Gauteng, which was then the PWV, held up for a recount, which was nonsense. A recount does nothing. There was no problem with the count, it was what had preceded the vote that they were complaining about, and that you could never reverse. The Nats were complaining about what was happening in the former homelands up in the north.

Even Cyril was very unhappy about the party not being able to go places, but he was the most realistic of them at the time. The most interesting one of them all, Zuma, came with his heavies, he came with his bodyguards. I may have listened to him a little bit more if I had not had the impression that he was trying to frighten me, and when that happens, I'm not a good guy to talk to.

You don't respond very well to being bullied.

But in the case of Peter Leon, my wife Betty actually typed a letter in my office at his dictation for him to take back to Zach de Beer to sign and say he wants to block the election because they want to go to court. I had the letter typed for him but sent him back a message that if he wants to go down in history as the person who blocked South Africa's peaceful transition, he must be my guest. I wouldn't resist.

And of course Leon came back and said, 'No – we are withdrawing our complaint,' and I think that applied to everybody, really, in the end. I have read elsewhere that Madiba actually spoke very firmly to Zuma and told him that they had miscalculated the depths of the support of the IFP in rural KwaZulu. That may well have been so, and that certainly was his attitude during the election: the game was more important than whether someone delivered a forward pass.

Essop says also that the way you ensured the elections were successful may have saved the country from a possible meltdown.

That point is a different one, really. There are people [who] say that regard[ing] the manifest administrative shortcomings of the electoral process and the fact that the election was run in less than four months where it should have taken at least three years is just too good to be true, and the result was a fiddled result; a negotiated result. Responsible people have said this, academics have said this, and I have always said this: If only, please God, we had had the competence to do that! We certainly couldn't, and to this day, nobody has come forward to say, 'I did this' or 'I did the other'. We couldn't do it.

[There] would have [had] to [have been[hundreds of people involved in that devious cunning plot. You see, the Nats got the Cape, the IFP got Natal, the ANC got sixty-two per cent (not sixty-six per cent – it couldn't amend the constitution on its own), but it got a very substantial majority, so everybody was happy – this is just too good a result. It's a result written in heaven, so Kriegler must have fiddled it.

But we did do this: we did cut corners. For instance, you may recall that you had to have marking ink on your finger, which is generally a safeguard against multiple voting. If you've stood in the queue for three hours, you are unlikely to want to stand in the queue for another three hours, so the mere incompetence of the election was a disincentive to multiple voting. But remember, because there were boycotters, it had to be invisible ink, visible only under ultraviolet. The ultraviolet lights broke down in places and ran out of ink. In most of the far north, around about day two, they had no ink left, and they were panicking. We ran out of ink in lots of places because instead of just dabbing, the polling station people stuck voters' fingers into the ink, so of course it ran out much faster than the Canadians had calculated. The ink had been made in the United States; it was a secret formula.

When we ran out of ink, the forensic lab made up the next lot in a couple of hours, we put in National Party-made ink, and we sent it up North. You know what you do: you use water. Who will know the difference? Your scanner breaks down and you say, 'Put your hand in,' and you nod sagely. They can't see on their side what you see.

On a lighter note, I had a phone call the day before the election, before the foreign voting, from our ambassador in Australia who also administered in New Zealand. And he's in a major panic and asks what to do. 'What's wrong?' I enquire. And he says:

> The prime minster of New Zealand's wife has a friend who claims she is Mandela's cousin and she's going to cast the first vote in the elections of liberation because New Zealand started first, right next to the dateline. And she's going to vote tomorrow morning and she is going to go to the polling station rigged out in ANC regalia, and she's going to vote.

'So, what's the problem?' I asked. He says, 'Well, she's a fraud. She is not Mandela's cousin, and she is not even a South African.' I asked again, 'What's the problem?' And he says, '*That's* the problem. She's going to vote!' 'Yes ... so?' I asked. To which the Ambassador replied, 'Well, what are you going to do about it?' 'Mr Ambassador,' I said, 'if it makes you feel better, I promise you I will deduct a vote from the ANC in [the] final count.'

But that makes no earthly Godly difference. We went through massive expense (for the foreign votes) and ultimately had 96,000 of them, which adds up to a drop in the ocean!

When the counting was finally finished and the results agreed, the ANC had received 62.6% of the vote, the National Party 20.4%, the IFP 10.5% and the DA 1.7%. I was, however, disappointed to learn that a majority of Indians and Coloureds had voted for the National Party.

As detailed in the section about Mandela in Chapter 6, after announcing our triumph, the ANC had a victory party in the ballroom of the old Carlton Hotel. The next step was to travel to Cape Town and be sworn in as an MP. All our travel arrangements and accommodation had been arranged by the ANC, and at that moment, Cape Town seemed even more spectacular and beautiful than usual.

The inauguration came next, which I also described in Chapter 6 but must mention here that my brother Aziz, as part of the organising committee, took part in satisfying the security demands and handling the difficult task of deciding the order in which guests representing countries from all over the world would be announced. Mohamed Tikly caught Meg and I on camera, recording one of the happiest and greatest moments of our lives. All of us from the ANC, its allies and the international community could take pride in knowing that we had in some way contributed to 'so glorious a human achievement'.

First Years of Our Democracy

A day or two after the inauguration, Mbeki asked me to accompany him to the Union Buildings so he could set up an office to fulfil his duties and responsibilities. We drove to Pretoria in his ANC car since he had not yet been given an official vehicle or security. On the way, I recounted to him my mother's recollection of the Women's March to the Union Buildings in 1956. We knew that Mandela had already set up an office with the help of the Department of Foreign Affairs (DFA). When we arrived, we were met by a few officials from the old Cabinet Office, one of whom, Smith, was to stay on and become an important part of Mandela's, and later Mbeki's, Cabinet Secretariat. It was their first encounter with Mbeki, and they suggested, without a hint of protocol, that they would take him around the East Wing and he could choose an office. I objected most strenuously to the idea that the deputy president should subject himself to this process and said that I would go around the building and choose an appropriate office.

I found one that looked great and had an interleading office that would be occupied by his still-to-be-found personal assistant (PA). It also had adjoining offices which could be occupied by his staff once they had been recruited. Mbeki, who doesn't care much for fancy frills, accepted my suggestion and wanted to start work immediately. But there was no office equipment, not even pens and paper. Fortunately for him, the DFA had seconded two people to assist him: a man and a woman, both Afrikaans-speaking and well-drilled in acquiring the necessary equipment and running an office. They were friendly, helpful, efficient and enabled Mbeki to begin his duties, such as signing the many official documents requiring the signatures of Mandela and both his deputies.

Before he appointed Nomsa Ngakane as his PA, I assisted in running Mbeki's office. By then, Mandela, on Mbeki's advice, had appointed Jakes Gerwel, former Vice Chancellor of the University of the Western Cape, as Director-General (DG) of the Office of the President. We had met Gerwel in Dakar, where he had been invited by Frederik Van Zyl Slabbert to the gathering of Afrikaans-speaking whites to meet the ANC in exile, and subsequently became good friends.

Nomsa was great. She carried out her tasks with a smile, great efficiency and some good laughs, but that office also required a head who would be responsible for the appointment of other officials. So I consulted Dave Stewart, head of De Klerk's office, and asked him for their organogram. They had already employed some sixty persons, mostly from his time as president of South Africa. Mbeki then decided to bring in Tebogo Mafole to head his office. Tebogo had worked under him at the ANC's International Department and knew him well. But at what level should he be appointed? Mandela had a DG, De Klerk had a DG, and my view was clear that, at the very least, Tebogo should be appointed at the level of a chief director. All those positions had to be cleared by the Public Service Commission, and I was tasked to raise the matter with them.

At the meeting were a group of white-haired men convinced of their superiority. When it was suggested that Tebogo be appointed at the level of a chief director, they bristled since he had no university degree. I argued my case, pointing out his experience working in ANC structures and his understanding of ANC policies, but they would not budge, insisting that he would not be placed higher than a director. In my frustration at this unseemly refusal, I retorted, 'But Tebogo has more political depth and understanding in his little finger than all of you put together!'

My insistence was grounded on the fact that in the bureaucracy, it would be extremely difficult for a director to deal as an equal with the DGs in the other two presidential offices and other government departments. My report to Mbeki was laced with anger at the behaviour of the officials in the Public Service Commission. However, Mbeki, as cool and calm as always, merely said, 'Let's appoint him as a director and sooner rather than later we will promote him to chief director.'

That was the beginning of Mbeki's office as deputy president. Once he appointed me as his parliamentary councillor, life became easier, as I had an official title, which seems to matter so greatly in a bureaucracy. The job was interesting, and I put all my energy into it. As it turned out, it was also setting the scope, perimeters and content of that position.

When we were in Cape Town during parliamentary sessions, going to work at Tuinhuis was fine. For the first two weeks, I stayed in a hotel within walking distance of Parliament and Tuinhuis. De Klerk then advised me that the president has a number of houses in the Groote Schuur estate that he can allocate to his staff, and the deputy president would also have at least two. I looked around and found a small but pleasant house just outside the main entrance to Groote Schuur. After a discussion with Mbeki, I approached Jeff Radebe, then-Minister of Public Works, and he agreed to allocate the house to me. That was fine, and Samson Phakgwayo, employed as a driver in Mbeki's office, would give me a lift every morning and, if needed, at the end of the day.

My life in Cape Town was made much more comfortable by the fact that my second cousin Yusuf Pahad and his wife, Shireen, lived there and welcomed me to their home. When we first arrived in Cape Town, Yusuf's parents were still alive and living with them. His father Ismail was my father Goolam's first cousin. I could visit at any time, was always given the most delicious food, and got to know a number of their friends who were also regular visitors, as well as their relatives who were also ours. When my family came down, Shireen and Meg would go for walks on Table Mountain and Shireen would show Meg the best places to buy food, swim or admire the beauty of Cape Town. Yusuf and Shireen have three children, Yasmin, Shenaaz and Fazel. Later in life, Shenaaz moved to Johannesburg, and she and her husband Rikki Barnes have become two of Amina's best friends. Shenaaz says that everyone assumes she is either Essop or Aziz's daughter, and she does indeed fit into our family like another daughter. Unfortunately, and to my great sadness, Yusuf died of Covid in December 2020.

So I was able to adjust to life in Cape Town, but working in Pretoria was exceptionally difficult. I had never had a car, and neither Aziz nor I ever learnt to drive, so every morning I would arrange for a lift from Mojanku Gumbi, Moss Ngoasheng or Thami Ntenteni, all of whom lived in Johannesburg. But returning home was a nightmare, as we all had very different programmes, and I had to go around the office asking for a lift from those who lived in Joburg. Few lived anywhere near me, and when we had meetings at night, Mbeki would arrange for one of his security to take me home. I was determined to ignore those obstacles and go to work every day in Pretoria. That problem only ended when I was appointed as a deputy minister and allocated an official car and driver in Cape Town and Pretoria, along with an office and a staff complement of five.

In mid-1996, I was on a trip with Mbeki when I received a call from a journalist just before six in the morning congratulating me on my appointment as the deputy minister in Deputy President Thabo Mbeki's office. I was stunned, as I had no inkling that this was on the cards. At breakfast, when I told Mbeki about the call, he replied nonchalantly, 'Oh, so now you know. Congratulations.' He was waiting for the official announcement and had not mentioned it to me earlier.

Ministers and deputy ministers were given accommodation in both Pretoria and Cape Town, so some people who already had homes in one (or both) of those places moved into the homes that went with their jobs and rented out their private property, which saved them a lot of money. However, Meg had a job in Johannesburg, the children were at school there, and most of my family and our friends were in Joburg, so we didn't even consider moving.

I had purchased our house in Bellevue East for R200,000, an unbelievably low price for someone who was used to the prices in Europe, and my family were delighted with it, as it had three bedrooms, a garden and even space to build a swimming pool. The children were able to fulfil their long-standing desire to get a dog, and we bought a beautiful cross-bred sheepdog which we called Ben, until Amina started to go out with Banele Levine, who was also called Ben. So the dog was renamed Benny-Boy, and he lived with us for fifteen years.

For a few months, Sandra Black, who had arranged to return to South Africa with Billy Nannan and their daughter Zinzile, joined us. They decided to move to Johannesburg even though Billy had tragically died, and Sandra asked Meg if they could stay with us until she was able to buy a place. Aziz, an occasional visitor, suddenly started spending a lot of time at our house. Eventually, he and Sandra got married and bought a house a few doors away from us, opposite where Wally Serote lived. Amina and Govan got on very well with Zinzi.

We lived in Bellevue East for about three years and then moved down the road to a smarter address in Observatory, where the prices had gone down before the first democratic election, with a number of white people leaving the country, so once more we had a bargain price.

We also had the good luck to employ Siphiwe Hlatshwayo as a domestic worker, and she proved to be loyal, hardworking and intelligent. She stayed with us in our various homes and was a tremendous help right up to her retirement. In 1995, Siphiwe had a baby daughter, Nokuthula, and the two of them stayed in our domestic quarters until Siphiwe retired. Nokuthula has a BA Honours degree from Wits University, where she is about to re-register for her LLB, which she could not complete because of difficulties caused by COVID and problems of funding.

Our first ANC branch served Bellevue East and Observatory, and several old and a few new ANC friends lived there, some attracted by Sacred Heart

College as a progressive school for their children to attend and others by the area's relative affordability. Those included Aziz, Geraldine (Fraser-) and Jabu Moleketi, Mac and Zarina Maharaj, Wally Serote and Thantshi Matsitari, Carol Marshall and Antonio Fernandes, Annie Orgill, Henry Magothi, Jessie Duarte, Richard and Thabisile Levine, Jonas and Violet Gwangwa, Mannie Brown, Cheryl Carolus and Graeme Bloch, Eric and Martha Molobi, Terry Oakley-Smith, Martin and Carmen Rall, Joe Slovo and Helena Dolny, Trevor and Thelma Fowler, Barbara and Trevor Watson, Saths Cooper and many others. For the first years, we all got on well and enjoyed the cheap but good restaurants and the dancing and jazz music at Tandoor in Yeoville. We often had parties and braais at the weekends, especially with Tony and Carol and our children, and we had a few great New Year's Eve parties at our house.

Later, some divisions gradually appeared amongst our ANC comrades, and the ANC branch meetings were never good. They always started incredibly late, and only a few people like Maurice Smithers bothered to immerse themselves in local needs. Most of us had national or provincial positions in the ANC or SACP or were professionals immersed in the work of transforming the health, education and public service systems, too busy to pay enough attention to our local branches, which turned out to be a bad mistake in the longer run.

The children settled in well at Sacred Heart, which was a Catholic School (Marist Brothers), but very tolerant and open to people from other religious beliefs and cultures, including Amina and Govan, who were agnostic or atheist. The director of the school was Brother Neil McGurk, who had transformed it gradually from 1976 to 1990 from a conservative whites-only boys' school to a progressive community school with boys and girls from all races. Brother Neil had helped many Black children and returned exiles to attend the school, and, for the first two years, he allowed Amina and Govan to attend without paying school fees, as we were not earning at the time.

Some of the teaching staff were initially nervous at the influx of the returned exiles' children. A teacher friend of Meg's, Carin Roux, told us with amusement how relieved some of the worried teachers were when they discovered that those children 'with strange names actually looked quite nice and normal', with one mentioning Amina Pahad as an example.

Govan overheard teachers discussing which maths group he should be put in; they had decided that children from London were usually poor at maths and put him in the bottom set. He did very badly and made mistakes all the time, so was made to repeat the same kind of work but never got it right because he was so bored. Eventually, someone rather smart decided to see how he would cope in the middle group. When he immediately improved, they put him in the top group, where he had absolutely no problems (but was never as good as his friend Miguel, who was upset if he got less than a 100 per cent). A couple of years later, when Govan entered the high school, Carin overheard some of Govan's teachers discussing his atrocious spelling and wondering where he should be put in terms of the English groups. She laughed at them for their worries, telling them that Govan was a voracious reader and an eloquent speaker and that his vocabulary was far larger than most of theirs. I'm sure she found a more tactful way of saying it than that, but she did know Govan well because her brilliant daughter Naomi was one of his friends.

Several of the offspring of returned exiles were recommended to attend speech therapy because of their unusual pronunciation in English, take Ritalin or do occupational therapy because they found it hard to sit still and keep quiet. But the school adapted fast, as it should, rather than forcing the children to make all the adjustments.

A fundraising event revealed some of the apartheid-era assumptions still held by at least one staff member. Concerned at the scarcity of parents who had volunteered to set up tables selling their contributions, she identified a gap and went to Govan's year and read out the names of children she wished to speak to after school. They were all mixed-race children, and she appealed to them to ask their mothers to make koeksisters. The problem was that those children had, for example, a Russian mother and a Zulu father, or an English mother and an Indian father ... and many other combinations that hardly fitted the imagined 'Coloured' parent.

Older children could choose between serious religious studies or community service, so our children both chose the latter. The school was very successful in creating a multiracial environment where friendships were developed, regardless of race. During the 1990s and 2000s, many university students and lecturers commented on the phenomenon that few of the students moved out of their segregated race groups in their casual friendship activities – with the noted exception of those from Sacred Heart and St Barnabas. Meg, Amina and Govan all attended Wits during that time, and they were shocked to notice how people clung to their apartheid-formed comfort zones, with, for example, students of Indian origin even splitting into Hindu and Muslim groups. One day when Amina accidentally bumped into her cousin Zayd Dadabhay, who was devout, his Muslim friends looked on in amazement when they hugged each other and chatted.

The Sacred Heart secondary school was blessed with an amazing group of teachers who pioneered integrated studies with an emphasis on language across the curriculum, an approach designed to accommodate mixed-ability classes, including those whose first language was not English. This initiative was, at first, hard to sell to the more conservative parents. However, when the students did well in the Senior Certificate and then excelled at universities, the resistance evaporated. Brother Neil supported and inspired those efforts and gave teachers the time and opportunity to write textbooks for schooling and attend conferences, discussions and user groups while still practising their profession. Emilia Potenza[183] and Steven Lowry ensured that the history was 'revisionist' – very anti-racist, anti-imperialist and class-conscious. Peter Ranby made a similar impact in the field of geography.

Govan found it harder to adjust than Amina, as the emphasis in their primary school on neatness and following rules in a rigid timetable did not suit his temperament, but he got used to it during his first year and then did fine. Once, after being forced to stay inside during playtime and copy out the Lord's Prayer over and over because his work was messy, he came home and told his mother, 'Well, there's one good thing about this, at least it puts people off religion!' He and Amina made good friends quickly, with some becoming friends for life.

Meanwhile, Meg had completed the coursework for her MEd in History of Education at Wits University in 1992, benefiting from excellent lecturers like Sue Krige, who revealed to her some of the most unpleasant aspects of the education given to white South Africans (she already knew about Bantu Education), and steady guidance from her inspiring supervisor, Professor Bram Fleisch. Once Meg took on a job, she struggled to finish her research report, but finally got her MEd in 1996, with a report entitled 'Issues of Assessment in Education in South Africa During the Period of Transition, 1989–95'.

While studying at Wits, Meg had the good fortune to be invited by Mary Metcalfe to join a small education discussion group composed mainly of people who had been active for years in the National Education Coordinating Committee's project entitled NEPI (National Education Policy Initiative), which included Pam Christie and Jonathan Jansen, who were the joint chairs of NEPI. They were interested in Meg's experience as an anti-

---

183. Emilia later became the CEO of the Apartheid Museum.

racist, anti-imperialist teacher with expertise in assessment and curriculum development in primary and secondary schools. Meg found that group immensely rewarding. In 1999, Christie and Jansen edited a book called *Changing Curriculum: Studies on Outcomes-based Education in South Africa*,[184] and Meg felt honoured when they asked her to contribute a chapter on outcomes-based assessment called 'The need for a common vision of what counts and how to count it.'

In 1993, Meg was on the verge of accepting a job as head of the Maths Centre for Primary Teachers, which terrified her. She had no expertise in maths education, and a major responsibility would be fundraising, which she hates, but then a fortuitous meeting occurred. I had been invited by Colleen Williams to a party to celebrate her father's eightieth birthday, and there we met David Adler, who had been recently appointed CEO of the Independent Examinations Board (IEB). Meg had applied to the IEB to see if there were any vacancies but had not received a response. When I introduced Meg to David and explained that she was looking for work, they had a long chat which culminated in David inviting her for an interview to work in the schooling section of the organisation. That was headed by Dodo Pitt, the brilliant former head of St Mary's School (which has a broadly Reggio Emilia approach to education), who knew all the most progressive teachers in the independent schools and was a great mentor. Meg took over the role of managing the schooling user groups from Melissa King, another seasoned contributor to the NEPI project, and she and Meg quickly became good friends. Melissa moved to the adult section of the IEB, where she also had an exceptional mentor in Ed French.

David gave his employees lots of rope to hang themselves but expected dedication to the transformation of education in South Africa, encouraging maximum participation in the major innovations which were developing rapidly at the time. Meg also replaced Melissa as the representative of the IEB on the Education Service Organisations Forum (ESOF), where she was elected as the secretary from 1993–1994. There, she got to know key people from all the education NGOs in what was still the Transvaal. In 1994, ESOF was reorganised to service the new province, Gauteng, and was renamed GETOA (Gauteng Education and Training Organisations Association), with fifty-four affiliated organisations. Much to her astonishment, she was proposed and elected as chair in May 1995 at a meeting with over 100 delegates.

---

184. Cape Town: Juta & Company, 1989.

Through many diverse channels, Meg became involved in the education policy development process, which included a National Education and Training Forum (NETF) set up as 'a consensus-seeking mechanism for addressing the crisis in education and creating stable conditions for the restructuring of education and training into a single national system'.

Meg would refer to the NETF, in which Mary Metcalfe took a leading role, as a mini-CODESA. She was absorbed into the whole process, attending numerous meetings and conferences, where she was fascinated by the polarity in the appearance and views of the participants. The people representing the Department of Education during that pre-democracy period astonished her:

> The women had bouffant hairstyles and sticking-out skirts filled by starched petticoats, like something out of a time warp. And the men were all in suits. Most of us were in jeans, our women in flat shoes, and some of our men had earrings, dreadlocks or ponytails.

Pretoria seemed to Meg to be very conservative and outdated.

David Adler was instrumental in advocating the need for a National Qualifications Framework (NQF) in South Africa, and the Adult Assessment Department of the IEB played a strong role in developing unit standards which could be used to measure achievements by adults in Adult Basic Education. They also pioneered the first adult assessments leading to a certificate that was understood and accepted as a reliable standard nationally by business, industry and the unions. They worked to achieve a framework that would facilitate movement between academia and the worlds of work and schooling and also assist in establishing the recognition of learning which had taken place outside of formal academic institutions (Recognition of Prior Learning and Experience, often referred to as RPL). This was particularly important in our country, as millions of Black people had been denied access to a decent education. When involved in making appointments, I insisted that job advertisements, when stating the minimum qualifications required, should always include the phrase 'or a demonstrated level of equivalent competence'. This was a concept that most Human Resources (HR) professionals appeared to be unable to grasp (and apparently now simply reject).

In 1994, a group of people decided that a document that would help people understand the thinking behind a National Qualifications

Framework was needed. Included were David Adler, Melissa King and Gail Elliott from the IEB. Other key participants Meg worked with later included Sam Isaacs from the Peninsula Technikon, Adrienne Bird from the Metal Engineering Industries Education and Training Board, Chris Vorwerk from the Plastics Industry Training Board, John Tyers from the Transnet Training Board, and Sam Morotoba from COSATU. The final outcome of that working group was an influential book released in September 1995 called *Ways of Seeing the National Qualifications Framework*.[185]

That book was seen by some as presenting clearly the views of Labour but neglecting somewhat the questions and challenges the NQF might pose for the Department of Education, an issue on which the Minister of Education decided work needed to be conducted. The result was the establishment of the Ministerial Committee for Development Work on the NQF and consisted of four people, including Sam Isaacs as its chair and Meg, who was seconded to it as a ministerial appointee. The South African Qualifications Authority (SAQA) was established to oversee the NQF, and Sam Isaacs was appointed as the chair of its board in 1996. After the establishment of the NQF, Meg was appointed to a Department of Education task team on quality assurance (1998) and then to a ministerial committee to investigate the Senior Certificate Examination.

In the IEB, Meg was asked to set up a department to conduct assessment training, a department she headed from 1997 to 2000, becoming a director. She was fortunate to employ Pauline Matlhaela and Dumisani Dlamini as her first trainers, and later Estelle Nel, all of whom were great colleagues and became good friends. Estelle took over the Assessment Education and Training Department when Meg left, and she has developed it into a highly respected training organisation.

That was an enormously exciting period, and we were both extremely busy.

❧

In my new role as deputy minister, I gradually put together a support team to make my work more effective. The most important position for me was chief of staff, occupied by Louis du Plooy, a young white Afrikaans-speaking man who was calm with a pleasant personality, outstanding leadership

---
185. Pretoria, HSRC, 1995.

abilities and a willingness to learn. He ran the Office of the Deputy Minister, and later that of the Minister, effectively, efficiently and without fuss. Indeed, the other staff members, all African, used to say that Louis was not white but 'one of us'. He also took care of my personal affairs, including my bank account. He was well-liked by all of us, including my family. He grew in the job and was well-versed in the way government functions and how to work with the other leaders in the presidency, such as Frank Chikane, Trevor Fowler, Mojanku Gumbi, Moss Ngoasheng and Wiseman Nkuhlu, who later replaced Moss as Mbeki's financial advisor.

Louis joined my office in 1998 and worked there for a decade. After he left the presidency, he worked as a consultant until August 2017, providing advice for the National School of Governance, Cooperative Governance and Traditional Affairs (CoGTA), the Demarcation Board, Eskom, and, through a Department for International Development (DFID)-funded programme, the Department of Health. Since 2017, he has done work for an NGO in the health sector, and in that year, graduated from UCT with an MPhil in Development Policy and Practice. Louis is an outstanding worker and leader who made an immense contribution to the successful operations and services rendered by the two positions I occupied in the presidency and government.

At this point, I should also like to express my gratitude and appreciation to the other people who worked in my Ministry, helping to ensure the smooth running of my office:

- Samson Pakgwayo, who began as a driver, became a personal assistant and then a private secretary;
- Vathiswa Mafana, who began as an administrative assistant and became Director for Parliamentary Liaison in the Presidency;
- Caroline Mangwane, who began as an administrative assistant and became an assistant private secretary;
- Emmanuel Kgomo, who was an administrative secretary, ANC activist, a branch leader and ran the Marx Library;
- Ricardo McKenzie, who was a private secretary and is now a Member of Parliament (MPL) for the DA in the Western Cape legislature;
- Qinsile Dela, who was a deputy director;
- Winnie (Khensani) Maluleke, who was the financial officer to assist with the National Youth Commission and oversee Public Finance Management Act (PMFA) compliance;

- Dan Machogo, who started as a driver and became an administrative clerk; and
- John Madela, who was a driver.

As deputy minister, I had access to all Cabinet memoranda and documents and attended meetings of a number of Cabinet committees. Issues as reflected in the Cabinet memos would first be processed and discussed at the Cabinet Committee, which would make recommendations to the Cabinet regarding decisions which needed to be taken. From the outset, I decided that the best way to serve the deputy president was always to put his interests and requests first, which meant that, on occasion, my work and that of the office had to be delayed. Although I had to work closely with the Office of the Deputy President, I had no administrative tasks there.

Among the responsibilities given to me was the enhancement of the work of the Office on the Status of Persons with Disability and the Office on the Status of Women, Youth and Children. Two other major tasks were also important priorities: to lead the government team responsible for conducting the first proper census in South Africa and to take steps to transform the old apartheid communications office into an effective information structure. In this section, I shall only reflect on the census, as I shall cover the other when I write about my work as Minister in the Presidency of Thabo Mbeki.

Pali Lehohla – later Statistician-General – was the lead person for that census. He was a tower of strength, using his intellectual depth, charm and wit to the fullest extent in carrying out the difficult and complex task of ensuring a credible outcome.

I recall that I went with Pali and Samson Pakgwayo to Tafelkop in Limpopo. The two chiefs in the areas who fell under the Elias Motsoaledi municipality were *Kgoši* Boleu Rammupudu and Chief Mahlangu. Many residents in those areas were opposed to participating in the census since they wanted to be part of Mpumalanga, not Limpopo. When we arrived in the area, a public meeting was organised in an open field. While I was speaking, a few young men starting writing slogans denouncing the census, one of which said, 'Go and do a census in India.' My immediate response was to exhort the crowd:

> Look at that young man; he has no manners, and he is asking me to go and do a census in India. Let me assure him that I will do no such

thing, and in any case, there are too many people in India who would have to be counted.

The crowd burst out laughing and the man quietly withdrew.

However, I was concerned that we had failed to observe the proper protocol by not informing the relevant chief of our intentions or seeking his permission to hold the meeting. So I asked Samson, who was from that province, to meet with the relevant people, apologise and indicate that the deputy minister would be pleased if he were given an audience. Fortunately, Chief Rammupudu agreed, and when our delegation arrived at his residence, we were each allocated a seat by his protocol staff. I was to sit next to the chief, who was an excellent host and very friendly, and he listened intently to my input. I pointed out the importance of the census for the distribution of government funding and resources in proportion to population density. I also emphasised that if his people did not register, we would take aerial photographs of the area and calculate the population based on the number of houses identified multiplied by a factor of four or five.

At the end of the convivial discussion, the chief organised tea, coffee, cakes and biscuits for all of us. I had earlier noticed the young man who had put up the slogan at the earlier meeting sitting comfortably on the floor, and I asked the *Kgoši* who he was. It turns out that he was one of his nephews. When I related to the *Kgoši* the rude behaviour and disrespect for elders shown by that youngster, the *Kgoši* called him over, told him off in my presence and ordered him to apologise to me. Despite the opposition of many of the residents, we had a successful campaign, and for some time, *Kgoši* Boleu Rammupudu kept in touch with me.

The other chief was Poni Jafta Mahlangu, who said to Samson that, out of respect for the deputy minister, he would come to my office at the Union Buildings. When he came, he brought a delegation from the Ndebele traditional authority with him. They wanted to be part of Mpumalanga since that part of the province was mainly populated by Ndebeles. He was friendly and modest and a good listener. I pointed out that South Africa was a unitary state, not a federation, and that the demarcation of provinces was essentially for administrative purposes – also that which province they were in had no impact on their identity as Ndebeles. They were Ndebele whether they were in Limpopo or in Mpumalanga. I also repeated the argument I had offered to *Kgoši* Boleu Rammupudu regarding the census, and Samson thought my intervention had positive results concerning both issues.

Under Pali's leadership, we successfully completed the census. For me, it was a great learning experience, visiting different parts of the country and deepening my understanding and knowledge of how difficult and time-consuming it is to conduct a census; also how invaluable the information gathered, processed and published is for the public and private sectors and the broad civil society.

Earlier in this memoir, I quoted extracts from interviews I had given to Padraig O'Malley, which reflect my views at the time on a wide range of issues and challenges, so I shall make use of them from the period 14 March 1996 to 29 July 1998.

In the interview of 14 March 1996 I said:

> If, in South Africa, the economic policies of those who call themselves liberal are basically around trying to reduce the amount of state intervention in the economy, then obviously what you are arguing for is that the status quo should remain ... the greatest amount of wealth and therefore influence in the political, economic and social [spheres] is vested in a minority ... The fact of the matter is that the whites could not have had the high standard of living they enjoy without the exploitation – the super-exploitation – of the majority of people in South Africa.[186]

On the thorny and complex issue of nationalisation, I commented that 'the issue is not nationalisation or not nationalisation. The fundamental issue is the level and depth of state intervention in the economy.'[187] In South Africa, we've gone for another route called the restructuring of state assets, in which you may sell parts of an enterprise but not the whole entity. I gave the example of Telkom, which should go beyond a million telephone lines and look at the information superhighway with fibre optics:

> Once you say that, then you are talking of investments of billions of rands ... But it has fantastic spin-offs ... you immediately transform the distance learning programmes in this country for a start. You make all kinds of things accessible to the remotest rural areas which need them most.[188]

---

186. '14 Mar 1996: Pahad, Essop', *O'Malley – The Heart of Hope*, O'Malley Archives, Nelson Mandela Foundation. Available at https://omalley.nelsonmandela.org/index.php/site/q/03lv00017/04lv00344/05lv00965/06lv00974.htm
187. Ibid.
188. Ibid.

I also argued that you would need a partner to raise that investment. And that restructuring also means changing the management patterns – for example, making the CEOs of parastatals more accountable to independent boards, in whom you have confidence and trust. Ultimately, they must be responsible to the majority shareholder – the government. My view then, as it remains, is that restructuring must include 'the involvement of the labour movement in the whole process and then ultimately in the running of these parastatals'. I also discussed the state's responsibility in providing essential services, using water as an example.

> There are a number of things one has to weigh up: are they just pure commercial ventures or are they essential for the improvement of the quality of life of our people in this country? ... Just access to clean water, it's not a matter for privatisation to get some private water company. Why should they be interested in whether or not an African woman in the rural areas must walk ten kilometres to get water for her daily needs? But we would be ... because that's why so many of us enlisted in the political struggle ... because we were genuinely driven ... to be involved in trying to improve the quality of the lives of our people. So it's quite clear the same would apply to electricity to which such a large part of our population is denied access.[189]

When asked about COSATU's criticism of the government's declaration on restructuring state assets, I pointed out that COSATU was right to complain since a process had begun in NEDLAC (the National Economic Labour and Development Council), and the government chose to announce its package without completing the process of consultation with COSATU. I was clear that blame should be apportioned to government as a whole and not to any specific minister or department.

I also ventured to say that in South Africa, you cannot hope to implement economic policies without having at the very heart the tacit support of labour and capital. I argued that a lot of confidence is vested in our economy because, 'by and large, people are convinced that at least we in South Africa are not easy-going, spending and throwing money around like confetti; that we are quite serious about an approach which is consistent with fiscal discipline.'[190]

This now takes me to GEAR, (a five-year plan for Growth, Employment

---
189. '14 Mar 1996: Pahad, Essop', *O'Malley – The Heart of Hope*.
190. Ibid.

and Redistribution announced in 1996,[191] which replaced the 1994 Reconstruction and Development Programme [RDP] of 1994),[192] which still provokes controversy, and in some quarters, deliberate misunderstanding or misinterpretation.

In an interview on 23 September 1997, I said that we in government had failed to communicate effectively what GEAR aimed to achieve and why it was devised. At that time, I was the political head of the South African Communication Service (later the Government Communication Information System: GCIS) and took some of the blame myself, as I still do. In the interview I explained:

> The Growth, Employment and Redistribution plan is not the economic policy of this country. It's basically the framework that seeks to deal with monetary and financial arrangements ... It's not designed to be a replacement for an industrial strategy policy [or] a job creation policy ... [GEAR] was going to be a contributing factor to economic growth because if you limited certain levels of public expenditure, if you didn't allow your deficit to grow ... more money would be freed for other things.[193]

In response to opponents of GEAR, I asked the question:

> What do we do with the debt? Now it's very easy for the government, 1999 is coming, to go and borrow billions. Who will pay? Ten, fifteen years down the line, when we are dead, somebody must pay. I think we are not getting enough credit for being courageous enough to try to deal with issues now ... but the ANC in 15 years' time, when it is still in power will have to bear the cost. I think it's wrong ... that we're paying for the sins of the apartheid regime – it went on this borrowing spree.[194]

For me, it was important that the critics of GEAR in COSATU and the SACP addressed that issue, which I believed they were not doing. If they were not happy with the industrial strategy, they should have come up with concrete proposals, including how to generate greater investment in the

---

191. Available at https://www.gov.za/sites/default/files/gcis_document/201409/gear0.pdf
192. Available at https://omalley.nelsonmandela.org/index.php/site/q/03lv02039/04lv02103/05lv02120/06lv02126.html
193. '23 Sep 1997: Pahad, Essop', *O'Malley – The Heart of Hope*, O'Malley Archives, Nelson Mandela Foundation. Available at https://omalley.nelsonmandela.org/index.php/site/q/03lv00017/04lv00344/05lv01092/06lv01158.htm
194. '14 Mar 1996: Pahad, Essop', *O'Malley – The Heart of Hope*

manufacturing sector instead of chasing paper money on the Johannesburg Stock Exchange.

I also pointed out that our unemployment figures cannot reflect the situation accurately for many reasons. I spoke about the non-unionised labour in South Africa. For example, at every building site:

> for every ten people working, you've got ten people standing outside the fence looking for a job. So simply supply and demand. Supply is very great, the demand not so great; therefore, the employers are in a far more powerful position with regard to this labour. But this is not reflected in the statistics because the employer is not going to tell you, 'I am employing fifty people at cut-rate wages and I am not offering them anything.' So the figures you get are from those honest employers who actually register workers, pay UIF (Unemployment Insurance Fund) … all of these benefits.[195]

Regarding the service sector, we think tourism has grown by about thirty to forty per cent over the last two or three years, which means many new jobs were created in the service sector by those tourists. But many employers avoid unionised labour. There is also the large informal sector of hawkers and people standing on the streets selling, earning some income, spending it, and thus contributing to the economy. So I argued that although GEAR may cause some job losses, it was too early to say whether or not it was achieving its longer-term aims.

On that topic, I should also like to point out that at successive ANC National Conferences, the overall policy of GEAR was adapted with amendments suggested by delegates from ANC branches, COSATU and the SACP. There were heated debates with arguments put forward from different perspectives, and at the end of the Conferences, resolutions were adopted that were consistent with GEAR. In spite of the sometimes sharp differences, those discussions were conducted in a friendly spirit with proper respect shown to the views of all participants.

On 14 March 1996, I responded to questions from O'Malley about constraints facing the ANC in a government of national unity, and I mentioned the problem of changing the civil service.

> We brought in a few Black people, that's fine, but basically the civil

---
95. '23 Sep 1997: Pahad, Essop', *O'Malley – The Heart of Hope*.

service is what it was before. I think there are some very good people from the old civil service who are genuinely interested in serving the government of the day. There are others who are lethargic and others who are hostile ... but we have inherited that civil service, and we have inherited just about the most corrupt system in the world ... We have an election in April 1994, you think this corruption is going to stop in May 1994? Of course not. If they were corrupt before April 1994 they remain corrupt now in 1996, but they are in their jobs ... take this police force at the present time – every time you're looking for a car hijacking ring or something, murders in KwaZulu-Natal, there are policemen involved, sometimes in leading positions. What do you do? There are so many of these things.[196]

In a follow-up interview on 27 March 1996, I added that:

We had a police force that was corrupt and corrupted by the apartheid regime, who asked them to do things no police force should be asked to do, which is to be the arm of the security police. Instead of policing crime they were policing us 'terrorists'. I didn't need an IDASA survey to tell me that we still face a severe problem with corruption. We absolutely do, because the old system was totally corrupt. If anybody thinks ... that we can deal with this problem in just two years, I think they are out of their minds ... but I must reiterate that the government is absolutely committed to do[ing] everything possible to root out corruption.[197]

I recall that when Geraldine Fraser-Moleketi was Minister of Public Service, she produced several Cabinet memoranda on that challenging and infectious disease. Despite the decisions we took to arrest its growth and eradicate the malevolent practices, it is clear that two-and-a-half decades later, things have become worse. Corruption's malignant impact and influence are felt within all spheres of government and in the structures of the ANC.

It is the responsibility of government, law enforcement, intelligence agencies, the courts, the private sector and civil society in all its formations to work together or separately to confront and eradicate this challenge. Let us not just focus on the lower rungs of the corrupted but identify, charge and

---
196. '14 Mar 1996: Pahad, Essop', *O'Malley – The Heart of Hope*.
197. '27 Mar 1996: Pahad, Essop', *O'Malley – The Heart of Hope*, O'Malley Archives, Nelson Mandela Foundation. Available at https://omalley.nelsonmandela.org/index.php/site/q/03lv00017/04lv00344/05lv00965/06lv00982.htm

imprison the corrupters. It is the corrupter with the means and resources to offer inducements who should be our main target.

On the attitudes of the (mainly white) critics and commentators from the media and academic circles towards the government, I said on March 14 1996:

> I think basically a lot of the commentators are politically conservative, which is fine ... because you need to have criticisms from different sides and different angles ... but sometimes I read them to say, 'Well, see now that these Blackies are there, you must be careful, we don't really trust them – look what's happened in the rest of Africa. Blackies will be more prone to authoritarianism.'[198]

Although they would not state those things openly, I feel that their comments and criticisms often carried a hidden implication of this attitude towards Black people. It didn't have a resonance with the majority of our population, although it might have had some kind of resonance with the chattering classes.

In the interview on 27 March 1996, I agreed that while the white private sector says what the government should do, it doesn't say what they themselves are going to do:

> They will not sit down and say, this is our plan for the next five years; this is the level of investment we're going to have for the next five years, not in shifting their money around the stock exchange but in actual productive use; and therefore if we go and invest so much money in such and such a plant, we will create so many jobs. They are not doing this and this is a fundamental problem we are facing here. ... I think that at the moment, they are showing less confidence than many foreign investors are showing in the South African political process. ... the problem we are facing is to some extent this lack of confidence [in] domestic South African capital. ... We are talking about people who are very powerful, very influential, and obviously any sensible government has to take into account the views, feelings and concerns of that sector. So my own view is that at the moment, they have not been playing ball with the government, they have not been playing ball with the country, they have not been playing ball

---

95. '14 Mar 1996: Pahad, Essop', *O'Malley – The Heart of Hope*.

with their own stated ideological positions that competition is good for capitalism.[199]

When asked what I thought about criticisms of De Klerk and the National Party accusing them of selling out the poorer Afrikaners, I characterised it as a nonsensical approach (23 September 1997), saying that the NP should be given credit for recognising the changes that had taken place in the course of the negotiating process. If the NP had stood stubbornly by its positions, I think the transition here would have been different and the NP critics would now be saying that their stubbornness led to a bloodbath in South Africa. So I conceded that credit must be given to the NP and De Klerk for the courage to move in the direction of an interim constitution.[200]

In the interview on 14 March 1996, O'Malley probed me on my attitude to Marxism, asking if I had moved away from it. My response was that what Marx called dialectical materialism is a theoretical and philosophical 'enriching methodology ... which helps me to understand some problems a bit more deeply than I might have done otherwise'.[201] Furthermore, I questioned the usefulness of interpreting Marxism and the work of a whole lot of other revolutionary writers in a dogmatic manner, explaining that I tried to use the framework, the methodology, to take as critical approach as possible to issues and not to be hidebound by some ideological stereotype. I asserted that I was a Marxist and not a pragmatist who just does a thing because it seems like a good thing at that moment in time or because it might benefit me personally. My approach is to look not only at the initial results of an action but to consider what might be the possible consequences in the longer term. This is what Marxism has helped me to do. For me, a Marxist has to be realistic in understanding the given context, circumstances and conditions in which one operates. In 1996, I said the reality was that we faced a huge problem of forty to fifty per cent unemployment and that the vast majority of our people were poor, destitute.

In the year 2021, I continue to regard myself as a Marxist and am convinced of its relevance as an organisational tool and methodology to critically analyse and understand challenges and problems, however complex they may appear.

On the thorny but important issue of informers and agents planted in the ANC, I agreed that we had such people but pointed out that those in the NP

---

199. '27 Mar 1996: Pahad, Essop', *O'Malley – The Heart of Hope*.
200. '23 Sep 1997: Pahad, Essop', *O'Malley – The Heart of Hope*.
201. '14 Mar 1996: Pahad, Essop', *O'Malley – The Heart of Hope*.

and apartheid structures who know the identities of those people are not giving us the relevant evidence but sometimes mischievously making allegations that a few senior leaders of the ANC worked for them. I was certain there were elements in the National Party who were behind that, and, for me, they were operating 'in the sewers of politics' and unable to work in an open, clean political environment.

I asserted that there was a 'third force', which could include elements from the old security, defence force, military intelligence and police force whose common interest was to undermine and weaken the ANC. That was 'a complex phenomenon and a more complex web of intrigue'. I was optimistic and confident that the ANC and its allies would withstand that onslaught and believed there was no way they would succeed in destroying the ANC. Given the present disarray and factionalism, my view appears to have been over-optimistic. I shall return to this subject in the last chapter of this memoir.

In the interview on 29 July 1998, I confidently stated that the new democratic government had not failed. I pointed out that provision and access to clean water 'makes a great difference to people's lives ... and regarding the programme of the Minister of Water Affairs, millions more, over the next few years, will have access to this clean water'.[202] And the provision of electricity is also of tremendous importance, using the example of young people who no longer have to study at night by candlelight. I also emphasised that 'the opening of clinics in many rural areas has also transformed people's lives'[203] and mentioned some other benefits of improved health care.

On the school feeding schemes, I admitted that there had been some corruption concerning some of the people who had been given contracts to feed the children but that this should not detract from the fact that millions of children were now sure of getting at least one meal a day at school. But in conclusion to my response to the accusation that the government had failed, I emphasised that 'the challenge remains immense because millions of our people are still suffering from poverty'.[204]

In the month of July 2021, South Africa was rocked by widespread violence, looting, damage to property and infrastructure, and hundreds of people were killed or injured during those grim and dreadful days. I am of the view that it was a counter-revolutionary attempt aimed at achieving

---

202. '29 July 1998: Pahad, Essop', *O'Malley – The Heart of Hope*, O'Malley Archive, Nelson Mandela Foundation. Available at https://omalley.nelsonmandela.org/index.php/site/q/03lv00017/04lv00344/05lv01183/06lv01214.htm
203. Ibid.
204. '29 July 1998: Pahad, Essop', *O'Malley – The Heart of Hope*.

some kind of uprising. In the interview of 29 July 1998, I said, 'Of course there is a counter-revolutionary threat in South Africa. Only a fool would think there isn't a counter-revolutionary threat.'[205] For me, there were certain forces who were not in favour of the changes taking place and who were 'determined to either reverse the progress that has been made or make it more difficult for further progress to take place'.[206] At that time, the threat emanated from the white community, who were highly trained and skilled militarily and heavily armed. I certainly did not foresee what happened in 2021, where some elements involved in the counter-revolutionary actions came from the formerly oppressed and some from the ranks of the ANC.

It is also important to recognise that continued widespread poverty, hunger, destitution and inequality of employment and living conditions were significant contributing factors. To prevent a recurrence of those kinds of actions, the ANC government has to deal decisively with the major underlying problems listed above and the individuals behind the organised disruption of our country's economy and social order.

In response to what O'Malley called increasing divisions straining the Tripartite Alliance and whether it was necessary to maintain it at all costs, I said that while the SACP had rejected GEAR, it had reasserted and emphasised the need for an alliance. I added that no alliance can ever be free of tension:

> ... there are differences inside the ANC itself and surely there must be differences between the Alliance partners ... I think it would be a terrible thing if we were to arrive at the day when the trade union movement, COSATU, doesn't have a difference with the SACP as well as the ANC. It would inevitably have this if it actually represents and articulates the interests of its own members, because its own members go beyond the members of the party and the ANC. There are many people who are in COSATU who might belong to other political parties, who might not belong to any political formation, but they are interested in the protection of their jobs, increasing their salaries, improvement of their working conditions and so on ...

So clearly, COSATU would have to adopt positions which would, at times, differ from those of the SACP and the ANC. I pointed out that such tensions and differences had been present since the beginning of the Tripartite

---

205. Ibid.
206. Ibid.

Alliance, and were inevitable. What I considered important was that 'We, as the leadership, have the capacity to manage these differences in a way that does not lead to schism.'[207]

I asserted that there was certainly a need for the Alliance, which had been created not just to get rid of apartheid but to bring about a national democratic revolution. Writing this in August 2021, I emphasise that since the objective remains the same, we still need an alliance of the ANC, the SACP and COSATU, led by the ANC.

In the same interview, some eleven months before the second democratic elections in our country, O'Malley raised some concerns relating to that election. One of them was the possibility of a low voter turnout. My response was that the ANC and its allies had the responsibility of getting the people to be enthusiastic about the elections and cast their votes, preferably for the ANC. I was categorical in my view that the ANC would win the elections handsomely with a massive majority. As the ANC leadership, we had agreed that we would go on a 'listen and learn' campaign in all nine provinces, where meetings would be held and people would be encouraged to speak out and speak the truth.

Indeed, large numbers of people came to those meetings and expressed their criticism of the government. Interestingly, their attacks were mainly directed at local councillors or the local branches of the ANC. I commented in the interview that 'ANC structures were not as vibrant and active'[208] as before. One of the main reasons being that many of our best cadres had gone to national institutions, which had weakened local and provincial structures. I pointed out that to address that issue, the National Working Committee of the ANC was going every Monday to a different province to meet with the Provincial Executive Committee (PEC) to discuss the major problems confronting that province. I was firm in my opinion that our structures did function and take up the issues raised by our people and gave the example of pensioners unable to access their pensions because they did not have an ID book. I said that in the North West, where I was an NEC deployee and did a lot of election campaigning, I encouraged ANC members to go out and assist pensioners with getting their IDs and thus also their pensions. I asserted:

> I personally am confident that we can get our structures enthused again ... that our own membership will become more active ... [and] we are not going to allow the NP, the DP or the UDM ... to come and

---
207. '29 July 1998: Pahad, Essop', *O'Malley – The Heart of Hope*.
208. Ibid.

replace the ANC. So I want you to understand that there are a lot of problems, there [is] a whole set of weaknesses which we have to deal with – but I don't think they are such that they can't be overcome.[209]

In response to O'Malley's statement that a massive majority would allow the amending of the Constitution – something that was repeatedly said in the print and electronic media and presented by the opposition parties as a threat to our young democracy – I made it clear that we were going to work for a massive victory but had no intention of changing the Constitution. Even if we had ninety per cent of the vote, we would not tamper with the fundamentals of the Constitution. The ANC had helped to draft the Constitution. 'It was not imposed on us. It's as much an ANC constitution as anybody else's, so the core values of the Constitution are there because we, the ANC, wanted them to be there.'[210] For me, that applied also to the independence of the Reserve Bank.

The five years between 1994 and 1999 were exceptionally difficult and required the fullest attention of the government and the ANC. As Deputy Minister in the Presidency, Member of the NEC of the ANC and CC, and politbureau member of the SACP, I was working a seven-day week, often for more than twelve hours a day. I enjoyed the work and gave it all my mental and physical energy and commitment. But something had to be sacrificed, and that was my family. I had less and less time for my two children and my extended family. Fortunately, as before, Meg took on the responsibility and ensured that our family remained a viable unit.

We had a functioning, well-oiled collective in the ANC NEC and in the government. In both, there were differences, conflicts and contradictions, sometimes sharp, but we remained a coherent united collective. However, the Tripartite Alliance was not fully functional, and on some major policy issues, especially GEAR, it was unable to act collectively.

The economy did well, and we were able to deliver important benefits to our people. One such area was the growth of the grant system. Yet, the majority of whites, including those within the business, manufacturing and financial sector, were still sceptical of an ANC government, an attitude that has endured to the present day.

During those years, we learnt the ropes of governing a country and developing policies and programmes to improve the living conditions of the people. We were also consciously playing a role in helping to build a better

---

209. '29 July 1998: Pahad, Essop', *O'Malley – The Heart of Hope*.
210. Ibid.

and more prosperous continent and strengthening the collective impact of international progressive forces. It was a huge learning exercise. As a leader of the ANC and SACP and a member of the governing executive, I endeavoured to make my contribution. The work was hard but worthwhile, and I thoroughly enjoyed the meetings of the NEC and SACP. As a deputy minister, I was not a member of the Cabinet but served on several Cabinet committees entrusted with the task of discussing Cabinet memos produced by the relevant minister. Those were meetings where amendments could be (and were) made to the memos. Ministers had to take them into account and, where necessary, redraft their proposals. Once adopted by the Cabinet Committee, the memos would be presented to the Cabinet, who, on most occasions, would approve them as presented. The Committee work involved a lot of reading and thinking while learning and digesting the work, policies, programmes and recommendations of the relevant departments.

On some occasions, I would raise issues and challenges that arose from the memos with the deputy president, and if he agreed, he would in turn raise those matters at Cabinet. However, Mbeki was such a voracious reader and had (as he still has) a remarkable ability to absorb information, analysis and recommendations with great speed. With his alert mind and intellectual capacity, he could spot weaknesses in the memos and defend ideas with which he agreed but which came under criticism. During this period, I also developed skill in reading memos and identifying gaps and weaknesses, which was a good foundation for my later work as a minister after the 1999 elections.

As the 1999 election date approached, the ANC structures and members from local to national level were confident of securing a massive majority. Still, we were fully aware that we had to work extremely hard and develop an election manifesto, slogans and campaigns that would resonate with the majority of our people.

The ANC electoral machinery at the national level met regularly to take stock of developments around the country, ran a successful media campaign and worked well as a collective. For that election, Thabo Mbeki was the main face and personality of the campaign. Mandela had declared that he was stepping down as president, and as president of the ANC, Mbeki had to be at the forefront. Given the massive role played by Mandela in the 1994 election, we understood that we had to double and redouble our efforts in his absence. I must say that Mbeki rose to the occasion splendidly.

Once more, I served as a member of the ANC election team and represented it on the Party National Liaison Committee; again, the wisdom of the decision of Kriegler and Moseneke to set up an MPC was demonstrated. When a party felt aggrieved by the behaviour of another party or an IEC official, the matter was raised, and in most cases, resolved at the Committee meetings. That process was, at times, difficult to navigate as there were several new parties with little or no experience of the work of the Committee or the IEC. However, we were able to function effectively and found commonly agreed solutions to most of the problems that arose.

I do recall that the DA was unhappy at the coverage given to their campaign by the SABC, and the matter was escalated to Cabinet level. I was invited to that Cabinet meeting to make an input into the government's understanding of the role of the SABC in covering the elections. As I was responsible for government communications at that time, and Joel Netshitenzhe was head of the GCIS, the two of us produced a document on the place, role and functions of the public broadcaster in covering the elections. Our document was based on the one we had adopted for the 1994 elections. In it, we clearly stated that the SABC should follow the guidelines used by the BBC for its coverage of elections in the UK and not favour one party or another.

Prior to that, I had not attended a Cabinet meeting and was nervous about my appearance. On the day of the meeting, the official car allocated to me, an old Mercedes Benz, broke down on the way to Pretoria, and I grew even more apprehensive, as I would be delayed. However, Louis was contacted and asked to inform Mbeki of my misfortune. But Zolile and I were stuck. Fortunately, a car from the Johannesburg Metro Police stopped and agreed to drive me to the Union Buildings, while Zollie stayed behind to sort out the car. When I arrived at the meeting, the ministers were waiting and so was Douglas Gibson of the DA, who was vociferous in his and his party's criticism of the SABC.

Mbeki, who was chairing the meeting, looked angry and criticised me for being late. But my apology was accepted, and I made my input. It seemed to me that the position I had outlined was accepted by Cabinet and also by Douglas Gibson. We had made it clear that the SABC had to be as objective as possible and give due coverage to the contesting parties. But the DA nevertheless lodged an official complaint with the Independent Broadcasting Authority (IBA) that a so-called SABC document was biased against it. However, the complaint referred to a much earlier draft that had no relationship to the final guidelines outlined by the SABC.

The ANC, with the assistance of our allies, ran a very successful election campaign. Mbeki addressed scores of meetings, large and small, and wherever he went, he was greeted by thousands of people. At times, much to the consternation of his security detail, he was surrounded, hugged and besieged by people who wanted to shake his hand. For me, it was a firm rebuff to those who claimed he was not comfortable with large crowds. I remember one crowd in the Northern Cape with many working-class Coloured women greeting him. One woman cried in Afrikaans, 'I have shaken his hand – I am not going to wash it!' and another kissed him smack on the lips and shouted, 'I have kissed him! I have kissed him!'

My role in the campaign was to address meetings, mainly in the North West, and I visited many places and experienced enthusiastic support for the ANC. I also held several meetings in Gauteng and KwaZulu-Natal.

In KZN, I worked within the Indian community, where I approached Anant Singh, the well-known film director, who suggested that I seek help from Nirode Bramdaw and Robbie Naidoo, two energetic ANC supporters who worked hard to ensure a victory for the ANC. Nirode introduced me to Saantha Naidu and Adam Mahomed, two prominent business people who were also of great help. Bala Naidoo, who was a police officer at the time, made it possible for me to work with the Tamil Federation, which was also of great assistance. I also roped in Saths Cooper, who supported us by arranging meetings with several Hindu temples. With the assistance of my cousin, the late Amin Vania, I met with some Muslim organisations, a few of which were sceptical of participating in elections at all, never mind voting for the ANC.

I recall one meeting at a mosque in Durban. Fortunately for me, while I was waiting, I saw a Muslim newsletter quoting a highly respected international Muslim leader calling on Muslims, wherever they resided, to participate in elections. In the course of our conversations, one of the Muslim clergy spoke out against Muslims participating in elections, especially in places where they were a minority. My response was to draw their attention to the newsletter they were distributing. After intense discussion, they were convinced not only to call on their congregants and followers to vote but to cast their votes for the ANC.

Meg and I became lifelong friends with many of the people we worked with in Durban and their families. Anant and Vanashree, with their children Gyana and Kiyan, are always generous and gracious hosts when we visit. Nirode and his wife Sangeetha aways looked after us when we were in Durban and took special care of Meg at events where she did not know many people. Saantha Naidu and his wife Saras and their family became good friends and always give us a warm welcome at their home and their hotels. Sadly, Saras died in 2021 after a long battle with cancer.

Aziz and I also became close to Adam Mahomed and his wife Noorjehan, who frequently invited us to stay and party with them in Durban. Before we met them, they lost their three young daughters in a car accident. The story of their struggle to move through life with dignity and purpose is told in their joint autobiography, *Journey into the Unknown*.[211] Many years after Noorjehan's passing, Adam has settled down happily with Chandra, who happens to be the sister of Angina Parekh, wife of my brother Aziz, which has brought our families even closer together.

The work we and others did within the Indian community paid huge dividends, as the ANC increased its share of the votes in KZN from 32.23% in 1994 to 39.38% in 1999. The IFP vote went down from 50.32% to 41.90%, which laid the basis for the ANC to later become the biggest party in KZN and govern that province. In that 1999 election, the ANC won a massive victory with 66.35% of the national votes.

Thabo Mbeki was now the president-elect and responsible for forming a new Cabinet. I had no idea what he had in mind for me and was anxious about whether he would offer me any position at all.

꒳

For the first Mbeki presidential inauguration in 1999, Nkosazana Dlamini-Zuma, Minister of Foreign Affairs, chaired the planning committee; I was a member, as was Aziz. We worked well as a team to plan the event in the grounds of the Union Buildings, but there were many logistical issues and challenges to iron out, including determining with the police and security officers the total number of people who could be accommodated at the venue, the accreditation process, seating arrangements, cultural programme and the menu for the lunch that would follow the official inauguration.

Foreign Affairs was responsible for drawing up the list of foreign leaders and guests. However, with the permission of Thabo and Zanele Mbeki, I submitted the names of some of Thabo's friends from his days in London and at Sussex University: Mel and Rhiannon Gooding; Peter Lawrence and Catherine, his wife at the time; Derek Gunby and Jenny; Mike Seifert and

---

211. Johannesburg: Real African Publishers, first published in 2010.

Caroline Conran; and the well-known poet Adrian Mitchell and his wife Celia. Mel, Rhiannon, Mike and Caroline stayed at our home in Observatory, and we found a pleasant bed and breakfast nearby for the others. This was wonderful as we all ate together and spent a lot of time talking, catching up on recent events and remembering past times. We also arranged for them to meet a few other people, and Meg and I got to know Adrian and Celia much better. They were very friendly and got on wonderfully with Amina and Govan, with Adrian giving them all his books for children and us several volumes of his poetry. Everyone was excited and happy to be invited to the Mbeki's home for dinner, and they enjoyed the inauguration and the lunch, which provided further opportunities to meet people they knew or knew about and admired.

Despite some glitches and shortcomings, the event was a huge success, and I felt some pride and satisfaction that I had been able to contribute to its organisation. However, I did not enjoy the lunch. I had been informed by the president's protocol that he wanted me to host Blaise Compaoré, Burkina Faso's head of state. To say the least, I was extremely disappointed. I had so much respect and admiration for Thomas Sankara since accompanying Mbeki to a meeting with him at his home in Ouagadougou, the capital of Burkina Faso. I was convinced that Compaoré had had a hand in Sankara's assassination and was a most reluctant host. (At the time of writing, Compaoré is on trial, accused of that crime.) Furthermore, during that lunch, like many other comrades, I was nervously waiting for a signal from Frank Chikane that the president wanted us to go to the Presidential Guest House.

Mbeki had decided that all of the people he was going to appoint should go to the Guest House and wait to be called, one by one, to his home, O. R. Tambo House. At the end of the inaugural lunch, when Frank Chikane and a few others asked the invitees to go there, I was overjoyed to be invited but still uncertain about what position I would be offered. All the prospective ministers and deputy ministers gathered at the Guest House, each anxious to know about their appointment. Then, one by one, we were called. At the end, early the next morning, only three of us remained: Jeff Radebe, Steve Tshwete and me. When Jeff was called before us, Steve and I made some small chit-chat as we waited. Eventually, I was called and heard that Steve had also been called, just a little later. When I got to O. R. Tambo House, I asked Frank where Steve was, and he said he didn't know. So I phoned him, and he said he was tired and on his way home. I told him that he must come and join us immediately.

When I entered the sitting room, Mbeki was accompanied by Secretary-General Kgalema Motlanthe and Mendi Msimang, Treasurer-General of the ANC. After a brief greeting, I was informed that I would be appointed Minister in the Presidency. I wanted to shout in joy, 'Hurrah! Hurrah!' but managed to stay calm and enquired about some aspects of the post.

Now from where I sat, I could see the front door and knew that Steve was probably not on his way home but coming to O. R. Tambo House, so I said I was sure Steve was about to open the door and walk straight into the sitting room and give a warm greeting to everyone. And that is what happened. When Steve walked in, I walked out. Later, when I was driving back to Johannesburg, Steve phoned me and asked about my appointment. I answered him, and he told me that he had been appointed Minister of Police. We were both happy and eager to meet once more at the official announcement of the Executive.

An important element of the 1999 elections was the slight improvement of women's representation in the National Assembly. The ANC had 266 MPs, out of which 96 were female (36.1% of the ANC MPs). In spite of this, there was a clear appreciation that it was not good enough and that at the next election in 2004, the ANC had to do much better. It has continued to improve, and at present, fifty per cent of its MPs are women.

Essop and Joel Netshitenzhe

Chapter 9
Minister in the Presidency

Minister in the Presidency

For a comprehensive summary of the 1999 general election, please refer to *The South African Election Update: November 1998–June 1999*, published by the Electoral Institute of Southern Africa (EISA). I must express my appreciation for their tremendous work in producing that report and others before and after 1999.

President Mbeki's first cabinet was composed of the following people:

Deputy President: Jacob Zuma

Ministers:
Minister in the Presidency: Essop Pahad (ANC)
Agriculture and Land Affairs: Thoko Didiza (ANC)
Arts, Culture, Science and Technology: Ben Ngubane (IFP)
Correctional Services: Ben Skosana (IFP)
Defence: Mosiuoa (Terror) Lekota (ANC)
Education: Kader Asmal (ANC)
Environmental Affairs and Tourism: Valli Moosa (ANC)
Finance: Trevor Manuel (ANC)
Foreign Affairs: Nkosazana Dlamini-Zuma (ANC)
Home Affairs: Mangosuthu Buthulezi (IFP)
Housing: Sankie Mthembi-Mahanyele (ANC)
Intelligence: Joe Nhlanhla (ANC)
Justice and Constitutional Development: Penuell Maduna (ANC)
Labour: Membathisi (Shepherd) Mdladlana (ANC)
Mineral and Energy Affairs: Phumzile Mlambo-Ngcuka (ANC)
Posts, Communication and Broadcasting: Ivy Matsepe-Casaburri (ANC)
Provincial and Local Government: Sydney Mufamadi (ANC)
Public Enterprises: Jeff Radebe (ANC)
Public Service and Administration: Geraldine Fraser-Moleketi (ANC)
Public Works: Stella Sigcau (ANC)
Safety and Security: Steve Tshwete (ANC)

Sport and Recreation: Ngconde Balfour (ANC)
Trade and Industry: Alec Erwin (ANC)
Transport: Dullah Omar (ANC)
Water Affairs and Forestry: Ronnie Kasrils (ANC)
Welfare and Population Development: Zola Skweyiya (ANC)

Deputy Ministers:
Agriculture and Land Affairs: Dirk du Toit (ANC)
Arts, Culture, Science and Technology: Brigitte Mabandla (ANC)
Defence: Nozizwe Madlala-Routledge (ANC)
Education: Smangaliso Mkhatshwa (ANC)
Environmental Affairs and Tourism: Rejoice Mabudafhasi (ANC)
Finance: Mandisi Sipho Mpahlwa (ANC)
Foreign Affairs: Aziz Pahad (ANC)
Justice and Constitutional Development: Cheryl Gillwald (ANC)
Mineral and Energy Affairs: Susan Shabangu (ANC)
Public Works: Busi Nzimande (IFP)
Safety and Security: Joe Matthews (IFP)
Trade and Industry: Lindiwe Ngwane (ANC)

The Minister in the Presidency was given special responsibility for the Office on the Status of Women, the Office on the Status of Persons with Disabilities, and the Office on the Rights of the Child. The presidency also had a youth desk, which held the responsibility for the National Youth Commission (established in 1996) and, from 2001, the *Umsobomvu* Youth Fund. Those were placed under the Minister in the Presidency, as the issues and challenges facing women, youth, children and persons with disabilities cut across many different departments. It was considered important that the response be coordinated, not fractured and piecemeal. In addition to the routine and normal duties performed by a minister, the other major responsibility was the GCIS.

The presidency published an annual report offering a comprehensive picture of its role, work, and performance, so anyone wishing to examine the work of the presidency should consult that report.

As Minister in the Presidency, I was also deeply involved in setting up and chairing the South African Democracy Education Trust (SADET) and the South Africa-Mali Timbuktu Manuscripts Trust. These two projects were undertaken with commitment, love and passion. Later, in 2005, I was appointed to the Board of Directors of the 2010 FIFA World Cup Organising Committee South Africa. As those three additional tasks involved a vast amount of time and energy and were not strictly part of my ministerial duties as defined, I have recorded them separately in Chapter 10.

My work as minister was time-consuming and filled with the usual stress and strain but hugely enjoyable and loaded with lessons rewarding me with new insights. I was also responsible for tabling memos from the president and deputy president, although on many occasions, Mbeki would introduce his ideas and proposals himself.

Cabinet and Cabinet Committee meetings were lively and I always looked forward to them. Preparation entailed reading, appreciating, analysing and critically appraising every Cabinet memo. I actively participated in the subsequent discussions and, when necessary, I would bring certain memos to the attention of the principals. Two ministers who assiduously read every one and commented on them were Trevor Manuel and Naledi Pandor. In the course of Cabinet Committee discussions, it was possible to detect which ministers and deputy ministers had read the memos. There were times when one could tell that a specific minister had not really read the memo but was participating in the discussions in response to what a colleague had said.

I also had the wonderful opportunity of attending meetings President Mbeki held with world leaders from France, the UK, Ghana, Palestine and Mozambique.

In addition, my work involved helping run the president's office and having political oversight of the Research and Monitoring Unit in the Presidency. We were fortunate to have Frank Chikane as the DG and Joel Netshitenzhe as the head of that unit. They were both extremely able, hardworking, dedicated and committed to their work and two of the most outstanding public officials ever to work for the democratic government. They were also members of the NEC of the ANC with profound knowledge and understanding of the history, policies and programmes of the governing party. I treasure my time working with those two comrades, brothers and co-workers. Although we were comrades and in the leadership of the ANC, the two of them never criticised me in the presence of other officials. Instead, they would wait until the meeting was over and request that I stay behind with just the two of them. At that point, they would explain whatever they might wish to criticise about my interventions, and when this happened, they were invariably correct, and I would make adjustments to what had been agreed upon, if necessary.

Other people who worked in the presidency during my time there included Trevor Fowler, Murphy Morobe, Anne Letsebe, Lorato Phalatse, Vusi Mavimbela, Moss Ngoasheng, Wiseman Nkuhlu and Mojanku Gumbi. The latter was the legal advisor with a sharp and incisive legal mind who remained faithful and committed to the Black Consciousness Movement.

Those varied and extensive responsibilities and duties gave me great joy, and I carried them out with diligence to the very best of my ability. In this memoir, I shall focus on the main tasks mentioned above.

The Government Communication Information System

When I was deputy minister under Deputy President Mbeki, with his agreement, we set up a Communications Task Group (COMTASK) to advise us and make recommendations on a new communication system suitable for a constitutional democracy. This had to take into account the context of ongoing political, social and economic developments and the importance of communicating better and faster with our people to respond rapidly to their needs, demands and aspirations.

As Chair of COMTASK, I invited well-known writers and journalists to join us. Included in the group were Mandla Langa (convenor), Raymond Louw, David Dison, Mathatha Tsedu, Sebiletso Mokone-Matabane, Tony Heard, Stephen Mncube, Val Pauquet, Tshepo Rantho and Willem de Klerk. Others who provided service and assistance included Paul Lusaka and Steve Godfrey from Canada. All were outstanding and respected people in the world of communications.

Over an eight-month period, COMTASK consulted with a wide variety of national and international institutions, bodies and government departments. I chaired every one of those COMTASK meetings, which received reports from the consultations and other work completed, including suggestions of other areas that needed to be considered. During this time, I learned a great deal about communications, journalism, the work of journalists and how to operate a new communications system. I am deeply grateful to the task team and appreciative of the work they did on a pro bono basis, which culminated in a most valuable and informative report: *Communications 2000*,[212] which was presented to Deputy President Mbeki in 1996. The report had an Executive Summary, which pointed out:

---

212. *Communications 2000: A vision for government communications in South Africa*, COMTASK, October 1996. Available at https://www.gcis.gov.za/sites/default/files/docs/resourcecentre/reports/comtask/com_rep.pdf

> The report delineates critical constraints which new policies should take into account. These are: the low status of government communications; a tradition of inflexible and inward-looking bureaucracy; a high level of concentration of media ownership; a journalism profession impoverished by apartheid; obsolete media legislation; and finally, the reality of severe resource restraints on government.[213]

It also made a powerful observation when it said:

> Overall, government lacks central coordination in messaging [and] adequate planning of information campaigns, and [government] communications has a low priority, as reflected by its budgets and the status of communicators.[214]

The report's main recommendations were setting up the GCIS and that each minister would appoint a head of communications who would be 'responsible for all aspects of departmental communications', and support for the 'community media sector' through a 'recognised media development agency'.[215]

Mbeki, an expert on communication needs, issues and challenges, had been kept abreast of the COMTASK work and adopted its report and recommendations with appreciation. I then took it to Cabinet, where it was adopted as government policy without any changes. That was the start of one of the democratic government's most important initiatives: the GCIS.

In writing about the GCIS, I shall concentrate on the areas in which I played a role, which were mainly the *Imbizo*, the Multipurpose Community Centres (MPCCs), the Media Development and Diversity Agency (MDDA) and *Vuk'uzenzele* magazine.

The establishment of the GCIS was a critical recommendation of the COMTASK, but how were we to set up a new institution with no management structure, building, plans or policy framework? The first thing we did was advertise for a CEO, and I recall that I chaired the selection panel, which included Ministers Kader Asmal and Jeff Radebe. We received applications from several highly qualified candidates and interviewed them in an intensive process, asking searching questions about how they would set

---

213. Communications 2000: A vision for government communications in South Africa, COMTASK, p. 5.
214. Ibid.
215. Ibid., pp. 7–9.

up a new structure that would be sustainable and earn the respect of government departments, ministers, and media practitioners and owners inside and outside South Africa. Amongst them, one candidate stood out: Joel Netshitenzhe, who was appointed, and the old South African Communication Service was replaced by the GCIS on 18 May 1998.

Joel recruited some really efficient, hard-working personnel, including Tony Trew and Ilva Mackay Langa.

I was the political head, and the GCIS made regular reports to me. I held frequent meetings with their senior management and attended their annual function – a meeting with the entire staff and a day of fun and relaxation at an outdoor venue. On those occasions, I thanked them all for their contributions to the success of the work done by the GCIS.

After discussions with Mbeki, we agreed that the CEO of the GCIS should attend Cabinet meetings and that after each such meeting, he would hold a press briefing. Often, Joel would consult me about which issue to concentrate on and would approach a minister to attend the briefing if the Cabinet had made a major decision impacting the work of their department. Prior to this innovation, under Mandela's presidency, the post-Cabinet briefings were conducted by Professor Jakes Gerwel, DG of Mandela's office and Cabinet Secretary.

A successful initiative of the presidency was to hold regular Cabinet *lekgotlas*[216] organised by Frank Chikane and senior managers in the presidency like Trevor Fowler and Anne Letsebe. A massive set of documents was produced by each department, and ministers, deputy ministers and premiers were expected to read and familiarise themselves with the contents of those documents. In my view, it was clear that some members of the executive were content to confine their reading and presentations to the work of their own departments. Given my responsibilities, I endeavoured to read, study and understand all the documents. At the *lekgotlas*, Mbeki's leadership was pronounced, and there were occasions when he would ask an offending minister and department to rework their documents and present a more credible product – usually the next day.

At the closing session of a *lekgotla*, I would present an opinion piece on communications, the importance of such, and polls and research carried out by private companies on the popular rating achieved by the president and his government. Those inputs would be prepared by the GCIS after discussions with me and included any suggestions I made for changes in the final

---

216. A broader meeting than a cabinet meeting – including deputy ministers, premiers and DGs. Traditionally, lekgotlas were held by leaders of Sotho and Tswana communities to discuss important matters or settle disputes.

version. The GCIS documents were high quality, and on every occasion, the *lekgotla*, including Mbeki, had no problem accepting them. My only gripe was that my presentation was the last item on the agenda, and one could sense that the participants were tired and ready to call it a day.

Another regular item I presented to the Cabinet was current affairs, a new initiative that enabled the Cabinet to have a free, open and valuable discussion on current affairs without being encumbered by departmental memos, limits and structures. It was quite successful. Although this input was also drafted by the GCIS, on many occasions, I added issues I thought warranted the Cabinet's attention. I thoroughly enjoyed this presentation and believe that the rest of the Cabinet felt the same way. It also gave the president and his deputy the chance to hear and learn from the views of their Cabinet colleagues, who also had the opportunity, as I did, to raise issues and questions I had not covered. It was a wonderful initiative that I believe had been prompted by Chief Buthelezi.

The Presidential *Imbizo*[217]

In writing about this important undertaking, I was assisted by an MA dissertation in Public Governance in the Faculty of Humanities at the University of Johannesburg by Odette Hartslief.[218]

If I am not mistaken, the Presidential *Imbizo* was first conceived and proposed by Joel Netshitenzhe and me. Joel had accompanied me on an official visit to India in which one of the matters we wanted to understand better was how Indian ministers and parliamentarians, particularly from the governing party, kept in regular contact with their constituencies, party members and the general public in such a vast country with its huge population. Following that trip, we came up with the *imbizo* idea, which we discussed with Mbeki and Frank Chikane. Once we secured their understanding and agreement, I presented the matter to Cabinet, it was adopted in 2000, and the first Presidential *Imbizo* took place. In the years 2000–2005, Mbeki had a Presidential *Imbizo* in each of the nine provinces and continued them until his recall by the ANC NEC in 2009.

Organising and holding a successful *imbizo* required a great deal of planning and hard work. The preparatory work was carried out by the

---

217. Imbizo is the isiZulu word for a gathering of the people called by a traditional or other high-level leader to discuss policy.
218. Odette Hartslief, 'The Presidential Public Participation Programme (*Imbizo*) as Participatory Policy-Making.' Dissertation in fulfillment of the requirements for the degree Master of Arts in Public Governance in the Faculty of Humanities at the University of Johannesburg, June 2008. Available at https://ujcontent.uj.ac.za/esploro/outputs/graduate/The-presidential-public-participation-programme-imbizo/9913679007691#file-0

presidency with the assistance of the GCIS. As Minister in the Presidency and political head of the GCIS, I was involved in all three phases: planning, the *imbizo* event, and the post-*imbizo* follow-up.

On the side of the presidency, Chikane led the team and was ably assisted by Anne Letsebe and Lorato Phalatse. As part of his responsibilities prior to and post- an *imbizo*, Chikane also acted as a troubleshooter when problems or challenges arose.

As Hartslief points out, the planning phase included setting dates for the provinces to be visited, liaising with the national, provincial and local government departments, and appointing a coordination team at the provincial level.

An *Imbizo* programme over two and a half days would include:

- a stakeholders' meeting (meetings with business, academics, civil society and religious leaders);
- two to three community imbizo gatherings (community-based, rural and semi-urban areas);
- three project/site visits per day;
- the *Imbizo* on Air radio programme ...[219]

I had the pleasure of accompanying Mbeki on every imbizo he attended. I enjoyed those events and once more learnt a great deal. Everywhere we went, the community came out in their numbers and jostled to get a chance to speak to the president directly. They raised important challenges confronting them, such as the lack of housing and other service delivery issues. It was fascinating and encouraging to hear the people speak up without fear. Their criticisms were mainly directed at their local government representative, and my experience is that on no occasion was the national government or the president the subject of their complaints.

Sitting next to Mbeki, I would take extensive notes. When I would write a paragraph, Mbeki had the skill to sum it up in one sentence. His note taking was impressive, and he responded to every question or statement directed at him. At times, he would request the representatives from the province or local municipality to respond. During the *Imbizo*, the officials from the presidency and the GCIS would also note what was said with the president's responses, so there was a detailed record to inform the post-*imbizo* process.

At the post-*imbizo* meetings, we would meticulously go through all the

---

219. Ibid., p. 135.

notes so the presidency could respond as adequately as possible to the numerous suggestions and criticisms that had been made. Together with the president, we were determined to ensure our responses were on time and adequate. However, Chikane and the teams from the presidency and GCIS did not always receive prompt, useful or informative responses from the relevant local municipalities. This was a matter of concern, as most of the challenges and problems could only be solved at that level.

The Presidential *Imbizo* programmes were a resounding success, and accompanying Mbeki gave me the opportunity to visit places to which I would otherwise not have gone and an insight into the sometimes appalling living conditions of our people. I developed a clearer picture of the service challenges that we as the government faced in endeavouring to improve the quality of life of the people. It gave me a great deal of pain and anxiety to understand that the prospect of improving the employment rates in the rural areas was seriously limited, as those places had very little capacity for development.

I was also moved by the support the people expressed for the ANC government. Mbeki was outstanding, demonstrating his capacity to engage with the masses in good spirits while being mobbed. People just wanted to be near him, hug him or touch him. His demeanour, readiness to engage, good humour and untiring stamina were a firm rebuff to those critics who labelled him aloof, too intellectual and not in tune with ordinary people.

The more imbizos I attended, the more I became convinced that the original idea of a Presidential *Imbizo* was not only correct but a valuable political learning experience. The research by Odette Hartslief, in her words, 'confirmed that this method provided accessibility to information … and also feedback on service delivery-related matters, amongst others, as information is shared with the president in an unmediated discussion', and she concluded that 'it can improve local democracy'.[220]

I feel a lot of satisfaction that Joel and I conceived of the Presidential *Imbizo* project and that I was able to make my contribution to the success of the Mbeki's *imbizos* as his Minister in the Presidency.

Multipurpose Community Centres (MPCCs)

From its inception, the new democratic government was concerned about the lack of communication and information with millions of our people, particularly those living in the rural and peri-urban areas. The COMTASK

---

220. Odette Hartslief, 'The Presidential Public Participation Programme (Imbizo) as Participatory Policy-Making', p. 150.

Team had recommended support for what they called multipurpose information centres. Later, the MPCCs were branded Thusong Centres. In a briefing note, the GCIS identified some of the roles the centres would play:

- Identifying community education needs and allowing a response to these needs from relevant government agencies in partnership with the community and other non-government groups.
- Building capacity at a local level by involving and training local leaders in identifying and responding to development information needs.
- Networking between local level structures and institutions. This creates an opportunity for partnerships between the public and private sectors to have a common place from where they can share information costs and activities for improving the lives of individuals and communities.
- Providing a 'government with a human face' so the MPCC can be seen as a platform for government representatives of all spheres to interact with communities and respond to their concerns in face-to-face discussions.
- Integrating services on offer by providing a mix of information needs and services of interest to each community to avoid duplication and save costs.
- Accessing universal service in the areas of post and telecommunications to provide cost-effective technology needs in a relevant manner.
- Acting as an institutional home for the promotion and support of community media (print, electronic and traditional) that will serve communities in their preferred languages and at opportune times. This will also allow a home and venue for certain community groups such as youth and women's groups.

The GCIS and I, as the political head, were determined that the MPCCs were also about embracing, enhancing and promoting two-way communication between the people and government. Thus, communities were encouraged to use them to communicate their views, needs, aspirations and criticisms of government service delivery, their programmes and promises. It was a much-needed initiative, as the MPCCs also enabled people to register births and deaths more easily and provided young people with access to information technology.

As Minister in the Office of the President, I opened a few centres and visited others. But they did not always play the role we envisaged. There were times when officials from government departments failed to show up when expected, and the services delivered were not of the required quality. Moreover, as a report by the Public Service Commission pointed out, some of the centres were in poor physical condition.

However, I would argue that, overall, the MPCCs played a useful role, and communities were happy that they could access services more easily than before. I feel some pride that I played my part in setting up those centres and endeavouring to ensure they functioned effectively.

The Media Development and Diversity Agency (MDDA)

Another media initiative I was involved in was the setting up and sustainability of the MDDA.

The COMTASK had recommended that the Independent Media Diversity Trust should be used as a funding administration agency for community radio stations. In one of our regular meetings, the senior management of the GCIS raised this issue and proposed that we set up the MDDA. I accepted their recommendations with great enthusiasm, as my interest and support for community radio stations preceded the COMTASK report. In my view, the South African government needed to take further initiatives with the private sector and broad civil society to increase funding and support for community radio stations, which play an important role in keeping communities informed about local news and events and bringing local music and culture to their listeners. They also provide a useful ground for the training and development of future media professionals. At present, more than 200 community radio stations are licenced by the Independent Communications Authority of South Africa (ICASA).

As the minister responsible for the GCIS, I worked very closely with them to ensure Cabinet and Parliamentary approval of the MDDA Act (No. 14 of 2002) and the creation of the MDDA in 2003.

In writing this memoir, I asked Lumko Mtimde to reflect on the MDDA, and he kindly obliged. A graduate of the University of the Western Cape, a student activist and leader, Lumko was deeply involved in the work of community radio stations, including setting up UWC's Bush Radio, the first community radio station in South Africa. He also served as a councillor of the IBA and ICASA, and after the late Libby Lloyd, he was CEO of the MDDA. After stints as Chief of Staff in the Office of the Minister of

Agriculture, Forestry and Fisheries, and Chief Director responsible for broadcasting policy at the Ministry of Communications, he was a special advisor to the Minster in the Presidency. Lumko played a pivotal role in ensuring the success of the MDDA. Some extracts from the reflections he sent to me are quoted below:

> The work leading to the establishment of the MDDA was led in President Mbeki's Cabinet by then-Minister in the Presidency, Dr Essop Pahad, a passionate and visionary leader who laid a foundation for the realisation of [the] ideals of media freedom in South Africa. Other Cabinet members of the time (the early post-1994 era) who strongly supported media diversity include Pallo Jordan, Jay Naidoo [and] the late Dr Ivy Matsepe-Cassaburi …
>
> I recall when I was still an IBA Councillor, prior to the 1999 elections, and the budget of the IBA was cut. Led by Mandla Langa, we went to … Dr Essop Pahad's house to explain to him the implications of the budget cuts to the IBA's mandate of monitoring broadcasters during elections and prescription of Election Broadcast Regulations. He welcomed us into his house and, despite our unhappiness, prepared us breakfast snacks. We left his house a little relieved, even though we didn't get [the] funding commitment we expected, just political support [for] doing our work without interference …
>
> The MDDA grew its budget from R10 million in 2004 up to more than R70 million in 2014 and awarded grants worth more than R275 million …
>
> Dr Essop Pahad was an easy-to-work-with minister, always available to support us whenever needed and [who] ensured we [we]re able to pursue our legislated mandate without hindrance. He provided clear leadership in terms of policy directives but understood the independence of the MDDA enshrined in the MDDA Act. The MDDA acted only through its board without fear, favour or prejudice.
>
> The MDDA is mandated to promote media development and diversity [and] support and fund community and small commercial media …

At its 10th anniversary, the MDDA listed a number of deliverables and successes, including ... 10 years of unqualified and clean audits, 570 supported media projects through grants worth R275 million, more than 247 bursaries awarded in media studies, advocating and ensuring [a] more than R30 million government adspend annually allocated to community and small commercial media ... reduction of signal distribution costs, production of ... research reports on media ownership and control, production of easy-to-use toolkits on governance, advertising and marketing.

As is evident from those extracts, the MDDA, with minimal resources, played a critical role in empowering community radio stations and small commercial enterprises and training media personnel. Its success is due to the untiring efforts of the board: the late Libby Lloyd; the late Govan Reddy; Lumko Mtide; Khanyi Mkhonza, the first chair of the MDDA; her successor Gugu Msibi; the GCIS and me.

I held regular meetings and briefings with the board during which we covered issues ranging from the work they were doing, the successes and weaknesses of their operations and the financial short-fall they continuously faced. Except for the employees of the MDDA, all the others gave their time, energy, and impressive know-how of the media landscape pro bono, which demonstrated that we had individuals prepared to lend their talent and skills to a project without any financial reward because they believed in it. It was a pleasure and a profound learning experience to work closely with all the individuals involved in the MDDA.

In reflecting on my time as the political head of the GCIS, I need to comment on two other important initiatives: the International Marketing Council and *Vuk'uzenzele* magazine.

The International Marketing Council

President Mbeki and his government were concerned that we did not have properly coordinated international marketing policies or an agency. After discussions with him, Netshitenzhe and Chikane and interactions with the corporate world and media, we concluded that South Africa needed an International Marketing Council (IMC). In December 1999, I raised the matter in Cabinet, and the idea was approved. As pointed out in a GCIS briefing note in August 2000:

The International Marketing Council, therefore brings together the government, corporate and non-government sectors. It will provide strategic advice to government on a broad range of international marketing initiatives, including investment, export and tourism promotion. The Council also has the power to take decisions within its mandate and to ensure implementation.

Given its mandate, Mbeki suggested that the Minister of Foreign Affairs, Dr Nkosazana Dlamini-Zuma, should chair it, and in her absence, the Minister of Trade and Industry, Alec Erwin, should have that responsibility. The GCIS serviced both the interdepartmental team and the IMC; however, a great deal of the work for ensuring the success of the IMC fell on my shoulders. In close consultation with the GCIS, we convened the first meeting and attended the board and Exco meetings.

The following impressive list of invitees attended the IMC's inaugural meeting: Paul Bannister, Koos Bekker, Irene Charnley, Salukazi Dakile-Hlongwane, Marinus Daling, Pam Golding, Steve Griessel, Hugh Harman, Danny Jordaan, Sibongile Khumalo, Wendy Luhabe, Nana Makaula, Barbara Masekela, James Motlatsi, Dr Sam Motsuenyane, Mavuso Msimang, Anant Singh, Michael Spicer and Dr Frederik van Zyl Slabbert.

From the government side, we had ministers from the following departments: Office of the Presidency; Foreign Affairs; Posts, Communications and Broadcasting; Sport and Recreation; Trade and Industry; and Tourism, and their departments were represented by their DGs. Frank Chikane, Joel Netshitenzhe, Moss Mashishi, Rafiq Bagus and I also represented the government.

I must emphasise that of all the ministers who played a leading role in securing the sustainability and success of the IMC, apart from myself, the most notable was Ivy Matsepe-Casaburri, who was a tower of strength and never missed a meeting. Another person who deserves a special mention is first CEO, Yvonne Johnston. She loved the work, was creative, industrious and a good leader who made an immense contribution to the successful work of the IMC.

I attended all the IMC Board and Exco meetings, briefed the president regularly and, with the GCIS, did what we were asked to do by the board. The IMC Board met annually with President Mbeki in the East Wing of the Union Buildings. Through the CEO, they would report on their work and propose new ideas and recommendations on improving the marketing of

South Africa internationally. We would then end up downstairs in the amphitheatre for a photo with the president. I think all of us present found those meetings valuable and enjoyable.

An insight into the work of the IMC can be gleaned from a report made by the CEO on the GCIS budget vote in 2004. In it, Yvonne Johnston spoke to the successes of the IMC in setting up and running several initiatives such as a Communications Resource Centre and the Brand South Africa Campaign, which utilises the new National Web Portal and has achieved significant corporate support. Another initiative promoted our country's achievements and attractions through the presentation of positive information in many formats, including the booklet *The South African Story* for our 'ambassadors', SAA and others, to change perceptions about South Africa. She noted that Professor Sinclair of Wits University had calculated the current value of Brand South Africa at R379.5 billion.

In concluding her report, Yvonne said, 'We have touched many lives, heard heart-warming stories … and have been surrounded by positive prospects, all aimed at making this country a better place for all of us who are lucky enough to live in it.'

I thoroughly enjoyed working with the board and staff of the IMC and the GCIS. At important moments, we were able to give strategic direction to the work of the IMC and help oversee the work of our brand managers in the UK, the USA and India. I attended the Exco meetings until asked not to so the participants could be more comfortable expressing views that were critical of government. After I stopped attending, the chair, Wendy Luhabe, would brief me after each Exco meeting. She was an excellent leader, giving well-considered advice and support to the IMC. As busy as she was as a leading business executive, she gave her time, intellect, insight and energy to her responsibilities at the IMC. It was an honour and a pleasure to work with Wendy, and she deserves credit for her enormous contribution to the IMC and Brand South Africa. I am also happy that I was able to make my contribution to their work.

Vuk'uzenzele

In 2004, the Cabinet requested that we consider producing a regular government publication that would enable the majority of our people to access information on what the government was doing and tell them about its various programmes. Following this directive, the GCIS recommended to me that we research the possibility of producing a bimonthly magazine,

Vuk'uzenzele,[221] with an initial print run of one million copies. In the ensuing discussions, I enquired whether the GCIS could distribute that many copies and was assured it would not be a problem. I think at the same meeting, it was agreed that, as well as publishing it in all eleven official languages, we could also produce an edition in Braille. We were determined that it be easy to read and understand and visually attractive and that an important focus would be to serve the rural areas, particularly the poor. I was excited by this development, as we were pursuing an objective close to my heart.

When writing about *Vuk'uzenzele*, I decided that the best person to refresh my memory would be Tony Trew, as he was actively involved with the magazine. Below I reproduce his input:

> A few years after its establishment, [the] GCIS reflected on a core part of its mandate, namely to empower citizens with the information they needed to work with government to implement programmes for the development of themselves and their communities.
>
> Surveying the media landscape, it was clear that there was a huge gap between the information people and communities needed to become agents in their own development and what they were getting access to. What was needed was a platform that combined not only a particular content but also format, language and reach that put the information in the hands of those who could use it and that made it shareable within the community.
>
> Out of that came *Vuk'uzenzele*, a magazine published every two months, using all the country's official languages and distributed through outlets close to where people lived. With its magazine format, it overcame the fleeting existence of information in newspapers and on radio and could be handed on from person to person.
>
> To get the formula right, the project team did research to test and refine it, from font to layout and language, and drew on the rich print and broadcast media experience of Govin Reddy.

---

221. Xhosa for 'Get up and do it yourself.'

Wanting to defray as much cost as possible through advertising, [the] GCIS registered the publication with the Audit Bureau of Circulations.

Vuk'uzenzele was launched in October 2005 at Constitution Hill to signal the intention to contribute to constitutional rights for development and reconstruction.

The first editor of *Vuk'uzenzele* was Rafiq Rohan, with years of print media experience, and the production team drew on GCIS capabilities in design and writing and knowledge of the country's languages. *Vuk'uzenzele* is partially translated into all official languages to ensure that readers receive government news in the language of their choice.

The formula proved to be a good one, and the publication has gone from strength to strength ...

By the time of the launch, [the] GCIS had started work in a partnership with SABC Education that resulted in a TV series informed by the same objectives as the magazine. *Azishe-Ke: Opportunity Knocks* was a thirteen-part series broadcast on SABC 2 on Saturday mornings. A description of the series by SABC Education matches the objectives and content of *Vuk'uzenzele*:

> The core content included different projects that the government had launched in an effort to change people's lives. It featured real stories of initiatives in which people had been trained to do different jobs and received helped in starting businesses. The government hoped thereby to work with media to reach more people, especially the economically poor, and to show them how they can take advantage of government-created opportunities to improve their lives.
>
> Specifically, the programme showed what Expanded Public Works Programme projects like Working for Water and road construction can do to empower people. It also looked at government support for Black-owned hotels, promotion of small business opportunities through the Umsobomvu Youth Fund, gender and women's empowerment, the National Development Agency, and the School Nutrition Programme.[222]

---

222. The Communication Initiative Network: *Azishe-Ke: Opportunity Knocks.*

Vuk'uzenzele started with a print run of one million copies every second month. In 2009, the SA Advertising Research Foundation (SAARF) published readership figures from its All Media Products Survey (AMPS) showing that 'emerging market publications are still charging ahead, outperforming their mainstream counterparts' and that *Vuk'uzenzele* was amongst those 'showing significant increases in readership'. Since then, it has gone through two transformations: in 2011, it changed from a bimonthly magazine to a monthly broadsheet, and in 2015, the frequency changed to twice a month with a fresh design.

> In keeping with the times, *Vuk'uzenzele* is available online at http://www.vukuzenzele.gov.za – and there is an app which allows it to be read on smartphones.

In the GCIS Budget Vote of 2006–2007, I said with a measure of pride and satisfaction:

> With a circulation of one million copies, the magazine has consistently elicited an enthusiastic response and requests for more copies than it has been possible to supply. What we can say with confidence is that the practical information it supplies in all official languages and Braille is clearly meeting a public need.[223]

In the GCIS Budget Vote of 2007–2008, I reported to Parliament:

> *Vuk'uzenzele*, our popular magazine, continues to extend its reach into second economy communities. It profiles real stories of people who have initiated projects with government support. The demand continues unabated, and the print run will increase this year from 1.2 million to 1.5 million. I should add that it has been especially rewarding to see the reaction of blind people to the Braille edition.[224]

In my years as a minister who reported to parliament on my work, including participating in the presidential budget vote, I most enjoyed the GCIS budget vote. The ANC MPs were always supportive and provided innovative suggestions for improvement. It was most pleasing to debate, and where

---

223. Available at https://www.gcis.gov.za/content/newsroom/speeches/minister/essop-pahad-gcis-budget-vote-2006-7
224. Available at https://www.gcis.gov.za/content/newsroom/speeches/minister/essop-pahad-gcis-budget-vote-2007-8

necessary disagree, with Dene Smuts of the Democratic Party. I had first met her at the CODESA negotiations, and our friendship and respect for each other did not diminish over the years.

The parliamentary budget votes of all the ministers are important, as they enable MPs from the ANC and the opposition to be informed about the ministers' and corresponding departments' major activities over the year and give them the opportunity to criticise the minister and the government s/he represents. During those years, I was aware of some of my colleagues getting quite a rough ride in their budget votes. For me, although there was criticism from the opposition, it was always friendly and helpful. It is a pity that those budget votes do not get the necessary publicity in the public and private mass media sectors.

Office on the Status of Disabled Persons (OSDP)

An important aspect of my responsibilities as the Deputy Minister in the Deputy President's Office (1996–1999) was to be the political head for the OSDP and Office on the Status of Women (OSW). These two responsibilities gave me a great deal of pleasure and the opportunity to absorb new knowledge and appreciate the fantastic talent possessed by persons with disabilities and the women of our country and continent.

With respect to the OSDP, I am grateful for the contributions of Shuaib Chalken and Zain Bulbulia. The first democratic government in South Africa set up the RDP Office in the presidency, headed by Jay Naidoo. That office established a disability desk with the late mercurial Maria Rantho as the head. When Maria took her seat in Parliament in 1994 (the first-ever wheelchair user MP), Shuaib Chalken was appointed to replace her, assisted by Charlotte McClain and Lidia Pretorius. That desk, following extensive consultation with persons with disabilities, including visits and meetings in all the provinces, developed a Green Paper in 1996. Fortunately, Shuaib remained at his post and was a formidable fighter for the rights of the disabled; he was highly respected within the disability movement in South Africa, Africa and internationally. When we established the OSDP, he was appointed as director, and with my assistance, he raised funds from the Swedish government to produce a White Paper entitled 'The Integrated National Disability Strategy',[225] which was, as Shuaib writes in a note to me:

> ... the first policy paper that adopted the social model of disability. It

---
225. Available at https://www.gov.za/sites/default/files/gcis_document/201409/disability2.pdf

became globally recognised for adopting the social model, where the emphasis was on the removal of barriers in society that prevent people with disabilities from participating fully in society, instead of a medical model that placed the burden on the individual with a disability that is akin to victim blaming.

This was groundbreaking and never fully recognised in SA. While the rest of the world either focused on expanding a welfare system or had no services for people with disabilities, South Africa was developing leading policy on employment, inclusive education, health care and housing, among others.

Together with the DPSA (Disabled People of South Africa), we succeeded in getting our government to recognise the struggle of the disabled as part of the struggle for human rights and democracy, which was later integrated into our constitution.

After my appointment as Mbeki's Minister in the Presidency, that work continued. Shuaib is generous when he writes:

> The Minister in the Presidency had an engaging approach to working with civil society, especially with DPSA. He had an open-door policy, and during this period, the most groundbreaking progress was made concerning people with disabilities in South Africa.
>
> Among the most significant policy decisions of the state was the inclusion of persons with disability in the Constitution, which outlawed discrimination on the basis of disability. Secondly, the new labour laws promoted affirmative action and included disability as a category for affirmative action. State-owned enterprises (SOEs) such as Telkom, Transnet, etc. began to employ people with disabilities for the first time. Government departments had a target of employing 2% of people with disabilities ...
>
> The media played a positive role, and positive stories on disability were carried on the front pages of major news outlets. The SABC appointed a disabled person on[to] their board, and local soap operas included characters with disabilities.
>
> The net result of all of these activities spearheaded by the state was

that there was suddenly a greater awareness of the rights of people with disabilities.

I was most pleased assisting in achieving those objectives. It was a difficult task, as it was groundbreaking, and one had to convince leaders in a whole range of categories that disabled persons were as good, if not better, than able-bodied persons in performing managerial tasks. We did succeed in our work, and many disabled persons were employed for the first time.

I was also part of the team in the presidency, with the full support of Mbeki, to persuade Cabinet to agree to a collective approach to bring together government departments to participate actively in developing and implementing the relevant policies. This coordination was crucial, but as Shuaib points out, 'In reality, there was still resistance by ministers to the idea of losing authority over their departmental turf, and this led to significant policy lag.' But by using the authority of the president and the presidency, I managed to convince my Cabinet colleagues that there was no other way to deal with that huge challenge. Sometimes there were objective barriers, such as no vacant positions or difficulty in finding the right person for a specific job.

Both the ministers and their senior managers in the departments played an important role in endeavouring to employ persons with disabilities and assisting the various organisations representing and articulating the interests of their constituencies. This also helped establish OSDPs in the offices of the premiers in all provinces, which led, as Shuaib points out, to 'a sharp increase in policy implementation at a provincial level'. One of our most enthusiastic adherents was Sam Shilowa, Premier of Gauteng. However, then as now, the majority of local governments were sadly not up to scratch, which is an area that needs the urgent attention of all three spheres of government.

The OSDP, through the hard work of Shuaib with my assistance, secured funding from Sweden and Belgium, which enabled the OSDP to expand its activities to the provinces and employ additional staff to augment its work capacity.

From the outset, I was keen to get more disabled persons elected to the National Assembly, the National Council of Provinces (NCOP) and provincial legislatures. This was not difficult, as the ANC leadership was responsive, and we were able to elect a few to become MPs. But once elected, those with disabilities faced a number of challenges, including how and where they would be seated in the National Assembly.

The late William Rowland, a blind activist, fighter and leader of the DPSA, writes in his informative book *Nothing About Us Without Us – Inside the Disability Rights Movement of South Africa*:[226]

> I have been invited to witness the briefing of the new disabled parliamentarians by Essop Pahad, Minister in the Presidency. Wilma is concerned about the positioning of her interpreter on the floor of the House. They need to face each other for good communication. Louis wants to know about the immediate surroundings. Whether there is a garden if he wants to take his guide dog outside. Joseph asks about transport and parking. As a wheelchair user, he has to be sure about the practical arrangements. Michael wishes to know what materials will be provided in Braille.

I listened attentively and undertook to raise those concerns and challenges with the Speaker of the National Assembly and Makhenkhesi Stofile, Chief Whip of the ANC.

Frene Ginwala, an influential fighter for women's rights, empowerment and emancipation, notable historian and member of the NEC of the ANC, was the first Speaker of the National Assembly. She acknowledged the problems faced by MPs with disabilities, in particular Wilma Duche, who was deaf. In terms of the rules and procedures governing who is allowed to be on the floor of the National Assembly, Wilma's interpreter could not be accommodated on the floor of the House. We inspected the floor and worked out that Wilma should be seated on the right of the Speaker's chair and opposite a section that was designed to accommodate very senior managers and advisors to the president and deputy president. We reserved a special place for the interpreter, which enabled Wilma to have eye contact with the interpreter to follow the debates when she wanted to address the house. The interpreter would be given a mike, and Wilma's speech would be relayed to the House. This was a groundbreaking solution which worked extremely well.

Together with Frene, we found solutions to all the problems raised by MPs with disabilities. Frene deserves credit for how she responded and found answers and solutions, no matter how difficult and complex the task. I was particularly pleased, as it demonstrated that our government, parliament and the ANC were alive and sensitive to the many acute challenges facing MPs

---

226. Pretoria: Unisa Press, 2004.

with disabilities and, indeed, visitors with disabilities who wanted to witness parliamentary proceedings.

I was greatly saddened when informed that Frene had passed away in January 2023.

Nothing About Us Without Us, the title of Rowland's book, is a fantastic slogan for the DPSA. As an activist and later leader of our movement, I have appreciated the value and mobilising power of well-crafted slogans. From the beginning, I was moved by that slogan, inspired by it, and it informed my work and interactions with the disability movement in South Africa and Africa. Any person interested in enhancing their knowledge and understanding of that movement should read and study Rowland's book. As he writes in the concluding paragraph:

> So, these are some of our adventures, but the point of it all was to spread the message that by organising ourselves, we could change things around us and the attitude of governments. This we have continued to do in the countries of South and Southern Africa for twenty years and more, and yet, the process is far from ended.[227]

I could not agree more and call upon all the political parties, governments in all three spheres, public servants and the private sector to pursue a relentless struggle together with the disability movement for the protection, promotion and enhancement of the human rights of persons with disabilities.

Let me also pay my respect and admiration to Hendrietta Bogopane-Zulu, a feisty no-nonsense fighter for the rights of women and persons with a disability. She has impaired vision, and by sheer hard work, endurance, creativity and intelligence, rose to become (at the time of writing) Deputy Minister for Social Development. I will forever cherish the memory that she was late for her own wedding, and when I chided her for that, she merely replied, 'But Comrade Pahad, who is getting married? You or I?' And that was that.

On reflecting upon my work concerning persons with disabilities, I have decided to write about two areas that gave me a lot of pleasure and had an impact on South Africa, Africa and the world. The first is about the United Nations Convention on the Rights of Persons with Disabilities, and the second is on the Paralympics and our Paralympians.

---

227. Wiliam Roland, *Nothing About Us Without Us*.

In 2001, at the UN Conference on Racism held in Durban, the Government of Mexico called for the drafting and adoption of such a convention. I fully backed that call and engaged with the governments of Mexico, Sweden and Canada to pursue with vigour the necessary process, and our collective endeavours led to the UN General Assembly establishing a task force to bring it to life.

With my full support, Shuaib joined that team and played an important role in helping to draft the Convention. Later, after she was appointed Head of the OSD, Sebenzile Matsebula led the South African team in the negotiations between member states that followed. Sebenzile was passionate about her work and an excellent communicator. My wife Meg was grateful to her for a number of insights into disability; for example, when they danced together, she demonstrated that being in a wheelchair does not prevent a person's body from responding to music and enjoying movement and rhythm.

I received regular briefings on the developments, and when necessary, edited the proposed texts and briefed the president and the government. The hard work of Sebenzile and Shuaib, assisted by our representatives at the United Nations and the government bore fruit when the UN General Assembly adopted the UN Convention on the Rights of Persons with Disabilities in December 2006. For that momentous and historic event, I was full of joy to be asked to represent the South African Government. We were one of the first signatories and one of the first to ratify. I believe those who shared the long road and arduous process which led to that point felt a shared pride at that historic achievement.

The UN Convention on the Rights of Persons with Disabilities contained forty-four articles covering critical areas impacting on the lives and livelihoods of persons with a disability. Both the Preamble and the Articles are fully consistent with the positions taken by the Mbeki Government, the OSD and me as the responsible minister. Let me quote the last paragraph [25] of the Preamble, which reflects the considered view of the member states:

> Convinced that a comprehensive and integral international convention to promote and protect the rights and dignity of persons with disabilities will make a significant contribution to redressing the profound social disadvantage of persons with disabilities and promote their participation in the civil, political, economic, social

and cultural spheres with equal opportunities, in both developing and developed countries … Have agreed as follows:[228]

The Preamble is followed by the Articles, all of which have been agreed upon.

When we first established the OSD and engaged with the DPSA and other bodies representing and giving voice to the interests and aspirations of people with disabilities, we never imagined that one day we, as a country and a people, would make a sterling contribution to a convention which gives hope and optimism to persons with disabilities in every corner of the world. That will remain a highlight of my life as an activist, leader and internationalist.

To move on to the Paralympics: one of the most pleasant and fulfilling responsibilities I have been given was to represent the South African Government at the Summer Paralympics in Sydney in 2000, Athens in 2004 and Beijing in 2008.

For the 2000 Paralympics in Sydney, at the request of the Paralympians, I asked Deputy President Zuma to lead our delegation. He agreed, and our athletes and the Australian Government were very happy, as this was, I believe, the first time a representative at the level of deputy president, outside of the host nation, had attended those games. When we arrived at the main venue, Zanele Situ, to our great delight, won gold in the women's javelin, later winning silver in the women's discus. At the same games, one of our greatest athletes, abled or disabled, Fanie Lombard, bagged three gold and one silver. All in all, we won thirteen gold, twelve silver and thirteen bronze – a total of thirty-eight medals. Never before had a representative South African team won so many medals. In Athens in 2004, Team South Africa won fifteen gold, thirteen silver and seven bronze – a total of thirty-five medals. In Beijing in 2008, we won twenty-one gold, three silver and six bronze – a total of thirty medals. These Paralympian achievements outshone those of our able-bodied Olympians.

It has always irked me that our print and electronic mass media do not pay sufficient attention to the Summer Paralympics and fail to celebrate some of our greatest athletes and swimmers. Let me mention just a few: Fanie Lombard, Zanele Situ, Natalie du Toit, Oscar Pistorius, Ernst van Dyk, Teboho Mokgalagadi, Scott Field, Malcolm Pringle and Hilton Langenhoven – my sincere apologies for not mentioning the many other outstanding Paralympians.

---

228. Available at https://www.un.org/development/desa/disabilities/convention-on-the-rights-of-persons-with-disabilities/preamble.html

At the Beijing Games, Oscar Pistorius was in a public verbal feud with some SA officials. I had to intervene, and after ascertaining his view of the conflict, I asked him to calm down and concentrate on his events. After a quiet discussion, he agreed to tone down his criticisms and help create a welcoming and friendly climate in our camp. At the same games, I recollect having the pleasure and honour of presenting a few winners with their medals. I was most proud of presenting a gold medal to that phenomenal swimmer, Natalie du Toit, who bagged five golds. Throughout the competition, she remained calm, humble and determined. It had been wonderful to witness Natalie, our flag bearer, leading our team into the stadium at the opening ceremony.

For years, I had been a fan of Fanie Lombard and asked if I could accompany him on the bus from their residence to the venue for the discus competition. As we were happily chatting, he suddenly said in a quiet voice, 'We have to go back – I forgot my leg!' We got off the bus, took another to the residence, collected his leg, and made it just in time for the discus competition. Undaunted, Fanie went on to win gold, a remarkable achievement by any standard!

Office on the Status of Women (OSW)

It is well to remember that during the long years of colonialism, racism and apartheid, women, including white women, were heavily discriminated against and treated as inferior to men. Patriarchy was also strong and prevalent in our revolutionary alliance. For too long, we took the position that the national liberation of the oppressed and exploited was the priority, and the fight for the empowerment of women was subsumed in the overall national struggle. It took some time before we understood the interconnection and inter-relationship between the national liberation struggle and the struggle for full women's rights and against patriarchy and sexism.

Although we fully recognised, spoke and wrote about the triple oppression of Black women in terms of race, class and gender, it was not until the late seventies, with ANC women activists and leaders taking a stand and responding to the worldwide movement for women's rights in every aspect of life, that our movement began to pay greater attention to this issue, including within our own structures. This fundamental shift gave a tremendous boost to our struggle inside the country, in exile, and in international anti-apartheid solidarity movements.

As detailed in Chapter 6, Comrade President Oliver Tambo gave a speech in 1981 at a conference in Luanda, Angola, which challenged men and women to understand and recognise that the struggle for the liberation of women was an integral part of our revolutionary struggle. In that speech, he said:

> Women in the ANC should stop behaving as if there is no place for them above the level of certain categories of involvement. They have a duty to liberate us men from our antique concepts and attitudes about the place and role of women in society and the development and direction of our revolutionary struggle.[229]

That speech was an inspiration to women and men in the movement and put to shame the sexists still lurking in our struggle. Reading that speech, I was moved to make a contribution to the struggle for women's rights and representation in the leadership echelons of the Alliance. The speech also laid the basis for the groundbreaking NEC statement of 2 May 1990 on the 'Emancipation of Women in South Africa', which ensured that women's rights, concerns and demands were taken seriously, and that their having greater representation at all levels of our structures was recognised as a priority. It also ensured more gender-balanced representation in the CODESA negotiations, the placing of more women on our electoral list for the 1994 elections and more women occupying leadership positions in the new democratic dispensation.

Before I write about the OSW, let me mention some of the women who played (and some who continue to play) a role in building a non-racial, non-sexist democratic society. These include: Ida Mntwana, Lilian Ngoyi, Helen Joseph, Dora Tamana, Albertina Sisulu, Adelaide Tambo, Blanche La Guma, Hetty September, Ayanda Dlodlo, Winnie Madikizela-Mandela, Thenjiwe Mtintso, Jackie Modise, Ivy Matsepe-Cassaburi, Ruth First, Hilda Bernstein, Gertrude Shope, Ruth Mompati, Cissie Gool, Dr Zainab Asvat, Zanele Mbeki, Amina Cachalia, Fatima Meer, Florence Mposha, Kate Molale, Maggie Resha, Sonia Bunting, Shanthie Naidoo, Frene Ginwala, Mavivi Manzini, Naledi Pandor, Cheryl Carolus, Sankie Mthembi-Mahanyele, Dr Nkosazana Dlamini-Zuma, Geraldine Fraser-Moleketi, Lindiwe Sisulu, Angie Motsheka, Dulcie September, Stella Sigcau, Phumzile Mlambo-Ngcuka, Barbara Masekela, Brigitte Mabandla, Thoko Didiza, and Baleka

---

229. Luli Callinicos, *Beyond the Engeli Mountains*, p. 439.

Mbete, Sally Motlana and Joyce Piliso-Seroke. My most sincere apologies to those freedom fighters I have not mentioned here. Earlier in this memoir, I wrote of my mother, Amina Pahad, and Ama Naidoo, two remarkable women. A special tribute is also paid to the women in the ranks of Umkhonto we Sizwe, who had to be twice as strong as the men in the MK camps in Angola.

Thabo Mbeki was one of the most vocal of the leaders. In theory and practice, he was a firm fighter for the empowerment of women in South Africa, Africa and the world. Thus, in 1997, with his guidance and full support as deputy president, I, as Deputy Minister in the Presidency, set up the OSW, the functions of which included developing a national gender policy, promoting affirmative action in government, supporting government bodies to integrate a gender perspective in all policies and programmes, and organising gender training for government departments.

That was a difficult task, but the OSW, led by Dr Ellen Kornegay and assisted by Susan Nkomo, played an instrumental role in giving life to those functions. Despite a lack of financial resources and personnel, they worked extremely hard in performing their duties and exercising their responsibilities. Dr Kornegay led from the front and was highly respected and admired by many gender activists inside and outside government. She had agreed earlier this year to meet me and help me to write up this section. However, her husband, Professor Francis Kornegay, also a good friend of mine and lifelong internationalist fighter against racism and colonialism and a brilliant journalist, tragically passed away on 11 June 2021. A few days later, on 4 July, Ellen died from COVID complications.

In paying tribute to Ellen, and in recognition of her prodigious contribution to the OSW and her national, continental and international struggle for the rights of women, I reproduce below extracts from her article 'The National Gender Machinery' (NGM), which she wrote for *The Thinker*, *Vol. 6*, 2009.

> Over the 15 years that South Africa has developed its gender machinery, this process has entailed a set of integrated structures located at various levels of state, civil society and within the relevant statutory bodies. When it was established, the NGM's institutional framework, at it's core, comprised the Office on the Status of Women (OSW) in the Presidency and the Chapter 9 Commission on Gender Equality (CGE) to serve as a link between government and civil

society. Responsibility for gender mainstreaming, however, in terms of realising gender equality was, and remains, the responsibility of all members of Cabinet and government entities. The apexes of the NGM were designed to be facilitating and coordinating agents. As such, they served important functions of oversight as well as monitoring and evaluation.

The choice to establish an OSW, as opposed to a Women's Ministry, was based on the need to ensure that the mainstreaming of gender considerations was approached in a seamless and uniform manner across all government sectors. Taking a lead from countries with experiences of similar socio-economic conditions, South Africa opted for an OSW, as it did not wish to have a situation where women's issues were isolated from all other issues or where a Women's Ministry was in competition with its peers at Cabinet level. Located in the presidency, it was elevated above mainline ministries with respect to the articulation, formulation and adoption of the National Policy Framework for Women's Empowerment and Gender Equality, reporting to international institutions, and monitoring and evaluating the implementation of government policies, projects and programmes.

In the study that preceded the establishment of the OSW, it was clear that the OSW would ideally form the apex of the gender machinery and provide integration and coordination for the entire NGM. By being placed at the apex of government, the OSW would draw from that authority to define norms and standards and ensure overall compliance with the constitutional imperative.

Consequently, the issue of the location of a number of apex points for the NGM was central in its formation. These provided the rest of the NGM with vision, direction and authority. This view is affirmed by the National Policy Framework for Women's Empowerment and Gender Equality, which lists those apex points as follows:

- Parliament: the Joint Committee on the Improvement of the Quality of Life and Status of Women, women's caucuses, Women's Empowerment Unit ... mandated to ensure that all parliamentary

committees would include gender considerations in their work.
- Government: Cabinet, the OSW in the Presidency, provincial OSWs in premiers' offices ... gender units and focal points in line departments ... and ... local government structures.
- Independent bodies: the Constitutional Court, other courts, and all Chapter 9 bodies, including the Commission for Gender Equality ...
- Civil Society: NGOs, religious bodies, the Congress of Traditional Leaders of South Africa, and the South African Local Government Association.

It is this founding version of the NGM that was universally acclaimed as global best practice and deemed to have outstripped the structures that informed it from other countries, including those of Australia, Canada and Uganda. It is the South African NGM, and in particular the OSW, that promoted the integration of gender as a prime consideration into the organisational structures of the African Union (AU).

After illustrating the progress made in terms of women representatives in leading government roles, nationally and provincially (to slightly over forty per cent), and senior managers in the public service (to just under thirty-five per cent), Ellen points out that there is still a persistent and protracted struggle ahead.

I felt that President Zuma's decision to move the work of the OSW out of the presidency was a mistake, as no single minister has the authority to coordinate inter-ministerial work effectively. Ellen also commented tactfully on this, saying:

> Under the new administration of President Jacob Zuma, the work, role and functions of the OSW are now located in the newly formed Ministry of Women, Youth and People with Disabilities. As long as this Ministry enjoys the full backing and authority of the president and the presidency, the change in its location should not impact adversely on the apex and points of coordination of the NGM.

Ellen and Susan were the main drafters of the SADC and AU documents and were greatly assisted by Athaliah Molokomme of SADC (from Botswana) and Joséphine Ouédraogo of the Economic Commission on Africa (from

Burkina Faso).

The Solemn Declaration of African Heads of State on Gender and Development was piloted and championed by President Mbeki. Getting the AU, with its powerful presence of Muslim-majority countries, to come to a common position was not easy, as some of those involved held the more conservative interpretations of Islamic laws. Susan Nkomo, in a note to me, pointed out that the OSW had excellent working relations with a number of Muslim civil society organisations, which made it easier to overcome the opposition offered by the more reactionary forces.

As the head of the OSW, I also made a contribution to the SADC and AU documents and the positions adopted. I recall that we had regular meetings with the ministers responsible for Women's Rights from Tanzania, Malawi, Angola and Namibia. The minister from Namibia was always cheerful with a ready smile and a hearty laugh. She was very well informed about sociopolitical and economic developments on the African continent and protocol matters regarding presidents and first ladies. I remember once in Malawi when the president was to address a meeting on the topic of women's development and rights, and I had been asked to speak on behalf of all the SADC countries present. She said to me, 'Now, Comrade Pahad, you see there are three microphones on the stage. The first one is for the president, the second is for the first lady and the third is for the rest of the speakers, including you. So go to the correct microphone.' And I did.

We had wonderful meetings in that ministerial group, and I was usually teased for being the only male. Those ministers also contributed to the texts that were adopted by SADC and the AU. I must say that, of all the ministerial meetings I attended or convened, those were the most congenial and comfortable. As a collective, we were driven by our common desire to take to higher levels the struggle for the empowerment of women in our countries and elsewhere.

One of the most serious and painful challenges we face is the fight against gender-based violence (GBV) in all its forms and manifestations. The National Policy Framework for Women's Empowerment and Gender Equality, produced by Ellen Kornegay for the OSW in the year 2000, contains this telling paragraph:

> Violence against women remains a serious problem in South African society. The high incidence of rape cases, as well as other forms of physical and psychological abuse of women and girls, are evidence of

this. The Criminal Justice and Safety and Security systems are now beginning to deal with this crisis in a gender-sensitive manner. It will continue to be a major challenge, especially as it is compounded by its interrelation with poverty and HIV/AIDS.

I wish I could say that great progress has been made in this crucial area, but unfortunately, this is not the case.

In the course of my years as deputy minister and minister, I had a relatively large number of duties and responsibilities. On reflection, I must conclude that the most worthwhile of all those tasks were my work with the OSW and the OSD, which have given me the greatest pleasure in the long term. My gratitude to all those who made it possible for me to perform that work is immense. Without those dedicated and fully committed officials and individuals, it would not have been possible to make the impact we made.

In the year 2022, it is a searing indictment of the private sector in our country that women do not get paid the same as men for the same work, that they are a miserable minority in boardrooms, face discrimination when applying for jobs or promotions, and after years of work, still retire with less income than men. That surely has to come to an early end. It remains the responsibility of the ANC, SACP, COSATU, civil society bodies and women's organisations to intensify the struggle at all levels of society for women's rights. This does not only mean legal and political emancipation but full equality in the social and economic spheres.

Women and people with disabilities are entitled to live with respect, dignity and the opportunity to fulfil their best potential. Self-fulfilling prophesies of low expectations are no longer acceptable. We must all learn to have high expectations for all our citizens and witness what people are capable of, enabling each person to flourish and achieve at the highest possible level.

༄

While I was Minister in the Presidency, my father, who had been living in Mayfair with his second wife, Zubeida, died in November 2001, aged ninety. Although it had been twenty-eight years since my mother Amina died, I don't think he had ever been genuinely happy in all those years. His marriage to Zubeida had been arranged in India by Molvi Cachalia, who hoped that

Zubeida would take good care of Goolam. It was not a success, and the Pahad family never became close to Zubeida and her relatives.

Meg was one of three people elected by a large meeting of education bodies in 2000 to establish a new Sectoral Education and Training Authority (SETA) for the education sector. The IEB seconded her, and this work continued for over a year. She was then seconded to the South African Certification Council (SAFCERT, now Umalusi) to work on quality assurance processes for Further Education and Training (FET), funded by German Technical Co-operation (GTZ) and later by the Department of Labour as a manager in the National Assessor Training Project funded by the European Union. In 2005, she retired from the IEB and became a quality assurance consultant for a series of projects over the next ten years, working mainly for SETAs, the Departments of Education, Labour, and Public Service, as well as some private companies. This kept her extremely busy until 2010, when she decided it was time to retire at the age of 65. Much of the little spare time she now has is spent in support of Project Literacy, a non-profit organisation whose board she joined as a non-executive Director in 2005 and became its Chair in 2012.

Amina was highly successful at school in both the arts and the sciences and had some difficulty in deciding what to study at university. She got into Wits to study medicine because people advised her that only people with marks as high as hers could get in. However, she found the programme unbelievably boring, with lecturers just going through the textbooks, which, as she pointed out, she could easily do at home without their help. So she changed to a BCom, and we made her finish the year before giving her a well-deserved year off.

During that break, Amina went to stay in London with her friends Lily and Jenny McNeil, whose parents, Anne and George, insisted that she stay there rent-free – and with a lot of food, too – for a whole year. They said it was their pleasure. For several years, Meg had taken Lily and Jenny to school at Paddington Green every day and brought them home to our place until their parents picked them up, and Anne had taken Amina and Govan to their adored gymnastics club twice a week after school and on Saturday mornings because we didn't have a car.

While in London, Amina's main pleasure was getting back into her old gymnastics club and with her friends there. To earn a living in London, she worked in an administrative job at a language school, which she later admitted had taught her that she needed a degree, as she found the work soul destroying and unfulfilling.

At the end of that year, Amina returned to Joburg and settled down to do a BCom degree at Wits, majoring in finance and economics. She went on to complete her Chartered Financial Analyst (CFA) certification while she was working full-time, which is not easy to do. After surviving an unrewarding year at JP Morgan, she joined Rand Merchant Bank in 2005, where she has worked ever since. For many years, she has been in its private equity division. Amina is a hard worker and a tough negotiator when doing deals for her unit, and she has earned a very good reputation as a sympathetic colleague and a successful financial manager.

Like his sister Amina, Govan had difficulty deciding what do but found a perfect start by doing his BSc and MSc at Wits in the APES (Animal, Plants and Environmental Sciences) department. He loved the field-based research, found the coursework well-designed, and the lecturers passionate about their work. He was also able to go to Costa Rica to look at flora and fauna of different rainforests.

Govan then completed a post-graduate certificate in education, but disliked the burden of administrative duties, so he qualified to teach English as a Foreign Language and went to Taiwan for a year, which he thoroughly enjoyed. His Kung Fu school in South Africa gave him permission to study Kung Fu at their top school in Taiwan, which is a great privilege rarely granted. Eventually, however, he decided to return to his interest in animal behaviour and completed his PhD at the University of Johannesburg in 2019. The title of his thesis is *Phylogeography and ecological niche modelling: reciprocal enlightenment.*

༄

I am adding a kind of postscript to this chapter, as I found a boxful of notes I had received during Cabinet meetings and in the Cabinet Secretariat. One of the most active message writers was Minister of Finance, Trevor Manuel. Because I was not consciously preserving them, I did not date any of the messages. However, I have decided that some of them are worth reproducing, as they illustrate the warm and cooperative relationships many of us shared.

Let me start with Deputy President Phumzile Mlambo-Ngcuka. During the time when Jacob Zuma was deputy president, I never received informal notes from him, as we did not have that kind of a relationship. However, his successor, Phumzile, was happy to communicate with me informally when she thought it would be helpful. In the context of the xenophobic attacks against many of the Africans already living in South Africa and the problems suffered by newly arrived refugees and immigrants (around 2008) she wrote:

> Cde Essop – President feels strongly about 1) Expediting prosecution; 2) Using the social mobilisation and mediation in a sustained manner; 3) 'Short lefts' by executive and MPs to explain and guide people and create our own stories; 4) Let's have a system to know where migrants are i.e. 'temporary exemption'; 5) We must not stop self-repatriation but resist deportation; 6) We must sort out without ambiguity the matter of provision of temporary shelter and do it asap. No people, especially children and women in the open rain; 7) The support of the army is retained; 8) Our short left must assist in re-integration back into communities. We must please ask the SABC and others to remove the provocative images which are offending viewers and hurting the country.

In another note she wrote:

> Hi Cde Essop, I ask that for introduction to your memo today you highlight that ... the response of the private sector call to employ unemployed graduates is positive. We want govt departments to be ahead of the private sector.

Some notes related to administrative problems around the residential arrangements for the president and deputy president. In one she enquired:

> Does it mean that the Tambo staff [at the official residence, O. R. Tambo House] that come to help at my home, which is where I spend most of my time, can no more do that? – i.e. to get support, I have to reside at Tambo? On p. 7, I think if you consider the work Sis Zanele [Mbeki] does, which we support and need, we cannot say there is no responsibility so emphatically ...

In the course of my work, I was asked to help Deputy President Mlambo-Ngcuka attend to several functions organised by individuals in the private sector, civil society organisations and religious groups. For example, I have a note from her agreeing to meet a well-known Guru from India at her home.

༶

The following are notes sent to me by Trevor Manuel – sixteen of them to give you a flavour of our relationship.

> Essop, I didn't properly respond to your question this morning. The issue of the exclusion of white women is actually a matter arising from the BEE codes compiled by the Department of Trade and Industry (DTI). I happen to disagree with their perspective (as you do), but we let the codes through without reading the details or properly debating them – and now we're stuck.
>
> Apropos your point on serving on the boards of private companies: I'm sure that you would deny Joel, Goolam or Louis from serving on the boards of, say, Anglo American. [I] would not allow any of my public servants to do so. It's worse if those serving on the private sector boards are DGs.
>
> We need a discussion on Murphy [Morobe – who had been appointed to work in the presidency] apart from handover. Murphy and I had a minor disagreement about the boards he serves on – SanParks, Old Mutual and Ernst & Young (which he chairs). Presumably you're aware of this and will deal with this aspect.
>
> A friendly word on press conferences: fewer, better but fewer – Eish, I always mix up the order of the words. But you get the drift.
>
> On the banquet, I know that my office did apologise early. I had an early engagement in Cape Town Tuesday morning. Did protocol act correctly? The latter was in response to my criticism of ministers [and] deputy ministers who failed to attend banquets in honour of visiting presidents or prime ministers.
>
> The YL (ANC) delegates remind me of you in your youth! They surely learnt this from senior leaders of the YL, and, in particular, Cde

> E. Pahad! Except that you never pulled down your pants in public.
>
> You remind me of what we used to say in Becker Street: 'Legal advice is worth what you pay for it.' This idea of cheap paluka (sic) lawyers doesn't work!
>
> Apropos the French election, the 2 candidates are not 'blue blood' French. Segolene was born in Dakaar, Senegal; Sarkozy's parents emigrated from Hungary, and he may have been born in Hungary.
>
> I thought you were a communist, of whatever shade – maybe even a light pink one. Why would you want to concession out a port – the most profitable port, actually? Somebody else would have to subsidise the rest of the ports whilst Temasek [from Singapore] hives off profits from Durban to Singapore. Where's the logic, Chief? Actually, my info has it that the president has instructed the end of the idea of sale/concessioning of ports.

That admonishment from Trevor was in response to my report to Cabinet on my visit to Singapore. I had been very impressed by the super efficiency of the port and the work of Temasek. I suggested that we learn from that experience and from Temasek. Certainly at that time, I would not have considered selling or concessioning out the work of our ports.

On another occasion, there had been a sharp disagreement between Trevor and then-Minister of Transport Jeff Radebe on whether it is better and cheaper to lease cars for the executive rather than buying them. The note I reproduce below also related to whether or not Cabinet had decided in favour of Jeff's proposal to lease, not buy. Trevor wrote:

> I trawled the Cabinet Minutes again yesterday. There was no decision to transfer either the Treasury Regs or Ministerial Handbook responsibilities to Jeff. He was asked to return to Cabinet after the detail of his memo; instead, he wrote to us: 1. There is no saving on leases – they're more expensive. 2. There are many ministers above the 70% benchmark.

My view was that ministers and deputy ministers had the authority to choose either to lease or buy a vehicle as long as it was within the financial limits set out in the Ministerial Handbook.

Many of Trevor's notes were light-hearted, like the two below:

> The reason why the National Treasury meets all the disability stats is that you, quite frankly, have to be crazy to work there. Mental disability is included amongst the other disabilities.

> Hey, Wena! You make me give so much money to Mali – and look how the ref behaved last night. That Malian referee robbed us! No more money for Timbuktu.

But he also raised salient issues which required attention:

> Would you please ask GCIS to examine the government website. I was looking for some info and found, for example, that the last legislation available on the Web was passed in 2002. The government website is also incredibly boring and needs a HUGE overhaul.

> I need to raise a matter relating to GCIS with you. [The] GCIS has requested finance for the Non-statutory Forces Pension 'buy-back scheme'. Regrettably, the scheme is only open to individuals who remained in the Protection Services and not to persons who were demobilised … I know that GCIS employs many former MK cadres – but they were demobilised and therefore excluded. Thanks.

> You are obviously correct about the IMC [International Marketing Council]. I attended yesterday, against my better judgement. The agenda arrived mid-morning and no documents were available until we got there. The presentation we discussed there until Rob [Davies] and I left at 4 p.m. was very, very different from the one brought here this morning. The issues I responded to were not in yesterday's presentation, were not discussed, so how do they enter the presentation this morning? Why is the IMC so undermined that within hours of its meeting you have new proposals? I advised them yesterday that the presentation carried no practical sense!

> My recollection is that the Dept of Health decided to have 18 sites

> around the country on mother-to-child transition using Nevarapine – these sites were supposed to give us clarity on the use of ARV[s] before expanding. [The] TAC [Treatment Action Campaign] then took us to court for universal access, which is what the court ruled.
>
> If I raise it, it looks sort of line function [intervention]. Please raise it. There is this sense of limitless resources, and while we're about it, spend it all on health. Properly costed programmes with measurable outcomes should be the route. H-E-L-P.

My guess is that that plea was about the National Health Insurance Scheme that Minister of Health Manto Tshabalala-Msimang was punting vigorously. Trevor was correct: the Department of Health memos failed to produce a viable financial and resource-based plan.

In response to a Cabinet memo from Marthinus van Schalkwyk, a leader of the National Party, Trevor sent me a note:

> When was M. J. Boonzaaier appointed as a Cabinet Minister? See memos 5.1, 5.2 and 5.3, etc. Should you not advise Marthinus that he should sign [the memo]? I raised the matter with Marthinus and he replied: 'Thank you for drawing my attention to it. I signed the cover letters, and I suppose the Cabinet Secretariat accepted it on that basis. It will be rectified.'

There were two messages from him on Zimbabwe on different dates. The first one reads:

> Apropos your 'messages on Zim', 2 points – firstly at 3.2, I do not believe that we can say, 'our approach ... is not to impose any conditions.' It will not fly. Our ability to hold off the IMF [International Monetary Fund] is in fact premised on the introduction of conditions, as in the president's note. Secondly, at 4.3, we 'note that the operation has been suspended'. It has in fact been extended according to the SABC yesterday and today. In its present guise, the notes, I submit, will not fly.

My recollection is that I agreed with Trevor on both those points and made the necessary changes to the current affairs notes I presented to Cabinet. The second note on Zimbabwe reads:

> I suppose you heard what happened at the ZANU Politbureau last week. The PB said to Uncle Bob, 'Comrade President, we think that you should bid farewell to the people.' His reply was, 'Sure I will, but pray, where might they all be going to?' On receiving this note, I looked at him and we both smiled.

༄

Another person with whom I exchanged regular notes was Minister Geraldine Fraser-Moleketi. Neither she nor Trevor sat particularly close to me, so we clearly enjoyed exchanging views on a wide range of topics. Below, I reproduce a sample of these.

> I will reflect on internship programmes in comments in Governance and Administration tomorrow.
>
> On a different note. We are launching the census of [the] PS [Public Service] project in Kinshasa tomorrow – Kabila will be involved. This is one of our biggest projects.
>
> You did speak a bit too long, but you raised important issues ... so thank you for that.
>
> There is an ANC Policy Conference Resolution that a Women's Ministry should be formed – supported by the Women's League and spearheaded by SAWID [South African Women in Dialogue]. This counters an incredibly progressive thrust of MAINSTREAMING gender/women's empowerment. What is your take on this?[230]
>
> I had expected different conduct from you – it is not appropriate to act instinctively. If I had wanted to share that information with Lindi [Sisulu], I would have sent it directly. I do not believe we have anymore/anything to discuss.

---

230. I fully agreed with Geraldine's view and still do.

Now, Essop, don't be so short-tempered! I acknowledged what you raised and merely tried to reflect that it was widespread ... that it was even prevalent in the Public Service and we attempted to remedy it! So, smile! And know your comrades and friends.

With your Prof. in Governance and Public Admin [Anver Saloojee] as an advisor, you have become more sensitive to matters of governance and the state, particularly the Executive-Administrative interface, Macro organisations of the state, etc.! I am hence surprised at your proposal at 6.1.1 in the Current Affairs document. 6.1.2 seems logical, as duplication will arise in view of [the] closeness of the updating of the POA [Programme of Action] and the *lekgotla*.

I greatly value your wisdom and advice. What I value above all is the ability to consider another point of view – critically and dispassionately! Including competence does not detract from the president's role but it enforces the need [of] ministers to have greater rigour in recommending certain appointments. In this round of appointments, there was undisputed evidence of fraudulent representation – in those instances, the insistence by ministers – and their arguments were incogent. If that means that 'I do not want to be helped' ... then so be it, but that is less compelling than what I would really have wanted

In a note in the National Assembly, she said, What a tribute! Brilliant! Thank you!

My friendship and comradeship with Geraldine and Jabu Moleketi, which started in July 1990, has continued to this day, and I have great respect and admiration for their political courage, acumen, incisive thinking and discipline. In addition, they are wonderful hosts in their home.

From the late Ivy Matsepe-Cassaburri, Minister of Communications, I retained a few notes and share three of them below:

In the next series of radio communications, allocate Naledi [Pandor] to Tswana, as I am not good at it. I'm better in Sotho.

Whatever you have heard re: Telkom and some local company offer,

I have had no discussions. They were advised to speak to [the] Board of Telkom and make an offer, which I am informed is not really serious. But private equity partnerships may also mean stripping of assets and sell-off. Why would I take a strategic RSA asset and sell off like that? Even all the noises and aggressive moves by Vodaphone for sell-off of [the] majority ha[ve] not been finalised by me. These assets are very, very, very important to RSA.

I hope you are aware of the three very successful gatherings we had in preparation for WSIS [World Summit on the Information Society] in Tunisia in Nov[ember]: ICT and Youth – Africa-wide; ICT and Women – Africa-wide; and People with Disabilities – SADC. The last was the most exciting.

❧

I first got to know about Ronnie Kasrils in 1960, when he waded into fascist thugs who were violently attacking our peaceful demonstration against the Sabotage Act outside the Johannesburg City Hall. Since then, we have remained close friends and comrades. Regrettably, I have only two notes from him, and one is amusing but not printable. The other is simple:

Best speech I've ever heard you make!

And in response to the same speech, the late Kader Asmal, a minister in the Mandela and Mbeki governments wrote:

This is the best speech you have made – whether in Dublin, London or in SA. I am proud of you. Congratulations!

❧

I will end this section with three notes from Frank Chikane, DG in the Presidency and Secretary of the Cabinet. At eleven a.m. on the morning of a Cabinet meeting, he wrote to me:

The Minister for Defence has asked us now to make copies of the above memo [on the Hawk Fighter Trainer Aircraft System] today, as per his agreement with the president (as he stated to me). It is difficult for me to say [no], especially where the name of the president is evoked. I thought that you needed to know about this.

As you may be aware, I have a regular scheduled meeting with you on the following matters (amongst others): 1. Privileges of former presidents 2. Manual of State and Official Funerals. I hope that these documents will reach you before the end of the day today. We can try to convene a meeting of the Ministers Committee on Privileges of Former Presidents as per Cabinet decision, say on Friday this week. Otherwise, we shall have to do so either on 23 or 24 May, as we have to distribute documents by 25 May (Wednesday).

I am of the view that we can't deal with current affairs without dealing with the so-called 'Arms Deal' story. It is a bad story, and it is meant to impact on the integrity and person of the president. Unfortunately, the Minister of Justice is not here. The DG: Justice only arrives in CT at 11 a.m., which might be too late. I think we should do without them and make a public statement at the post-Cabinet media briefing.

Frank was always accessible and open to discussion. Like the other note-writers above, we developed a close relationship, especially when we worked together in the presidency.

MINISTER IN THE PRESIDENCY

The Road to
DEMOCRACY
in South Africa
Volume 5, African Solidarity
Part 2

The Road to
DEMOCRACY
in South Africa
Volume 3, International Solidarity
PART 2

South African Democracy Education Trust

Chapter 10
Timbuktu, SADET and the FIFA World Cup

TIMBUKTU, SADET AND THE FIFA WORLD CUP

As I explained in the previous chapter, alongside my work as the Minister in the Presidency, I was deeply involved in three projects that were very close to my heart and took up huge amounts of time and energy. Not long after I was appointed, the president asked me to do my best to follow up on his promise to the President of Mali concerning the preservation of the Timbuktu manuscripts. This work was completed successfully in 2009, soon after my resignation. The second massive undertaking was the South African Democracy Education Trust, which I chaired for nearly thirteen years. The board completed its mandated task and then handed over the project to the Thabo Mbeki Foundation (TMF) in 2013. The TMF is still actively pursuing further work in this context. And the third special commitment I made was to assist in ensuring South Africa's winning the bid to hold the 2010 FIFA World Cup and follow this by demonstrating to the whole world that we were capable of managing that event with outstanding success. I was active throughout the process, even though by 2010, I was no longer in the Cabinet. Below is an outline of those special projects.

The Timbuktu Manuscript Project

When writing about this project, I was fortunate to be able to utilise the rich information contained in the book *Building an African Partnership: The Ahmed Baba Institute's New Library Archive in Timbuktu*, published by the South Africa-Mali Timbuktu Manuscript Trust.[231]

The marvellous journey of that project began after President Mbeki's state visit to Mali and Timbuktu in November 2001. He was moved by the vast collection of critical and irreplaceable written materials stored in the Ahmed Baba Institute, which had collected about 19,000 ancient manuscripts, many of which had been saved in private homes for centuries. But, as he says in the foreword to the book, Mbeki was also shocked at the 'poor storage conditions in which the Centre's great and invaluable store of knowledge contained in

---

231. Shamil Jeppie, 2011.

its books and manuscripts was kept'. He raised the matter with then-President of Mali, Alpha Oumar Konaré, and agreement was reached that South Africa would do what it could to help rebuild and preserve that library. South Africa would provide assistance in three main areas: a 'proper housing' solution for the manuscripts; conservation training; and promotion of awareness of the manuscripts through research, publication and exhibitions.

On his return to South Africa, Mbeki raised the matter with several of us working in his office and with Rick Menell, who immediately agreed to donate some money to kick-start the project. But there needed to be a dedicated structure to conceptualise the steps to be taken and to raise funds to construct the new building, so I approached Mbeki. When I said that it was vital that we set up the necessary mechanism and that I would be most willing to lead such a process, he gave me the go-ahead.

After consulting with several people, we set up the South Africa-Mali Timbuktu Manuscripts Trust, whose members were:

Dr Essop Pahad (Chairperson)
HE Sinaly Coulibaly – Ambassador of Mali to South Africa
Ntombazana Botha – Deputy Minister of Arts and Culture
Ebrahim Rasool
Rick Menell
Mary Slack
Dr Snowy Khoza
Shaheen Ebrahim
Adnaan Mia
Akhtar Thokan
Shaboodien Roomaney.

My deepest gratitude goes to members of the Trust and COESSA Holdings for their time, energy, resources and drive; COESSA agreed to participate and lead the team in every facet of putting up such a building without any payment. Throughout the project, they at times had to use their own funds and never asked to be reimbursed – a wonderful gesture of solidarity and selflessness. Special credit should go to Shaboodien Roomaney and Adam Essa for assembling the building team and ensuring the success of the project.

I would like to record our appreciation of the technical building team from South Africa, which was made up of people from the following firms:

Target Projects, dhk Architects, Twothink Architecture, LDM Quantity Surveyors, Letshabile Consultants, Goesain Johardien and Associates, WBHO (formerly Wilson Bayly Holmes) and COESSA. And the team from Mali: Sandy Construction, Socotec and Baba Cissé.

Some of the individuals who played a prominent role and without whom the project could not have succeeded include: HE Oupa Mokou, Ambassador to Mali from South Africa and former Ambassador, Thomas Mathoma; Riason Naidoo, Graham Dominy and Alexio Motsi of the National Archives and Records Service; Louis du Plooy and Anver Saloojee from my office as Minister in the Presidency; Irma Weenink from the Development Bank of South Africa; Terence Smith; Graham Clarence; Mark Stone; Jerome Voller; Jako van Heerden; Goesain Johardien; Ashley Ruiters; Andre Spies; Faghmie Christians; Hanief Dollie; Shabir Ismail; Adam Essa; A. K. Lockhat; Dr Shamil Jeppie; Najmie Benjamin; Abdullah Toefy; Abubakker Davids; Armien Hartley; Salie Benjamin; Anwa Benjamin; Saliem Peters; Ebrahim Sapud; Seydou Traoré; Issa Traoré; and Ibrahim Cissé.

The names of the professionals, artisans, technicians and construction workers who participated are listed in the book about the Timbuktu Library project.

Many thanks are due to all the sponsors who made generous donations to support this monumental project. The major donors are listed below:

South African Government departments: The Presidency, Arts and Culture, Foreign Affairs, Treasury, Office of the Western Cape Premier.

Ministries of the Republic of Mali: The Presidency, Higher Education and Secondary Research, Foreign Affairs, International Co-operation.

Private donors: Oasis Group Holdings, Mary Slack, the Development Bank of South Africa, the Oppenheimer Trust, South African Airways, MTN, Midas Earthcote, Mvelaphanda, Transnet, Media 24, South African Breweries, BHP Billiton, BSA Bank, Cell C, LNM Holdings, Tata Afrika, African Rainbow Minerals, AngloGold, Annex Midrand, Telkom, SDPS, Eskom, HBZ Bank, Iscor, Standard Bank, Interair, Sahara, BMW, Toyota.

The Kingdom Foundation in Saudi Arabia and the International Financial Advisors in Kuwait were also donors.

We also raised significant amounts of money from the Muslim communities in Gauteng, Durban and Cape Town and are proud of them and their generosity.

One of my first tasks as the chairperson was to visit Bamako, capital of Mali, and sign the joint cooperation agreement. Brigitte Mabandla, Deputy Minister of Arts and Culture, was part of our delegation. Our Malian counterpart was their Minister of Education, the late Mamadou Lamine Traoré, who was a gracious and welcoming host. One of my heroes had been the former leader of Mali and its first president, Modibo Keïta. I was hesitant to express my admiration for Keïta, not knowing what my host's reaction would be, but he responded by saying that Keïta was one of Mali's great liberation heroes and directed me to his statue and library. I duly went and found a massive statue of him, put up by the North Koreans in their idealised socialist realist style. I visited the library and was moved by the recognition given to Keïta for being one of the first African leaders to support and train our MK cadres.

It is important to give credit to Riason Naidoo, who was employed by the Department of Arts and Culture to head and oversee the operations of this project. He came into the project bilingual in English and French, had worked in museums, taught art at Wits University and managed cultural projects involving French and South African artists. And he loves Mali – the country, its people, Timbuktu and the Ahmed Baba Institute. Without his dedication, commitment, hard work and willingness to often act as an interpreter, the project would not have seen the light of day. He wrote an article for *The Thinker, Vol. 9*, 2009, entitled 'The South Africa-Mali Project: Timbuktu Manuscripts', which gives the reader a valuable account of the project.

The Department of Arts and Culture started in 2003 by funding and organising conservation training for five Malians identified by their government. Each trainee spent two months of each year between 2003 and 2005 in Pretoria and Cape Town under the supervision of Alexio Motsi of the National Archives, and Riason and Alexio (along with conservators Mary Minicka and Oswald Cupido) went each year to Mali to work with the group on-site in Timbuktu. Protective cases were made for the rare manuscripts using acid-free imported cardboard, paper and buckram.

As Riason explains in his article:

> But the task of constructing a new building for the manuscripts was much more difficult than anyone had imagined. Local building capacity in the capital in Bamako is limited to Chinese, Russian and French companies operating there. And in the desert in Timbuktu, there are no cranes, no sophisticated machinery and hardly any skilled labour for modern architecture. Modern building materials are a scarcity and have to be imported from the capital ... Last but not least, in the summer, the heat in Timbuktu reaches 50 degrees Centigrade.
>
> Timbuktu's remoteness also affected the project in more ways than one. While most of the nearly 1,000 km of road from the capital to Timbuktu is a tarred single lane, the last 198 km is desert – no road ... Material not available in Mali had to be transported in containers from Cape Town to Abidjan by ship and then by road to Bamako.

From 2003, Riason made twenty-two trips to Timbuktu, including the official opening of the building in 2009. After that, he went on to direct the South African National Gallery for six years (2009–2015) and is presently in France doing a PhD focusing on contemporary African Art. He is also an independent curator of a public art project entitled Neuf-3 in the cosmopolitan Saint-Denis suburb of Paris, where many people with African roots live. Participating artists are from Nigeria, Algeria, Central African Republic, Ivory Coast, Zimbabwe, Cameroon, Senegal, France and South Africa.

> I also made quite a few trips to Bamako and Timbuktu to check on the progress being made and to iron out problems that arose in the course of the work. On my first visit to that great city of learning, I was thrilled to see and marvel at the beauty of the Sankoré Mosque, both inside and outside. It was built over 700 years ago and continues to be used as a place of learning (Madressa), institute of higher education and prayers. It is also a UNESCO World Heritage Site, along with the magnificent Djingareyber Mosque, constructed in 1327.
>
> It was most fortunate that the President of Mali later appointed the Minister of Culture, Cheick Oumar Sissoko, to work with me. He was not a member of the ruling party but a member of a small party in alliance with

the president. He had a great respect and admiration for South Africa, its people and the ANC, and one of the several films he has made is a documentary about women in our country. He is a well-known film director, not only in Mali.

I remember that on one of the visits we made together, we were informed by the South African builders that the Malian company contracted to do some of the building had done a shoddy job. We were shown a wall so badly built you could make a hole in it by poking it with your finger. The Malian contractor was adamant that his company had done good work, in spite of the glaring evidence to the contrary. He thought his purported close friendship with the president would protect him, but Sissoko would have none of it. He insisted, together with me, that rebuilding had to be done at the contractor's cost, which indeed happened.

I had agreed with Mbeki that we should raise as much funding as possible from the South African public, and to that end, I organised a fundraising event on the grounds of the president's residence in Pretoria. That raised R13.5 million and was attended by the Presidents of Mali and South Africa. I have already mentioned the major donors. I think the whole project cost about R60 million. Of course, this does not take into account the enormous amount of money saved by the project due to the many individuals who gladly contributed their services and expertise free of charge.

The Trust had regular meetings in Pretoria and Cape Town, during which we received reports and updates on the project progress and the numerous difficulties and problems faced by the South African building team. But no challenge fazed the members of the Trust, who went beyond their original aims, which were to renovate the building, train conservators and equip the Ahmed Baba Institute with the latest equipment. Following our involvement, the manuscripts were safe and preserved and gradually being made accessible to researchers and scholars through digitisation. The library also has air conditioning and reading areas and a sophisticated climate control system for the storage and conservation areas located underground, preserving the manuscripts in a naturally cool environment. Culturally appropriate furniture was also provided and work stations established. Equipped and furnished individual studios were included in the new building, which can host a dozen visiting researchers at a time, for any length of time, who can now come to Timbuktu to study the contents of the manuscripts in situ and be hosted in comfortable lodgings.

After I resigned as a minister in September 2008, we continued with the

Trust with the agreement and support of President Motlanthe. In January 2009, the monumental Timbuktu project was celebrated with the opening of the new building by the President of Mali, Amadou Toumani Touré, and President Kgalema Motlanthe of South Africa.

On every visit to Mali, I learned something new. Sissoko was a wonderful host, warm, friendly and engaging. On one visit, he organised a dinner on the Timbuktu dunes. It was a warm evening, with locally spun traditional cotton blanket carpets on the ground and Malian musicians and dancers to entertain us. The Malians were wearing their national dress, including a kind of turban known as a *litham* in Arabic. Sissoko took one of these and carefully wrapped it round my head. As we were enjoying that lovely evening, one of our delegation came to me and whispered, 'Look inside the turban.' I did, and saw a label 'Made in China'. Later, at an appropriate moment, I asked Sissoko why their traditional headgear was not made in Mali. Indeed, why was it that Mali, which grows and produces high-quality cotton, did not have even one textile factory. He was embarrassed by my questions and merely said that the one attempt at opening a textile manufacturing enterprise had failed, and no one had tried again. We both agreed that Mali should beneficiate its raw materials.

That day in January 2009, when the building was officially opened by the two presidents in the presence of a South African delegation, including former President Thabo Mbeki, members of the Trust, the building team and me, will forever remain in my memory. I was thrilled and overwhelmed with emotion, just managing to hold back my tears until the ceremony was over and I was in my hotel room. I was so proud of all the South Africans who had contributed to the project, demonstrating that African unity and cohesion were possible and a worthwhile engagement. In his article in *The Thinker*, Riason Naidoo captures the mood most eloquently:

> A lively reception of music and festivity greeted us as we walked off the planes onto the tarmac ... local dignitaries in colourful and intricately embroidered boubous (the elegant West African male attire) lined the red carpet ... The short route from the airport to the city was lined with scores of Touareg men dressed in traditional warrior costume and accessories, majestically mounted on camels.

The large South African delegation included South African musicians, with a solo performance by Thandiswa Mazwai. As the author of the book *Building an African Partnership* put it so succinctly:

> The opening was a great celebration, a moment of joy. But for many of the South Africans involved, it was also a moment of sadness. Many had spent years involved in various stages of the project. Some had spent months living in Timbuktu and had made new friends in the town. It had become a home from home. Now they were preparing to pack up and move on to the next project ... back home in South Africa.[232]

In my preface to the Timbuktu book, I expressed my gratitude to all who contributed to the success of the project and also captured my own feelings:

> As Chairman of the South Africa-Mali Timbuktu project, I have been intimately involved in the endeavour to preserve the awe-inspiring manuscript collection in Timbuktu. It has been one of the most satisfying undertakings I have ever been involved in.
>
> My own participation in the struggle against colonialism, imperialism, racism and apartheid was always imbued with a passionate commitment to African unity and to the struggle against neo-colonial domination of the continent's economic, political and cultural development. From the outset of this project, we were driven by the imperative that the inspiring African cultural, educational, artistic, intellectual and literary heritage reflected in the manuscripts of Timbuktu should be communicated to the people of South Africa; that we should utilise the project to enhance and deepen the knowledge of South Africans about the rich history and heritage of our continent. Conserving the manuscripts and improving the facilities and conditions for the study of these works became a driving force for the members of the Trust.
>
> It is hoped that the struggle to combat negative, racist stereotyping of Africa, its history, culture, languages and traditions will be strengthened by the publication of this book. In it we reflect on our cooperation with the Malians, the design and architecture, the building process, with all the pain, anxiety and pleasure this entailed,

---

232. Shamil Jeppie, *Building an African Partnership*.

and the voices of some of those who devoted themselves to building this centre of learning, research, meditation and prayer.

The project was inspired by the ANC's vision, as well as that of our democratic government, to build and sustain solidarity and friendship amongst the people of our continent. It is our hope that the project, so vividly captured in this book, will further enhance and deepen the bond of friendship and mutual respect between the people of Mali and the people of South Africa.

As the project evolved and took shape, the distance that separates Timbuktu from our cities and towns was often forgotten; Timbuktu became part of our lives. The venture was given greater prominence when it was adopted as NEPAD's first cultural project. ...

This book celebrates one of the most tangible and rewarding outcomes of our wonderful engagement with our Malian sisters and brothers, and we thank Andre Spies, Shamil Jeppe and Irma Weenik for ensuring its publication. Please read and enjoy it in the name of African unity and the African Renaissance![233]

As part of our endeavours to inform, educate and inspire South Africans about Timbuktu and the manuscripts, Dr Shamil Jeppie convened a conference in Cape Town at UCT, where he brought together Arab manuscript experts from Timbuktu and other parts of the world. After long negotiations, we were able to convince the authorities at the Ahmed Baba Institute to allow us to bring an exhibition of about forty manuscripts to South Africa. They were very correct in expressing their fear that these irreplaceable and invaluable documents could be damaged. However, we knew exactly how to care for these treasures and were able to exhibit them and return them to Timbuktu in exactly the same state with no damage at all. The exhibition was hosted by IZIKO at the Castle of Good Hope, and many thousands of South Africans took the opportunity to see those priceless documents. I remain proud to have been part of the team that arranged it.

Ahmed Baba (1556–1627) was a great scholar, producing some fifty-six works on law, governance, philosophy, race and slavery. In 1591, during the invasion of Timbuktu by Morocco, he was arrested and taken to Marrakesh

---

233. Shamil Jeppie, *Building an African Partnership*.

as a prisoner. But his fame was so widespread that he was allowed to teach and lecture to scholars while imprisoned. Those involved in the Timbuktu project hoped that their work would bring to the attention of South Africans the life and profound works of that great son of Africa. As Thabo Mbeki wrote in the foreword to the book:

> Through the extraordinary literature in its collection, the Ahmed Baba Institute makes the unequivocal statement that Africa had established great traditions and institutions of learning. Eurocentric racism and colonialism denigrated our past and our institutions, even claiming that Africa has no history to speak of. We have the task and obligation to reclaim our past, to delve deep into all repositories of knowledge to rediscover the truth about ourselves. Thus should we respond to the challenge to interrogate the dominant narrative about Africa and create the possibility for us to imagine ways of making our past speak to the present.[234]

Much-publicised reports in 2012 of the destruction of the Ahmed Baba Institute's library by Al Qaeda's affiliate, AQIM (Al-Qa'ida in the Lands of the Islamic Maghreb), have proved to be false. When AQIM occupied Timbuktu, there was some destruction, aimed mainly against Sufi monuments and sacred tombs, and around 4,000 of the manuscripts already housed in our specially designed archive were burnt, but the new museum/archive created through our project was not destroyed. In fact, the leaders of AQIM chose to live in the museum, as they saw that it was the most modern and comfortable building they could find. The great majority of the manuscripts have been preserved, many of them now moved to Bamako. Also, many of the families who have treasured these texts for centuries still keep them in their hiding places.

However, the research and care that is still required has been interrupted, as the area remains volatile and access is restricted. The manuscripts are fragile, and we hope that it will soon become safe to restore them to their home.

Manuscripts which have already been digitised continue to be studied at the University of Cape Town, the Ahmed Baba Institute temporarily located in Bamako, and other institutions of Higher Education.

---

234. Ibid.

The South African Democracy Education Trust (SADET)
After he became president, Thabo Mbeki once more raised his concern about the lack of authentic voices and writers chronicling, critically analysing and telling the stories of the rich history of our struggle for national liberation, democracy and freedom from the scourge of racism and sexism. Responding to that concern, Seth Phalatse, then working for BMW, Professor Yvonne Muthien, then working at the Human Science research Council (HSRC), and I met at my office in the Union Buildings and agreed to respond to Mbeki's concerns. Yvonne undertook to prepare a concept paper and Seth to raise the initial funding. Both performed their tasks diligently, and after further discussions, we took the decision to set up the SADET Board of Trustees. Core funding to cover a two-year period was provided by Nedcor and MTN. The board comprised: Essop Pahad (chair); Professor Yvonne Muthien and Jacques Sellschop of MTN; Ivan May of Nedcor; Seth Phalatse; Isaac Makopo of the MK Veterans' Association; General Andrew Masondo, formerly of MK and SANDF; Vincent Maphai of South African Breweries; Minister Lindiwe Sisulu; and Professor Bernard Magubane. Sellschop left the board after his resignation from MTN in 2002. Selby Baqwa, a former public protector, replaced Ivan May in June 2003. Dr Meshack Khosa replaced Yvonne Muthien as MTN representative briefly in 2006, to be replaced in the same year by Nkateko Nyoka. Dr Eddy Maloka joined the board in 2005, and Joe Matthews in 2006.

The board appointed a project management and research team consisting of Ben Magubane (Project Leader), Dr Gregory Houston (Project Coordinator), Dr Sifiso Ndlovu (Senior Researcher) and Elsa Kruger (Administrator). In 2004, Houston was appointed Executive Director and Magubane Editor-in-Chief. In 2006, Ndlovu was appointed Director of Research.

The SADET moved into offices in the Nedbank building in Church Street, Pretoria, on 1 September 2000. Interestingly, Nedcor's office was once the Dutch Embassy where Klaas de Jonge, a Dutch freedom fighter, sought refuge from the apartheid regime. That office was offered to us rent-free. We also received donations in kind from the Strategic Fuel Fund, Tarsus and Compaq.

The project management and research teams travelled to various parts of the country to set up groups of researchers, which they did successfully. Their endeavours, supervised by the board and ably assisted by Elsa Kruger, enabled us to be ready for President Mbeki to launch the Road to Democracy

Project on 21 March 2001 at the Presidential Guest House in Pretoria. The launch was attended by leading business people, the deputy president, Cabinet ministers, representatives of political parties, members of the diplomatic corps, freedom fighters and members of the public.

All those involved in the project were elated to have achieved our successful launch in such a short time. In addition to assisting the management and research teams, the board had to draw up the deeds of the Trust, conditions and contracts of employment, establish bank accounts and find and equip office space. The board met every two months, and I chaired every meeting. We scrutinised and adopted research reports and financial statements and addressed administrative issues. We had embarked on a mission in which other countries had invested a great deal of money, but we had to operate with a small budget. Furthermore, all board members served pro bono and never raised the question of payment for their services.

It was a pleasant responsibility and a learning experience to chair those meetings, and I cannot recall a single time when we had acrimonious discussions or disagreements. After Joe Matthews joined us, we benefited greatly from his deep knowledge, understanding and appreciation of our history, and he would regale us with anecdotes about his past experiences. I found particularly interesting his stories about the fundraising for the Congress movement by leading Indian political figures such as Dr Dadoo, Molvi Cachalia, Yusuf Cachalia and Goolam Pahad. At that time, Joe was a member of the IFP but remained a firm, honest and trustworthy raconteur of the history and development of the Congress Alliance and the SACP.

As chair of the board, I read every research report with due care and attention, which enabled me to contribute both in theory and practice to the work of producing a monumental history of our struggle. Without the energy, drive and selfless contributions of Yvonne Muthien and Seth Phalatse, the project would not have succeeded.

All of us were over the moon when we published Volume 1 of *The Road to Democracy* in 2004, which represented years of unrelenting work, especially by the team led by Prof. Magubane. Volume I consists of 756 pages, made up of sixteen chapters and six appendices and covers the activities of the ANC, PAC, African Resistance Movement, the African People's Democratic Union of Southern Africa, and rural resistance and peasant struggles in Matlala, Zeerust, Mpondoland and Thembulani and on Robben Island. I had read every chapter in manuscript form and suggested a few changes. Volume 1 set a very high standard, and the board and the two teams were fully aware of the daunting task that lay ahead: to produce many more volumes of the same excellence.

In Volume 1, Mbeki wrote the foreword, and I contributed the preface. Below are some extracts from Mbeki's foreword:

> The superior lord, our antithesis, had a history he obliged us to learn and commit to memory. We, for our part, had to have no history except as secondary, peripheral, inferior and lesser beings, dependent for the discovery of our past on what our betters decided was our past.
>
> Thus it was that it was said, 'The hunters will always be victors until the lions have their own historian.' We too, the colonised and lesser human beings, could not be liberated and our humanity restored until we had our own historians to tell us the truth about our past.
>
> And it is only when we have discovered our own past and defined our own role in the making of human history that we will cease to be a great many different but inferior things in many places at many times. If we had not discovered and recorded our past, as we have begun to do with this book, we would have perpetuated the fate with lasting, indeed grotesquely unfair results of entrenching a definition of ourselves as having no identity except as the inferior antithesis of our former overlord, whom we would thus continue to worship as our overlord, even as we pretended that we had liberated ourselves.

And in relation to the outlook for the future after Sharpeville and the banning of the ANC and PAC:

> The irreconcilable contradiction between repression and revolution communicated the powerful message that the titanic conflict would be resolved either by the defeat and destruction of one of the contenders for a victory that could not be shared or the mutual annihilation of both.
>
> And yet, history was to produce yet another paradoxical outcome. In the end, the moment of defeat of one force over the other never came. Neither did the eventuality materialise that both should perish, locked in an embrace of death.

Rather, the belligerents sat down in conference and negotiated an historic compromise that gave the oppressed their freedom and the former oppressors their immunity from retribution by the victorious majority.

And for the future of SADET:

The history related in this book and its future companion volumes must therefore tell a story of the shared thoughts and untied action of leaders and masses, the combined organised force that took to the field of battle to defeat the sustained effort of consigning an entire people to secondariness, peripherality, inferiority and dependency.

I quote from the preface I wrote for the first volume:

SADET's mission is to examine and analyse events leading to the negotiated settlement and democracy in South Africa, with special attention to:

- The events leading to the banning of the liberation movements;
- the various strategies and tactics adopted in pursuit of the democratic struggle;
- the events leading to the advent of democracy;
- the dynamics underpinning the negotiation process from 1990 to 1994.

The study will result in the publication of five volumes, each covering a separate decade in the run-up to the first democratic elections.

The Road to Democracy project is a chronological analysis ... and covers the following aspects:

- The political dynamics of each decade, including the banning of the liberation movements, formation of insurgency structures, exile and [the] containment of resistance in the 1960s.
- The formation of key organisations, policies and objectives, membership and activities during each decade, and the historical role of individuals.

- The evolution of strategy and tactics of key organisations, including debates about and the impact of strategy and tactics on revolutionary developments.
- The response of the apartheid regime to the activities of the liberation movements, including changes to the nature of the state and the evolution of counter-revolutionary strategy and policies to contain resistance.
- The role of the international community in the liberation of South Africa and global events and processes that impacted on the liberation struggle.
- Regional events and processes that had an impact on the liberation struggle and the decision to adopt a negotiation strategy and studies of provincial and local involvement in the liberation struggle.
- The major outcomes at the end of each decade.

The banning of the liberation movements in the 1960s and the subsequent launch of an armed struggle led to dramatic change in the lives of millions of South Africans. Participation in the sabotage campaign and other underground activities, exile, military training and action, imprisonment, death in detention, banishment, constant surveillance and harassment, and general involvement in the struggle against apartheid characterised the lives of many of our people for the next 30 years. Recording this history is a major task and a serious responsibility that has been given to SADET.

From the outset, it was decided that this should be a truly South African project, drawing on the expertise of as many people as possible.

The successful publication and launch of Volume 1 nourished our determination and commitment to continue this important work. Three years later, we published Volume 2 (1979–1980), which has 963 pages and contains seventeen chapters covering the Black Consciousness Movement, the PAC and ANC, the Soweto uprising and the revival of the labour movement. Referring to the latter, I wrote in the preface:

> The revival of the workers' movement in the factories, mines and stores was arguably the most important development of the 1970s.

The mass Durban strike of some 60,000 workers in January 1973 was a catalyst event that reignited mass struggle and spurred the formation of trade unions. Together with the school student movement in 1976 that sparked the uprisings in Soweto and around the country and led to the first political general strikes since 1961, the Durban strikes – of which the organised workers were the backbone – opened the way towards the mass revolutionary uprisings that took place in the 1980s against brutal racial oppression and the intolerable economic exploitation.

In the foreword to Volume 3, I wrote that the Worldwide Anti-Apartheid Movement (WAAM) 'grew into the most successful global solidarity movement in human history. It demonstrated that collective action in solidarity with the victims of injustice can be a very powerful force for social change on a global scale'. In the last paragraph I said:

> This dialectic of struggle and solidarity is, without question, one of the most important contributions that the Anti-Apartheid Movement has left on the global terrain of the fight for social Justice. The WAAM, in initiating local, national and global political actions, redefined global spaces of protest and solidarity, and in doing so, made a lasting contribution to the development of global movements of solidarity in the twentieth century.

Progressive forces throughout the world should use the WAAM as a shining example of what needs to be done to embrace, promote and strengthen the international solidarity movement.

When I penned the foreword and preface to Volume 3 on International Solidarity, I had no idea that soon thereafter I would resign as an MP and Minister in the Presidency in September 2008. My resignation was in response to the unjust demand by the NEC of the ANC that Mbeki should resign as president of South Africa. In a later chapter, I shall write more about this event.

Since the SADET Board was an independent body, it was crucial that I continue in my role as its chair and that we publish further volumes of *The Road to Democracy* in South Africa. Mbeki was fully supportive of this decision. By that, time Sifiso Mxolisi Ndlovu (executive director) and Elsa Kruger (project administrator) comprised the project management team.

Their hard work, complemented by the contributions of the board, enabled us to publish Volume 4 (1989–1990), Parts 1 and 2, in 2010. Volume 4 consists of 1,693 pages with thirty-two chapters. Professor Magubane and Gregory Houston remained on the board and contributed chapters to that volume. I wrote both the foreword and the preface. In the former I wrote:

> Volume 4 is bound to have a significant impact on the historiography of South African revolutionary movements and will influence future generations of scholars in South Africa and abroad. The 1980s were characterised, to paraphrase Dickens, as the 'best of times', the 'worst of times', the 'age of wisdom', the 'age of foolishness', the 'season of light', the season of darkness', the 'spring of hope', the 'winter of despair'.[235]
>
> That decade of struggle, heroism and unprecedented mass mobilisation in the face of brutal and murderous repressive measures made it possible to secure the release of political prisoners, including Nelson Mandela, to obtain the unbanning of the ANC, PAC, SACP and other organisations. It opened the road to a negotiated resolution of a seemingly intractable racial conflict and conflagration.

After my resignation as minister, Sifiso and I discussed the SADET project with President Zuma. However, as former deputy president of South Africa and the ANC, he was well-informed about the work of the board and its published volumes. He agreed that Collins Chabane, who was then Minster in the Presidency, should be a member of the board and the links with the presidency should continue. The board was pleased when we gave them this information. But Sifiso and I were in for a rude shock.

We arranged to see Minister Chabane in his office in the Union Buildings (my previous office) to hand over SADET volumes to him to pass on to Zuma and discuss the arrangements for the launch of Volume 4 in the Presidential Guest House, where all previous launches had taken place.

When Sifiso and I arrived at Chabane's office at the time agreed to by him and his office staff, he kept us waiting for about two hours. I considered leaving after one hour had passed but I convinced myself that in the interest of SADET and not to seem rude as a former minister, I stayed. When Chabane did arrive, he was rude – and abrupt. He did not even apologise for

---
235. Charles Dickens, *A Tale of Two Cities*.

coming so late and merely informed us that he was about to leave for Cape Town and that we should also leave. However, I managed to get a few minutes with him to hand over the volumes and obtain his agreement to attend the launch and secure the presence of Zuma. Due to the minister's attitude, his staff were also not helpful.

Bypassing the minister and his staff, which I was most reluctant to do, I contacted Lakela Kaunda, a senior manager in the president's office, who undertook to brief Zuma about our request. Zuma had earlier consented to participate in the launch, which was set for a Friday evening – but on that morning, Sifiso was informed by Chabane's office that Zuma was not feeling well and that the event would not take place.

We ignored the warning, and Sifiso and Elsa continued their efficient work to ensure an effective launch. They were fortified by the knowledge that Zuma's office was supportive of the event and assured us that it would take place at the Presidential Guest House.

Remembering the occasion, Sifiso commented:

> I think for the event not to be cancelled, Dr Pahad directly got in touch with President Zuma's office, wh[o] w[ere] really supportive and made it a point that the event would take place at the Presidential Guest House at the Union Buildings.
>
> The only 'real problem and scandal' was that a majority of members of the audience kept on referring to Dr Pahad as 'Minister'; they were not spiteful to Minister Chabane, it was just a natural habit which needed to be 'checked'… they were not used to the word 'former' …
>
> As usual after these SADET book launches, 'Minister' Pahad was elated, as he was in [the] company of 'friends he has not seen for a very long time' – they attended the book launch event at the Presidential Guest House. But this was supposed to be Minister Chabane's event!

Following the publication of Volume 4, the board resolved that we should now publish at least one volume on African Solidarity. As it turned out, this was a complex and difficult task that Sifiso, with the assistance of Elsa, worked tirelessly to achieve. Sifiso, with some help from the board, first had to identify the authors and then persuade them to make their contributions.

Volume 5 was produced in two parts, with 997 pages comprising twenty chapters. Published in 2013, it covered Ghana, Algeria, Tanzania, Zambia, Egypt, Nigeria, Botswana, Zimbabwe, Lesotho, Ethiopia, Swaziland, Namibia, Mozambique and Angola. It also had a chapter on Caribbean and African solidarity and the role of the OAU, as well as the 2010 FIFA World Cup held in South Africa. Once more, I contributed the foreword and the preface. As a firm and committed fighter for pan-African unity, I was very pleased with the publishing of Volume 5.

In the foreword I wrote:

> The awe-inspiring words of the former head of state of Algeria, [Ahmed] Ben Bella, that Africa should open a 'blood bank' for the revolutionary movements in Southern Africa could currently serve to inspire and mobilise the international solidarity movement in support of the just cause of the Palestinians ...
>
> The OAU was instrumental in mobilising international solidarity and material assistance for the ANC and PAC. Yet, there were times when some African leaders, such as Hastings Banda of Malawi, Houphouët-Boigny of the Ivory Coast and K. A. Busia of Ghana were seduced by the overtures of the apartheid regime and succumbed to the subtle – and not so subtle – pressures of major Western powers to find common ground with Portuguese colonialism, racist Rhodesia and apartheid South Africa ...
>
> The solidarity movement in Africa had a global impact on the imposition of sports, cultural, academic, economic and trade boycotts as well as sanctions. One of the most powerful sports boycotts was the withdrawal of African athletes supported by Iraq and Guyana from the 1976 Montreal Olympics in response to New Zealand's continued courting of sports relations with racist South Africa.
>
> This was a magnanimous act of solidarity from Olympians who had sacrificed years of hard work and training as well as prospects of winning medals for a great humanitarian cause. The expulsion of white South African football from FIFA had a powerful impact on the sports boycott of South Africa ...

Volume 5 will enable generations to come to understand and appreciate the immeasurable contribution of African solidarity to the struggle for freedom, democracy, human rights and dignity in South Africa.

Following the launch of Volume 5, an unspoken feeling on the board was that our work was coming to an end, but we were convinced that we had to produce one more volume to cover the period 1990–1996. Sifiso and Elsa, with great enthusiasm, undertook this task, and through their outstanding work, we published Volume 6, Parts 1 and 2, also in 2013.

In the foreword to Volume 6, the last one I wrote as chair of the board, I said:

> The six volumes published contain contributions from leading South African historians, political scientists, academics, cultural workers and researchers. Hopefully, their contributions will enhance the study and theory of history. G. A. Cohen, in his book Karl Marx's *Theory of History: A Defence* writes:
>
> 'We may attribute to Marx, as we cannot to Hegel, not only a philosophy of history but what deserves to be called a theory of history, which is not a reflective construal, from a distance, of what happens, but a contribution to understanding its inner dynamic. Hegel's reading of history as a whole, and of particular sciences, is just that, a reading, an interpretation which we may find more or less attractive. But Marx offers not only a reading, but something more rigorous. The concept of productive power and economic structure (unlike those of consciousness and culture) do not serve only to express a vision. They also assert their candidacy as the leading concepts in a theory of history, a theory to the extent that history admits of theoretical treatment, which is neither entirely nor not at all.'[236]

I also quoted from the publishers' note in the book by Engels and Marx, *The Individual and Society* as follows:

> ... Marx's starting point is society, a definite social system which

---
236. Princeton, NJ: Princeton University Press, 1978, p. 27.

forms man. This does not mean that he ignores the individual. It means that the analysis of man should begin with the study of the social system since the latter provides the key to understanding the nature of man as a social being, a being that can manifest its distinctive individuality only in the framework of definite social relations. Man's essential features, his entire personality, reflect the totality of social relations that have produced him in his specific individuality. This discovery of Marx's made it possible to see man in the context of history as the product, and, at the same time, the bearer and originator of definite social relations. It put an end to speculation on the nature of man 'in general' and explained why different epochs produce quite different types of men.[237]

In that foreword, I also stated 'the SADET volumes demonstrate that, as important as political leaders are, it is the conscious masses, in action, that are the true makers of history,' and:

This is the last volume that will be overseen and published by the SADET Board. It is our earnest desire that the six volumes produced by SADET will serve to inform the people of South Africa, Africa and the world about our brutal, violent, complex, rich and inspiring history.

Our history should enable us to look at the future with confidence and optimism, imbued with creativity and a deep and everlasting spirit of Ubuntu.

Volume 6, Parts 1 and 2 comprise 1,480 pages made up of thirty-two chapters covering, amongst other things, the violence in KZN and the PWV region, the Bantustans, CODESA, the National Party, the IFP, the SACP and some issues around sports and culture.

Members of the board were satisfied with their work. The board had fulfilled its undertaking to former President Mbeki to produce at least five volumes dealing with the rich tapestry as well as the evil and ugly aspects of our history. It was therefore with great sadness that the board decided to dissolve and hand SADET over to the Thabo Mbeki Foundation.

Prior to that decision, I had discussions with Zanele Mbeki, who had first

---

237. Moscow: Progress Publishers, 1984, pp. 11–12.

suggested that the Thabo Mbeki Foundation might be interested in continuing the work. Sifiso remembers that at one of the meetings at the Mbeki home in preparation for the handover, where Zanele was accompanied by Mojanku Gumbi and Thoko Didiza (then acting CEO of the TMF), I said to them, 'I am handing over a warm human body (Sifiso) – look after him.'

For nearly thirteen years, the SADET Board carried out its responsibilities with commitment, passion and dedication. Throughout that period, Seth Phalatse played a monumental role, and, as chair, I pay a well-deserved tribute to him and the other board members. Credit also goes to Elsa Kruger, who worked so hard to ensure the smooth running of our venture. However, the greatest credit for the work of SADET goes to Sifiso Ndlovu. Without his commitment and unflagging energy, we would probably have ended up with three volumes. He took over in 2010 and single-handedly led the team of contributors who produced Volumes 4, 5 and 6, each with two parts. Thereafter, with the backing of UNISA and the TMF, he published Volumes 7 and 8, and in November 2021, Volume 9. Sifiso has also overseen the production of the SADET volumes in a more popular abridged form, suitable for, amongst others, school-going young people.

Sifiso is undoubtedly a leading historian in South Africa and the African continent, and my admiration for his patience, fortitude, intellectual abilities and research capacity, as well as his dedication to the publication and launching of the work, is immeasurable. I hope one day, the South African government will recognise his outstanding contribution to the historiography of our country with a suitable national award.

As I write this memoir, rereading the contributions I made and reflecting on the commitment we made in 2000, I feel a great sense of pride and pleasure at our remarkable achievement. As the years go by and recollections of our history fade, these volumes will remain a source of knowledge, enabling future understanding and appreciation of the immense resolve and willpower shown by our people, our movements, our trade unions and civil society. Let the values we fought for triumph!

The 2010 FIFA World Cup

The South African Football Association (SAFA), led by Danny Jordaan, Irvin Khoza and Molefi Oliphant, bid for the 2006 World Cup. They were supported by Issa Hayatou, President of the Confederation of African Football (CAF) and the Mbeki government of South Africa. We lost by one vote, that of Charles Dempsey of New Zealand. As Sifiso Ndlovu points out in his chapter on the 2010 FIFA World Cup in South Africa entitled 'Ke Nako! Celebrate Africa's Humanity':[238]

> FIFA was bankrupted by the shenanigans and corruption of its marketing partner, an organisation called International Sport and Leisure (ISL), which collapsed in 2001 with debt totalling GB£153 million ...

... and therefore, Germany was a safer bet to plug that financial lacuna.[239] On the same page, he quotes me as a member of the Local Organising Committee (LOC):

> 2006 was very painful. And I was there when the announcement was made ... Danny has said over and over again: we were the equal of Germany in preparations and the FIFA inspection team that came did not rate Germany much higher than us ... So it was heartbreaking. But the first thing we did was we went and congratulated the Germans.[240]

Danny Jordaan, Irvin Khoza, Molefi Oliphant, Thabo Mbeki, his government and Issa Hayatou were even more convinced and determined that South Africa should bid for the 2010 World Cup, that Africa's time had come. (*Ke nako!* means It's time! in SeSotho.) The Minister of Sport and Recreation then was Ngconde Balfour, a burly, well-built warm and genial person. He and I participated in the bidding process.

As part of that process, we were in Zurich at a FIFA meeting, and I approached Joseph 'Sepp' Blatter to seek his support. His response was swift: 'Minister, you have my support, but start with the head of the Union of European Football Associations (UEFA), which has a lot of votes.' So I lobbied Nils Lennart Johansson from Sweden, who was the head of UEFA.

---

238. *The Road to Democracy, Volume 5*, Part 2, Chapter 20.
239. Ibid. p. 905.
240. Ibid.

He was very friendly and assured me of his vote but then advised me to go and lobby other members of UEFA. As part of our bidding, Danny and I went on tour to Brazil, Argentina and Paraguay. We were warmly received in all three countries – by Julio H. Grondona of Argentina, Ricardo Terra Teixeira of Brazil and Juan Ángel Napout of Paraguay, who all assured us of their support. In an interview I conducted for *The Thinker*, Vol. 5, 2009, Blatter said:

> Passion isn't enough. We [FIFA] had to work extremely hard to overcome the negative view that no country in Africa is ready to host an event of this magnitude. ... To overcome this resistance we had to change certain regulations and introduce a system of rotation [which] was critical to South Africa winning the bid for 2010 and Brazil for 2014.

The bidding team was emboldened by the firm and enthusiastic support of Nelson Mandela and Thabo Mbeki. It was hard, unrelenting work. Morocco was in the mix and had strong support from France and other countries, including Senegal. The South African Football Association had produced a powerful bid book which included letters of support from the different spheres of government and the private sector.

In a letter to Sepp Blatter in support of our bid as an African bid, Mbeki wrote:

> The foundation of this bid lies in our resolve to ensure that the twenty-first century unfolds as a century of growth and development in Africa. This is not a dream. It is a practical policy. ... the successful hosting of the FIFA World Cup will provide a powerful irresistible moment to this resolute African Renaissance. ... We want to ensure that one day, historians will reflect on the 2010 World Cup as a moment when Africa stood tall and resolutely turned the tide on centuries of poverty and conflict. We want to show that Africa's time has come.[241]

D-Day was 15 May 2004, when FIFA was to announce the winner. Prior to that, we had the support of three Nobel Peace Prize winners: Nelson Mandela, F. W. de Klerk and Archbishop Desmond Tutu. All three of them

---

241. Sifiso Ndlovu, *The Road to Democracy*, Vol. 5, Part 2, Chapter 20, p. 920.

agreed to be in Zurich as part of our bidding team, which also featured three of Africa's greatest football players: Kalusha Bwalya of Zambia, George Weah of Liberia and Abedi Pele of Ghana. No other country in the world could field such a combination of world-renowned personalities.

Yet, as formidable as our bidding team was, we were anxious and nervous about the outcome. After both Morocco and South Africa had made their presentations, the FIFA executive retired to debate the issues and make a decision. Mbeki had decided to return to South Africa, confident that we would win, and he wanted to celebrate the occasion with our people.

As our team, which included Irvin Khoza, Kaizer Motaung, Michael Katz and Michael Spicer, anxiously waited in a holding room, the ever ebullient Archbishop Desmond Tutu said, 'Let us pray and form a circle.' Then he turned to me and said, 'Minister, I know you are not a believer, but right now you are going to pray.' I readily joined the circle, and Tutu said, 'Oh God, I command you. I instruct you that you give us this World Cup or I will give you a …' [I will not tell you what he said!] That was a memorable moment, with our Archbishop instructing God in the presence of believers and non-believers.

My anxiety dissipated when I saw Mandela entering the hall for the announcement. I was of the view that Blatter and his team would not want to embarrass him by announcing Morocco as the winner. True to form, Madiba gave nothing away, and we waited for Blatter to open the envelope.

Blatter arrived with his team, beaming, white envelope in hand. Our hearts were pounding Then he pulled out the card for all the world to see the name 'South Africa', and the country erupted in joy and celebration. At last, the African continent would host the most popular international sporting event, comparable to the Olympic Games. Tears rolled down my face, and my delight was enhanced when Mandela stepped onto the stage to hold the World Cup aloft.

I immediately asked Balfour to lead us in shaking hands with the Moroccan delegation and praising them for their powerful bid. Then I resumed my seat, and the enormity of what had happened hit me. I wanted to jump up and down and shout, 'We did it! We did it!' But good sense prevailed, and with all the others attending the event, I stood up to cheer Mandela to the rafters.

Having won the bid, the real hard work was now to begin.

Allow me to add one negative comment. Michel Platini, one of the great football players of his generation and a French international, had supported

Morocco's bid, which was fine. But he bad-mouthed South Africa, exaggerating the crime rate and talking of the violence awaiting those who attended the games. In my view, his negative attitude toward South Africa tarnished his reputation on the continent. Let me note, however, that once the World Cup started, he became supportive.

Alas, large sections of the British media, including the BBC, continued their negative reporting about our preparedness to host the games – in ways which, at times, degenerated into racism. Sifiso commented on this in Chapter 20, Part 2, Volume 5 of *The Road to Democracy*, saying that one report claimed 'body armour was on sale with the team colours of your choice' and that English fans 'could be caught up in a machete race war'. Also that the designated training ground chosen by the English Football Association posed a danger because of the 'wild animals' and 'deadly snakes' that awaited them at the Bafokeng Sports Campus. However, it was not only the British and other international media who displayed hostility to our hosting the World Cup. As Sifiso points out, 'atavistic views about the African continent and African people in general ... were also articulated by the white-controlled South African media.' (p. 925)

With Sepp Blatter at the helm, FIFA over and over again stressed that there was no 'Plan B', only Plan A, which is South Africa. He also said that Mbeki had played a pivotal role in bringing the World Cup to the country.

Mbeki suggested, and Blatter agreed, that the Local Organising Committee (LOC), which was composed of persons involved in football, government and business, should contain Cabinet Ministers to enable close and speedy cooperation with all three spheres of government. Those included, over the years at different times: Sydney Mufamadi, Jeff Radebe, Jabu Moleketi, Nathi Mthethwa, Nhlanhla Nene, Maite Nkoana-Mashabane, Charles Nqakula, Nkosazana Dlamini-Zuma, Tokyo Sexwale, Susan Shabangu, Fikile Mbalula, Sicelo Shiceka, and myself. Sibusiso Ndebele, former premier of KwaZulu-Natal, served as director for about ten months. Since Nkosazana, as foreign minister, was frequently abroad, it was agreed that she would be substituted by her deputy, Aziz Pahad.

When Mbeki informed me that he was nominating me as one of the ministers, I was overjoyed. Never in my life had I imagined that one day we would host the World Cup and I would be a member of the LOC. When the LOC appointed its Executive Committee, Sydney Mufamadi, Jabu Moleketi and I were elected to serve on it. As the Exco had to process and discuss many issues before they were tabled at the LOC, which remained the main decision-making structure, this put us at the very heart of it. Attending those meetings was great since we were involved in all the details of hosting a World Cup and delivering one of the best that has ever been held. I was appointed a director on the LOC on 29 August 2005. Following my resignation as a minister, I resigned from the LOC on 26 January 2009 but was reappointed on 8 September that same year, When our task was completed, all board members resigned on 13 December 2010.

As a board member, and for the period I was on the Exco, I attended all meetings and was an active participant in all the discussions and debates on how to deal with challenges, such ensuring that our hotels did not increase their rates unduly. I also served on two subcommittees: the Legacy and Legal Committee and the Marketing and Communications Committee. I shall briefly touch on the work of the latter, which I chaired before my resignation in 2009. When I returned to the board, I once more joined that committee, which was then chaired by Selwyn Nathan.

Since I was the political head of the GCIS and Brand South Africa (IMC), cooperation was made easier. Both bodies played an important role in the marketing and communication endeavours and campaigns undertaken by the LOC and FIFA. We also had extensive reports back and discussions on the hosting and preparations of fan parks, which were an important FIFA initiative for people to enjoy watching the games as part of a crowd, viewing matches on a big screen. That committee, after much deliberation, adopted the Slogan 'Ke Nako! Celebrate Africa's Humanity', to which Tim Modise and I had made contributions, and it was agreed to by FIFA and the LOC. The Marketing and Communications Committee undertook a public participation exercise which led to the adoption of the main posters. Our strategic priorities in marketing were governed by the requirement 'to plan, manage and execute a world class event' and to 'protect, expand and enhance the utility of the brand' as well as 'develop an effective stakeholder management plan'.

As chair of that committee, I worked with several wonderful people, such as Rich Mkhondo, Tim Modise, Jerome Craig, and Vivian Casaletti, who later married Kalusha Bwalya. We had to interrogate and update the reports of those who were given responsibilities that included a media tour by ten influential journalists, preparations for 2010 events given as the preliminary, the main draw, fan parks, campaigns aimed at schools, football development, arts and culture, and areas of cooperation with various interest groups. Our work was overseen by the LOC and FIFA, and the recommendations and reports were well received. As chair, it was encouraging to find that the Committee's work was appreciated.

I remember well one particular LOC meeting when FIFA presented to us a proposal for the 2010 mascot, and Jérôme Valcke, its Secretary-General, was there. Fortunately, we had delayed taking a final decision to give everyone an opportunity to critically examine the proposal. On looking at the mascot image, I was struck by its similarity to the 'golliwog' once used on Robertson's jam bottles in England. Anti-racist organisations in the UK had campaigned against that trademark with measurable success. At our next meeting, I objected to that proposed mascot because it resembled a golliwog, my main argument being that it would be most improper and open us to harsh criticism and ridicule for pandering to a symbol which was a racist caricature of Black people. More so since the 2010 event was taking place in a country with such a terrible past resulting from the racist policies, programmes and practices of colonial and racist regimes.

The other committee members had no difficulty in understanding and accepting my arguments, and the persons responsible were asked to go back to the drawing board. They did so, and we adopted the mascot Zakumi.

Cape Town had to host some first-round games – at the very least, a quarter-final – but it did not have a stadium that could host a semi-final. My preference was that we upgrade Athlone Stadium to host first-round matches and that an upgraded Newlands could host a quarter-final. However, Blatter had other ideas. He made it very clear that FIFA was determined and adamant that Cape Town have a new stadium at Green Point. For him and FIFA, Cape Town, with its natural beauty and the magnificent Table Mountain, would be the centrepiece for attracting tourists and supporters. I argued my case, but Blatter and FIFA had made up their minds, and we had no choice but to agree.

I was keen on Athlone, as that suburb was composed mainly of Coloureds and was a hotbed of resistance to apartheid and close to Langa and Nyanga. I also felt that an upgraded Athlone would demonstrate to its inhabitants and the adjoining areas that an ANC government was sincere in its commitments to improving the lives and livelihoods of the people and making it easier and more accessible for them to watch some workday matches. Moreover, it would have been a lasting legacy. Nevertheless, that stadium wasn't chosen but upgraded, and some participating teams, if they so chose, could use it for training purposes.

While the ANC's Ebrahim Rasool was premier of the Western Cape, we had no hassles, and discussions and preparations proceeded smoothly. However, when Helen Zille replaced him, the discussions, at least with me, became more intense and robust. Notwithstanding our differences, her provincial government came to the party and made a notable contribution to building the new stadium at Green Point. Her administration was also helpful in dealing with the negative sentiments of the mainly white population living in that suburb.

As a member of the Board of Directors of the 2010 FIFA World Cup Organising Committee I was acutely aware that we had a responsibility and duty to the people of South Africa and Africa to ensure that the media coverage met high international standards. In this context I first met Walter Mokoena in 2010, but I was already familiar the high quality of his work in both the public and private electronic media, and I was impressed by his profound knowledge of football and sports in South Africa, the African Continent and the World.

Walter, as the main host of our public broadcaster's coverage, did an outstanding job. We became good friends and after he returned to South Africa in 2014 from a period spent in France we started to meet regularly. At the time of writing we have a fortnightly lunch date with Maurizio Mariano which we have usually managed to keep over the last five years.

I have always been impressed by Walter's determination to achieve whatever he sets his sights upon. After I got to know him well I found out a bit about his childhood. Below is an extract from the story he told me when we were discussing his background:

> I was born in Carolina in Mpumalanga. My father drove a delivery van for the baker and my mother was a domestic worker. I started primary schooling at the age of 5, in the village of Bushbuckridge. For the first four years our 'classroom' was under a tree. I matriculated in 1996 at Mphanama High School, where I was involved in student politics, culminating in being elected the youngest ever President of the Student Representative Council at the age of 16. Like most South African school leavers my English was poor, so I taught myself to communicate effectively by reading English newspapers every day from cover to cover, listening to English radio programmes and practicing at every opportunity. I paid for the newspapers by selling sweets at school and went to Johannesburg each month to buy the papers from the profit. I was determined to improve my communication skills.

Walter combines his love of sport and his talent for working effectively in the media with boundless energy and constant hard work. Since 2016 he has created and popularised both *Joburg Post* and *My Sports Book*, and he is currently returning to the problem of managing water, which he studied in France. His success is well deserved.

The LOC organised a Kick-Off Celebration Concert at Orlando Stadium for the evening of 10 June. Despite the cold, all of us present had a most enjoyable time listening to the great music performed by renowned international artists including Alicia Keys, Angélique Kidjo, the Black Eyed Peas and Shakira. From South Africa, we had Hugh Masekela, Freshly Ground, Vusi Mahlasela and a host of other great performers. That concert was a fine curtain-raiser to the opening ceremony and opening match the next day when LOC members and other VIP guests were transported by bus from Sandton to the Soccer City stadium. The LOC members, who had given their energy, drive and time to host the event, the first on our continent, were in a joyful mood. We were more nervous about how our team would perform that evening than the opening ceremony. I was thrilled that we were about to make history and that I would be an integral part of it.

The opening ceremony featured some fantastic performers from South Africa and the continent, including Femi Kuti, Osibisa, Hugh Masekela and Thandiswa Mazwai. We had twenty heads of state and about eighteen eminent world personalities, including Ban Ki-moon, the UN Secretary General, who were seated in a special VVIP section next to the VIP section. From our country, we had Desmond Tutu, Thabo Mbeki and President Zuma in that section. When we arrived at the VIP section, I noticed Evo Morales, President of Bolivia, standing in one corner of that room. I was surprised that he was not in the VVIP section and went over to greet him. Since I was not a minister at that time, I asked Jeff Radebe to accompany him to the VVIP section, which Jeff did with grace and enthusiasm.

Soccer City was rocking with the vibrancy of 90,000 fans singing, shouting and using the vuvuzelas. You can imagine how we all reacted when Siphiwe Tshabalala scored the first goal in the first FIFA World Cup on the African continent. Alas, Mexico equalled, and we had to make do with a draw.

After the game ended, LOC members and a few other invited guests had to endure the bitterly cold night for more than an hour, as our transport was late. But for us, that mishap could not spoil our evening. We had pulled it off and emphatically rebuffed the Afro-pessimists and racists who doubted South Africa's ability and capacity to organise the tournament.

On my way back to Sandton, I could not help but reflect on my youth, playing football in Becker Street and on the dusty grounds for Dynamos and other teams. I was so consumed in my thoughts that I hardly conversed with the other passengers. But when I got home that night, Meg was awake, waiting to hear about that historic night, and the words gushed out of my mouth. Twelve years later, I remain proud that I was able to contribute to hosting the 2010 FIFA World Cup. I am filled with memories of our LOC and other meetings, the ups and downs inherent in organising such an event, and the camaraderie amongst us in the LOC, the management team and our inter-ministerial team. For me, those ranked with my feelings when we celebrated our victory in the 1994 elections.

To conclude this section, I reproduce a contribution written by the Chair of the LOC and the Head of the Premier League in South Africa, the indomitable Irvin Khoza, whose kind words about me I highly appreciate:

> As a South African, it is near impossible to encounter Essop Pahad and not be struck by his height. He towers above everybody he stands with in the room. So tall he stood, it reminded me of my youth in Alexandra Township. We used to differentiate between tall and long. People who were referred to as lank – long – were so tall it was considered a special work of God that they could stand up and walk. They needed to lie on the ground for us to determine their height. Alexandra is famous for its naming culture. Something about you will earn you a nickname. Your height or lack thereof, how you talk, your skin pigmentation, your brow, how you walk, your shoe size, something about you will earn you a sufficiently descriptive name. Essop Pahad would have earned a name like *Malankana* – the long one.
>
> It does not take long after meeting Essop Pahad before it becomes evidently clear that it is not only his height that is towering. He is driven by towering ideas and action. He takes his interactions with people seriously, so he prepares. You better come prepared when you are going to engage him. For this part, in Alexandra he would have earned himself the name, *Touch* – touch is a move. This is derived from Draughts, a board game. When you play against a Touch, you require skill and planning, otherwise you will be guaranteed to lose your shirt.

Armed with a resolution appointing me to lead the bid to host the FIFA World Cup in South Africa, I had our first meeting with our government. Essop Pahad was the Minister in the Presidency. Until then, my encounter was from a distance. The Essop Pahad I knew was mainly through the media. The media played on and presented him as abrupt. The Essop Pahad I met was thorough and methodical. A thinker. A student of history and the world. An activist who never missed a chance to intervene where he sensed inequity, exclusion or any form of injustice. Yes, he was abrupt at times. He could not help it, he does not suffer fools gladly.

Right from the beginning, Minister Essop Pahad realised [what] the opportunity of hosting the FIFA World Cup would mean for South Africa and the continent. Every continent has good and bad things that happen, both natural and man-made. If you used the media around the world as your only measure, you will not be wrong in concluding that Africa is singled out as a continent where the worst of the human condition would occur. This is a continent that is not spared from natural disasters and bad weather. Like an evangelist, Minister Pahad would repeat, at every turn, the opportunity we had during the bid and how we would have an even bigger opportunity if we won the bid and successfully hosted the FIFA World Cup. This was the opportunity to change the narrative that Africa is where bad things happen to people, especially its citizens. He remained true and kept us awake to this opportunity throughout the bidding process, but more so when we prepared to host the 2010 FIFA World Cup. I thought of Essop Pahad first when FIFA officially announced [that] the South Africa 2010 FIFA World Cup was the best ever. I said to myself, Essop was right, we did succeed in addressing pessimism about Africa – our version, South Africa and Africa's version of the FIFA World Cup, was the best ever.

The 2010 Bid to host the FIFA World Cup was different in that all the contesting countries were African. Essop Pahad made it clear that we are not going to run a negative campaign. When the negativity started, he reminded us of our commitment not to rubbish any of our fellow competitors.

Minister Pahad took up the role of moderating the tone and manner of the campaign and preparation for the 2010 FIFA World Cup. This was over and above his active involvement in the meetings and the requisite travelling. He travelled to Brazil to consolidate the sixteen votes we had classified as being in the bag. The meeting provided a commitment that Brazil would vote for South Africa, but intelligence told us that the sixteen votes were not as firmly in the bag as we had been made to believe. Alas, the Dempsey fiasco was upon us again. It was time to pull out our biggest draw card. We requested for Madiba to travel to Trinidad and Tobago to meet Jack Warner. It would be a long and arduous flight that Madiba's doctors had advised he lessen. In the meeting, government officials, Minister Nkosana Dlamini-Zuma, Minister Essop Pahad, Minister Ngconde Balfour and Reverend Frank Chikane pushed back on Madiba travelling. Mention was made that if Madiba were to die on this trip, [it] would be a disaster. I remember thinking, if there is one thing Madiba was prepared to give his life for, it is South Africa. So I said, 'We will take the doctors with; we will use an air ambulance.' Then the words came out, 'What if Madiba died?' The part that I did not say out loud was, 'If there is one thing Madiba was prepared to give his life for, it is South Africa.' Minister Pahad responded in an agitated and disappointed manner, 'Are you mad?' he asked. 'He went to jail for twenty-seven years.' [But] I had not finished. 'You are mad and insensitive,' Minister Pahad concluded. The meeting was over.

Using another of our trump cards, Madiba did go to Trinidad and Tobago. There were numerous of those kind[s] of responses from Minister Pahad. After the announcement that South Africa would host the 2010 FIFA World Cup, Sepp Blatter called us to a meeting in Zurich, where he announced that he had a gift for us – the MATCH package. Selwyn Nathan's immediate response was a quip saying all the money will go to FIFA, and South Africa will be left with experience. Minister Pahad accosted him, kicking his leg under the table. 'How rude of you,' he said to Selwyn.

Minister Pahad's commitment to the winning bid and successful hosting of the 2010 FIFA World Cup was self-evident. He enabled and fast-tracked the legislation that made it possible for South Africa to deliver on the onerous FIFA guarantees without changing the republic's constitution. Sepp Blatter had a desire to see Cape Town hosting one of the semi-finals because of Cape Town's attractiveness to the rest of the world. Minister Pahad was instrumental in [getting] the Cape Town Stadium built – [in spite of] the pushback from the Mayor of Cape Town. Always an advocate for letting management work [proceed] without interference from the board, he once called for the whole management of the Local Organising Committee to be fired after a presentation he found to be lacklustre. The management team responded with an energy that was vindicated by FIFA declaring that the 2010 FIFA World Cup was the best ever.

In the last meeting of the Local Organising Committee, Sepp Blatter commended me for being a good Chairman. Essop Pahad responded by requesting that the commendation be specifically recorded in the minutes. That was kind of him.

The Government Minister in the highest office; the Activist; the Change Agent; the Liberation Struggle Hero; the Diplomat and Internationalist – thank you for throwing everything into our winning the bid and successfully hosting the 2010 FIFA World Cup. I remember the board meetings; our bus ride to Alexandra Township after returning from Zurich, where we won the right to host the FIFA World Cup; the impromptu prayer Bishop Tutu encircled us into just before the announcement of our winning bid; your phone being glued to your ear before the announcement – we suspected it was to the president. South Africa does not see how much you fight for it at every turn. They should have seen the fight you mounted to arrive at a representative mascot. Your welcome lesson on how imagery can be offensive gave birth to the presentative and inspiring Zakumi.

As a football man and a born and bred Alexandra boy, my best salute is captured best in your football name, Bra Stretch – the defender.

Sydney Mufamadi, Fazel Randera and Frank Chikane.

Chapter 11
Developments in the ANC and SACP

DEVELOPMENTS IN THE ANC AND SACP

I always looked forward to meetings of the NEC, which I thoroughly enjoyed, as they gave me the opportunity to meet, greet and socialise with comrades, in particular those who came from the provinces. We had in-depth and at times robust but not antagonistic discussions and exchanges of views on a wide range of problems and challenges confronting South Africa, the government and the ANC. In this chapter, I shall recall details of one NEC meeting and one *lekgotla*, which, hopefully, will give the reader some insight into the political overview given by the president and a flavour of the ensuing debate and discussions. I have refreshed my memory of these events by reading the notes I made at the time.

At the NEC meeting of 21 July 2006, President Mbeki said that the most contentious issues surrounded Deputy President Jacob Zuma – JZ. He stressed, as he did in subsequent NEC meetings, that there was no division and no fight for leadership between the two of them. Nevertheless, it was the first time in its history that the ANC had had to deal with such issues relating to an official. Mbeki said that it was the view of the deputy president that he (Zuma) was the victim of a conspiracy. President Mbeki then covered a wide range of issues, but I will only mention four that I think are important.

Firstly, our movement was elected by the masses on the basis of a detailed mandate, and Mbeki expressed confidence that the ANC would honour its undertakings and implement tasks arising from that.

Secondly, an urgent and central revolutionary task was to unite the entire movement under the leadership of the ANC and faithfully implement our mandate, which was to bring about a better life for all our people by being a caring government. This meant to improve the quality of life of our people, fight racism and sexism, uphold the rule of law, reduce unemployment, reduce poverty by half and ensure that vulnerable groups enjoy full rights and dignity.

Thirdly, on international issues, Mbeki spoke about the importance of the renaissance of Africa, calling on ANC structures to give life to government programmes since government cannot implement its programmes without the active participation of the ANC. The ANC is the principle driver of socio-economic transformation; and mass mobilisation is critical in taking forward the movement's duty to change the world – not only to interpret it.

And fourthly, the NEC was not elected or voted into power to engage in meaningless and destructive fights for leadership and pursue personal agendas but to serve the people. Mbeki stressed the point that ANC branches should be in the forefront of defeating corruption and maladministration.

That overview was received with acclaim and led to very interesting discussions. One of the first to take the floor was Jeremy Cronin, who was also a leader of the SACP. He said that the core issues raised by the president were also those that the SACP wished to raise.

Cronin spoke of the lack of capacity in the ANC to carry out its mandate and tasks. He said that in the terrain of politics, we have high levels of unemployment and poverty, which means that the struggle is also about escaping grinding poverty. He raised the issue of the need to develop career paths for young people joining the ANC and that we needed to build the organisation around campaigns.

Alec Erwin thanked President Mbeki for taking us back to fundamental tasks, pointing out that the positions and arguments of the Alliance partners created an impression of disunity and ill-disciplined factions. He raised the issue of differences on economic policies within the Alliance and gave one factual account of the gains and successes in some areas of socio-economic development in the country. Charles Nqakula, also a leader of the SACP, said that the political overview was a rallying call to unify our movement and decide what contributions NEC members should make to bring this about.

For Smuts Ngonyama, a fundamental weakness in the relationship between the government and the ANC was a lack of coordination. He raised the question of whether we could have a structure able to mobilise branches in support of Cabinet decisions. He also called for a meeting of the communications structures of the Alliance and spoke about the role of the ANC in Africa.

In her contribution, Naledi Pandor posed the question of whether or not the ANC headquarters had the capacity to execute the function of leading the organisation. Frene Ginwala stressed the importance of empowering branches to monitor and evaluate the work of government regarding all three spheres of government, pointing out that NEC sub-committees should be involved in this work. On the impact and influence of the ANC internationally, she recounted an incident of Brazilian students invading a conference in their country to raise their demands. They followed this action by singing our national anthem, *Nkosi Sikelel' iAfrika*.

Aziz Pahad criticised the Alliance partners for hypocrisy in their attacks on the ANC's so-called dominant capitalist path project and its popular mobilisation campaigns, designed to ensure that the ANC implements its manifesto. When giving input, he posed two questions: 1) Have we fully understood what it means to govern? 2) What is the level of political consciousness of the cadres in the movement?

Jabu Moleketi spoke about the role of the Secretary-General and that of the Secretary-General's office (SGO), calling on the SGO to focus on tasks arising and to come up with an organising plan, also pointing out the weakness of provincial secretaries and the uneven implementation of tasks across the provinces.

Nosiviwe Mapisa Nqakula spoke about the potential of ANC volunteers and the real prospect of turning them into cadres of a special type, pointing out that on our continent, people say that you have the best president and that Home Affairs has good immigration practices. Mathews Phosa agreed with the president's position on unity and cohesion within the movement and called on the Secretary-General to give us our marching orders. He said that we needed further discussions on the role of the ANC in government.

In my contribution I applauded the president for his political overview and said that this important contribution had to be made available to all ANC members. Regarding international issues, I informed the meeting about developments concerning Bolivia and the huge respect and admiration President Morales had for the ANC and the South African government. I also told them about his wish that a high-level delegation led by Bolivia's deputy president would visit South Africa to learn some important lessons. I then spoke about the struggles waged by Palestinians against Israeli occupation and domination, and mentioned the bravery and courage of one of its martyrs, Leila Khaled, even though I did not agree with some of her actions, such as hijacking aeroplanes.

The SG, Kgalema Motlanthe, in his contribution, said that the overview helps us to focus on our tasks and responsibilities. He called on the ANC to integrate veterans into their work and structures and recognise the importance of political training, ethics, values, and door-to-door work and campaigning. He stressed that no other political party in South Africa could mobilise the people like the ANC. He also said that we had a mobilising unit and that the SGO was undertaking a review of organisational design. My view is that ministers should be involved in policy decisions and refrain from attempting to run SOEs.

The second political overview I will mention is the one President Mbeki gave to the NEC lekgotla held on 19 January 2007, when COSATU and the SACP were invited to attend as partners in the Alliance. There, Mbeki called on the Alliance to examine what existing socialist countries were doing and the lessons we could learn from them. In that context, he had an extensive look at the People's Republic of China and found that their programmes were not very different from ours – and in some aspects, they were behind us. The People's Republic wanted to sustain high economic growth rates and build a moderately prosperous society by 2020. They had a weak social security system and had undertaken to do a lot more work to improve it. Indeed, in this area, they were behind us, as we already had a viable social security system. President Mbeki pointed out that the Chinese Communist Party and government had had extensive discussions on what a socialist market is, in form and content; however, they were clear that ministers should not run state-owned enterprises (SOEs), as those should be run independently to function effectively. To that end, they were going to have a discussion we have already had in our country – about the relations between the state and SOEs. My own view is that ministers should be involved in policy issues and should refrain from attempting to run SOEs.

Thereafter, Mbeki raised issues and challenges confronting us and called for a reaffirmation of the general framework on the struggle against poverty. The central task, he said, was to ensure the implementation of our programme. To achieve this he pointed out the importance of bringing about higher economic growth rates, as well as growing investments in the economy.

Other issues he raised were: the balance of payments deficit; the need to speed up the delivery of houses; the need to speed up job creation, which would come mainly through SMMEs; examining the links between a comprehensive social security system, health system and fighting poverty; improving the capacity of state institutions; and the importance of mobilising cadres of the movement and ANC branches to intensify the struggle against poverty.

In the context of consummating the national democratic revolution, Mbeki made the critical theoretical and methodological point that the dictatorship of the proletariat cannot be an instrument of the transitional phase but is an outcome of a socialist revolution.

Following that overview, Jabu Moleketi, Deputy Minister of Finance and member of the NEC, made an extensive political input, making reference to some of Lenin's writings, such as *Two Tactics*,[242] *What is to be Done?*,[243] *Left-Wing Communism – An Infantile Disorder*,[244] and *The Communist Manifesto*,[245] penned by Marx and Engels. Moleketi spoke about how distinct the national democratic and socialist revolutions are and made the point that the national democratic revolution cannot be a democratic revolution and a dictatorship of the proletariat. He also gave an outline of the distinguishing features of socialism, and in so doing, remarked that you cannot achieve socialism by proclamation.

In his contribution Moleketi characterised some COSATU resolutions as unsound, lacking a Marxist-Leninist theoretical approach and at times descending into a vulgar application of that theory. He said that we cannot consider issues in the abstract but have to do so in national, specific and distinct circumstances and conditions.

In his assessment, the decision of the SACP to become a mass party meant that it would no longer be a party of the most advanced cadres, including those from the trade union movement. In that context, it would be difficult for the SACP to play its vanguard role in the political and economic spheres, and he warned against the phenomenon of tailism. He referred to the 1962 SACP programme and the one adopted later in Cuba, which recognised the ANC as the leader of the Tripartite Alliance.

Jabu's well-considered and thoughtful contribution was welcomed by the ANC delegates but not by COSATU. I regret that I do not recall the position of the SACP.

Zwelinzima Vavi, speaking on behalf of COSATU, said that they were ready to discuss any issues, including COSATU resolutions. However, it was an error for the ANC to discuss those resolutions in that fashion and make COSATU members feel that they were in the wrong place and that COSATU was being ridiculed. Still, the ANC hoped to lead them. COSATU would

---

242. V. I. Lenin, *Two Tactics of Social-Democracy in the Democratic Revolution*, first published as a pamphlet in Geneva in July 1905 and later that month as a book published in Russia by the Central Committee of the R. S. D. L. P. Available at https://www.marxists.org/archive/lenin/works/1905/tactics/index.htm

243. V. I. Lenin, 'What Is to Be Done? Burning Questions of Our Movement', *Lenin's Selected Works, Volume 1*, pp. 119-271. First published as a separate work in March 1902. Available at https://www.marxists.org/archive/lenin/works/1901/witbd/

244. V. I. Lenin, 'Left-Wing' Communism: an Infantile Disorder. First published as a pamphlet in June 1920, then as part of *Collected Works, Vol. 31*, pp. 17–118, Progress Publishers, USSR, 1964. Available at https://www.marxists.org/archive/lenin/works/1920/lwc/

245. K. Marx and F. Engels, *The Communist Manifesto*. First published in February 1848. Also in *Marx/Engels Selected Works, Vol. One*, Progress Publishers, Moscow, 1969, pp. 98–137. Available at https://www.marxists.org/archive/marx/works/download/pdf/Manifesto.pdf

meet and decide what to do.

It was agreed that the president's political overview and all other contributions would be discussed in the commissions following Joel Netshitenzhe's input on strategy and tactics. Joel's contribution led to an invigorating and interesting discussion in which some speakers made detailed suggestions on various programmes contained in the document.

In my input, I said that if we were to meet all the challenges that had been outlined, we had to involve SANCO in our endeavours. I then made five points:

1. To improve service delivery, ANC structures, including NEC and PEC deployees, would have to be involved; also that we had to eradicate the bucket system within the next few years, ensure supply and access to electricity in every home and enhance the building and delivery of homes.
2. I mentioned the critical role played by ward committees and proposed that provincial and regional leaders should utilise the potential of the ward committee, which would also enable them to perform their task of monitoring and evaluation.
3. I spoke about the importance of a National Youth Service and called for ANC members to be more directly involved in programmes pertaining to that service.
4. We were not optimally using the provincial MPLs to perform ANC work in their areas of residence and in the given regions and provinces.
5. I also called for a more effective use of provincial portfolio committees in the work of the ANC as well as that of oversight and the monitoring and evaluation of provincial and national programmes.

꒛

My responsibilities also entailed duties and activities as an NEC deployee to a province, and I was first assigned to the North West and later to the Free State. In this context, I had my parliamentary constituency office first in Klerksdorp and later in Welkom. As an NEC deployee, I attended PEC and REC meetings on a regular basis, got involved in some of their work and campaigns and resolved disputes amongst some of their members and structures. This was hard work and meant going to those areas on weekends, but it was most interesting and a continuous process of learning and facing new experiences.

When possible, I visited my constituency office one day each week to perform my tasks there as best I could. I had to attend to issues affecting members of the community, including businesses, which were brought to my attention, as well as problems and challenges confronting ANC structures in those regions. Thanks to parliamentary support, I was able to employ one person to work in both of the constituency offices. That person had to be in touch with the issues facing the people, not only in the cities but, more importantly, in the townships outside the cities, where the overwhelming majority of our people resided. The work of an MP allowed me to learn, and learn fast, the severe problems of poverty, unemployment, destitution and lack of housing, which were widespread. I was also able to interact regularly with the communities in the township areas. My one regret is that I was unable, owing to other commitments, to spend more time with ANC members and structures and the township communities in the area covered by my two consecutive constituencies.

In addition to my ANC work, I fully participated in meetings of the CC and PB of the SACP; I enjoyed those meetings and the robust discussions we had. Unfortunately, because of my other commitments and work as an MP, Minister, NEC member and NEC deployee, I was unable to be as actively involved as I wished in the work and activities of the SACP at local, regional and provincial levels. My main responsibility as a CC member was to head up the international department, which enabled me to keep in touch with Communist and Workers' Parties internationally, as well as several of their leaders.

I found my work in the party pleasant, refreshing and an ongoing learning experience, and it enabled me to raise my level of political understanding, consciousness and discipline. But there were some in the party leadership who were dissatisfied with me, along with a few of the other ministers and deputy ministers who were members and leaders of the SACP. Detractors started mobilising party structures and members against some of us, alleging that we were more interested in defending government positions than those of the party. They also claimed that we were neglecting our party duties and responsibilities.

In my view, those allegations were baseless, as our work as ministers was also directed at enhancing the work, interests and positions of the SACP.

Indeed, I thought it was to the credit of the party that so many of us were elected to leading positions in the ANC and government. They also attacked Mbeki again, against all the evidence, for pursuing neo-liberal policies and positions. And by association, they linked a number of us to him and the so-called GEAR economic policy.

The campaign against Mbeki and those who supported him was intensified in the period prior to the 11th SACP Congress held in July 2002 in Rustenburg, North West Province. A number of us, Jabu Moleketi, Geraldine Fraser-Moleketi, Sydney Mufamadi, Jeff Radebe, Ronnie Kasrils, Sam Shilowa and I were vilified and unjustly attacked with the accusations just mentioned. In the runup to the 11th Congress, it became clear that some, if not all of us, would not be elected to the Central Committee (CC). Knowing this, I attended the Congress, since I was still head of the International Department and responsible for attending to our international guests. I was of the opinion that it is always the democratic right of delegates to elect or not elect a person to the CC, and that my membership of the party for more than thirty-five years was a critical part of my political life and activities.

At that 11th Congress, many international delegates had been briefed by some in the party that several of us would not be re-elected to the CC. They were concerned and raised the matter with me.

One concerned person was the Chief Minister of West Bengal, who was also a PB member of the Communist Party of India-Marxist. He had met me before coming to South Africa and held me in high regard. He asked me what was happening and expressed concern and disappointment at the prospect of a split in the SACP and worried about my future work and role in the party. I explained to him that, as he well knew, communist parties around the world have splits and crises, including his own, which had split from the Communist Party of India, following the disputes and difficulties between the Communist Parties of the Soviet Union and China. The CPI-M were more favourably disposed to the positions of the CPC and its leader Mao Tse-tung. I took him through the difficulties some SACP leaders had with those of us who were ministers or deputy ministers. He understood and appreciated what I said, more so because the CPI-M had been the ruling party in West Bengal for twenty years and had had to deal with the challenges that arise from having leading party members serving in a government. He was saddened when I told him that there was a real possibility that I would not be re-elected to the CC.

Some of the other international guests from fraternal parties like Iraq, Iran and Portugal raised the same concerns, and I offered the same explanation. They also expressed their disappointment at the probability of my not being elected to the CC.

Those party members who opposed us had done their work of maligning and undermining us well, with the result that not one of the seven members mentioned above were elected to the CC. The organisers of that move had placed some of their supporters outside the polling booth to hand out a list of names of those they wanted to be elected, which, to me, was one of the lowest forms of organising and mobilising.

Nevertheless, we accepted the result without any recriminations, knowing full well that it would lead to malpractice and other insidious developments in the party. What I did not know at that time was that Rustenburg was the precursor to what would take place at the ANC's 52nd National Conference in Polokwane in December 2007.

Following the Rustenburg Congress, I was no longer an active member of the SACP but did attend party events, seminars and conferences, if invited. Today, although I am still not an active member of the SACP, my deep passion and commitment to the science of Marxism-Leninism, the World Communist Movement and the struggle for socialism in South Africa, Africa and the world remains as strong as ever.

One of the greatest difficulties and challenges confronting the ANC arose after President Mbeki asked Jacob Zuma to step down as deputy president in 2005. So I need to say something about my relationship with Zuma when we were both in the presidency.

For those who want a better understanding of the personality and politics of JZ and the relationship between Mbeki and Zuma, I recommend the book, *Time is Not the Measure – A Memoir*, by Vusi Mavimbela.[246] Vusi has a fine writing style and his story, logic and arguments are easy to follow. He worked closely with Mbeki and Zuma and, in his book, gives an honest and candid personal assessment of both leaders while recounting incidents and events in which I was involved but, in some cases, had forgotten. Vusi was the DG of the National Intelligence Agency (NIA) from 1999-2004. (NIA is currently

---

246. Johannesburg: Real African Publishers, 2018. Mavimbela was DG of the National Intelligence Agency from 1999–2004.

called the State Security Agency)

Joe Nhlanhla, a leader of the ANC I had known since about 1959, was Dullah Omar's Deputy Minister of Justice. According to Vusi, Nhlanhla approached him and enquired about 'who was advising Thabo on who to consider as his deputy president?'[247] They agreed that a structure should be set up for this purpose and that Vusi should discuss the matter with me. I agreed with Vusi's suggestion, and for this informal advisory structure, Vusi convened Joe Nhlanhla, Joel Netshitenzhe, Joe Modise, Steve Tshwete, Jacob Zuma, Aziz Pahad and me, with Nhlanhla and I as co-chairpersons. Vusi recounts that Nhlanhla, Essop Pahad and he had discussed 'the difficulty of involving Zuma in such a discussion'[248] but concluded that it was best to involve him since he was Deputy President of the ANC and, in any event, would hear of such a meeting. At that meeting, Nhlanhla 'opened the floor for discussion but there was dead silence'.[249]

> Essop Pahad broke the ice. He suggested that we start by characterising the kind of leader we envisaged before coming back to the names. That helped to thaw the atmosphere, but not for long ... However, the characterisation would inevitably point towards or away from certain individuals.[250]

Vusi then outlined his characterisation of the qualities required by a leader, which was accepted by the group. But then we still had to find a name. Somebody cracked a joke and there was 'controlled laughter'. But Zuma's laughter was different.

> It was classic Zuma, true to his African name of Gedleyihlekisa, which, loosely translated means 'rough them up while you laugh with them' – in other words, lull them into a false sense of comfort while you pursue your campaign against them by all possible means. In the 23 years I had known Zuma, I came to understand that his extravagant laughter was a defence mechanism and an antidote – in this case, against the incommodious atmosphere the discussion had generated.[251]

---

247. Vusi Mavimbela, *Time is Not the Measure*.
248. Vusi Mavimbela, *Time is Not the Measure*.
249. Ibid.
250. Ibid.
251. Ibid. p. 282.

Vusi then proposed the name of Joel Netshitenzhe, but he demurred. Nevertheless, the meeting agreed to his name, which Vusi then conveyed to Thabo Mbeki. Mbeki thanked him and said, 'Your meeting does not expect me to say yes or no.' Vusi is of the view that 'Mbeki was not comfortable about appointing Zuma as his deputy.'[252]

Zuma was unhappy about the recommendation made by the meeting and conveyed this to Lindiwe Sisulu, who in turn told Vusi. As it transpired, Mbeki had wanted Buthelezi, who rejected the offer. Thereafter, as Vusi points out, Mbeki appointed Zuma as his deputy (1999–2005).

As the Minister in the Presidency I had to work closely with both the president and his deputy. I met Zuma on many occasions, during which we discussed issues and challenges relating to the Presidency, the government and the ANC. Zuma always received me warmly with a ready smile and hearty greeting. However, I had the impression that he remained suspicious of me as someone he saw as close to Mbeki and not to be confided in. This became clearer to me as time went by, for example on his official visit to the Ukraine, which included Aziz and me. Without trying to hide it, Zuma would meet the rest of his delegation, excluding the two of us. When I pointed this out to Aziz, he merely smiled and shrugged his shoulders. Thereafter, in my many meetings with Zuma, I was conscious that he did not trust my views or motives.

I first met Zuma in 1984 when he addressed the ANC structure in London on the Nkomati Accord, signed by the Mozambique government with the South African apartheid regime. He spoke eloquently and, with clear logic, spelt out the consequences of that accord for the ANC and the struggle as a whole. He also spelt out and defended the decision of the NEC not to publicly criticise Samora Machel or FRELIMO. I and the other ANC comrades who attended the meeting were hugely impressed by Zuma and the briefing he gave us. From then on, I had respect and admiration for his deep understanding of the political issues and challenges facing the ANC, SACP, FRELIMO and the Mozambican Government. Indeed, we were both on the CC of the SACP and elected to that position at the Party Congress in Cuba in 1989. However, despite his warm and cordial manner, he kept his distance from me and very seldom confided in me about his views on the Cabinet, the ANC or the Tripartite Alliance. While reflecting on that relationship, I am reminded of the words of Vusi Mavimbela, which I quoted earlier, on the meaning of Gedleyihlekisa.

---

252. Ibid. p 287.

Although Mbeki and Zuma professed to a good working relationship, many members of the NEC and people working with them in government doubted their assertions and detected an underlying hostility. Nevertheless, I tried to serve Zuma as best I could in the government, presidency and ANC. My position was clear: Zuma was the Deputy President of South Africa and the ANC, and therefore one of my leaders in both structures.

Yet, I was concerned, but kept it to myself, about Zuma's financial position since he took on so many commitments to his nuclear and extended families. Given what has since emerged about his economic plight, difficulties and associates, and knowing his salary and the number of wives and children he had, I should have been more concerned. I regret that I did not use the opportunities I had to raise those matters with the president and within the official structures of the ANC and SACP.

Below are a few more comments from Vusi Mavimbela's book which are relevant to my work at that time. He writes:

> Shortly after joining Mbeki's office, Essop Pahad and I had an animated discussion. I had great respect for Pahad's encyclopaedic knowledge of the history of communist and workers' parties around the world. His time in Prague ... enriched his knowledge immensely.[253]

Vusi goes on to say that we discussed the drafting of the new constitution, in which I was involved. In his view the 'Constitution would have the effect of disarming the ANC from radically transforming society', was 'a worrying liberal document' and that 'people like him [Essop Pahad] had allowed themselves to be diluted by liberal constitutional experts in the ANC.'[254] He continues:

> Pahad argued that the Constitution did not prevent transformation if the ANC had the political will ... He made the point that the world had a great hope that South Africa would become a beacon of progressive thought, not only in Africa but in the developing world. The Constitution, he argued, was a good starting point in demonstrating our leadership in the progressive world. We agreed to disagree.[255]

---

253. Vusi Mavimbela, *Time is Not the Measure*.
254. Ibid. p. 253.
255. Ibid. p 255

He also commented:

> I appreciated Essop Pahad's continued participation in the SACP ... There was a need for a left ideological orientation in the Alliance to keep ideological drift in the ANC in check. Working people needed a voice that would continue to provide Marxist instruments of analysis in understanding human developments.[256]

To return to the growing tensions and differences between President Mbeki and Deputy President Zuma, I was aware of this problem and, together with Frank Chikane and Vusi, we tried to arrange regular meetings between the two, but as Vusi records in his memoir, this was not successful and the 'tensions continued to fester'.[257]

Following Judge Hilary Squires' judgement in the Schabir Shaik case, where Zuma was mentioned as benefiting from large sums of money over a long period, Mbeki addressed the National Assembly on 15 June 2005 and announced that he was relieving Zuma of his position as deputy president. As I understand it, Mbeki had hoped that Zuma would voluntarily step down, but since he refused to do so, Mbeki felt that he had to release Zuma from his positions as deputy president and member of the Cabinet.

So the die was cast, and Zuma felt free to engage in a multipronged attack on Mbeki within the ANC and the Alliance structures. Within the latter, he was sowing seeds on fertile soil, and the SACP and COSATU started wrongly accusing Mbeki – without presenting a shred of evidence – of undermining democratic processes in the ANC and government. They became Zuma's willing allies in his endeavours to undermine Mbeki.

Around that time, Zuma's image suffered further damage from a charge of rape. On 2 November 2005, Fezekile (Fezeka) Kuzwayo, a thirty-one-year-old woman whose father had spent ten years on Robben Island with Zuma and whose parents had often given food and shelter to him and Ronnie Kasrils when they were working underground in Swaziland, accused Zuma of rape. Her father had died in a car accident when she was ten years old, and she regarded Zuma and Kasrils as trusted uncles. Zuma was acquitted of the rape charge in 2006 after the court found that the sexual intercourse was consensual. He said he knew Fezeka was HIV-positive but took a shower afterwards to protect himself. This foolish statement led to his becoming the butt of a permanent joke inspired by the cartoonist Zapiro, who forever after

---

256. Ibid, p. 255.
257. Ibid.

depicted Zuma with a showerhead appendage.

The trial brought about some disturbing behaviour from Zuma supporters, many of them leading figures in the ANC Women's League, who attacked and vilified Fezeka like demented avengers, shouting slogans like, 'Burn the bitch.' They appeared to be totally unaware of the serious problems faced by women in our society, such as rape, patriarchy and gender-based violence. The 'One in Nine Campaign' against sexual violence, formed in 2006 in the aftermath of Zuma's trial stated:

> Despite the characterisation in the mainstream corporate media and in court, Fezeka, to us, was a feminist, an activist, a teacher, a sister, a friend, [and] a colleague who inspired people close to her and women who only knew her as Khwezi.[258]

Zuma continued to receive support from those who were basically determined to get rid of Mbeki, although many in the ANC were disgusted by Zuma's behaviour, despite the verdict.

Ronnie Kasrils reacted to the news of Fezeka's death in October 2016, saying:

> We should never forget her name. Fezeka Kuzwayo. Her life was completely smashed in 2005 and 2006. She was abused, hounded and castigated. It broke her. Her house was burnt down. But she was rebuilding her life again with a small group of friends who supported her and her ailing mother. ... She stood as a symbol for all of us who are abused in this violent, disgusting and patriarchal way. She is an example of what we must not do. We must show solidarity with those who are vilified for speaking out. I grieve her passing as I know we have been robbed of someone who could have made a fantastic contribution to society.[259]

The anti-Mbeki campaign intensified in the months preceding the ANC's 52nd National Conference held in Polokwane from 16–20 December 2007. Given my positions and role in the ANC and the government, I could confidently reject the accusations; from my experience and vantage point, I

---

258. Available at https://www.dailymaverick.co.za/article/2016-10-09-rememberkhwezi-zumas-rape-accuser-dies-never-having-known-freedom/
259. https://www.dailymaverick.co.za/article/2016-10-09-rememberkhwezi-zumas-rape-accuser-dies-never-having-known-freedom/

knew that they were baseless – and there were many leading figures in both structures who shared my views.

In his book, *Eight Days in September: the Removal of Thabo Mbeki*, Frank Chikane writes about the 'vicious anti-Mbeki crusade' and the divisions in the ANC, saying:

> To intensify this division and conflict, devious and unscrupulous intelligence projects were devised to deepen the crisis within the ANC, to break it from inside. ... All these projects shared two key elements: the collaboration of the worst of the old and the new intelligence operatives, and the hand of foreign intelligence elements. ... I have also seen the frightening spectre of factions within the party battling to control or corrupt elements of the intelligence services to ensure that they served their party factions or individuals, rather than the security interests of the state and the people of South Africa.[260]

I could not have put it better.

Mbeki had responded to the call from some ANC structures to stand for the position of president of the ANC, but according to the Constitution, he could not serve more than two terms as president of South Africa. His willingness to stand for the post of ANC president remains a controversial decision and was used by the Zuma backers as a rallying point. Mbeki's aim was to retain some political power and isolate Zuma. I fully supported him and made that clear to the structures in the Free State, to which province I was an NEC deployee at that time, and also to any person who sought my opinion. I pointed out that several ANC structures were determined that the Polokwane Conference should adopt resolutions to strengthen the ANC's capacity to impact on and influence even more strongly government policies and actions.

For that to happen, I believed it would be in the best interest of the country for Mbeki to retain his position as president of the ANC and Zuma to retain his as deputy. This would mean that Zuma would become the ANC's president-elect for South Africa and Mbeki would be more hands-on in the ANC. But as it turned out in Polokwane, the majority of ANC delegates were in favour of Zuma, who was duly elected president of the ANC.

Although I do not have strong evidence, I remain convinced that there was

---

260. Johannesburg: Picador Africa, 2012, pp. 4–5.

a lot of skulduggery and manipulation in the selection of delegates to Polokwane and in the elections to the positions of the top six. The delegation from the Western Cape was convinced that this was so, and their members were ready to initiate some processes that would lead to a review of the legitimacy of the elections. A few of them sought my opinion, and I told them that while I agreed with them, the die had been cast, and Mbeki had gone onto the stage to congratulate Zuma on his election. Moreover, I was of the view that those not in favour of Zuma would be seen as splittist and anti-democratic diehards who put their own interests above those of the ANC. For me, it was important that Mbeki supporters, and there were many in the ANC, should continue our work and activities in the organisation and contribute to achieving unity and cohesion within it, the Alliance and the government. Some of Zuma's supporters, not satisfied with winning the election, found it necessary to jeer at Mbeki's supporters, some even spitting and making rude gestures, which shocked the older comrades who had never before witnessed such behaviour at an ANC Conference.

Once Zuma was elected president of the ANC, I was convinced that some of us who were seen to be close to Mbeki would not be re-elected to the NEC, and I was correct. But since I had been elated when I had been, I felt that I should be equally happy and supportive to those who had now been elected.

But the Zuma supporters in the ANC were not done yet, and they started agitating and mobilising for the NEC to recall Mbeki. It was a difficult undertaking, the NEC was divided, and only after an intense all-night meeting did they arrive at their decision.

Early the next morning on 19 September 2008, Smuts Ngonyama informed me via a phone call that the NEC had decided to recall Mbeki. I thanked him for the information and started thinking of my public response. I informed Meg about what had happened and suggested that we not discuss any action I might take, as I wanted to be wholly responsible for my decision. She graciously agreed, even though any action I took would impact upon her and the children. After much soul-searching, I came to the conclusion that I should go to Mbeki's official residence later that morning and inform him that I had decided to resign as a minister and MP.

That morning, I found several people at the Mbekis', and Thabo was jovial and in a good mood. I communicated my feelings and decisions to him, and his response was, 'But I have not asked you to resign.' I replied, 'But Comrade President, I did not come to seek your permission but to inform you that I have decided to resign, both as a minister as well as an MP'. He asked, 'But why do you want to resign from your positions?' My answer was, almost word for word, as follows:

> Chief, for many years, we have agreed, including Madiba, that whatever position we hold in the government is due to the ANC and the SACP. If it [were] not for those organisations, we would be doing something else. You would probably have been an outstanding academic, Madiba a chief in the Transkei, and myself ... I shudder to think. Given the unjust, wholly wrong and unwarranted decision to recall you, I find it impossible to serve the ANC in an honest and meaningful way. However, I will remain a member of the ANC. Meg understands my reasons and is very supportive.

Except for my pension, which was difficult to obtain immediately, the only money other than my savings was a gratuitous payment from parliament. Once more, we were going to have to rely on Meg's income until and unless I found a job. My resignation was dictated by my conscience and principle. In reflecting on those momentous events, I remain angry and dissatisfied that the leadership of our movement took such a decision without offering Mbeki the opportunity to express his views and wishes.

Following Mbeki's resignation, Kgalema Motlanthe was elected president of the Republic of South Africa by parliament.

I first met Kgalema when I was working for the SACP and he was the political education officer for the NUM. I found him affable, warm and courteous, and he was a fine raconteur. His depth of political understanding of domestic and international issues and events was impressive, and he loved reading political tracts as well as English literature and poetry. One of his favourite poets was Bertolt Brecht. When young, he was a good football player and took a keen interest in following the game in South Africa and internationally. Given my own love of sport, we naturally exchanged views and joked with each other about what was happening to our teams.

Listening to Kgalema's stories and anecdotes about life on Robben Island was most interesting. He had joined the ANC underground in 1974, was arrested in April 1976, and, together with his close friend Stan Nkosi, sentenced to an effective ten years imprisonment. As Ebrahim Harvey, in his political biography *Kgalema Motlanthe – A Political Biography* records, 'Kgalema, together with Stan Nkosi, S'bu Ndebele, George Mashamba, Kehla Shubane, Ephraim Butshingi and Isaac Seko, arrived at Robben Island on 2

August, 1977. It was a cold, drizzly, winter morning.'[261]

Kgalema did not see himself as a leader, nor did he actively solicit being one. However, his personality, deep political understanding, commitment and discipline were recognised by the ANC, and he was later elected to the post of Secretary-General at the 50th National Conference held in Mafikeng in December 1997.

Prior to that election, Kgalema was also a member of the CC of the SACP, and I attended meetings which included him. He listened attentively to the debates and discussions in both organisations, and when he did speak, his views and suggestions were highly respected. He was determined to strengthen the unity and cohesion of the ANC and that of the Tripartite Alliance. When he was elected as SG of the ANC, Kgalema resigned from the CC, as he wanted to devote his energy and time to fulfil his duties and responsibilities in the ANC.

In 2008, Mbeki had appointed Kgalema as Minister in the Presidency and Leader of Government Business, so there were then two Ministers in the Presidency. For me, there was no doubt that he was the more senior, given his position and authority as SG. I had many meetings with him where we discussed the developments in the ANC and the Alliance, government work, parliament and the presidency. I treasure those times and meetings and continue to have the greatest respect for him, and do try to see him from time to time. He has always agreed to see me and greeted me warmly at his home. I was also very happy to be invited to his wedding with Gugu. They are a wonderful couple, always ready to receive friends and comrades. Meg and I were honoured when they attended my 80th birthday party and gave us a much treasured gift.

Once I had resigned as a minister and MP, my life completely changed, and suddenly, I had a great deal of free time to spend with family and friends. Often, since then, I have been asked whether I miss those times, and the perks that go with being a minister. Let me address that question.

To start with the easiest part: the perks. I have not regretted, and do not regret losing the perks available to ministers. More complex are my feelings about missing meetings of the ANC NEC, those of the Cabinet Committees and Cabinet. I certainly miss those, as I relished meeting my comrades and finding time for small talk as well as intense, robust comradely discussions. Often one learns a great deal during those informal discussions, becoming wiser and better informed while enhancing the bonds of comradeship and

---

261. Johannesburg: Jacana Media, 2012.

friendship. Again, I do indeed miss those meetings.

To be a minister is a high calling, and from the outset, I had decided that at all costs, I must treat my staff with care, consideration and respect. This applied equally to the staff working in the presidency. They knew that my door was open to any of them at all times. My political upbringing had taught me that I could, and should, learn from persons occupying the highest to the lowest posts. This was reinforced, as I wrote earlier, by my experiences in the National Archives in Delhi, India.

My wife tells me that several of the staff members in the presidency told her (and it seems Anver also) that I would be tough on anyone who did not do their job to the best of their ability. If called out, I would explain to that person exactly what was required regarding punctuality and completing agreed tasks. However, they all knew that, thereafter, unless the same problem was repeated, everything was absolutely fine: no grudges were held and from the next day, relations were cordial and easy. They also appreciated that I included different staff members on those foreign trips where we needed assistance.

Similar messages were given to Meg by some of the drivers, especially Zolile, who was very loyal to me and happy that I insisted he be retained, even after I ws advised that he was not fit enough to offer protection. Zolile had suffered injuries as a captured member of AZAPO, which led to his incapacity, and I was not prepared to add to his suffering. He was an excellent driver and a very decent human being.

While a minister, I tried my utmost to meet any person who wanted to see me, whether I knew them or not. I was unhappy when told stories of persons, whether in high positions or not, who had to wait a long time to get an appointment with a minister. There are ministers who may remember that when asked for help, I would urge them, and if necessary, push them, to meet those who were requesting an audience. I saw the responsibility of a minister or deputy as one of service: service to the movement, service to the government, service to my superiors, and above all, service to the people. We occupy positions of leadership and authority as the result of the recognition, support and votes of the people.

It is my mantra that no political leader should ever take for granted the support of the masses. That has to be earned on a regular basis, day by day and must be demonstrated by the way we undertake our responsibilities and the manner in which we relate to our people and those undertaking arduous responsibilities in serving people with a disability, children, the vulnerable and the poorest of the poor. It is the opportunity to meet those responsibilities that I miss.

Let me go back to perks for a moment. Once a person is removed or resigns as a minister or deputy minister, s/he is given one month to remain in an official residence and retain the use of a car and the services of a driver. With the assistance of Louis and other members of my office, my response was to vacate my offices in Cape Town and Pretoria immediately.

While a minister, I tried my utmost to meet any person who wanted to see me, whether I knew them or not. I was unhappy when told stories of persons, whether in high positions or not, who had to wait a long time to get an appointment with a minister. There are ministers who may remember that when asked for help, I would urge them, and if necessary, push them, to meet those who were requesting an audience. I saw the responsibility of a minister or deputy as one of service: service to the movement, service to the government, service to my superiors, and above all, service to the people. We occupy positions of leadership and authority as the result of the recognition, support and votes of the people.

It is my mantra that no political leader should ever take for granted the support of the masses. That has to be earned on a regular basis, day by day and must be demonstrated by the way we undertake our responsibilities and the manner in which we relate to our people and those undertaking arduous responsibilities in serving people with a disability, children, the vulnerable and the poorest of the poor. It is the opportunity to meet those responsibilities that I miss.

Let me go back to perks for a moment. Once a person is removed or resigns as a minister or deputy minister, s/he is given one month to remain in an official residence and retain the use of a car and the services of a driver. With the assistance of Louis and other members of my office, my response was to vacate my offices in Cape Town and Pretoria immediately and refrain from using the official car or driver. To me, it was important to adjust to a life without those perks and return to the life of a citizen with immediate effect. Moreover, those privileges were offered to me because of my position in the Cabinet, and therefore should be available immediately to the person who would replace me. I mention this because, although it is the obvious course of action, some people clung to their perks for as long as they could.

I sometimes regret the fact that there were times when I was too robust and even aggressive in debates with comrades, colleagues, friends and people I didn't know. It is a weakness that I recognise but was not able to deal with satisfactorily during my time in the leadership of our government and movement.

I am what I am because of my work and activities in the ANC and SACP. That is what gave me the opportunity to accept the responsibilities and hold the positions I was given. The ANC has been and remains my mother, father, brother and sister. It is extremely painful to witness the degeneration of my party into warring factions laced with greed and corruption, and it is excruciatingly distressing to witness, hear and read about ANC public representatives putting the interests of their own pockets and those of their collaborators above those of the masses of our people and our country. It is agonising to see that by their nefarious activities, they are bringing shame and disrepute to our glorious movement. How can our movement be glorious if led in the various spheres of government by corrupt and greedy individuals?

But the ANC can and must be saved. I continue to believe that South Africa, the African continent and progressive humanity want a strong and united ANC totally committed to serving progressive causes at home and internationally. As a veteran of the ANC, I shall continue my efforts, however minor, to strengthen our movement and defeat those counter-revolutionary forces, inside and out, who are hell-bent on destroying everything we continue to stand for.

Thabo Mbeki

In this memoir, I have mentioned some of the extraordinary leaders who had a substantial impact on my life and so influenced my political journey and development. One of these was my peer, leader and mentor, Thabo Mbeki, who appointed me to the position of Parliamentary Councillor and later Minister in the Presidency. I am aware of how he stood by me when some of my detractors wanted me to be removed from my position. He taught me a great deal, more than he will ever know, so in concluding this memoir, I pay respect and deep admiration to him by reproducing parts of an interview I gave to Sifiso Ndlovu and Miranda Strydom for their book *The Thabo Mbeki I Know*. As that interview included much that has already been covered in earlier chapters, I have selected a few passages that shed light on aspects of Thabo's character, talents and gifts that are less well-known.

I first met Thabo at Macosa House when Tata Sisulu and others sent him and Sindiso Mfeyana to me to discuss the formation of the African Students' Association, which was formally launched on 16 December 1961.

My first impression of Thabo was of a very young, handsome-looking fellow with a warm personality and already at that time you could tell that he had a sharp political brain. He is three years younger than I am, so I was involved in the struggle before him. By the time I met him, I was already on the executive committee of the Transvaal Indian Congress as well as the TIYC. ... We went to a number of parties together in the white suburbs in those days. I am not sure that he wants to remember this, but one of the songs we used to sing was 'We will take the country the Castro way'. So that was where we established a friendship and a political relationship ...

Thabo and I clicked immediately, at least from my side. I was impressed by this young man's depth of political thinking and his sense of fun and enjoyment. I think this is very important to note because people think that, from a young age, he was always a very serious person, which is just not true, not even in his old age. He loved to party and he loved to sing freedom songs. He denies it but, hell, he can sing! When we were in exile he used to sing bass in our youth choir ...

To come back to his other skills that emerged later on: when he reads documents or articles or books, Thabo Mbeki has a greater capacity to really get to grips with the content and central points more quickly than most people I know ...

[In 1969] ... he was in London and we were having a general discussion about the post-independence South African economy. He asked me if I had read Lenin. I responded that of course I had read Lenin. He then asked me if I had read Lenin's book entitled *The Impending Catastrophe and How to Combat It*. ... He was the first person to point me in that direction and it was remarkable because it was one of Lenin's significant works, which most people have ignored although it is in his Collected Works. It is where Lenin argues about a new economic policy. When I read it, I thought this chap is quite right. Another example: I was asked by the Party to attend a conference on Engels in Berlin ... sometime in the 1970s. Thabo happened to be in London so I asked him, 'Chief, what do you think, what should one say at the conference?' He said 'Have you read Engels on *The Second Peasant War in Germany*? I said no. He suggested I read it and that I would then know what to talk about regarding Engels ...

... Thabo Mbeki had the capacity to find things that were not that well-known but that had a profound impact if you read them carefully. That is Thabo's strength and it distinguished him from us even though we were of the same generation. It was something that enabled him to grow, develop and mature politically much faster than most of us. ....

In my view, Thabo must take credit for creating the Youth and Students Section and using it to broaden the South African struggle and popularise the ANC abroad. With a number of others, he also played a very important role in getting the ANC projected internationally as the dominant liberation movement and not the Pan Africanist Congress or the Unity Movement. ...

When we moved into the ANC Office in Rathbone Place in London, it was filthy, and he said that what we needed to do was go down on our hands and knees and scrub... and we scrubbed for nearly two weeks to make it relatively presentable. Of course, we could have hired people to do the scrubbing, but we thought that it was part of our own political work and training. ...

... Of course, Comrade Oliver Tambo was a stickler and even more difficult than Thabo to write speeches for. We would go to conferences and sit up all night writing, and he would say, but why is the comma there and why the full stop there – and what about that word? A lot of the time Oliver Tambo would say the speech was OK and then write his own. I think that was when Thabo began to be more careful with words; what you say and what you write must be something you are able to defend, and so you would write with caution and not with anger. In the end, Thabo was the only one who could write speeches for Oliver Tambo that O. R. did not change. Oliver Tambo had full confidence that what Thabo Mbeki wrote was what Oliver Tambo thought. The same thing applied to Mandela; he also had such confidence in Thabo who wrote some of his main speeches before he became President. ...

> One of Thabo's greatest strengths is his unbelievable ability to put himself in another person's shoes. He is a very good listener and by putting himself in the other person's shoes he was able to understand, even if he did not agree, why the person had a particular viewpoint. He would respond on the basis of an understanding of what they were saying. But he was also able to bring them round to a position that was very different from where they had started the conversation. This is a very challenging skill: to lend a sympathetic ear even if you do not agree with the other side. I think that this helped him a great deal in all his interactions when he became president of South Africa:

whether it was President Chirac of France, Prime Minister Blair of the UK or President Bush of the US, he could really use this skill. They would come with preconceived positions on Zimbabwe and a whole range of issues, but Thabo was able to bring them round without using anger in his arguments. I never heard him say to a person, I do not agree with you.[262]

One of the greatest achievements of the Mandela and Mbeki ANC governments was bringing Africa onto the world stage as a continent with a voice and a value not just as something to be exploited. Thabo's speech-writing skills have been discussed already, but when he was president, his early public speeches to mass audiences were often criticised for his delivery, which sometimes lacked the liveliness and expression to retain interest and sometimes because the content was too dense and the speeches needed to be read later to be fully appreciated. But Mbeki learned to choose a key phrase as a vehicle for his main message and repeat it at intervals while developing his theme.

Perhaps his greatest speech was 'I am an African', addressed to the National Assembly: a great work of poetry and a manifesto for the African Renaissance which still stands as a monument to our hopes and dreams of the possibility of a new, united and strong Africa – something which seemed to be emerging during our Timbuktu project and Mbeki's presidency. Hopefully that vision is not lost.

> Whatever the setbacks of the moment, nothing can stop us now! Whatever the difficulties, Africa shall be at peace! However improbable it may sound to the sceptics, Africa will prosper! Whoever we may be, whatever our immediate interest, however much we carry baggage from our past, however much we have been caught by the fashion of cynicism and loss of faith in the capacity of the people, let us err today and say – nothing can stop us now!

---

262. Sifiso Ndlovu and Miranda Strydom, *The Thabo Mbeki I Know* (Johannesburg: Pan Macmillan, 2016).

HIV and AIDS

I will now address two very controversial issues on which many people ask my opinion. The first concerns Mbeki's handling of the HIV and AIDS crisis; the second is about his stance regarding South Africa's position on the problems in Zimbabwe.

Mbeki's attitude to the HIV and AIDS pandemic which ravaged our country, causing the death of hundreds of thousands of people, is probably seen by many as the least successful part of his presidency.

At the outset, let me state clearly that Mbeki never said that HIV does not cause AIDS and that he was not an AIDS dissident. During his presidency, he was pilloried and vilified as an AIDS denialist, which was an outrageous lie that was unfortunately given a lot of credence by some sections of the media, both inside South Africa and internationally. A credible account of Mbeki's position on HIV and AIDS is given by Ronald Suresh Roberts, who explores Mbeki's intellectual tradition and details his policies and the reasons behind them in his book *Fit to Govern, The Native Intelligence of Thabo Mbeki*.[263] It is no secret that I encouraged and assisted Roberts in writing the book and had the opportunity to read it in manuscript form and suggest changes. Some of my comments and suggestions were accepted by the author and the publisher.

In his book, Roberts devotes a chapter each to 'the medical politics of AIDS' and 'the racial politics of AIDS'. My own understanding of AIDS is captured by Helen Epstein in the *New York Review of Books*, 20 July 2009. Roberts quotes Epstein who wrote:

> AIDS is caused by the HIV virus [sic], which is passed from person to person through sexual fluids, blood or blood products or from mother to unborn child in the womb or through breastfeeding. The virus destroys the immune system that protects the body from infectious diseases.[264]

I concurred with Mbeki's questioning of the drugs pushed by the Big Pharma companies and the role of co-factors such as nutrition and poverty in helping to deal with the deadly virus. It should be noted that when antiretrovirals were first introduced, the adverse side effects and impact on people taking them had not been fully researched. We also did not know how effective they would be for people who needed regular monitoring to ensure they took the

---

263. Johannesburg: STE Publishers, 2007.
264. Ronald Suresh Roberts, *Fit to Govern*, p. 181.

drugs consistently, nor how effective they were for people with poor nutrition or serious co-morbidities like TB. At the same time, we were also anxious to explore the possibility of other treatments being developed in other parts of the world, like India, which might be made available more cheaply than those offered by Big Pharma and therefore provide a more sustainable solution.

At a time when COVID is impacting the health and well-being of people throughout the world, I believe that prevention is better than cure.

As the political head of the GCIS, I also bore responsibility for government communication on HIV and AIDS and their impact on our country. As the GCIS, we provided regular pamphlets and leaflets on that issue based on the premise that HIV causes AIDS. Roberts points out that government spending on that disease from the time that Mbeki was deputy president and president grew from year to year.[265]

That growth was huge, given that we faced tremendous health problems, including the fact that more people in South Africa died of TB and diabetes than of AIDS. The government also faced other socio-economic challenges that demanded urgent financing and attention.

It is well-known that Mbeki is a voracious reader, and his intellectual quest was to endeavour to understand as comprehensively as possible the economic, social, political, cultural and health issues that impact on the people of South Africa and the continent. It was this quest for a better understanding of the science behind HIV and AIDS that led to his setting up the advisory panel of world-renowned scientists to air and discuss their differing opinions and views about solutions to the HIV and AIDS pandemic.

Mbeki had asked me to meet, greet and welcome the panellists and present the terms of reference to them for consideration, which I did, emphasising that they were at liberty to discuss and analyse issues raised by Mbeki and any others they wished to consider. In his book, Roberts quotes from the terms of reference, which pose questions about what causes 'the immune deficiency that leads to death by AIDS', 'what is the most efficacious response to this cause or causes' and the 'role of therapeutic interventions in the context of developing countries'. I concur with the words of Roberts: 'Mbeki's sin was to reject a drug-based intellectual protectionism in favour of a free exchange of ideas on the proper solution to the AIDS pandemic, including but not limited to drugs alone.'[266]

---

265. Ronald Suresh Roberts, Fit to Govern, p. 181.
266. Ronald Suresh Roberts, Fit to Govern, p. 195.

I agreed with Mbeki's views and positions and was disappointed and angry that they were so cuttingly misrepresented and that he was subjected to a campaign of vituperative and vitriolic attacks. In all the meetings I addressed in my capacity as a minister or NEC member where solutions to the pandemic featured, I frankly expressed my opinions.

I did point out to Mbeki that the GCIS budget was miniscule compared to that of the major pharmaceutical companies and that, consequently, we could not win the debates in the mass media in South Africa and internationally.

One of the lessons I learned was that at those ANC meetings or rallies, there were always groups of young people shouting slogans like 'Viva ANC!' 'Viva SACP!' 'Viva COSATU!' and 'Viva Essop Pahad!' But as soon as I raised the issue of taking precautions such as using contraceptives or possibly refraining from having multiple partners, I lost their attention, and they would indulge in loud interactions which disrupted my message and the meeting.

Later, Mbeki announced that he would back off from commenting on that issue, but Cabinet members did not agree with this approach and told him that he should continue to engage in the debates around HIV and AIDS, as the government position that HIV does cause AIDS was clear to everyone.

Zimbabwe

The other major issue which is still regularly raised when evaluating Mbeki's presidency is the position he took on Zimbabwe. Below I summarise my views on this.

Zimbabwe is our neighbour and a very important economic and trading partner. Moreover, what does or does not happen in that country has a massive impact on us. For example, unrest, troubles, violence, poverty, unemployment and political instability in that country affect South Africa and its people in myriad ways. Over the last two decades, we have already witnessed a large number of Zimbabweans entering South Africa legally and illegally. They are hard-working, disciplined people and a reliable workforce. They work in South Africa as professionals, gardeners, waiters, domestic workers and other occupations and without a doubt make a substantial contribution to the economic growth and development of this country.

Zimbabweans have been coming to South Africa for many decades, and some of them have become activists and leaders in the worlds of sports and culture. Furthermore, there are many Zimbabweans who have lived and worked in South Africa since 1910 and have become South African citizens. The ANC had close fraternal relations with ZAPU, which was demonstrated during the MK campaigns in Wankie (1967) and Sipolilo (1968). ZAPU, like the ANC, received help from the Soviet Union and its allies, and its main support base was in the south of Zimbabwe, in Matabeleland. The other important liberation movement was ZANU, with a pro-Chinese political orientation. After Zimbabwe's independence in 1980, ZANU won elections, and its leader, Robert Mugabe, became the president. Joshua Nkomo, ZAPU's leader, was in Zimbabwe's first cabinet but was fired in 1982.

From 1983–87 ZANU-PF[267] carried out a brutal campaign of torture, rape and murder against the Ndebele people of Matabeleland, ostensibly to remove the threat posed by disgruntled ZAPU soldiers. This has been described by many historians as attempted genocide, resulting in between 20,000 and 80,000 deaths. Naturally, many Ndebele people from Zimbabwe fled to South Africa and made this country their home. In 1987, ZANU and ZAPU officially merged and the genocide stopped. However, acts of violence perpetrated against Mugabe's political opponents have continued sporadically, and poverty and unemployment have continued to provide good reasons for Zimbabweans to seek refuge in South Africa.

Since its independence, Zimbabwe allowed the ANC to use their country to enhance and escalate South Africa's freedom struggle. Thus, unlike the former British colonial power, today's South Africa has a far greater interest in helping to ensure that Zimbabwe is a stable and truly independent country, economically, politically and socially. There is a close fraternal and sisterly bond that ties our people and countries together.

Let us recall that when the racist Ian Smith made his Unilateral Declaration of Independence (UDI) for Rhodesia in 1965, British Labour Party Prime Minister Harold Wilson refused to send British troops to put to an end the illegal regime because, in his words, they were 'kith and kin'. He obviously meant the white Rhodesians – it is hard to imagine a more blatantly racist statement.

Mbeki's preference for 'quiet diplomacy' with Zimbabwe was severely attacked, and what few South Africans and Zimbabweans appeared to be aware of was the determination of the British government to use South Africa to help them induce regime change in Zimbabwe. The media, local and international, criticised Mbeki and his government's policies, positions

---

267. In 1975, ZANU split into two wings loyal to Robert Mugabe and Ndabaningi Sithole, later respectively known as ZANU-PF and ZANU-Ndonga. The two subdivisions ran separately in the 1980 general election, where ZANU-PF has been in power ever since and ZANU-Ndonga a minor opposition party.

and actions concerning Zimbabwe. These attacks were orchestrated by political and other leaders in the UK and assiduously promoted by influential white South Africans through the media they controlled and operated.

As the ANC government, we firmly and categorically rejected attempts by the British government to seek our assistance in the overthrow of President Mugabe. We consistently refused, and without the involvement of the government of South Africa, they were unable to achieve their objective of bringing about regime change in the interest of the Western powers and big capital. Those who doubt this intent should look at how many African governments have been overthrown in the interest of the former colonial powers and the USA and how little the people of those countries have benefited from such regime change.

All of us in the Cabinet understood why regime change in Zimbabwe would have had devastating consequences for us in South Africa. Most importantly, the same thing could be done to us if they did not like our policies: they could initiate regime change against us.

Mbeki was concerned that Zimbabwe should remain a democratic country with regular free and fair elections, free expression of political views, and a strong and stable economy. He was opposed to some of the disastrous spending sprees and other activities which had driven Zimbabwe into an economic crisis, partly occasioned by and sustained due to the economic sanctions imposed on Mugabe and Zimbabwe by the UK, supported by the USA and the EU.

An aspect of Mbeki's approach can be gleaned from this quote from Roberts's book, where Mbeki says:

> To come out of this crisis, the people of Zimbabwe will have to make serious sacrifices and take a lot of pain … The longer the problem of Zimbabwe remains unresolved, the more entrenched poverty will become. The longer this persists, the greater will be the degree of social instability, as the poor try to respond to the pains of hunger. The more protracted this instability, the greater will be the degree of social and political conflict. To respond to this, the state will inevitably have to emphasise issues of law and order, even as it has ever fewer means to address the needs of the people.[268]

I attended a few of the meetings with other heads of state and economic and

---

268. Ronald Suresh Roberts, *Fit to Govern*, p. 175.

political leaders in which Mbeki patiently, with facts and figures and a deep understanding of the Zimbabwean socio-economic situation, explained his and his government and party's position on Zimbabwe.

In my view, his position and analysis was appreciated and in many cases accepted. An interesting example was provided when President Bush, after a meeting with Mbeki in Pretoria, publicly declared in a press conference that Mbeki was his 'point man' on Zimbabwe.

Mugabe was the bogeyman pilloried by the British political establishment and the EU. But in South Africa and Africa, he was popular and had mass support for many years. We saw this on three occasions in South Africa: firstly at Mandela's inauguration; secondly, at Mbeki's inauguration; and thirdly at the funeral of our revered leader Walter Sisulu.

Let me recount one experience where I was involved to a limited extent. At a meeting with a large business delegation, Mbeki spent considerable time explaining his position and that of the ANC and the South African Government on Zimbabwe. The delegation accepted his views and positions and adopted a joint communiqué with our government. Saki Macozoma let the business delegation working on the communiqué. At the end of that meeting, Mbeki and I agreed that I, as the political head of GCIS, should contact Professor Jonathan Moyo, head of communications in the Mugabe government, and explain to him the importance of that communiqué for Zimbabwe, its government and people. I followed his instructions and suggested to Professor Moyo that his government might use the communiqué in their efforts to deal with the negative and highly critical view of Zimbabwe in circles in Western Europe and the USA. But he prevaricated, much to my consternation, and merely repeated that 'your principal should contact my principal', which was an absconding of responsibilities, and I had to supress my response. I duly informed Mbeki about this one-sided conversation but do not know if he followed up on it or not.

Mbeki's intervention in Zimbabwe was also appreciated at times by the main opposition leader, Morgan Tsvangirai, leader of the Movement for Democratic Change, who said that the 'dialogue between the MDC and the African National Congress' leaders had been 'very positive', and the latter 'had made its opposition to lawlessness in Zimbabwe clear'.[269] Roberts is very critical of Mugabe, saying that his conduct was 'atrocious and self-defeating'[270] and that 'Mugabe is a politician who has created a wretched plight in his country through the pursuit of unsustainable and populist economics and politics.'[271]

---
269. Ibid. p. 158.
270. Ibid. p. 170.
271. Ibid. p. 172.

Mbeki and his team, which included Mojanku Gumbi and Frank Chikane, were instrumental in getting ZANU-PF and the MDC to engage in the talks which eventually led to the formation of a government of national unity. Aziz Pahad, Deputy Foreign Minister at the time, was much more directly involved than I was in the South African Government's endeavours to help resolve the crisis in Zimbabwe. It is my hope that those more directly involved in the controversial elections held in that country, the complexities of the negotiations, the controversial land policies and invasions and other germane matters will enlighten us on some of those important issues.

However, let me reiterate my fierce opposition to any manifestation of anti-Zimbabwean sentiments, voices and activities. This also applies to xenophobic expressions and attitudes aimed at other non-South Africans, often labelled 'foreigners', despite a long and lawful association with our country often including legal residency, work and raising their families in this country as their home. I continue to hold firmly to the view that for SADC to be a comprehensive, integrated, united and powerful economic and political force, it must encompass the free movement of goods and services and also the free movement of labour.

As South Africans, we must pursue with vigour, transparency and honesty the comprehensive unity and integrity of SADC, for, in the long run, our own socio-economic development and stability requires this.

I would like to end with another quotation from the interview I gave in the book, *The Thabo Mbeki I Know*:

> Notwithstanding what happened in Polokwane, Thabo Mbeki still commanded a great deal of respect and support within the ANC leadership and obviously in the country among the majority of our people. Upholding his own principles of always respecting the decisions arrived at by the leadership of the ANC, he complied with a decision, however badly it might affect him. Again, at that moment in time, he demonstrated his capacity to take rational decisions, even though they impacted negatively on his own life. He did not know what he was going to do after that; in fact, none of us knew what we were going to do after we had resigned.
>
> In the end, we needed to respect the way President Mbeki handled the matter and the way that he went onto national television and the calm manner in which he announced that he was stepping down. ...

It was very painful and tragic – in my view not only for us and Thabo Mbeki – it was painful because the top leadership of this organisation that we had given our lives to and that we still continue to love and respect behaved in the manner they did. The organisation had taken a step that had never before been taken in its history, and it was really tragic that the NEC could arrive at that decision not fully understanding its enormity.

I think that when historians look at this event later with an objective approach ... we will see that the decision was arrived at mainly because there were some people who were determined to see the humiliation of Thabo Mbeki. For me, the humiliation was not Thabo Mbeki's, the humiliation was the ANC's, and that is what makes it so much sadder: it remains true to this day.

Epilogue

In this memoir, I have endeavoured to trace aspects of my life as a political activist and leader in the ANC, SACP and the democratic government of our beloved country. The memoir ends at the time of my resignation as an MP and the Minister in the Presidency as a result of the recall of Mbeki by the NEC of the ANC. Thereafter, my life changed, and I had to find a new job at the age of seventy. However, I remain a member of the ANC branch in Ward 90, Johannesburg.

The ANC National Conference of 2008 in Polokwane marked a turning point for the worse in the history of the ANC and for our democratic government. That conference paved the way for charlatans, opportunists, factionalists and sectarians to insert themselves into the heart of the movement and all spheres of government.

At present, the ANC is trying to recover from over a decade of weak governance, corruption and malfeasance. This malaise has led to a loss of electoral support. Indeed, the ANC leadership has accepted that if it does not renew and revitalise the movement, returning it to its core basic values, culture and traditions, there looms a real possibility of losing the 2024 national and provincial elections.

Greed and factionalism have had a searing impact on the unity and cohesion of the ANC and the Alliance. Instead of building mass support based on ideology, policy and programme delivery, the ANC is torn apart by destructive and debilitating battles at all levels for power and privilege. For some, the fight is for opportunities to loot the state and its SOEs. These people put their own interests above those of the people of South Africa, while others put what they perceive as the interests of the ANC above the well-being of the people, which also damages our country.

Sectarianism is characterised by a narrow-minded – even thoughtless – adherence to the interests, views and standpoint of a group (or sect) against that of the collective. There can be no substitute for a collective leadership if an organisation is to be successful. Embracing factionalism is the very antithesis of revolutionary action, for a revolutionary subsumes her or his personal interests and ambitions in the collective constituted in the party and the government.

Unfortunately, the wrong, even abhorrent behaviour of many delegates and leaders in Polokwane has sunk deep roots inside the ANC and has impacted the organisation at branch, regional, and provincial level, as well as nationally. A weak and divided ANC has also led to a weakened Alliance, a deterioration that prevents the ANC from playing its proper role as a leading force for progressive, revolutionary change and socio-economic transformation in South Africa and the continent.

The Tripartite Alliance has to be better organised and functional to help the ANC rid its ranks of factionalism and self-interest and jointly bears the responsibility to assist it in achieving the objective of a better life for all – for our people and the people of Africa.

As I conclude, let me reflect briefly on the closest members of my family, who have been alongside me in my life's journey, sharing the impact of my commitment to the struggle. They contribute greatly to my ability to face the future with hope, in spite of my sorrow at the state of my party and my country.

Meg and I are very proud of our two children, Amina Zanele Pahad and Govan Timol Pahad.

Amina is still working successfully at RMB, where she has consistently helped to empower women in the organisation. She married Menzi Mbatha in 2006, they had two children and got divorced in 2016. Throughout these times, which were sometimes hard, she was helped by her wonderful housekeeper, Dayina, who was later joined by her adult daughter, Gracious. These two have become part of Amina's family and are always smiling and radiating calm and warmth. In 2020, just before the first COVID lockdown, Amina married Muhammed Asad Moosa.

Our daughter Amina has a wonderful temperament: generous, warm and friendly with a beautiful smile. She has brought up two lovely children who are a real credit to her – kind, polite, thoughtful and caring. She has a very loyal group of friends, and they all support each other. She doesn't pretend or lie to people but always acts with complete integrity. She is a wonderful mother to both her children, Asani and Dania, as well as to Saliha and Sana, the daughters of Muhammed. Muhammed is kind and has a generous spirit. He is calm, very intelligent and usually quite reserved. He can also be amusing and entertaining. He is wonderful with Amina and has strengthened the sense of stability and happiness in her and her children.

Amina is also a caring and fantastic daughter, and Meg and I can rely on her support whenever we need anything. Although very busy, she manages to make time to spend with us and brings her children to see us regularly and organises holidays with us from time to time.

Asani Kalusha Mbatha and Dania Zinhle Mbatha are a source of great joy and pride to us. Both attend Redhill School in Morningside, Johannesburg and are doing well in their studies. Asani, who was born in 2010, loves playing football at school and for a local club and was doing very well in gymnastics but had to give it up to fit in basketball. He is mature and confident for his age, and one can have adult conversations with him (which I do regularly and enjoy immensely!). He is kind and funny and makes friends easily. He loves maths and IT, and I am sure he will do well at school and in further studies.

Dania, who was born in 2013, is full of verve and vitality. Her face is very expressive, as is her body language, and her laughter is infectious. She is very keen on sports and good at them. She excels at gymnastics and is typically the youngest competitor in her level. She also loves netball and hockey. She is both sensitive and sensible, full of feeling but well-balanced, very kind and considerate and loves to write thoughtful messages, draw endlessly, design Lego homes, read and joke.

Govan is now a lecturer in the Zoology Department at the University of Johannesburg, where he works hard and is interested and concerned about his students' welfare and understanding. By all accounts, he is respected by his students and peers there. His favourite sports are Kung Fu and Tai Chi, and he has achieved high levels of proficiency in both these and is a Tai Chi instructor.

Govan married Aimee Topp in 2015, and they have three lovely and adorable children: Xavier Henry Goolam Pahad (born 2016), Hugo Melt Martin Pahad (born 2018), and Tau Topp Shorrock Pahad, (born 2020). They live in the cottage of our house, so we see them all the time, and they bring us joy and keep us younger than we would otherwise be. Fortunately, both Govan and Aimee are wonderful parents, as having three tiny children is a lot of work, but they really love being with their crazy 'Pahad Boys' and don't go mad, even when they are exhausted.

Aimee is amazing with children and reminds us of a 'Pied Piper', with children all immediately attracted to her and running after her, calling for her attention. She first worked as an au pair and later qualified as a Montessori teacher and was very popular in her two Montessori schools. She is now also a highly experienced and respected teacher using the Reggio Emilia approach and works at the lovely Small World School in Roosevelt Park, Johannesburg. She is particularly wonderful with children who have learning, sensory or social difficulties and charms them into being able to listen, play and learn. Her parents live nearby in Blairgowrie, and the Pahad Boys are lucky enough to have Granny Annie and Grandad (John) as well as Granny Meg and me (Papa). Aimee's family provide support as well as a crowd of cousins to play with.

Govan is a very composed, intelligent, warm and friendly. He is completely genuine and unaware of what impression he might be making. When he's not fully engaged, his mind sometimes drifts off, and he does not notice people staring at him when he is absent-mindedly practicing Tai Chi moves. When you have his attention, he is very entertaining and a mine of information. Like his Uncle Aziz, he has a fine sense of humour.

We are proud that Govan walks around the house or garden holding his baby or toddler, reciting poetry to him while trying to put him to sleep. Meg did this with Govan when she was in the hospital with him when he was tiny. We are pleased with how our children have grown into adulthood and parenthood and happy that both of them are honest, genuine and responsible.

Govan's son Xavier has been a very unusual boy from early days. He has an astonishing memory and wants to have books read to him for hours each day. Never much interested in fiction, he soaks up facts. He also loves documentaries, like those of David Attenborough, and has developed an extensive vocabulary. He constantly asks questions, so he not only remembers things but understands them and can explain them. His brain works exceptionally well, especially regarding dinosaurs, mammals, reptiles, birds, the solar system, trees and plants, etc., where his knowledge is really phenomenal. He has been able to swim almost from birth and can do tricks on the trampoline like a front flip. I hope he will retain his interest in the natural sciences. He is currently at an excellent primary school called Kairos School of Inquiry, in Parkview, Johannesburg.

Govan's second son Hugo is a happy and attractive little boy, full of energy. People tend to love him at first sight, and he responds happily to their attention. He climbs trees fearlessly, is strong and flexible and has great balance, so we expect him to be good at gymnastics. He is very imaginative and loves to pretend to be different animals, copying their sounds and movements and making up stories about them. He likes fiction and can listen to the same story a hundred times. He also enjoys drawing, creating and building things and doing puzzles. He loves going to the school where his Mummy works.

The third son Tau is only two, but he is growing up fast because he copies his brothers and learns from them. He now understands that when he wants to have a tantrum, he can just walk away and lie down for a few minutes and then go back to normal, which is quicker and easier than screaming and crying for hours. He seems to enjoy everything and can now often play well with Hugo, interacting with him for quite long periods. He is also happy to play by himself, which not all small children are able to do.

My brother Aziz Pahad, born in 1940 and eighteen months younger than me, was Deputy Minister of Foreign Affairs from 1994–2008 and a key figure in the negotiations which led to the unbanning of the ANC and the start of the CODESA negotiations. He has maintained his relationship with many of his former colleagues and is regularly in touch with a host of former diplomats, ambassadors and intelligence people around the world. He continues to be held in high esteem by the ANC's international department, the Department of International Relations and Co-operation (DIRCO), and by Thabo and Zanele Mbeki. Aziz is the recipient of an honorary doctorate from the University of Pretoria and the O. R. Tambo Lifetime Achievement Award from DIRCO.

Aziz is also an active member of the Concerned Africans Forum (CAF) and Chair of the Tambo-Dadoo Palestinian Solidarity Committee, a much-needed group he set up with Mohammed Dangor. The Board includes Fazel Randera, Wally Serote, Ronnie Kasrils, Roshan Dadoo, Dali Tambo, Na'eem Jeenah, Brigalia Bam, Horst Kleinschmidt, Shaukat Fakie and myself. This committee seeks to link up South African families with the families of Palestinian prisoners and should become an important source of solidarity with the embattled and oppressed Palestinians and deserves the support and assistance of South Africans.

Aziz has had two previous marriages (Gloria and Sandra) but is now, fortunately, married to Angina Parekh, who recently retired from her position of Deputy Vice-Chancellor of the University of Johannesburg. She has captured all our hearts, and everyone agrees that Aziz was very lucky to capture hers, as marrying her was one of the best things he has ever done. Angina has a Master's degree in clinical psychology as well as an MPhil in Psychology, which perhaps equips her well for her life with Aziz, but it seems more likely that her calm, happy and patient disposition is a major factor, as it helps her to get on well with the whole family. With a distinguished career in Higher Education, she continues to work as a consultant.

Aziz has been by my side for most of my life and has become my best friend.

Yasmin and Shehnaaz Dadabhay, our two special nieces, remain very close to us, and always show us the kindness and consideration we would deserve if we were their parents. Indeed, Yasmin has always been a daughter to us, and we are so glad she has had a successful career and is the centre of a close and happy family. Both she and her sister have achieved wonders through sheer hard work and determination, backed by their good brains and strong, caring personalities.

Yasmin and Yusuf 'Dada' Dadabhay have a very loving marriage and are blessed with three children, Zakiya, Zayd and Muhamed (known as Mo D). Zakhiya is a successful medical doctor and lives with her husband Zahir and their three children, Danyal, Ziyad and Sabreen in Australia, near Brisbane. The children all know their South African family well, having stayed with Yasmin for long periods. Zayd is married to Fatima, and they have three children, Aadam, Imaan and Mohammed-Ilyaas. 'Mo D' is married to Nadia, and they expect to go to Australia with their children, Zaidaan and Hamzah soon, where Mo D will work as an industrial psychologist.

Shehnaaz, who works in foreign exchange at Rand Merchant Bank, was married to Dada's first cousin, also named Yusuf Dadabhay, known as 'Georgie', and they have two children, Zeenat and Zaeem. Zeenat is a well-known and respected anaesthetist and is ever ready to assist any of her friends or relatives when they are ill (and even when they are fine). She is married to Mohammed Saloojee, and they have two children, Taariq and Tahiyyah. Zaeem is married to Nabilla, and they have a son named Danyaal.

My other special cousin is Shenaaz Pahad, whom I wrote about in Chapter 8. She and Rikki are another bright spot in our lives and are always good company and ready to help in hard times. Shenaaz has really become like a daughter to us, and we are missing her at the time of writing as she is busy with some post-graduate studies in the UK.

While I pay my respect and deepest gratitude to all those who helped shape my life and political activism, I must mention my wife, Meg. We first met in September 1965 and married in 1971. She has been a bulwark in my life and brought up our children Amina and Govan with much love, joy and a sound value system – on many occasions as a single parent when my work took me away from home. For years, she was the main breadwinner in the family. Because of her, we are a solid family unit with two wonderful children and lovely grandchildren. My respect and admiration for her know no bounds.

⁂

As mentioned previously, I am deeply pained and disappointed that my beloved ANC is consumed by debilitating factionalism and sectarianism. In the more than sixty-five years of involvement in the Congress movement and the struggle for national liberation, peace, democracy and human rights in South Africa, I have remained a loyal, committed and disciplined member and leader, so it is extremely painful to witness the deterioration within the ANC and in the ranks of the SACP and COSATU. It is important that honest, hardworking and highly committed members and leaders of the ANC fully support the seemingly intractable struggle to renew, revive and refresh the ANC. Fortunately, I know many people who are doing their best to achieve this aim. They are too many to name, but I must mention Wally Mongane Serote and Fazel Randera in that context. Our country, Africa and progressive forces throughout the world need a strong, healthy and cohesive ANC – an internationalist ANC that is free from corruption.

Since my retirement from active politics, I have been asked many times if I regret anything.

I certainly regret that I was not a better and more accomplished football player and that I was at times rude and intemperate to political friends, comrades, allies and opponents. I do regret that I was not always patient, understanding and comradely.

It is my ambition to publish a book containing articles that appeared in my journal, *The Thinker*. In that book, I intend to update my life following my resignation and comment on political developments, including the Zuma years, the Gupta family, and international developments involving the US and the NATO-led Ukrainian conflict with Russia. Thankfully, at the time of writing, South African foreign policy under Naledi Pandor recognises the importance of resisting a unipolar world where the USA can act in the interest of its military and industrial corporations with impunity. Organising regime change against countries who do not toe the US line has become a commonplace occurrence. Together with the BRICS countries and much of the developing world, we are refusing to support the demands of the US and NATO to isolate Russia. This stand is maintained, despite daily opposition and misinformation from a massive worldwide media campaign.

I fully support the statement made by the Prime Minister of Namibia, Saara Kuugongelwa-Amadhila at the Munich Security Conference on 18 Feb 2023 on the subject of the Ukraine:

We are promoting a peaceful resolution of that conflict … so that the entire world and all the resources of the world can be focused on improving the conditions of people around the world instead of being spent on acquiring weapons, killing people and actually creating hostilities.

I hope to be able to record some revival of the ANC's commitment to contributing to the consolidation, defence and promotion of progressive forces in the world. The party has to intensify its internationalist, anti-imperialist positions and its stand against neocolonialism.

In that context, it is essential that the ANC and the government resolutely oppose xenophobic actions like those of Operation Dudula and protect the human rights of Zimbabweans and others who are living in South Africa legally, working hard, obeying the law, and bringing up their children who were born here legally but are denied their rightful citizenship.

We must also give comprehensive support to the struggle of the Palestinians for national liberation, democracy and freedom from the shackles of the apartheid Israeli regime. Some of Israel's vile anti-Palestinian actions are even worse than those perpetrated by the hated South African apartheid regime. As I am deeply involved in the work of the Palestinian political prisoners' support group, the Tambo-Dadoo Palestine Solidarity Committee, I believe that it is imperative that we connect South African families to Palestinian political prisoners' families as a tangible act of international solidarity. It is non-negotiable that we become part of the campaign to declare Israel an apartheid state.

Postcript

Essop intended to write another book but near the end of March he felt unwell and tests revealed that he had terminal lung cancer. His health declined very rapidly but fortunately he was able to be cared for at home and he passed away peacefully in his sleep on 6 July, having spent his last days surrounded by family and friends.

We decided that it would be appropriate to include a few extracts from some of the many tributes to Essop that the family received after his death.

Essop Pahad played a vital role in 1994 as chair of the political party liaison committee, which was crucial in the provision of the flawed yet universally welcomed national elections. It was his clarity of vision and persuasive powers, his resolute leadership and interpersonal skill and, above all, his tireless dedication to the cause of liberty, that empowered and guided the committee. In the result, the committee proved indispensable in resolving and even anticipating bottlenecks and deadlocks in the electoral process, and ensured the practically universal buy-in without which the IEC could not have delivered the elections.

In a very real sense, Essop Pahad was one of our founding fathers, an example to the current role-players in the political arena.
— **Johann Kriegler, retired Justice of the Constitutional Court and founding Chair of Lawyers for Human Rights**

I shall never forget our friendship and especially the lively discussions we had with Comrade Essop for almost 50 years. I will always remember the help he gave me during the most difficult days.

To quote Nikolai Ostrovsky, 'Man's dearest possession is life. It is given to him but once, and he must live it ... so that, dying, he might say: all my life, all my strength were given to the finest cause in all the world – the fight for the Liberation of Mankind.' Dear Essop, we'll never forget you, and we'll never forget your contribution to that finest cause – the liberation of your country and the liberation of the whole of mankind. *Hamba Kahle*, Comrade Essop.
— **Vladimir Shubin, former Secretary of the Soviet Afro-Asian Solidarity Committee of the Soviet Union: Recipient of the Order of Companion of OR Tambo in Silver**

I worked with Essop from the early 1970s in London when I was editor of the Young Communist League's newspaper, *Challenge*, and through many years in the Anti-Apartheid Movement. One fond memory was when Essop renamed St George's Place in Glasgow after Nelson Mandela in 1986 and we were speakers at the rally in the City Chambers afterward. This was much to the annoyance of the apartheid regime, whose consulate was in a building in the renamed square, the place of many pickets and demonstrations. They refused to use the new address and instead used a PO box!

Essop Pahad made a singular and invaluable contribution to the overthrow of apartheid and the building of a new democratic, non-racial,

non-sexist South Africa. It was an honour and a privilege to have worked with him.
— **Brian Filling, Chair of the Scottish AAM from 1976-1994, Honorary Consul for South Africa in Scotland; Recipient of the National Order of Companions of OR Tambo, 2012**

Essop was an indefatigable fighter with an unwavering lifelong commitment to the ANC and the struggle against apartheid. His frank and fearless expressions were a testimony to his character and endeared him to his friends and comrades… He has left a proud legacy.
— **From Anand Sharma, former Union Cabinet Minister, India**

We will pick up your spear, Essop, and the struggle continues. You have made an indelible contribution to the liberation of our people. A constitutional democracy to be proud of, an independent judiciary and media, and a Bill of Rights for us ordinary folk. Challenges remain, but we will endeavour to continue the transformation of the society to a just, equitable and prosperous one. *Hamba Kahle* anti-apartheid struggle veteran and my friend, Essop Goolam Pahad.
— **Dr Oscar van Heerden, senior research fellow for African Diplomacy and Leadership at the University of Johannesburg**

I was always slightly in awe of this lanky, straight talking, bold and uncompromising leader… I found that under his gruff exterior, lurked a gentleness that was willing to guide and mentor, but also equally willing to fight with unmatched fierceness when it was required. … I cannot claim any special friendship with him, but he was able to take your measure quickly and accurately and push you further than you ever imagined for yourself. All that we can do now, is to bow our heads to Essop Pahad; he passed among his loved ones, but what a life he lived.
— **HE Ruby Marks, South African Ambassador to Benin (and former Mandela scholar at Sussex University). Received from Prof Sasha Roseneil, Vice Chancellor and President of Sussex University as part of a tribute posted by the University**

The most memorable personal experience we shared was when we were both in the South African delegation, led by Madiba, to the FIFA headquarters in May 2004 where South Africa was announced as the host of country for the

2010 FIFA World Cup, bringing this global event for the first time to Africa.

I was fortunate to have developed a close friendship with Essop and his family over the years. I admired Dr Pahad for his wit, his political expediency, his commitment to South Africa and his sense of humour. He was also a raconteur of note who could keep one engaged for hours.
— **Anant Singh, film producer and member of the International Olympic Committee**

Throughout his life, Comrade Essop demonstrated an unwavering commitment and dedication to the cause of freedom, justice and equality. As a fervent internationalist, that commitment extended not only to South Africa, but also to all other oppressed people throughout the world, including in occupied Palestine. His passing is a significant loss, not just for South Africa, but also for the Palestinian people.
— **Dr Mousa Aba Marzouq, HAMAS, Palestine**

When uncle Essop believed in you, he believed you could move mountains! If he trusted you, he gave you challenges to bring out the best in you: he could persuade you to do things which seemed impossible.
— **Faith Isiakpere & Firdoze Bulbulia, Moments Entertainment SA**

I met Essop for the first time in 2003 at FIFA House when he was leading a government delegation and the 2010 bid committee and I was covering the event for the SABC. I was 25 years old. Sport, and in particular football, would become our connective tissue.

Over the last nine years or so, we started meeting, with Maurizio Mariano, every second Monday for lunch. Maurizio would often play referee in the numerous verbal sparring sessions during our many hard fought debates. However the real essence of these sessions was for us to learn from Essop about life and politics. Essop became my close friend and advisor – the kind every person needs.
— **Walter Mokoena, SABC sports anchor, commentator of 2010 FIFA World Cup and editor of** *Joburg Post* **and** *My Sports Book*

From the early 2000s we engaged with Essop and also partnered with him on projects that were important for him. This included the historically significant Timbuktu Manuscript Project as well as the thought provoking *The Thinker* magazine. Essop will be remembered for his selflessness, his

intellect, his humour, his forgiving nature and his tireless efforts to achieve justice and freedom for all South Africans. Indeed, we take from his life numerous valuable examples of how to live our own lives and salute the amazing gift he has given to our country and all its citizens.
— **the Ebrahim family, Oasis Holdings**

Essop Pahad's … commitment to fighting oppression and discrimination, regardless of race, religion or nationality, exemplified his unwavering dedication to the betterment of society. We are forever grateful for his tireless efforts in advocating for a just social order that uplifted the marginalised and brought about positive change.

As we mourn the loss of Essop Pahad, let us also take solace in the exceptional life he lived as a freedom fighter, visionary, and champion of social justice. His legacy will continue to inspire us, urging us to strive for a better South Africa, one where equality, justice, and compassion prevail.
— **Haroon Kalla of Awqaf**

Known to have a strong-arm approach to making things work, Essop had a softer side to him that many MPs and ANC activists never really saw. He could talk leisurely about Dynamos Football Club, for which he and all his brothers played during the early 1960s. He would stroll along the Zoo Lake on Eid Day and meet family and friends, caring little for VIP protection. And in the parliamentary restaurant, he would dunk his samoosa in his tea without thinking twice. That was Essop Pahad. He was devoted to his work but never missed an opportunity to be with family. His children and nephews and nieces meant everything to him.
— **Ismail Vadi, published in the *Lenasia Rising Sun***

Index

A Glimpse into the Future 51
A View From Moscow 190
Ackerman, Laurie 208
Action for Southern Africa (ACTSA) 239–240
Adam, Ebrahim 32, 50, 61
Adam, Essop 32
Adam family 32
Adam, Feroza 32
Adam, Goolam 32
Adam, Mohammed 32
Adam, Rashid 'Mousie' 82
Adam, Suleiman 32
Adams, Faried 62–63
Adler, David 55, 379–381
Adler, Margrit See: Pittman, Margrit (née Adler) 125–126
Adler, Ray See: Harmel, Ray
Adom, Aman 174
Africa
   Communist Call to Africa 141, 166, 168, 170, 270
     adoption 168
     countries involved 166–167, 172
     Maputo Declaration non-adoption reasons 171
     Maputo Manifesto, Africa and the Struggle for Socialism 171
        Pahad facilitation role 166–173
     Pahad's visits 173–188
   solidarity movement 468–469
   support to ANC 227, 468
Africa Notes and Comment 107
African National Congress (ANC), anti-imperialist demonstrations 96–97, 100
   armed struggle impetus (1960) 53, 63
   armed struggle stance 189, 198, 206–207
   banning (1960) 52–53
   bleak period (1963-1966) 92
   Chairman O. R. Tambo 306
   Conferences See: conference concerned
   decisions for SA post-unbanning 208–209
   elections (1994), campaign & results 289–290
   Ferreirastown office 31
   Group of Eight expulsion 90
   history 464, 466
   IDASA meeting (1987) 201
   international student body contact 96
   leadership issues 486–487, 495–496
   Macosa House office 31
   Mandela inauguration (1994) 369
   membership opening to non-Africans 188
   National Conference (48th, 1991) 305–306
   National Conference (50th, 1997) 503
   NEC decision to examine problems 188
   NEC *lekgotla* overview (2007) 489–491
     Chinese socialism comparison 489
     COSATU and SACP invited to attend 489
     COSATU stance 490–491
     Essop Pahad contribution 491
     SANCO possible involvement 491
   NEC overview (2006) 486–489
     Aziz Pahad contribution 488
     branch empowerment necessity 487
     Essop Pahad contribution 488, 491
     Mbeki on need for an African Renaissance 486
     Mbeki on need for party unity 486
     SACP stance on ANC 487
   NEC overview (2006) Zuma issues 486
   negotiations with National Party 206–208
   Operation Mayibuye adoption debate 296–297
   Politico Military Commission 198–200
   Presidential inauguration (1999) 399
     Aziz Pahad role 399
   propaganda campaigns 94
   recruits 95
   relations with Cuba 221
   relations with GDR parties 224–225
   relations with Indian National Congress (INC) 251–252
   rugby as a factor for change 201–202
   Sechaba launch (1967) 91
   Soviet Union training 218
   support from,
     African countries 227–228
     India 251-254
     Frontline States 227–228
     HIP 245-246
     German Democratic Republic 224-225

Reggio Emilia (Italy) 242–246
Sweden 229–231
torture and solitary confinement of twenty-two members by SA government (1969) 92–93
unbanned (1990) 208
See also; *Umkhonto we Sizwe*, SACP, COSATU
African Rainbow Minerals 452
African Renaissance concept 486, 509
African Resistance Movement 57
African Students Association (ASA) 59–60, 507
Afrikaner Weerstandsbeweging (AWB) 349
Afro-Asian Solidarity Movement 93
Ahmed Baba Institute 450, 453, 455, 458–459
  Library occupation and damage by AQIM 459
AIPSO 253
al-Dulaimi, Naziha Jawdet Ashgah 137
Alexander, Neville (*pseud* Nosizwe) 107
All India Peace and Solidarity Organisation (AIPSO) 251
All-India Youth Federation 126
Allende, Salvador 113
Amadhila, Saara Kuugongelwa- See: Kuugongelwa-Amadhila
Anand, Zenobia (née Asvat) 251
ANC Women's League 499
ANC Women's Section 308
ANC Youth League (ANCYL) 49, 301, 311
ANC Youth and Students Section 89, 91, 94–96, 99–100
  association with CPGB and other communist affiliates 91
  discussion and formation 88–89
  inclusive of non-Africans 88
  shunned by British National Union of Students 91
ANC-SACP Alliance 216
  consolidation 94
Anderson, Larry 51
Andersson, Muff 200
Andrews, Bill 215
AngloGold 452
Angola
  Call to Africa, party participation 168, 170
  liberation struggles 221

Pahad visit 185–188
SANDF invasion (1975), Cuban support 220–221
solidarity with ANC 228
solidarity with SWAPO 228
Annex Midrand 452
Anti-Apartheid Movement 91–92, 92–93, 95, 99, 101, 105, 206, 232, 234, 241–242, 302
Anti-Apartheid Movement (Ireland) 152
Anti-Apartheid News 102, 240
Arafat, Yasser 112, 290
Arellano, Oswaldo López 73
Arloff, Steve 154
Arloff, Sue 154
Armatrading, Joan 237
Armscor, arms deals 254
Artists Against Apartheid campaign 75, 237
Asmal, Kader 152, 188, 202, 233, 327, 404, 408, 445
Asmal, Louise 152, 202
Association of Cinematograph, Television and Allied Technicians (ACTT) 154
Association of Teachers of Mathematics 81
Assoyan, Boris 218
Asvat, Zainab 430
Asvat, Zaynab 38
Asvat, Zenobia See: Anand, Zenobia (née Asvat)
Atchuthan, *Comrade* 154
Attenborough, Richard 237
Ausberg, Pavel 123
Averyanov, Boris 151
awards, Vyacheslav (Slava) Tetekin from President Cyril Ramaphosa (2018) 219
Axel, Hermann 167
Ayob, Ismail 206
Azad, Ahmed (Pahad, Essop, *pseud*) 106–107, 216
Azishe-Ke: Opportunity Knocks 420
Aziz, Haroon 324, 324–325

Baba, Ahmed 458–459
Bafokeng, *Queen of the* 354
Bagus, Rafiq 417
Bahula, Julian 238
Bakdash, Khalid 129
Balfour, Ngconde 405, 472, 474, 482
Bam, Brigalia 523

533

Banda, *President* Hastings 468
Bandung Conference (1955) 128
Bannister, Paul 417
Baqwa, Selby 460
Barnard, Niel 207
Barnes, Rikki 374
Barre, Mohamed Siad 174
Barry, Kevin 153
Bastomsky, Saul 55
Basu, Jyoti 253
Batista, Fulgencio 219
Bauer, Roland 143–144
Bedford, Tommy 201
Bee Gees 237
Before They Can Speak of Flowers 132
Beggar Your Neighbours: Apartheid Power in Southern Africa 227–228
Behra family 66
Bekker, Koos 417
Belafonte, Harry 206, 237–238
Bella, Ben 150, 468
Benin, Communist Call to Africa party participation 168, 171
Benjamin, Anwa 452
Benjamin, Najmie 452
Benjamin, Salie 452
Benson, Mary 295
Berlins, Marcel 55, 67
Bernstein, Hilda 44, 277, 430
Bernstein, Lionel (Rusty) 44, 62, 105–106, 277
Bernstein, Toni 51
Beukes, Gina 193
Beukes, Johan 193
Bhaba, Kaliq 78
Bham, Abdul 50, 79, 89, 100
Bhamjee, Ismail 182
Bharatiya Janata Party (BJP) 77
Bhayat, Zohra 38
Bhayet, Ahmed (Archie Boy) 32, 60–61
Bhikhoo, Fatima See: Bhyat, Fatima (née Bhikhoo)
Bhikhoo, Mohammed 43
Bhikhoo, Shamim (née Bhyat) 43
Bhowan, Amrit 50
BHP Billiton 452
Bhyat, Alice (née Sweetnam) 43
Bhyat, Farouk 72
Bhyat, Farouk Mohammed 43

Bhyat, Fatima (née Bhikhoo) 43
Bhyat, Hamid 43, 72
Bhyat, Shamim 72
Bhyat, Zaheer 43, 72, 100
Bhyat, Zaibie (née Patel) 35, 43, 72
Bidenko, Ivan 158, 161–162
Bidenko, Jiří 158–159
Bidenkova, Eugenie 158, 162
Bidenkova, Evuška 158–159
Biko, Steve 231–232
Bird, Adrienne 381
Birley, *Sir* Robert 74
Bisho Massacre (1992) 341
Black Consciousness Movement (BCM) 407, 464
Black Consciousness student organisations 60
Black Eyed Peas 479
Black, Sandra See: Pahad, Sandra (née Black)
Blair, Tony 101
Blatter, Joseph (Sepp) 472–475, 477, 483
Bloch, Graeme 376
BMW 452
Bogopane-Zulu, Hendrietta 426
Bogoslovsky, V. 107
Boipatong Massacre (1992) 340
Boigny, Felix Houphouët- See Houphouët-Boigny, Felix
Boonzaaier, M. J. 442
Booysens Indian High School 47
Bopape, David 285
Boraine, Alex 207
Botha, Ntombazana 451
Botha, P.W. 179
Botswana, Pahad visit 180–185
Bouneaud, Hélène 154
Bramdaw, Nirode 398
Brandaw, Sangeetha 398
Brand South Africa 418
Breytenbach, Breyten 208
British Anti-Apartheid Movement 69, 88, 232–241
British National Union of Students 74, 91
Brockway, Fenner 111
Brodie, *Mr* 47
Brooks, Alan 105, 106
Brown, Mannie 96, 376
Brown, Richard 75, 77–78

Brutus, Dennis 55, 56, 234
Brutus, May 95
BSA Bank 452
Building an African Partnership 456–457
Building an African Partnership: The Ahmed Baba Institute's New Library Archive In Timbuktu 450
Bulbulia, Ahmed 82
Bulbulia, Firdoze 530
Bulbulia, Zain 422
Bundy, Colin 295–297
Bunting, Brian 63, 102, 105–106, 108, 188–189, 204
Bunting, Sonia 63, 102, 104–106, 224, 346, 430
Bunzl, Tony 77, 210, 329
Burns, Emile 62–63
Bush, *President* 515
Busia, K. A. 468
Buthelezi, *Chief* Mangosuthu (Gatsha) 340, 364–365, 404, 410, 496
Buthelezi, Pule 329
Butshingi, Ephraim 502
Bwalya, Kalusha 476
Bwalya, Vivian (née Casaletti) 476

Cabaco, José 242
Cachalia, Ahmed 247
Cachalia, Amina 430
Cachalia, Azar 336, 350
Cachalia, Miriam 38, 247
Cachalia, Molvi 45, 47, 182, 247, 249, 251, 261, 285, 435, 461
Cachalia, Saad 182
Cachalia, Yusuf 47, 182, 261, 461
Cajee, Amin 30
Cajee, Imtiaz 87
Call to the Communists 226
Call to the People of South Africa 189
Call to the People of the World 189
Call to the South African People 103
Callinicos, Luli 301
Camay, Phiroshaw 336
Cape Verde and São Tomé, liberation struggles 220
Carolus, Cheryl 207, 376, 430
Carrera, Jeronimo 222
Casaburri, Ivy Matsepe- See: Matsepe-Casaburri, Ivy

Casaletti, Vivian See: Bwalya, Vivian (née Casaletti)
Castro, Fidel 143, 219, 221, 223, 290
Castro, Raúl 143, 221–222
Cell C 452
Central Indian High School 48, 50
Central Intelligence Agency (CIA) 54, 57
Chabane, Collins 466–467
Chalken, Shuaib 422, 422–424, 427
Challenge 101
Changing Curriculum: Studies on Outcomes-based Education in South Africa 379
Channock, Martin 55
Chapman, Graham 237
Chapman, Tracy 237
Charnley, Irene 417
Chavez, Hugo 76, 222
Cheadle, Thomson and Haysom 336
Chetty, Mana 233
Chiba, Laloo (Isu) 92, 280
Chikane, Frank 312–313, 400, 406, 409–412, 416–417, 445–446, 482, 498, 500, 516
Christians, Faghmie 452
Christie, Pam 378–379
Churchill, Winston 273
Cisse, Ibrahim 452
Cissokho, Seydou 269
Clarence, Graham 452
Class, Race and Black Liberation 315, 320
Coetzee, Kobie 207, 338–339
Cohen, G.A. 469
Cohen, Robin 55
Collure, Chandra 141
Collure, Raja 141–142
Comintern
  obligation to help those under colonial rule 215
  SA members 215
Comintern (1st Congress, 1919) 215
Comintern (6th Congress, 1928) 215
Commission on the National Liberation Struggle in Asian and African Countries 126
Communications (2000) 407
Communications Resource Centre 418
Communications Task Group (COMTASK) 407–408, 412, 414

Communist Call to Africa 141, 166, 168,
  170, 270
  adoption 168
Communist International See: Comintern
Communist Manifesto 214
Communist Party of Great Britain (CPGB)
  101
Communist Party of South Africa (CPSA)
  banning (1950) 105
  launch (1990) 330, 334
  reconstituted as SACP (1953) 105
Communist Party of the Soviet Union
  Congress (CPSU) (1976) 166
Communist Party of the USA (CPUSA)
  Henry Winston role 314–318
Communist and Workers' Parties of Tropical
  and Southern Africa 141, 166
Community Support Initiatives for Refugees
  (COSIR) 154
Compaore, Blaise 400
Concerned Africans Forum (CAF) 523
Congo, Call to Africa, party participation
  168, 170
Congress Alliance 42, 46, 219
Congress of the Communist Party of Cuba
  (1975) 173
Congress of the CPSU (25th, 1976) 166
Congress of Democrats 46, 49
Congress of the People (COP) 51–52
Conran, Caroline 400
Convention for a Democratic South Africa
  (CODESA, 1991) 66, 209, 289, 337-338
  ANC balance of power shift 341
  ANC negotiations committee 339–340
  AWB attack on World Trade Centre 349
  Bisho massacre effect 340–341
  Boipatong massacre effect 340–341
  election decision 349–350
  Interim Constitution ratified 349
  SACP representation 338–341
  Working Groups 338–339
Cooper, Saths 376, 398
Coovadia, Ahmed (Popeye) 327
Coovadia, Ismail 88–89
COP 52
Corbett, Michael 337
Corrigall, Jimmie 198
COSATU 386, 393, 490–491
Coulibaly, Sinaly 451

Cox, Idris 138–139
Craig, Jerome 476
Craven, Danie 201–202
Creecy, Barbara 200
Cronin, Jeremy 209–210, 329–330, 342,
  348, 487
Cry Freedom 90
Cuba, assistance to liberation struggles 219–
  221
Cupido, Oswald 453
Curran, Chris 195, 198
Curran, Maryvonne 195, 198
Curran, Stephanne 195, 198

Dadabhay, Aadam 524
Dadabhay, Abdul Haq (Freeman) 29
Dadabhay family 31, 82
Dadabhay, Fatima 524
Dadabhay, Hamzah 524
Dadabhay, Imaan 524
Dadabhay, Mohammed 210
Dadabhay, Mohammed (MoD) 328, 524
Dadabhay, Mohammed-Ilyaas 524
Dadabhay, Nadia 524
Dadabhay, Shehnaaz (née Pahad) 41, 82,
  210, 324, 327–328, 374, 524
Dadabhay, Tickey 326
Dadabhay, Yasmin (née Pahad) 79, 82, 99–
  100, 183, 192, 210, 324, 327–329, 524
Dadabhay, Yusuf (Dada) 82, 183, 192, 210
Dadabhay, Yusuf (Georgie) 210, 524
Dadabhay, Zaeem 328, 524
Dadabhay, Zaidaan 524
Dadabhay, Zakkiya 183, 210, 328, 524
Dadabhay, Zayd 210, 328, 378, 524
Dadabhay, Zeenat 328, 524
Dadoo, Ahmed 327
Dadoo, Roshan 266, 523
Dadoo, Winnie 266, 268
Dadoo, Yusuf 36, 38, 42–44, 46–47, 69, 73,
  77–78, 83, 85, 90, 94, 105, 108, 111, 122,
  170, 181, 184–185, 214, 233, 247, 255,
  260–269, 273, 294, 302–303, 318, 325,
  345, 461
  biographical and SA struggle information
  260–269
Dadoo-Xuma-Naicker Pact (1947) 262
Daily Worker 234
Dakile-Hlongwane, Salukazi 417

Daling, Marius 417
Dammers, Jerry 237
Dangor, Mohammed 523
Daniels, Enver 289, 337
Daniels, John 139
Dansokho, Amath 124, 141, 150, 152, 166–169, 260, 269–272, 282, 284
  biographical and Senegal struggle information 269–272
Dansokho, Babette 140, 270
Dansokho, Laurence 270
Dansokho, Yacine 270
Darnborough, Anne 75
Davids, Abubakker 452
Davidson, Apollon 118
Davidson, Basil 177
Davies, Anne 83, 195–196
Davis, Angela 126, 318–319
De Beer, Zach 366
De Jonge, Klaas 460
De Keyser, Ethel 232–233
De Klerk, F.W. 171, 202, 208, 279, 289, 331, 337, 341, 373, 391, 473
De Klerk, Willem 407
De Villiers, Mila 30
Defiance Campaign (1952) 39, 41, 45, 47, 285, 294
Dela, Qinsile 382
Delrio, Graziano 246
Dempsey, Charles 472
Development Bank of South Africa 452
Dibango, Manu 271
Didiza, Thoko 404, 430, 471
Dinat, Issy 79, 96, 196
Dinat, Natalya 196
Dinat, Ramnie 95–96
Dinat, Sean 196
Dingale, Michael 180
Diouf, Abdou 269, 271
Disabled People of South Africa (DPSA) 423
Dison, David 407
Dlamini, Chris 287, 342
Dlamini, Dumisani 381
Dlamini, Martha 93
Dlamini, Steve 190
Dlamini-Zuma, Nkosazana 60, 399, 404, 417, 430, 475, 482
Dlodlo, Ayanda 430

Docrat, Farida (née Patel) 43
Docrat, Rashid 43
Docrat, Sharifa (née Patel) 43, 44
Docrat, Yusuf 43
Docrat, Zarina 43
Dollie, Hanief 452
Dolny, Helena 376
Dominy, Graham 452
Dos Santos, Marcelino 178, 352
Dos Santos, Pam (née Beira) 178, 352
Douglass, Frederick 317
Doyle, Charlie 101
Doyle, Micky 101
Drabek (*contact with Communist Party of Czechoslavakia*) 154–155
Drum magazine 50, 59
Du Bois, W.E.B 317
du Plooy, Louis 222, 381–382, 452, 505
Du Toit, Dirk 405
Du Toit, Natalie 428–429
Duarte, Jessie 253, 290, 355, 376
Duche, Wilma 425
Dyani, Johnny 90
Dynamos Football Club (Moscow) 115, 216
Dynamos Football Club (SA) 29, 32, 56, 80, 276, 480, 531

Ealing Anti-Apartheid Movement 197
Ebrahim, Ebrahim 253
Ebrahim family 531
Ebrahim, Gora 277
Ebrahim, Shaheen 451
Echeverria, Luis 112
Eight Days In September: The Removal of Thabo Mbeki 500
elections (1994)
  Electoral Commission established 350
  Johann Kriegler interview on 356–368
  Multiparty Liaison Committee 357–358, 365
  Party Liaison Committee 350, 356, 364–365
  preparations 350–351, 353–368
  results 368–369
elections (1999)
  Essop Pahad role 396–399
  KZN results 399
  preparations 396–397
  SABC coverage issue 397

537

Elliott, Gail 381
Engels, Friedrich 214–215, 469, 490, 507
Epstein, Helen 510
Eriksson, Lars-Gunner 231–232
Erwin, Alec 254, 334, 405, 417, 487
Esakjee, Suliman 62–63
Eskom 452
Essa, Adam 451–452
Ethiopia
  Communist Call to Africa party participation 168, 170–171
  Pahad visit 174–176

Faik, Nevin 83, 96, 195–196
Faik, Shay 196
Faik, Zed 196
Fakie, Shaukat 523
Farrell, Mairéad 203
Farrell, Niall 132, 203
Fast, Howard 62
Fatogun, Dapo 171–173
Faux, Andrew 81
Faux, Geoffrey 81, 197
Faux, Jill (née Shorrock) 81, 197, 210, 329
Faux, William 81
Federation of South African Women (FEDSAW) 47
Feinberg, Barry 105–106
Feni, Dumile 90, 191
Fernandes, Antonio 346, 351, 376
Ferreirastown 31
  Becker Street gang 32–33
  gangs 30–33
Feza, Mongezi 90
Field, Scott 428
FIFA World Cup (2010) 406, 450, 468, 472, 472–483
  bidding process 472–475, 481–483
  Cape Town as a host city 477–478, 484
  Irvin Khoza tribute to Essop Pahad 480–483
  Kick-Off Celebration Concert 479
  Local Organising Committee (LOC) 475–480, 483
  mascot Zakumi 477, 483
  media coverage 478–479
  opening ceremony 479
  result 479
  SA wins host bid 474

slogan 476
Fifty Fighting Years – The South African Communist Party 1921-1971 48, 104
Filling, Brian 101, 235, 239, 298, 529
Filling, Mary 101, 239
First International 214
First, Ruth 179, 430
Fischer, Abraham (Bram) 92
Fischer, Ilse 51
Fischer, Molly 48, 50
Fischer, unknown 61
Fischer, Abraham (Bram) 40, 56, 68, 260
Fit to Govern: The Native Intelligence of Thabo Mbeki 510
Fowler, Trevor 319, 376, 407, 409
Franklin, Aretha 319
Fraser, Malcolm 235–236
Fraser-Moleketi, Geraldine 209, 329–330, 342, 350, 376, 389, 404, 430, 443–445, 493
Free Nelson Mandela Campaign 206, 236, 237
Freedom Charter (1955) 51–54, 60, 199, 246, 325, 330
French, Ed 379
Freshly Ground 479
Frontline States, support to ANC 227–228
Funde, Eddie 208

Gabriel, Peter 237
Gaetsewe, John 149
Gandhi, Indira 251, 265
Gandhi, Mahatma 36, 43, 231, 248, 250, 262, 265, 306
Gandhi, Rajiv 251
Gandhi, Sonia 253–254
gangs 30–33
Gani, Ahmed 326
Gani, Farida See: Pahad, Farida (née Gani)
Gani, Farouk 326–327
Gani, Zaida 326
Gani, Zayd 326–327
Gani, Aaminah See: Loonat, Aaminah (née Gani)
Garner, Lesley 76, 81
Garro, Yacoub 128–130
Garvey, Chloe 193
Garvey, Micky (Marietjie) (née Beukes) 193, 195

Gaster, Polly 177
Gawe, Stephen 244
Gay, Lionel 92
Gaye, Marvin 288
GEM (Meg Pahad, *pseud*) 107
Gensous, Pierre 150
Gere, Richard 237
German Democratic Republic (GDR), party support to liberation struggles 224
Gerwel, Jakes 197, 292, 372, 409
Gibson, Douglas 397
Gifford, *Lord* Tony 131–132, 177, 198
Gill, Ken 102
Gill, Tess 102
Gillwald, Cheryl 405
Ginwala, Frene 248, 267, 425–426, 430, 487
Ginwala, Gene 244
Girginov, Girgin 145–146
Giuffredi, Armando 245
Godfrey, Steve 407
Goga, *Dr* 43
Goga, Feriel (nee Patel) 43
Goldberg, Denis 64, 287
Goldberg, Whoopi 237
Golding, Marcus 350
Golding, Pam 417
Goldreich, Arthur 64
Gomomo, John 342
Gonsharov, Viktor 218
Gooding, Francis 196
Gooding, Mel 76, 91, 96, 196, 200, 399–400
Gooding, Rhiannon (née Richards) 76–77, 91, 96, 196, 200, 399
Goodluck, Wahab 171, 171–173
Gool, Cissie 430
Gorbachev, Mikhail 135, 144, 218, 284
Gordhan, Ketso 200, 350
Gordon, Anne J. 336
Govan Mbeki 295
Govan, *Reverend* William 297
Govender, Bommie 51
Government Communication Information System (GCIS) 252
  CEO selection 409
  COMTASK recommendations 407–408, 412–414
  current affairs initiative 410

imbizo initiative 410–412
  IMC role 416–418
lekgotla initiative 409–410
  MDDA role 414–416
  MPCC role 412–413
Graham, Bruce 75
Gray, Robert 235
Griessel, Steve 417
Grigorian, Arkady 114–119
Grigorian, Nadia 114
Grondona, Julio H. 473
Groot Schuur Talks 209
Growth, Employment and Redistribution (GEAR, 1996) 386–388
Guinea Bissau, liberation struggles 220
Gumbi, Mojanku 374, 407, 471, 516
Gunby, Derek 76–77, 399
Gurney, Bethan 240
Gurney, Christabel 91, 102, 195–196, 232, 240–241
Gwala, Harry 197–198, 226, 334, 339
Gwangwa, Jonas 238, 376

Hain, Peter 234
Hall, Gus 314, 318–319
Hall, John 336
Hanekom, Trish 342
Hani: A Life Too Short 343
Hani, Chris 93, 100, 186–187, 190, 221, 223, 252, 294, 302, 306, 334, 337–338, 340–347, 356
  biographical information 343–347
Hani, Khwezi 346
Hani Memorandum 93, 302, 344–345
Hanlon, Joseph 228
Hanna, Anton 154
Harare Declaration 304–305
Harman, Hugh 417
Harmel, Barbara 51
Harmel, Michael 41, 51, 73
Harmel, Michael (A. Lerumo, *pseud*) 48, 104–106, 122, 138, 224, 268
Harmel, Ray (née Adler) 55
Harriman, Leslie O. 243
Harris, Brian 153–154
Harris, Kevin 152, 154
Harris, Noel 152–154, 203
Harris, Rhona 152, 154
Hartley, Armien 452

Hartslief, Odette 410–412
Harvey, Ebrahim 502
Hassani, Haider 150–152
Hassani, Maj 152
Hassani, Sarah 152
Haxton, Jan 77
Haxton, Jan See: McColl, Jan (née Haxton)
Haxton, Wendy 77, 84, 197
Hayatou, Issa 472
Hayden, Robert 317–318
HBZ Bank 452
Heard, Tony 407
Hellenic (Greek or Cypriot, Italian, Portuguese Alliance of South Africa (HIP) support to ANC 245–246
Hepple, Bob 286
Hernandez, Esteban Lazo 223
Higgs, Vivian 93
Hill, Joe 85
Hlatshwayo, Nokuthula 375
Hlatshwayo, Siphiwe 375
Hlongwane, Salukazi Dakile- See: Dakile-Hlongwe, Salukazi
Hodgson, Jack 41, 94
Hodgson, Rica 40
Hogan, Barbara 238, 253, 280
Holland, Eva 240
Hollingsworth, Tony 237, 238
Honecker, Erich 144
Houphouët-Boigny, Felix 468
Houston, Gregory 343, 460, 465
Huddleston, Father Trevor 51, 236, 238, 263
Hughes, Bob 236
Hulett, *Sir* Liege 35
Hume, A.O. 250
Hunger March, Washington DC, 1931 314
Hutchinson, Alfred 48–51
Hutchinson, Hazel (née Weiler) 49

IBSA (India, Brazil, SA) 252
Imbizo 408
Independent Communications Authority of South Africa (ICASA) 414
Independent Examinations Board (IEB) 55
Independent Media Diversity Trust 414
India
  academic contact with SA 257
  ANC support 251-254
  donation to ANC after Mandela visit
  (1990) 251
  INC association 250-254
  Kolvad importance to freedom fighters 255–256
  relations with SA 251–252
  arms trade resuscitation attempt with SA 254
  trade embargo and sanctions on SA support 250–251
Indian Congress 40, 42, 46
Indian National Congress (INC, India) 250-254, 257
Indian population (SA) early history (SA) 33–35
Indian Youth Congress 60
  anti-apartheid movement 251
Innis, Roy 316
Inside BOSS: South Africa's Secret Police – An Ex-Spy's Dramatic and Shocking Expose 202
Institute for Democratic Alternatives in South Africa (IDASA) 201, 207–208
Insurgent Diplomat – Civil Talks or Civil War? 206
Interair 452
International Defence and Aid Fund (IDAF) 192
International Financial Advisors (Kuwait) 453
International Marketing Council 416–418
  Brand South Africa campaign 418
  Communications Resource Centre 418
  Yvonne Johnston observations 418
International Marxist Tendency 76
International Meeting of the Communist and Workers' Parties (Turkey, 2019) 141
International Monetary Fund (IMF) 442
International Organisation of Journalists 148
International Scientific Conference (1980) 169
International Union for the Conservation of Nature 81
International Union of Students (IUS) 57, 93, 148, 214
International University Exchange Fund (IUEF) 73, 231–232
International Working Men's Association 214
Iraqi Women's League 137

Irish Anti-Apartheid Movement 202
Isaacs, Sam 381
Iscor 452
Isiakpere, Faith 530
Island in Chains: Ten Years on Robben Island 64
Ismail, Fazel 200
Ismail, Shabir 452
Iswe Lomzi 295
Italy See: Reggio Emilia
Ives, Burl 62

Jack, Joseph 296
Jackson, George 319
Jackson, James 318–319
Jacobs, Jessica 171
Jagan, Cheddi 133–134, 136, 260, 272–275
   biographical and Guyana struggle information 272–275
Jagan, Janet (née Rosenburg) 133, 275
Jaiswal, Abha 255
Jaiswal, Randhir 255–256
Jana Sakthi 267
Jansen, Jonathan 378–379
Jassat, Abdulhai (Charlie) 52, 62–64, 95–96
Jassat, Essop 52, 62, 277, 324–325
Jassat, Harlene (nee Pillay) 52, 79, 95–96
Jassat, Isa See: Pahad, Isa (née Jassat)
Jeenah, Na'eem 523
Jele, Josiah 178, 244
Jeppie, Shamil 452, 458
Joffee, Joel 79
Joburg Post 479
Johannesburg African Football Association 60
Johansson, Nils Lennart 472–473
Johardien, Goesain 452
John Paul II, *Pope* 243
Johnston, Yvonne 417–418
Jones, Ivan 215
Jordaan, Danny 417, 472–473
Jordan, Nandipah 192, 238
Jordan, Pallo 79, 86, 90, 179, 190, 192, 302, 305, 308–309, 311, 350
Joseph, Dasoo 72
Joseph, Helen 430
Joseph, Paul 62–63, 79
Journey into the Unknown 399
Junior Dynamos 326

Kabwe Conference (1985) 188–189, 191, 207, 303, 345
   NEC changes 189–190
   resolutions 189
Kajee, (Joe) 50
Kajee, Ruki 210
Kaka, Ahmed Suliman (Ronnie) 77-80, 82, 86, 196, 326
Kalla, Haroon 531
Karodia, Dawood 43
Karodia, Fowzia (née Patel) 43
Kasrils, Ronnie 94, 102, 105–106, 209, 255, 337, 340–342, 405, 445, 493, 499, 523
Kathrada, Ahmed (Kathy) 30-31, 39–40, 45, 47–48, 55, 59, 62–64, 105, 108, 214, 238, 253, 260, 266, 273, 275–280, 283, 285–287, 297, 301, 327
   biographical and SA struggle information 275–280
Katz, Michael 474
Kaunda, Kenneth 231, 305
Kaunda, Lakela 467
Keable, Ken 94
Keita, Modibo 453
Keita, Salif 237
Keitseng, Fish 189
Kemp, Stephanie 83
Kena, Mokhafisi 171–173
Kerr, Jim 237
Keshwani, *Miss* 247–249
Keys, Alicia 479
Kgalema Motlanthe – A Political Biography 502
Kgokong, Alfred 94
Kgomo, Emmanuel 382
Khan, Sherief 30–31, 33
Khanyile, Eleanor 178
Khanyile, Lenki 312
Khanyile, William 178
Khayinga, Wilson 92
Khosa, Meshack 460
Khota, Ahmed (Quarter) 327
Khota, Mohamed 82
Khoza, Irvin 472–474, 480–483
Khoza, Snowy 451
Khumalo, Sibongile 417
Kidjo, Angélique 479
King, Coretta Scott 289
King, Jane 97–98

King, Martin Luther 289
King, Melissa 38, 379, 381
Kingdom Foundation (Saudi Arabia) 453
Kingsolver, Barbara 125
Kitson, David 92
Klaaste, Aggrey 59
Kleinschmidt, Horst 523
Knox, Arthur 80
Kodesh, Wolfie 79
Kollapen, Jody 38
Kolvad House 44, 52
Kolvad Madressa 44
Konare, Alpha Oumar 451
Kornegay, Ellen 431–434
Kornegay, Francis 431
Kosukchin, N. 107
Kotane, Moses 26, 294, 302–303, 315, 318
Kriegler, Betty 366
Kriegler, Justice Johann 350, 528
  interview on 1994 elections 356–368
Kriel, Hernus 338–339
Krige, Sue 378
Kruger, Elsa 460, 465–467, 469
Kruger, Paul 28
Kunene, Raymond 75
Kuper, Adam 55
Kuper, Richard 55
Kuti, Femi 479
Kuugongelwa-Amadhila, Saara 526
Kuzwayo, Fezekile (Fezeka/Kwezi) 498–499

La Guma, Alex 79
La Guma, Blanche 430
Lagu, Lennox (Mongameli Tshali) 177, 344
Lamb, Jeff 55
Laher, Amin 178
Langa, Ilva Mackay 409
Langa, Mandla 108, 407
Langenhoven, Hilton 428
Lava, Jesus 281–282
Lava, José (Peping) (Philip Malaya, *pseud*) 124, 260, 281-283
  biographical and Phillipines struggle information 281–284
Lava, Vicente 282
Lawrence, Catherine 399
Lawrence, Peter 76–77, 399
Left-Wing Communism – An Infantile Disorder 490
legislation
  90-Day (later 180-Day) 64, 65
  Act of Union (1910) 28
  Asiatic Land Tenure Act (1946) 262
  Bantu Education Act (1953) 48
  Extension of University Education (1959) 52
  Group Areas Act (1950) 45, 47–48, 67
  Immorality Act (1950) 49
  Natal Coolie Law (1859) 33
  Terrorism and Internal Security Act 150
Lehohla, Pali 383, 385
lekgotlas 409–410
Lekota, Mosiuoa (Terror) 350, 404
Lembede, Anton 285, 301
Lenasia, Indian township 48
Lenin, Vladimir 215, 490, 507
Lennon, John 319
Leon, Peter 365, 366
Lerumo, A. (Michael Harmel, *pseud*) 48
Lesotho, Communist Call to Africa party participation 166
Lestor, Joan 233, 239
Letsebe, Anne 407, 409, 411
Letters from Robben Island 275, 278
Levine, Banele 375
Levine, Richard 376
Lewin, Julius 74
Lewis, Rupert 107
Leys, Colin 75
Lhamsuren, Badamyn 146–147
Liberal Party 54
Lings family 84
Lings, Lesley 85
Lings, Martin (Abu Bakr Siraj ad-Din) 85
Lings, Mary See: Shorrock, Mary (née Lings)
Little Rivonia Trial (1964) 92
Lloyd, Libby 414, 416
LNM Holdings 452
Lockhat, A. K. 452
Lombard, Fanie 428–429
London, Jack 62
Long Walk to Freedom 284–285
Longoni, Ruth 87
Loonat, Aaminah (née Gani) 326–327
Loonat, Maryam 327
Loonat, Mohammed 326–327

Loonat, Yusuf 327
Louw, Tony 74, 75, 77–78, 247–248
Louw, Raymond 407
Ludi, Gerald 56
Luhabe, Wendy 417, 418
Lusaka, Paul 407
Lutchman, Ramhori 61
Luthuli, *Chief* Albert 36–37, 53, 260, 263, 286, 301
Luyt, Louis 201–202

Mbalula, Fikile 475
Mabandla, Brigitte 405, 430, 453
Mabhida, Moses 149, 170, 190–191, 303
Mabiletse, Martin 54
Mabudafhasi, Rejoice 405
Mabuza, Lindiwe 312–313
McAlpine, *Mr* 46
McClain, Charlotte 422
McColl, Jan 192 (née Haxton) 192
McColl, Max 192, 195
McGregor, Chris 81
McGurk, *Brother* Neil 210–211, 376–377
Machel, Graça 246
Machel, Samora 177, 179, 242, 496
Machogo, Dan 383
McKenzie, Ricardo 382
Macmillan, Hugh 227
McNeil, Anne 195, 436
McNeil, George 195, 436
McNeil, Jenny 194–195
McNeil, Lily 194–195
Macozoma, Saki 513
Madagascar, Communist Call to Africa party participation 166–167
Madela, John 383
Madikizela-Mandela, Winnie 92, 238–239, 293–294, 334, 430
Madlala-Routledge, Nozizwe 405
Madumo, Tom 58
Maduna, Penuell 209, 291–292, 305, 404
Maerdhal, *Professor* 168
Mafana, Vathiswa 222, 382
Mafole, Tebogo 373
Mafunjwa, Dayina 520
Mafunjwa, Gracious 520
Magothi, Henry 376
Magubane, Ben 460–461, 465
Magubane, Bernard 460

Magubane, Peter 93
Mahanyele, Sankie Mthembi- See: Mthembi-Mahanyele, Sankie
Maharaj, Mac 92, 190, 209–210, 233, 334, 376, 3278
Mahjub, Abdel Khaliq 139
Mahlangu, *Chief* 383
Mahlangu, Poni Jafta 384
Mahlasela, Vusi 479
Mahlathini and the Mahotella Queens 238
Mahlaule, Jackson 92
Mahomed, Adam 398, 399
Mahomed, Ismail 337
Mahomed, Noorjehan 399
Maimane, Theresa 89
Makana, Simon 190
Makathini, Johnny 89–90, 188, 190
Makaula, Nana 417
Make, Cassius 190
Makeba, Miriam 237
Makgothi, Henry (Squire) 65, 182, 190, 209
Makhubu, Vincent 51
Makhura, David 246
Makiwane, Tennyson 94
Makopo, Isaac 182, 460
Makwana, Boysie 51
Makwetla, Thabang 185–186
Malaya, Philip See: Lava, José 9 (*pseud*)
Malebane-Metsing, Rocky 290, 353–354
Mali, Thami 343
Maliba, Alpheus 92
Maloka, Eddie 204, 205, 335, 341, 460
Maluleke, Winnie (Kensani) 382
Mamkhala, Nomwe 92
Manchka, (from International Dept of CPSU) 166
Manci, Robert 190
Mandela, Nelson 31, 36–37, 37, 39–40, 47, 64, 89, 136, 207, 208, 225, 236–237, 238–239, 243, 244, 251, 260, 266, 279–280, 283, 284–294, 297, 301, 305–307, 334, 337–338, 340–342, 346–349, 353–355, 367, 369, 373, 409, 473–474, 482, 501, 508, 509, 515
    biographical and SA struggle information 284–289
    death 293
    electoral system views 291–292
    inauguration as President of SA (1994)

543

290–291
reconciliation policy 291
retirement 292–293
Mandela United Football Club 294
Mandela, Winnie Madikizela- See:
  Madikizela-Mandela, Winnie
Mandela, Zindzi 294
Mangope, Lucas 290, 353, 353–354
Mangwane, Caroline 382
Mantashe, Gwede 221
Manuel, Trevor 207, 326, 404, 406, 437,
  439–443
Manzini, Mavivi 430
Maope, Keith 181
Maphai, Vincent 460
Maputo Declaration 171
Marcus Garvey, Anti-Colonial Champion
  107
Marcus, Gill 95, 246, 350
Mariam, Mengistu Haile 174, 176
Mariano, Celia See: Pomeroy, Celia (nee
  Mariano)
Mariano, Maurizio 246
Marks, J. B. 36, 149, 260, 292, 294, 302–
  303, 315
Marks, Ruby 529
Marks, Shula 78
Marshall, Carol 346–347, 351, 376
Marx, Karl 214–215, 320, 469, 490
Marzouq, Mousa Aba 530
Masekela, Barbara 201, 417, 430
Masekela, Hugh 237–238, 479
Masetlha, Billy 198, 202–203
Mashabane, Maite See: Nkoana-Mashabne,
  Maite 256
Mashamba, George 502
Mashishi, Moss 417
Masondo, Andrew 343, 460
Matabane, Sebiletso Mokone- See:
  Mokone-Matabane, Sebiletso
Mathoma, Thomas 452
Matigari 107
Matlhaela, Pauline 381
Matsebula, Sebenzile 427
Matsepe-Casaburri, Ivy 404, 417, 430, 444
Matshaba, Paulos 93
Matshikiza, John 90, 191
Matthews, Joe 94, 105, 405, 460–461
Mavimbela, Vusi 407, 494–495, 495–496

Mawani, Amin 196–198
Mawani, Susi 196–198
May, Ivan 460
Mayekiso, Caleb 92
Mayet, 'Chummy' 61
Mazwai, Thandiswa 456, 479
Mbatha, Asani 280, 293, 521
Mbatha, Dania Zinhle 521
Mbatha, Menzi 255–256, 293, 520
Mbeki, Epainette (Piny) 295, 300
Mbeki, Govan 64, 105, 198, 260, 285–286,
  335, 342, 343
  ANC/SACP/MK membership 294
  awards 294–295
  character 300
  Deputy President of the Senate 299
  MK role 296
  political life 294–300
  Sechaba International Conference
    attendance (1990) 298–299
  stance on the masses 299
Mbeki, Jama 300
Mbeki, Kwanda 300
Mbeki, Linda 300
Mbeki, Moeletsi 83, 300
Mbeki, Thabo 32, 59, 69, 75–77, 79, 83,
  86–90, 94, 96–97, 102, 105, 107, 112,
  114, 118, 119, 182–183, 185, 189–190,
  201, 207–208, 221, 222, 225, 230, 246,
  252–253, 275, 279, 283, 287–289, 290–
  291, 293, 295, 297, 299–300, 304–305,
  307, 311–312, 327, 333, 336–337, 339,
  347, 348, 353–354, 372–374, 374–375,
  396, 397–398, 399–401, 406–408, 410–
  412, 415, 417, 423–424, 427, 431, 434,
  450–451, 455–456, 459–460, 460, 462,
  465, 470, 472, 473, 475, 479, 486–487,
  489, 493–495, 496–501, 501, 503, 507-
  508, 523
  African Renaissance ideal 509
  ANC as dominant liberation movement
    508
  character 506–509
  Deputy-President 292
  first cabinet members 404–405
  HIV/AIDS issue 510–511
  political life and biograhical information
    506–509
  President (1999) 251-252, 292, 399

anti-Mbeki campaign 493,499–500
cabinet (1999) 400–401, 404–405
campaign against 501–502
criticism by SACP leaders for neo-
liberal policies 493
GCIS initiatives 409–422
I am an African speech 509
NEC *lekgotla* review (2007) 489–490
recall 501-502, 516-517
relationship with Zuma 497–498
stance on
HIV/ Aids 510–512
liberation struggle history 460
Zimbabwe 510, 512-515
Mbeki, Zanele 312, 399,430, 437, 470–471, 523
Mbete, Baleka 246, 355, 431
Mboweni, Tito 198, 201
Mbulu, Letta 238
Mda, A. P. 285, 301
Mdladlana, Membathisi (Shepherd) 404
Media (24) 452
Media Development and Diversity Agency (MDDA) 408, 414–416
Lumko Mtimde observations 414–415
Meer, Fatima 34, 430
Meer, Ismail 40, 63, 261, 285
Meli, Francis 91, 105–106, 190, 201, 204, 225–226
Memoirs (Kathrada) 40, 275–276, 280
Menell, Rick 451
Menon, Krishna 253
Metcalf, Mary 378, 380
Methuen, *Lord* Paul 28
Metsing, Rocky Malebane- See: Malebane-Metsing, Rocky
Meyer, Roelf 336, 341
Mfenyana, Sindiso 59, 507
Mhlaba, Raymond 64, 296-297, 335, 342
Mhlambiso, Thami 90
Mia, Adnaan 451
Midas Earthcote 452
Miners' Strike (UK, 1984-1985) 139
Mini, Vuyisile 92
Minicka, Mary 453
Minty, Abdul 50, 51, 69, 233, 234
Mitchell, Adrian 400
Mitchell, Celia 400
Mitchell, Charlene 126, 318–319

Mitra, Sandra Prasad 126–127
Mkaba, Zinakile 92
Mkhatshwa, Smangaliso 405
Mkhomdo, Rich 476
Mkhonza, Khanyi 416
Mkwayi, Wilton 92, 149
Mlambo-Ngcuka, Phumzile 404, 430, 437–439
Mlangeni, Andrew 64
Mncube, Stephen 407
Mngoma, Venus 93
Mngqikana, Lindiwe 96
Mngqikana, Sobizana (Bizo) 79, 85-86, 89-90, 96, 100, 229, 345
Mntwana, Ida 47, 430
Mnumzana, Neo 244
Mnyele, Thamsanqa (Thami) 184
Moabi, Max 244
Modi, Narendra Damodardas 77
Modise, Billy 188
Modise, Jackie 430
Modise, Joe 187–188, 190, 292, 354, 495
Modise, Tim 476
Mofolo, Tebogo 181
Mofutsanyana, Thabo 295
Morogoro Conference (1969) 94-95, 199, 264–265, 303, 345
decisions 94
impetus to cadres 104
post-Conference attacks on Tambo 94
post-Conference stimulation to liberation struggle 94–95
Revolutionary Council established 199
Mohamed, Feroze 134
Mohamed, Ismail 66–68, 289
Mohammed, Ali 61
Moholo, Louis 90
Mokae, Zakes 90
Mokgalagadi, Teboho 428
Mokoena, Julius 346
Mokoena, Walter 478–479, 530–531
Mokone-Matabane, Sebiletso 407
Mokou, Oupa 452
Mokwebo, George 93
Mokwena, Thabo 182
Molale, Kate 430
Molefe, Popo 290, 350, 354
Molefe, Sidney 251
Moleketi, Geraldine Fraser- See: Fraser-

Moleketi, Geraldine
Moleketi, Jabu 209, 342, 376, 444, 475, 488, 490, 493
Molife, Mancy 51
Molobi, Eric 376
Molokomme, Athaliah 433
Mompati, Ruth 190, 243, 430
Mongalo, Antonio/Anthony 102, 145, 190, 225, 242–244, 246
Monteiro, Oscar 171
Moola, Ebrahim, 62
Moola, M. H. 249
Moolla, Mohammed 327
Moolla, Moosa (Mosie) 32, 62–64, 66, 214, 251, 253
Moonsamy, Kesval (Kay) 231, 335
Moosa, Valli 404
Moosajee, 50
Moposho, Florence 190
Morales, Evo 479, 488
Morning Star 97, 101–102, 234
Morobe, Murphy 238, 407, 439
Morotoba, Sam 381
Moseneke, Dikgang 350
Mosikare, Simon 93
Motala, Chota 63, 285
Motau, David 92
Motaung, Kaizer 474
Motaung, Simon 51
Motlana, Sally 431
Motlanthe, Gugu 503
Motlanthe, Kgalema 246, 401, 488, 502–504
   ANC Secretary-General (1997) 503
   political life and biographical information 502–503
   President of SA (2008) 502
Motlatsi, James 351, 417
Motsepe, Godfrey 244
Motshabi, Doreen 40
Motsheka, Angie 430
Motsi, Alexio 452–453
Motsoaledi, Caroline 277
Motsoaledi, Elias 64, 277
Motsuenyane, Sam 417
Moyo, Jonathan 515
Mozambique
   Call to Africa, party participation 168, 170-171

FRELIMO support from Reggio Emilia (Italy) 242
liberation struggles 220
Pahad visit 176–180
Mpahlwa, Mandisi Sipho 405
Mphahlele, Memory 51
Mposha, Florence 430
Msibi, Gugu 416
Msimang, Agnes 251
Msimang, Manto Tshabalala- See: Tshabalala-Msimang, Manto
Msimang, Mavuso 417
Msimang, Mendi 251, 301, 401
Mthembi-Mahanyele, Sankie 404, 430
Mthembu, Theo 55
Mthethwa, Nathi 475
Mtimde, Lumko 414–416
Mtintso, Thenjiwe 337, 342, 430
MTN 452, 460
Mtshali, Eric (Stalin) 148–150
Mufamadi, Sydney 185, 336–337, 342, 404, 475, 493
Mugabe, Robert 442, 513–515
Muhammad: His Life Based on the Earliest Sources 85
Mukherjee, Praneed, 256
Multipurpose Community Centres (MPCCs) 408, 412–414
Murray, Hugh 207
Muthien, Yvonne 199–200, 460, 461
Mvelaphanda 452
Mvemve, Douglas 93
Mxadana, Mary Ntswaki 312
My Fight Against Apartheid 180
Myburgh, Tertius 207

Naicker, G. M. 46, 78, 261
Naicker, M. P. 78, 91, 102, 105, 191, 224, 261, 267
Naidoo, Ama 38, 42, 431
Naidoo, Bala 398
Naidoo, H. A. 261
Naidoo, Indres 63–64, 96, 330
Naidoo, Jay 197, 334, 422
Naidoo, Krish 199–200
Naidoo, M. D. 244, 261
Naidoo, Nandha 233
Naidoo, Naransamy 261
Naidoo, Riason 452, 453–454, 456

Naidoo, Robbie 398
Naidoo, Shanthie 92, 95, 430
Naidu, Saantha 398–399
Naidu, Saras 399
Nair, Billy 149
Namibia, liberation struggles 220
Nanabhai, Jasmat 261
Nanabhai, Shirish 63 330
Nannan, Billy 59, 79, 83, 89, 96, 100, 102, 195, 267–268, 276, 375
Nannan, Nadine 196
Nannan, Nicky 196
Nannan, Theresa 95-96, 101, 195–196
Nannan, Vanessa 196
Nannan, Zinzile 195, 375
Napout, Juan Angel 473
Natal Indian Congress 91
M.P. Naicker as a leader 91
Nathan, Selwyn 482
National Conference of Solidarity for the Peoples of Southern Africa Against Colonialism, Racism and Apartheid (1978) 243
National Development Agency 420
National League of Young Liberals 234
National Party (NP)
negotiation demands 206–207
unbans ANC, SACP and other political organisations (2 February 1990) 208
National Peace Accord (NPA) (1991) 336–337
National Qualifications Framework (NQF) 380
National Union of Journalists 152
National Union of Mineworkers (NUM) 196
National Union of South African Students (NUSAS) 57, 91, 214
National Union of Teachers (NUT) 101
National Youth Commission 405
Nato, Benny 244
Ncube, Tembi 51
Ndamase, Bonke 61
Ndebele, Sibusiso 475, 502
Ndlovu, Sifiso Mxolisi 338, 460, 465–467, 469, 471–472, 475, 506
Ndou, Samson 92
N'Dour, Youssou 237
Ndzanga, Lawrence 92

Ndzanga, Rita 92
Neame, Sylvia 56
Nedcor 460
Nehru, Jawaharlal 36, 253–254, 265, 306
Nel, Estelle 381
Nelson Mandela Foundation 330
Nene, Nhlanhla 475
Neruda, Pablo 108
Netshitenzhe, Joel 204, 252, 338–339, 350, 406, 409–410, 412, 416-417, 491, 495–498
New Age 59
New Horizon 172
New York Review of Books 510
Ngakane, Lionel 75
Ngakane, Nomsa 372–373
Ngcuka, Phumzile Mlambo- See: Mlambo-Ngcuka, Phumzile
Ngculu, James 343
Ngoasheng, Moss 200, 374, 407
Ngonyama , Smuts 487, 501
Ngoyi, Lilian 430
Ngubane, Ben 404
Ngudle, Looksmart 92, 343
Ngwane, Lindiwe 405
Nhlanhla, Joe 89–90, 100, 178, 190, 207, 346, 404, 495
Nhlapo, Welile 181
Nichol, Jim 240
Nicholson, Anne 56, 83, 112, 114
Nicholson, Fergus 91
Nicolaou, Stavros 245–246
NICRA 152
Nigeria, Communist Call to Africa party participation 166–167, 171
Nigeria Labour Congress (1975) 172
Nimir, Hanin 129
Nixon, *President* Richard 319
Nkadimeng, John 190, 342
Nkoana-Mashabane, Maite 256, 475
Nkobi, Poloka 198
Nkobi, Thomas 45, 190, 231, 244
Nkomati Accord (1984) 180, 496
Nkomo, Joshua 513
Nkomo, Susan 431, 433–434
Nkomo, William 285, 301
Nkosi, Stan 502
Nkuhlu, Wiseman 207, 407
Nobanda, Joseph 93

547

Nokwe, Duma 49, 51, 54, 90, 94
Nokwe, Poppy 90
Nokwe, Tiny 90
Non-Aligned Movement (NAM) 128
Non-Capitalist Development 107
Northern Ireland Civil Rights Association (NICRA) 132
Nosizwe (Neville Alexander, *pseud*) 107
Nothing About Us Without Us – Inside the Disability Rights Movement of South Africa 425–426
Nqakula, Charles 341–342, 353, 475, 487
Nqakula, Nosiviwe Mapisa 488
Ntenteni, Thami 374
Ntithe, Peter 37
Nujoma, *President* Sam 155, 243
Nxumalo, Jabulani (Mzala) 105, 148, 204
Nyanda, Siphiwe 225
Nyoka, Nkateko 460
Nzimande, Blade 205, 342
Nzimande, Busi 405
Nzo, Alfred 83, 112, 175, 183, 190, 201, 244, 247, 251, 267–268, 306

Oasis Group Holdings 452, 531
O'Callaghan, Kate 122
Odendaal, Andre 197
O'Dowd, Tony (Phineas Malinga *pseud*) 102, 105–106
Office on the Status of Disabled Persons (OSDP) 422–429
 disabled MPs assistance 424-
 Disabled People of South Africa role 423, 425–426, 428
 overseas funding 424
 Paralympics 428–429
 Shuaib Chalken observations 422–424
 William Rowland observations 425–426
Office on the Status of Women (OSW) 422, 429–430
 Ellen Kornegay observations 431–433
 establishment (1997) 431
 incorporated into Ministry of Women, Youth and People with Disabilities 433
O'Flaherty, Tommy 132
Oliphant, Molefi 472
Oliver Tambo: Beyond the Engeli Mountains 301
Oliver Tambo Remembered 301–302

Oliver Tambo Speaks 302, 312
O'Malley, Padraig 330, 333, 385, 388, 391, 393–395
Omar, Dullah 405, 495
One in Nine Campaign 499
Ono, Yoko 319
Oppenheimer Trust 452
Organisation of African Trade Union Unity (OATUU) 172
Orgill, Annie 376
Orient House 52
Osibisa 479
Ouédraogo, Joséphine 433

Pan Africanist Congress (PAC) 464, 466
 Freedom Charter stance 53–54
Pačes, *Dr* 157–158
Pachai, Bridglal 106
Padayachee, Links 61
Padayachee, Pickie 61
Padayachee, Roy 200, 325
Pahad, Aisha 42–43
Pahad, Adam 326
Pahad, Ahmed 325–326
Pahad, Aimee (née Topp) 242, 521–522
Pahad, Aisha See: Patel, Aisha (née Pahad)
Pahad, Amina See: Patel, Amina (née Pahad)
Pahad, Amina (née Tilly) 35, 37–38, 44, 79, 99, 276, 431, 435
 character 35–40
 death (1973) 42, 99
 Defiance Campaign participation 41
 Indian Congress participation 40
 London sojurn 42
 Passive Resistance participation 37–39
 politicisation 37–39
 posthumous award by President Mbeki 42
 returns to India 79
 visits London (1966) 79
Pahad, Amina Zanele 43, 126–127, 139, 142, 145, 155-159, 185, 193–194, 209–211, 222, 238, 254–255, 298, 328–329, 375, 375–378, 400, 436–437, 520-521
Pahad, Angina Parekh 181, 327, 399, 523–524
Pahad, Arshad 325–326
Pahad, Azad 326
Pahad, Aziz 29, 38, 41, 47–48, 51–52, 60,

63, 66–68, 72–73, 76, 79–80, 82–83, 86–89, 89, 94, 96, 100, 102–103, 116, 181, 183, 185, 190, 192, 195, 198–199, 201, 204–207, 209, 229, 234, 240, 246, 249, 267–268, 276, 278, 280, 290, 293, 311–312, 326–327, 333, 335, 337, 369, 374–376, 399, 405, 475, 488, 495–496, 516, 523–524
  awards 523
  Concerned African Forum (CAF) membership 523
  Deputy Foreign Minister (1994-2008) 523
  marriages 523–524
  marries Gloria Wilkinson (1971) 85–87
  military combat training 100, 116
  role in 1994 inauguration 369
  Tambo-Dadoo Palestinian Solidarity Committee chair 523
  Young Tigers Football Club 32
  Zimbabwe crisis role 516
Pahad, Essop 106
  African Communist involvement 106–111
  arrests
    (ANC strike 1961) 65–66
    (breaking banning order 1964) 66–67
  ASA involvement 60
  attends,
    COP 51–52
    IDASA meetings 207
    Marxist classes at Wits 56
    Marxist-Leninism classes arranged by TIYC 62
  awards
    Pravasi Samman Award (2015) 256
    Pravasi Bharatiya Samman Award (2015) 136
  awareness of mother's political stance 38
  banning (1964) 66–68
  Becker Street gang 32–33
  birth 29
  bridge player 56, 96
  census involvement 383–385
  Central Committee election 191, 204
  character 504–506
  CIA and security police at Wits 56-57
  death (2023) 527
  declines position of Premier of North West Province 290
  Deputy Minister to Deputy President (1996) 292, 373-374, 381–383, 395–396
  Dynamos Football Club involvement 56, 60–61, 80, 116, 276
  early political associations 47, 49, 51–52
  exile, early days 73–74, 88–89
  exile decision 67–69
  early days 73–74, 88–89
  family holiday in Maputo (December 1993) 351–353
  Family Tree 18–19
  Father See: Pahad, Goolam
  FIFA World Cup role 472–483
  first democratic election involvement (1994) 350–351, 353–356, 363–364
  football interest See: Dynamos Football Club
  Free Mandela Campaign and other concerts 206
  friendship with British communists 102
  GCIS budget vote 421–422
  Grandparents 42–43
  imbizo role 410–412
  IMC role 416–418
  informal notes from
    Chikane, Frank 445–446
    Fraser-Moleketi, Geraldine 443–444
    Kasrils, Ronnie 445
    Manuel, Trevor 437, 439–443
    Matsepe-Cassaburri, Ivy 444–445
    Mlambo-Ngcuka, 437–438
  interviewed by Padraig O'Mally 330–333
  Leeds University debate 95
  lekgotla role 409–410
  Lenin Party School (Moscow) training 100, 112–119, 114–119
  London exile
    early days 73–74, 88–89
    Maida Vale days 99
    North End House days 78–83, 95–96
    Shirland Road days 194–195
  Mandela's US speech-writing delegation 287–298
  marries Meg Shorrock (1971) 85–86
  MDDA role 414–416
  meets Meg Shorrock 76
  mentors
    Ahmed (Kathy) Kathrada 275–280
    Amath Dansokho 269–272
    Cheddi Jagan 272–275

Govan Mbeki 294–300
Henry Winston, 313–321
José (Peping) Lava 281–284
Mandela, Nelson Rolihlahla 284–289
O. R. Tambo 301–313
Yusuf Dadoo 260–269
military training in Angola 185–188
Minister in the Mbeki Presidency (1999) 292, 401, 404
   responsibilities 405–407
   See also: responsibility concerned
Mother See: Pahad Amina (née Tilly) 35–42
MPCC role 412–413
NEC deployee 491–492
NEC overview (2006) contribution 488
Orient House 30–31
OSDP role 422–428, 435
OSW role 431–435
Paralympics role 428–429
parliamentary councillor to Mbeki 373
PhD research in India 247–249
post-Prague
   London return 191–198
   work 198–206
Prague years 123–148
   continued focus on Africa 166–173
   visit to, Angola 185–188
      Botswana 180–185
      Ethiopia 174–176
      Mozambique 176–180
      Somalia 173–174
   WMR colleagues and friends
      al-Dulaimi, Naziha Jawdet Ashgah 137–138
      Bauer, Roland 143–144
      Collure, Chandra 141–142
      Collure, Raja 141–142
      Cox, Idrcs 138–139
      Garro, Yacoub 128–130
      Girginov, Girgin 145–146
      Harris, Noel 152–155
      Hassani, Haider 150–152
      Lhamsuren, Badamyn 146–147
      Mitra, Sarada Prasad 126–127
      Mtshali, Eric (Stalin) 148–150
      Pittman, John 124–125
      Pittman, Margrit 125–126
      Ramotar, Donald 134–137

Rohee, Clement 133
Salim, Ahmed Salim 139–142
Salim, Thoraya 139–141
Stanishev, Dimitar 144–145
Stavrou, Agamemnon 127–128
Sudiman, Satyadjaya 128
Thomas, Elean Roslyn 130–132
Vivó, Raúl Valdés 142–143
Wushdan, Abu 138
Yazeji, Nawal 128–130
Presidential inauguration (1999) role 399–400
Regional Political Military Council deployment 198
relationship with Zuma 496–497
resignation as Minister in the Presidency 465–466, 479, 501–503
returns to SA 209–210, 324–329
RPMC secretary 199–200
rugby as a factor for change 201–202
SACP treasurer 329, 335
SACP, CC, non re-election (2002) 493–494
   non-active member 494
   recruitment and participation 102–105
SADET role 461–471
SANROC connection 55–56
schooling 47–51
stabbing (1993) 347–349
stance on
   African anti-apartheid support 227–228
   ANC counter-revolutionary forces 506
   ANC post-Mbeki recall 519–520, 525–526
   anti-Mbeki campaign 500
   CC members open declaration 333–334
   civil service change 388–389
   clean water access 392
   clinics 393
   Communist Party of China visit to SA (1992) 333
   constitutional amendment 395
   corruption 389–390, 392, 525
   COSATU 331, 334
      criticism of restructuring state assets 386
   counter-revolutionary threats 392–393
   CPSU suspension 331–332
   Cuba 219–224

de Klerk and NP selling out poorest
Afrikaners 391
electricity provision 392
first democratic elections 331
formation of SACP branches 334
Freedom Charter 330
GEAR 386–388
German Democratic Republic 224–227
government critics 390–391, 394–395
informers planted in ANC 391–392
international solidarity 214–224
liberal economic policies 385
Marxism 391
Mbeki recall as President 516–517, 519
membership recruitment 334–335
National Peace Accord 336–337
nationalisation 385–386
non-unionised labour 388
Palestinian struggle 526
Pass Laws 98
power-sharing 331
Russia 525–526
Russia-Ukraine conflict 525–526
SA economy 330
SACP issues (1990-1994) 333–336
school feeding schemes 392
second democratic elections (1994) 394
socialism 331–333
Soviet Union 216–219
student mobilisation 58–60
Tripartite Alliance tensions 393–395
worker representation at board level 330–331
xenophobia 516, 526
student associations 54–55
teaching career 98–99
Timbuktu Manuscript Project role 450, 453–459
TIYC, Central Branch founding 47
political activism influence 62, 214
tribute to
  Ahmed Timol 87–88
  Jawaharlal Nehru 253–254
  Meg Pahad 524–525
  Seth Phalatse 471
  Sifiso Ndlovu 471
tributes by
  Anand, Sharma 529
  Anant Singh 530
  Brian Filling 529
  Ebrahim family 531
  Faith Isiakpere 530
  Firdoze Bulbulia 530
  Haroon Kalla 531
  Irvin Khoza 480–483
  Ismail Vadi 531
  Johann Kriegler 528
  Mousa Aba Marzouq 530
  Oasis Holdings 531
  Oscar van Heerden 529
  Ruby Marks 529
  Vladimir Shubin 528–529
  Walter Mokoena 530–531
UCL studies 73–74
UN Convention on the Rights of Persons with Disabilities role 428
University of Sussex MA studies 74–77
University of Sussex PhD studies 77–78
visits to
  Bulgaria (1966) 89-90
  Cuba 221–224
  India 247–256
Vuk'uzenzele report 421
World Festival of Youth and Students attendance 100
World Marxist Review deployment and contribution 122–124 See also: Pahad, Essop, Prague Years
Pahad, Faeeza 326
Pahad, Farida (née Gani) 326–327, 327, 347
Pahad, Fazel 374
Pahad, Gloria (née Wilkinson) 80, 82-83, 86, 96 Wilkinson, Gloria 80, 82
Pahad, Goolam Hoosein Ismail 35, 42-46,78, 97, 180, 255, 261, 268, 273, 293, 324, 326, 435–436, 461
arrest 46
character 42
political stance 45–47
Kholvad Madressa association 44
Mahatma Gandhi association 43–44
SAIC leader 45
TIC leader 45
Pahad, Govan Timol 126, 154-155, 157-158, 161–162, 185, 193–194, 198, 209, 210, 211, 255, 271, 298, 328, 346, 375–376, 377–378, 400, 437, 521–522
character 522

551

Pahad, Hala 326
Pahad, Hugo Melt Martin 521–523
Pahad, Iman 326
Pahad, Isa (née Jassat) 325
Pahad, Ismail 29, 32–33, 47, 61, 79, 82, 97, 324, 326, 329
Pahad, Ismail (Goolam's cousin) 374
Pahad, Ismail (Zombie) 197
Pahad, Kulsie 97, 324, 329
Pahad, Meg (née Shorrock) 76–77, 79, 80–87, 96, 99–102, 107, 114, 119, 122, 124-126,, 130, 135, 140, 145, 151–155, 158, 160–161, 178, 181, 185, 187, 191–193, 195–196, 197, 209–210, 238, 254–255, 268, 271–272, 282, 290, 298, 328–329, 346, 348, 349–350, 356–369, 374–381, 398, 427, 436, 480, 501–503, 520–521, 524–525
  Assessment Education and Training Department head 381
  chapter in book entitled *Changing Curriculum* 379
  editorial work at Trade Union News Prague 151
  ESOF (GETOA) representative 379
  family holiday arrangements 197
    returns to SA 211
  GETOA chair 379
  IEB schooling section post 379
  joins
    CPGB 101
    NEPI initiative 378–379
  MEd degree studies 210, 378
  National Assessor Training Project 436
  NETF involvement 380
  NQF role 381
  Project Literacy role 436
  quality assurance consultant 436
  Sectoral Education and Training Authority role 436
  South African Certification Council role 436
  supportive role 85, 122, 169–170, 209–210, 395, 398–399, 480, 501–502, 524–525
  teaching career (UK) 97, 99, 122, 191–193, 209
  trip to Moscow 114
  trips to India with Essop 254–255
Pahad, Nallifoi See: Vania, Nallifoi 43 (née Pahad)
Pahad, Nassim 29, 48, 178, 195, 197, 293, 324–325
Pahad, Reyad 324
Pahad, Rouhana See: Pestana, Rouhana (née Pahad)
Pahad, Rukeya (Ruki) 79, 82
Pahad, Sam 195–196, 210, 240
Pahad, Sandra (née Black) 195, 375
Pahad, Shenaaz, 524
Pahad, Shireen 374
Pahad, Tau Topp Shorrock 521, 523
Pahad, Xavier Henry Goolam 521–522
Pahad, Yasmin 33, 41, 79, 82
Pahad, Yasmin See: Dadabhay, Yasmin (née Pahad)
Pahad, Yasmin 374
Pahad, Yumna 324
Pahad, Yusuf 183, 197, 37
Pahad, Zubeida 435–436
Pahad, Zuneid (Junaid) 29, 48, 78, 178, 195, 324, 326–327
Paine, Thomas 260
Pakendorf, Harald 207
Pakgwayo, Samson 382, 383–384
Palme, Olof 229–232
Palmer, *Mrs* 48
Pan Africanist Congress (PAC)
  armed struggle impetus 53
  banning (1960) 53
Pandor, Naledi 406, 430, 444, 487, 525
Panfilov, Yevgeny 146
Paralympics 428–429
Parekh, Angina See: Pahad, Angina (nee Parekh)
Parekh, Chandra 399
Parker, Kenny 75–76
Pascucci, Hanna 192–193
Pass Laws 58
Passive Resistance Council 46
Passive Resistance Campaign (1946) 37, 37–41, 45, 262
Patel, Abdul 43
Patel, Ahmed 30, 43
Patel, Aisha (née Pahad) 43–44
Mbatha, Amina Zanele (née Pahad) 43, 126–127, 139, 142, 145, 155-159, 185, 193–194, 209–211, 222, 238, 254–255,

298, 328–329, 375, 375–378, 400, 436–437, 520-521
Patel, Amina See: Saloojee, Amina (née Patel)
Patel, Anisa 43
Patel, Anver 43
Patel, Ebrahim 201
Patel, Farida See: Docrat, Farida (née Pahad) 43
Patel, Farouk 43
Patel, Feriel See: Goga, Feriel (née Pahad)
Patel, Fowzia See: Karodia, Fowzia (née Patel) 43
Patel, Haroon 61
Patel, Iqbal 30
Patel, Khairoonisha 51
Patel, Mohammed Amin 43
Patel, Rabia 43
Patel, Rukshana 43
Patel, Shamim See: Bhikhoo, Shamim (née Patel)
Patel, Sharifa See: Docrat, Sharifa (née Patel)
Patel, Yasmin 43
Patel, Zaibie 44
Patel, Zubeida 38, 43
Patheguey, Semu 135
Pauquet, Val 407
People's World 124
Pertini, Sandro 243
Pestana, Albert 325
Pestana, Rouhana (née Pahad) 325
Peters, Saliem 452
Phakgwayo, Samson 374
Phalatse, Lorato 407, 411
Phalatse, Seth 460-461, 471
Phillips, Maud 95
Pholoto, Samuel 93
Phosa, Mathews 488
Piliso, Mzwai 93, 190, 345
Piliso-Seroke, Joyce 431
Pillay, Harlene 277
Pillay, Herbie 52, 62, 95, 102, 277
Pillay, *Mrs* 277
Pillay, Patsy 233
Pillay, Vella 69, 233
Pinochet, Augusto 113
Pinsie, Saul 238
Pistorius, Oscar 428–429

Pitt, Dodo 379
Pittman, Carol 126
Pittman, John 124–126, 318–319
Pittman, Margrit (née Adler) 124–126, 319
Pityana, Barney 60
Platini, Michel 474
Pochee, Ahmed 82
Pochee, Willie 327
Political Affairs 124
Polokwane Conference (2008), NEC recalls Mbeki 500-501, 518
Zuma as President of ANC 256
Pomeroy, Celia (née Mariano) 281
Pomeroy, William 281–283
Ponomarev, Boris 168
Porter, *Lady* 195
Portside 126
Potenza, Emilia 378
Press, Ronnie 94
Pretorius, Lidia 422
Pringle, Malcolm 428
Prior, Mike 77
Problems of Peace and Socialism See: *World Marxist Review* 123
Pukwana, Dudu 90
Putin, Vladimir 219
Putini, Diza 49, 51

Rabkin, David 150
Rabkin, Franny 150
Rabkin, Sue 150
Radebe, Jeff 149, 225, 374, 400, 404, 408, 440, 475, 479
Radebe, Zinto 149
Radebe, Jeff 493
Radical Students Alliance (RSA) 236
Rajbansi, Amichand 338, 349
Rall, Martin 376
Rama, Vijay 78, 79, 89
Ramaphosa, *President* Cyril 306, 340–341, 366
Ramathlodi, Ngoako 287, 305
Ramelson, Bert 101, 139
Ramelson, Nina 101
Rammupudu, *Kgoši* Boleu 383–384
Ramos, Abraham Benatton 73
Ramotar, Alexei 134
Ramotar, Alvaro 134
Ramotar, Diolatchmee 134

Ramotar, Donald 134–137, 137, 256
Ramotar, Lisavita 134
Ramsamy, Sam 55, 234
Ramurula, Obed 51
Randera, Fazel 348, 523, 525
Randina, *Professor* 114
Ranku, Lucky 238
Ranthi, Maria 422
Rantho, Tshepo 407
Rashtriya Swayamsevak Sangh (RSS) 77
Rasool, Ebrahim 451, 477
Rayjack, Harry 55
Reconstruction and Development Plan (RDP, 1994) 387
Reddy, Govan 416, 419
Reeves, Peter 77-78
Reggio Emilia (Italy)
  relations with FRELIMO 242
  support to ANC 242–246
Relly, Gavin 207
Remembering Jawaharlal Nehru 253
Remembers Chris Hani: The Sun that Set Before Dawn 343
Reneke, *Field Cornet* 28
Resha, Maggie 430
Resha, Robert 42, 45
Reuben, Neville Z. 227
Reunion, Communist Call to Africa party participation 166–167
Review of African Political Economy 76
Revolutionary Communist at Work: A Political Biography of Bert Ramelson 139
Revolutionary Democracy in Africa: Its Ideology and Policy 107
revolutionary movements historiography 466 See also: organisations concerned
Ramjee, Jivan 50
Rhodesia, Wankie and Sipolilo Campaigns (1967-1968) 93
Richards, Ceri 76
Richards, Frances 76
Richards, Rhiannon See: Gooding, Rhiannon (nee Richards)
Risquet, Jorge 143
Rivonia Trial 64, 68, 79, 92, 277–278, 294, 297
Rivonia Trial (1964) 286
Road to Democracy Project 460–461
Road to Democracy in South Africa 224, 227, 229
Road to South African Freedom 122, 215
Roberto, Holden 220, 316
Roberts, Colin 101
Roberts, Ronald Suresh 510, 511, 514–515
Robeson, Paul 317
Rohan, Rafiq 420
Rohee, Clement 133, 134, 274
Rolling Stones 319
Roomaney, Shaboodien 451
Roth, Carolyn 192
Rosenburg, Janet See: Jagan, Janet (née Rosenburg)
Routledge, Nozizwe Madlala- See: Madlala-Routledge, Nozizwe
Roux, Carin 376–377
Roux, Edward 295
Roux, Naomi 377
Rowland, Tiny 305
Rowland, William 425–426
Ruiters, André 452
Rybakov, Vsevolod 124

Sachs, Albie 64, 83, 180, 189
Sachs, Johnny 102
Sacred Heart College Johannesburg 210–211, 375–378
Sader, *Dr* 261
SADET
  funding 460
  research team 460–461, 465–466, 471
  Road to Democracy
  mission and aspects covered 463–464
  vol. 1 461–464
  vol. 2 464–465
  vol. 3 465
  vol. 4 466–467
  vol. 5 468–469
  vol. 6 469–470
  vol. 7-9 471
Sahara 452
Salim, Salim Ahmed (*pseud*) 139, 166–168
Sall, Macky 271–272
Salooje, Suliman (Babla) 67–68, 92
Saloojee, Aboobaker 60
Saloojee, Aisha (née Vania) 38, 43
Saloojee, Amina (née Patel) 43
Saloojee, Anver 100, 222, 444, 452
Saloojee, Dawood 43

Saloojee, Hamed 326
Saloojee, Kadir 324
Saloojee, Mohammed 52
Saloojee, Riaz 200
Saloojee, Suliman (Babla) 40, 62, 255
Saloojee, Taariq 524
Saloojee, Yusuf (Charles) 79-80, 82–83, 85, 192, 196, 210, 326, 328
Saloojee, Yusuf (JoJo) 62, 100, 244, 326-327
Saloojee,Tahiyyah 524
Sands, Bobby 203
Sankara, Thomas 108, 400
Sapud, Ebrahim 452
Savimbi, Jonas 316
Scargill, Arthur 139, 196
Schleicher, Hans-Georg 224, 226
School Nutrition Programme 420
Schoon, Fritz 185
Schoon, Jeanette 185
Schoon, Katryn 185
Schoon, Marius 185
Schreiner, Barbara 200
Schreiner, Olive 48
Schutte, Danie 338
Schweizer, *Captain* 28
Schweizer-Reneke 28–30, 47
  destruction by British 28–29
  families of Indian origin 30
Scottish Anti-Apartheid Movement 101, 240
SDPS 452
Seamen's Strike (UK, 1966) 101, 139
Sechaba 91, 224, 243
Sechaba International Conference and Festival: Cultural Resistance to Apartheid (1990) 298
Seck, Idrissa 272
Second International (1889) 215
Sectoral Education and Training Authority (SETA) 436
Seedat, Tony 100, 233, 244
Sehanavis, Chinmohan 250
Sehanavis, Uma 250
Seifert, Mike 102, 196, 399–400
Seifert, Roger 139
Seifert Sedley 102
Sekgaphane, Thembi 312
Seko, Isaac 502
Sellschop, Jacques 460

Sellstrom, Tor 229, 231
Seme, Vusizwe (Essop Pahad, *pseud*) 106, 313
Semenya, Caiphus 238
Senegal, Communist Call to Africa party participation 166–167
Senghor, Léopold Sédar 269
Sepple, Ralph 79
September, Dulcie 191–192, 430
September, Hetty 430
September, Reg 102, 190, 198
Sere, M. (*pseud*) 171
Seroke, Joyce Piliso- See: Piliso-Seroke, Joyce
Serote, Mongane Wally 108, 132, 184, 198, 200–201, 205, 238, 310–312, 375–376, 523, 525
Sexwale, Tokyo 475
Seyd, Nicola 96
Shabangu, Elliot Goldberg 92
Shabangu, Susan 405, 475
Shabort, Petrus 337
Shaik, Schabir 498
Shakira 479
Sharma, Anand 251–255, 529
Sharpeville massacre (1960) 53, 285
Shiceka, Sicelo 475
Shilowa, Sam 221, 342, 493
Shope, Gertrude 190, 308, 430
Shope, Mark 149
Shorrock, Amabel 81
Shorrock, Celia 81
Shorrock, Chris 81
Shorrock family 83–84
Shorrock, Heidi 81
Shorrock, Jill See: Faux, Jill (née Shorrock)
Shorrock, Jim 83–85, 156
Shorrock, Luke 81
Shorrock, Marianne 81
Shorrock, Mary (née Lings) 83–84
Shorrock, Matthew 81
Shorrock, Meg See: Pahad, Meg (née Shorrock)
Shorrock, Michael 80–81, 210
Shorrock, Rosie 81
Shubane, Kehla 502
Shubin, Vladimir 118, 190, 218, 528–529
Sibeko, Archie 343
Sibley, Tom 139

Sigamoney, *Reverend* 55
Sigcau, Stella 404, 430
Sigxashe, Sizakele 190
Sikahlel'u-OR: A Praise Poem for Oliver Tambo 311
Sikhakhane, Joyce 92
Silverman, Roger 75
Simons, Jack 189
Simpson, Elaine 193–195
Sinclair, Elizabeth (Betty) 132, 203
Sinclair, *Professor* 418
Sindelo, Thami 244
Singh, Anant 398, 417, 528, 530
Singh, Debbie 261
Singh, Eric 224
Singh, Gyna 398
Singh, Kiyan 398
Singh, Vanashree 398
Sissoko, Cheick 454–455
Sisulu, Albertina 40, 244, 430
Sisulu, Lindiwe 430, 443, 460, 496
Sisulu, Walter 36, 39, 47, 51, 54, 59, 64, 283, 285–286, 296–297, 301, 306–307, 334, 342, 347–348, 353, 507, 515
Sisulu, Zwelakhe 238
Sita, Nana 261
Situ, Zanele 428
Sjöwall, Maj 125
Sklyarov, Yuri 124
Skosana, Ben 404
Skweyiya, Zola 225, 405
Slabbert, Frederik van Zyl 207, 372, 417
Slack, Mary 451–452
Slovo, Joe 40, 94, 105, 136, 170–171, 187–190, 266, 286, 289, 297, 303, 329, 335, 337, 339–340, 342, 345, 348, 356, 376
Smith, Ian 513
Smith, Janet 343
Smith, *Mr* 372
Smith, Terence 452
Smith, Terry Oakley- See: Oakley-Smith, Terry
Smithers, Maurice 376
Smuts, Dene 422
Smuts, *General* Jan 46
Sobukwe, Robert Mangaliso 53
Socialism and the Newly Independent Nations 107
Socialist Ideas in Africa 138

Socialist Unity Party (SED, GDR) 10th Congress, 1981 170
Solodnikov, V. 107
Somalia, Pahad visit 173–174
Soncini, Giuseppe 242–244, 245–246
South Africa-Mali Timbuktu Manuscripts Trust 405, 450–451
South African Airways 452
South African Breweries 452
South African Coloured Peoples' Organisation 46
South African Communist Party (SACP) 207
  armed struggle impetus 63
  armed struggle stance 296
  CIA interest on university campuses 57
  Congress
    (6th, Moscow, 1984) 190–191
    (11th, Rustenburg, 2002) 493–494
  emergence (1961) 53
  Essop Pahad responsibilities 492
  Internal Leadership Group (ILG) 297
  low membership reasons 205
  mass party decision 490
  Mbeki criticism for so-called neo-liberal policies 493
  M.P. Naicker as a leader 91
  Party Congress (7th, 1989) 205, 207
  Party Congress (8th, 1991) decisions 341–342
  party leaders dissatisfaction with Pahad and others 492–493
  reconstituted (1953) 105
  recruitment African intellectuals 205
  relations with Cuba 221
    GDR parties 224–225
  role 205–206
  Soviet Union training 219
  unbanned (1990) 208
South African Congress of Trade Unions (COSATU) 46
South African Democracy Education Trust (SADET) 405, 450, 460, 463–471
South African Indian Congress (SAIC) 42, 45, 46
South African Non-Racial Olympic Committee (SANROC) 55
South African Students Organisation (SASO) 60

South Africa-Mali Timbuktu Manuscripts Trust 405 See also: Timbuktu Manuscripts Project
Soviet Afro-Asian Solidarity Committee 219
Soviet Red Army Ensemble 62
Soviet Union, assistance to liberation struggles 216–219
Soweto Uprising (1976) 303, 464
Spartacus 62
Spicer, Michael 417, 474
Spies, Andre 452, 458
sports boycott 55
Squires, Hilary *Judge* 498
Standard Bank 452
Stanishev, Dimitar 144–145
Stanishev, Dina 145
Stanishev, Georgi 145
Stanishev, Sergey Dmitrievich 145
Starushenko, Gleb 218
State of Emergency (1960) 46, 53, 63, 294–295
Stavrou, Agamemnon 127–128
Stavrou, Dana 127
Stewart, Dave 373
Stofile, Makhenkhesi 425
Stone, Mark 452
Stop the Seventies Tour campaign 234
Stout, Rex 125
Strachan, Harold 295, 296
Strategic Problems in South Africa's Liberation Struggle: A Critical Alliance 107
Strategy for a Black Agenda – A Critique of New Theories of Liberation in the United States and Africa 315, 318
Straw, Jack 91, 236
Strydom, Miranda 506
Stuart, James (Hermanus Loots) 190
Stuart, Susan 298
Subbotin, Alexander 124
Sudan, Communist Call to Africa party participation 167, 171
Sudiman, Satyadjaya 127–128
Sukupova, Barbara 160
Suliman, Hamid (Tossie) 32
Sunmonu, Hassan 172
Suzman, Helen 67
Swart, Derek 200

Swartz, *Policeman and Dynamos team member* 67
Sweden, support to ANC 229–231
Sweetnam, Alice See: Bhyat, Alice (née Sweetnam)

Tamana, Dora 430
Tambo, Adelaide 40, 86, 88, 302, 305, 311–313, 430
   ANC MP (1994-1999) 313
Tambo, Dali 237, 309, 311, 523
Tambo, Nomatemba 246
Tambo, O. R. (Oliver Reginald) 31, 47, 86, 88–90, 93–94, 177–178, 189–190, 198, 204, 207, 225, 229–231, 242–246, 260, 264, 285, 287, 301–313, 344–345, 347, 430, 508
   ANC President re-election (1969) 303
   character 303–304
   death 306, 347
   hands over ANC Presidency to Nelson Mandela 306
   political life 301–311
   speech-writing 508–509
   stance on. environment 309
      Hani's assassination 306
      negotiations 304–305
      women 308
   tributes by
      Dali Tambo, 309
      Gertrude Shope 308
      Mongane Wally Serote 310–311
      Nelson Mandela 307
      Pallo Jordan, 308–309
      Thabo Mbeki 307–308
      Walter Sisulu 307
Tambo, Thembi 311
Tambo, Tselane 311
Tambo-Dadoo Palestinian Solidarity Committee 523, 526
Tamil Federation 398
Tarimo, Elias C. 227
Tata Afrika 452
Teachers Against Racism campaign 101
Teixeira, Ricardo Terra 473
Telkom 452
Temba, Can 50
Tenerini, Louis 151
Terry, Mike 91, 95, 100, 236, 238–239, 241

Tetekin, Vyacheslav (Slava) 119, 219
Thabo Mbeki Foundation 450, 470–471
Thandaray 50
Thatcher, Margaret 237
The African Communist 90, 104–106, 122, 148, 172, 174, 198, 204–205, 216–217, 224, 313, 329–330
The Blood Knot 90
The Comedians 90
The Communist Manifesto 490
The Compassionate Healer: A Biography of Dr Essop Jassat 324
The End of a Regime? An Anthology of Scottish-South African Writing Against Apartheid 298
The Forest 281
The Fundamentals of Marxism-Leninism 63
The Hungry Half – A Study in the Exploitation of the 'Third World' 138
The Impending Catastrophe and How to Combat It 507
The Individual and Society 469
The International Aspects of the South African Indian Question, 1860-1971 106–107
The London Recruits 94
The Lusaka Years: The ANC in Exile in Zambia, 1963 to 1993 227
The National Policy Framework for Women's Empowerment and Gender Equality 2000 434–435
The Passion of Sacco and Vanzetti 62
The Peasants' Revolt 295–296
The Road to Democracy in South Africa 232
The Road to Ghana 48
The Second Peasant War in Germany 507
The Socialist Way of Life 103
The Solemn Declaration of African Heads of State on Gender and Development 434
The South African Communist Party: Exile and After Apartheid 204, 335, 341
The South African Story 418
The Sowetan 59
The Story of an African Farm 48
The Struggle is My Life 243
The Thabo Mbeki I Know 506, 516
The Thinker 76–77, 219, 260, 309, 431, 453, 456, 473, 525, 530
The West on Trial – My Fight for Guyana's Freedom 273
The World 59
Theory of History: A Defence 469
Thiong'o, Ngũgĩ wa 107–108, 132
Thokan, Akhtar 451
Thomas, Elean Roslyn 130–132, 198
Thomas, Gareth 193
Thompson, Jeremy 341
Thoraya, (*pseud*) 139–140
Three Doctors Pact (1947) 262
Thusong Centres 413
Tikly, Mohammed 267, 369
Tilly, Ahmed (Dadiseth) 44
Tilly, Amina See: Pahad, Amina
Tilly, Ebrahim 249
Tilly, Essop 249
Tilly, Ismail 249
Tilly, Suleiman 249
Tilly, Zohra 249
Timbuktu Manuscript Project
  book project 457–459
  Cape Town conference 458
  COESSA role 451–452, 457
  damage by AQIM 459
  digitisation 459
  donors 452–453
  fundraising 453, 455
  logistics 453–455
  Mali technical building team 452, 455
  opening 456–457
  President Mbeki stance towards 450–451
  SA technical building team 452
Time is Not the Measure – A Memoir 494
Time Longer than Rope 295
Timol: A Quest for Justice 87
Timol, Ahmed 62, 68, 72, 74, 79, 82–83, 87–88, 100–101, 112, 114, 209, 255
  posthumously awarded Isitwalandwe Medal (2019) 88
  tribute by Essop Patel 87–88
Timol, Mohamed 82
Tloome, Dan 49, 147, 182, 190–191, 342
Toefy, Abdullah 452
Topp, Aimee See: Pahad, Aimee (née Topp)
Topp, Ann 521
Topp, John 522
Toyota 452
trade union development 465
  See also: COSATU

Trade Union News 151
Traikova, Marina 218
Transkei in the Making 295
Transnet 452
Transvaal Indian Congress (TIC) 31, 42, 45, 48, 214, 286, 324–325
   Ferreirastown office 331
   Macosa House office 32
   Nassim Pahad involvement 29, 324–325
   resuscitation 29
Transvaal Indian Youth Congress (TIYC) 31, 47, 49, 51–52, 54, 275–276, 286
Traoré, Issa 452
Traoré, Mamadou Lamine 453
Traoré, Seydou 452
Treason Trial (1956-1961) 50, 63–64, 285
Trew, Tony 409, 419
Trial of Twenty-two 93
Triesman, *Baron* David 101–102
Tripartite Alliance tensions 393–395
Tromp, Beauregard 343
Trotskyite New Unity Movement 54
Truth and Reconciliation Commission 232
Tsedu, Mathatha 407
Tselapedi, Reverend 354
Tshabalala, Manto 187
Tshabalala, Siphiwe 479
Tshabalala-Msimang, Manto 442
Tshwete, Steve 201, 305, 340, 400–401, 404, 495
Tsoletsi, David 93
Tsvangirai, Morgan 515
Turok, Ben 63, 98, 107
Turok, Mary 102
Tutu, *Archbishop* Desmond 244, 473–474, 479–480
Two Tactics 490
Tyres, John 381

UB 40 237
Ulyanovsky, R. 107, 166
Umkhonto we Sizwe (MK)
   formation (1961) 63
   Rhodesia Campaigns (1967-1968) 93
   unrest in ANC camps leading to Morogoro Conference 94
Umsobomvu Youth Fund 405, 420
UN Centre Against Apartheid 243
UN Conference on Racism (Durban, 2001) 427
UN Convention on the Rights of Persons with Disabilities (2006) 426–428, 427
UN High Commissioner for Refugees (UNHCR) 210
United Democratic Front (UDF), launch 29
   Nassim Pahad involvement 29

Vadi, Ismail 280, 531
Vajpayee, Atal Bihari 77, 251–252
Valcke, Jerome 477
Van Dyk, Ernst 428
Van Heerden, Jako 452
Van Heerden, Oscar 529
Van Schalkwyk, Marthinus 442
Van Tonder, *Officer* 66
Vandeyar, Reggie 63
Vania, Aisha See: Saloojee, Aisha (née Vania) 38
Vania, Amin 398
Vania, Fatima 43
Vania, I. A. 43
Vania, I. M. 43
Vania, Nallifoi (née Pahad) 43
Vania, Zayboon 43
Vanqa, Owen 93
Varachia, Ayob 82
Vassan, Bobby 95, 276
Vassan, Tommy 95
Vavi, Zwelinzima 490
Verwoerd, Hendrik 48
Vierra, Sergio 170
Virges, Paul 167
Vivó, Raul Valdés 142–143
Voices of Liberation – Chris Hani 343
Voller, Jerome 452
Vorster, B. J. 67
Vorwerk, Chris 381
Vuk'uzenzele magazine 408, 416, 418–422
   objectives 420
   Tony Trew observations 419–420

Wade, Abdoulaye 269–271
Wahlöö, Per 125
Walsh, *Professor* 75
Walus, Janusz 346
Wankie Campaign (Rhodesia) 344
Wolfenden, Tom 101
Wardle, Marlene 193

Watson, Trevor 376
Ways of Seeing the National Qualifications Framework 381
Weenink, Ira 452, 458
Weiler, Hazel See: Hutchinson, Hazel (née Weiler)
Weinberg, Mark 51, 79
Weinberg, Sheila 51
West, Audrey 126
West, Jim 126
Wier, Ingrid 72
Wilkinson, Gloria See: Pahad, Gloria (née Wilkinson)
Williams, Colleen 379
Williamson, Craig 185, 231–232
Wilson, Harold 101, 139, 233–234, 513
Winston, Fern 314, 317–318
Winston, Henry 108, 260, 313–321
  CUPSA role 314–318
  political life 313–321
  tribute by Essop Pahad 313–314
Winter, Gordon 202–203
Wolpe, Harold 56, 64
women
  CODESA negotiations 430
  Frene Ginwala fighter for 425
  gender-based violence 434–435
  Hendrietta Bogopane-Zulu fighter for 426
  National Policy Framework for Women's Empowerment and Gender Equality 434
  NEC statement (1990) 430
  O. R.Tambo stance 308, 430
  Race and Class 319
  Solemn Declaration of African Heads of State on Gender and Development 434
  Thabo Mbeki stance 431
Woods, Alan 75–76
World Assembly for Peace and Life and Against Nuclear War (Prague, 1983) 111–112
World Assembly of Youth (WAY) 214
World Federation of Democratic Youth (WFDY) 89, 93, 214
World Federation of Democratic Youth 57
World Federation of Trade Unions (WFTU) 93, 148, 150
World Marxist Review 64, 104, 123, 139, 203, 263 See also: Pahad, Essop, Prague Years

World Peace Council 93
World Youth Festival (Berlin, 1973) 100–101, 346
Worldwide Anti-Apartheid Movement (WAAM) 465
Worrall, Denis 206
Wright, Nick 101, 192
Xuma, A. B. 46

Yashin, Lev 216
Yawa (*NUM leader*) 354
Yazeji, Nawal 128–130, 140
Yeltsin, Boris 218, 284
Youth Action Committee 49
Yutar, Percy 297

Zapiro 498–499
Zaradov, Konstantin 124
Zikalala, Joseph (Snuki) 92, 181, 183–184
Zikalala, Pinky 183–184
Zille, Helen 478
Zolile, *driver* 504
Zulu, Hendrietta Bogopane- See: Bogopane-Zulu, Hendrietta
Zuma, Jacob 138, 190, 207, 209, 256, 333, 365–367, 404, 428, 431, 433, 437, 466–467, 479, 486, 494–501, 499
  ANC president (2008) 501
  rape charge 498–499
  SA president 433
Zuma, Nkosazana Zuma- See: Dlamini-Zuma, Nkosazana
Zungu, Cap 88–89